Unsustainable World

T0383088

Using a cross-disciplinary, science- and economics-based approach, this book provides a sobering and comprehensive assessment of the multifaceted barriers to achieving sustainability at a global level.

Organized into three parts, the book defines sustainability in part I and sets the context of the historical and current difficulties facing the world today. In parts II and III, it outlines the sustainability challenges faced in transportation, manufacturing, and agriculture, and then in turn addresses the solutions, conditional solutions, and nonsolutions to these challenges. These include electric and autonomous automobiles, nuclear power, renewable energy, geoengineering, and carbon capture and storage. The author attempts to differentiate among those proposed solutions and discusses which are most promising and which are infeasible, counterproductive, and potentially a waste of time and money. In each of the book's chapters, the scientific evidence is presented in detail, in keeping with the advice of the young Swedish climate activist, Greta Thunberg, to let the science speak for itself. The author outlines why sustainability is unlikely to be achieved in several key areas of human endeavor and readers are challenged to weigh the scientific evidence for themselves.

Using an economic business–based approach, this book introduces students and general readers to the challenges of sustainability and the environmental difficulties facing humanity today.

Peter N. Nemetz received a PhD in Economics from Harvard University and is Professor Emeritus of Strategy and Business Economics in the Sauder School of Business at the University of British Columbia, Canada. For twenty-nine years he held a visiting research position in the Department of Health Sciences Research at Mayo Clinic in Rochester, Minnesota. He has published more than one hundred books, academic articles, and consulting reports in the areas of natural disaster economics, natural resource and environmental economics and policy, international business, sustainability, and epidemiology.

Unsustainable World

Are We Losing the Battle to Save Our Planet?

Peter N. Nemetz

LONDON AND NEW YORK

from Routledge

First published 2022
by Routledge
4 Park Square, Milton Park, Abingdon, Oxon OX14 4RN

and by Routledge
605 Third Avenue, New York, NY 10158

Routledge is an imprint of the Taylor & Francis Group, an informa business

© 2022 Peter N. Nemetz

British Library Cataloguing-in-Publication Data
A catalogue record for this book is available from the British Library

Library of Congress Cataloging-in-Publication Data
A catalog record has been requested for this book

ISBN: 978-1-032-05862-7 (hbk)
ISBN: 978-1-032-05858-0 (pbk)
ISBN: 978-1-003-19954-0 (ebk)

DOI: 10.4324/9781003199540

Typeset in Bembo
by Newgen Publishing UK

To my dearest wife, Roma, and daughter, Fiona, the grandest stars in my universe—may they continue to burn bright for many years to come.

Contents

Figures

Tables

Boxes

Other books by the author

Economic Incentives for Energy Conservation (with Marilyn Hankey), New York: Wiley-Interscience, 1984.
Business and the Sustainability Challenge: An Integrated Perspective, New York: Routledge, 2013.
The Economics and Business of Sustainability, Abingdon, UK; New York: Routledge, 2021.
Corporate Strategy and Sustainability, Routledge, 2022, forthcoming.

Books edited by the author

Editor, *Energy Policy: The Global Challenge*, Montreal: Institute for Research on Public Policy, 1979.

Editor, *Resource Policy: International Perspectives*, Montreal: Institute for Research on Public Policy, 1980.

Editor, *Energy Crisis: Policy Response*, Montreal: Institute for Research on Public Policy, 1981.

Editor, *The Pacific Rim: Investment, Development and Trade*, Vancouver: UBC Press, 1987.

Editor, *The Pacific Rim: Investment, Development and Trade*, Vancouver: UBC Press, 2nd revised edition, 1990.

Editor, *Emerging Issues in Forest Policy*, Vancouver: UBC Press, 1992.

Editor, *The Vancouver Institute: An Experiment in Public Education*, Vancouver: JBA Press, 1998.

Editor, *Bringing Business On Board: Sustainable Development and the B-School Curriculum*, Vancouver: JBA Press, 2002.

Editor, *Sustainable Resource Management: Reality or Illusion?*, Cheltenham: Edward Elgar, 2007.

Co-editor, *Reflections of Canada. Illuminating our Opportunities and Challenges at 150+ Years* (with Philippe Tortell and Margot Young), Vancouver: Peter Wall Institute for Advanced Studies, 2017.

Cover photo courtesy of NASA

Preface

This book has emerged from more than four decades of teaching, research, and publishing in the areas of environmental economics and policy and, more recently, the broader and emerging discipline of sustainability. In my most recent work on sustainability (Nemetz 2013, *Business and the Sustainability Challenge*), the principal thrust was the contention that business buy-in is a necessary although not sufficient condition for achieving global sustainability. In fact, the challenge is much more complex than mere considerations of active business participation, and this forms the core of this current work.

The pedagogical approach adopted herein differs radically from most of the numerous books on the subject which, while defining the problems at hand, focus on how these problems *might* be solved and relegate scientific evidence to their footnotes. In each of the subsequent chapters of this book, the scientific evidence is presented in detail in keeping with the advice of the sixteen-year-old Swedish climate activist, Greta Thunberg, to "let the science speak for itself." I outline why sustainability is unlikely to be achieved in several key areas of human endeavor and readers are challenged to weigh the scientific evidence for themselves. The motivation for this approach is derived from recent evolution in the theory and practice of risk analysis which, in the context of climate change, now includes more expansive study of extreme values—that is, what have been termed zero-infinity dilemmas—which entail low probability events with potentially catastrophic consequences. (see Chapter 8 for a more detailed discussion of this issue in the context of the coevolution of modern risk theory and the development of commercial nuclear power.) Of course, I would be delighted to receive a successful rebuttal of the theses outlined in this work, but I suspect it will not be easy.

It is conventional wisdom that studies of future sustainability should not be unduly bleak lest they encourage a sense of helplessness and engender apathy and inaction. Nothing could be further from the truth. The strategy that puts a positive spin on future prospects runs a real risk of promoting a sense of complacency and satisfaction with marginal and cosmetic changes to business as usual. This is counterproductive in the extreme in light of the steady deterioration of our ecological systems, and ultimately the economic and social systems that depend on them. If, in fact, the presentation of the brutal facts in the face of an existential threat is considered unnecessary and counterproductive, then Winston Churchill would be remembered for his famous speech: "no blood, no toil, no tears and no sweat." In contrast, the approach adopted in this book is to present the unvarnished facts and convey a strong sense that unless drastic action is undertaken, the survival of our way of life is in serious jeopardy.

As unpalatable as it may seem on first blush, what is required is a radical transformation in our patterns of production and consumption, specifically the energy and materials we use and how they are produced. This transformation must be led by an informed electorate, business community, and government, the last of which must be willing and able to facilitate this transformation using the many levers—economic and noneconomic—available to them. Nothing less will suffice.

Some have argued that we have all the scientific and policy tools necessary to solve the climate crisis (Wallace-Wells 2019; Friedman and Gabriel 2019) and that the challenge is changing human attitudes and behavior. If that is indeed the case, then the challenge we are facing is indeed momentous. Such attitudes and behavior are notoriously hard to change for several critical reasons. Humanity has a decision framework with a relatively short time horizon; it has difficulty processing risk, especially risks that will materialize in the medium to distant future. But, perhaps, most importantly, there are deep biological roots for this problem. In his work "Is humanity fatally successful" (2007, p. 392), William Rees concludes that:

> we humans have a long evolutionary history and many of the traits that we've acquired along the way, traits that were adaptive 50,000 years ago, are with us still. But now some of these once desirable qualities may threaten humanity's future prospects. That is, some characteristic human qualities and behaviours may well now be maladaptive … these ancient traits are such that techno-industrial society in particular is inherently unsustainable. The world is ecologically full – but evolution has not provided us with inhibitions against extinguishing other species, against eliminating competing human groups or, indeed, against destroying our earthly habitat(s).

The subtitle of this book is "Are we losing the battle to save our planet?" In fact, this is misleading. The more appropriate subtitle would be: "Are we losing the battle to save humanity?" as nature is supremely indifferent to the fate of humanity, only one of the many species that inhabit the earth. In fact, if one could anthropomorphize nature and impute emotions to it, then we might find that it would be exceedingly relieved to be rid of a species that has done more than any other to destroy the fabric of the global ecosystem.

This book is divided into three parts: the first, a brief introduction, outlines several critical definitions and theories in economics and ecology that are essential for understanding the flow of the arguments. The second is composed of several chapters, each devoted to a major source of greenhouse gases. More than one-third of this second part is devoted to the subject of agriculture as the prospect of its unsustainability poses the greatest threat to the continued prosperity and survival of modern civilization. Finally, the third section considers the viability of several technological and policy options that have been offered to address the monumental task faced by humanity in attempting to secure a viable future for the species and the rest of the ecosystem. The book ends with an afterword devoted to the emerging threat of pandemics and their significance for sustainability.

In writing this book, I must acknowledge the central role that my students over four decades have played in helping me form my opinions. They have raised critical questions and forced me to examine the validity of conventional wisdom that occasionally has been voiced by me and others in the incubator of ideas that is the university classroom. I am particularly indebted to the following individuals for their advice and assistance in this research project: the late W.H.L. (Bert) Allsopp, the late Ray Anderson, Ms. Bruna Angel, Professor Joel Bakan, Ms. Dyhia Belhabib, Professor Francesca Bray, Dr. William Cheung, Dr. Fiona Danks, Mr. Patrick Dore, Ms. Liz Doyle, Professor Leonard Foster, Mr.

Buddy Hay, Dr. Cristina Infante, Mr. Bob Johnston, Dr. Les Lavkulich, Dr. Jane Lister, Dr. Todd Litman, Mr. Robert MacDonald, Professor Bill McKibben, Mr. Ling Meng, Mr. Chris Milly, Dr. Liz Minne, Mr. Brian Moghadam, Dr. Jane Pan, Dr. Daniel Pauly, Ms. Gwen Pitman, Ms. Jennifer Potter, Dr. Juan Reyero, Ms. Fei Song, Professor Rashid Sumaila, Professor Scott Valentine, Dr. Frank von Hippel, and Dr. Andy Yan. I am especially grateful to Matt Shobbrook at Routledge for his thoughtful editorial advice and assistance and Katherine Demopoulos for her meticulous copyediting. I hold neither them nor my colleagues responsible for any errors, omissions, or misinterpretations in the material contained herein.

PNN
Vancouver

Disclaimer

Writing a book on sustainability presents an unusual challenge as the field is advancing rapidly both theoretically and empirically. During manuscript preparation, it has been necessary to revise each chapter on a near-weekly basis. This experience brings to mind the words of Lewis Carroll's Red Queen in *Through the Looking Glass*: "It takes all the running you can do, to keep in the same place" (Carroll 1945, p. 42). Facing this challenge requires a certain degree of caution about making predictions on future prospects, for fear that future events—both near and medium term—will render them irrelevant. The author hopes the reader will bear this caveat in mind given the inevitable delay between submission of the final manuscript to the publisher and the moment the book reaches the reader.

References

Carroll, Lewis (1945) *Through the Looking Glass and What Alice Found There*, London: The MacMillian Company.

Nemetz, Peter N. (2013) *Business and the Sustainability Challenge*, New York: Routledge.

New York Times (2019) "A Green New Deal is technologically possible: Its political prospects are another question," February 21.

Rees, William (2007) "Is humanity fatally successful?" in Peter N. Nemetz (ed.) *Sustainable Resource Management: Reality or Illusion?* Cheltenham: Edward Elgar.

Wallace-Wells, David (2019) *The Uninhabitable Earth: Life After Warming*, New York: Tim Duggan Books.

Part I

Introduction and critical concepts

1 Introduction

The nature of the challenge

Few concepts have had such a major impact on recent public discourse as sustainable development. Since the publication of the Brundtland Report in 1987 (WCED 1987), a vast array of initiatives has been taken by governments, business, nongovernmental organizations (NGOs), and individuals to advance the cause of sustainability. While there are numerous examples of relatively successful policies and practices, the achievement of sustainability at the level that matters most—the global scale—has been an unmitigated failure. Evidence in support of this discouraging conclusion has been provided by several international scientific reports. Recent reports from the Intergovernmental Panel on Climate Change (IPCC 2018, 2019, 2021a and b) have painted a bleaker picture than a previous report of 2014, highlighting greater impacts and a foreshortened deadline in which to act in order to forestall potentially catastrophic results. The Sixth Assessment Report by the Intergovernmental Panel on Climate Change (IPCC 2021b) predicts faster warming than previously anticipated and increasing ecological changes in all regions of the globe. "There will be increasing heat waves, longer warm seasons and shorter cold seasons. At 2°C of global warming, heat extremes would more often reach critical tolerance thresholds for agriculture and health" (IPCC press release August 9, 2021). The principal conclusions of the Sixth Assessment Report are presented in Box 1.1.

Box 1.1 IPCC *Sixth Assessment Report (2021): Headline Statements from the Summary for Policymakers*, August 9

A The Current State of the Climate

A.1   It is unequivocal that human influence has warmed the atmosphere, ocean and land.
Widespread and rapid changes in the atmosphere, ocean, cryosphere and biosphere have occurred.

A.2   The scale of recent changes across the climate system as a whole and the present state of many aspects of the climate system are unprecedented over many centuries to many thousands of years.

A.3   Human-induced climate change is already affecting many weather and climate extremes in every region across the globe. Evidence of observed changes in extremes such as heatwaves, heavy precipitation, droughts, and tropical cyclones, and, in particular, their attribution to human influence, has strengthened since the Fifth Assessment Report (AR5).

DOI: 10.4324/9781003199540-2

A.4   Improved knowledge of climate processes, paleoclimate evidence and the response of the climate system to increasing radiative forcing gives a best estimate of equilibrium climate sensitivity of 3°C, with a narrower range compared to AR5.

B Possible Climate Futures

B.1   Global surface temperature will continue to increase until at least the mid-century under all emissions scenarios considered. Global warming of 1.5°C and 2°C will be exceeded during the 21st century unless deep reductions in carbon dioxide (CO2) and other greenhouse gas emissions occur in the coming decades.

B.2   Many changes in the climate system become larger in direct relation to increasing global warming. They include increases in the frequency and intensity of hot extremes, marine heatwaves, and heavy precipitation, agricultural and ecological droughts in some regions, and proportion of intense tropical cyclones, as well as reductions in Arctic sea ice, snow cover and permafrost.

B.3   Continued global warming is projected to further intensify the global water cycle, including its variability, global monsoon precipitation and the severity of wet and dry events.

B.4   Under scenarios with increasing CO_2 emissions, the ocean and land carbon sinks are projected to be less effective at slowing the accumulation of CO_2 in the atmosphere.

B.5   Many changes due to past and future greenhouse gas emissions are irreversible for centuries to millennia, especially changes in the ocean, ice sheets and global sea level.

C Climate Information for Risk Assessment and Regional Adaptation

C.1   Natural drivers and internal variability will modulate human-caused changes, especially at regional scales and in the near term, with little effect on centennial global warming. These modulations are important to consider in planning for the full range of possible changes.

C.2   With further global warming, every region is projected to increasingly experience concurrent and multiple changes in climatic impact-drivers. Changes in several climatic impact-drivers would be more widespread at 2°C compared to 1.5°C global warming and even more widespread and/or pronounced for higher warming levels.

C.3   Low-likelihood outcomes, such as ice sheet collapse, abrupt ocean circulation changes, some compound extreme events and warming substantially larger than the assessed *very likely* range of future warming cannot be ruled out and are part of risk assessment.

D Limiting Future Climate Change

D.1   From a physical science perspective, limiting human-induced global warming to a specific level requires limiting cumulative CO_2 emissions, reaching at least net zero CO_2 emissions, along with strong reductions in other greenhouse gas emissions. Strong, rapid and sustained reductions in CH_4 emissions would also limit the warming effect resulting from declining aerosol pollution and would improve air quality.

D.2 Scenarios with low or very low greenhouse gas (GHG) emissions (SSP1–1.9 and SSP1–2.6) lead within years to discernible effects on greenhouse gas and aerosol concentrations, and air quality, relative to high and very high GHG emissions scenarios (SSP3–7.0 or SSP5–8.5). Under these contrasting scenarios, discernible differences in trends of global surface temperature would begin to emerge from natural variability within around 20 years, and over longer time periods for many other climatic impact-drivers (high confidence). (IPCC 2021a)

These comprehensive studies by the IPCC, representing the consensus views of thousands of scientists, have concluded that greenhouse gas (GHG) emissions (especially carbon dioxide and methane) continue to increase, the temperature of the atmosphere and oceans continues to rise, land and sea ice continues to melt, sea levels and ocean acidification continue to rise, and climate extremes have begun to materialize and will continue to worsen (see also NAS 2016; BAMS 2018; NOAA 2019a and b; Nisbet et al. 2019; Blunden and Arndt 2019; WMO 2019a and b, 2020, 2021a and b; IPCC 2018; IPCC 2019; Cheng et al. 2021; Hooijer and Vernimmen 2021; IPCC 2021). In their annual survey of several dozen anthropogenic global risks, the World Economic Forum (WEF 2019) identifies climate change with all its manifestations as the risk most likely to occur and also threatening the greatest impact.

In May 2019, it was reported that carbon dioxide levels in the atmosphere had reached levels higher than those recorded in the past 800,000 to 2 million years (Smithsonian.com 2019; *Washington Post* May 14, 2019). Symptomatic of this phenomenon was the extraordinary temperature of 84 degrees Fahrenheit (°F) or 29 degrees Celsius (°C) recorded near the entrance to the Arctic Ocean in northwest Russia, approximately 30–40°F higher than average (Smithsonian.com 2019; *Washington Post* May 14, 2019). One year later, the Arctic Circle saw its highest ever recorded temperature with the Siberian town of Verkhoyansk reaching 100°F on June 20, 2020 (BBC June 22, 2020). It is accepted fact that the Arctic is experiencing the effects of global warming at a much faster rate than the rest of the world (AMAP-SWIPA 2017; Jeong et al. 2018; Francis 2018; Struzik 2015; *Washington Post* July 3, 2019a and b; Fischetti 2019; Hu et al. 2020; Lai et al. 2020; Landrum and Holland 2020; Garbe et al. 2020; King et al. 2020; Previdi et al. 2020; Dickie 2021). Jansen et al. (2020, p. 714) conclude that "warming rates similar to or higher than modern trends have only occurred during past abrupt glacial episodes. We argue that the Arctic is currently experiencing an abrupt climate change event, and that climate models underestimate this ongoing warming."

These dramatic changes in the Arctic provide the equivalent of a crystal ball for scientists to see what lies in store for the rest of the world in the years to come, as there are significant climatological linkages between the Arctic and midlatitudes (Francis and Vavrus 2012; UNEP 2019). A report from the United Nations Environment Programme (UNEP 2019) concluded that a sharp rise in Arctic temperatures in the order of 3–5°C is now inevitable. In 2018 the world experienced the breaking of all-time global heat records (*Washington Post* July 5, 2018). These provide clear signals of the direction and magnitude of changes that the globe is undergoing with profound implications for the future. Similar dramatic changes are occurring in Greenland and Antarctica with the threat of rapid loss of ice cover and subsequent sea-level rise (Alley 2019; Lai et al. 2020; Garbe et al. 2020; King et al. 2020; Aschwanden 2020; Gilbert and Kittel 2021; Pan et al. 2021). DeConto et al. (2021) have forecast that rapid and unstoppable sea-level rise from Antarctica will be triggered by mid century if Paris Agreement targets are exceeded. However, other recent research by Hugonnet et al. (2021) has found that "glaciers currently lose more mass, and at similar or larger acceleration rates, than the Greenland or Antarctica ice sheets taken separately."

In May 2021 the US Environmental Protection Agency (EPA) released a comprehensive update of critical indicators of climate change after a hiatus of four years during which the Trump administration downplayed the scope and impact of the issue. The EPA classified these groups of indicators under six headings: (1) GHGs, (2) weather and climate, (3) oceans, (4) snow and ice, (5) health and society, and (6) ecosystems. Some of these general indicators are supplemented with regional or local case studies. A list of all indicators is provided in Table 1.1. In most cases, these indicators are pointing in the

Table 1.1 US Environmental Protection Agency's indicators of climate change

Categories	Nature of change since 2005
Greenhouse gases	
US GHG emissions	Decreased
Global GHG emissions	Increased
Atmospheric concentration of GHGs	Increased
Climate forcing (i.e. warming effect)	Increased
Weather and climate	
US and global temperature	Increased
Season temperatures	Increased
High and low temperatures	Extremes more common
Heat waves	More frequent
US and global precipitation	General increase with some regional decreases
Heavy precipitation	More frequent
Tropical cyclone activity	Increased
River flooding	Greater in some regions, lower in others
Drought	US West has experienced more; the Southwest and Rockies less
Temperature and drought in the Southwest	Increased
Oceans	
Ocean heat	Increased
Sea surface temperature	Increased
Sea level	Increased
Coastal flooding	More frequent
Ocean acidity	Increased
Land loss along the Atlantic coast	Increased
Snow and ice	
Arctic sea ice	Decreased
Antarctic sea ice	Net decrease
Ice sheets (especially Greenland and Antarctica)	Decreased
Glaciers	Accelerated shrinkage

Table 1.1 Cont.

Categories	Nature of change since 2005
Lake ice	Shorter periods
Great Lakes ice cover	Decreased
Snowfall	Decreased
Snow cover	Decreased
Snowpack	Decreased
Permafrost temperature	Increased
Freeze-thaw conditions (i.e. unfrozen days)	Increased
Glaciers in Glacier National Park	Shrunk
Ice breakup in three Alaskan rivers	Earlier
Ecosystems	
Wildfires	Increased
Streamflow	Runoff earlier where fed by snowmelt
Stream temperature	Increased
Lake temperature	Increased
Great Lakes water levels and temperatures	Moderate temperature increases with mixed results re water levels
Bird wintering ranges	Moving north and inland
Marine species distribution	Moving north
Leaf and bloom dates	Generally earlier in the North and later in the South
Trends in stream temperature in the Snake River	Increased
Cherry blossom bloom dates in Washington, DC	Slightly earlier
Black guillemots of Cooper Island, Alaska	Decrease
Health and society	
Heat-related deaths	Increased when related to age
Heat-related illnesses	Increased
Cold-related deaths	Possible increase
Heating and cooling degree days	Heating degree days decreased and cooling days increased in US North and West; the opposite in the South
Residential energy use	Mixed results
Lyme disease	Increased
West Nile virus	No trend
Length of growing season	General increase
Growing degree days	Increased
Ragweed pollen season	Increased

Source: US EPA 2021

wrong direction, suggesting that climate change is getting worse and having a greater impact on the country's citizens and its ecosystems.

Most climate-related changes are marked by positive feedback loops, lags, potential abrupt shifts (so-called tipping points) and irreversibilities that pose a direct threat to humanity if left uncontrolled (US CCSP 2008, 2009a and b; Barnosky et al. 2012; Steffen et al. 2018). A similar bleak outlook is reflected in the work of the Intergovernmental Science-Policy Platform on Biodiversity and Ecosystem Services (IPBES 2019), which states that "nature's dangerous decline [is] 'unprecedented'; [as] species extinction rates [are] 'accelerating'" (see also UN 2019).

While the sustainability challenge is multifaceted, encompassing economic and social as well as ecological variables, it is climate change that has assumed preeminence with its potentially massive direct and indirect effects on the fabric of our economic and social systems. The threat to global sustainability appears to rest on three variables: (1) rising population, (2) increasing industrialization and wealth with its concomitant rise in demand for food and other natural resources, and (3) technological innovations that may have environmentally detrimental effects. Total pollution can increase from any one of these factors. If the goal is to decrease humanity's environmental impact on the planet, it is clearly insufficient to tackle only one or two of these factors; a worsening in the remainder may offset any beneficial changes in the others.

In light of the depth of intellectual resources devoted to addressing the problem of climate change, the question remains as to why global climate change not only continues unabated but also appear to be accelerating, pushing the limits of planetary boundaries (Steffen et al. 2015b; see also Nerem et al. 2018; WMO 2019b; NASA 2018). The principal agents capable of addressing this issue are the governmental and corporate sectors with the help of civil society but, to date, the record has been mixed at best. At least part of the problem has been the existence of powerful and pervasive myths that have had a broad influence on public opinion, corporate strategy, and government policy. These include: the myth that countries can grow their way out of pollution; the myth that international trade and globalization have an unambiguously positive effect on sustainability; the myth that humankind's technological ingenuity will overcome any barriers to sustainability; and the myth that humankind can adapt to continuing climate change (Nemetz 2015).

Of course, sustainability is much more than climate change and includes a broad range of concerns relating to fisheries, forestry, biodiversity, agriculture, fresh water, the oceans, and human health. All of these threats, however, have linkages to climate change.

Before addressing these issues, it is important to identify the core of relevant theory bearing upon the analysis. The first, and perhaps the most important, is the distinction between sustainable development and sustainability. In their original treatise, Brundtland et al. (WCED 1987) were principally motivated by the desire to help impoverished developing countries to raise their standard of living without jeopardizing the welfare of future generations. Thus was borne the concept of sustainable development, which to all intents and purposes meant sustainable growth. Herein lies the major problem. The de facto iron law of sustainability is that growth cannot under any circumstances continue indefinitely in a closed system such as the earth. And yet, growth is the fundamental foundation of current economic theory and government policy. As cogently stated by Ronald Colman (2002, p. 142):

> Scientists recognize that the only biological organism that has unlimited growth as its dogma is the cancer cell, the apparent model for our conventional economic theory. By contrast, the natural world thrives on balance and equilibrium, and recognizes inherent limits to growth. The cancer analogy is apt, because the path of limitless growth is profoundly self-destructive. No matter how many cars we have in the driveway or how many possessions we accumulate, the environment will not tolerate the growth illusion even if we fail to see through it.

The challenge remains to redefine sustainability in a manner which is operational. There are numerous studies of sustainable development, many with their own more precise definition than the Brundtland Commission. Several common conceptual threads run through these studies of sustainability:

1 A direct or indirect articulation of the concept of natural capital, where maintenance of a constant natural capital stock (including the renewable resource base and the environment) yields an indefinite stream of output or "income." This is a direct analog of the business concept of interest from capital. In his recent study on *The Economics of Biodiversity*, Partha Dasgupta (2021) makes the argument that saving our natural environment is essentially an asset management problem. Only by treating nature as an asset to be preserved can we successfully address the multifaceted threats to global ecosystems. The central concept of sustainability is the proposition that the current generation must leave the next generation a stock of capital no less than this generation has now. Implicit in this proposition is that we must, to the best of our ability, live off the "interest" on this capital stock and not draw it down. If part of this capital is drawn down, it must be replaced by substitute capital. The ability to achieve this goal hinges on which of two major definitions of "sustainable development" one adopts: "weak" sustainability or "strong" sustainability. Under what is called the "weak sustainability constant capital rule," society can pass on less environment to future generations so long as this loss is offset by increasing manufactured (physical) capital stock such as roads and machinery. In contrast, the "strong sustainability constant capital rule" states that perfect substitution among different forms of capital is not a valid assumption. Some elements of natural capital stock cannot be replaced by manufactured capital, except on a very limited basis. Some functions and services of ecosystems are essential to human survival; they are life support services (e.g., biogeochemical cycling) and cannot be replaced.

  Yamaguchi et al. (2019) have measured inclusive wealth (i.e. comprising produced, human, and natural capital) for 140 countries over the period 1990–2014 (see also Managi and Kumar 2018). They find that only 60 percent of these countries show nondeclining wealth over this period (Yamaguchi et al. 2019, p. 101).

  Most countries, both developed and developing, fall into the group of running down natural capital and increasing produced and, to a lesser extent, human capital … Globally, aggregated produced and human capital per capita increased 94% and 28%, respectively, while natural capital per capita declined by 34%.

  While these results may suggest acceptable results using the weak sustainability rule, they clearly fail the strong sustainability criterion. The distinction between these two criteria is critically important, for failure to achieve strong sustainability means that we are continuing to slowly destroy the ecological system that sustains life on our planet. To achieve sustainability, we need to have more accurate measures of the various types of capital (natural, human, produced). Without these measures, it is impossible to make the right decisions.

2 A focus on social stability, empowerment, and equity with particular emphasis on reducing poverty and assuring an adequate quality of life for all global inhabitants alive and to be born (i.e. both intragenerational and intergenerational equity).

3 A critical distinction between qualitative and quantitative changes in the utilization of our technology and natural resource base (i.e. expressed as development versus growth); for example, technological advances which may permit us to raise our standard of living without increasing the throughput of material and energy resources—a process sometimes defined as "dematerialization." Figures 1.1 and 1.2 provide historical data on the inexorable historical rise in the use of both materials and energy. Projections of existing trends (Hatfield-Dodds et al. 2017; European

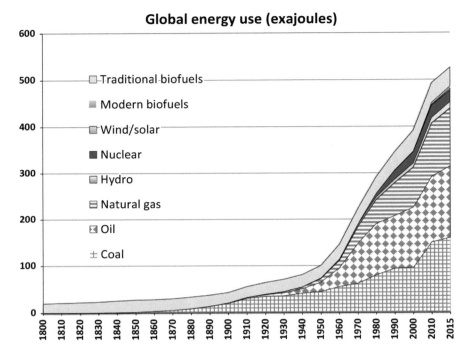

Figure 1.1 Global energy use (exajoules).
Source: Smil 2017.

Commission 2018) suggest that, by 2050, global energy use could increase by 69 percent and material resource extraction may increase by as much as 119 percent, with
the biggest increase in nonmetallic minerals.

4   The adoption of the "precautionary principle," which states that one cannot wait
    for definitive scientific proof of a potential threat to the global ecosystem before
    acting, if that threat is both large and credible (UNESCO 2005). Although this
    principle can be applied to relatively minor potential risks, it is particularly ger-
    mane to what are called "fat-tail" or "zero-infinity" cases, meaning cases where
    there is a relatively low probability of a catastrophic event. The underlying theory
    is based on scientific principles, largely associated with the pioneering work of
    ecologists such as C.S. (Buzz) Holling (1973, 1978 , 2005; Holling and Gunderson
    2002; Holling and Peterson 2008), which includes exponential change, positive
    feedback loops, irreversibilities, and tipping points (see also Steffen et al. 2018;
    Alley 2004; Lenton et al. 2008; Bathiany et al. 2018). The sum of these theories
    suggests that by the time one recognizes or begins to feel the tangible effects of
    certain types of ecological threat, such as climate change, it may be too late to act.
    The concept of zero-infinity cases has been popularized by Nasim Nicholas Taleb
    in his 2010 book *The Black Swan: The Impact of the Highly Improbable*, which outlines
    the theory of rare events with enormous effects. It is noteworthy that when Taleb's
    work first appeared, the probability of runaway climate change was deemed to be
    very low. Only more recently has the probability of such an event increased in

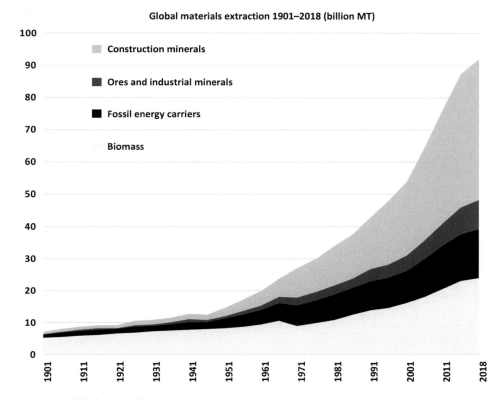

Figure 1.2 Global materials extraction 1900–2009.
Sources: Maddison Historical Statistics (n.d.); European Commission 2018.

light of the current trajectory of GHG emissions (Wagner and Weitzman 2015). In conversations with *New York Times* columnist and author Thomas Friedman (Friedman 2014), the environmentalist Adam Sweidan enunciated the concept of a "black elephant"—a high probability event with serious consequences, which people are reluctant to address.

A central challenge to addressing the issue of climate change is the difficulty people experience in recognizing nonlinear change in human and ecological systems; the human mind has been conditioned by millennia of relatively incremental change. For most of human history, at the moment of an individual's death, the earth and its society looked very much the same as it did at his/her birth. This has been the conditioning that has infused our social and economic institutions and worldviews until relatively recent times. One of the first works recognizing the phenomenon of nonlinear change was written by the late editor of the *Scientific American*, Gerard Piel, and entitled *The Acceleration of History* (1972). More recent explications of this concept include James Gleick's *Faster: The Acceleration of Just About Everything* (2000); Steffen et al. "The trajectory of the Anthropocene: The Great Acceleration" (2015a); McNeill and Engelke's *The Great Acceleration: An Environmental History of the Anthropocene since 1945* (2016); Friedman's *Thank You for Being Late: An*

Optimist's Guide to Thriving in the Age of Accelerations (2016); and Robert Colville's *The Great Acceleration: How the World is Getting Faster, Faster* (2017).

While some have posited that the Great Acceleration began during England's industrial revolution, McNeill and Engelke (2016) present a compelling case for its birth in the immediate postwar period. The following quote from their book supports this hypothesis:

> Within the last three human generations, three-quarters of the human-caused loading of the atmosphere with carbon dioxide took place. The number of motor vehicles on Earth increased from 40 million to 850 million. The number of people nearly tripled, and the number of city dwellers rose from about 700 million to 3.7 billion. In 1950 the world produced about 1 million tons of plastics but by 2015 that rose to nearly 300 million tons. In the same time span, the quantities of nitrogen synthesized (mainly for fertilizers) climbed from under 4 million tons to more than 85 million tons.
>
> (p. 4)

The authors' hypothesis is given further credence by the graphical analysis of almost two dozen socioeconomic and earth system variables from 1750 to 2010 in Steffen et al. (2015a). Mark Carney, the former governor of the Bank of England (2021, pp. 263–5), provides several examples to illustrate the nature of this acceleration. To quote:

> Our oceans have become 30 percent more acidic since the Industrial Revolution. Sea levels have risen 20 centimetres over the past century, with the rate doubling in the past two decades. The pace of ice loss in the Arctic and Antarctic has tripled in the last decade … Current extinction rates are around a hundred times higher than average over the past several million years. Since I was born, there has been a 70 per cent decline in the population of mammals, birds, fish, reptiles and amphibians … It took 250 years to burn the first half-trillion tons of carbon. On current trends, the next half-trillion will be released into our atmosphere in less than forty years.

It should be noted, however, that not all observers feel that this acceleration will continue. Professor Danny Dorling (2020) of Oxford University has posited a slowdown and even end of the Great Acceleration. The author has presented evidence that suggests that many recent rapid changes are decelerating. However, the author candidly admits that one exception to his findings is the continued rapid rise in global temperatures, yet this is clearly the area that matters most; all other areas are secondary. As such, increased concerns over the critical issue of accelerating climate change remain front and center among the challenges facing humanity.

The latest reports of the World Meteorological Organization (WMO 2019a and b, 2020, 2021b) confirm the findings that global warming is accelerating (see also BBC September 16, 2019). Nowhere is this phenomenon of rapid change more apparent than in the Arctic, which in many respects is the canary in the coal mine, a part of the globe that provides a premonition of the rest of the earth on fast forward (NOAA 2018; see also Patel and Fountain [2021] for an example of the speed of transition). Two particularly insidious forms of positive feedback in the Arctic are provided by the melting of both sea ice and permafrost, the former by reducing the albedo of the Arctic Ocean, which then absorbs more heat rather than reflecting it back into space, and the latter by releasing entrained methane, a GHG approximately twenty-eight times as powerful as carbon dioxide, thereby further accelerating the process of global warming (Anthony et al. 2012; Pistone et al. 2014; Herndon 2018; IPCC 2014; Etminan et al. 2016; Chadburn et al. 2017; Natali et al. 2019; Martens et al. 2020; Turetsky et al. 2020; Zhang et al. 2019). A similar threat of methane release from permafrost also appears to originate in the high–latitude/altitude northern hemisphere areas such as the Tibetan plateau (Wang et al. 2020). Another major Arctic and subarctic sink for carbon is peat in Northern Canada. Wilkinson et al. (2020) report that peat deposits, particularly those no thicker than 0.66 meters (m) where water tables have fallen, are particularly vulnerable to wildfires, posing the threat of significant releases of carbon in light of the fact that peatlands store almost one-third of global organic soil carbon.

There is continued surprise among the scientific community attending each new finding of the rapidity of global climate change (see Appendix to this chapter). This could possibly be attributed to a misinterpretation of the data. As stated above, much of history can be characterized by either little or slow incremental change, captured by a simple linear extrapolation of past trends. Such projections can be misleading in the presence of exponential change driven by a multitude of positive feedback loops. Figure 1.3 represents a hypothetical linear projection of past trends and several possible exponential growth curves. The problem of early identification of exponential change is that the first phases of this growth are difficult to distinguish from linear change. Even when the existence of nonlinear change is recognized, errors in projection may occur when the exponent of the exponential function is underestimated. Some examples of ecological nonlinearity are provided in Chapter 6 on agriculture.

If one were to seek a definition of sustainability by using an online search, one would find literally dozens. The phrase has passed into common currency and is now ubiquitous. In an Orwellian twist, this descriptor is now considered an essential ingredient in

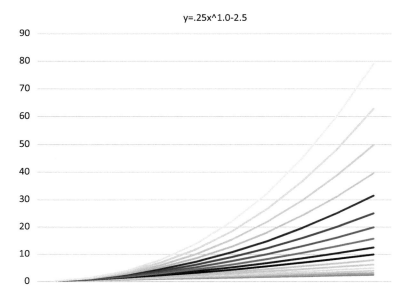

Figure 1.3 Alternative exponential growth paths.

any corporate mission statement and has been used by some corporations whose practices are the antithesis of sustainability. In some cases, these corporations have been included in one or more of the numerous indexes of sustainable businesses. As Farley and Smith (2014)have stated, when a term such as sustainability is used so widely it can mean anything, it in essence ends up meaning nothing. As such, this book attempts to provide a sober and realistic assessment of sustainability absent spin and terminological obfuscation.

Finally, since sustainability is in essence a multidisciplinary study, any analysis must recognize the contributions from a range of other disciplines, including, inter alia, psychology, political science, sociology, economics and, most importantly, ecology. One of the most important challenges to traditional economic theory has emerged from this last discipline. After describing some of the more relevant ecological principles that apply to sustainability, Chapter 2 also reviews briefly the contribution of this hybrid discipline to the study of economics as now embodied in the new field of ecological economics.

Before proceeding any further, however, it is useful to step back and hypothesize about the uniqueness of the human condition. In 1950, the physicist Enrico Fermi was the first to apply scientific reasoning to the question of whether we are alone in the universe, given the absence of any information to the contrary (Sagan 1963). More recent informed speculation emerges from the new field of astrobiology. Frank and Sullivan (2016; Frank 2015, 2018) have hypothesized that any and all technological civilizations—if they exist in the universe—must inevitably face an insurmountable barrier to the assimilation of energy and material waste. The most extreme interpretation of this hypothesis suggests that all such civilizations will expire or self-destruct before they reach the point of extraplanetary communication and travel. This is indeed a sobering thought and its lack of resolution at this point must give us pause in our approach to the accelerating pace of global economic development. Stephen Hawking (2018) has his own take on the existence of other intelligent life in the universe. He has postulated that if such life has developed elsewhere in the universe, at some point it may become unstable and destroy itself.

Overview of this work

Because of the magnitude of subject material to be covered in an adequate treatment of sustainability and its challenges, this work focuses on the four sectors that contribute most to GHG emissions: industry, transportation, food produced by agriculture, and energy production (see Figure 1.4). There are several other major issues that threaten the future sustainability of the world and these are touched upon in this work. They include loss of biodiversity, ocean acidification, and deforestation. Brief commentary on these issues follows below. This volume ends with a tentative look at some potential solutions to the challenge of sustainability.

Biodiversity

Biodiversity is arguably the most important factor in ecosystem health, supporting ecosystem function, resilience, redundancy, integrity, and intactness (see Dasgupta 2021). Swiss Re (2020, p. 2) has concluded that:

> Over half (55%) of global GDP, equal to USD 41.7 trillion, is dependent on high-functioning biodiversity and ecosystem services. However, a staggering fifth of

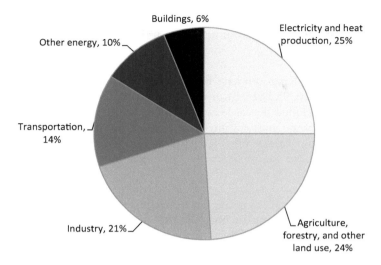

Figure 1.4 Global greenhouse gas emissions by sector.

countries globally (20%) are at risk of their ecosystems collapsing due to a decline in biodiversity and related beneficial services.

The Convention on Biological Diversity defines biodiversity as "the variability among living organisms from all sources including, inter alia, terrestrial, marine and other aquatic ecosystems and the ecological complexes of which they are part; this includes diversity within species, between species, and of ecosystems" (www.thegef.org). As the late E.O. Wilson (2016, p. 14), one of the world's leading experts on ecology and biodiversity, has observed: "biodiversity as a whole forms a shield protecting each of the species that together compose it, ourselves included. … As extinction mounts, biodiversity reaches a tipping point at which the ecosystem collapses."

Recent scientific research has demonstrated that the earth is currently undergoing its sixth mass extinction since the first such event approximately one-half billion years ago (Kolbert 2014). This crisis of ongoing extinction covers most living species including marine and terrestrial life forms such as birds, mammals, and insects (see also Diaz et al. 2019; Dickie 2021; Arctic Council 2021) The decline is so severe that some scientists are warning that such losses, referred to as "biological annihilation" (Ceballos et al. 2017 and 2020), threaten a catastrophic collapse of natural ecosystems (see also Wilson 2016; WWF 2020, 2021; Sanchez-Bayo and Wyckhuys 2019). Bradshaw et al. (2021, p. 6) summarize "predictions of a ghastly future of mass extinction, declining health, and climate-disruption upheavals (including looming massive migrations) and resource conflicts this century."

Rosenberg et al. (2019) have reported on the loss of three billion birds in North America over the last forty-eight years, representing 29 percent of their 1970 abundance. The authors observe that:

Slowing the loss of biodiversity is one of the defining environmental challenges of the 21st century. Habitat loss, climate change, unregulated harvest, and other forms of human-caused mortality have contributed to a thousandfold increase in global extinctions in the Anthropocene compared to the presumed prehuman background rate, with profound effects on ecosystem functioning and services.

(p. 1)

Comparable data for the United Kingdom have been reported by the Royal Society for the Protection of Birds (RSPB 2020). The Nature Conservancy is the coauthor of a study (Deutz et al. 2020) which concluded that at least $700 billion is required to reverse the global biodiversity crisis. One of the most comprehensive efforts to track the state of biodiversity loss and its threat to the planet is provided by the World Wildlife Fund's biennial *Living Planet Report*. The Executive Summary to the latest version (2020, p. 4) paints a grim picture. To quote:

The global Living Planet Index [LPI] continues to decline. It shows an average 68% decrease in population sizes of mammals, birds, amphibians, reptiles and fish between 1970 and 2016. A 94% decline in the LPI for the tropical subregions of the Americas is the largest fall observed in any part of the world. Why does this matter? It matters because biodiversity is fundamental to human life on Earth, and the evidence is unequivocal—it is being destroyed by us at a rate unprecedented in history. Since the industrial revolution, human activities have increasingly destroyed and degraded forests, grasslands, wetlands and other important ecosystems, threatening human well-being. Seventy-five percent of the Earth's ice-free land surface has already been significantly altered, most of the oceans are polluted, and more than 85% of the area of wetlands has been lost. Species population trends are important because they are a measure of overall ecosystem health. Measuring biodiversity, the variety of all living things, is complex, and there is no single measure that can capture all of the changes in this web of life. Nevertheless, the vast majority of indicators show net declines over recent decades. That's because in the last 50 years our world has been transformed by an explosion in global trade, consumption and human population growth, as well as an enormous move towards urbanisation. Until 1970, humanity's Ecological Footprint was smaller than the Earth's rate of regeneration. To feed and fuel our 21st century lifestyles, we are overusing the Earth's biocapacity by at least 56%.

Virtually all of this loss in biodiversity is anthropogenic, and it has been estimated that 70 percent is due to agriculture (UN 2014). Future projections to 2050, short of major changes in agricultural systems, appear even worse (Williams et al. 2020, p. 314). To quote:

The projected loss of millions of square kilometres of natural ecosystems to meet future demand for food, animal feed, fibre and bioenergy crops is likely to massively escalate threats to biodiversity. Reducing these threats requires a detailed knowledge of how and where they are likely to be most severe. We developed a geographically explicit model of future agricultural land clearance based on observed historical changes, and combined the outputs with species-specific habitat preferences for 19,859 species of terrestrial vertebrates. We project that 87.7% of these species will lose habitat to agricultural expansion by 2050, with 1,280 species projected to lose ≥25% of their habitat. Proactive policies targeting how, where, and what food is produced could reduce these threats, with a combination of approaches potentially preventing almost all these losses while contributing to healthier human diets. As international biodiversity targets are set to be updated in 2021, these results highlight the importance of proactive efforts to safeguard biodiversity by reducing demand for agricultural land.

Plumptre et al. (2021) have found that no more than 2.9 percent of the earth's land surface can be considered to be faunally intact, posing a serious threat to the maintenance of global biodiversity. This topic is addressed in greater detail in Chapter 5.

Ocean acidification

Much of the current climate change research has focused on atmospheric concentrations of GHGs and their effect on global social, economic, and ecological systems. Of equal importance is the effect of these gases, carbon dioxide in particular, on global oceans. The continued health of the world's oceans is vital to the functioning of global ecosystems as these massive bodies of water are responsible for a significant proportion of our food supply and assimilation of waste, as well as influencing—both positively and negatively—atmospheric weather patterns, producing a significant proportion of atmospheric oxygen, and providing recreation opportunities, transportation routes and, perhaps most importantly, carbon sequestration. Two variables stand out as critical to the survival of healthy oceans: the temperature of the water, which affects the health and survival of fish species and other components of ocean ecosystems, and the acidity. As global temperatures rise, the oceans have less capacity to store CO_2 and any resulting off-gassing will induce a positive feedback loop, accelerating the process of global warming. Recent research has also demonstrated that as ocean pH falls, dramatic changes occur in ocean ecological systems not only from increased acidity, but also from decreased carbonate availability, which interferes with the ability of life-forms that rely on carbonate-based shells and skeletons (US EPA 2016). It has been estimated that "ocean acidification is now happening at a faster rate than at any point in the last 66 million years, and possibly in the last 300 million years" (UCS 2019, p. 3). One of the most pronounced effects of changes in both temperature and acidity is on coral reefs which:

> are among the most biologically diverse and valuable ecosystems on earth. An estimated 25 percent of all marine life, including over 4,000 species of fish, are dependent on coral reefs at some point in their life. … Approximately half a billion people globally depend on coral reef ecosystems for food, coast protection and income from tourism and fisheries.
>
> (US EPA 2018, p. 3)

Since acidification can affect the functioning of all levels of the complex ocean ecosystem, there is also an accompanying and reinforcing ripple effect where even negative effects can be amplified through passage up the food chain (US EPA 2016, 2019). The threat of ocean acidification essentially precludes from consideration one of the major types of global geoengineering: solar radiation management, including injecting sulfate or seawater aerosols into the atmosphere or stratosphere, cloud brightening or seeding, and the placement of giant reflectors in orbit around the Earth. This approach to geoengineering, while decreasing incoming sunlight, can leave the current path of GHG emissions untouched, thereby exposing the oceans to further acidification. This topic is addressed further in Chapter 10.

Deforestation

Forests have played a central role in human history, providing wood for construction, heating, and cooking. Only recently has this commodity-oriented approach been reexamined and recognition been granted to the multifaceted contributions forests make to human welfare and ecosystem health. Described as the lungs of the world, forests provide a diverse and essential range of benefits, including (US Forest Service n.d., p. 1):

- **Provisioning services:** the goods or products people obtain from ecosystems, such as food, fresh water, timber, and fiber. These services are often directly used by humans and are typically goods included in our market economy.
- **Regulating services:** the benefits that come from an ecosystem's effect on natural processes, such as pollination of crops, storm damage mitigation, and climate stabilization.
- **Cultural services:** nonmaterial benefits people obtain from ecosystems, such as recreation, aesthetic and intellectual enjoyment, and spiritual renewal.
- **Supporting services:** the underlying ecosystem processes necessary to maintain and allow production of the previously mentioned services, such as nutrient cycling and soil formation.

Despite these essential contributions, the world continues to experience high rates of deforestation, especially in tropical and subtropical forests (*New York Times* March 31, 2021). In 2014, governments, companies, and civil society entered into a nonbinding political declaration endorsing a global timeline to cut natural forest loss in half by 2020 and strive to end it by 2030 (UN 2014). Despite this agreement, recent data suggest that there has been a 50 percent increase in deforestation of tropical woodlands since the 2014 declaration (Gustin 2021). The loss of forests can lead to cascading effects on ecosystem services across soils, freshwater, and ocean sediments and increase vector-based and zoonotic diseases (Ineson et al. 2021; Morand and Lajaunie 2021; MacDonald and Mordecai 2019; Van Grinsven et al. 2020; Conflict and Environment Observatory 2021). The reasons for deforestation are markedly diverse and include: conversion of land for agricultural purposes, use of wood as a traditional fuel for cooking and heating, forest removal in conflict and post-conflict areas, the use of used cooking oil as a biofuel feedstock in the European Union, and the removal of lumber, harvested both legally and illegally. A major report by UNEP and Interpol (2012, p. 6) concluded that:

> The vast majority of deforestation and illegal logging takes place in the tropical forests of the Amazon basin, Central Africa and Southeast Asia. Recent studies into the extent of illegal logging estimate that illegal logging accounts for 50–90 per cent of the volume of all forestry in key producer tropical countries and 15–30 per cent globally. Meanwhile, the economic value of global illegal logging, including processing, is estimated to be worth between US$ 30 and US$ 100 billion, or 10–30 per cent of global wood trade.

Major areas of continued deforestation include Southeast Asia, the Amazon region of Brazil, parts of Central America, and Russian Siberia (see, for example, Dummett and Blundell 2021; Davidson 2021). The Rainforest Action Network Norway (2021) reports that two-thirds of tropical rainforest has been destroyed or downgraded. Each region of deforestation has its own particular driver: Russia, Cambodia, and Laos to provide timber for China and other global markets, Indonesia and Malaysia to provide land for palm oil plantations, Central America to facilitate the transportation of illegal drugs to the United States (McSweeney et al. 2014; Sesnie et al. 2017), and Brazil to convert land for cattle grazing and soybean production (BBC News July 18, 2020; Trase 2019 and 2020; *Guardian* May 19, 2021). A recent report (Qin et al. 2021) on the state of the Brazilian Amazon, which accounts for almost 50 percent of global rainforests, has found that forest degradation has become the largest process driving carbon loss and "should become a high policy priority." Clearly one of the most important functions of forests is to act as a carbon sink, yet, in a recent research paper published in *Nature*, Gatti et al. (2021) concluded that Amazonia has recently been transformed into a net carbon source due to deforestation and climate change. Unfortunately, this is not the only critical forest region that has shifted its carbon profile. North America's boreal forests, including those in British Columbia, have also been transformed either directly or indirectly by climate change (Lamers et al. 2014; Zhao et al. 2021). In addition, UNESCO (2021) has reported that at least ten world heritage forests have been transformed into carbon emitters. Among other resulting challenges, this presents a major challenge for countries attempting to offset their carbon emissions with natural carbon sinks and increases pressure on them to accelerate the reduction of GHG emissions.

The World Resources Institute (2021) has reported that just seven commodities replaced an area of global forest twice the size of Germany over the period 2001–15. Thirty-six percent of forest lost to agriculture was due to cattle raising. In addition to deliberate removal of forest by logging or burning, there are several other threats to forest health and survival—from heat, drought, increased disease, and insect predation to the increased size, frequency, and intensity of natural forest fires. All of these phenomena are either directly or indirectly driven by climate change.

Chapter 5 describes in greater detail the ecological repercussions of the continuing deforestation in Southeast Asia for plantation-grown palm oil and the loss of Amazonian forests to ranching and farming.

In sum, the next five chapters of this book describe in detail the nature and extent of current and future threats to sustainability across several key areas of human activity, while the final chapters consider the range of potential solutions and their anticipated effectiveness. It is concluded that the challenges are immense and their successful resolution is by no means guaranteed.

References

Alley, Richard B. (2004) *Scientific American*, "Abrupt climate change," November.

Alley, Richard B. (2019) *Scientific American*, "Is Antarctica collapsing?" February.

AMAP-SWIPA (Arctic Monitoring and Assessment Program) (2017) *Snow, Water, Ice and Permafrost in the Arctic (SWIPA) 2017.*

Anthony, Katey M. Walter, et al. (2012) *Nature Geoscience*, "Geologic methane seeps along boundaries of Arctic permafrost thaw and melting glaciers," May 20.

Arctic Council (2021) *State of the Arctic Terrestrial Biodiversity Report*, May.

Aschwanden, Andy (2020) *Nature,* "The worst is yet to come for the Greenland ice sheet," October 1.

BAMS (*Bulletin of the American Meteorological Society*) (2018) "Explaining extreme events from a climate perspective," December.

Barnosky, Anthony D. et al. (2012) *Nature,* "Approaching a state shift in Earth's biosphere," June 7.

Bathiany, S. et al. (2018) *Scientific Reports,* "Abrupt climate change in an oscillating world," March 22.

BBC News (2019) "Faster pace of climate change is 'scary', former chief scientist says," September 16.

BBC News (2020) "Arctic Circle sees 'highest ever' recorded temperatures," June 22.

BBC News (2020) "Amazon soya and beef exports 'linked to deforestation'," July 18.

Blunden, Jessica, and Derek S. Arndt (eds.) (2019) *State of the Climate in 2018*, special supplement to the *Bulletin of the American Meteorological Society* 100 (9).

Bradshaw, J.A. et al. (2021) Frontiers in Conservation Science, "Underestimating the challenges of avoiding a ghastly future," January 13.

Carney, Mark (2021) *Values(s): Building a Better World for All*, New York: Public Affairs.

Ceballos, Gerardo et al. (2017) *PNAS,* "Biological annihilation via the ongoing sixth mass extinction signaled by vertebrate population losses and declines," July 10.

Ceballos, Gerardo et al. (2020) *PNAS,* "Vertebrates on the brink as indicators of biological annihilation and the sixth mass extinction," June 16.

Chadburn, S.E. et al. (2017) *Nature Climate Change,* "An observation-based constraint on permafrost loss as a function of global warming," May.

Cheng, Lijing et al. (2021) *Advances in Atmospheric Sciences,* "Upper ocean temperatures hit record high in 2020," January 13.

Colman, Ronald (2002) "Measuring genuine progress," in Peter N. Nemetz (ed.) *Bringing Business on Board: Sustainable Development and the B-School Curriculum,* Vancouver: JBA Press.

Colville, Robert (2017) *The Great Acceleration: How The World is Getting Faster, Faster,* London: Bloomsbury.

Conflict and Environment Observatory (2021) *Deforestation in Conflict Areas in 2020,* April.

Dasgupta, Partha (2021) *The Economics of Biodiversity: The Dasgupta Review,* February.

Davidson, Helen (2021) "From a forest in Papua New Guinea to a floor in Sydney: how China is getting rich off Pacific timber," Judith Nelson Institute for Journalism and Ideas, May 31.

DeConto, Robert M. et al. (2021) *Nature,* "The Paris Climate Agreement and future sea-level rise from Antarctica," May 5.

Deutz, A. et al. (2020) *Financing Nature: Closing the Global Biodiversity Financing Gap,* Nature Conservancy, September.

Diaz, Sandra et al. (2019) *Science,* "Pervasive human-driven decline of life on earth points to the need for transformative change," December 18.

Dickie, Gloria (2021) "The polar crucible," *Scientific American,* June.

Dorling, Danny (2020) Slowdown: *The End of the Great Acceleration—and Why It's Good for the Planet, the Economy, and Our Lives,* New Haven, CT: Yale University Press.

Dummett, Cassie and Arthur Blundell (2021) *Illicit Harvest, Complicit Goods: The State of Illegal Deforestation for Agriculture,* Forest Trends, May.

Etminan, M. et al. (2016) *Geophysical Research Letters,* "Radiative forcing of carbon dioxide, methane, and nitrous oxide: A significant revision of the methane radiative forcing," December 27.

European Commission (2018) Raw Materials Scoreboard, European Innovation Partnership on Raw Materials.

FAO (Food and Agriculture Organization of the United Nations) (2020) *The State of the World's Forests: Forests, Biodiversity and People.*

Farley, Heather M. and Zachery A. Smith (2014) *Sustainability: If It's Everything, Is It Nothing?* London: Routledge.

Fischetti, Mark (2019) "Divide or conquer," *Scientific American,* August.

Francis, Jennifer and Stephen J. Vavrus (2012) *Geophysical Research Letters*, "Evidence linking Arctic amplification to extreme weather in mid-latitudes," 39(6).

Francis, Jennifer A. (2018) "The Arctic is breaking climate records, altering weather worldwide," *Scientific American*, April 1.

Frank, Adam (2015) "Is a climate disaster inevitable?" *New York Times*, January 17.

Frank, Adam (2018) *Light of the Stars: Alien Worlds and the Fate of the Earth*, New York: W. W. Norton.

Frank, Adam and W.T. Sullivan (2016) *Astrobiology*, "A new empirical constraint on the prevalence of technological species in the universe," October 19.

Friedman, Thomas (2014) "Stampeding black elephants," *New York Times*, November 12.

Friedman, Thomas (2016) *Thank You for Being Late: An Optimist's Guide to Thriving in the Age of Accelerations*, Farrar, Straus and Giroux.

Garbe, Julius et al. (2020) *Nature*, "The hysteresis of the Antarctic Ice Sheet," September 23.

Gatti, Lucian V. et al. (2021) *Nature*, "Amazonia as a carbon source linked to deforestation and climate change," July 14.

Gilbert, E. and C. Kittel (2021) *Geophysical Research Letters*, "Surface melt and runoff on Antarctic ice shelves at 1.5C, 2C and 4C of future warming," April 8.

Gustin, Georgina (2021) *Inside Climate News*, "Trees fell faster in the years since companies and governments promised to stop cutting them down," May 19.

Gleick, James (2000) *Faster: The Acceleration of Just About Everything*, New York: Vintage.

Guardian (2021) "Food giants accused of links to illegal Amazon deforestation," May 19.

Hatfield-Dodds, Steve et al. (2017) *Journal of Cleaner Production*, "Assessing global resource use and greenhouse emissions to 2050, with ambitious resource efficiency and climate mitigation policies," 144: 403–14.

Hawking, Stephen (2018) *Brief Answers to the Big Questions*, New York: Bantam.

Herndon, Elizabeth M. (2018) *Nature Climate Change*, "Permafrost slowly exhales methane," April 8.

Holling, C.S. (1973) *Annual Review of Ecological Systems*, "Resilience and stability of ecological systems."

Holling, C.S. (1978) "Myths of ecological stability: Resilience and the problem of failure," in C. F. Smart and W.T. Stanbury (eds.) *Studies on Crisis Management*, Montreal: Institute for Research on Public Policy, 97–109.

Holling, C.S. (2005) *Adaptive Environmental Assessment and Management*, Caldwell, NJ: Blackburn Press.

Holling, C.S. and L. Gunderson (eds.) (2002) *Panarchy: Understanding Transformations in Human and Natural Systems*. Washington, DC: Island Press.

Holling, C.S. and Garry D. Peterson (2008) "Panarchies and discontinuities" in Craig R. Allen and C.S Holling (eds.) *Discontinuities in Ecosystems and Other Complex Systems*, New York: Columbia University Press.

Hooijer, A. and R. Vernimmen (2021) *Nature Communications*, "Global LiDAR land elevation data reveal greatest sea-level rise vulnerability in the tropics," June 29.

Hu, Siyu et al. (2020) *Geophysical Research Letters*, "Marine heatwaves in the Arctic region: Variation in different ice covers," August 6.

Hugonnet, Romain et al. (2021) *Nature*, "Accelerated global glacier mass loss in the early twenty-first century," April 28.

Ineson, Phillip et al. (2021) "Cascading effects of deforestation on ecosystem services across soils and freshwater and marine sediments: Ecosystem processes," ClimatePolicyWatcher.org, January 6.

IPBES (Intergovernmental Science-Policy Platform on Biodiversity and Ecosystem Services) (2018) "Worsening worldwide land degradation now 'critical', undermining well-being of 3.2 billion people," press release, March 27.

IPBES (Intergovernmental Science-Policy Platform on Biodiversity and Ecosystem Services) (2019) "Nature's dangerous decline 'unprecedented': Species extinction rates 'accelerating'," press release, May 7.

IPCC (Intergovernmental Panel on Climate Change) (2014) *Climate Change 2014: Synthesis Report. Contribution of Working Groups I, II and III to the Fifth Assessment Report of the Intergovernmental Panel on Climate Change*, R.K. Pachauri and L.A. Meyer (eds.), IPCC, Geneva, Switzerland.

IPCC (Intergovernmental Panel on Climate Change) (2014) *Fifth Assessment Report*, AR5 Reports.

IPCC (Intergovernmental Panel on Climate Change) (2018) "Summary for policymakers of IPCC Special Report on Global Warming of 1.5°C approved by governments."

IPCC (Intergovernmental Panel on Climate Change) (2019) "Summary for policymakers," in H.-O. Pörtner et al. (eds.) *IPCC Special Report on the Ocean and Cryosphere in a Changing Climate.*

IPCC (Intergovernmental Panel on Climate Change) (2021) "Climate change widespread, rapid and intensifying—IPCC," press release, August 9.

IPCC (Intergovernmental Panel on Climate Change) (2021a) "Headline statements from the Summary for Policymakers," Sixth Assessment Report, August 9.

IPCC (Intergovernmental Panel on Climate Change) (2021b) *Climate Change 2021, The Physical Science Basis, Summary for Policymakers*, Sixth Assessment Report, August 9.

Jansen, Eystein et al. (2020) *Nature Climate Change* "Past perspectives on the present era of abrupt Arctic climate change," August, 714–21.

Jeong, Su-Jeong et al. (2018) *Science Advances*, "Accelerating rates of Arctic carbon cycling revealed by long-term atmospheric CO_2 measurements," July 18.

King, Michalea D. et al. (2020) *Communications Earth & Environment*, "Dynamic ice loss from the Greenland Ice Sheet driven by sustained glacier retreat," August 13.

Kolbert, Elizabeth (2014) *The Sixth Extinction: An Unnatural History*, New York: Henry Holt & Company.

Lai, Ching-Yao et al. (2020) *Nature*, "Vulnerability of Antarctica's ice shelves to melt-driven fracture," August 26.

Lamers, Patrick et al. (2014) *Global Change Biology: Bioenergy*, "Damaged forests provide an opportunity to mitigate climate change," January.

Landrum, Laura and Marika M. Holland (2020) *Nature Climate Change*, "Extremes become routine in an emerging new Arctic," September 14.

Lenton, Timothy Y. et al. (2008) *PNAS*, "Tipping elements in the Earth's climate system," February 12.

MacDonald, Andrew J. and Erin Mordecai (2019) *PNAS*, "Amazon deforestation drives malaria transmission, and malaria burden reduces forest clearing," October 29.

Maddison Historical References (n.d.) www.ggdc.net/maddison.

Managi, Shunsuke and Pushpam Kumar (eds.) (2018) *Inclusive Wealth Report 2018: Measuring Progress Towards Sustainability*, Routledge.

Martens, Jannik et al. (2020) *Science Advances*, "Remobilization of dormant carbon from Siberian-Arctic permafrost during the three past warming events," October 16.

McNeill, J.R. and Peter Engelke (2016) *The Great Acceleration: An Environmental History of the Anthropocene since 1945*, Cambridge, MA: Belknap Press.

McSweeney, Kendra et al. (2014) *Science*, "Drug policy as conservation policy: Narco-deforestation," January 31.

Morand, Serge and Claire Lajaunie (2021) *Frontiers in Veterinary Science*, "Outbreaks of vector-borne diseases are associated with changes in forest cover and oil palm expansion at global scale," March 24.

NAS (National Academy of Sciences) (2016) *Attribution of Extreme Weather Events in the Context of Climate Change.*

NASA (2018) "Ramp-up in Antarctic ice loss speeds sea level rise," June 13.

Natali, Susan M. et al. (2019) *Nature Climate Change*, "Large loss of CO_2 in winter observed across the northern permafrost region," October 21.

Nemetz, Peter N. (2015) "Reconstructing the sustainability narrative: Separating myth from reality," in Helen Kopnina and Eleanor Shoreman-Ouimet (eds.) *Sustainability: Key Issues*, Abingdon; New York: Routledge.

Nerem, R.S. et al. (2018) *PNAS*, "Climate-change-driven accelerated sea-level rise detected in the altimeter era," February 27.

New York Times (2021) "Tropical forest destruction accelerated in 2020," March 31.

Nisbet, E.G. et al. (2019) *Global Biochemical Cycles*, "Very strong atmospheric methane growth in the 4 years 2014–2017: Implications for the Paris Agreement," March 18.

NOAA (National Oceanic and Atmospheric Administration) (2018) "Executive summary" in *Arctic Report Card: Effects of Persistent Artic Warming Continue to Mount*.

NOAA (National Oceanic and Atmospheric Administration) (2019a) ESRL Global Monitoring Division: Global Greenhouse Gas Reference Network, February.

NOAA (National Oceanic and Atmospheric Administration) (2019b) *Global Climate Report: State of the Climate,* National Centers for Environmental Information, January.

Pan, Linda et al. (2021) *Science Advances*, "Rapid postglacial rebound amplifies global sea level rise following West Antarctic Ice Sheet collapse," April 30.

Patel, Jugal K. and Henry Fountain (2021) "The Muldrow Glacier in Alaska is moving 100 times faster than normal," New York Times, April 13.

Piel, Gerard (1972) *The Acceleration of History*, New York: Knopf.

Pistone, Kristina et al. (2014) *PNAS*, "Observational determination of albedo decrease caused by vanishing Arctic sea ice," March 4.

Plumptre, Andre J. et al. (2021) *Frontiers in Forests and Global Change*, "Where might we find ecologically intact communities?" April.

Previdi, Michael et al. (2020) *Geophysical Research Letters*, "Arctic amplification: A rapid response to radiative forcing," September.

Qin, Yuanwei et al. (2021) *Nature Climate Change*, "Carbon loss from forest degradation exceeds that from deforestation in the Brazilian Amazon," April 29.

Rainforest Action Network Norway (2021) *Banking on Climate Chaos: Fossil Fuel Finance Report*.

Rosenberg, Kenneth V. et al. (2019) *Science*, "Decline of the North American avifauna," October 4.

RSPB (Royal Society for the Protection of Birds) (2020) *The State of the UK's Birds*.

Sagan, Carl (1963) *Planetary and Space Science,* "Direct contact among galactic civilizations by relativistic interstellar spaceflight," May.

Sanchez-Bayo, Francisco and Kris. A.G. Wyckhuys (2019) *Biological Conservation* "Worldwide decline of the entomofauna: A review of its drivers," April.

Sesnie, Steven E. et al. (2017) *Environmental Research Letters*, "A spatio-temporal analysis of forest loss related to cocaine trafficking in Central America," May 16.

Smil, Vaclav (2017) *Energy Transitions: Global and National Perspectives*, Santa Barbara, CA: Praeger.

Smithsonian.com (2019) "Carbon dioxide levels reach highest point in human history," May 15.

Steffen, Will et al. (2015a) *Anthropocene Review*, "The trajectory of the Anthropocene: The great acceleration," January 16.

Steffen, Will et al. (2015b) *Science*, "Planetary boundaries," February 13.

Steffen Will et al. (2018) *PNAS,* "Trajectories of the Earth system in the Anthropocene," August 14.

Struzik, Edward (2015) *Future Arctic: Field Notes from a World on the Edge*. London: Island Press.

Swiss Re (2020) *Biodiversity and Ecosystem Services: A Business Case for Re/insurance*.

Taleb, Nasim Nicholas (2010) *The Black Swan: The Impact of the Highly Improbable*, London: Random House.

Trase (2019) *Decoupling China's Soy Imports from Deforestation Driven Carbon Emissions in Brazil*, December.

Trase (2020) "China's exposure to environmental risks from Brazilian beef imports," June.

Turetsky, Merritt R. et al. (2020) *Nature Geoscience*, "Carbon release through abrupt permafrost thaw," February.

UCS (Union of Concerned Scientists) (2019) "CO2 and ocean acidification: causes, impacts, solutions," February 6.

UN (United Nations) (2014) *Global Biodiversity Outlook 4.*

UN (United Nations) (2019) "Sustainable Development Goals," press release, May 6.

UNEP (United Nations Environment Programme) et al. (2019) *Global Linkages: A Graphic Look at the Changing Arctic.* UN Environment and GRID-Arendal.

UNEP (United Nations Environment Programme) and Interpol (2012) *Green Carbon, Black Trade: Illegal Logging, Tax Fraud and Laundering in the World's Tropical Forests; A Rapid Response Assessment.*

UNESCO (United Nations Educational, Scientific and Cultural Organization) (2005) *The Precautionary Principle.*

UNESCO (United Nations Educational, Scientific and Cultural Organization) (2021) *World Heritage Forests: Carbon Sinks under Pressure.*

US CCSP (Climate Change Science Program) (2008) *Abrupt Climate Change.* US Climate Change Science Program and the Subcommittee on Global Change Research.

US CCSP (Climate Change Science Program) (2009a) *The Effect of Climate Change on Agriculture Land Resources, Water Resources, and Biodiversity in the United States.*

US CCSP (Climate Change Science Program) (2009b) *Thresholds of Climate Change in Ecosystems.*

US EPA (Environmental Protection Agency) (2016) "Effects of ocean and coastal acidification on marine life," December 21.

US EPA (Environmental Protection Agency) (2018) "Basic information about coral reefs." www.epa.gov/coral-reefs/basic-information-about-coral-reefs.

US EPA (Environmental Protection Agency) (2019) "Effects of ocean and coastal acidification on ecosystems," October 4.

US EPA (Environmental Protection Agency) (2021) "Climate change indicators"

US Forest Service (n.d.) "Key ecosystem services provided by forests," Fact Sheet 5.10.

Van Grinsven, Anouk et al. (2020) *Used Cooking Oil (UCO) as Biofuel Feedstock in the EU*, CE Delft for Transport & Environment, December.

Wagner, Gernot and Martin L. Weitzman (2015) *Climate Shock: The Economic Consequences of a Hotter Planet*, Princeton, NJ; Woodstock: Princeton University Press.

Wang, Taihua et al. (2020) *Science Advances*, "Permafrost thawing puts the frozen carbon at risk on the Tibetan Plateau," May 6.

Washington Post (2018) "Red-hot planet: All-time heat records have been set all over the world during the past week," July 5.

Washington Post (2019) "It was 84 degrees near the Arctic Ocean this weekend as carbon dioxide hit its highest level in human history," May 14.

Washington Post (2019a) "Alaska heat wave: Parts of state face hottest weather ever recorded," July 3.

Washington Post (2019b) "A giant heat dome over Alaska is set to threaten all-time temperature records," July 3.

WCED (World Commission on Environment and Development) (1987) *Our Common Future.*

WEF (World Economic Forum) (2019) *The Global Risks Report 2019: 14th Edition.*

Wilkinson, S.L. et al. (2020) *Environmental Research Letters*, "Shallow peat is most vulnerable to high peat burn severity during wildfire," September 22.

Williams, David R. et al. (2020) *Nature Sustainability* "Proactive conservation to prevent habitat losses to agricultural expansion," December 21.

Wilson, Edward O. (2016) *Half-Earth: Our Planet Fights for Life*, New York: Liveright Publishing.

WMO (World Meteorological Organization) (2018) *WMO statement on the State of the Global Climate in 2018.*

WMO (World Meteorological Organization) (2019a) *Climate Statement 2018.*

WMO (World Meteorological Organization) (2019b) *The Global Climate in 2015–(2019.*

WMO (World Meteorological Organization) (2021) *State of the Global Climate 2020.*

WMO (World Meteorological Organization) (2021a) *State of Climate in 2021: Extreme Events and Major Impacts.*

WMO (World Meteorological Organization) (2021b) *Decadal Climate Update.*

World Resources Institute (2021) "Deforestation linked to 7 agricultural commodities."

WWF (World Wildlife Fund) (2020) *Living Planet Report 2020: Bending the Curve of Biodiversity Loss,* R.E.A. Almond, M. Grooten, and T. Petersen (eds).

WWF (World Wildlife Fund) (2021) *Feeling the Heat: The Fate of Nature Beyond 1.5°C of Global Warming.*

Yamaguchi, Rintaro et al. (2019) *Letters in Spatial and Resource Sciences,* "Inclusive wealth in the twenty-first century: A summary and further discussion of *Inclusive Wealth Report 2018,*" May 7.

Zhang, Rudong et al. (2019) *PNAS,* "Unraveling driving forces explaining significant reduction in satellite-inferred Arctic surface albedo since the 1980s," November 11.

Zhao, Bailu et al. (2021) *Scientific Reports,* "Northern American boreal forests are a large carbon source due to wildfires from 1986 to 2016," April 8.

Appendix: Recent ecological surprises

News reports

New Scientist (2011) "Warmer oceans release CO2 faster than thought," April 25.

Guardian (2014) "Australia's heat wave frequency tops projections for 2030," February 18.

Science News (2014) "Fertilizer produces far more greenhouse gas than expected," June 9.

New York Times (2017) "More permafrost than thought may be lost as planet warms," April 13.

US NOAA (National Oceanic and Atmospheric Administration) (2017) "Alaskan North Slope climate just outran one of our tools to measure it," December 6.

Guardian (2018) "Microplastic pollution in oceans is far worse than feared, say scientists," March 12.

AOL Weather (2018) "Drastic Arctic warm event stuns scientists, as record-breaking temperatures reach the North Pole," April 5.

Voice of America (2018) "UN: World temperatures rising faster than predicted," April 5.

BBC (2018) "Scientists shocked by mysterious deaths of ancient trees," June 11.

CBC (2018) "3 trillion tons of Antarctic ice lost since 1992, seas rising, study suggests," June 13.

New York Times (2018) "Antarctica is melting three times as fast as a decade ago," June 14.

New York Times (2018) "Report finds industrial chemicals more toxic than thought," June 20.

New York Times (2018) "Federal study: Chemicals toxic at levels EPA thought safe," June 21.

UNSW Sydney (2018) "Global warming may be twice what climate models predict," July 5.

New York Times (2018) "Taking the oceans' temperature, scientists find unexpected heat," November 1.

New York Times (2018) "Greenhouse gas emissions accelerate like a 'speeding freight train' in 2018," December 5.

New York Times (2019) "Ocean warming is accelerating faster than thought, new research finds," January 10.

GRIST (2019) "Ocean temps rising faster than scientists thought," January 11.

CBC (2019) "Expect more extreme hurricanes on the East Coast due to faster ice melts in Greenland, study says," January 21.

New York Times (2019) "Greenland's melting ice nears a 'tipping point' scientists say," January 21.

Guardian (2019) "Cavity two-thirds the size of Manhattan discovered under Antarctic glacier," February 6.

New York Times (2019) "The plague killing frogs everywhere is far worse than scientists thought," March 28.

Science (2019) "Earlier springtime disrupts insect and bird lives—and it's worse than expected," April 1.

CBC (2019) "Global warming is shrinking glaciers faster than thought," April 8.

CBC (2019) "Permafrost is thawing in the Arctic so fast that scientists are losing their equipment," May 2.

BBC (2019) "Climate change: Global sea level rise could be bigger than expected," May 20.

New York Times (2019) " 'Earthworm dilemma' has climate scientists racing to keep up," May 20.

Guardian (2019) "Latest data shows steep rises in CO2 for seventh year," June 4.

Guardian (2019) " 'Frightening' number of plant extinctions found in global survey," June 11.

Guardian (2019) "Energy industry's carbon emissions rise at fastest rate in nearly a decade," June 11.

Weather.com (2019) "Arctic permafrost melting 70 years sooner than expected, study finds," June 14.

Reuters (2019) "Scientists shocked by Arctic permafrost thawing 70 years sooner than predicted," June 18 (updated June 24).

Guardian (2019) " 'Precipitous' fall in Antarctic sea ice since 2014 revealed," July 2.

Science (2019) "Major U.S. cities are leaking methane at twice the rate previously believed," July 19.

HuffPost (2019) "Greenland loses staggering amount of ice in July heat wave," August 2.

Scientific American (2019) "Scientists have been underestimating the pace of climate change," August 19.

HuffPost (2019) "Scientist astonished after finding microplastics in Arctic snow," August 19.

Stanford News (2019) "Stanford researchers use vintage film to show Thwaites Glacier ice shelf in Antarctica melting faster than previously observed," September 2.

BBC News (2019) "Climate change: Extreme weather events are happening sooner than expected," September 16.

Climate Central (2019) "Report: Flooded future; Global vulnerability to sea level rise worse than previously understood," October 29.

New York Times (2019) "A methane leak, seen from space, proves to be far larger than thought," December 16.

CBC News (2020) "Greenhouse gas 12,000 times worse than CO2 shows surprise rise in the atmosphere," January 21.

Guardian (2020) "Sea levels could rise more than a metre by 2100, experts," May 8.

CNN (2020) "Greenland's glaciers could lose more ice than previously thought, raising concerns for sea level rise," November 17.

Guardian (2021) "Sea level rise could be worse than feared, warn researchers," February 2.

Washington Post (2021) "We're underestimating the destructive power of tornadoes, study shows," March 22.

Guardian (2021) "One of Earth's giant carbon sinks may have been overestimated—study," March 24.

Guardian (2021) "Antarctic 'doomsday glacier' may be melting faster than was thought," April 30.

CNN (2021) "Sea levels may rise much faster than previously predicted, swamping coastal cities such as Shanghai, study finds," May 21.

Daily Mail (2021) "Antarctica's Pine Island glacier could collapse within 20 years, study warns," June 16.

Guardian (2021) "Climate crisis: Dangerous thresholds to hit sooner than feared, UN report says," June 23.

CNN (2021) "Scientists are worried by how fast the climate crisis has amplified extreme weather," July 20.

Washington Post (2021) "Siberia's 'methane bomb' may be worse than scientists thought," August 2.

CNN (2021) "Earth is warming faster than previously thought, scientists say, and the window is closing to avoid catastrophic outcomes," August 9.

Scientific references

Stroeve, Julienne et al. (2007) *Geophysical Research Letters*, "Arctic sea ice decline: Faster than forecast," May 1.

Lubbers, Ingrid M. et al. (2013) *Nature Climate Change*, "Greenhouse gas emissions from soils increased by earthworms," March.

Shcherbak, Iurii, et al. (2014) *PNAS*, "Global metaanalysis of the nonlinear response of soil nitrous oxide (N_2O) emissions to fertilizer nitrogen," June 9.

Lubbers, Ingrid M. et al. (2015) *Scientific Reports*, "Reduced greenhouse gas mitigation potential of no-tillage soils through earthwork activity," September 4.

Phoenix, Gareth K. and Jarle W. Bjerke (2016) *Global Change Biology* "Arctic browning: Extreme events and trends reversing Arctic greening," September.

Arneth A. et al. (2017) *Nature Geoscience* "Historical carbon dioxide emissions caused by land-use changes are possibly larger than assumed," January 30.

Ceballos, Gerardo et al. (2017) *PNAS*, "Biological annihilation via the ongoing sixth mass extinction signalled by vertebrate population losses and declines," July 10.

Lara, Mark J. et al (2018) *Scientific Reports*, "Reduced arctic tundra productivity linked with landform and climate change interaction," February 5.

Scientific American (2018) "The Arctic is breaking climate records, altering weather worldwide," April 1.

Hurley, Rachel et al. (2018) *Nature Geoscience*, "Microplastic contamination of river beds significantly reduced by catchment-wide flooding," April 1.

Shepherd, Andrew et al. (2018) *Nature*, "Mass balance of the Antarctic Ice Sheet from 1992 to 2017," June 14.

Fischer, Hubertus et al. (2018) *Nature Geoscience,* "Paleoclimate constraints on the impact of 2 degrees C anthropogenic warming and beyond," July.

Scientific American (2018) "New climate report was too cautious, some scientists say," October 11.

Resplendy, L. et al. (2018) *Nature*, "Quantification of ocean heat uptake from changes in atmospheric O_2 and CO_2 composition," November 1.

Trusel, Luke D. et al. (2018) *Nature*, "Nonlinear rise in Greenland runoff in response to post-industrial Arctic warming," December 5.

Science (2018) "Discovery of recent Antarctic ice sheet collapse raises fears of a new global flood," December 18.

Bevis, Michael et al. (2019) *PNAS*, "Accelerating changes in ice mass within Greenland, and the ice sheet's sensitivity to atmospheric forcing," January.

Rignot, Eric et al. (2019) *PNAS*, "Four decades of Antarctic ice sheet mass balance from 1979–2017," January.

Cheng, Lijing et al. (2019) *Science*, "How fast are the oceans warming?" January 11.

Science (2019) "East Antarctica's ice is melting at an unexpectedly rapid clip, new study suggests," January 14.

Milillo, P. et al. (2019) *Science Advances*, "Heterogeneous retreat and ice melt of Thwaites Glacier, West Antarctica," January 30.

Alley, Richard, (2019) "Is Antarctica collapsing?" *Scientific American*, February.

Scheele, Ben C. et al. (2019) *Science*, "Amphibian fungal panzootic causes catastrophic and ongoing loss of biodiversity," March 1.

Greenberg, Dan A. and Wendy J. Palen, (2019) *Science*, "A deadly amphibian disease goes global," March 29.

Zemp, M. et al. (2019) *Nature*, "Global glacier mass changes and their contributions to sea-level rise from 1961 to 2016," April 8.

Voosen, Paul (2019) *Science*, "New climate models forecast a warming surge," April 19.

Turetsky, Merritt R. (2019) *Nature*, "Permafrost collapse is accelerating carbon release," May 2.

Bamber, Jonathan L. et al. (2019) *PNAS*, "Ice sheet contributions to future sea-level rise from structured expert judgment," May 20.

Voosen, Paul (2019) *Science*, "A 500-million-year survey of Earth's climate reveals dire warning for humanity," May 22.

Bell, James R. et al. (2019) *Global Change Biology*, "Spatial and habitat variation in aphid, butterfly, moth and bird phenologies over the last half century," June.

Bamber, Jonathan L. et al. (2019) *PNAS*, "Ice sheet contribution to sea level rise from structured expert judgement," June 4.

Farquharson, Louise M. et al. (2019) *Geophysical Research Letters*, "Climate change drives widespread and rapid thermokarst development in very cold permafrost in the Canadian high arctic," June 10.

Parkinson, Claire L. (2019) *PNAS*, "A 40-y record reveals gradual Antarctic sea ice increases followed by decreases at rates far exceeding the rates seen in the Arctic," July 1.

Plant, Genevieve et al. (2019) *Geophysical Research Letters*, "Large fugitive methane emissions from urban centers along the U.S. East coast," July 15.

Sutherland, D.A. et al. (2019) *Science*, "Direct observations of subsurface melt and subsurface geometry at a tidewater glacier," July 26.

Preshing, Andrew J. et al., (2019) *PNAS*, "Challenges to natural and human communities from surprising ocean temperatures," September 10.

Kulp, Scott A. and Benjamin H. Strauss (2019) *Nature Communications*, "New elevation data triple estimates of global vulnerability to sea-level rise and coastal flooding," October 29.

Stanley, K.M. et al. (2020) *Nature Communications*, "Increase in global emissions of HFC-23 despite near-total expected reductions," January 21.

Ceballos, Gerardo et al. (2020) *PNAS*, "Vertebrates on the brink as indicators of biological annihilation and the sixth mass extinction," June 16.

Jansen, Eystein et al. (2020) *Nature Climate Change*, "Past perspectives on the present era of abrupt Arctic climate change," August.

Wu, Wenbo et al. (2020) *Science*, "Seismic ocean thermometry," September 16.

Khan, Shfaqat et al. (2020) *Nature Communications*, "Centennial response of Greenland's three largest outlet glaciers," November 17.

Bradshaw, Corey J.A. et al. (2021) *Frontiers in Conservation Science*, "Underestimating the challenges of avoiding a ghastly future," January 13.

Grinsted, Aslak and Jens Hesselbjerg Christensen (2021) *Ocean Science*, "The transient sensitivity of sea level rise," February 2.

Wurman, Joshua et al. (2021) *PNAS*, "Supercell tornadoes are much stronger and wider than damage-based ratings indicate," April 6.

Wahlin, A.K. et al (2021) *Science Advances*, "Pathways and modification of warm water flowing beneath Thwaites Ice Shelf, West Antarctica," April 9.

Joughin, Ian et al. (2021) *Science Advances*, "Ice-shelf retreat drives recent Pine Island glacier speedup," June 11.

Schweiger, Axel J. et al. (2021) *Communications Earth & Environment*, "Accelerated sea ice loss in the Wandel Sea points to a change in the Arctic's last ice area," July 1.

Science (2021) "Europe's deadly floods leave scientists stunned," July 20.

IPCC Sixth Assessment Report, *Climate Change 2021, The Physical Science Basis, Summary for Policymakers,* August 9.

McCrystall, Michelle R. et al. (2021) *Nature Communications*, "New climate models reveal faster and larger increases in Arctic precipitation than previously projected," November.

2 The economics–ecology nexus

A rudimentary understanding of basic economics and ecologic principles, at the least, is essential to interpreting and understanding what is happening to our planet today. A key pillar of ecology is systems theory. This theory is an inherent part of sustainability within and across each of its three major pillars (ecology, economics and society), and was originally articulated in a business context by Elkington (1998) as the *triple bottom line*. The study of systems theory within ecology itself has enhanced and informed analysis within the spheres of economics and society by illustrating how principles which illuminate the understanding of one discipline have cross-disciplinary relevance.

Stability, resilience, nonlinearities, thresholds, and tipping points

One of the founders of ecological theory, C.S. Holling, was instrumental in elucidating concepts that have played a pivotal role in our modern understanding of the functioning of ecological systems and how they are influenced by anthropogenic behavior. Among the concepts developed by Holling are principles of stability and resilience, nonlinearities, irreversibilities, thresholds, and tipping points. (See also US CCSP 2009; Schneider 2003 for general principles; and Robel et al. 2019 for a specific example of potential irreversibility of glacial melting in Antarctica).

Stable systems are systems not easily disturbed by shocks from their current state or path. In contrast, *resilient systems* are those which, if disturbed by shocks, tend to return to their previous state or path. Figure 2.1 presents one of Holling's classic representations of types of ecological systems (Holling 1973). In this model, there is a central domain of attraction (demarcated by the shaded area within the dashed line) where disturbances of sufficiently small magnitude move the system only temporarily away from the point of equilibrium. The system has a certain amount of resilience. However, with a sufficiently large shock, the system passes a threshold and jumps from one equilibrium state to another (i.e. there is a nonlinear response). The crucial point is that this second state may be less desirable from a human perspective than the first.

The measurement of resilience presents an interesting challenge, but Arani et al. (2021) have developed a mathematical model using "exit time" as a measure of ecological resilience. To quote the authors:

> We propose to use "life expectancy" as a measure of resilience, which can be formalized as the mean exit time from an attraction basin (i.e., the expected time required to cross the border of the basin). This approach has the advantage of taking

DOI: 10.4324/9781003199540-3

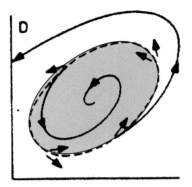

Figure 2.1 Holling's domain of attraction.
Source: Holling 1973.

the natural variability of real complex systems explicitly into account. If we have many observations of shifts, we can calculate the mean exit time simply as the average time the system spends in each given state. However, such data are rare. Moreover, the permanent fluctuations also contain information about the system, which would be lost if one considers only the rare occasions at which a shift occurs. In the approach we outline, this information is used as we infer the deterministic and stochastic components of the underlying dynamical system from observed fluctuations. Applying techniques from statistical mechanics, we show how one can subsequently use the reconstructed empirical model to compute the expected mean exit time for each basin of attraction.

(p. 1168)

A simple example of a nonlinear response is the phase change when water freezes/thaws or boils/condenses. The critical question is whether such a sudden change at the threshold is reversible over some relevant time period. In the case of water the answer is clearly yes. Water/ice and water/steam change back and forth easily with modest changes in temperature.

An equally relevant question is posed by transformations associated with global warming, such as possible changes in sea level. Figure 2.2 portrays the effect of two possible drivers of sea-level rise: (1) a steady expansion in volume due to warming, and (2) a possible sudden increase in sea level driven by catastrophic loss of land-based Antarctic or Greenland ice sheets. In this figure, L = sea level, and T = global temperature. The critical question is again one of reversibility and, in this case, the answer is different. The figure contrasts the potentially rapid sea-level rise accompanying global warming with the slow reversal of this trend should there be a subsequent cooling trend. The point of inflection is often referred to as a tipping point which, in layperson's terms, represents a sudden, non-linear, and usually unfavorable, change, one that is not reversible in the short to medium term. One of the critical questions facing climate science today is the exact timing of potential tipping points and whether there is enough time to forestall the potentially devastating results (NAS 2013).

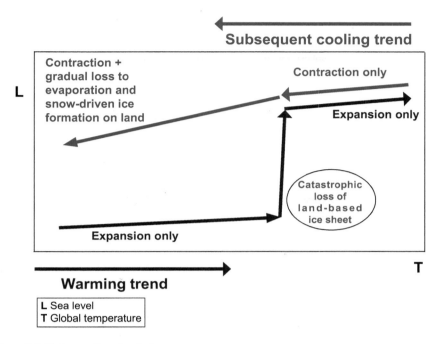

Figure 2.2 Drivers of sea-level rise.

Feedback loops are critical contributors to nonlinear system dynamics, and they can be either negative or positive. An archetypal example of a negative feedback system is the homeostatic system which regulates body temperature. There is a natural tendency to return to the equilibrium temperature of 98.6 degrees Fahrenheit (°F; or 37 degrees Celsius [°C]) after any deviation—as long as this deviation is not too large (i.e. the temperature does not fall outside the domain of attraction which brings it back to normality).

In contrast, a positive feedback system can occur when a shock sets up a process where the system continues to move further away from the point of equilibrium, frequently at an increasing velocity (i.e. the response is nonlinear). Figure 2.3 presents a graphical representation of several major positive feedback loops. Recent examples related to greenhouse gases (GHGs) include melting Arctic ice and permafrost (Francis 2018; Chadburn et al. 2017; Farquharson et al. 2019). Most recently, it has been posited that tropical wetlands may also represent a positive feedback source of GHG in the form of methane (Nisbet et al. 2019). In the case of Arctic ice, increasing global temperature reduces ice cover on the Arctic Ocean, thereby reducing its albedo (i.e. its capacity to reflect sunlight). As a consequence, the ocean absorbs more heat and the melting of sea ice is accelerated. This process is self-reinforcing and nonlinear. Pistone et al. (2019, p. 7474) have concluded that "additional heating due to complete Arctic sea ice loss would hasten global warming by an estimated 25 years." Economic estimates of the costs of the nonlinear decline in Arctic sea ice and permafrost run as high as \$66.9–\$90 trillion dollars (Yumashev et al. 2019). Some other examples of nonlinear processes include the effects of nitrogen fertilizer (Shcherbak et al. 2014), Greenland runoff in

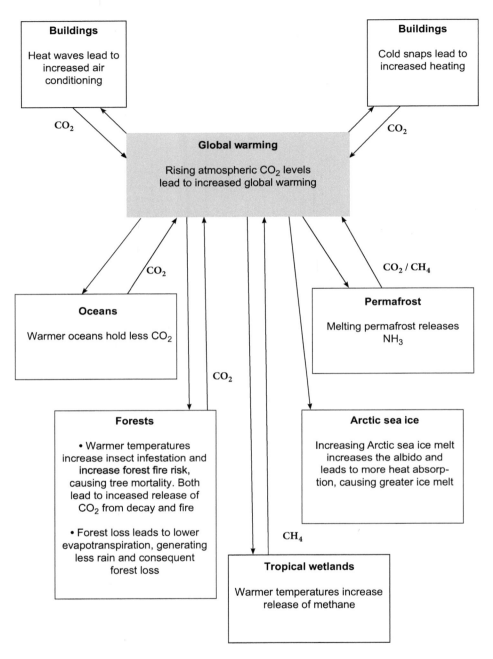

Figure 2.3 Some major positive feedback loops.

response to Arctic warming (Trusel et al. 2018), and melting of the Thwaites Glacier in West Antarctica (Milillo et al. 2019).

A similar mechanism is posited to exist in Siberia and other Arctic regions with large areas of permafrost covering peat bogs (Ise et al. 2008; Swindles et al. 2015; *New York Times* April 13, 2017; MacFarquhar and Ducke 2019). The concern is that global warming will melt the permafrost, releasing large quantities of entrained methane, which is twenty times more powerful than carbon dioxide as a GHG. Research has suggested the existence of potentially massive methane reservoirs beneath Antarctica which, if released by global warming, could also lead to a strong positive feedback loop on climate change (Wadham et al. 2012). These scenarios are still the subject of ongoing scientific debate, but have non-zero probability; this includes potentially catastrophic events which could lead to a rapid and uncontrolled rise in global temperature, threatening many vulnerable parts of the world. Because of its importance, the study of future sea-level rise has received significant scientific attention and much remains to be learned. Two forestry-related feedback loops have been included in Figure 2.3. The first entails the effect of warmer temperatures on insect infestation and forest fire risk, leading to tree mortality. The net result is the release of CO_2 from decay and fire.

The second potential feedback loop is based on the fact that agricultural intensification and forests can effectively create their own rain through the process of evapotranspiration. It has been posited that the loss of forest cover due to a multitude of causes can lead to less rainfall which, in turn, can cause increased forest mortality (see, for example, Cox et al. 2000; Stickler et al. 2013; Balch et al. 2015; Aragao et al. 2008). In the worst-case scenario, referred to as "forest dieback," this positive feedback loop can lead to total forest loss (*New York Times* August 30 2019).

While the positive feedback loops described above entail purely ecological feedbacks, the chief economist of British Petroleum (BP), Spencer Dale (2019), has described a feedback loop which directly involves human response to more extreme weather associated with global warming. Specifically, he raises "the possibility of a worrying vicious cycle: increasing levels of carbon leading to more extreme weather patterns, which in turn trigger stronger growth in energy (and carbon emissions) as households and businesses seek to offset their effects" (p. 10). In essence, increases in the number and degree of heat waves would elicit a great use of energy-intensive air conditioning and, conversely, more frequent instances of extreme cold snaps would involve greater use of energy for heating. With respect to heating, the extensive use of air conditioning in the developed world, most particularly the United States, is now being replicated in such major developing countries such as China and India (IEA 2018, 2019). In its analysis (2018), the International Energy Agency (IEA) predicts that the number of air conditioning units globally will rise from 1.6 billion units today to 5.6 billion by 2050, representing a growth in demand from 6,200 gigawatts (GW) in 2016 to 23,000 GW in 2050 (pp. 59–60).

Recent research has suggested the existence of a *negative* feedback loop that may slow down, but not stop, the loss of ice from Antarctica (Larour et al. 2019). A cautionary note is provided, however, in an accompanying commentary (Steig 2019, p. 937) to the research in the journal *Science*:

> For those concerned about potentially catastrophic sea-level rise, the results of Larour *et al.* might be taken as welcome news. But it is important to recognize that Larour *et al.* do not make a specific prediction. There are too many unknowns about the topography of the glacier bed at the finest spatial scales, the process of glacier calving,

and how winds and ocean currents will change. Rather, the results should serve as a guide to the magnitude and sign of the uncertainty in existing predictions, and as a road map for future research. Accounting for solid-Earth feedbacks suggests that although the greatest effects may be delayed by a few decades, Antarctic ice sheet retreat remains virtually certain.

Recent studies of possible ecological tipping points (abrupt shifts between alternative ecological regimes) include a broad range of examples from across the globe. These include the Amazon rainforest, the Greenland ice sheet, the ozone hole, the Antarctic circumpolar current, the Sahara desert, the Tibetan plateau, the Asian monsoon, methane clathrates, ocean acidity levels, El Niño, Antarctic ice sheets and shelves, salinity valves, and the North Atlantic "conveyor" current (Broecker and Kunzig 2008; WWF and Allianz 2009; Kopp et al. 2016, *Economist* August 1, 2019; Staal et al. 2020; Landrum and Holland 2020; Jansen et al. 2020; Joughin et al. 2021). While many of these examples remain the subject of speculation with an indeterminate timeframe, several local or regional ecological tipping phenomena have already been identified. Some of these concern rapid loss of forests in Alaska, the southwest United States, and British Columbia (Kurz et al. 2008; Natural Resources Canada 2018; Alaska Department of Natural Resources 2019) due to predation by massive insect outbreaks attributed to the effects of global warming. A well-documented case of a significant phase shift associated with a tipping point concerns coral reefs in the Caribbean. Hughes (1994) documents how overfishing, inter alia, led to a virtually total collapse of reefs near Jamaica and the emergence of an altered ecosystem dominated by fleshy macroalgae. This dramatic change has major impacts on ecotourism and other revenue streams associated with healthy coral reef–based ecosystems (see also Pandolfi et al. 2011). Boers and Rypdal (2021) conclude that the western Greenland ice sheet is close to a tipping point, and the World Meteorological Organization (WMO) predicts that there is an increased likelihood that the world itself will reach a tipping point of +1.5°C in the next five years (WMO 2021). One of the most threatening tipping points is associated with the Atlantic Meridional Overturning Circulation (also known as the Gulf Stream), where recent research has found numerous early warnings of its collapse (Boers 2021). The significance of this cannot be underestimated, as

> such an event would have catastrophic consequences around the world, severely disrupting the rains that billions of people depend on for food in India, South America and West Africa; increasing storms and lowering temperatures in Europe; and pushing up the sea level in the eastern North America. It would also further endanger the Amazon rainforest and Antarctic ice sheets.
>
> (*Guardian* August 5, 2021)

In a significant elaboration on the theory of tipping points, Kinzig et al. (2006) posit the existence of "cascading thresholds," where the crossing of an individual threshold in a social–ecological system can induce the subsequent crossing of other thresholds. Trisos et al. (2020, p. 496) expand on this approach by concluding that:

> future disruption of ecological assemblages as a result of climate change will be abrupt, because within any given ecological assemblage the exposure of most species to climate conditions beyond their realized niche limits occurs almost simultaneously.

Under a high-emissions scenario (representative concentration pathway RCP 8.5), such abrupt exposure events begin before 2030 in tropical oceans and spread to tropical forests and higher latitudes by 2050.

Wunderling et al. (2021) conclude that interacting tipping elements increase the risk of climate domino effects under global warming. Lenton et al. (2019, p. 595) conclude that "we are in a state of planetary emergency: both the risk and urgency of the situation are acute." To support this conclusion, the authors have developed a simple but powerful mathematical model of the emergency the planet faces. Their critical equation is as follows:

$$E = R \times U = p \times D \times \tau / T$$

Where:

E = emergency, the product of risk (R), and damage (D).
U = urgency, defined in emergency situations as reaction time to an alert (τ)
T = the intervention time left to avoid a bad outcome
p = probability

They conclude that:

> The situation is an emergency if both risk and urgency are high. If reaction time is longer than the intervention time left ($\tau / T > 1$), we have lost control. We argue that the intervention time left to prevent tipping could already have shrunk towards zero, whereas the reaction time to achieve net zero emissions is 30 years at best. Hence, we might already have lost control of whether tipping happens. A saving grace is that the rate at which damage accumulates from tipping—and hence the risk posed—could still be under our control to some extent.
>
> (p. 595)

A recent study on the economic impacts of tipping points identifies the largest effects associated with dissociation of ocean methane hydrates and thawing permafrost (Dietz et al. 2021).

A major issue is the concept of planetary boundaries; planetary boundaries are limits beyond which the planet risks serious if not catastrophic consequences. A study undertaken in 2009 (Rockstrom et al. 2009) identified and attempted to quantify nine such planetary boundaries. The authors admitted the existence of a large degree of uncertainty in this initial research effort but were, nevertheless, able to draw a number of important conclusions. First, they estimated that three planetary boundaries had already been crossed (climate change measured as atmospheric CO_2 concentrations; the rate of biodiversity loss measured as the extinction rate per year; and the nitrogen cycle measured as the amount of N_2 removed from the atmosphere for human use). In addition, it is estimated that our planet may be approaching boundaries for four other categories: global freshwater use, change in land use, ocean acidification, and interference with the global phosphorous cycle. Subsequent research (Steffen et al. 2015, 2018) concluded that the earth has already crossed four boundaries: climate change, loss of biosphere integrity, land-system change, and altered biogeochemical cycles (phosphorus and nitrogen).

A more recent study focused on planetary boundaries for more than 150 countries (O'Neill et al. 2018, p. 88) and quantified the resource use associated with meeting basic human needs. They found that:

> no country meets basic needs for its citizens at a globally sustainable level of resource use. Physical needs such as nutrition, sanitation, access to electricity and the elimination of extreme poverty could likely be met for all people without transgressing planetary boundaries. However, the universal achievement of more qualitative goals (for example, high life satisfaction) would require a level of resource use that is 2–6 times the sustainable level, based on current relationships.

A critical question revolves around the ecological, economic, and social effects of crossing a tipping point. By way of example, the consequences of losing a keystone species or central system component can be momentous.

System interdependencies and boundaries

Central to the study of systems—be they in ecology, economics, business, or society—is the understanding of system interdependencies. Systems are characterized by such interdependencies, both obvious and counterintuitive. A trophic level is the position in a food chain inhabited by an organism. Trophic cascades are the effects of additions or deletions of an apex predator (i.e. a predator at the top of a food chain), which ripple through an ecosystem and alter it. In a typical food chain, each trophic level feeds on the level below and is fed upon by the level above. To understand the complexity of trophic cascades and system interdependencies, consider several recent examples drawn from the American Midwest, East Coast, and Pacific regions. The underlying similarity in all of these cases is the unexpected linkages—unexpected due to our limited understanding of the complexity of ecosystems and our interactions with them.

The first example illustrates the unanticipated system effects of the controversial reintroduction of wolves into Yellowstone National Park. While the impact on domestic and farm animals was partially anticipated, little was known about the direction and extent of possible effects on a range of other species. The rather complex chain of events which followed led to a decrease in the wolves' principal competitor, the coyote, and principal prey, elk. Accompanying this, however, were the somewhat surprising and unanticipated increases in magpies, ravens, yellow warblers, Lincoln sparrows, voles, mice, willow, cottonwood, aspen, beaver, red foxes, and trout (Ripple et al. 2013).

The second example, with unpredicted but tangible economic impacts on commercial fisheries, focuses on the loss of sharks off the east coast of the United States. Sharks have largely been considered undesirable because of their tendency to predate on more valuable species and the occasional human. Myers et al. (2007) traced the trophic cascade associated with loss of the shark as apex predator. The intentional and unintentional killing of eleven species of large sharks that typically feed on rays, skates, and smaller sharks led to an explosion in the population of these prey, which were no longer under predator pressure. This, in turn, led to a massive predation of bay scallops, the next lowest trophic level. The result was the total physical and economic collapse of the scallop fishery, which had existed for more than a century. To place this in context, the value of total scallop landings in the United States in 2005 was approximately $400 million (NEFMC n.d.). In sum, sharks serve a critical role as an apex species maintaining ecological balance within the complex food chain they dominate.

The third example is also related to a commercial fishery with significant economic benefits: the Pacific salmon, whose range extends from California in the south to Alaska in the north. Considered a keystone species, the salmon play an essential role in the maintenance of a thriving ecosystem. Salmon of the Pacific Northwest and Alaska are under increased stress from global warming as they require relatively cool water temperatures in which to reproduce and thrive. The loss of this apex species would have a cascading and detrimental effect on a large array of mammals, insects, and plants that rely on its central ecological role (Cederholm et al. 2000). Included among these are many creatures from which humans gain tangible economic benefits from hunting or tourism, including the grizzly and black bear, bald eagle, Caspian tern, coon merganser, harlequin duck, killer whale, and osprey, as well as 129 other mammals, birds, reptiles, and amphibians.

The correct delineation of system boundaries can lead to vastly different problem definitions and possible solutions. Eating locally, together with its perceived benefits, is a concept that has received wide currency after the publication of the national bestseller *The 100-Mile Diet: A Year of Local Eating* (Smith and MacKinnon 2007). A key concept in this public debate is the concept of food miles, meaning the distance food has to travel from point of production to point of consumption. Central to this calculation is the amount of energy expended (and the associated GHGs produced) in the transportation of this food. In general, the conclusion is that locally produced food is better, since less energy is consumed—and fewer GHGs are produced—in the transportation of the food.

A study from New Zealand critically reexamined this theory by expanding the boundaries of the analysis and looking at the total system effects of transporting lamb from that country to the United Kingdom (Saunders et al. 2006). If one relies solely on food miles as the desideratum, then clearly it makes more sense for consumers in the United Kingdom to eat domestically produced lamb. The thrust of the New Zealand study was that food miles is an incomplete measure of environmental impact. It includes only the distance food travels and is misleading because it does not consider total energy use throughout the production process. In contrast, Saunders et al. take a much broader view of the environmental impact of lamb and some other major food exports. The environmental impact calculations are based upon a life-cycle assessment and include the energy use and CO_2 emissions associated with production and transport to the United Kingdom. This is a much more valid comparison than just distance traveled as it reflects differences in the production systems of the two countries. This system-wide reanalysis reveals the counterintuitive result that New Zealand lamb has a lower total energy and CO_2 profile than UK lamb even after transportation of imported lamb to the United Kingdom is factored into the analysis. Clearly, in order to assess the true overall effect and sustainability of a product, it is necessary to develop a methodology that looks at the problem from a systems perspective. One major type of this approach is that of the ecological footprint discussed later in this chapter; another is life-cycle analysis described in Nemetz (2022).

Revenge theory

In 1996, Edward Tenner of Harvard University published a book entitled *Why Things Bite Back: Technology and the Revenge of Unintended Consequences*. The central hypothesis advanced by Tenner was that we know very little about the complexity of natural systems and even some made by humans. As a consequence, any attempt to intervene in one location to fix a problem can lead to another totally unanticipated problem elsewhere. Through casual observation it is possible to see a plethora of supporting examples of this persuasive theory.

One of the most famous of these is the story of malaria control in Borneo. While several variants of this tale have been related in the literature, the message is the same: unintended consequences—sometimes very serious—can emerge from what are considered benign interventions designed to cure major problems; in this case, a global disease that affects more than one-quarter of a billion people and kills almost one-half million annually (WHO 2019). In the immediate postwar period, the World Health Organization (WHO) encouraged the widespread use of dichlorodiphenyltrichloroethane (DDT)— considered a benign pesticide—for the control of malaria. Vast swaths of the developing world, including Borneo, were sprayed with this chemical—with little understanding of its ultimate ecological effects. The initial result was a marked reduction in the number of mosquitoes and consequent incidence of malaria (Conway 1972). However, the spraying of DDT, especially in homes, led to the mortality of both cats and small lizards, which controlled rats and caterpillars respectively. This led, in turn, to a marked increase in the numbers of both these pests, the former carrying such diseases as plague and typhus, the latter feeding on thatched roofs, leading to roof collapse. Finally, through the process of Darwinian natural selection, the most resistant mosquitoes were able to continue reproducing. On balance, this initial attempt to eliminate malaria was counterproductive, leading ultimately to the return of the disease accompanied by several other pests and diseases.

There are numerous, more recent examples of revenge theory—all the consequences of well-intentioned but ill-informed interventions as matters of public policy. They are summarized in Table 2.1. One of the best known examples is China's one-child policy, devised in an attempt to control the multifaceted negative consequences—political, economic, social, and ecological—of uncontrolled population growth in a country with a population already exceeding 1.25 billion (Ebenstein and Sharygin 2009). China was recently forced to abandon this policy for several reasons, most notably the potentially serious social consequences of the emergence of a large number of "bare branches", or excess males with no prospect of marriage (Hudson and Den Boer 2004; *New York Times* November 4, 2015).

One of the most graphic examples of revenge effects is associated with hydroelectricity—long considered one of the most benign of all energy supply alternatives. As with all energy sources, benefits come with associated costs, and large hydroelectric dams are no exception (Ackermann et al. 1973; Goldsmith and Hildyard 1984; Scudder 2005). The archetypal illustration of the law of unintended consequences is the Aswan High Dam, which was completed in Egypt in 1965. The benefits to this large but underdeveloped country were substantial—in excess of 10,000 megawatts (MW) of electricity capacity and conversion of more than 700,000 acres from flood to canal irrigation, permitting double and triple cropping. The construction costs exceeded $1 billion but the dam was expected to yield benefits many times that in magnitude. It soon became apparent, however, that there were numerous unanticipated externalities from the dramatic change in water flows and drastically reduced sediment transport in the Nile River: (1) the loss of natural river water flushing of salts from the soils of the fertile Nile Delta, requiring the construction of an extensive network of drainage tile systems costing $1 billion; (2) loss of soil-building and natural fertilizing in the Delta, which then required chemical fertilization costing more than $100 million per year; (3) increased salinity and seawater intrusion

Table 2.1 Examples of revenge theory

Revenge theory example	Original goal	Policy/action	Unintended consequence
Bangladesh drinking water	To find alternative sources of water when surface water contaminated with fecal coliform and other pollutants	Deep well drilling	Deep well water in Bangladesh contains arsenic, a known carcinogen, which is present in subsurface strata.
Mississippi River levees	To reduce the incidence of flooding	Installing and raising the levees	Levees trap sediment which would normally flow over the banks during flooding and restock local soils; to counter the rise of river levels from the buildup of silt, constant dredging is required along with levee raising. As levees become higher, there is a greater risk of breeching and undermining.
Lyme disease	To eliminate wolves	Wolf kills	Reduction in wolves leads to explosion in deer population and rodents which host Lyme disease vectors.
China's former population control policy	To control population growth	One-child policy	Rural populations, in particular, require male children for labor. Female children are aborted or abandoned; this led to thirty million excess males known as "bare branches" with potentially disruptive influence on social stability.
Mad cow disease	To find cheaper food and faster ways to fatten cattle	Adding animal byproducts (including spinal and neurological tissue) to the diet of cattle	Turning herbivores into carnivores has unintended effects, one of which was the inadvertent contamination of cattle feed with scrapie virus, leading to bovine spongiform encephalopathy (BSE/mad cow disease) and possible transmission to humans in the form of Creutzfeldt-Jakob disease.
Forest fire prevention	Desire to reduce forest fires, especially in national parks	Intensive effort to extinguish fires, even those from natural sources such as lightning	The interruption of the natural cycle of forest fires, which can play a critical role in forest and ecosystem regeneration, leads to the build up of old trees and inflammable waste on the forest floor. When a spark starts a fire, there is a resulting conflagration because of the unnatural accumulation of flammable material.

in the Delta; (4) increased coastal erosion; (5) increased riverbank and bottom scouring, which threatened the integrity of more than five hundred bridges built over the previous decade, requiring $250 million in mitigation measures; (6) reduction in plankton and organic carbon levels in the eastern Mediterranean which had traditionally sustained a large and productive sardine fishery; (7) less water downstream because of evaporation and seepage; and (8) loss of dry periods between floods: dry periods normally controlled the prevalence of water snails which carry schistosomiasis (or bilharziasis), a debilitating disease which affected a significant proportion of the rural Egyptian population (Sterling 1973; Stanley and Warne 1993; Vörösmarty and Sahagian 2000; Abd-El Monsef et al. 2015).

In a related manifestation of the revenge effect, a cascade of consequences affected the productivity of fisheries off the mouth of the Nile Delta in the decades following the construction of the Aswan High Dam. First, the initial collapse in the fishery was reversed in the late 1980s as the dual impact of fertilizer and sewage runoff produced a surge in nutrient levels and fish populations. But it has declined once again from increased levels of eutrophication (low oxygen) due to the accumulated impacts of the aforementioned fertilizer and sewage discharges (Oczkowski and Nixon 2008; Oczkowski et al. 2009).

The most recent example of electricity-related revenge issues is associated with the world's largest hydroelectric installation—on China's Yangtze River. The Three Gorges Dam, built at a cost of more than $24 billion to provide 20,000 MW of electricity and prevent the reoccurrence of historically devastating floods, has been deemed an environmental catastrophe. The dam required the displacement of 1.2 million people, but also reduced biodiversity, altered weather patterns, and created landslides, seismicity, water pollution, drops in downstream water tables with saltwater intrusions, jellyfish blooms, and a rise in the number of cases of schistosomiasis (Hvistendahl 2008; CNN August 1, 2020).

In a controversial new book entitled *Techno-Fix: Why Technology Won't Save Us or the Environment,* Huesemann and Huesemann (2011) detail the unintended consequences of technological advances in a broad range of areas including industrial agriculture, genetic engineering, automobiles, high-technology warfare, and high-technology medicine.

Some other important ecosystem characteristics

As already noted, ecosystems are characterized by nonlinear dynamics and tipping points. One related characteristic is the presence of lags or delayed effects. A graphic example of this phenomenon is provided by the lasting impacts of DDT and polychlorinated biphenyls (PCBs) long after the cessation of their use (Breivik et al. 2002; Davis 2014).

Two other concepts are of particular relevance to global fauna—including humans: bioaccumulation and biomagnification in food chains. Bioaccumulation represents the gradual accumulation of toxic chemicals in fish or animals as they age, whereas biomagnification represents the increasing concentration of toxics as they rise through the food chain. By way of example, the concentrations of organochlorines such as DDT and PCBs in a north Pacific food chain can range from seven to eight orders of magnitude from the top to bottom of the food chain (based on data in Tanabe et al. 1984; Noble and Elliott 1986). What may appear to be a harmless concentration in seawater becomes potentially toxic at upper levels of the food chain—frequently fish consumed as food by humans. In 2005, the US Environmental Protection Agency (EPA) issued guidelines for eating fish. They recommended that people not consume shark, swordfish, king mackerel, or tilefish because of bioaccumulated levels of mercury, a known neurotoxin.

The ecological footprint

While many of the theories discussed above remain largely in the realm of scientific discourse, one concept that has gained wide currency among public agencies, nongovernmental organizations (NGOs), and even the general public is that of the ecological footprint, which is an attempt to create a summary, system-level measure of the impact of human activity on the ecosystem. (See www.footprintnetwork.org.) The ecological footprint is a measure of the actual physical stocks of natural capital necessary to sustain a given human population within a given geographic region such as a city. It is sometimes expressed as a ratio; for example, if the ecological footprint of an urban area is 10.0, this implies that the land "consumed" by the urban region is ten times greater than contained within its political boundaries. A full definition of the ecological footprint for a region—its ecological footprint or appropriated carrying capacity—is the land (and water) area in various categories required exclusively by the people in this region: (1) to continuously provide all the *resources* they currently consume, and (2) to continuously absorb all the *wastes* they currently discharge. This land is either borrowed from the past (e.g., through the use of fossil fuels), or appropriated from the future (e.g., as contamination, plant growth reduction through reduced ultraviolet radiation, soil degradation, etc.; see Rees 2007).

While the ecological footprint is frequently used to measure the impact of urbanization, it is also applicable to larger geographic areas such as regions or nations. Consider the ecological footprint of a larger geographic area such as the Netherlands. This country now consumes six times its domestically available biocapacity, up from two times in 1961 (www.footprintnetwork.org).

Perhaps the most important level of ecological footprint analysis is at the global level which measures the total impact of all human activity on our earthly environment. The National Footprint Accounts list the total land area of the earth as 12.2 billion hectares (ha), of which 10.7 billion ha in 2014 was productive cropland, pasture, or forest (www.footprintnetwork.org). The most important observations flowing from this global-level ecological footprint analysis are that the industrialized world appropriates far more than its fair share of global carrying capacity, and if the developing world were to achieve living standards comparable to those experienced in the developed world, we would require two additional planet Earths (WWF 2010).

The precautionary principle

In light of the complexities associated with the diverse range of threats faced by modern society, especially rare but catastrophic outcomes, the challenge is to find a decision rule that can help protect the ecosystem and current and future generations of humanity. The precautionary principle is one such rule. Simply stated, it is based on the premise that we live in an uncertain world and that society cannot wait for definitive scientific proof of a potential threat before acting if that threat is both large and credible. The underlying theory is based on scientific principles largely associated with the work of ecologists such as C.S. Holling. One consequence of Holling's theory is that by the time one recognizes or begins to feel the tangible effects of certain types of ecological threats, it may be too late to forestall or reverse the negative effects.

Variations of the precautionary principle have already been incorporated into legislation and regulation in several countries within the Organisation for Economic Co-operation and Development (OECD)—mostly in Europe but also in the United States (Harremoes et al.

2001; Tickner 2003; UNESCO 2005). One of the most important potential applications of the precautionary principle concerns the assessment of the large number of new chemical compounds introduced in Europe and the United States in the postwar period. There are in excess of one hundred thousand such chemicals currently in use in the world today, and their production had increased from 1 million metric tons (MT) in 1930 to more than 400 million MT by 2001 (CEC 2004). A US EPA report (1998) on the availability of data concerning potential chemical hazards reported that 2,863 organic chemicals (i.e., excluding polymers or inorganic chemicals) were either produced or imported at or above 1 million pounds per year in the United States. The report observed that

> EPA's analysis found that no basic toxicity information, i.e., neither human health nor environmental toxicity, is publicly available for 43% of the high volume chemicals manufactured in the US and that a full set of basic toxicity information is available for only 7% of these chemicals. The lack of availability of basic toxicity information on most high volume chemicals is a serious issue.
>
> (p. 2)

A more recent article found that

> only about 15% of premanufacture notifications for new chemicals submitted to EPA include any health or safety data at all and EPA's own statistics show that only 10% of the new chemicals entering commerce between 1979 and 2016 involved restrictions or testing orders.
>
> (Gold and Wagner 2020, p. 1068)

The impact of chemicals on human health has led to the emergence of an entirely new field of research: environmental neuroscience, which studies the potentially multifaceted impact of chemicals on brain function and pathogenesis (NAS 2020b).

At least three major classes of chemicals have emerged in the last several decades which entail unknown but potentially significant risks to human health and the environment and are, as a consequence, candidates for the application of the precautionary principle: plastics, endocrine mimickers, and nanomaterials.

Plastics (and particularly microplastics): Geyer et al. (2017) have estimated that

> 8300 million metric tons (Mt) of virgin plastics have been produced [from 1950] to date. As of 2015, approximately 6300 Mt of plastic waste had been generated, around 9 percent of which had been recycled, 12 percent was incinerated, and 79 percent was accumulated in landfills or the natural environment. If current production and waste management trends continue, roughly 12,000 Mt of plastic waste will be in landfills or in the natural environment by 2050.

Plastics have become a central part of modern manufacturing and are ubiquitous. The United Nations reports that as many as fifty-one trillion microplastic particles litter the sea, representing five hundred times more than the number of stars in our galaxy (UN 2017). Borelle et al. (2020) have concluded that the predicted growth in plastic waste exceeds efforts to mitigate plastic pollution. Most plastics do not biodegrade and continue to accumulate in the environment, posing a threat of unknown magnitude to human health and the functioning of ecosystems (*Lancet* 2017; Prata et al. 2020; Vethaak and Legler 2021; NIH 2020). As Brahney et al. (2021, p. 1) state:

> Plastic pollution is one of the most pressing environmental and social issues of the 21st century. … Akin to global biogeochemical cycles, plastics now spiral around the globe with distinct atmospheric, oceanic, cryospheric, and terrestrial residence times. … Our data suggest that extant nonbiodegradable polymer will continue to cycle through the earth's systems.

Recent research has found that 50 percent of the world's single-use plastic is made by twenty companies, and one hundred companies produce 90 percent (Minderoo Foundation 2021). Another study has found ten plastic products (mainly food and drink litter) account for up to 75 percent of all ocean plastic (Morales-Caselles et al. 2021). Recent research has found that one thousand rivers account for 80 percent of all global riverine plastic emissions into the ocean and small urban rivers are among the most polluting (Meijer et al. 2021).

Science magazine devoted its July 2, 2021 special issue to plastics, covering a diverse range of subjects including their distribution and accumulation, their effect in the environment, their ingestion by wildlife, the potential for upcycling and enzyme-based recycling, the history of bioplastics, next-generation material design, and the potential role of plastics in a circular bioeconomy. In summary, given the extraordinary range and quantity of global plastic pollution and its largely ignored but potentially enormous impact, this represents an archetypal example of massive uninternalized externalities.

Endocrine mimickers: According to the US NIH (n.d., p. 1),

> Many chemicals, both natural and man-made, may mimic or interfere with the body's hormones, known as the endocrine system. Called endocrine disruptors, these chemicals are linked with developmental, reproductive, brain, immune, and other problems. Endocrine disruptors are found in many everyday products, including some plastic bottles and containers, liners of metal food cans, detergents, flame retardants, food, toys, cosmetics, and pesticides. Some endocrine-disrupting chemicals are slow to break down in the environment. That characteristic makes them potentially hazardous over time. Endocrine-disrupting chemicals cause adverse effects in animals. But limited scientific information exists on potential health problems in humans. Because people are typically exposed to multiple endocrine disruptors at the same time, assessing public health effects is difficult.

Common endocrine disruptors include bisphenol A, dioxin, perfluoroalkyl and polyfluoroalkyl substances, which are most commonly associated with the production of Teflon, as well as phthalates, phytoestrogens, polybrominated diphenyl ethers, PCBs, and triclosan. In 2012, the European Environment Agency (EEA) strongly recommended the adoption of a precautionary principle with respect to the introduction and use of chemicals with endocrine-disrupting properties in light of their potentially devastating impact on hormonal systems within humans and other animal species.

Nanomaterials: Another major technological development that has prompted calls for the application of the precautionary principle is in the emerging area of nanotechnology and nanomaterials. While present in the environment since the earth's formation, only recently has our natural background of nanomaterials been supplemented by human-engineered counterparts for use in medicine, electronics, energy, water, and food production (Hochella et al. 2019). They are generally in the range of millionths of a millimeter in size (i.e. nanometer size). The challenge is identifying and quantifying the risk to human health and the environment of the proliferation of these anthropogenic materials. One review study on exposure to workers found that certain types of nanoparticles may impact the immunological system and may cause inflammation of the lungs, signs of asthma, interstitial fibrosis, genotoxicity, and possible human cancer (Pietroiusti et al. 2018). There is a clear need to extend our understanding of biological and pharmacological properties and effects of these substances in order to create a clearer picture of the risk-benefit trade-offs in the general population (NAS 2012). Valued at $1.055 trillion in 2013, the global nanotechnology-enabled market was expected to grow to $3.4 trillion by 2018 (NAS 2016 and 2020a).

The application of the precautionary principle is not an arbitrary exercise, but one that must follow strict rules of logic and proof. To demonstrate the usefulness of the principle, in 2001 and 2013 the EEA published two landmark studies that reexamined the history of almost three dozen controversial cases—many involving the introduction of new chemicals—from the late 1800s to this century (Harremoes et al. 2001; EEA 2013). Included among these case studies were major public policy and regulatory decisions concerning fisheries, radiation, benzene, asbestos, PCBs, halocarbons, the drug diethylstilbestrol (DES), antimicrobials such as antibiotics added to animal feed as growth promoters, sulfur dioxide, the gasoline additive methyl tert-butyl ether, Great Lakes contamination, tributyltin antifoulants, estrogen mimickers, and mad cow disease. Table 2.2 lists these technologies and their revenge effects. It was concluded that in many of the cases (1) "early warnings" and even "loud and late" warnings were clearly ignored; (2) the scope of hazard appraisal was too narrow; and (3) regulatory actions were taken without sufficient consideration of alternatives, or of the conditions necessary for their successful implementation in the real world.

Table 2.3, based on the EEA report (Harremoes et al. 2001), illustrates how the precautionary principle could be applied to the three major categories and examples of risk originally conceptualized by Frank Knight (1921). Two additional studies by Raffensperger and Tickner (1999) and Tickner (2003) provide numerous examples where the principle has been applied in a diverse range of industries and countries. Perhaps the most persuasive use of the precautionary principle is in the area of global warming. Despite these diverse applications of the precautionary principle, some decision makers, policy analysts, and business persons have expressed concern that the general principle is too imprecise to permit an economically efficient determination of the appropriate timing and magnitude of anticipatory action (Marchant and Mossman 2004). In contrast to these concerns, Pittinger and Bishop (1999 p. 960) from Procter & Gamble state that

> neither the practice of risk assessment nor the elements of the precautionary principle are "new" or "revolutionary." For decades, they have been important elements in the design, manufacture and marketing of new consumer products. They also have long been embodied in the frameworks used to regulate the introduction of new products, globally. Due precaution is entirely consistent with sound, cost-effective management of the risks and uncertainties inherent in new technologies.

Table 2.2 Technologies with revenge effects

Item	Intended effects	Revenge effects
Modern industrial fishing technology	To increase efficiency of fishing	Depletion of fish stocks
X-rays	For diagnosis and treatment	Increased incidence of cancer
Benzene	Industrial solvent—starting material for inorganic synthesis—in petroleum products and in blending of motor fuel	Leukemia, aplastic anemia, multiple myeloma
Asbestos	Fire and boiler insulation and brake linings	Asbestosis, lung cancers, especially mesothelioma
Polychlorinated biphenyls (PCBs)	Insulating compound in electrical equipment, used in heat-transfer and hydraulic fluids, paints, adhesives, lubricants, sealants, carbonless copy paper, PVC plastics	Global contamination and persistence, bioaccumulation and biomagnification, omnipresent in food chain, toxic to animals (especially affecting reproductive systems), neurological and hepatic toxicity, and hormonal disruption in humans
Halocarbons	Refrigerant and aerosol propellant	Damage to ozone layer leading to increasing ultraviolet radiation and skin cancer incidence
Diethylstilbestrol (DES)	Multiple medical uses in humans, especially to prevent spontaneous abortion, menopausal symptoms, and prostate cancer, also used as postcoital contraception and growth promoter in livestock	Teratogen, transplacental carcinogen (vaginal cell adenocarcinoma), widespread incidence of reproductive tract abnormalities in DES daughters (women exposed in utero), increased rate of genital abnormalities in men
Antimicrobials for livestock	Growth promoter for livestock and prophylactic against disease spread in high stocking environments (feedlots)	Increased bacterial resistance to antimicrobials through multiple pathways
Methyl tert-butyl ether	Antiknock agent instead of lead	Fouling of groundwater and drinking water, possible carcinogen, risk factor for asthma and endocrine disruption
Organochlorines (e.g., dichlorodiphenyl-trichloroethane [DDT], aldrin, chlordane, heptachlor, etc.)	Pesticides	Toxic to nontarget species and affecting reproduction in wildlife; effects on humans include carcinogenesis, acute neurotoxicity, endocrine disruption; promotes insect resistance to these organochlorines
Tributyltin and booster biocide antifoulants	Antifoulant biocide as marine paint additive	Environmental bioaccumulation, toxic to nontarget species, especially commercially valuable molluscs such as oysters
Hormones for livestock	Growth promoter in livestock	Endocrine disruption in wildlife after entering water bodies and food chain; possible negative effects on humans to immune system and endocrine system, as well as cancer

(continued)

Table 2.2 Cont.

Item	Intended effects	Revenge effects
Use of rendered animal remains including neuro-spinal tissue as feed for livestock	To increase recycling, reduce waste, and lower costs	Bovine spongiform encephalopathy (BSE/mad cow disease), Creutzfeldt-Jakob disease in humans
Lead additive to gasoline	Antiknock quality	Neurotoxic to humans
Tetrachlorethylene	Plastic linings for drinking water distribution pipes, dry cleaning fluid	Contamination of water supplies, carcinogenicity, teratogenicity
Mercury	Industrial catalyst, used in medicines, lighting, and cosmetics	Neurotoxic
Beryllium	Used in nuclear weapons, large area mirrors for telescopes, speakers, semiconductors, and lightweight structural components	Irreversible inflammatory lung disease
Vinyl chloride	Used to produce a wide range of polyvinyl products such as shower curtains, food containers, floor coverings, pipes, packaging, wire coating, and resins	Hepatotoxic, liver cancer, damage to skin and bone
1,2, Dibromo-3-chlorpropane	Pesticide	Contamination of drinking water, endocrine-disrupting chemical with adverse effects on reproduction
Bisphenol A	Used to make polycarbonate plastics used in common products such as baby bottles, household electronics, medical devices, and coatings on food containers	Endocrine disruptor
Ethinyl estradiol	Birth control	Endocrine disruptor
Some seed dressings (e.g. imidacloprid, neonicotinoids)	Insecticides	Toxic to bees and other nontarget species (see Chapter 6 on agriculture)
Flood levees	Flood control	Frequently degrade local ecosystems and can increase the effects of flooding
Nuclear power	See Chapter 8 on nuclear power	
Genetically modified crops	Well suited to high-input monocultural agricultural systems that are highly productive	Largely unsustainable in their reliance on external, nonrenewable inputs; with patent protection can reduce other innovation; potential impact on nontarget fauna
Introduction of invasive alien species	Deliberate introduction frequently used to control plants or animals considered undesirable	Can cause ecological disruption due to unanticipated effects on biodiversity

Table 2.2 Cont.

Item	Intended effects	Revenge effects
Nanotechnology	Applications in energy, textiles, paints and coatings, fuel catalysts, additives, lubricants, cosmetics, food packaging, medicine	Potential increased emissions and toxicity of nanoscale material compared to bulk forms of the same materials, concern over emergent risks to human health and ecosystems

Source: EEA 2013.

Table 2.3 Generic applications of the precautionary principle

	Examples	Possible actions
Risk	Known impacts and known probabilities; for example, asbestosis, lung cancer especially mesothelioma	Prevention: reduce known risks, such as asbestos dust
Uncertainty	Known impacts and unknown probabilities; for example, antibiotics in animal feed and development of bacterial resistance	Precautionary prevention: reduce potential hazards by reducing or eliminating human exposure to antibiotic residues in animal feed
Ignorance or "wicked" problems	Unknown impacts and therefore unknown probabilities; for example, surprises of chlorofluorocarbons (CFCs) and their destruction of the ozone layer	Precaution: action taken to anticipate, identify, and reduce the impact of surprises. For example, use properties of chemicals such as persistence or bioaccumulation as predictors of possible harm; use of robust, diverse, and adaptable technologies

Source: EEA 2013.

In response to the concern over issues of operationalizing what appears to be a vague principle, numerous researchers have proposed several methodologies to bring analytical rigor to the study and application of the precautionary principle (see, for example, Sandin 1999; Sandin et al. 2011; Sandin and Hansson 2011; Vardas and Xepapadeas 2010). Those engaged in continuing debate over the principle sometimes lose sight of the fact that it is not a one-size-fits-all approach that can hamper the development of potentially useful new technologies and products but is instead a more nuanced concept with several dimensions. Cameron (2006) and others (Cooney 2005; Peterson 2006; Wiener and Rogers 2002) have identified three distinct versions (weak, moderate, and strong) of the precautionary principle, each tied closely to different evidentiary standards. To quote Cameron (2006, pp. 12–13):

Weak Version

The weak version is the least restrictive and allows preventive measures to be taken in the face of uncertainty, but does not require them. To satisfy the threshold of harm, there must be some evidence relating to both the likelihood of occurrence and the severity of consequences. Some, but not all, require consideration of the costs of precautionary measures. Weak formulations do not preclude weighing benefits against the costs. Factors other than scientific uncertainty, including economic considerations, may provide legitimate grounds for postponing action. Under weak formulations, the requirement to justify the need for action (the burden of proof) generally falls on those advocating precautionary action. No mention is made of assignment of liability for environmental harm.

Moderate Version

In moderate versions of the principle, the presence of an uncertain threat is a positive basis for action, once it has been established that a sufficiently serious threat exists. Usually, there is no requirement for proposed precautionary measures to be assessed against other factors such as economic or social costs. The trigger for action may be less rigorously defined, for example, as "potential damage," rather than as "serious or irreversible" damage as in the weak version. Liability is not mentioned, and the burden of proof generally remains with those advocating precautionary action.

Strong Version

Strong versions of the principle differ from the weak and moderate versions in reversing the burden of proof. Strong versions justify or require precautionary measures, and some also establish liability for environmental harm, which is effectively a strong form of "polluter pays." Reversal of proof requires those proposing an activity to prove that the product, process, or technology is sufficiently "safe" before approval is granted. Requiring proof of "no environmental harm" before any action proceeds implies the public is not prepared to accept any environmental risk, no matter what economic or social benefits may arise. At the extreme, such a requirement could involve bans and prohibitions on entire classes of potentially threatening activities or substances.

There is clearly a continuum, from weak to strong, along which the various forms of the precautionary principle may apply. Shamir et al. (2007) have linked two locations on this continuum in particular to accepted rules of evidence: the midpoint is equivalent to the "balance of probabilities" concept typical of civil litigation, while the strong point is equivalent to use of "beyond reasonable doubt" in criminal law. The fundamental challenge is determining which point on the continuum (i.e., which degree of precaution) is appropriate for any given problem. The incorrect placement of any particular problem on this continuum can lead *in extremis* to one of two pathologies: suppression of a course of action that would have net benefits to society, or accession to a course of action that poses a serious threat.

The precautionary principle and risk–risk trade-offs

One of the principal challenges to the use of the precautionary principle has been the emergence of the concept of risk–risk trade-offs. Simply stated, this theory states that any action or policy to curtail or prevent the use of a product or technology motivated by the desire to reduce potential risks by invoking the precautionary principle must be tempered by the consideration of the risks associated with abandoning or not adopting such technology (Graham et al. 1997). While superficially appealing, the application of the theory of risk–risk trade-offs can be problematic if system boundaries are incorrectly defined, as illustrated in Chapter 5 on agriculture.

Ecological economics

The publication of Rachel Carson's pioneering work, *Silent Spring*, in 1962 led to the blossoming of a new subdiscipline of neoclassical economics—environmental economics. The great contribution of this new discipline to the traditional model of an economic system was inclusion of a component to reflect wastes generated by both producers and consumers of goods and services. The principal normative goal was to internalize externalities in order to reduce economic inefficiency from a social perspective. However, the overall goal of maximizing economic growth to increase human welfare remained the central thrust.

This new theoretical modification of neoclassical economics appeared to go a long way in identifying the sources of and potential remedies for a myriad of environmental problems. However, ecologists and a subset of members of the economics profession felt that the model was still an imperfect representation of reality and hence provided insufficient insight into problem genesis and resolution. Hence was born the transdisciplinary field of ecological economics in the 1980s (Spash 1999; Røpke 2004, 2005).

Figure 2.4 captures the essence of the ecological economics model, which makes three major modifications to the environmental economics model: (1) waste products generated by both consumers and producers have a feedback loop, which means that

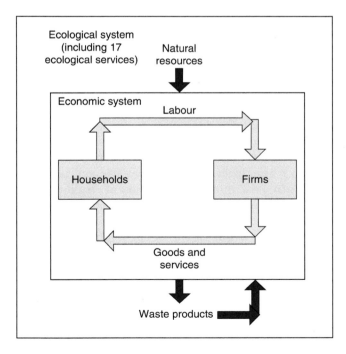

Figure 2.4 The ecological economics model.

such products have the capacity to negatively impact the production system from which they are generated; (2) there is a specific inclusion of certain natural resources as inputs such as clean air, clean water, and assimilative capacity; and (3) most importantly, there is an ecological system which includes at least seventeen ecological services, as described by Costanza et al. (1997). The fundamental premise of this major conceptual revision is that the economic system is embedded in the ecological system, cannot function without it, and is ultimately subject to the same laws and constraints applying to natural systems.

The import of this schematic is captured in the words of Herman Daly, a former senior economist at the World Bank and one of the founders of the new discipline of ecological economics. Daly states:

> It is interesting that such a huge issue should be at stake in a simple picture. Once you draw the boundary of the environment around the economy, you have implicitly admitted that the economy cannot expand forever. (Daly 1996), p. 7
>
> The notion of an optimal scale for an activity is at the very heart of microeconomics. Yet for the macro level, the aggregate of all microeconomic activities ... there is no concept of an optimal scale. The notion that the macroeconomy could become too large relative to the ecosystem is simply absent from macroeconomic theory. The macroeconomy is supposed to grow forever. Since GNP [gross national product] adds costs and benefits together instead of comparing them at the margin, we have no macro-level accounting by which an optimal scale could be identified. Beyond a certain scale, growth begins to destroy more values than it creates—economic growth gives way to an era of anti-economic growth. But GNP keeps rising, giving us no clue as to whether we have passed that critical point!
>
> (Daly 1999, pp. 6–7)

Daly's work represented the transfer of the concept of optimal scale from microeconomics to macroeconomics (Daly 2005). Past the point of optimal production and consumption, we enter an area of what Daly terms "uneconomic growth," where disutility exceeds utility and where humankind may face a potential ecological and economic catastrophe. This critical problem is confounded by the fact that it is not clear at which point this transfer will occur.

One of the principal challenges posed by ecological economics is that it forces us to examine the specific interlinkages and interdependencies of our economic and ecological systems. What does the ecological system provide that we need? There are at least four components: (1) a natural resource base, including both renewable and nonrenewable resources. Note that "renewable" may be a misnomer as it is just as easy, if not easier, to deplete a renewable as a nonrenewable resource base; (2) a set of natural goods, such as landscape and amenity resources; (3) a waste assimilation capacity which is finite in extent; and, most importantly, (4) a life support system.

In May 1997, a multidisciplinary research team composed of scientists and social scientists under the leadership of Robert Costanza published a landmark article in the leading English scientific journal, *Nature*. The article, entitled "The value of the world's ecosystem services and natural capital," was the first major and comprehensive effort to attach a dollar figure to the ecological services sustaining the planet. To place the total estimated value of $33 trillion in context, the global GNP in that year was estimated at $18 trillion.

The study by Costanza et al. was a meta-type analysis which relied largely on extracting economic estimates from dozens of studies using a broad range of analytical methodologies, and focused on such common methodologies as contingent valuation, hedonic pricing, travel and replacement costs, and option value. The authors recognized that the value of some ecosystem services will be infinite (i.e. no life would be possible on earth without them). As a consequence, Costanza et al. focused on changes in incremental value from the goods and services provided by existing natural capital resources.

The authors (Costanza et al. 2014) updated their study for the year 2011 and arrived at a recalculated value for total ecosystem services of $125–145 trillion per year in 2007 US dollars.

Comparing environmental and ecological economics

Table 2.4 summarizes three critical differences between environmental and ecological economics. It has been commonly assumed that while the theoretical interpretations of distribution and scale differ markedly between the two fields, the basic neoclassical concept of allocative efficiency remains the same in both areas. In fact, it can be argued that this accepted theory is incorrect and that ecological economics brings a critically important modification (called resilience) borrowed from the field of ecology to the concept of allocative efficiency. Resilience encompasses three related concepts: resistance, recovery, and robustness (Grafton et al. 2019) and focuses on the ability of natural systems to rebound from shocks. The problem created by focusing solely on the traditional definition of allocative efficiency is that it may be achieved by decreasing system resilience. There is a trade-off between efficiency and resilience, and ecological economics specifically recognizes this distinction (see, for example, Goerner et al. 2009). Consider two simple examples drawn from the fields of ecology and economics: advanced agricultural production, and the global trading and financial system.

As will be discussed in greater detail in Chapter 5 on agriculture, the modern system typical of American farming, often referred to as "industrial agriculture," has achieved extraordinary levels of productivity, creating vast surpluses of food available for both domestic and international consumption. One of the principal characteristics of industrial agriculture, which contributes to its productivity, is a reliance on monoculture. This highly efficient system of agricultural production relies on a cropping protocol which has little, if any, resilience. It is highly vulnerable to insect attacks and plant diseases. As such, economic efficiency—narrowly defined to exclude systemic considerations—is achieved at the expense of resilience.

Table 2.4 Environmental versus ecological economics

	Environmental economics	Ecological economics
Allocative efficiency	Principal focus	Must be tempered by recognition of the trade-off between efficiency and resilience
Distribution	Secondary focus (essentially left to the political process)	Prominent focus (both intragenerational and intergenerational)
Scale (macro level)	The more, the better	Central concept entails limits to physical volume of throughput —Daly's concept of optimality

One can argue that a similar sacrifice of resilience for the sake of efficiency has been achieved through the use of just-in-time inventory control where such systems are extremely vulnerable to breakdowns at any point in the supply chain. A cogent example of this phenomenon has been provided by the disruptions caused by the COVID-19 pandemic of 2019–22 (see Chapter 11). But, perhaps, the most important example of the critical trade-off is the inherent characteristics of the vast and complex international systems of trading and finance, often referred to as globalization. These highly efficient institutions and processes for the movement of large amounts of goods and services and the concomitant vast daily financial flows which make this possible are also extremely vulnerable to system shocks. Examples in the last two decades (including, inter alia, the Mexican peso crisis of 1994–95, the 1997 Asian financial flu, and the subprime market meltdown of 2008 and its sequelae) demonstrate how the consequences of events which in previous times could be geographically isolated to the locus of their generation now have the capacity to threaten the functioning of the entire global financial system.

The field of ecological economics is still in its infancy and major conceptual advances are being made annually. There are, however, at least four basic points of consensus in ecological economics. As summarized by Costanza et al. (1997), these are: (1) the earth is a thermodynamically closed and nonmaterially growing system. This implies that there are limits to biophysical throughput of resources; (2) the future goal is a sustainable planet with a high quality of life for all its inhabitants (humans and other species). This includes both present and future generations; (3) a complex system, such as the earth, where fundamental uncertainty is large and irreducible and certain processes are irreversible, requires a fundamentally *precautionary* stance; and (4) institutions and management should be proactive rather than reactive, and this should result in simple, adaptive, and implementable policies based on a sophisticated understanding of the underlying systems which fully acknowledges their inherent uncertainties.

The socioeconomic challenge of income inequality

Gross domestic product (GDP) and its growth are considered the *sine qua non* of the economic health of a nation. However, Table 2.5 illustrates how the most common measure of well-being, GDP per capita, can lead to a seriously skewed interpretation of the relative well-being of alternative countries. In this table, two pairs of countries have been chosen with relatively similar per capita GDP. It should be apparent from a cursory examination of this table that there are profound differences between the two sets of countries despite their superficial similarity based on an average economic value (UNDP 2019). One of the most important distinctions is related to the level of income inequality. There are two common methods for measuring this variable: the Gini coefficient and comparative shares of income between the highest and lowest decile or centile. The World Bank (n.d.) defines and illustrates the Gini concept as follows:

> [The] Gini index measures the extent to which the distribution of income (or, in some cases, consumption expenditure) among individuals or households within an economy deviates from a perfectly equal distribution. A Lorenz curve plots the cumulative percentages of total income received against the cumulative number of recipients, starting with the poorest individual or household. The Gini index measures the area between the Lorenz curve and a hypothetical line of absolute equality, expressed as

Table 2.5 Pairwise comparisons of GDP/capita

	Namibia	*Ukraine*	*South Africa*	*Albania*
GDP/capita ($)	9,683	7,994	11,756	12,300
Gini	59.1	25	63	29
Bottom 40% share	8.6	24.5	7.2	22.1
Top 10% share	47.3	21.2	50.5	22.2
Top 1% share	n.a.	n.a.	19.2	6.4
Human Development Index	0.645	0.75	0.705	0.791
Rank	129	88	111	69
Life expectancy at birth	63.4	72	63.9	78.5
Expected years of schooling	12.6	15.1	13.7	15.2
Mean years of schooling	6.9	11.3	10.2	10.1
Happy Planet Index	21.6	26.4	15.9	36.8
Rank	103	70	128	13
World Happiness Index	4.571	4.561	4.814	4.883
Rank	122	123	109	105
Gender Development Index	n.a.	0.995	0.984	0.971
Gender Inequality Index	n.a.	0.284	0.422	0.234
Rank	n.a.	60	97	51

Source: UNDP 2019.

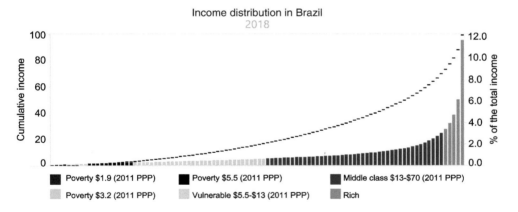

Figure 2.5 Lorenz curve for Brazil.
Note: PPP is purchasing power parity.

a percentage of the maximum area under the line. Thus a Gini index of 0 represents perfect equality, while an index of 100 implies perfect inequality.

The Lorenz curve for Brazil in 2018 is displayed in Figure 2.5 and its Gini index for 2017 is 53.3 (World Bank World Development Index). Figure 2.6 maps GDP per capita versus the Gini coefficient for seventy-five countries for which data were available in 2015. It is noteworthy that countries with remarkably different GDP per capita can have similar Gini indices, but even more remarkable is the number of countries with similar GDP per capita and widely divergent Gini indices.

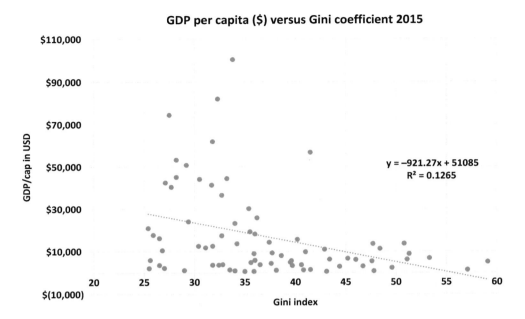

Figure 2.6 GDP/capita versus Gini coefficient 2015.
Data Source: World Bank (n.d.).

Alternatively, as stated above, a quicker assessment of income or wealth inequality may be generated by a simple comparison of upper and lower deciles, percentiles, or any other similar statistical category. For example, the Federal Reserve Bank of St. Louis (2019) has reported that income inequality in the United States rose from 1989 to 2016 with the share of the top 1 percent of income earners rising from 42 percent to 50 percent and the share of the bottom 50 percent of income earners falling from 15 percent to 13 percent. The Bank also concludes that wealth is even more inequitably distributed: the top 10 percent of Americans increased their share of total wealth from 67 percent in 1989 to 77 percent in 2016. This change has been accompanied by a largely non-ameliorated, white–black wealth gap. Similar gaps have continued to exist for whites and Hispanics, educational attainment, and older versus younger families. Other findings are even more striking. *Forbes* (October 8, 2020) reports that the top 1 percent of US households hold fifteen times more wealth than the bottom 50 percent combined, and an earlier study from the National Bureau of Economic Research (Saez and Zucman 2014, abstract) found that:

> Wealth concentration has followed a U-shaped evolution over the last 100 years: It was high in the beginning of the twentieth century, fell from 1929 to 1978, and has continuously increased since then. The rise of wealth inequality is almost entirely due to the rise of the top 0.1% wealth share, from 7% in 1979 to 22% in 20—a level almost as high as in 1929. The bottom 90% wealth share first increased up to the mid-1980s and then steadily declined. The increase in wealth concentration is due

to the surge of top incomes combined with an increase in saving rate inequality. Top wealth-holders are younger today than in the 1960s and earn a higher fraction of total labor income in the economy.

Time series analysis conducted for the Resolution Foundation (Advani et al. 2020) in the United Kingdom found that while the share of wealth held by the richest 1 percent and 10 percent of UK citizens fell during the early and mid-twentieth century, these shares have stabilized or slightly increased since 1985. The authors observe that this trend has been largely replicated across many countries according to the monumental study of inequality authored by Thomas Piketty (2014) and entitled *Capital in the Twenty-First Century*.

The fundamental question is why this matters. The clearest and most articulate answer to this question has been provided by the Nobel Laureate in Economics, Professor Joseph Stiglitz, who has devoted much of his academic career to the study of the extent and impact of income inequality. He has concluded that

> much of America's concentration of wealth at the top was the result of rent seeking … We are paying a high price for our inequality—an economic system that is less stable and less efficient, with less growth, and a democracy that has been put into peril.
>
> (Stiglitz 2013, p. xiv)

He also observes that:

> These disturbing trends in income and wealth inequality were outdone by even more disturbing evidence about inequalities in health. … Today, women in the United States, on average, have the lowest life expectancy of women in any of the advanced countries. Educational attainment, which is often tied in with income and race, is a large and growing predictor of life span. … Decreases in income and decline in standards of living are often accompanied by a multitude of social manifestations— malnutrition, drug abuse, and deterioration in family life, all of which take a toll on health and life expectancy. Indeed these declines in life expectancy are often considered more telling than income numbers themselves.
>
> (p. xiii)

An interesting historical footnote to the subject of income inequality comes from the 1914 decision of Henry Ford, one of America's most prominent industrialists, to double the wages of his workers compared to the average wage for automakers. He voiced the following justification for his action (*Saturday Evening Post* 2014, pp. 3–4):

> The owner, the employees, and the buying public are all one and the same, and unless an industry can so manage itself as to keep wages high and prices low it destroys itself, for otherwise it limits the number of its customers. One's own employees ought to be one's own best customers. … We increased the buying power of our own people, and they increased the buying power of other people, and so on and on … It is this thought of enlarging buying power by paying high wages and selling at low prices that is behind the prosperity of this country.

Ford was articulating a concept generally accepted in the economics profession that one cannot have a healthy economy without sufficient purchasing power in the working and middle classes. And yet, in recent times, a not insignificant proportion of the population has experienced just the opposite: trapped in a vicious circle of low-paying work and unable to purchase anything but cheap goods from companies unable to pay decent wages. In her book *Cheap: The High Cost of Discount Culture*, Shell (2009, p. 161) states: "As Woolworth himself pronounced in 1892, cheap goods cannot be had without 'cheap help'. America is now awash in cheap help who distribute the cheap goods." In the same vein, Barbara Ehrenreich (2011) in her book *Nickel and Dimed: On (Not) Getting By in America*, presents a graphic portrayal of the lives of those Americans on the lowest rung of the socioeconomic ladder earning "poverty-level wages." In his landmark book, *Bowling Alone*, Robert Putnam (2000, updated to 2020), a Harvard social scientist, described the loss of many institutions, such as churches, clubs, and bowling leagues, that had traditionally provided the social glue helping to hold communities together. Several causes were identified, but foremost among these has been the increasing financial pressures on a significant proportion of the population.

Compounding the financial and social burdens on the poorest members of society are the findings that pollution, in general, and climate change in particular have the greatest impact on this group, which also has the least ability to mitigate these impacts (Carson et al. 1997; Hajat et al. 2015; Islam and Winkel 2017; Muller et al. 2018; US Fourth National Climate Assessment 2017). In their innovative research, Muller et al. (2018) adjust the distribution of income data in the United States for both 2011 and 2014 by deducting damages due to exposure to air pollution from reported market income. Their findings suggest that the distribution of income is worse when air pollution is taken into consideration. Their conclusion was:

> The Gini coefficient for this measure of adjusted income is 0.682 in 2011, as compared to 0.482 for market income. By 2014, we estimate that the Gini for adjusted income fell to 0.646, while the market income Gini did not appreciably change. The inclusion of air pollution damage acts like a regressive tax: with air pollution, the bottom 20% of households lose roughly 10% of the share of income, while the top 20% of households gain 10%.
>
> (p. 1)

To this point, the discussion has largely focused on the extent and significance of domestic level inequality in the developed nations such as the United States and United Kingdom. Of even greater potential import is the level of income and wealth inequality across nations, particularly the contrast between the developed world and developing nations. The extent of poverty in the developing world has varied by study and time. In 2005, the World Bank estimated that 2.5 billion people earned less than $2 per day and 11 billion less than $1 (Collins et al. 2009; see also Collier 2007). More recent estimates from the United Nations (UNDP 2019) estimate that some 600 million people currently live below the $1.90 poverty line and this number increases to 1.3 billion when measured by the UN's Multidimensional Poverty Index. Yet, as the UNDP reports, significant progress has been made in the past few decades in addressing some of this inequality, recognizing that simple measures of per capita GDP fail to capture the true nature and extent of these disparities.

The UNDP report presents five key messages: (1) while many people are stepping above minimum floors of achievement in human development, widespread disparities remain;

(2) a new generation of severe inequalities in human development is emerging, even if many of the unresolved inequalities of the twentieth century are declining, (3) inequalities in human development can accumulate through life, frequently heightened by deep political imbalances, (4) assessing inequalities in human development demands a revolution in metrics, and (5) redressing inequalities in human development in the twenty-first century is possible—if we act now, before imbalances in economic power translate into entrenched political dominance.

The report stresses the existence of two seismic shifts that will shape the twenty-first century: technological transformation and climate change. In order to address the challenges of technological change, the report concludes that "having a set of basic capabilities—those associated with the absence of extreme deprivations—is not enough. Enhanced capabilities are becoming crucial for people to own the 'narrative of their lives'" (p. 6). Despite the fact that inequalities in basic capabilities are slowly narrowing, inequalities in enhanced capabilities are widening (typified by life expectancy at age seventy, population with a tertiary education, and the extent of fixed broadband subscriptions).

The potential impact of climate change is equally momentous. To quote (UNDP 2019, p. 17):

> Climate change will hurt human development in many ways beyond crop failures and natural disasters. Between 2030 and 2050 climate change is expected to cause an additional 250,000 deaths a year from malnutrition, malaria, diarrhea and heat stress. Hundreds of millions more people could be exposed to deadly heat by 2050, and the geographic range for disease vectors—such as mosquitoes that transmit malaria or dengue—will likely shift and expand. The overall impact on people will depend on their exposure and their vulnerability. Both factors are intertwined with inequality in a vicious circle. Climate change will hit the tropics harder first, and many developing countries are tropical. Yet developing countries and poor communities have less capacity than their richer counterparts to adapt to climate change and severe weather events. So the effects of climate change deepen existing social and economic fault lines. There are also effects in the other direction, with evidence that some forms of inequality may make action on climate harder.

Other studies have produced similar results, describing "extreme carbon inequality" among nations (Oxfam 2015) and concluding that global warming has increased global inequality (Diffenbaugh and Burke 2019).

This raises a fundamental question: to what extent should the developed world divert resources required for domestic climate change preparedness to the much greater pool of population in the developing world? There are clearly humanitarian reasons for doing so. All of humanity faces the similar threat of global climate change. Yet there are also many more mainstream arguments why extending, and indeed augmenting, aid to the developing world is in the interest of the industrial nations. The developing world has traditionally been a supplier of raw materials and offered a market for goods produced by the developed world. Unfortunately, this relationship has historically been profoundly asymmetrical, with subsidies and tariff and nontariff barriers imposed by the industrialized world significantly diminishing the capabilities of many nations of the developing world to fully capitalize on their natural comparative advantage.

There is at least one more justification for increasing the level of assistance to developing nations in light of recent events. The emergence of the latest pandemic to afflict humanity in the form of COVID-19 has highlighted what Laurie Garrett (1994, 2000) has referred to as the global petri dish, one capable of incubating and transmitting new, or even preexisting, pathogens at a global scale. As discussed in Chapter 11 of this book, the phenomenon has been intensified by increased population pressure and density, certain agricultural practices, and conversion and destruction of natural habitat which place humanity in closer contact with domesticated and wild animals, as well as other disease reservoirs in the natural environment.

Summary

While economy, ecology, and society form the three pillars of sustainability, it is evident that all three are intimately intertwined. In an attempt to explicitly recognize and measure this interdependence and progress towards global sustainability, in 2015 the United Nations developed a series of Sustainable Development Goals, a list of seventeen goals to guide nations' assessment of their progress towards sustainability (UN 2020a). Every year, the international agency produces a detailed progress report on each goal. The latest report, issued in 2020, paints a mixed picture. UN Secretary-General Antonio Guterres has recently stated that

> global efforts to date have been insufficient to deliver the change we need, jeopardizing the Agenda's promise to current and future generations. … Now, due to COVID-19, an unprecedented health, economic and social crisis is threatening lives and livelihoods, making the achievement of Goals even more challenging.
>
> (UN 2020b)

To quote a summary (UN 2020b):

> Yet even these advances were offset elsewhere by growing food insecurity, deterioration of the natural environment, and persistent and pervasive inequalities. Now, in only a short period of time, the COVID-19 pandemic has unleashed an unprecedented crisis, causing further disruption to SDG progress, with the world's poorest and most vulnerable affected the most.

Table 2.6 (UN 2020a) summarizes the status of the seventeen goals in the immediate pre-COVID-19 period. Clearly much more remains to be accomplished in achieving these diverse and ambitious goals.

Table 2.6 Status of UN Sustainable Development Goals

#	Goal	Before COVID-19
1	End poverty in all its forms everywhere	The world is off track to end poverty by 2030 (current projection is 6% still in poverty in 2030, although down from 15.7% in 2010)
2	End hunger, achieve food security and improved nutrition, and promote sustainable agriculture	Population affected by moderate or severe food insecurity rose from 22.4% in 2014 to 25.9% in 2019
3	Ensure healthy lives and promote well-being for all at all ages	Progress in many health areas continues but needs acceleration

Table 2.6 Cont.

#	Goal	*Before COVID-19*
4	Ensure inclusive and equitable quality education and promote lifelong opportunities for all	More than two hundred million children will still be out of school in 2030
5	Achieve gender equality and empower all women and girls	Despite improvements, full gender equality remains unreached
6	Ensure availability and sustainable management of water and sanitation for all	2.2 billion people lack safely managed drinking water, and 4.2 billion people lack safely managed sanitation
7	Ensure access to affordable, reliable, sustainable, and modern energy for all	789 million people lack electricity and 1 in 4 lives without electricity in some developing countries
8	Promote sustained, inclusive, and sustainable economic growth, full and productive employment, and decent work for all	Global GDP per capita growth slowed from 2.0% in 2010–18 to 1.5% in 2019
9	Build resilient infrastructure, promote inclusive and sustainable industrialization, and foster innovation	Manufacturing growth declining due to tariffs and trade tensions
10	Reduce inequality within and among countries	Income inequality falling in some countries (the Gini index fell in thirty-eight out of eighty-four countries in the period 2010–17)
11	Make cities and human settlements inclusive, safe, resilient, and sustainable	Share of urban population living in slums rose to 24% in 2018
12	Ensure sustainable consumption and production patterns	Global material footprint was 73.2 billion MT in 2010 and rose to 85.9 billion MT in 2017
13	Take urgent action to combat climate change and its impacts	Before Covid-19, global community shied away from commitments to reverse the climate crisis (global temperatures are projected to rise by up to 3.2°C by 2100)
14	Conserve and sustainably use the oceans, sea, and marine resources for sustainable development	A 100–150% rise in ocean acidity projected by 2100, affecting half of all marine life
15	Protect, restore, and promote sustainable use of terrestrial ecosystems, sustainably manage forests, combat desertification, halt and reverse land degradation, and halt biodiversity loss	More than 31,000 species threatened with extinction, which is 27% of more than 116,000 assessed species in the International Union for Conservation of Nature Red List
16	Promote peaceful and inclusive societies for sustainable development, provide access to justice for all, and build effective, accountable, and inclusive institutions at all levels	Every day one hundred civilians are killed in armed conflicts
17	Strengthen the means of implementation and revitalize the global partnership for sustainable development	Net official development assistance totaled $147.4 billion in 2019, almost unchanged from 2018, but aid to Africa rose by 1.3% from 2018, and aid to the least-developed countries rose by 2.6% from 2018

Source: UN 2020a.

References

Abd-El Monsef, Hesham et al. (2015) *Water Resources Management*, "Impacts of the Aswan High Dam after 50 years," January 21.

Ackermann, William C. et al. (1973) *Man-Made Lakes: Their Problems and Environmental Effects*, Washington, DC: American Geophysical Union.

Advani, Arun et al. (2020) *The UK's Wealth Distribution and Characteristics of High-Wealth Households*, Resolution Foundation, December.

Alaska Department of Natural Resources (2019) "What's bugging Alaska's forests? Spruce beetle facts and figures."

Aragao, Luiz Eduardo O.C et al. (2008) *Philosophical Transactions of the Royal Society B*, "Interactions between rainfall, deforestation and fires during recent years in the Brazilian Amazonia," May 27.

Arani, Babak M.S., et al. (2021) *Science*, "Exit time as a measure of resilience," June 11.

Balch, Jennifer, et al. (2015) *Bioscience*, "The susceptibility of Southeastern Amazon forests to fire: Insights from a large-scale burn experiment," September.

Boers, Niklas (2021) *Nature Climate Change* "Observation-based early-warning signals for a collapse of the Atlantic-Meridional Overturning Circulation," August.

Boers, Niklas and Martin Rypdal (2021) *PNAS* "Critical slowing down suggests that the western Greenland Ice Sheet is close to a tipping point," May 25.

Borelle, Stephanie B. et al. (2020) *Science* "Predicted growth in plastic waste exceeds efforts to mitigate plastic pollution," September 18.

Brahney, Janice et al. (2021) *PNAS*, "Constraining the atmospheric limb of the plastic cycle," April 20.

Breivik, Knut, et al. (2002) *Science of the Total Environment*, "Towards a global historical emission inventory for selected PCB congeners—A mass balance approach: 2. Emissions," May 6.

Broecker, Wallace and Robert Kunzig (2008) *Fixing Climate: What Past Climate Changes Reveal About the Current Threat—and How to Counter It*, New York: Hill and Wang.

Cameron, Linda (2006) *Environmental Risk Management in New Zealand: Is There Scope to Apply a More Generic Framework?* Policy Perspectives Paper 06/06, New Zealand Treasury, July.

Carson, Rachel (1962) *Silent Spring*, Boston: Houghton Mifflin Harcourt.

Carson, Richard T. et al. (1997) *Environment and Development Economics*, "The relationship between air pollution emissions and income: US data," 2: 433–50.

Cederholm, C. Jeff et al. (2000) *Pacific Salmon and Wildlife: Ecological Contexts, Relationships, and Implications for Management*, Washington Department of Fish and Wildlife.

Chadburn, S.E. et al. (2017) *Nature Climate Change*, "An observation-based constraint on permafrost loss as a function of global warming," April 11.

CEC (Commission for Environmental Cooperation) (2004) *Taking Stock 2001: North American Pollutant Releases and Transfers*, CEC Secretariat, Montréal, June.

Charles, D. et al. (2021) *The Plastic Waste Makers Index: Revealing the Source of the Single-Use Plastics Crisis*, Minderoo Foundation.

CNN (2020) "China's Three Gorges Dam is one of the largest ever created: Was it worth it?" August 1.

Collier, Paul (2007) *The Bottom Billion: Why the Poorest Countries Are Failing and What Can Be Done About It*, Oxford; New York: Oxford University Press.

Collins, Daryl et al. (2009) *Portfolios of the Poor: How the World's Poor Live on $2 a Day*, Princeton, NJ: Princeton University Press.

Conway, Gordon R. (1972) "Ecological aspects of pest control in Malaysia," in M. Taghi Farvar and John P. Milton, *The Careless Technology: Ecology and International Development; The Record of the Conference on the Ecological Aspects of International Development Convened by the Conservation Foundation and the Center for the Biology of Natural Systems, Washington University, December 8-11, 1968, Airlie House, Warrenton, VA*, Garden City, NY: Natural History Press.

Cooney, Rosie (2005) "From promise to practicalities: The precautionary principle on biodiversity conservation and sustainable use," in Rosie Cooney and Barney Dickson (eds.)

Biodiversity and the Precautionary Principle: Risk and Uncertainty in Conservation and Sustainable Use, London: Earthscan, 3–17.

Costanza, Robert et al. (1997) *Nature*, "The value of the world's ecosystem services and natural capital," May 15.

Costanza, Robert et al. (2014) *Global Environmental Change*, "Changes in the global value of ecosystem services," May 20.

Cox, Peter M., et al (2000) *Nature*, "Acceleration of global warming due to carbon-cycle feedbacks in a coupled climate model," November 9.

Dale, Spencer (2019) "Energy in 2018: An unsustainable path." Speech at the launch of the BP Statistical Review of World Energy 2019, London, June 11. www.bp.com/en/global/corporate/news-and-insights/speeches/bp-stats-review-2019-spencer-dale-speech.html

Daly, Herman E. (1996) *Beyond Growth: The Economics of Sustainable Development*, Boston: Beacon Press.

Daly, Herman E. (1999) *Ecological Economics and the Ecology of Economics: Essays in Criticism*, Cheltenham: Edward Elgar.

Daly, Herman E. (2005) "Economics in a full world," *Scientific American*, September.

Davis, Frederick Rowe (2014) *Banned: A History of Pesticides and the Science of Toxicology*, New Haven, CT: Yale University Press.

Dietz, Simon et al. (2021) *PNAS*, "Economic impacts of tipping points in the climate system," August 24.

Diffenbaugh, Noah S. and Marshall Burke (2019) PNAS, "Global warming has increased global economic inequality," May 14.

Ebenstein, Avraham and Sharygin, Ethan Jennings (2009) *World Bank Economic Review*, "The consequences of the 'missing girls' of China," November 5.

Economist (2019) "The Amazon is approaching an irreversible tipping point," August 3.

EEA (European Environment Agency) (2012) *The Impact of Endocrine Disruptors on Wildlife, People and Their Environments*, May.

EEA (European Environment Agency) (2013) *Late Lessons from Early Warnings: Science, Precaution, Innovation*. EEA Report No. 1/2013, European Environment Agency.

Ehrenreich, Barbara (2011) *Nickel and Dimed: On (Not) Getting By in America,* New York: Picador Modern Classics.

Elkington, John (1998) *Cannibals with Forks: The Triple Bottom Line of the 21st Century Business*, Gabriola Island, BC: New Society Publishers.

Farquharson, Louise M. et al. (2019) *Geophysical Research Letters*, "Climate change drives widespread and rapid thermokarst development in very cold permafrost in the Canadian high arctic," June 10.

Federal Reserve Bank of St. Louis (2019) "What wealth inequality in America looks like: Key facts & figures," August 14.

Forbes (2020) "Top 1% of U.S. households hold 15 times more wealth than bottom 50% combined," October 8.

Francis, Jennifer A. (2018) "Meltdown," *Scientific American*, April.

Garrett, Laurie (1994) *The Coming Plague: Newly Emerging Diseases in a World out of Balance,* New York: Farrar, Strauss and Giroux.

Garrett, Laurie (2000) *Betrayal of Trust: The Collapse of Global Public Health,* New York: Hyperion.

Geyer, Roland, et al (2017) *Science Advances*, "Production, use and fate of all plastics ever made," July 19.

Goerner, Sally et al. (2009) *Ecological Economics*, "Quantifying economic sustainability: Implications for free-enterprise theory, policy and practice," August 28.

Gold, Steve C. and Wendy E. Wagner (2020) *Science* "Filling gaps in science exposes gaps in chemical regulation," June 5.

Goldsmith, Edward and Nicholas Hildyard (1984) *The Social and Environmental Effects of Large Dams*, San Francisco: Sierra Club Books.

Grafton, R. Quentin et al. (2019) *Nature Sustainability*, "Realizing resilience for decision-making," October.

Graham, John D. et al. (1997) *Risk vs. Risk: Tradeoffs in Protecting Health and the Environment*, Cambridge, MA: Harvard University Press.

Guardian (2021) "Climate crisis: Scientists spot warning signs of Gulf Stream collapse." August 5.

Hajat, Anjum et al. (2015) *Current Environmental Health Reports*, "Socioeconomic disparies and air pollution exposure: A global review," December.

Harremoes, Poul et al. (2001) *Late Lessons from Early Warnings: The Precautionary Principle 1896–2000*. Environmental issue report no. 22, European Environment Agency, Copenhagen.

Hochella, Michael F. et al. (2019) *Science*, "Nanomaterials impact on Earth system," March 29.

Holling, C.S. (1973) *Annual Review of Ecology and Systematics*, "Resilience and stability of ecological systems," November.

Hudson, Valerie and Andrea M. den Boer (2004) *Bare Branches: The Security Implications of Asia's Surplus Male Population*, Cambridge, MA: MIT Press.

Huesemann, Michael and Joyce Huesemann (2011) *Techno-Fix: Why Technology Won't Save Us or the Environment*, Gabriola Island, BC: New Society Publishers.

Hughes, Terence P. (1994) *Science*, "Catastrophes, phase shifts, and large-scale degradation of a Caribbean coral reef," September 9.

Hvistendahl, Mara (2008) "China's Three Gorges Dam: An environmental catastrophe?" *Scientific American*, March 25.

IEA (International Energy Agency) (2018) *The Future of Cooling: Opportunities for Energy-Efficient Air Conditioning*, May.

IEA (International Energy Agency) (2019) *The Future of Cooling in China*: Delivering on Plans for Sustainable Air Conditioning, June.

Ise, Takeshi, et al. (2008) *Nature Geoscience*, "High sensitivity of peat decomposition to climate change through water-table feedback," October 12.

Islam, Nazrul and John Winkel (2017) "Climate change and social inequality." DESA Working Paper No. 152, UN Department of Economic & Social Affairs, October.

Jansen, Eystein et al. (2020) *Nature Climate Change*, "Past perspectives on the present era of abrupt Arctic climate change," August.

Joughin, Ian et al. (2021) *Science Advances*, "Ice-shelf retreat drives recent Pine Island glacier speedup," June 11.

Kinzig, Ann P. et al. (2006) *Ecology and Society*, "Resilience and regime shifts: Assessing cascading effects," 11(1): 20.

Knight, Frank H. (1921) *Risk, Uncertainty and Profit*, reprinted by Cornell University Library.

Kopp, Robert E. et al. (2016) *Earth's Future*, "Tipping elements and climate-economic shocks: Pathways toward integrated assessment," August 25.

Kurz, W.A. et al. (2008) *Nature*, "Mountain pine beetle and forest carbon feedback to climate change," April 24.

Lancet (2017) "Microplastics and human health—an urgent problem," October.

Landrum, Laura and Marika M. Holland (2020) *Nature Climate Change*, "Extremes become routine in an emerging new Arctic," September 14.

Larour, E. et al. (2019) *Science*, "Slowdown in Antarctic mass loss from solid earth and sea-level feedbacks," June 7.

Lenton, Timothy M. et al. (2019) *Nature*, "Climate tipping points—too risky to bet against," November 27, correction April 9, 2020.

Marchant, Gary E. and Kenneth L. Mossman (2004) *Arbitrary and Capricious: The Precautionary Principle in the European Union Courts*, Westport, CT: Praeger.

Meijer, Lourens J.J. et al. (2021) *Science Advances*, "More than 1000 rivers account for 80% of global riverine plastic emissions into the ocean," April 30.

Milillo, P. et al. (2019) *Science Advances*, "Heterogeneous retreat and ice melt of Thwaites Glacier, West Antarctica," February.

Morales-Caselles, Carmen et al. (2021) *Nature Sustainability*, "An inshore-offshore sorting system revealed from global classification of ocean litter," June.

Muller, Nicholas Z. et al. (2018) *PLoS One,* "The distribution of income is worse than you think: Including pollution impacts into measures of income inequality," March 21.

Myers, Ransom A. et al. (2007) *Science,* "Cascading effects of the loss of apex predatory sharks from a coastal ocean," March 30.

NAS (National Academy of Sciences) (2012) *A Research Strategy for Environmental, Health, and Safety Aspects of Engineered Nanomaterials.*

NAS (National Academy of Sciences) (2016) *Triennial Review of the National Nanotechnology Initiative.*

NAS (National Academy of Sciences) (2020a) *A Quadrennial Review of the National Nanotechnology Initiative.*

NAS (National Academy of Sciences) (2020b) *Environmental Neuroscience: Advancing the Understanding of How Chemical Exposures Impact Brain Health and Disease: Proceedings of a Workshop.*

National Research Council (2013) *Abrupt Impacts of Climate Change: Anticipating Surprises.*

Natural Resources Canada (2018) *The State of Canada's Forests: Annual Report 2018.*

Nemetz, Peter N. (2022) *Corporate Strategy and Sustainability,* Routledge, forthcoming.

NEFMC (New England Fishery Management Council) (n.d.) "The trends in scallop landings, revenue, and prices."

New York Times (2015) " 'One child' culture is entrenched in China," November 4.

New York Times (2017) "More permafrost than thought may be lost as planet warms," April 13.

New York Times (2019) "Russian land of permafrost and mammoths is thawing," August 4.

New York Times (2019) " 'It's really close': How the Amazon rainforest could self-destruct," August 30.

Nisbet, E.G. et al. (2019) *Global Biochemical Cycles,* "Very strong atmospheric methane growth in the 4 years 2014–2017: Implications for the Paris Agreement," March 18.

Noble, David G. and John E. Elliott (1986) "Environmental contaminants in Canadian seabirds 1968–1985: Trends and effects," Ottawa, Canadian Wildlife Service.

Oczkowski, Autumn and Scott Nixon (2008) *Estuarine, Coastal and Shelf Science,* "Increasing nutrient concentrations and the rise and fall of a coastal fishery: A review of data from the Nile Delta, Egypt," April.

Oczkowski, Autumn et al. (2009) *PNAS,* "Anthropogenic enhancement of Egypt's Mediterranean fishery," February 3.

O'Neill, Daniel W. et al. (2018) *Nature Sustainability,* "A good life for all within planetary boundaries," February 5.

Oxfam (2015) *Extreme Carbon Inequality: Why the Paris Climate Deal Must Put the Poorest, Lowest Emitting and Most Vulnerable People First,* December 2.

Pandolfi, John M. et al. (2011) *Science,* "Projecting coral reef futures under global warming and ocean acidification," July 22.

Peterson, Deborah C. (2006) "Precaution: Principles and practice in Australian environments and natural resource management." Presidential address at the fiftieth annual Australian Agricultural and Resource Economics Society Conference, Manly, New South Wales, 8–10 February.

Pietroiusti, Antonio et al. (2018) *WIREs Nanomedicine and Nanobiotechnology* "Nanomaterial exposure, toxicity, and impact on human health," February 23.

Piketty, Thomas (2014) *Capital in the Twenty-First Century,* Cambridge, MA: Harvard University Press.

Pistone, Kristina et al. (2019) *Geophysical Research Letters,* "Radiative heating of an ice-free Arctic Ocean," June 20.

Pittinger, Charles A. and William E. Bishop (1999) *Human and Ecological Risk Assessment: An International Journal,* "Unraveling the chimera: A corporate view of the precautionary principle," June 3.

Prata, Joana Correia et al. (2020) *Science of the Total Environment,* "Environmental exposure to microplastics: An overview on possible human health effects," February 1.

Putnam, Robert D. (2000, updated to 2020) *Bowling Alone: Revised and Updated; The Collapse and Revival of American Community,* New York: Simon and Schuster.

Raffensperger, Carolyn and Joel Tickner (1999) *Protecting Public Health and the Environment: Implementing the Precautionary Principle,* Washington, DC: Island Press.

Rees, William (2007) "Is humanity fatally successful?" in Peter N. Nemetz (ed.) *Sustainable Resource Management: Reality or Illusion?* Cheltenham, UK: Edward Elgar.

Ripple, William J. et al. (2013) *Journal of Animal Ecology*, "Trophic cascades from wolves to grizzly bears in Yellowstone," July 16.

Robel, Alexander A. et al. (2019) *PNAS*, "Marine ice sheet instability amplifies and skews uncertainty in projections of future sea-level rise," July 8.

Rockstrom, Johan et al. (2009) *Nature*, "A safe operating space for humanity," September 24.

Røpke, Inge (2004) *Ecological Economics*, "The early history of modern ecological economics," 50(3–4): 293–314.

Røpke, Inge (2005) *Ecological Economics*, "Trends in the development of ecological economics from the late 1980s to the early 2000s," 55(2): 262–90.

Saez, Emmanuel and Gabriel Zucman (2014) "Wealth inequality in the United States since 1913: Evidence from capitalized income tax data." Working paper 20625, National Bureau of Economic Research, October.

Sandin, Per (1999) *Human and Ecological Risk Assessment*, "Dimensions of the precautionary principle," August 9.

Sandin, Per and Sven Ove Hansson (2011) *Human and Ecological Risk Assessment: An International Journal,* "The default value approach to the precautionary principle," September 27.

Sandin, Per et al. (2011) *Journal of Risk Research*, "Five charges against the precautionary principle," April 15.

Saturday Evening Post (2014) "Why did Henry Ford double his minimum wage?" January 3.

Saunders, Caroline et al. (2006) "Food miles: Comparative energy/emissions performance of New Zealand's agricultural industry," Lincoln University, July.

Schneider, Stephen H. (2003) *Abrupt Non-linear Climate Change, Irreversibility and Surprise,* Organisation for Economic Co-operation and Development.

Science (2021) *Special Issue: Our Plastics Dilemma,* July 2.

Scudder, Thayer (2005) *The Future of Large Dams: Dealing with Social, Environmental, Institutional and Political Costs,* Hoboken, NJ: Routledge.

Shamir, Mirit et al. (2007) *Artificial Intelligence and Law,* "The application of fuzzy logic to the precautionary principle," November.

Shcherbak, Iurii et al. (2014) *PNAS*, "Non-linear response of soil nitrous oxide missions to fertilizer nitrogen," June 14.

Shell, Ellen Ruppel (2009) *Cheap: The High Cost of Discount Culture,* New York: Penguin.

Smith, Alisa and J.B. MacKinnon (2007) *The 100-Mile Diet: A Year of Local Eating,* Toronto: Vintage Canada.

Spash, Clive (1999) *Environmental Values,* "The development of environmental thinking in economics," November.

Staal, Arie et al. (2020) *Nature Communications,* "Hysteresis of tropical forests in the 21st century," October 5.

Stanley, D.J. and A.G. Warne (1993) *Science,* "Nile delta: Recent geological evolution and human impact," April 30.

Steffen, Will et al. (2015) *Science,* "Planetary boundaries: Guiding human development on a changing planet," February 13.

Steffen, Will et al. (2018) *PNAS*, "Trajectories of the earth system in the Anthropocene," August 14.

Steig, Eric J. (2019) *Science,* "How fast will the Antarctic ice sheet retreat?" June 7.

Sterling, Claire (1973) "The trouble with superdams," in *Britannica Yearbook of Science and the Future, 1974,* Chicago; London: Encyclopaedia Britannica, 112–27.

Stickler, Claudia M. et al. (2013) *PNAS*, "Dependence of hydropower energy generation on forests in the Amazon Basin at local and regional scales," June 4.

Stiglitz, Joseph (2013) *The Price of Inequality: How Today's Divided Society Endangers Our Future,* New York: W.W. Norton.

Swindles, Graeme T. et al. *Scientific Reports,* "The long-term fate of permafrost peatlands under rapid climate warming," December 9.

Tanabe, Shinsuke et al. (1984) *Archives of Environmental Contamination and Toxicology,* "Polychlorobiphenyls, ΣDDT, and hexachlorocyclohexane isomers in the western North Pacific ecosystem," November 1.

Tenner, Edward (1996) *Why Things Bite Back: Technology and the Revenge of Unintended Consequences,* New York: Vintage.

Tickner, Joel A. (ed.) (2003) *Precaution, Environmental Science and Preventive Public Policy,* Washington, DC: Island Press.

Trisos, Christopher H. et al. (2020) *Nature,* "The projected timing of abrupt ecological disruption from climate change," April.

Trusel, Luke D. et al. (2018) Nature, "Nonlinear rise in Greenland runoff in response to post-industrial Arctic warming," December 6.

UN (United Nations) (2017) "Factsheet: Marine pollution," The Ocean Conference, New York, 5–9 June.

UN (United Nations) (2020a) *Sustainable Development Goals Report.*

UN (United Nations) (2020b) "Sustainable Development Goals," press release, July 7.

UNDP (United Nations Development Programme) (2019) Human Development Report: Beyond Income, Beyond Averages, Beyond Today; Inequalities in Human Development in the 21st Century.

UNESCO (United Nations Educational, Scientific and Cultural Organization) (2005) *The Precautionary Principle.*

US CCSP (Climate Change Science Program) (2009) *Thresholds of Climate Change in Ecosystems,* January.

US EPA (Environmental Protection Agency) (1998) *Chemical Hazard Data Availability Study: What Do We Really Know About the Safety of High Production Volume Chemicals?* Office of Pollution Prevention and Toxics, April.

US Fourth National Climate Assessment (2017) Executive summary: Climate Science Special Report, Highlights of the Findings of the U.S. Global Change Research Program Climate Science Special Report.

US NIEHS (National Institute of Environmental Health Sciences) (2020) "Microplastic pollution and human health," Partnerships for Environmental Public Education, podcast, June 22.

US NIH (National Institutes of Health) (n.d.) "Endocrine disruptors."

Vardas, Giannis and Anastasiois Xepapadeas (2009) *Environmental and Resource Economics,* "Model uncertainty, ambiguity and the precautionary principle: Implications for biodiversity management," August 13.

Vethaak, Andre Dick and Juliette Legler (2021) Science, "Microplastics and human health," February 12.

Vörösmarty, Charles J. and Dork Sahagian (2000) *Bioscience,* "Anthropogenic disturbance of the terrestrial water cycle," September.

Wadham, J.L. et al. (2012) *Nature,* "Potential methane reservoirs beneath Antarctica," August 30.

WHO (World Health Organization) (accessed 2019) "Disease, injury and causes of death: Country, regional and global estimates, 2000–2015."

WHO (World Health Organization) (2019) *World Malaria Report 2019.*

Wiener, Jonathan B. and Michael D. Rogers (2002) *Journal of Risk Research,* "Comparing precaution in the United States and Europe," 5(4): 317–49.

WMO (World Meteorological Organization) (2021) *WMO Global Annual to Decadal Climate Update for 2021–2025.*

World Bank (n.d.) Databank, metadata glossary, indicator name: Gini index (world Bank estimate.)

World Bank (various years) World Development Index.

Wunderling, Nico et al. (2021) *Earth System Dynamics,* "Interacting tipping elements increase risk of climate effects under global warming," June 3.

WWF (World Wildlife Fund) (2010) *Living Planet Report 2010: Biodiversity, Biocapacity and Development.*

WWF (World Wildlife Fund) and Allianz (2009) *Major Tipping Points in the Earth's Climate System and Consequences for the Insurance Sector.*

Yumashev, Dmitry et al. (2019) *Nature Communications*, "Climate policy implications of nonlinear decline of Arctic land permafrost and other cryosphere elements," April 23.

Part II

Greenhouse-gas-intensive sectors

3 Unsustainable industry

Business is a key player in any attempt to achieve sustainability given its central position in our economic system, and its role as a producer of goods and services. The word "sustainability" has entered the lexicon of the modern corporation as most of the largest companies in North America and many in Europe have incorporated the concept into either their annual reports or into standalone reports devoted exclusively to a discussion of the subject. Corporate acceptance of this concept can be mapped on a continuum all the way from full-throttled embrace to begrudging and mere token reference. In an insightful analysis, Scott Valentine (2006) created a typology of corporate environmental governance coupled with an empirical metric for signaling the level of commitment based on qualitative and quantitative content of annual corporate reporting documents. Table 3.1 defines the five levels of corporate buy-in. Level 1 companies—the most committed—are deemed leaders who have embraced the thrust of Porter and Van der Linde's landmark *Harvard Business Review* article of 1995. In this seminal work, the authors discard the traditional false dichotomy between pollution control and corporate profitability. Their thesis is that corporate strategy that recognizes, addresses, and incorporates issues of sustainability can yield significant and "sustainable" competitive advantage.

At the other end of Valentine's spectrum are Level 5 companies—avoiders—who make passing reference to the concept or avoid mentioning it altogether. On balance, the evidence would seem to suggest that the distribution of firms along this response spectrum has shifted somewhat toward Level 1. However, this shift is not monotonic. Some companies wear their commitment to sustainability very lightly and can change course opportunistically. A case in point is the American agricultural corporation, Cargill, which received praise for agreeing to a moratorium on buying soybeans from deforested lands in the Amazon. Since then, the company has refused to agree to a similar moratorium in another major soy producing area in Brazil (*New York Times* July 29, 2019). This prompted one environmental nongovernmental organization to issue a scathing report entitled *The Worst Company in the World* (Mighty Earth 2019), calling out the company for its checkered record on pollution control and meat contamination as well as deforestation.

There are a multitude of factors and actors that influence corporate policy on sustainability. Included among these are, most obviously, government regulatory agencies but also, to no less degree, suppliers, customers, competitors, banks, insurance agencies, nongovernmental organizations (NGOs), financial markets, and the court of public opinion reflected in the formal and informal media.

There are several critical issues that lie at the heart of assessing the extent of sustainability within the corporate sector and these include: how the concept is defined,

DOI: 10.4324/9781003199540-5

Table 3.1 Corporate levels of sustainability buy-in

Level	Defined as:	Which appears in environmental reports as:
Level 1—leaders	Firms committed to setting quantitative benchmarks in environmental initiatives.	Quantitative progress indicators related to environmental issues
Level 2—contenders	Firms that have adopted externally accredited environmental management systems.	Specific reference made to ISO14000 or accreditation under the EU Eco-Management and Audit Scheme
Level 3—talkers	Firms that are currently experimenting with the effectiveness of environmental management initiatives.	Qualitative standalone environmental reports
Level 4—pretenders	Firms that understand the threat posed by poor environmental governance. These firms, therefore, endeavor to demonstrate that they meet all binding regulations.	Qualitative environmental disclosure of more than fifty words in annual report or on website
Level 5—avoiders	Firms that obey environmental regulations because they must. However, they do not see a need to strategically address any environmental issues.	Empty space. Firms classified as avoiders do not disclose any information on environmental issues

Source: Valentine 2006.

measured, and incorporated into corporate decision-making. Each of these issues is discussed below with reference to several bellwether case studies.

Defining corporate sustainability

Translating the Brundtland Report's definition of sustainability in the context of the corporate sector poses a unique challenge. In theory, to be truly sustainable, a corporation should have a zero ecological footprint into the indefinite future. Whether this is in fact obtainable in light of the laws of thermodynamics remains an open question. One radical approach to reaching this goal has been advanced by McDonough and Braungart (1998, 2002) who propose a new industrial revolution. This would entail a complete redesign of the production process from raw material extraction, through production to final consumption and disposal. The current system of production has been labeled "cradle to grave" (Figure 3.1a). In contrast, the "cradle-to-cradle" approach advocated by McDonough and Braungart is illustrated in Figure 3.1b. In this model, raw materials are drawn exclusively from renewables; production byproducts are either biological nutrients that can be recycled in the environment or technical nutrients that can be reincorporated into a closed loop production process; and the final product is returned by the consumer to the producer for reuse. A variant of this model has been termed the circular economy (Ellen MacArthur Foundation 2015) in contrast to the traditional linear model of production.

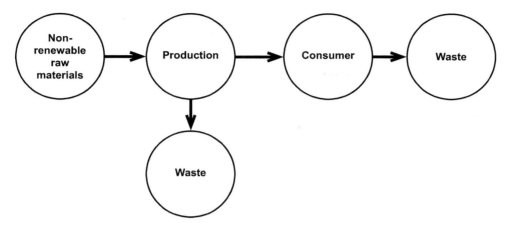

Figure 3.1a Cradle-to-grave production.

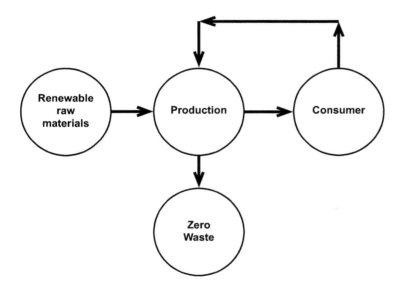

Figure 3.1b Cradle-to-cradle production.
Source: McDonough and Braungart.

Case study 1: Interface Carpets

The archetypal example of the attempted application of the circular model is Interface Inc, the world's largest producer of carpets for the commercial sector. The critical individual in Interface was the late Ray Anderson who founded the company in 1973. Anderson wrote several books and articles (1999 and 2007; Anderson and White 2009; Anderson et al. 2010) explaining his radical conversion to the cause of sustainability when he realized that he and his company were both a "plunderer of the earth." They "were part of the endemic process that is going on at a frightening, accelerating rate worldwide to rob our children and all their descendants of their futures" (Anderson 2007, p. 91). Anderson described this revelation as tantamount to a "spear through the heart" and he undertook to convert his company into the world's most sustainable enterprise. Anderson identified seven fronts on which serious change is needed for sustainability to be achieved: waste, with the goal of moving to zero waste; emissions, the goal being benign emissions; renewable energy; closed loop recycling; resource-efficient transportation; a "sensitivity hookup," which includes service to the community and closer relations with employees, suppliers, and customers; and a redesign of commerce itself, which entails:

> the acceptance of entirely new notions of economics, especially prices that reflect full costs. To us, it means shifting emphasis from simply selling products to providing services; thus, our commitment to downstream distribution, installation, maintenance, and recycling. These are all aimed at forming cradle-to-cradle relationships with customers and suppliers, relationships based on delivering, via the Evergreen Service Agreement™, the services our products provide, in lieu of the products themselves.
>
> (2007, pp. 104–105)

In sum, Anderson's conceptualization of the prototypical company of the twenty-first century is that it is "strongly service-oriented, resource-efficient, wasting nothing, solar-driven, cyclical (no longer take–make–waste linear), and strongly connected to our constituencies—our communities (building social equity), our customers, and our suppliers—and to one another" (p. 105). Figures 3.2 and 3.3 illustrate Anderson's conception of the typical company of the twentieth century and his view of how modern corporations should be redesigned for sustainability.

Two central parts to operationalizing Interface's sustainability strategy are: first, the adoption of a leasing system (called an Evergreen Lease) whereby the carpet is not owned by the customer but by Interface instead; and, second, the use of carpet tiles. When a carpet starts to show signs of fading, wear or damage, individual tiles are removed, rather than the entire carpet, and returned to Interface for recycling into new carpet. This is a type of "reverse logistics" defined by Sarkis (2010, p. 19) as a system "for the recovery of products or packaging from the consumer, or supply chain member." This process is formalized in Clause 6 of Interface's Evergreen Lease, which reads: "During the lease term [7 years], nothing contained herein shall give to [the] Customer any right, title or interest in or to the Carpet except as a lessee. At all times, legal title to the Carpet shall remain with Interface, and the Carpet shall not be considered a fixture for any purpose regardless of the degree of its installation in or affixation to real property" (Anderson and White 2009, p. 288).

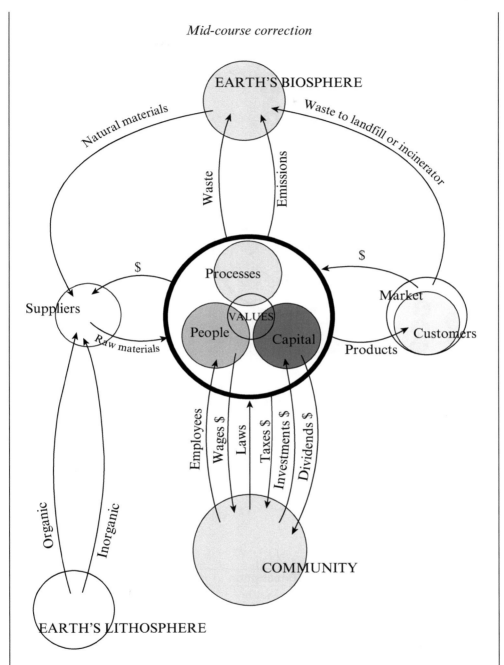

Mid-course correction

EARTH'S BIOSPHERE

Natural materials

Waste to landfill or incinerator

Waste

Emissions

$

Processes

$

Suppliers

Market

VALUES

People

Capital

Customers

Raw materials

Products

Employees

Wages $

Laws

Taxes $

Investments $

Dividends $

Organic

Inorganic

COMMUNITY

EARTH'S LITHOSPHERE

Figure 3.2 Anderson's conception of the modern corporation.
Source: Anderson 2007.

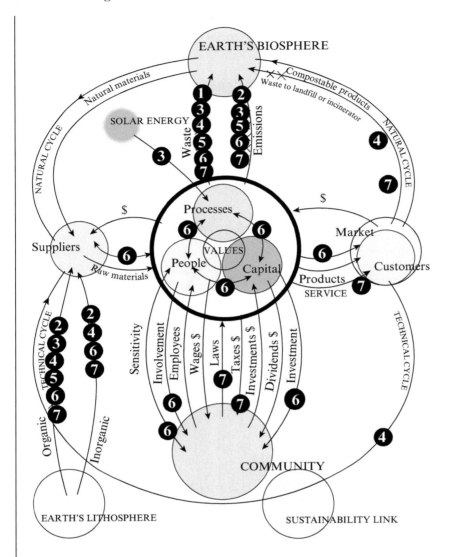

Link #	Description
1	Zero waste
2	Benign emissions
3	Renewable energy
4	Closing the loop
5	Resource-efficient transportation
6	Sensitivity hookup (service to community), closer relations among stakeholders
7	Redesign of commerce itself

Figure 3.3 Anderson's proposed redesign for corporate sustainability.
Source: Anderson 2007.

Interface's achievements

On Interface's corporate website (Interface.com), the company presents an annual update of progress towards the goal of zero total ecological impact. The company was ranked fourth (after Unilever, Patagonia, and IKEA) in the Globescan 2020 Sustainability Survey. The latest sustainability data for Interface available (personal correspondence with Interface) include the following highlights:

> **Carbon footprint:** the average carbon footprint of Interface's carpet has fallen 66 percent since 1996, and is the lowest in the industry
>
> **Energy:** energy efficiency at Interface's manufacturing sites has improved by 43 percent since 1996
>
> **Renewable energy**: 88 percent of energy used at Interface's manufacturing sites is derived from renewable sources
>
> **Greenhouse gas (GHG) emissions**: GHG emissions intensity at Interface's manufacturing sites has fallen 9 percent since 1996
>
> **Raw materials**: 58 percent of raw materials used to make Interface carpet are either recycled or bio-based
>
> **Water:** total water intake intensity at Interface manufacturing sites has fallen 88 percent since 1996
>
> **Waste:** waste sent by Interface to landfills has fallen 91 percent since 1996
>
> **Reuse**: 13 million pounds of used carpet have been diverted from landfills
>
> **Recycling**: 163,000 pounds of fishing nets have been collected and shipped to Interface's recycling partner
>
> **Safety performance**: total accident frequency rate is down 77 percent from 1999.

Several graphics on Interface's website support these accomplishments: total energy use by source 2016; energy use per unit of finished product; renewable energy use at manufacturing sites; and waste to landfills (see Interface n.d. a).

Anderson's reconceptualization of the modern corporation

Reengineering a major industrial corporation and reconceptualizing its strategic mission is a daunting undertaking, but Ray Anderson adopted a radical approach to business and economics. The standard economic model subdivides the products of a modern industrial economy into two categories: goods and services. Anderson was among the first to realize that this categorization represents a false dichotomy. With the exception of purchases motivated by concerns over appearance and personal prestige, consumers do not buy goods for their physical presence—they buy them for the services they provide. Does one buy a refrigerator, for example, because one likes a large colored metal box in one's kitchen? The answer is no. This good is bought because of the service it provides in the form of refrigeration of food.

By adopting this insightful new and unified view of goods and services, it is possible to focus on the nature of the service provided rather than the physical good itself. Instead of selling carpet per se, Interface made the conceptual jump to selling services. To Interface, the key carpet services that consumers were buying included color, design, texture, warmth, acoustics, comfort under foot, cleanliness, and improved indoor air quality. The customer benefits from Interface's novel approach in several ways: a smaller amount of carpet is replaced, there is no requirement for waste disposal by the customer, and the carpet can be expensed rather than capitalized. By reclaiming and recycling carpet tiles, Interface is able to lower its material costs, reduce its environmental impact, and lock customers into a longer-term leasing relationship rather than a one-off sale.

Anderson envisaged the emergence of the truly sustainable corporation, a modern industrial corporation relying exclusively on renewable inputs (both material and energy) and producing zero waste.

The competitive environment

A crucial question is whether a company, such as Interface, which adopts a radically different business model can survive and prosper in a highly competitive marketplace. The answer depends on the nature and direction of the competitive environment. If the market is moving towards more sustainable products and the company has a leadership role in sustainability, then the assessment of its prospects is more positive. This is congruent with Michael Porter's thesis that a sustainability strategy is an important route to building a strong competitive advantage.

The two most significant competitors to Interface are Mohawk Industries and Shaw Industries, the former being a public company, the latter a private entity. The critical question is whether either of these firms has an equally strong sustainability strategy which could threaten Interface's potential competitive advantage.

Mohawk Industries

Mohawk Industries' first sustainability report in 2009 (Mohawk 2009; Mohawksustainability. com) laid out the company's goals in four key areas: reductions in energy use, water use, GHG emissions, and waste to landfill. The stated intention was to improve upon the performance in each area by 25 percent by 2020. This is in marked contrast to Interface's "Mission Zero," which aimed for a zero environmental impact by 2020. In Mohawk's report for 2016, it listed eight metrics it used to measure its progress towards sustainability: pounds of recycled waste, water consumption reduction, GHG intensity reduction, energy intensity reduction, water intensity reduction, number of products containing recyclable material, number of plastic bottles recycled annually, and pounds of tires recycled into doormats. The interpretation of these data is somewhat problematic since, in some cases, there is no denominator or baseline against which to measure the degree of progress. Four figures in their 2019 *Sustainability Report*, however, do provide data on the degree of achievement of their four goals from 2010. In only one case did they achieve their goal of 35 percent or greater reduction from 2010: GHG emissions intensity 18.8 percent, energy intensity 7.23 percent, waste to landfill 53.9 percent, water intensity 8.1 percent.

Shaw Industries

The fact that Shaw Industries is privately held poses a major challenge to the assessment of corporate sustainability. However, one very important piece of information is available which bears upon the corporation's commitment to, and movement towards, sustainable production. For reasons of cost, many companies in this industry and numerous others rely to a certain degree on recycled rather than virgin material. An excellent example is provided by the pulp and paper industry where recycled paper products are part of a profitable international market. The principal trade-off is a result of the recycling process itself where the fibers tend to degrade with each recycling loop. As such, it is always necessary to make up for this deficiency by supplementing the production process with virgin feedstock. This phenomenon, referred to as downcycling, appears superficially to be related to the laws of thermodynamics and has appeared to impose a major constraint on industrial processes.

Recent technological advances have led to the emergence of upcycling, where waste products are converted into higher value products. Shaw Industries was an early adopter of upcycling, using old carpet fiber to produce new carpet material with no loss of quality. While Interface is experimenting with upcycling, Shaw Industries may have already achieved sustainable competitive advantage with this technological advance. In a case study of Shaw Industries, the Investor Environmental Health Network (IEHN 2010b) claimed that Shaw Industries was prompted to pursue its intensive research into technological innovations to pursue sustainability by the very public commitment to this cause by Ray Anderson and Interface.

It is instructive to ask if it is possible to conceive of an existing carpet manufacturing process which meets Anderson's criteria for true sustainability. Somewhat tongue in cheek, one possible answer would be a carpet that relies for its raw material on pasture-bred sheep, natural organic dyes, human labor, and wooden looms and produces biodegradable waste. In fact, such carpets have been produced— and continue to be produced—in countries such as Turkey, Iran, Pakistan, and India. On reflection, this model may entail two possible problems with achieving sustainability: (1) the output is limited, although a major ramping up of production for the global market might go a long way towards solving the endemic problem of unemployment and underemployment in the developing world; and (2) the carpets must be shipped from their locus of production to global markets by modern and energy-intensive transport. Since the delivery of the products is not time dependent, one solution might be the adoption of wind-driven sea transport or novel hybrid versions thereof recently demonstrated in the shipment of wine (Willner 2021). Of course, wine tends to mature with age, so extra time on the high seas might not be an unfavorable economic issue.

Assessing Interface's current and future competitive and sustainability situation

There are at least two critical issues to consider when attempting to assess this situation: (1) the existence and sustainability of Interface's competitive advantage, and (2) the prospects that the company will achieve its sustainability goals in the immediate future. A useful concept to use in conducting this analysis was developed by Hamel and Valikagnas (2003) and is called "strategic decay." The authors outline four metrics to assess a firm's performance: (1) Replication: Is the company's strategy losing its distinctiveness? (2) Supplantation: Is the company's strategy in danger of being superseded? (3) Exhaustion: Is the company's strategy reaching the point of exhaustion? and (4) Evisceration: Is increasing customer power eviscerating the company's margins?

First, it appears that Interface may be facing strategic decay risk on replication as its principal competitors increasingly adopt sustainability initiatives. And second, the problem of potential exhaustion can be manifested if the pace of improvement in key performance metrics is slowing. A hint of this problem is indicated by some of Interface's current and past graphed eco-efficiency metrics. Some of these metrics display initially rapid technological achievements followed by a leveling off. These include the latest metrics for waste to landfills from manufacturing sites and energy use per unit of finished product, although this latter problem is tempered by the increasing use of renewable energy. More revealing, however, would be the trend of Interface's metrics for which it no longer publishes historical figures, including water intake for both modular and broadloom carpet. Interestingly, a similarly mixed pattern in historical trends of some eco-efficiency metrics is characteristic of some of Mohawk's results as well, including water intensity and waste-to-landfill intensity (Mohawk 2016). What this seems to suggest is that for some aspects of production the low-hanging fruit have already been picked and further advances will require a change in or modification of technology. Interface and its competitors have clearly made remarkable strides towards remolding their corporate strategies and technology towards greater sustainability. The issue, instead, revolves round the prospects of making significant new strides in the immediate future.

In gauging sustainability, one must also make a system-wide assessment as opposed to focusing only on the production process per se. In making an assessment, it is useful not only to closely examine the financial statements of the company, but also to consult filings by the corporation required by the US Securities and Exchange Commission (SEC). Of these filing requirements, the 10-K form is frequently the most informative as it requires the corporation to disclose, among other things, all major current and anticipated risks. It is important to bear in mind, however, that a corporation may be inclined to include or overstate risks solely for the purpose of avoiding any future legal challenges that they have not disclosed all material facts. In spite of this caveat, however, the 10-K provides critical information on the state of the corporation. The most significant entry in a recent 10-K section on risk for Interface (US SEC Interface-10K, p. 14) is as follows:

Item 1a. Risk factors

"*Large increases in the cost of petroleum-based raw materials could adversely affect us if we are unable to pass these cost increases through to our customers.* Petroleum-based products comprise the predominant portion of the cost of raw materials that we use in manufacturing. While we attempt to match cost increases with corresponding price increases, continued volatility in the cost of petroleum-based raw materials could adversely affect our financial results if we are unable to pass through such price increases to our customers.

Unanticipated termination or interruption of any of our arrangements with our primary third party suppliers of synthetic fiber could have a material adverse effect on us. We depend on a small number of third party suppliers of synthetic fiber and a single supplier for our LVT [luxury vinyl tile] products. The unanticipated termination or interruption of any of our supply arrangements with our current suppliers of synthetic fiber (nylon) or sole supplier of LVT, including failure by any third party supplier to meet our product specifications, could have a material adverse effect on us because we do not have the capability to manufacture our own fiber for use in our carpet products or our own LVT."

Clearly, a reliance on fossil-based synthetics represents an additional obstacle to achieving the corporate goal of long-term zero impact. Table 3.2 lists the energy consumption and, by extension, the GHG profile of alternative textile fibers.

In this regard, however, Interface has recently achieved a remarkable advance in the GHG profile of one of its products: it is carbon negative. As Interface reports in describing the creation of a carbon negative product (Interface 2020):

Table 3.2 Textile fiber energy use

Textile	Energy consumption (MJ/kg fiber)
Nylon	250
Acrylic	175
Polyester	125
Polypropylene	115
Viscose	100
Cotton	55
E: Wool	63

Source: Barber and Pellow 2006. Reproduced with permission.

A carbon negative carpet tile is one that has a negative carbon footprint for its entire manufacturing phase—measured from cradle to gate, which starts with the extractions of the raw materials and continues through the manufacturing process all the way until it leaves our dock for customers. Through this entire phase, our carpet tile stores more carbon than it emits without the use of offsets. We currently lead the industry in low carbon footprint products, so we had a good platform upon which to build these products. A carbon footprint of a carpet tile made with 20 oz of yarn on our existing recycled backing is 4.4 kg of CO_2 per square meter. Contrast this to our new backings that allow us to make a product with a carbon footprint of -0.3kg of CO_2 per square meter using 12 oz of yarn on our CQuestBioX backing.

They then explain how it is possible for products to have negative embodied carbon (Interface n.d. b):

Some materials are made from atmospheric carbon either through photosynthesis or direct air capture of CO_2 and other GHGs, so they remove carbon from the atmosphere. If the emissions of carbon from the handling, transport, and processing the material are less than the carbon they have removed from the atmosphere, the result is net negative Embodied Carbon. When we say negative carbon backings, we mean the material used in our CQuest™ backings (measured on a stand-alone basis) [is] net carbon negative. Not every carpet made with CQuest ™ backing is carbon negative. It is only when CQuest™BioX backing is paired with specialty yarns and tufting processes that the end result is a cradle to gate carbon negative carpet tile.

While Interface is one of the leaders in the creation of net carbon negative products, there is an emerging industry doing the same. As reported in the *New York Times Magazine* (Payne and Gertner 2021):

Interface is far from the only company trying to "embed" large amounts of carbon within commercial merchandise. For the past few years, a number of start-ups have begun developing products that aim to fold in carbon dioxide captured from smokestacks and other sources of pollution, in an attempt to reach a new level of environmentally friendly manufacturing: one in which greenhouse-gas molecules are not only kept out of the atmosphere but also repurposed. This undertaking, usually characterized as carbon utilization, goes well beyond flooring—to plastics, jet fuels, diesel, chemicals, building materials, diamonds, even fish food. Advocates of carbon utilization, or carbontech, as it's also known, want to remake many of the things we commonly use today. But with one crucial difference: No emissions would have been added to the environment through their fabrication.

Siegel (2018, p. 2) has categorized the companies making up the carbon negative supply chain into three groups:

> The first group is focused on direct air carbon capture (as opposed to capture from exhaust streams, which can be carbon neutral at best). The second is focused on using captured CO_2 to create raw materials. And the third is focused on creating products directly from captured CO_2.

This is clearly one of the principal pathways to a sustainable industrial future.

Interface takeaway lessons

There are several lessons that emerge from the analysis of Interface's revolutionary approach. First is that buy-in from senior management is absolutely essential. Without Ray Anderson's leadership, it is unlikely that Interface would have pursued its current course of action but notably, since his death, senior management has continued, if not accelerated, his commitment. Second is the importance of intercorporate transferability of technology, whether through sharing or competitive pressure. Mohawk and Shaw Industries have been clearly motivated to respond to some of Interface's past initiatives. Third is the underlying challenge of technological barriers in production which can limit the progress of a firm on the road to total sustainability. Overcoming such barriers requires a concerted research effort to move to the next stage. Fourth, the Interface model produces highly competitive returns for its shareholders. In 2018, its stock market performance significantly outpaced the S&P 500, Dow Jones Industrial Average, and Nasdaq. And, finally, this case study highlights the importance of the contribution of a firm's supply chain to the total GHG releases associated with its products. In many cases, the supply chain contributions far exceed those of the firm's own operations. An excellent data source for tracking these system data on an industry-by-industry basis is the EIO-LCA (Environmental Input–Output–Life Cycle Analysis) database produced by Carnegie Mellow University (www.eiolca.net/). While a corporation such as Interface has made significant strides in reducing their own carbon footprint, these data highlight the need to identify and attempt to reduce the supply chain contributions of suppliers across all industries. These approaches are described briefly in the case studies on Walmart and Puma.

Case study 2: Rohner Textil

Another remarkable transformation in technology driven by both government regulation and market opportunities is provided by the small Switzerland-based textile company, Rohner Textil AG. The company faced many similar environmental problems to those experienced by other companies in the industry (IEHN 2010a). It was under regulatory economic pressure because of the need to treat its

Table 3.3 Interface versus Rohner sustainability

Characteristic	Interface	Rohner	Handwoven
Fiber	Nylon	Natural (wool)	Natural (wool)
Source of fiber	Fossil fuels	Pasture-bred sheep	Pasture-bred sheep
Type of dyes	Synthetic	Natural	Natural
Major inputs	Capital and energy intensive	Capital and energy intensive	Labor intensive
Energy source	Renewable	Renewable	Labor
Looms	Metal	Metal	Wooden
Toxic wastes	Some	None	None

wastewater and dispose of carpet trimmings deemed toxic by regulatory authorities. The impetus for change came from a textile designer in the United States who requested that the company consider producing a completely biodegradable commercial fabric for office furniture. McDonough Braungart Design Chemistry was employed as a consultant to the project to transform Rohner's production technology and the nature of the final product. The project was challenging as it involved not only finding new raw material for the textile itself—wool from pasture-bred sheep replaced cotton—but also the much more imposing task of finding environmentally benign dyes. Only one major chemical company, Ciba-Geigy, was prepared to share its industrial secrets with the company, resulting in the identification of sixteen environmentally benign chemicals out of a total of eight thousand possibilities.

The result of this reengineering process was remarkable, as formerly toxic carpet waste could now be recovered and sold to local farmers as mulch, toxic wastewater was eliminated, and costs were reduced by the elimination of the need to filter out dyes and chemicals. The new product, called *Climatex Lifecycle*™ became a major contributor to the company's bottom line. This is a classic example of Michael Porter's thesis that sustainability and profitability can be one and the same. Table 3.3 compares the achievements of Interface and Rohner with the pure model of sustainability posited earlier for handwoven carpets. In the case of Rohner Textil, many of the basic ingredients of sustainability have been successfully transferred into a modern, high-volume commercial product capable of meeting the large demands of the international market.

Moving along the sustainability spectrum

While Interface and Rohner Textil made state-of-the-art advances towards sustainability, there are other companies whose claims to sustainability pose conceptual problems. Several companies in particular are worthy of mention since they bear directly on the question of how the concept of sustainability is used in practice. There are two principal issues: (1) to what extent are firms sustainable if their sustainability practices are not systemic? and (2) can sustainability be used as a relative term, or is it an absolute?

Case study 3: H&M

The fashion industry has one of the largest environmental impacts in the world—more than one hundred billion units sold in 2015—and the negative impacts of this output are projected to dramatically increase by 2050 (Ellen MacArthur Foundation 2017; Niinimaki et al. 2020). A Swedish multinational, H&M is the second-largest global clothing retailer with annual sales in 2020 of $20.2 billion (H&M 2020). In 2017, the company introduced a new sustainability strategy partly in response to negative publicity about two of the foundational elements of sustainability: environment and social factors. In 2010 it was revealed that the corporation was disposing of excess clothing in New York City (*New York Times* January 5, 2010). Garments had been rendered unfit to wear by slashing with box cutters or razors. Just two years later, a disastrous fire in a Bangladesh sweatshop killed more than one hundred workers (*New York Times* November 25, 2012). Although H&M did not buy from this factory, it was a general wake-up call for the clothing industry. In its 2017 comprehensive sustainability strategy, H&M articulated three principal goals: (1) to provide good and fair opportunities for workers, (2) to transform the production process to become 100 percent circular and climate positive. This entails "the continued quest for more recycled and sustainably sourced materials, improved design, production processes and product lifespan," and (3) to further develop customer engagement around sustainability. This involves a clear commitment to the Higg Index developed by the Sustainable Apparel Coalition (H&M interview with Anna Gedda, n.d.).

> The Higg Index is a suite of tools that enables brands, retailers, and facilities of all sizes—at every stage in their sustainability journey—to accurately measure and score a company or product's sustainability performance. The Higg Index delivers a holistic overview that empowers businesses to make meaningful improvements that protect the well-being of factory workers, local communities, and the environment.
>
> (apparelcoalition.org—The Higg Index).

While H&M has received its fair share of criticism for its business practices relating to sustainability, it is only one company in an industry with many other businesses facing the same challenges. The United Nations Economic Commission for Europe (UNECE 2018) has stated that the fashion industry is an "environmental and social emergency." To quote:

> The fashion industry is responsible for producing twenty per cent of global wastewater and ten per cent of global carbon emissions—more than the emissions of all international flights and maritime shipping combined. Cotton farming is responsible for 24 per cent of insecticides and 11 per cent of pesticides despite using only 3 per cent of the world's arable land. In addition, the textiles industry has been identified in recent years as a major contributor to plastic pollution in the world's oceans. It was estimated that around half a million tonnes of plastic microfibers shed during the washing of plastic-based textiles such as polyester, nylon, or acrylic end up in the ocean every year. In

addition to the negative environmental impacts, fashion is also linked to dangerous working conditions due to unsafe processes and hazardous substances used in production.

(p. 1)

A recent major research report into the environmental impact of the global apparel and footwear industries (Quantis 2018, p. 3) provides a detailed breakdown of these impacts at all stages of the production process, focusing on the contribution to GHG release. The life-cycle analysis finds that "the apparel industry alone represents 6.7% of global GHG emissions … [and] more than 50% of emissions come from three stages: dyeing & finishing, yarn preparation and fiber production."

In response to the environmental and social challenges facing the industry, H&M's 2017 and 2019 sustainability reports (H&M 2017, 2019) provided detailed historical data as well as future goals for two of its main strategic thrusts: 100 percent circular and renewable production, and fairness and equity in the labor market. These goals, along with recent and target results, are reproduced in Table 3.4. These are ambitious goals which will require further advances in technology as well as a pervasive reordering of the labor market, especially in the developing world where the bulk of clothing is now manufactured.

Table 3.4 H&M sustainability indicators

Goal	2014	2017	2019	Ultimate goal
100% circular and renewable				
Recycled or other sustainably sourced material of total material used (commercial goods) (%)	13	35	57	100 by 2030
Water recycled out of total water consumption (%)	—	—	13	15 by 2022
Recycled or other sustainably sourced cotton (certified organic, recycled, or Better Cotton) (%)	22	59	97	100 by 2020
Garments collected (MT)	7.684	17.771	29.005	25,000 per year by 2020
Stores with recycling systems for main types of store waste (%)	58	64	62	100
Own operations with water efficient equipment (%)	24	51	67	100 by 2020
Business partner factories in compliance with wastewater quality requirements as defined by Business for Social Responsibility (%)	71	84	—	100
Renewable electricity in own operations (%)	27	96	96	100 by 2030
Change in CO_2 emissions from own operations (Scope 1 and 2) compared with previous year, including renewables (%)	−4	−21	8	Climate positive by 2040 at the latest

(continued)

Table 3.4 Cont.

Goal	2014	2017	2019	Ultimate goal
Electricity consumption intensity (kWh/sq m per operating hour compared with 2016) (%)	n/a	−2.70	−10.1	−25 by 2025 (2016 baseline)
100% fair and equal				
Number of supplier factories using Fair Wage Method (% of product volume covered)	3	227 (40)	—	(50% of product volume by 2018)
Number of supplier factories that have implemented democratically elected worker representation (% of product volume covered)	—	458 (52)	—	(50% of product volume by 2018)
Business partners regarding H&M group as a fair business partner (%)	76	94	—	90 by 2018
Employees agreeing with the statement "People here (at H&M group) are treated fairly regardless of age, ethnicity, sex, sexual orientation and disabilities" (%)	89	90	—	Continuous increase
Remediated issues (defined by the Bangladesh Accord) (%)	—	90	—	100

Source: H&M 2017 and 2019.

There is a major threat to the attainment of corporate sustainability in the fashion industry. H&M, along with fellow retailer Zara, have been pioneers in the field of fast fashion. This production and marketing philosophy is based on the large-scale production of relatively low-value goods with a very short fashion cycle, sometimes numbering only several weeks. The net result of this approach is the de facto encouragement of consumer overconsumption in constant pursuit of rapidly changing fashion. The concomitant high levels of production lead in turn to a markedly increased and negative impact on the environment and working conditions (Forbes July 26, 2017; *Independent* January 8 2018; Taplin 2014a and b; Hobson 2013; Cline 2012). Symptomatic of this problem was a $4.3 billion pile of unsold clothing held by H&M, as reported by the *New York Times* (March 27, 2018).

Despite H&M's attempt to burnish its image after the reports it had damaged perfectly usable clothing in 2010, it was revealed that the company provided fifteen tons of discarded products to a power plant in a small Swedish city in 2017 (*New York Times* March 27, 2018). The *New York Times* report suggested that the destruction of unsold consumer goods was endemic to the industry and cited the practices of several prominent companies: Burberry had destroyed more than £90 million worth of goods over the preceding five years; the Swiss watch maker, Richemont, destroyed more than £400 million worth of watches in two recent years; Nike slashed unwanted running shoes before disposal; and Urban Outfitters poured green paint on unsold Toms shoes.

The bottom line is that despite H&M's laudable efforts at improving their sustainability indicators, there is a fundamental incompatibility between their business model and the goal of sustainability, a problem faced by all other players in both the fast and slow fashion marketplaces. The Council for Textile Recycling (n.d., p. 3) reported that the amount of post-consumer textile waste was estimated to grow from 25.6 billion pounds in 2009 to 35.4 billion pounds in 2019. "Between 1999 and 2009 the volume of PCTW [post-consumer textile waste] generated grew by 40%, while the diversion rate only increased by 2%."

Case study 4: Walmart

Walmart, the world's largest company, with more than two million employees and annual revenues of almost one-half trillion dollars, is a much more complex example of the paradoxical juxtaposition of a clearly articulated sustainability policy and the underlying business model.

On October 24, 2005 Lee Scott, Walmart's chief executive officer, delivered his "Twenty-first century leadership lecture" (Scott 2005), billed as a major reorientation of the company's strategy towards sustainability. Scott began his speech by molding Hurricane Katrina into a metaphor for the crisis facing our physical and business environment. To quote:

> We should view the environment as Katrina in slow motion. Environmental loss threatens our health and the health of the natural systems we depend on. The challenges include: increasing greenhouse gases that are contributing to climatic change and weather-related disasters; increasing air pollution which is leading to more asthma and other respiratory diseases in our communities; water pollution which is increasing while safe fresh water supplies are shrinking; water-borne diseases causes [sic] millions of death each year, mostly among children; destruction of critical habitat, causing unprecedented threat to the diversity of life, the natural world and us. And that's just to name a few. As one of the largest companies in the world, with an expanding global presence, environmental problems are OUR problems. The supply of natural products (fish, food, water) can only be sustained if the ecosystems that provide them are sustained and protected. There are not two worlds out there, a Walmart world and some other world.
>
> (p. 4)

Scott then enunciated Walmart's environmental goals and outlined the intimate relationship between environmental stewardship and good business practice. The principal goals were: (1) to be supplied 100 percent by renewable energy, (2) to create zero waste, and (3) to sell products that sustain resources and the environment. Scott (p. 5) stated that: "These goals are both ambitious and aspirational, and I'm not sure how to achieve them … at least not yet. This obviously will take some time. But we do know the way. There is a simple rule about the environment. If there is waste or pollution, someone along the line pays for it."

Scott then presented specific examples in four environmentally related areas to illustrate the nature and magnitude of the potential savings: trucking, store design and operation, waste generation, and product design and sourcing. To assist the multitude of firms in their supply chain to coordinate their activities with

Walmart's sustainability programs, Walmart (n.d.) has published an extensive *Supplier Sustainability Assessment* manual. This document asks each supplier to answer fifteen basic questions in the four areas of energy and climate, material efficiency, nature and resources, and people and community; scores these responses depending on the level of performance; explains some of the benefits of improving their scores in each of the four areas; and finally, lists a group of tools and resources suppliers can use to improve their performance.

Several years have passed since the declaration of new goals for Walmart and the company is now under different leadership. In 2016, the corporation published a scorecard on its progress entitled "Global Responsibility Report." This was updated in 2018 and subsequently relabeled as its "Environmental, Social and Governance Report." Examples of explicit goals and their status according to Walmart's 2021 report are provided in Table 3.5. Whether its ambitious goals will be fully attainable in the near- to medium-term future remains an open question, but the contents and import of Scott's talk are remarkable.

Table 3.5 Walmart sustainability scorecard

Target area	Goal	Metric	FY 2021 results unless otherwise noted
GHG emissions	Zero emissions across global operations by 2040	CY2019: Million metric MT of CO_2e	Total: 17.56 Scope 1: 6.48 Scope 2: .08
Energy	Power 50% of operations with renewables by 2025 and 100% by 2035	CY2020 percentage	36%
Supply chain	Reduce or avoid 1 billion MT of CO_2e from Scope 3 by 2030	Avoided emissions reported by suppliers cumulatively from CY2017 to CY2020	>46 million MT of CO_2e
		Avoided emissions reported by suppliers in CY2020	>186 million MT of CO_2e
Commodities	By 2025 all fresh and frozen seafood sourced from suppliers who are third-party certified as sustainable or working towards	Percentage of sustainably sourced fresh and frozen wild-caught and farmed seafood	US 100% Canada 89% Mexico 61% Central America 73%
	By 2022 source apparel and home textile products only from suppliers who use Higg Index	Percentage of net product sales sourced from suppliers reporting at least one facility has completed the Higg assessment	>82%

Table 3.5 Cont.

Target area	Goal	Metric	FY 2021 results unless otherwise noted
	100% of palm oil sourced from Roundtable on Sustainable Palm Oil–certified suppliers by end of 2020	Percentage certified as sustainable by RSPO	~90%
	Source pulp and paper products with zero net deforestation in 100% of Walmart global private brand products by 2020	Percentage that is recyclable or certified as sustainable by third parties	97%
Animal welfare	100% cage-free egg supplied by 2025	Percentage of cage-free shell eggs as percentage of total shell egg net sales	Walmart US 18% Sam's Club US 30%
Operational waste	Zero waste to landfill and incineration by 2025	Percentage of waste materials diverted from landfill and incineration by country (CY2020)	US 82% Canada 88% Japan 79% UK 89% Mexico 75%
Packaging	100% of global private brand packaging to be recyclable, reusable, or industrially compostable by 2025	Estimated percentage of packaging	62%
Social sustainability	Between 2013 and 2023 purchase an incremental $250 billion in products supporting American jobs	Dollars purchased (cumulative since 2013)	$145 billion
	Between 2018 and 2022 to invest $25 million to strengthen farmer organizations and farm yield in India	Dollars invested (cumulative since 2018)	>$20 million
Product safety	By 2022, reduce footprint of "priority chemicals" by 10% from 2017	Percentage change CY2019 versus CY2017	5% decrease
Food safety	Invest $25 million in projects to advance food safety in China over five years	Amount invested to date	On track to meet goal by end of 2021

Source: Walmart 2021.

Note: FY is full year; CY is calendar year.

Walmart's unique role in the diffusion of sustainability technology and policy

There is a clear role for government in facilitating the diffusion of sustainable technology, policy, and practices throughout the economy by providing a level playing field to allow these initiatives to compete freely with existing technologies and strategies. Prime examples of this approach can be found in the area of renewable energy sources and demand-side management. However, an equally important phenomenon is the diffusion of sustainability within the corporate sector itself. Figure 3.4 presents models of diffusion

Model A: Horizontal diffusion

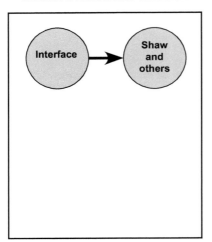

Model B1: Vertical diffusion—up

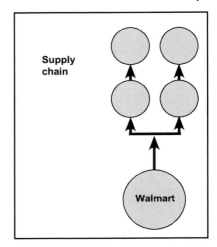

Model B2: Chained vertical diffusion

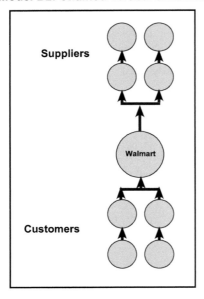

Model C: Vertical diffusion—down

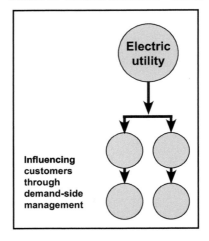

Figure 3.4 Models of sustainability diffusion.

which may be applied to the challenge of moving the industrial system closer to the goal of sustainability. Model A represents horizontal diffusion, Model B vertical diffusion up the supply chain, and Model C vertical diffusion down the supply chain. Each is briefly described in turn below.

Model A: Horizontal diffusion

There are several ways in which sustainability innovation and policy can be transferred either directly or indirectly among competitors. The first, illustrated by the case of Interface Inc and Shaw Industries, is where one company sets the standard and forces other companies to respond. The second involves the direct transfer of technology either through licensing for a fee or without charge. In the case of Rohner Textil, for example, the company offered to share its new nonpolluting technology with other companies in the same industry.

Model B: Vertical diffusion up the supply chain

In some respects, this model potentially represents the most successful model of diffusion for sustainable production technology and strategy. Despite the proliferation of exhortative literature for the corporate sector on the benefits of sustainability, it is not realistic to expect all companies to adopt sustainable practices into their business models, especially when they are operating in highly competitive, low profit margin industries. Suggestions that these firms should adopt new practices that might, on balance, cost many of them lost profits in the short run is not a viable suggestion and is, in fact, counterproductive as it lowers the credibility of sustainability advocates within the business community.

However, this environment can change radically when a major corporation mandates that its suppliers must meet sustainability criteria in order to continue to receive orders. Once this *greening of the supply chain* (Sarkis 2010) occurs, the vast array of suppliers who previously might not have been able to afford sustainability initiatives can now not afford *not* to do so. The prime example of this phenomenon is Walmart, which has moved aggressively in this area to demand more ecologically friendly products from its approximately one hundred thousand suppliers. As a consequence, Walmart has been termed a "private regulator," achieving within the business sector what government might be unwilling or unable to attempt. This model represents one of the critical keys to the diffusion of sustainability throughout the economic system, as Walmart has come to realize that sustainable business is the key to sustainable profits (Humes 2011).

Model C: Vertical diffusion down the supply chain

In this model, corporations sitting atop or amidst a supply chain adopt practices and policies that induce their customers to follow suit. One example of this phenomenon is the adoption by electric power utilities, as early as the 1980s, of innovative rate structures such as marginal cost pricing (Nemetz and Hankey 1984), which provide a strong incentive to customers within the industrial and commercial sectors to alter their energy use—and perhaps input or product mix—in a more sustainable direction.

Bearing in mind that if Walmart were a country it "would be the 20th largest in the world," (Scott 2005) the corporation has an extraordinary capacity to leverage the nature of global business practices, but no company has had such a polarizing effect on public discourse in the United States. While its social impacts on small businesses, urban cores, and labor have been a lightning rod for criticism, its massive presence in the American economy entails less visible but extraordinary impacts on material throughput and energy use throughout its supply chain. Because of its virtually unique role, Walmart has the ability to dramatically change the face of commerce not only in the United States, but also globally.

So, if Walmart is able to achieve its stated sustainability goals and induce similar responses among its many international suppliers, where is the problem? In two thought-provoking books entitled *Eco-Business: A Big Brand Takeover of Sustainability* (Dauvergne and Lister 2013) and *Will Big Business Destroy Our Planet?* (Dauvergne 2018) the authors articulate the nature of the paradox. Big business is engaging in what the authors call eco-business—which is labeled "sustainability" by corporations but is more about corporate sustainability than environmental sustainability. The principal driver is increased efficiencies and more secure markets, which guarantee larger sales and profitability. The authors argue that:

> recent brand company efforts through their global supply chains are achieving environmental gains in product design and production. Yet, these advances are also fundamentally limited. Total environmental impacts of consumption are increasing as brand companies leverage corporate sustainability for competitive advantage, business growth, and increased sales. Big brand sustainability, while important, will not on its own resolve the problems of global environmental change.
>
> (Dauvergne and Lister, 2013, p. 36)

This is the paradox of the Walmart business model that renders it ultimately incompatible with sustainability.

Case study 5: Suncor

At the other end of the corporate sustainability spectrum are firms that claim to be sustainable but cannot show any persuasive evidence to support this. Located in northern Alberta, Canada, Suncor is a leading producer of synthetic crude oil extracted from large oil sand deposits. This company and other oil sands producers have assumed particular importance because they sit on massive petroleum deposits rivaling those of Saudi Arabia, and because they offer a unique opportunity for the United States to access large supplies of oil from a friendly neighbor with minimal risk from disruption due to political, social, or military factors.

Suncor originally began exploiting the oil sands in the mid 1960s under the name of Great Canadian Oil Sands Ltd. Corporate profitability is directly related to global petroleum prices, so prospects for the large-scale development of the oil sands had to await the run-up in prices within the last few decades. The raw material, called bitumen, is contained in a sand matrix which has been traditionally extracted in a manner similar to conventional surface mining and heated with reactants to create synthetic crude. This process relies on extensive use of natural gas (approximately 750 cubic feet [cu ft] per barrel of bitumen) in order to provide the fuel for this energy-intensive technology (Alberta Chamber of Resources 2004). Since most of the deposits of bitumen are inaccessible by conventional surface mining, the oil sands industry has also invested large sums of capital into developing an alternative method of extraction called *in situ* mining. This recovery process can access deeper deposits by drilling holes into the underground strata and using large quantities of heated water and reagents to force the bitumen to the surface. This process is estimated to require approximately 1500 cu ft of natural gas per barrel of bitumen (Alberta Chamber of Resources 2004). The advent of higher priced oil permitted the development of the oil sands which, because of their nature, are considerably more expensive to exploit than conventional crude oil.

It is interesting to note that Suncor has been listed in at least four sustainability indexes: the Dow Jones Sustainability Index for North America, the TD Global Sustainability Fund, the Corporate Knight's Report on Clean Capitalism, and the Fortune list of green giants. In 2011, the oil sands industry began a public relations campaign to label its output as "ethical oil" to contrast it with petroleum from nations with dubious social and political policies that impact human rights (*New York Times* September 25, 2011). A major impetus for this campaign was to counter emerging concerns in both Europe and the United States about the environmental impacts of petroleum produced from the oil sands (*New York Times* December 8, 2010; Canada. com 2011). This campaign has been largely abandoned after pushback even from some major supporters of oil sands development because of the incongruous nature of the claim (Findlay 2012).

The process of upgrading bitumen to synthetic crude oil has numerous environmental impacts in addition to land disturbance from the removal of boreal forest and soil overlaying the deposits. Emissions of SO_2, NOx, and GHGs, as well as water use, are greater on a per barrel basis than those associated with conventional petroleum recovery (National Pollutant Release Inventory 2012). A recent study by Dietz et al. (2018) identifies Suncor's GHG emission intensity as the highest among fifty-two major international energy companies. This is in no small part due to the nature of bitumen, the principal product. In fact, the oil sands of Alberta represent one of the largest sources of carbon dioxide emissions on the planet. Estimates of direct emissions from the production process must be supplemented by estimates of the impact of mining on carbon storage and sequestration by lost boreal forest and peatlands. It has been estimated that landscape changes due to currently approved surface extraction will release 11.4–47.3 million metric tons (MT) of stored carbon (equivalent to 41.8–173.4 MT of CO_2) (Rooney et al. 2012). Even *in situ* extraction leads to significant damage to the landscape due to wellheads, piping, and access roads (Schindler 2009).

Tailings ponds can be a significant source of methane (CH_4), a GHG with a global warming potential twenty-three times that of carbon dioxide (Alberta Auditor General 2011). Recent research suggests that the carbon dioxide emissions from the oil sands sector have been underestimated by almost 64 percent (Liggio et al. 2019). This is a significant error, given the major contribution of oil sands emissions to national GHG output.

In addition, the oil sands process produces large quantities of wastewater contaminated with toxic pollutants, which requires storage in large tailings ponds for lengthy periods of time to facilitate settling and evaporation. Canada's National Pollutant Release Inventory—the equivalent of the American Toxic Release Inventory—lists several dozen pollutants of concern. There is continuing debate over the existence and severity of leakage from the tailings ponds (CEC 2020) as well as downwind deposition of pollutants, which can influence water quality, aquatic biota, and possibly the health of Indigenous peoples in downstream communities (Timoney and Lee 2009; Kelly et al. 2009 and 2010).

Suncor is extremely sensitive to concerns over the environmental impacts of its operations and the public reaction thereto, since these impacts are a potential threat to both current and future markets for its synthetic crude, as well as being a possible threat to its social license to operate. A large degree of negative international publicity resulted from the death of several hundred ducks which had landed on the surface of the tailings ponds of another major oil sands producer, Syncrude Ltd (*New York Times* March 10, 2010). Oil sands tailings ponds, some as high as 300 feet above the adjacent Athabasca River, currently cover more than 170 square kilometers (sq km), of which Suncor accounts for approximately 40 sq km (Grant et al. 2010; see also National Geographic 2009). It has been estimated that six cubic meters of tailings are created for every cubic meter of bitumen recovered (Griffiths 2006).

The company's public image is enhanced by its inclusion in the sustainability indexes, an outcome which appears to be based on corporate policies in a number of related areas. These are listed below in Table 3.6 with accompanying commentary that provides perspective on these activities under the heading "critique."

Table 3.6 Suncor sustainability policies and critique

Suncor's sustainability policies	Critique
1. Use of Global Reporting Initiative (GRI) indicators	The choice of which indicators to include and publicize is at the discretion of each company. Some important environmental indicators currently not chosen by Suncor include: 302–5: reductions in energy requirements of products and services; 303–4 and 5: water discharge and consumption; 304–4: International Union for Conservation of Nature Red List species and national conservation list species with habitats in areas affected by operations; 305–6: emissions of ozone-depleting substances; 306–4: transport of hazardous waste; 308:1: new suppliers that were screened using environmental criteria; and 308–2: negative environmental impacts in the supply chain and actions taken. In general, however, while the reporting of indicators is a first step, it does not imply that a corporation is becoming any more sustainable or, in the case of Suncor, any less unsustainable. See the items below relating to land cover restoration, investment in renewables, hiring of Indigenous people, intensity of greenhouse gas (GHG) emissions, and water use.
2. Use of triple bottom line	As is common practice, the three accounts (financial, environmental, and social) are presented separately without integration, thereby eliminating the opportunity to assess economic issues of materiality and risk (Nemetz 2013).

Table 3.6 Cont.

Suncor's sustainability policies	Critique
3. Intention to restore land cover	As of 2010, the company had achieved only 0.2% restoration (*Journal of Commerce* 2010). The company reported 10% land reclamation in their 2018 sustainability report, however, an independent estimate places it closer to 0.1% (Pembina Institute 2017). There is also the question of whether the original ecosystem can be replicated to any significant degree.
4. Investments in wind power and ethanol	As of 2020, Suncor's investment in wind power equals approximately 2% of its last 5 years of capital expenditures. Its estimated revenue from the sale of ethanol is no more than 1% of total revenue.
5. Use of carbon offsetting	The use of carbon offsetting has raised several major conceptual problems including concerns over the degree of additionality (Alberta Auditor General 2011).
6. Hiring local Indigenous people and funding local initiatives	This must be offset against destruction of traditional hunting habitat, and concern over toxic chemicals in river water, fish, and wildlife (Kelly et al. 2010; Timoney and Lee 2009; CBC 2010) and possible links to cancer in a downstream Indigenous community (McLachlan 2014).
7. Shift to *in situ* recovery from surface mining	This entails much higher releases of GHGs (Gosselin et al. 2001).
8. Commitment to lower GHG intensity of production	Most of the major reductions in total GHG emissions and GHG intensity occurred in the early years of operation and the company forecasts no significant changes over the next few years (Nemetz 2013; Suncor 2021).
9. Commitment to reduce water use	The water intensity of oil sands production is approximately four times that of conventional crude oil. The company reported a drop in water consumption in 2017 after three consecutive years of increases. Surface water withdrawals are up however.
10. Commitment to seek replacement for natural gas in production process	It is unclear which fuel source would replace the intensive use of a high energy source to produce a lower quality energy product. At one point the idea of building nuclear reactors for the oil sands was floated and continues to receive occasion mention (CBC 2019).
11. Plans to use carbon capture and storage	Carbon capture and storage is yet to achieve credible economic viability anywhere in the world (Greenpeace 2016, 2021; Alberta Views 2015; Smil 2010). See Chapter 10 in this work.

Source: Suncor and author.

The Suncor case raises several issues which bear directly on the goal of corporate sustainability: standards for sustainability reporting, process versus performance measures, triple bottom line accounting, pollutant-intensity measures versus total output, sustainability indexes, and best-in-class versus absolute measures of sustainability. Each is addressed in turn.

Sustainability reporting

Suncor is one of many corporations that have chosen to report not only financial results but also their performance in the two other aspects of sustainability, namely environment and society. The standard procedure for so doing is to separately list results for a selection of performance indicators in each of these two major areas. In their annual reports on sustainability, Suncor has highlighted their results on such key environmental indicators as air emissions, water consumption, and land use, and social variables such as occupational injuries. These types of indicator have been developed by a wide range of organizations—including commercial rating agencies, NGOs, standard-setting bodies, governments, international organizations, and multiple-stakeholder groups—in order to standardize the process of reporting and guarantee comparability both temporally and across companies.

One of the largest of these organizations is the Global Reporting Initiative (GRI), which issues sustainability guidelines for reporting on the economic, environmental, and social dimensions of activities, products, and services to a broad array of entities in addition to corporations. The choice of indicators is left to each organization and it is up to that organization to seek third-party certification of the reported data if so desired. This latitude can lead to key information being unavailable to the public, withheld either unintentionally or intentionally (Sridhar and Jones 2013).

In addition to the GRI, there are several other prominent agencies with promulgated guidelines or standards, including the United Nations, the Organisation for Economic Co-operation and Development, AccountAbility, and the International Organization for Standardization (ISO). There are three basic types of standards (Oakley and Buckland 2004, pp. 134–35): (1) *principle-based* standards, which set out "broad principles of behavior but do not specify how they are to be achieved or how conformity with them can be assessed," (2) *performance* standards which measure the actual achievements of the organization on the selected indicator, and (3) *process* standards, which outline processes an organization should follow in order to achieve sustainability. The conceptual difficulty of relying on process measures is that while they may indicate good corporate intentions and activities, they fail to reflect whether the corporation has achieved any notable results with respect to sustainability. The ultimate measure in assessing a corporation's record on sustainability must be a measure of its performance.

Triple bottom line accounting

A corporation or other organizational entity that chooses to report on environmental and social effects of their operations is generally considered to have adopted triple bottom line accounting but, clearly, the choice of standard system, number of indicators and their level of detail, existence of temporal comparative data, and presence or absence of third-party certification all bear upon the question of validity. Perhaps the most critical conceptual difficulty with triple bottom line accounting as currently practiced is that the three accounts—financial, environmental, and social—are standalone lists or statements that lack any form of integration. Under these circumstances, it can be difficult, if not impossible, for shareholders or other stakeholders to obtain any sense of the impact of these variables not only on the financial performance of the company, but also on broader society, the economy, and the environment in which the corporation operates.

Pollutant intensity versus total pollutant output

The ambiguous impact on the environment of reductions in pollutant intensity has prompted many governmental regulatory agencies to abandon this type of requirement in favor of performance measures that track total pollutant output. Pollutant-intensity reductions are a necessary but not sufficient criterion for reduced impact on the environment—the ultimate goal of any sustainability policy—because any reduction in pollution intensity can be offset by a compensating increase in product output.

Suncor and sustainability indexes

Suncor is currently listed on at least four sustainability indexes, perhaps the most prominent of which is the Dow Jones Sustainability Index. The Index lists the criteria and weights adopted for inclusion. The criterion of environmental reporting receives a weight of 3 percent and environmental performance, as measured by eco-efficiency, receives a weight of 7 percent. The central question is whether Suncor should be listed on a sustainability index. The inclusion must rest on either one of two criteria: absolute or relative performance.

If Suncor's inclusion is based on its relative performance, then there are five possible comparisons: all extractive and manufacturing industries, extractive industries only, the energy industry, the oil and gas sector, or the oil sands industry. Because of the pollution intensity of its production process, the only category in which Suncor could achieve any relative classification of sustainability would be among the subset of oil sands companies. This essentially renders the appellation of sustainability meaningless. If Suncor could be called sustainable, then any company in any industry could satisfy this criterion. Several authors, including Ray Anderson (1999); Robert (2008); and McDonough and Braungart (2002), have developed lists of absolute criteria which define a sustainable corporation. These are summarized in Table 3.7 and ultimately can be the only criteria that define true corporate sustainability.

Table 3.7 Sustainability criteria

Anderson	Strongly service oriented Resource efficient Solar driven Wasting nothing Cyclical, not linear Strongly connected to constituencies
Robert	No increase in concentrations of substances extracted from the earth's crust No systematic increase in concentrations of substances produced as a byproduct No systematic increasing of degradation by physical means People not subject to conditions that systematically undermine their capacity to meet their needs
McDonough and Braungart	Waste can be reused Use of current solar income Respect for diversity Lack of product and byproduct toxicity, bioaccumulation, or persistence

Sources: Ray Anderson (1999); Robert (2008); McDonough and Braungart (2002).

In sum, Suncor has received its designation as a sustainable corporation on two conceptually indefensible propositions: first, that it has a marginally better environmental record than other oil sands companies; and second, that it has devoted only a miniscule percentage of its resources to renewable energy projects. Its dominant core business results in exceptionally high pollution of air, land, and water. The future of oil sands production hinges precariously on the future demand for and price of oil. Scenarios about the potential for an acceleration in the adoption of electric vehicles (EVs) suggest that oil could be displaced by electrification in this and other sectors in the next few decades (Helm 2017). Under these circumstances, as one of the highest cost sources of petroleum (Dale 2015), the oil sands can be expected to face the greatest threat to financial viability among alternative supplies of petroleum.

The politics of oil sands

The future prospects for the oil sands are uncertain for at least three climate-related reasons: the cancellation of the Keystone pipeline intended to carry Alberta bitumen to American markets, the decision by the Norwegian government and seven oil multinationals to pull out of the oil sands (Environmental Defense 2017; *Financial Post* January 12, 2021), and the decision by several major financial investors to back off funding what is perceived to be "dirty oil" (*New York Times* February 12 and 14, 2021; Funds Europe 2021). It has been estimated that up to $13.4 billion of oil sands assets are possible candidates for sale by the international majors to domestic producers due to pressures to cut emissions and invest in renewable energy (*Vancouver Sun* July 14, 2021). Added to these factors is the difficult political and economic calculation facing the US federal government in light of the pledges made by Canada and other governments at President Biden's climate summit on April 22, 2021 and the COP26 conference in Glasgow in November 2021. During the former meeting, Canada pledged to reduce their GHG emissions by at least 40 percent by 2030 (CBC April 22, 2021). This is a particularly ambitious goal in light of the fact that Canada is the only G7 nation whose GHG emissions rose after the Paris Agreement of 2015, in no small part due to the expansion of the country's oil sands operations in Alberta.

The oil sands have been a cornerstone of Alberta's energy policy since the decline in conventional oil and gas reserves, which were first discovered in 1947 at Leduc. This commitment to oil sands has continued despite the changing financial and environmental situation for fossil fuels at the global level. In fact, the Alberta government made a strategic blunder by investing $1.5 billion in the Keystone pipeline in 2020 at a time when it was clear that a future US Democratic administration, if elected, would renew President Obama's cancellation of the project (Berman 2020; *Calgary Herald* September 2, 2020; CTV News January 17, 2021). This is part of a larger picture of the province's budgetary philosophy. While both Norway and Alberta established special savings funds with revenues from their energy sector, Norway adopted special measures to insulate these funds from the domestic economy in order to provide for future generations and avoid the "resource curse," which affects many oil and gas producers, especially in the developing world. As of 2017, Norway's Sovereign Wealth Fund was valued at $1.32 trillion (SWFI accessed April 4, 2021), while Alberta's was only $16.3 billion in March 2020 (CBC July 13, 2020). Alberta buffers the gap between low taxes (including low royalties, no sales tax, and low income taxes) and high spending with oil and gas revenues. It appears that the Albertan government has made the strategic decision to make an unqualified commitment to what will eventually become a sunset industry. The wisdom of this decision remains to be seen but, at a minimum, it has created a serious fiscal situation for the provincial government, which is now faced with low energy prices and significant pushback over the ecological consequences of oil sands production.

In a renewed effort to rebrand the industry and maintain its social license to operate in the face of increased global pressure to reduce GHG emissions, the five largest oil sands producers, including Suncor, announced an alliance in June 2021 to achieve net zero output of carbon dioxide from their operations by 2050 using carbon capture and storage (Suncor June 9, 2021). This initiative entails several controversial components. First, if it is accepted by the Canadian government, it guarantees the right of the industry to continue operating for three more decades despite its dominant contributions to Canada's GHG emissions. Second, it calls for the Canadian government to make major financial contributions to the project at a time when scarce national resources should be spent on more immediate, effective, and less expensive initiatives to restructure the economy to meet Paris GHG commitments. Third, as discussed in Chapter 10 of this volume, the technology is extremely costly and has several inherent environmental risks associated with it. Finally, even if the stated goals were to be achieved, net zero output of GHG from the production process accounts for at most 20–30 percent of total life-cycle emissions, and does not address the problem of the residual 70–80 percent of emissions associated with the downstream combustion of the fuel itself (Natural Resources Canada n.d.; Dietz et al. 2021).

In Suncor's latest *Climate Report* (Suncor 2021), it articulates several policies to reduce carbon emissions in addition to carbon capture and storage (CCS): energy efficiency improvements, fuel switching, and implementation of new technologies. Included in this package of proposed measures are investment in low-carbon power, renewable fuels such as wind and ethanol, and electric charging stations. A principal critique of these specific proposals is that they are incompatible with the firm's principal business model and run the risk of being labeled cosmetic exercises to protect social license for the continued production of bitumen. The company's relatively minor scale of current investments in wind and ethanol is outlined in Table 3.6.

Case study 6: A cautionary tale (I): Ephemeral commitment and climate change denial

The Ford Motor Company

Few companies have displayed the deep philosophical commitment to sustainability demonstrated by Interface, which has not only sought to revolutionize its business model by transforming its technology, but also to fundamentally change the nature of the market in which it operates. Most other firms that have sought to move closer to a sustainable business model have done so opportunistically. This is not a bad thing per se, as it embodies Porter's message that the combination of sustainability and profitability are not only possible, but also advantageous. The critical ingredient in this type of corporate transformation from one business model to another is the existence of a favorable environment marked by either changes in consumer tastes, regulatory pressures, or some combination of changes in the relative prices of inputs and outputs.

A perfect example of this is the remarkable success of the Ford Motor Company, which escaped the bankruptcies that afflicted its main American competitors in

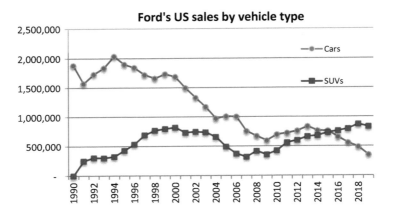

Figure 3.5 Ford's US sales by vehicle type.
Source: Ward's, multiple years. Data reproduced with permission.

2009. After the crude oil price shock of the 1970s and the emergence of imports of small Japanese automobiles as a major threat to business as usual, Ford made the historic decision to cast itself as a green company by focusing on smaller and more fuel-efficient cars. But the market changed: consumer tastes moved towards larger, less fuel-efficient SUVs. This was facilitated by the absence of any significant increasing trend in real gasoline prices, higher profit margins on SUVs, and a shift in the nature of the service economy in favor of greater self-reliance. Ford recently announced its imminent departure from the American passenger car market, with the exception of the Mustang, in order to focus on building more trucks, SUVs, and crossovers (*New York Times* May 24, 2018). Figure 3.5 explains the motivation: passenger car sales have been steadily declining and Ford's SUV sales now exceed those of its passenger cars. Reinforcing this decision is the low to negative profit margins on most of the company's standard automotive products and the much higher profit margin on SUVs (*New York Times* May 24, 2018). While the decision was clearly motivated to generate higher profit levels in the short to medium term, this strategy could be counterproductive in the future if gasoline prices increase (*New York Times* May 1, 2018).

In 2021, Ford undertook a major strategic reorientation in one of its markets by announcing its intention to phase out gasoline-powered cars in Europe by 2030 (*New York Times*, February 17, 2021). However, the newspaper reported that Ford would continue to sell *commercial* vehicles with gasoline or diesel engines in Europe "for years to come." This shift in focus, albeit in one of Ford's smaller markets, reflects major changes in the industry with several other major players, including GM, Volvo, and Volkswagen, signaling their intention to convert production to EVs. This move can only be reinforced by the announcement of the Biden administration that the adoption of EVs will be actively promoted in the United States (*New York Times* March 31, 2021). The impact of this shift on the environment is complex, and this issue is explored in Chapter 7. The recent history of industry strategy and government response unambiguously demonstrates the necessity of a system-wide economic and political environment that is supportive of corporate sustainability initiatives and provides an opportunity for profitability and sustainable competitive advantage.

Fossil fuel companies

While changes in the economic environment can induce corporations to scale back or abandon their commitment to sustainability, these changes can be a double-edged sword. There have been recent changes in the relative prices of alternative fossil fuels and warnings from the investment community about the effect of climate change on "stranded assets" (i.e. fossil fuels that cannot be extracted without further accelerating climate change) in the oil and coal sector (Ansar et al. 2013; Caldecott et al. 2015; Carbon Tracker 2020b). These developments will ultimately force major producers to make major changes in their business models. This is already happening in the coal sector where several companies have filed for bankruptcy or are facing serious financial problems (*New York Times* April 13, 2016; Carbon Tracker 2018).

The oil sector, however, remains relatively resistant to these considerations at the moment in light of the continued global reliance on liquid fuels. Several reports on companies in the energy and utility sectors (Welsh et al. 2018; Brulle 2018; HuffPost December 28, 2019; Forbes March 25, 2019; *New York Times* November 11, 2020) found that they have actively engaged in lobbying and election spending to forestall both the federal and state governments from enacting clean energy standards, improving energy efficiency, and closing fossil fuel tax loopholes. This involves both direct funding as well as indirect initiatives through financial support to selected nonprofit groups and what is called "astroturf" activity, where the impression is one of a legitimate grassroots organization.

Two companies, ExxonMobil and Shell Oil, are prime examples of this phenomenon (HuffPost February 25, 2021). Both have engaged in lobbying, election spending, and astroturf activity. Both have consistently denied the existence of global warming and, in the case of both Mobil and Exxon (before and also after the merger), have funded a campaign of misinformation reminiscent of the tobacco industry in its long fight against the regulation of cigarettes (Brulle 2013; Otto 2016; Oreskes and Conway 2010; Michaels 2008). It has been reported that BP has also participated in the funding of anti-climate lobby groups despite their public posture in support of sustainability (HuffPost September 28, 2020). It is particularly noteworthy that corporate documents (Supran and Oreskes 2017; Franta 2018; *Guardian* June 12, 2019; HuffPost December 3, 2019; *Inside Climate News* 2015) have revealed that both ExxonMobil and Shell have known for a considerable time that human-induced climate change does in fact exist and poses a threat to their ultimate survival. It is ironic that this behavior is perfectly rational from a purely private perspective of profit maximization in the short to medium term as fossil fuel firms attempt to perpetuate a business model that has been so profitable in the past. The problem is that such private pursuit of profit represents a classic case of market failure, reflecting a serious disconnect between private and social costs and benefits through the generation of massive negative externalities.

This attempt to shape public perception and government policy has been accompanied, at least in the case of ExxonMobil, by a conscious effort to deceive current and potential investors. In October 2018, the New York State's attorney general initiated an ultimately unsuccessful lawsuit against the company, claiming that Exxon had engaged in a longstanding fraudulent scheme to deceive investors and the investment community concerning the risks posed to its business by climate change regulation (Reuters October 24, 2018; *New York Times* December 10, 2019). The Appendix to this chapter includes excerpts from New York State's case against ExxonMobil.

A recent report (Influence Map 2019) has calculated that the five largest publicly traded oil and gas companies (ExxonMobil, Shell, Chevron, BP, and Total) "have invested over $1Bn of shareholder funds in the three years following the Paris Agreement on misleading climate-related branding and lobbying." This involves "carefully devised campaigns of positive messaging combined with negative policy lobbying on climate change" with the tactical use of social media such as Facebook and Instagram.

Recent statements by the fossil fuel industry purporting to support the concept of sustainability lack credibility given recent reports (Carbon Tracker 2019; Wang et al 2019) that no major oil company has invested to support the Paris goals of keeping the global temperature rise below 2°C. In fact, the industry has just approved $50 billion worth of major projects that undermine climate targets and risk shareholder returns. At risk is the continued vitality of the fossil fuel industry with stranded assets in excess of one trillion dollars (Caldecott et al. 2014, 2015; IRENA 2017; Jakob and Hilaire 2015; McGlade and Ekins 2015). It has recently been revealed that ExxonMobil lobbyists were quoted as saying that the company's support for a carbon tax as a key component of climate action was a public relations ploy (*Guardian* June 30, 2021; *New York Times* June 30, 2021). This is a damning indictment of a major energy multinational but is certainly in keeping with the company's longstanding record of secretly funding initiatives to counter governmental efforts to combat climate change.

The significance of energy megaprojects, both conventional and nonconventional

As stated, despite public policy pronouncements from the fossil fuel sector concerning a reorientation of strategy towards sustainability, the actions of many of these energy giants appear inconsistent with these stated objectives. The principal manifestation of this apparent paradox is the continued planning and development of major fossil fuel megaprojects. In a 2019 report, the NGO, Global Witness, detailed planned capital expenditures on new oil and gas development over the period 2020–2029. Figure 3.6 summarizes these planned expenditures by major companies. The report reached three critical conclusions:

- Any production from new oil and gas fields, beyond those already in production or development, is incompatible with limiting warming to 1.5°C.
- All of the $4.9 trillion forecast capital expenditure in new oil and gas fields is incompatible with limiting warming to 1.5°C.

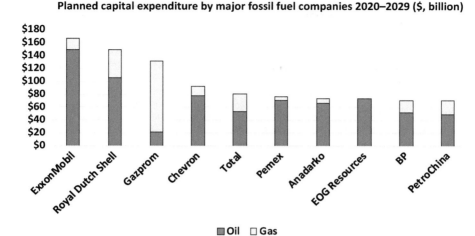

Figure 3.6 Planned capital expenditure by major fossil fuel companies 2020–2029.
Source: Global Witness 2019.

- 9 percent of oil and 6 percent of gas production forecast from existing fields is incompatible with limiting warming to 1.5°C.

Since the publication of this report, some of these projects, especially for liquified natural gas, have been rescheduled in light of climate concerns, pandemic delays, and the recent state of energy markets (Global Energy Monitor 2020; Reuters July 6, 2020). However, in light of projected increases in global energy demand, there remains a strong incentive for major fossil fuel producers to stay the course. This is especially the case for ExxonMobil, which has made the decision to focus on megaprojects at the expense of reducing carbon emissions (*Economist* 2019; Nasdaq 2019; Bloomberg October 5, 2020; *New York Times* September 21, 2020). As the Bloomberg report observes: "The largest US oil producer has never made a commitment to lower oil and gas output or set a date by which it will become carbon neutral. Exxon has also never publicly disclosed its forecasts for its own emissions." Whether this major strategic decision will stand remains to be seen, as there are already signs of tangible costs to this strategy. The company has been dropped from the Dow after nearly a century (CBS News August 25, 2020) and the NGO, Carbon Tracker (2020a), has concluded that chasing growth has destroyed shareholder value in the company.

Two other major fossil fuel companies have publicly announced a different strategic direction from ExxonMobil (*New York Times* September 21, 2020) . Both Royal Dutch Shell and BP have undertaken to move towards a more sustainable corporate strategy. In a press release on February 11, 2021, Shell announced that it was accelerating its "drive for net-zero emissions with a customer-first strategy," expanding on its commitment to become a net-zero-carbon company by 2050 (*Guardian* April 16, 2020; Royal Dutch Shell February 11, 2021), although skepticism has been voiced over whether this goal is attainable in the stated time frame (BBC May 11, 2020). As part of this strategy, Shell has recently bought Ubitricity, one of the biggest vehicle charging networks in Europe (*Week* January 30, 2021; Ubitricity.com).

Shell has invested several billion dollars to develop a clean energy business but has fallen at least $3 billion short of its announced spending target of $6 billion over the past three years (*Guardian* January 3, 2020). This figure pales in comparison to its announced plans to invest a further $149 billion in oil and gas development over the period 2020–29. (See Figure 3.6 and *New York Times* February 11, 2021). Perhaps the most critical commentary on Shell's original plans was presented by George Monbiot (June 26, 2019) when he observed that:

> Shell's "cash engines", according to its annual report, are oil and gas. There is no sign that it plans to turn the engines off. Its "growth priorities" are chemical production and deep water oil extraction. It does list low-carbon energy among its "emerging opportunities" in future decades, but says it will develop them alongside fracking and liquefied fossil gas technologies. In the future, the company says, it will "sell more natural gas". But as an analysis by Oil Change International explains, "there is no room for new fossil fuel development—gas included—within the Paris agreement goals". Even existing gas and oil extraction is enough to push us past 1.5C of global heating. Shell is a company committed for the long term to fossil fuel production.

BP has also announced its intention to become net zero by 2050 (BP 2020; *Guardian* February 12, 2020). While admirable in their stated goals, there are several qualifications required when interpreting these undertakings. BP went down this route once before over a decade ago, for example. Under the leadership of Lord John Browne from 1995 to 2007, the company attempted to rebrand itself as "Beyond Petroleum" by planning a major transition to renewable energy. This policy was reversed, however, by his successor, Tony Hayward, who reestablished the company focus on petroleum. Jonathan Watts, writing in the *Guardian* (February 12, 2020), has provided a detailed critique of BP's recently announced plans by noting that:

> there is nothing in the statement to suggest that BP will move away from previous plans to increase oil and gas production by 20% over the next 10 years … There are no concrete details here about scaling down production of fossil fuels or scaling up renewables. This will raise concerns that the company thinks it can just plant trees or use other offsets to make up for ever greater petrochemical production. This would not be enough to stabilize the climate.

Other analysts have also expressed concern over the difficulty BP will face in achieving its announced targets (Reuters August 9, 2020). BP has joined the French oil company, Total, however, in spending £879 million to purchase options to build offshore wind farms in the United Kingdom. It has been estimated that the total budget of this project could amount to tens of billions of dollars. The company has also paid $1.1 billion for a 50 percent share in an offshore wind facility off the US east coast (*New York Times* February 8, 2021). Included in its proposed new energy portfolio are plans to invest heavily in solar power (Bloomberg September 16, 2020).

Coupled with outsized environmental impacts of continued funding of energy megaprojects by the major fossil fuel companies is their concomitant depressing effect on the development of renewable energy sources. The large capital investments involved in megaprojects and their long lifespan displaces renewable energy projects and technologies necessary to achieve global climate goals. It has been reported that the energy industry is planning to construct 235 gas-fired power stations in the United States at a cost of more than $100 billion (*New York Times* November 12, 2020). It is remarkable that many such projects are being planned by industry with the tangible risk that the resources may have to be left in the ground as renewable energy technology evolves in an attempt to keep the global temperature rise below the IPCC's 1.5°C benchmark. If renewables do evolve sufficiently, the entire fossil fuel industry faces shut-ins and stranded assets and will ultimately have to undergo profound and sweeping structural realignment (McKinsey 2021). What is equally remarkable is that funding for these projects continues to be provided by major international banks and some Western governments such as France (CTV News November 15, 2020). While most Western banks tend to focus on oil and natural gas projects, several major Chinese, Japanese, and American banks have been funding the continued development of coal projects in countries still heavily dependent on this fuel as a significant source of electricity and/or export earnings. In their annual fossil fuel finance report, the Rainforest Alliance and partners (RAN et al. 2020) provided a detailed list of thirty-five international banks and their investments of $2.7 trillion in the four years following the Paris Agreement. Included in this list was financing of oil sands, Arctic oil and gas, offshore oil and gas, fracked oil and gas, liquified natural gas, coal mining, and coal power.

In an attempt to retard this trend towards greater fossil fuel production, particularly in the coal sector, the G7 nations agreed in June 2021 to stop international funding of any coal-fired power stations that lack CCS technology, although there was no agreement on a specific end date for the use of coal (*New York Times* June 14, 2021). It has been reported that the G7 ministers were heavily influenced by a report on pathways to net zero from the International Energy Agency (IEA 2021b), which concluded that "beyond projects already committed as of 2021, there are no new oil and gas fields approved for development in our pathway, and no new coal mines or mine extensions are required" (p. 21). At the COP26 conference in November 2021, a preliminary version of the final agreement called for the *phasing out* of coal, but a last-minute intervention by India, with the concurrence of China, forced a wording change to *phasing down* (*Guardian* November 13, 2021). Since China and India consume more than half the world's coal, the potential impact of this agreement remains to be seen. It has also been reported that oil and coal-rich countries were lobbying to weaken United Nations' climate reports in the lead-up to COP26 (*Guardian* October 21, 2021).

The year 2020 was a watershed for fossil fuel companies as seven, including Shell, Exxon, Chevron, and BP, downgraded their assets by a combined $87 billion in nine months (Reuters June 30, 2020; *Guardian* August 14, 2020) and lost billions of dollars resulting from the negative impact of the COVID-19 pandemic on energy prices as a result of the declining demand for gasoline, diesel, and jet fuel (*New York Times* December 10, 2020 and February 2, 2021). This raised expectations that a major strategic realignment might occur in the fossil fuel industry away from its traditional reliance on oil and natural gas. BP did take the unprecedented step of writing off $17.5 billion in assets not only due to COVID-19 but also because it recognizes that these may become stranded assets in the future (*Oil Change International* June 16, 2020). It has also been reported that oil and gas companies in North America and Europe wrote down roughly $145 billion in the first three-quarters of 2020 (*Wall Street Journal* December 27, 2020). The steep drop in global CO_2 emissions that accompanied this decline in energy demand also suggested that the fossil fuel industry, and the world, might be on a new path to a more sustainable energy future. Unfortunately, the IEA reported on March 2, 2021 that global emissions of carbon dioxide have rebounded sharply (IEA 2021a), suggesting that "we are returning to carbon-intensive business-as-usual."

On balance, it is easy to understand why a corporation would be reluctant to abandon a business model that has proved to be so remunerative for decades. However, it is difficult to imagine a starker example of the divergence between private and social costs and benefits than is provided by the business decision to continue down the same path, potentially increasing even further the emissions of GHGs and resulting global warming. The problem is compounded by the existence of corporate incentive structures which "trap companies in a loop of fossil growth" (Carbon Tracker 2020a and b). As Kenner and Heede (2021, p. 9) observe in their study of the role of executive compensation at BP, Chevron, ExxonMobil, and Shell: "what the executives and directors share in common is a desire to maintain demand for oil and gas, and to defend their company's social license to operate. They are paid to run fossil fuel supply chains—with large greenhouse gas emissions."

Several recent events may change the current path of fossil fuel development, even if at a relatively slow pace. In May and June 2021, three climate activists were elected to the board of ExxonMobil, much to the surprise of management (*New York Times* June 2, 2021). To quote the *New York Times* (May 26, 2021),

> The success of the campaign, led by a tiny hedge fund against the nation's largest oil company, could force the energy industry to confront climate change and embolden Wall Street investment firms that are prioritizing the issue. Analysts could not recall another time that Exxon management had lost a vote against company-picked directors.

The *New York Times* also described the unusual confluence of events that led to this outcome (*New York Times* June 9, 2021):

> An activist investor successfully waged a battle to install three directors on the board of Exxon with the goal of pushing the energy giant to reduce its carbon footprint. The investor, a hedge fund called Engine No. 1, was virtually unknown before the fight. The tiny firm wouldn't have had a chance were it not for an unusual twist: the support of some of Exxon's biggest institutional investors. BlackRock, Vanguard and State Street voted against Exxon's leadership and gave Engine No. 1 powerful support. These huge investment companies rarely side with activists on such issues.

Nevertheless, another article by the *New York Times* (May 27, 2021) presented a somewhat more somber appraisal of the potential consequences:

> But it is not clear if the activists can deliver on their dual goals—reducing the emissions that are warming the planet and lifting the profits and stock price of Exxon. The potential tensions between those objectives could doom the investor effort to transform the company and the oil industry. Getting Exxon, a behemoth company with $265 billion in revenue in 2019 and oil and gas fields around the world, to switch to cleaner energy will be a yearslong and difficult process. It is

unlikely to produce quick returns and could sap profits for a while as the company spends a small fortune to retool itself. And the biggest investment firms, which lent critical support to the activists and control a lot of Exxon's stock, may be too timid to keep the pressure on company executives and board members who are determined to resist big changes.

Perhaps more significant was the decision of a Dutch court ordering Royal Dutch Shell to cut its carbon dioxide emissions by 45 percent by 2030 from 2019 levels (CNN Business May 26, 2021). This ruling was preceded by a shareholder rebellion led by Britain's biggest fund manager, Legal & General Investment Management, over the credibility of its plans to reduce GHGs (*Guardian* May 24, 2021). It is hoped that the shareholder-led activism and the court decision may set a precedent influencing the behavior of other major polluters.

Adding further impetus to this reorientation of corporate strategic direction has been the recent decision of seventeen major British insurance companies to support the transition to a less carbon-intensive economy by "expanding insurance coverage for projects such as offshore windfarms, and partnering with governments to provide better disaster protection cover in countries facing serious risks like extreme weather caused by global heating" (*Guardian* June 24, 2021). Foremost among these companies is Lloyd's, the world's biggest insurance market, which made a decision in late 2020 to quit fossil fuel insurance by 2030 (*Guardian* December 17, 2020; see also *New York Times* February 13, 2020). This shift in attitudes in the financial community was also reflected in a recent letter signed by 450 major investors, managing more than $41 trillion in assets, calling on governments to set more ambitious emission reduction targets focusing on decarbonizing pollution-intensive industry and implementing mandatory climate risk disclosure requirements (CNN Business June 10, 2021).

Case study 7: A cautionary tale (II): Blindsided by new technology and products: Patagonia

Along with Interface Carpets, Patagonia, the outdoor clothing company, is one of the few companies that has demonstrated a deep, company-wide philosophical commitment to the principle of sustainability based on the passionate beliefs of its founder, Yvon Chouinard. Again, in parallel with Interface, Patagonia has achieved a solid financial record where sustainability provides its differentiation strategy and consequent competitive advantage. First and foremost, the company clearly recognizes the challenges it faces. To quote:

> Our work has always begun first by acknowledging that Patagonia is part of the problem. We make products using fossil fuels, built in factories that use water and other resources, create waste and emit carbon into the air. We ship our products around the world in boxes and plastic bags. We consume electricity— some generated using renewable resources and some not—at our corporate offices, distribution centers and stores. We drive cars and ride on airplanes. As individuals, we consume products of all shapes and sizes—probably more than we need. Knowing we are part of the problem, we must also recognize that climate change—as a deadly condition of infinite human actions—is not an

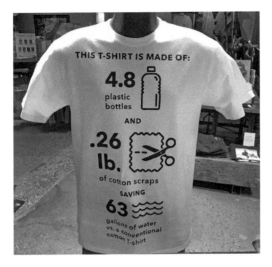

Figure 3.7 Patagonia T-shirt.

issue we can tackle outright. That's why we try to stay focused on specific things Patagonia can do to reduce, neutralize, or even reverse the root causes of climate change. We believe in extending our mission to cause no unnecessary harm to every area where Patagonia has influence. That way, as Patagonia grows in size, our efforts to meet the challenge of our mission can be amplified exponentially.

(Patagonia 2018, pp. 1–2)

Patagonia has undertaken specific actions including measuring and tracking the carbon footprint of their global operations, using renewable energy wherever possible, improving existing buildings rather than constructing new ones for their retail operations, using monetary incentives to encourage their employees to drive less, using sustainable paper, developing a program to help manage the chemicals and environmental impacts in their global supply chain, and relying wherever possible on natural fibers (e.g., hemp, organic cotton, Tencel Lyocell, and Yulex) to supplement their use of recycled nylon, polyester, cotton wool, and down fibers. (Patagonia 2018). (See Figure 3.7)

As indicated in its online statements of philosophy, Patagonia is not only committed to transforming the company into a truly sustainable enterprise, it has also actively promoted similar initiatives in its own industry by helping to fund the Sustainable Apparel Coalition, an alliance of thirty companies from the clothing and footwear industries; has helped to fund like-minded charities and grassroots organizations by donating 1 percent of its annual sales; and has backed a fund called $20 Million & Change which assists start-up companies bring benefits to the environment (Patagonia n.d.).

To achieve all of these multifaceted goals, Patagonia has registered as a B corporation, a new approach to business which focuses less on maximizing shareholder returns and more on achieving social and environmental goals (Benefitcorp.net). While there are now more than 1,200 companies worldwide with B-corporation status, this strategic reorientation does not obviate the longstanding legal requirement of first duty to shareholders. Patagonia is able to skirt this legal requirement because of its status as a privately held corporation. The status of this strategy remains unclear for public companies, despite the fact that a small number of such entities (such as the Brazilian toiletries company, Natura) have announced this type of strategic change. It has been reported that Unilever is giving serious consideration to becoming a B corporation as well, and their subsidiary, Ben and Jerry's, has already moved in this direction. What made the latter move possible, however, is that Ben and Jerry's is a wholly owned entity within the panoply of Unilever companies (Fast Company 2012; Unileverusa.com).

In essence, Patagonia's approach stands in stark contrast to the business model used by H&M and Zara. Patagonia's mantra is "reduce, repair, reuse and recycle." The company focuses on durable long-lasting products, and encourages their customers to return their old Patagonia wear to the store for a credit, after which the company will repair or recycle the goods. The corporate approach is summed up in the words of the late environmentalist David Brower: "There is no business on a dead planet" (Dilley 2014).

And yet, it is one of the underlying themes of this book that the achievement of sustainability is more elusive than once thought and this is no more apparent than in the corporate sector. Within the last decades, numerous research studies have identified a new and consequential environmental problem associated, in part, with the production and use of synthetic fibers (e.g., Napper and Thompson 2016), the output of which has risen dramatically within the last several decades (*Textile World* 2015). Vast quantities of microplastics, of which microfibers are a part, have been released into the environment and threaten the ocean-based food chain. The effects are at least twofold: first, filter feeders such as oysters and mussels incorporate these fibers into their tissue, and this tissue progresses up the food chain to human consumers; and, second, synthetic fibers tend to absorb chemicals, many of which are toxic and/or carcinogenic, and these also move up the food chain (Varinsky 2016; Cox et al. 2019; Mishra et al. 2019).

Recent estimates suggest that the United States may be releasing as much as 750,000 pounds of fibers into waterways every day (Varinsky 2016). This is of particular relevance to Patagonia in light of their significant production and sale of fleece jackets with the potential to release large quantities of microfibers during washing. To their credit, this unexpected result of the widespread use of synthetic fibers prompted the company to commission a study of the quantities released by their products (Hartline et al. 2016). The results were astonishing, suggesting that a single fleece jacket sheds as many as 250,000 synthetic fibers during laundering (*Guardian*, February 12, 2017). Patagonia has been devoting considerable resources to address and reduce this problem. Nevertheless, it is symptomatic of the general dichotomy between early benefits and delayed costs of new technologies. Given the projected increase in the production of polyester (see Figure 3.8), the fiber and clothing industries now face a major challenge in addressing the environmental consequences of its use.

With this monumental challenge facing the fashion industry, several niche companies have seized the initiative and adopted radically new business models. One of these is Tonle, with production based in Cambodia. Ninety percent of the company's raw materials are discards from major companies in the fashion industry, composed of cut waste, quality

Textile mill consumption: actual and estimates ('000 MT)

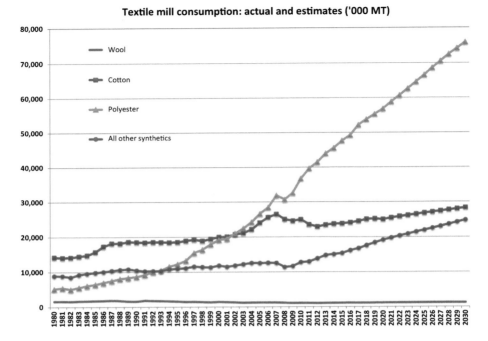

Figure 3.8 Fiber production and projections by type.
Source: PCI Wood Mackenzie 2018. Data reproduced with permission.

control failure, overstock, and dead stock (Tonle.com). Coupled with the use of natural dyes and inks, and recycled packaging, the company has drastically reduced the ecological footprint of clothing production. The increasing production of garments in Cambodia has not been without major environmental challenges, however. The French environmental organization, Geres (n.d.) reports that the industry is the country's largest contributor to GHG emissions, largely through the destruction of old growth forests as an energy source.

Measuring corporate sustainability and incorporating it into business strategy

Ever since the introduction of the concept of sustainability in the 1980s, a pressing concern has been the search for appropriate sustainability indicators, principally in the field of ecology, in order to measure the direction and magnitude of change towards this critical goal. A similar quest is now underway to find reasonable correlates in the allied fields of economics and business.

Several systems of metrics have been developed and have garnered wide international acceptance and use: for example, the Global Reporting Initiative Guidelines (GRI) discussed in the Suncor case; and eco-efficiency metrics developed by the World Business Council for Sustainable Development (WBCSD 2005a and b). The latter are generally expressed as a ratio of product service or value and environmental effect. Their use is illustrated in the Interface and Mohawk cases with such measures as energy, water, and GHG intensity of production.

Within the corporate sector, there are two distinct audiences for these data, reflecting the traditional dichotomy of financial and managerial accounting. Financial accounting is designed to provide information to all the firm's stakeholders (i.e. outside the corporation), while managerial accounting is designed to aid managers within the company to make better decisions. As such, there are two comparable types of environmental accounting information/techniques/methodologies which are largely—but not completely—independent, each targeting a different audience.

With respect to information aimed at external stakeholders, an increasingly common tool used by many corporations is triple bottom line accounting, where traditional financial statements are accompanied by both quantitative and qualitative indicators on ecological and social dimensions of corporate activity. Where such data have been presented for several years, it is possible to determine any trends towards greater or lesser corporate sustainability. These indicators can also be used to highlight goals for the corporation at a specified future date, as illustrated in the H&M case study.

There are two principal drawbacks to triple bottom line accounting as currently employed: first, the lack of monetization makes it difficult to deduce the financial impact on the corporation of individual products, production processes, or any other activity that has either positive or negative environmental or social consequences. For example, financial institutions such as banks, insurers, and investment houses have become increasingly concerned about the exposure of corporations to future liabilities associated with climate change. There have already been several initiatives to identify and monetize these risks (Bloomberg January 22, 2019). A second, and related, drawback is that with triple bottom line reporting, the ultimate focus remains on financial statistics to the exclusion of other potentially important costs and benefits facing the company. In other words, a truly *integrated* bottom line would be far preferable to a *triple* bottom line.

Case study 8: Puma

Perhaps one of the most innovative approaches to overcoming some of the challenges identified above has been offered by Puma, the third largest sportswear manufacturer in the world. In collaboration with PriceWaterhouseCoopers and the environmental research group, Trucost, Puma created and published what they termed an environmental profit and loss (EP&L) statement in 2011. This analysis attempted to monetize all the company's major environmental and social impacts, not only in the company itself but also throughout its extensive supply chain.

The results demonstrated that 94 percent of Puma's environmental costs were attributable to the production of raw materials in its supply chain. The PriceWaterhouseCoopers consultant observed that:

> fundamentally, this analysis is about risk management for the environment, and for business, because you cannot separate the two. . . . This is a first for a company to measure and value the impact of its business in this way and gives PUMA a unique and challenging insight into their supply chain. It's a game-changing development for businesses to integrate environmental issues into their current business model like this, because it provides a basis for embedding their reliance on ecosystem services into business strategy.
>
> (Puma and PPR Home 2011, p. 2)

The total environmental impact measured in the first phase of the multistage analysis yielded a figure of €145 million. To place this in the context of total corporate operations, Puma had profits in 2010 of €202.2 million on sales of €2,706.4 million. It was proposed that the following phase would attempt the more conceptually challenging task of estimating the impact of social factors such as fair wages, safety, and working conditions. Finally, the creation of an integrated profit-and-loss analog that includes environmental, social, and economic components requires the measurement of any offsetting benefits related to the creation of jobs, tax contributions, philanthropic initiatives, and other value-adding elements.

Puma has focused initially on five environmental impacts: water use, GHGs, land use, air pollution, and waste. Three categorizations have been used: (1) principal product lines, (2) global markets by region, and (3) tiers in the supply chain. Puma core operations include offices, warehouses, stores, and logistics; Tier 1 is the manufacturing of corporate products; Tier 2 represents outsourced processes such as embroiderers, printers, and outsole production; Tier 3 is the processing of raw materials, such as leather in tanneries, chemicals, and oil refining; and Tier 4 is raw material production such as cotton cultivation and harvesting, natural rubber production, oil drilling, and cattle ranching for leather, with the last contributing the most to land-use impacts. The company has also reported that the most important contributors to air pollution are ammonia emissions from animal waste and fertilizers used in agricultural processes.

The development of this innovative methodology has allowed Puma to structure its operations in a more sustainable manner and measure its degree of success on each of the component initiatives. A critical part of this reorientation of its business model and corporate strategy will clearly require extensive collaboration with suppliers. To quote:

> PUMA and PPR Home [Puma's parent company] will look to play a catalytic role in raising awareness that the current business model is outdated and needs decisive reforms, forging partnerships and collaborations to explore new and innovative ways to differentially attribute the responsibilities and equitably share the costs of these, while building capacity at suppliers' factories and developing new materials and products. PUMA and PPR HOME are sharing the results of the EP&L with other industry players and corporations to leverage adopting a new business model that takes the costs of using natural resources within business operations into account. This analysis will also help to better assess the relative environmental impacts of sourcing from different countries and regions. Down the line it will allow PUMA to improve supply chain management and reduce supply chain risks.
>
> (Puma and PPR HOME 2011, p. 4)

From a managerial perspective, the benefits derived from recognition and integration of relevant social and ecological factors can be substantial. The challenge facing the corporation is often the task of teasing out these costs and benefits from conventional accounting data. For example, it is frequently the case that environmental costs are buried in overhead or other ancillary accounts and cannot be easily attributed to any specific product or production process. There are several methodologies which can be used in an attempt to address this problem, note-worthy among them is activity-based costing (Emblemsvag and Bras 2001; Kaplan and Anderson 2007). One company which has successfully addressed this problem is Spectrum Glass, a privately owned company in Washington State that manufactures about 30 percent of the world's specialty sheet glass (i.e. colored sheet glass for stained-glass windows or lamps). Cadmium oxide and other pigments used in the manufacture of yellow, orange, and red glass are highly toxic, hazardous chemicals. The coloring chemicals are the primary source of the two environmental issues— hazardous wastes and air emissions.

Although ruby-red glass, which relies on cadmium-based pigments, generates more hazardous wastes than other colors, the company had allocated environmental costs equally across all its different glass products, and had not charged a premium for ruby-red glass. The company was paying approximately $3,500 per short ton (about $32,500 a year) to dispose of its hazardous waste. The net result of the trad-itional accounting practice used by the company was that ruby-red glass appeared profitable while, in reality, it was actually making a loss. The exercise of correctly allocating all relevant costs associated with products allowed the company to alter its pricing structure and increase profitability (Ditz et al. 1995).

A final critique

One of the most commonly used metrics for measuring corporate sustainability is the aforementioned group of eco-efficiency measures advanced by the World Business Council for Sustainable Development (WBCSD 2005a and b; www.wbcsd.ch), which is used by many of the corporations discussed in this chapter. This metric is not without controversy however: there are two principal criticisms. First, a firm may be achieving an improved eco-efficiency metric by lowering its GHG emissions per unit of output but, if output is increasing sufficiently, the total level of GHG emissions will rise. Ultimately, from the perspective of society and the ecosystem, it is the total output which matters. This is a nontrivial distinction which lies at the heart of the Suncor case study. The second critique is even more substantive and lies at the philosophical heart of how we design our modern industrial system. This critique is based on the work of William McDonough and Michael Braungart (1998, 2002, 2004, 2013).

McDonough, an architect and planner, and Braungart, a chemical engineer, first laid out their radical proposals for a total redesign of our modern industrial system of production in an article in the October 1998 edition of *Atlantic Monthly*, entitled "The next indus-trial revolution." This was followed by an in-depth elaboration of their proposal in a book published in 2002 called *Cradle to Cradle: Remaking the Way We Make Things*. They proposed a transformation away from our current linear, once-through "cradle-to-grave" production system, which is profoundly inefficient and generates massive amounts of waste. To quote:

> Cradle-to-grave designs dominate modern manufacturing. … Many products are designed with 'built-in obsolescence,' to last only for a certain period of time. … Also, what most people see in their garbage cans is just the tip of the material iceberg; the product itself contains on average only 5 percent of the raw materials involved in the process of making and delivering it.
>
> (pp. 27–28)

The central thrust of the innovation proposed by McDonough and Braungart is to redesign our production systems so they mimic nature where there is no waste per se, where virtually all byproducts of natural production—with the exception of energy—are recycled into nutrients for the production of other organisms. The industrial challenge is to alter the design process of modern industrial products so that their waste products can be recycled into two streams: what the authors call "biological nutrients" and "technical nutrients." As briefly described in Figure 3.1b, there is a key distinction between these two waste streams: the first can reenter the ecosystem without synthetic or toxic components and are thus able to be recycled without altering or contaminating natural cycles; in contrast, the second are recycled in closed loop systems within the production process so that no toxins are released into the environment. This is the essence of the cradle-to-cradle system.

The fundamental critique advanced by McDonough and Braungart of current sustainability efforts is that eco-efficiency is focused on reducing the negative environmental impacts of industrial production but does not induce producers to change the basic design of the production process or the products themselves. In the words of the authors, "efficient is not sufficient." Improved technologies that reduce the flow of energy and materials in the cradle-to-grave system do not ultimately eliminate the wastes and toxic products. The approach proposed by McDonough and Braungart is twofold: to replace eco-efficiency with *eco-effectiveness,* and change downcycling to upcycling—a step which Shaw Industries and some other companies such as Honeywell (McDonough and Braungart 2004) have already undertaken. The authors observe that "in our next Industrial Revolution, regulations can be seen as signals of design failure."

In a reconceptualization similar in spirit to Interface's partial substitution of a service for a good, McDonough and Braungart (1998, p. 90) state:

> Imagine what would happen if a chemical company sold intelligence instead of pesticides—that is, if farmers or agro-businesses paid pesticide manufacturers to protect their crops against loss from pests instead of buying dangerous regulated chemicals to use at their own discretion.

To advance their agenda of transforming industrial production, McDonough and Braungart formed a consulting company called McDonough Braungart Design Chemistry, which offers their services worldwide. While the company has had a number of both successes and failures (Fastcompany.com mentions some of the failures), one of the earliest and most important early success stories was the case of Rohner Textil in Switzerland discussed in this chapter.

Summary

Every year, GreenBiz publishes its *State of Green Business*. Its 2021 report includes five general categories of achievements: the big picture, natural capital impacts, climate risk, positive impact, and corporate performance. The reported highlights are mixed and summarized as follows:

The big picture

- 90 percent of major US companies published a sustainability report in 2019, up from 86 percent in 2018 and 20 percent in 2011.

- 16 percent of public US companies mentioned environmental, social, and governance (ESG) considerations in their SEC filings.
- >1,500 companies backed the Task Force on Climate-Related Financial Disclosures reporting framework in 2020, five times the number to do so in 2011.

Natural capital impacts

- In 2019, natural capital costs were 90 percent higher than net income for major global companies and 5 percent higher for major US companies.
- 64 percent of major global companies (up from 7 percent) and 58 percent of major US companies (up 6 percent) publicly disclosed carbon targets.
- For the first time, major global and US companies reported year-over-year declines in water use of 6 percent and 8 percent respectively.

Climate risk

- Major global companies are on track for >3°C warming, falling 72 percent short of emissions reductions required to achieve the goals of the Paris Agreement.
- Major global companies face $284 billion carbon pricing costs in 2025, representing 13 percent of earnings.
- Nearly 95 percent of major US companies and 80 percent of major global companies will face moderate physical risk by 2050.

Positive impact

- 53 percent of revenues of major US companies and 49 percent of revenues of major global companies are generated in business activities that support the United Nations Sustainable Development Goals.
- 27 percent of revenues generated by major US companies and 31 percent of revenues generated by major global companies are aligned to the EU Taxonomy for Sustainable Activities (EU n.d.).

Corporate performance

- Major US companies achieved an average S&P Global ESG score of 40/100 in 2019, while major global companies achieved 47/100.

A sober assessment of corporate promises of selected major companies on climate change was provided in a *New York Times* article of February 22, 2021:

- Costco and Netflix have not provided emissions reduction targets despite saying they want to reduce their impact on climate change.
- Others, like the agricultural giant Cargill and the clothing company Levi Strauss, have made commitments but have struggled to cut emissions. The emissions from Levi's supply chain grew by 13 percent between 2016 and 2019.
- Technology companies like Google and Microsoft, which run power-hungry data centers, have slashed emissions, but even they are finding that the technology often does not yet exist to carry out their moon-shot objectives.

- Just over one-third of the 500 companies in the S&P 500 stock index have set ambitious targets while 215 had no target at all. The rest had weak targets.
- Reducing impact on climate change gets even harder when companies begin the process of reducing so-called scope 3 emissions—pollution caused by suppliers and customers. At oil companies, for example, scope 3 would include emissions from cars that use gasoline.
- Cargill, one of the largest privately owned US companies and a major middleman that works with farmers and food companies around the world, has attempted to become a strong voice on climate change but has struggled to meet its goals.
- Google wants all its operations to be consistently powered by renewable energy by 2030, but that could be difficult to achieve because the output of wind and solar farms is still small in some countries.
- Microsoft wants to be carbon negative by 2030 even including scope 3 emissions. That goal will almost certainly require the company to extract carbon dioxide from the atmosphere. Those technologies are nascent and could be very expensive.

On a positive note, 310 major businesses and investors signed an open letter to President Biden in April 2021 calling for deep GHG emission cuts to combat climate change (*New York Times* April 13, 2021). The signatories represent more than $3 trillion in annual revenue and more than $1 trillion in assets (We Mean Business Coalition and Ceres 2021).

In conclusion, because of its predominant role in the production of goods and services, the corporate sector must be a critical player in moving an economy towards greater sustainability. Yet, companies cannot do this alone. Their efforts require the establishment of a favorable regulatory and economic environment which allows them to maintain or increase profits while pursuing a more sustainable path. This provides the clear case for a critical government role to facilitate this transition.

References

Alberta Auditor General (2011) *Report of the Auditor General of Alberta*, Edmonton, Auditor General of Alberta, November.

Alberta Chamber of Resources (2004) *Oil Sands Technology Roadmap: Unlocking the Potential*, Edmonton, Alberta Chamber of Resources, January 30.

Alberta Views (2015) "Pipe dream: The failure of Alberta's carbon-capture experiments," July 1.

Anderson, Ray (1999) *Mid-Course Correction: Toward a Sustainable Enterprise: The Interface Model*, Atlanta: Peregrinzilla Press.

Anderson, Ray (2007) "Mid-course correction: Toward a sustainable enterprise" in Peter N. Nemetz (ed.) *Sustainable Resource Management: Reality or Illusion?* Cheltenham: Edward Elgar, 88–114.

Anderson, Ray and Robin White (2009) *Confessions of a Radical Industrialist: Profits, People, Purpose; Doing Business by Respecting the Earth.* (Reissued in 2011 in paperback as *Business Lessons from a Radical Industrialist.*) Toronto: McClelland & Stewart.

Anderson, Ray et al. (2010) "Changing business cultures from within," in *State of the World 2010: Transforming Cultures; From Consumerism to Sustainability,* Worldwatch Institute, Washington, I, 96–102.

Ansar, Atif et al. (2013) *Stranded Assets and the Fossil Fuel Divestment Campaign: Report,* Smith School of Enterprise and the Environment, Oxford University.

Barber, A. and G. Pellow (2006) "LCA: New Zealand merino wool total energy use." [5]th Australian Life Cycle Assessment Society Conference, 16 Melbourne, November, 22–24.

BBC (2020) "Climate change: Study pours cold water on oil company net zero claims," May 11.

Berman, Tzeporah (2020) "Kenney's billions for Keystone XL is ballast for a sinking ship," *National Observer*, April 7.

Bloomberg (2019) "Corporate America is getting ready to monetize climate change," January 22.

Bloomberg (2020) "BP's clean energy push starts with five-year dash on solar, wind," September 16.

Bloomberg (2020) "Exxon's plan for surging carbon emissions revealed in leaked documents," October 5.

BP (2020) "BP sets ambition for net zero by 2050, fundamentally changing organisation to deliver," press release, February 12.

Brulle, Robert J. (2013) *Climate Change* "Institutionalizing delay: Foundation funding and the creation of U.S climate change counter-movement organizations," December 21.

Brulle, Robert J. (2018) *Climatic Change* "The climate lobby: A sectoral analysis of lobbying spending on climate change in the USA, 2000 to 2016," July 19.

Caldecott, Ben et al. (2014) "Stranded assets and scenarios." Discussion paper, Smith School of Enterprise and the Environment, Oxford University, January.

Caldecott, Ben et al. (2015) *Stranded Assets and Subcritical Coal: The Risk to Investors and Companies,* School of Enterprise and the Environment, Oxford University, March.

Calgary Herald (2020) "Alberta burned for billions in energy investment gambles," September 2.

Canada.com (2011) "Canada fighting EU plans to label oilsands world's dirtiest crude source," October 19.

Carbon Tracker (2018) "42% of global coal power plants run at a loss, finds world-first study," press release, November 30.

Carbon Tracker (2019) *Breaking the Habit,* September.

Carbon Tracker (2020a) *Fanning the Flames*, March.

Carbon Tracker (2020b) *Fault-Lines: How Diverging Oil and Gas Company Strategies Link to Stranded Asset Risk*, October.

Carbon Tracker (2020c) *Groundhog Pay: How Executive Incentives Trap Companies in a Loop of Fossil Growth*, December.

CBC (2010) "Oilsands poisoning fish, say scientists, fishermen," September 16.

CBC (2019) "Small nuclear reactors could make Alberta's oilsands cleaner, industry experts suggest," May 21.

CBC (2020) "Alberta's Heritage Savings Trust Fund hits lowest value in eight years," July 13.

CBC (2021) "Trudeau pledges to slash greenhouse gas emissions by at least 49% by 2030," April 22.

CBC (2021) "Keystone XL is dead, and Albertans are on the hook for $1.3B," June 9.

CBS News (2020) "Exxon Mobil dropped from the Dow after nearly a century," August 25.

CEC (Commission for Environmental Cooperation) (2020) *Alberta Tailings Ponds II: Factual Record Regarding Submission ESM-17-001, North American Environmental Law and Policy 36*, Montreal: Commission for Environmental Cooperation.

Cline, Elizabeth (2012) *Over-Dressed: The Shockingly High Cost of Cheap Fashion*, New York: Portfolio.

CNN Business (2021) "Court orders Shell to slash CO2 emissions in landmark climate ruling," May 26.

CNN Business (2021) "Investors holding $41 trillion demand action on climate—now," June 10.

Council for Textile Recycling (n.d.) "The facts about textile waste."

Cox, Kieran D. et al. (2019) *Environmental Science and Technology*, "Human consumption of microplastics," June 5.

CTV News (2020) "Public money guarantees 'risky' fossil fuel projects: Experts," November 15.

CTV News (2021) "Alberta 'big loser' on Keystone XL; NDP says Kenney made a bad investment," January 17.

Dale, Spencer (2015) "BP, economics of oil," Society of Business Economists Annual Conference, London, October 13.

Dauvergne, Peter (2018) *Will Big Business Destroy Our Planet?* Cambridge, Malden: Polity Press.

Dauvergne, Peter and Jane Lister (2013) *Eco-Business: A Big Brand Takeover of Sustainability*, Cambridge, MA: MIT Press.

Dietz, Simon et al. (2018) *Science*, "How ambitious are oil and gas companies' climate goals," October 22.

Dilley (2014) "Patagonia's new, decentralized approach to sustainability management," Triple Pundit, November 23.

Ditz, Daryl et al. (eds.) (1995) *Green Ledgers: Case Studies in Corporate Environmental Accounting,* World Resources Institute.

Economist (2019) "Bigger oil," February 9.

Ellen MacArthur Foundation (2015) *Towards a Circular Economy.*

Ellen MacArthur Foundation (2017) *A New Textiles Economy: Redesigning Fashion's Future.*

Emblemsvag, Jan and Bert Bras (2001) *Activity-Based Cost and Environmental Management*, Boston, MA: Springer.

Environmental Defense (2017) "Seven oil multinationals that are pulling out of Canada's tar sands," March 14.

EU (European Union) (n.d.) "EU taxonomy for sustainable activities."

Fast Company (2012) "When Unilever bought Ben & Jerry's: A story of CEO adaptability," August 14.

Financial Post (2021) "Norwegian oil company to quit Alberta, focus on offshore activities in Atlantic Canada," January 12.

Findlay, Martha Hall, (2012) "Please stop calling it 'ethical oil'," *Globe and Mail*, April 20.

Forbes (2017) "Fast fashion is a disaster for women and the environment," July 26.

Forbes (2019) "Oil and gas giants spend millions lobbying to block climate change policies," March 25.

Franta, Benjamin (2018) *Nature Climate Change*, "Early oil industry knowledge of CO_2 and global warming," December 18.

Funds Europe (2021) "BlackRock vows to divest from climate change laggards," January 27.

Geres (n.d.) "Fueling the low carbon development of Cambodian manufacturing industries."

Global Energy Monitor (2020) *Gas Bubble: Tracking Global LNG Infrastructure*, July.

Global Witness (2019) *Overexposed: How the IPCC's 1.5°C Report Demonstrates the Risk of Overinvestment in Oil and Gas*, April 23.

Globe & Mail (2012) "Rebuilding land destroyed by oil-sands may not restore it, researchers say," March 11.

Globescan (2020) *Sustainability Survey 2020.*

Gosselin, Pierre et al. (2010) *Environmental and Health Impacts of Canada's Oil sands Industry*, Royal Society of Canada, December.

Grant, Jennifer et al. (2010) *Northern Lifeblood: Empowering Northern Leaders to Protect the Mackenzie River Basin from Oil Sands Risks*, Pembina Institute, Calgary.

GreenBiz (2021) *State of Green Business 2021*, March 11.

Greenpeace (2016) *Carbon capture and storage a costly, risky distraction*, July 1.

Greenpeace UK (2021) *Net Expectations: Assessing the Role of Carbon Dioxide Removal in Companies' Climate Plans*, January.

Griffiths, Mary (2006) "Water use in the oil patch: The motivation for innovation," PTAC Water Innovation in the Oil Patch conference, June 21, Pembina Institute, Calgary.

Guardian (2017) "Microfibers are polluting our food chain. This laundry bag can stop that," February 12.

Guardian (2019) "Revealed: Mobil sought to fight environmental regulation, documents show," June 12.

Guardian (2020) "Royal Dutch Shell may fail to reach green energy targets," January 3.

Guardian (2020) "BP's statement on reaching net zero by 2050—what it says and what it means," February 12.

Guardian (2020) "Shell unveils plans to become net-zero carbon company by 2050," April 16.

Guardian (2020) "Seven top oil firms downgrade assets by \$87bn in nine months", August 14.

Guardian (2020) "Lloyd's market to quit fossil fuel insurance by 2030," December 17.

Guardian (2021) "Influential investor joins shareholder rebellion over Shell's climate plan," May 24.

Guardian (2021) "Top insurers join Prince Charles to fight climate crisis," June 24.

Guardian (2021) "ExxonMobil lobbyist filmed saying oil giant's support for carbon tax a PR ploy," June 30.

Guardian (2021) "Oil and coal-rich countries lobbying to weaken UN climate report, leak shows," October 21.

Guardian (2021) "Cop26 ends in climate agreement despite India watering down coal resolution," November 13.

H&M (2017 and 2019) *Sustainability Performance Report.*

H&M (2020) *Annual Report.*

H&M (n.d.) Interview with Anna Gedda, head of sustainability (hmgroup.com).

Hamel, Gary and Liisa Valikagnas (2003) *Harvard Business Review,* "The quest for resilience," September, 52–63.

Hartline, Niko L. et al. (2016) *Environmental Science & Technology,* "Microfiber masses recovered from conventional machine washing of new or aged garments," September 30.

Helm, Dieter (2017) *Burn Out: The Endgame for Fossil Fuels,* New Haven, CT: Yale University Press.

Hobson, John (2013) *Occupational Medicine,* "To die for? The health and safety of fast fashion," July.

HuffPost (2019) "28 years ago, big oil predicted it would take a high price on carbon to stop warming," December 3.

HuffPost (2019) "Fossil fuel giants claim to support climate science, yet still fund denial," December 28.

HuffPost (2020) "Revealed: BP and Shell back anti-climate lobby groups despite pledges," September 28.

HuffPost (2021) "Despite its pledges, Shell funded anti-climate lobbying last year," February 25.

Humes, Edward (2011) *Force of Nature: The Unlikely Story of Wal-Mart's Green Revolution,* New York: Harper Business.

IEA (International Energy Agency) (2021a) "After steep drop in early 2020, global carbon dioxide emissions have rebounded strongly," March 2.

IEA (International Energy Agency) (2021b) *Net Zero by 2050: A Roadmap for the Global Energy Sector.*

IEHN (Investor Environmental Health Network) (2010a) "Rohner Textiles: Cradle-to-cradle innovation and sustainability,"

IEHN (Investor Environmental Health Network) (2010b) "Shaw Industries: Ecoworx and cradle-to-cradle innovation in carpet tile."

IEHN (Investor Environmental Health Network) (2011) (www.iehn.org).

Independent (2018) "The environmental costs of fast fashion," January 8.

Influence Map (2019) *Big Oil's Real Agenda on Climate Change,* March.

Inside Climate News (2015) "Exxon's own research confirmed fossil fuels' role in global warming decades ago," September 16.

Interface (2020) "From carbon neutral to carbon negative", Erin Meezan, vice president and chief sustainability officer, October 20.

Interface (n.d. a) "A look back: Interface's sustainability journey."

Interface (n.d. b) "Carbon Negative FAQs."

Interface (n.d. c) "Mission zero: Measuring our progress."

IRENA (International Renewable Energy Agency) (2017) *Stranded Assets: How the Energy Transition Affects the Value of Energy Reserves, Buildings and Capital Stock,* July.

Jakob, Michael and Jerome Hilaire (2015) *Nature,* "Unburnable fossil-fuel reserves," January 8.

Journal of Commerce (2010) "Suncor Energy's tailings-pond reclamation claims questioned," September 29.

Kaplan, Robert and Steven Anderson (2007) *Time-Driven Activity-Based Costing: A Simpler and More Powerful Path to Higher Profits,* Boston: Harvard Business Review Press.

Kelly, Erin N. et al. (2009) *PNAS,* "Oil sands development contributes polycyclic aromatic compounds to the Athabasca River and its tributaries," December 29, 22346–51.

Kelly, Erin N. et al. (2010) *PNAS*, "Oil sands development contributes elements toxic at low concentrations to the Athabasca River and its tributaries," September 14, 16178–82.

Kenner, Dario and Richard Heede (2021) *Energy Research & Social Science*, "White knights or horsemen of the apocalypse? Prospects for Big Oil to align emissions with a 1.5C pathway," April 15.

Liggio, John et al. (2019) *Nature Communications*, "Measured Canadian oil sands CO_2 emissions are higher than estimates made using internationally recommended methods," April.

McDonough, William and Michael Braungart (1998) "The next industrial revolution," *Atlantic Monthly*, October, 82–92.

McDonough, William and Michael Braungart (2002) *Cradle to Cradle: Remaking the Way We Make Things*, New York: North Point Press.

McDonough, William and Michael Braungart (2004) "The cradle-to-cradle alternative," in *State of the World 2004*, Worldwatch Institute, 104–5.

McDonough, William and Michael Braungart (2013) *The Upcycle: Beyond Sustainability—Designing for Abundance*, New York: North Point Press.

McGlade, Christophe and Paul Ekins (2015) *Nature*, "The geographical distribution of fossil fuels unused when limiting global warming to 2°C," January 8.

McKinsey (2021) "Global oil outlook to 2040," February.

McLachlan, Stéphane M. (2014) *"Water is a living thing": Environmental and Human Health Implications of the Athabasca Oil Sands for the Mikisew Cree First Nation and Athabasca Chipewyan First Nation in Northern Alberta*, Fort Chipewyan, AB: Athabasca Chipewyan First Nation; Beaconsfield, QC: Canadian Electronic Library.

Michaels, David (2008) *Doubt Is Their Product: How Industry's Assault on Science Threatens Your Health*, Oxford University Press.

Mighty Earth (2019) *Cargill:* The Worst Company in the World, July.

Mishra, Sunanda et al. (2019) *Marine Pollution Bulletin*, "Marine microfiber pollution: A review on present status and future challenges," January.

Mohawk (2009, 2016, 2016, 2019) *Sustainability Report*.

Monbiot, George (2019) "Shell is not a green saviour: It's a planetary death machine," *Guardian*, June 26.

Napper, Imogen E. and Richard C. Thompson (2016) *Marine Pollution Bulletin*, "Release of synthetic microplastic fibres from domestic washing machines: Effects of fabric type and washing conditions," November.

Nasdaq (2019) "Exxon aims to sell $25 billion of assets to focus on megaprojects—sources," November 21.

National Geographic (2009) "The Canadian oil boom," March.

National Pollutant Release Inventory (2012) Government of Canada, Canada.ca.

Nemetz, Peter N. (2013) Business and the Sustainability Challenge: An Integrated Perspective, New York and London: Routledge, 410.

Nemetz, Peter N. and Marilyn Hankey (1984) *Economic Incentives for Energy Conservation*, New York: John Wiley & Sons.

New York Times (2010) "Clothes discarded by H & M in Manhattan are first destroyed," January 5.

New York Times (2010) "Alberta's tar sands and the dead duck trial," March 10.

New York Times (2010) "Backers rev up oil sands campaign," December 8.

New York Times (2011) "A Canadian oil ad vexes the Saudis," September 25.

New York Times (2012) "Bangladesh fire kills more than 100 and injures many," November 25.

New York Times (2016) "Peabody Energy, a coal giant, seeks bankruptcy protection," April 13.

New York Times (2018) "H&M, a fashion giant, has a problem: $4.3 billion in unsold clothes," March 27.

New York Times (2018) "Opinion: Why is a 'green' car company pivoting back to S.U.V.s?" May 1.

New York Times (2018) " 'Mustang means freedom': Why Ford is saving an American icon," May 24.

New York Times (2019) "From environmental leader to 'worst company in the world'," July 29.

New York Times (2019) "New York loses climate change fraud case against Exxon Mobil," December 10.

New York Times (2020) "Global financial giants swear off funding an especially dirty fuel," February 13.

New York Times (2020) "Digging into oil sands divestment," February 14.

New York Times (2020) "U.S. and European oil giants go different ways on climate change," September 21.

New York Times (2020) "How one firm drove influence campaigns nationwide for Big Oil," November 11.

New York Times (2020) "When will electricity companies finally quit natural gas?" November 12.

New York Times (2020) "'Is Exxon a survivor?' The oil giant is at a crossroads," December 10.

New York Times (2021) "After a bruising year, the oil industry confronts a diminished future," February 2.

New York Times (2021) "Oil giants win offshore wind leases in Britain," February 8.

New York Times (2021) "Shell, in a turning point, says its oil production has peaked," February 11.

New York Times (2021) "Digging into oil sands divestment," February 14.

New York Times, (2021) "Ford says it will phase out gasoline-powered vehicles in Europe," February 17.

New York Times (2021) "What's really behind corporate promises on climate change?" February 22.

New York Times (2021) "Biden's push for electric cars—$174 billion, 10 years and a bit of luck," March 31.

New York Times (2021) "Executives call for deep emission cuts to combat climate change," April 13.

New York Times (2021) "Climate activists defeat Exxon in push for clean energy," May 26.

New York Times (2021) "Activists crashed Exxon's board, but forcing change will be hard," May 27.

New York Times (2021) "Exxon board to get a third activist pushing cleaner energy," June 2.

New York Times (2021) "Exxon's board defeat signals the rise of social-good activists," June 9.

New York Times (2021) "G7 nations take aggressive climate action but hold back on coal," June 14.

New York Times (2021) "In video, Exxon lobbyist describes efforts to undercut climate action," June 30.

Natural Resources Canada (n.d.) "Oil sands: GHG emissions."

Niinimaki, Kirsi et al. (2020) *Nature Reviews Earth & Environment,* "The environmental price of fast fashion," April 7.

Oakley, Ros and Ian Buckland (2004) "What if business as usual won't work?" in Adrian Henriques and Julie Richardson (eds.) *The Triple Bottom Line: Does It All Add Up?* London: Earthscan, 131–41.

Oil Change International (2020) "'Historic moment' as BP writes-off billions of reserves as stranded assets," June 16.

Oil Sands Magazine (2020) "In situ bitumen extraction," June 3.

Oreskes, Naomi and Erik M. Conway (2010) *Merchants of Doubt: How a Handful of Scientists Obscured the Truth on Issues from Tobacco Smoke to Global Warming,* New York: Bloomsbury Publishing.

Otto, Shawn (2016) *The War on Science: Who's Waging It, Whit It Matters, What We Can Do About It,* Vancouver and Berkeley, CA: Milkweed Editions.

Patagonia (2018) "Our business and climate change," May 11.

Patagonia (n.d.) "Introducing '$20 Million & Change' and Patagonia Works—A holding company for the environment."

Payne, Christopher and Jon Gertner (2021) "Has the carbon tech revolution begun?" *New York Times Magazine,* June 23.

PCI Wood Mackenzie (2018) *Fibres Global Supply Demand Report 2017.*

Pembina Institute (2017) "Fifty years of oilsands equals only 0.1% of land reclaimed," October 13.

Porter, Michael and Claas van der Linde (1995) *Harvard Business Review,* "Green and competitive: Ending the stalemate," September/October, 120–34.

PUMA and PPR HOME (2011) "PUMA and PPR HOME announce first results of unprecedented environmental profit & loss account," May 16.

Quantis (2018) *Guiding Insights for the Fashion Industry.*

RAN (Rainforest Action Network) et al. (2020) *Banking on Climate Change. Fossil Fuel Finance Report 2020.*

Reuters (2018) "New York sues Exxon for misleading investors on climate change risk," October 24.

Reuters (2020) "Shell to cut asset values by up to $22 billion after coronavirus hit," June 30.

Reuters (2020) "Global LNG projects jeopardized by climate concerns, pandemic delays—report," July 6.

Reuters (2020) "BP's green energy targets will be tough to meet," August 9.

Robert, Karl-Henrik (2008) *The Natural Step Story: Seeding a Quiet Revolution*, Gabriola Island, BC: New Society Publishers.

Rochon, Emily et al. (2008) *False Hope: Why Carbon Capture and Storage Won't Save the Climate*, Greenpeace.

Rooney, Rebecca C. et al. (2012) *PNAS*, "Oil sands mining and reclamation cause massive loss of peatland and stored carbon," March 27.

Royal Dutch Shell (2021) "Shell accelerated drive for net-zero emissions with customer-first strategy," February 11.

Sarkis, Joseph (2010) *Greening the Supply Chain Eco-efficiency*, London: Springer.

Schindler, David (2009) "The environmental impacts of exploiting the Alberta tar sands," lecture delivered to The Vancouver Institute, March 7.

Scott, Lee (2005) "Twenty first century leadership," speech, Walmart, October.

Siegel, B.P. (2018) *Energy & Sustainability*, "Manufacturing goes carbon negative," May 7.

Smil, Vaclav (2010) *Energy Myths and Reality: Bringing Science to the Energy Policy Debate*, Washington, IDC: AEI Press.

Sridhar, Kaushik and Grant Jones (2013) *Asian Journal of Business Ethics*, "The three fundamental criticisms of the triple bottom line approach: An empirical study to link sustainability reports in companies based in the Asia-Pacific region and TBL shortcomings," 2: 91–111.

Suncor (2021) "Canada's largest oil sands producers announce unprecedented alliance to achieve net zero greenhouse gas emissions," press release, June 9.

Suncor (2021) *Climate Report.*

Supran, G. and N. Oreskes (2017) *Environmental Research Letters*, "Assessing ExxonMobil's climate change communications 1977–2014," August 23.

SWFI (Sovereign Wealth Fund Institute) (accessed April 4, 2021) "Top 95 largest sovereign wealth fund rankings by total assets," (www.swfinstitute.org).

Taplin, Ian M. (2014a) *Competition and Change*, "Global commodity chains and fast fashion: How the apparel industry continues to re-invent itself," June 1.

Taplin, Ian M. (2014b) *Critical Perspectives on International Business*, "Who is to blame? A re-examination of fast fashion after the 2013 factory disaster in Bangladesh," 10(1–2): 72–83.

Textile World (2015) "Man-made fibers continue to grow," February 3.

Timoney, Kevin P. and Peter Lee (2009) *The Open Conservation Biology Journal*, "Does the Alberta tar sands industry pollute? The scientific evidence," October.

UNECE (United Nations Economic Commission for Europe) (2018) "Fashion is an environmental and social emergency, but can also drive progress towards the Sustainable Development Goals."

US SEC Interface 10-K (2017) 10-K, United States Securities and Exchange Commission Report, January 1.

Valentine, Scott (2006) "An empirical test of the corporate environmental governance-financial performance relationship," MSc thesis, National University of Singapore.

Vancouver Sun (2021) "$13.4B of oilsands assets seen as candidates for sale," July 14.

Varinsky, Dana (2016) "The US may be releasing over 64,000 pounds of tiny synthetic clothing fibers into the water every day," Yahoo Finance, November 1.

Wall Street Journal (2020) "2020 was one of the worst-ever years for oil write-downs," December 27.

Walmart (2021) *Environmental, Social and Governance Report.*

Walmart (n.d.) *Supplier Sustainability Assessment: Full Packet.*

Wang, Pei et al. (2019) *Journal of Cleaner Production,* "Estimates of the social cost of carbon: A review based on meta-analysis," February 1.

Ward's (multiple years) *Motor Vehicle Facts and Figures,* Ward's Communications.

WBCSD (World Business Council for Sustainable Development) (2005a) *Eco-efficiency: Creating More Value with Less Impact.*

WBCSD (World Business Council for Sustainable Development) (2005b) *Measuring Eco-efficiency: A Guide to Reporting Company Performance.*

We Mean Business Coalition and Ceres (2021) "310 business and investors support U.S. federal climate target in open letter to President Biden," press release, April 13.

Week (2021) "Shell/Ubitricity: Charging ahead," January 30.

Welsh, Heidi et al. (2018) *Spending Against Change: 50-50 Climate Project Report,* 5050climate.org.

Willner, Andrew (2021) "New age of sail looks to slash massive maritime carbon emissions," Mongabay, March 15.

Appendix

Excerpts from New York State's lawsuit against ExxonMobil: October 2018; The People of the State of New York, by Barbara D. Underwood, Attorney General of the State of New York, Plaintiff, against Exxon Mobil Corporation, Defendant.

Nature of the action

1. This case seeks redress for a longstanding fraudulent scheme by Exxon, one of the world's largest oil and gas companies, to deceive investors and the investment community, including equity research analysts and underwriters of debt securities (together, "investors"), concerning the company's management of the risks posed to its business by climate change regulation. Exxon provided false and misleading assurances that it is effectively managing the economic risks posed to its business by the increasingly stringent policies and regulations that it expects governments to adopt to address climate change. Instead of managing those risks in the manner it represented to investors, Exxon employed internal practices that were inconsistent with its representations, were undisclosed to investors, and exposed the company to greater risk from climate change regulation than investors were led to believe.

2. For years, and continuing through the present, Exxon has claimed that, although it expects governments to impose increasingly stringent climate change regulations, its oil and gas reserves and other long-term assets face little if any risk of becoming stranded (i.e., too costly to develop or operate) due to those regulations, and reassured investors that it would be able to profitably exploit those assets well into the future. In particular, to simulate the impact of future climate change regulations, Exxon has claimed that, since 2007, it has rigorously and consistently applied an escalating proxy cost of carbon dioxide (CO_2) and other greenhouse gases (together, "GHGs") to its business, including in its investment decisions, business planning, company oil and gas reserves and resource base assessments, evaluations of whether long-term assets are impaired (i.e., have net present value lower than book value), and estimates of future demand for oil and gas.

3. Exxon's proxy cost representations were materially false and misleading because it did not apply the proxy cost it represented to investors. This was especially true of investments with high GHG emissions, where applying the publicly represented

proxy cost would have had a particularly significant negative impact on the company's economic and financial projections and assessments.

7. Exxon misled investors by presenting a deceptive analysis that concluded that the company faced little risk associated with a "two degree scenario," in which the production and consumption of fossil fuels is severely curtailed in order to limit the increase in global temperature to below two degrees Celsius compared to pre-industrial levels. Exxon's analysis of the costs associated with a two degree scenario was based on assumptions it knew to be unreasonable and unsupported by the sources upon which it purported to rely.

8. Exxon's fraud was sanctioned at the highest levels of the company.

11. When confronted with the negative impact to its economic and financial assessments that would result from applying proxy costs in a manner consistent with the company's representations to investors, Exxon's management directed the company's planners to adopt what an employee called an "alternate methodology." . . . By applying this "alternate methodology," Exxon avoided the "large write-downs" it would have incurred had it abided by its stated risk management practices, and failed to take into account "massive GHG costs" resulting from expected climate change regulation.

12. For example, Exxon's decision not to apply the publicly represented proxy costs in connection with fourteen oil sands projects in Alberta, Canada resulted in the under-statement of those costs in the company's cash flow projections by approximately $30 billion CAD (Canadian dollars), or more than $25 billion USD (US dollars). For one of these projects, an investment at Kearl, a 2015 economic forecast shows that the company understated projected undiscounted costs of GHG emissions by as much as 94%—approximately $14 billion CAD ($11 billion USD)—by applying lower costs to GHG emissions than those publicly represented.

13. Exxon's decision not to apply the publicly represented proxy costs in its company oil and gas reserves assessments enabled the company to avoid "large write-downs" in reserves that it would have had to take had it abided by its public representations. For example, at Cold Lake, an oil sands asset in Alberta, the company's own planners noted that applying a proxy cost consistent with Exxon's public representations would shorten the asset's projected economic life by 28 years and reduce company reserves by more than 300 million barrels of oil equivalent—representing billions of dollars in lost revenues. When presented with these facts, Exxon management instructed the planners to apply a lower cost projection based on existing regulations, contrary to the company's public representations.

19. Through its fraudulent scheme, Exxon in effect erected a Potemkin village to create the illusion that it had fully considered the risks of future climate change regulation and had factored those risks into its business operations. In reality, Exxon knew that its representations were not supported by the facts and were contrary to its internal business practices. As a result of Exxon's fraud, the company was exposed to far greater risk from climate change regulations than investors were led to believe.

20. Indeed, rather than protecting against the risk of future climate change regulation by reducing investment in GHG-intensive assets, Exxon expanded its investments in such assets. Between 2008 and 2016, the percentage of Exxon's oil and gas devel-opment and production (i.e., upstream) projects in GHG-intensive heavy oil and oil

sands increased from less than 20% to more than 30% in oil–equivalent barrels. This increased the GHG intensity of the company's upstream operations and, in turn, increased the company's exposure to future climate change regulation.

21. The State brings this action to enforce General Business Law § 352 et seq. (securities fraud) and Executive Law § 63(12) (persistent fraud or illegality), and for common law fraud.

4   Unsustainable automobility

The internal combustion engine (ICE) and the vehicles that use it are on the short list of inventions that have had a profound impact on the structure and functioning of our modern society. In fact, the introduction of the modern gas-driven automobile has created an indelible impact on our social, political, economic, and ecological systems. The reason is beguilingly simple—the benefits of automobile ownership and use are multifaceted and include, inter alia, convenience, speed, comfort, security, flexibility, fun, and prestige.

And yet, these benefits come with significant costs: air pollution in the form of acid rain, and emissions that directly affect human health such as nitrogen dioxide, ultrafine particles, black carbon, and ozone (SOCAAR 2019). Emissions are not restricted to the operation of internal combustion engines by themselves; additional negative externalities are generated by tire wear, the degradation of asphalt roads, and the production of the car and its components (Khare et al. 2020; Evangeliou et al. 2020). Other negative effects include global warming, urban sprawl, massive infrastructure and energy requirements, and a negative impact on social cohesiveness by facilitating increased isolation in living spaces and transportation. The *New York Times* (October 10, 2019) has provided a detailed map of automobile emissions in the United States and reports that transportation is the largest source of planet-warming greenhouse gases (GHGs) in the United States today and the bulk of those emissions comes from driving in cities and suburbs. (See also EPA 2021.) The International Energy Agency (IEA) has reported that the increasing preference for SUVs is challenging emission reductions in the passenger car market (IEA 2019). Added to these externalities is an inordinate number of accidents, injuries, and fatalities. The World Health Organization (WHO 2021) has estimated that approximately 20–50 million people suffer injuries each year in road traffic accidents and about 1.3 million people are killed. It is estimated that these crashes cost most countries as much as 3 percent of their gross domestic product (GDP). In the United States in 2020, there were 38,680 fatalities from automotive accidents (NHTSA 2021). Humes (2016b) reported that car crashes are the leading cause of death for Americans between the ages of one and thirty-nine. He observes that "if US roads were a war zone, they would be the most dangerous battlefield the American military has ever encountered." Despite this toll, the American public has become generally inured to this annual carnage. To put it in perspective, this is equivalent to one Boeing 737-100 crashing every day with an average loss of life of 102 people per crash. If this latter scenario were to occur, most people would probably refuse to fly after a relatively small number of such accidents despite the fact that, from a simple risk perspective, the automobile and airplane scenarios are superficially equivalent. The explanation for this apparent disjunction lies in modern risk analysis, specifically

DOI: 10.4324/9781003199540-6

the role of risk perception among the general public. Extensive empirical studies have demonstrated that individuals will assess risks differently depending on a broad range of factors such as perceived controllability, ordinary versus catastrophic events, continuous versus occasional occurrences, and degree of voluntariness.

In addition to road fatalities, researchers from the Massachusetts Institute of Technology (Caiazzo et al. 2013) calculated that road transportation causes a significant number of annual pollutant-related deaths: approximately 53,000 premature deaths from $PM_{2.5}$ and approximately 5,000 additional early fatalities per year due to ozone (see also CDC 2016).

As one of the world's most complex and advanced technologies, the modern automobile sector consumes more resources than any other industry. In the United States, for example, the manufacturing of cars directly used the following percentage of all US consumption in 2014: lead 76.3 percent; rubber for tires 93 percent (2007); rubber for non-tire products 40 percent (2007); aluminum 38.3 percent; iron 17.5 percent; zinc 23 percent; steel 14.6 percent; and copper and its alloys 19 percent (Ward's 2010, 2016). Transportation accounts for 29 percent of all US energy use, and light- and heavy-duty vehicles account for the lion's share at approximately 25 percent (US BTS 2018; US EIA 2019).

The American love affair with the automobile comes with an enormous price tag. Estimates for the entire US transportation system exceed $9 trillion, of which the automobile accounts for a significant amount (Winston 2013). As much as $124 billion is attributable to lost productivity due to traffic jams (CEBR 2014). Humes (2016a) has observed that our private automobiles are our least productive asset, spending an average of twenty-two hours a day unused.

Despite the broad range of costs associated with the production and use of the automobile, the international demand for this convenience continues to grow at a rapid rate. Figure 4.1 shows the inexorable increase in global automotive production and registration

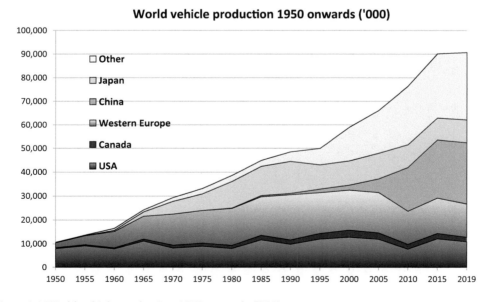

Figure 4.1 World vehicle production 1950 onwards ('000).
Source: Ward's historical data. Reproduced with permission.

since the early 1900s (Ward's, multiple years). It has been predicted that there may be as many as two billion motor vehicles on the road by 2030, the bulk of these being light-duty vehicles such as private automobiles (Sperling and Gordon 2009). American domination of the global industry in the first half of the twentieth century was eventually superseded by a truly integrated multilocational, global manufacturing system. This lengthy process of integration was accompanied by a steady pace of consolidation. Since the dawn of the auto age, more than 3,000 makes of cars and trucks have been produced by approximately 1,500 manufacturers in the United States (AMA 1968; Clymer 1950; Flink 1950; Heasley 1977; Humes 2016a; Musselman 2011). As of 2016, there were only four major American companies (with the recent addition of Tesla) producing cars in the United States, but they were accompanied by ten foreign manufacturers from Japan, Korea, and Germany (Ward's 2017b).

Figure 4.2 graphs the number of persons per car versus GDP per capita for a range of countries where such data are available. The message is unmistakable: as income rises there is a rapid increase in car ownership driven by the emergence of a middle class with disposable income. Table 4.1 shows the increase in the number of vehicles in use for selected countries over the period 1996 to 2016 (Ward's 2017b), indicating that while the Western industrialized countries have reached a relative level of saturation of automotive ownership, numerous developing countries have observed rapid increases in ownership. Figure 4.3 illustrates that the increase in car ownership far exceeds the growth rate of

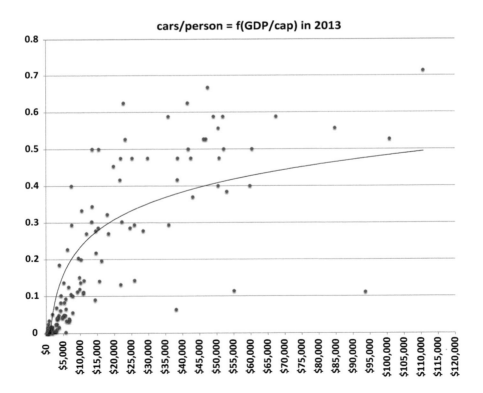

Figure 4.2 Cars per person as function of GDP per capita.

Table 4.1 World vehicle use 1996–2016

Country	Cars (units)			Increase (%)		Persons/car 2016	Population in 2016
	1996	2006	2016	1996–2006	2006–16		
Bangladesh	18,400	37,500	164,432	104	338	991.0	162,951,560
Brazil	12,666,000	19,446,000	33,888,100	54	74	6.1	207,652,865
Canada	13,300,000	18,738,935	22,410,030	41	20	1.6	36,286,425
China	2,050,000	11,000,000	165,600,000	437	1405	8.3	1,378,665,000
France	25,500,000	30,400,000	32,390,000	19	7	2.1	66,896,109
Germany	41,045,217	46,569,657	45,804,000	13	–2	1.8	82,667,685
Hong Kong	619,300	500,000	536,000	–19	7	13.7	7,346,700
India	2,025,500	8,100,000	34,361,000	300	324	38.5	1,324,171,354
Indonesia	691,400	4,100,000	13,481,000	493	229	19.4	261,115,456
Japan	53,525,800	57,521,043	61,403,630	7	7	2.1	126,994,511
Malaysia	2,292,200	6,600,000	11,335,000	188	72	2.8	31,187,265
Mexico	4,850,000	15,566,300	28,182,000	221	81	4.5	127,540,423
Nigeria	589,600	725,000	997,700	23	38	186.4	185,989,640
Pakistan	395,700	425,000	2,627,000	7	518	54.9	144,342,396
Philippines	612,600	793,100	971,750	29	23	106.3	103,320,222
Russia (1994)	13,549,000	26,800,000	44,696,000	98	67	3.2	144,342,396
Singapore	427,000	440,583	628,791	3	43	8.9	5,607,283
South Korea	8,370,200	11,607,000	17,338,000	39	49	3.0	51,245,707
Sweden	3,494,000	4,202,463	4,776,744	20	14	2.1	9,802,000
Taiwan	4,217,500	5,698,324	6,729,124	35	18	3.5	23,395,600
Thailand	1,296,200	3,700,000	8,286,000	185	124	8.3	68,863,514
UK	26,131,200	30,920,000	34,378,388	18	11	1.9	65,637,239
USA	124,672,920	135,046,706	123,552,650	8	–9	2.6	323,127,513
Vietnam	82,900	145,000	279,000	75	92	332.3	92,701,100
World	470,586,613	635,284,155	973,352,643	35	53	7.2	7,008,810,000

Source: Ward's, multiple years.

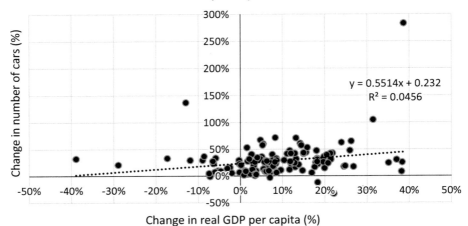

Figure 4.3 Growth in car ownership versus growth in real GDP per capita.

GDP/capita for most countries. This has profound environmental implications for both the national and global levels, as discussed below.

Parenthetically, it is interesting to note that of the Western industrialized countries, only the United States has experienced a decline in the number of total registrations of automobiles in the last decade. (In fact, German registrations fell from 2006 to 2007 but rose consistently after that. One possible explanation is an administrative reclassification.) While it has been posited that the marked decline in the United States represents a change among the young to a less materialistic lifestyle, a more persuasive argument emerges from the observation that American registrations have declined steadily since 2008. Following the financial meltdown of that date, more than ten million households lost their homes and other assets such as cars to foreclosure, and the aftereffects of this financial crisis remain today in the United States.

The rapid rise in global ownership is clearly explained by the multitudinous benefits enumerated earlier. Was this ordained? The late Ezra Mishan, one of the fathers of cost-benefit analysis, had a unique take on this phenomenon. To Mishan (1967, 1993), the invention of the automobile was a curse; once societies made the choice to move to private automobile use, there was little opportunity to change. In modern parlance, this can be referred to as a form of path dependence. The adoption of the private automobile as the principal form of personal transportation mandated the installation of a vast, distributed infrastructure which promotes the continued use of cars. In the words of Freund and Martin (1993, p. 3), "the forms that urban development have taken in this century reflect the functional needs of auto transport." In a sense, the proliferation of freeways designed to provide rapid transport for automobiles is the one valid example of the discredited Say's Law in economics, which stated that supply creates its own demand.

In a somewhat tongue-in-cheek assessment, Professor Vaclav Smil (2014), an acknowledged global expert on energy and energetics, has described the weight-to-payload ratio of the modern automobile as "the worst since mahouts rode elephants."

A selection of his data include: a bicycle (0.1), modern buses (5.0), Model T car (7.7), Smart Car (12), the Ford F-150 (32), and Cadillac Escalade EXT (39). In other words, we currently rely extensively on "the worst weight-to-payload ratios for any mechanized means of personal transportation in history" (p. 2).

The environmental burden of the automotive sector

The principal focus of the modern concern with the automobile is its contribution to global warming, although its other environmental impacts are widespread and multifaceted. These include direct emissions of carbon monoxide, nitrogen oxides, particulates, hydrocarbons, and some heavy metals as well as significant indirect effects such as ozone production. Recent US estimates of the transportation sector's contribution to carbon dioxide emissions suggest as much as 28 percent, of which 59 percent is attributable to light-duty vehicles (US EPA 2020). This is principally, but not completely, due to the direct combustion of fossil fuels, primarily refined petroleum. One research study (Unger et al. 2010) concluded that motor vehicles have the largest net contribution to global warming despite the apparent higher output of GHGs in the electric power sector. This is due to the fact that the power sector releases a high proportion of sulfates and other cooling aerosols that partially offset the release of GHGs. In contrast, the automotive sector produces relatively few aerosols that counteract the warming effect of this sector.

In fact, a more accurate picture of the environmental impact of automobiles must employ a systems analysis that considers production itself and all its processes and inputs. In pioneering engineering process–based studies conducted in 1972 and 1973 (a and b), Berry applied the relatively new methodology of energy analysis to the production of automobiles by examining energy requirements from raw material extraction to final assembly and disposal. This early analysis found that the bulk of the system-wide energy inputs to automotive production could be attributed to the manufacture of metallic materials, of which the cold rolling of steel was the largest component. One of the most interesting corollaries of this research was the conclusion that the total energy input into automotive construction accounted for no more than one year's worth of automotive use.

At least three important changes have occurred since Berry's original research. First, the composition of the modern automobile has shifted: the percentage of iron and steel has fallen by approximately one-third from 94 percent to approximately 60 percent and a broader range of other components is used (Ward's 2019). Second, process-based analysis has been supplemented with input–output based calculations which can capture entire economy-wide impacts. The significant contribution of this sector to overall global warming has led to a new focus on the relatively new systems methodology of GHG footprinting. This methodology suggests that the current ratio of GHG emissions from annual driving use to automotive production is approximately 87:17 (Ricardo.com 2011). Finally, pathbreaking work on life-cycle analysis of the automobile has been continued at Carnegie Melon by MacLean and Lave (1998, 2003) and at the Norwegian University of Science and Technology by Hawkins et al. (2012). The latter focus on comparisons between conventional and EVs, as discussed in Chapter 7.

A case study of China

Within the last decade, China has emerged as a major player in the global automobile industry as it is now the largest and fastest growing market for cars in the world. The

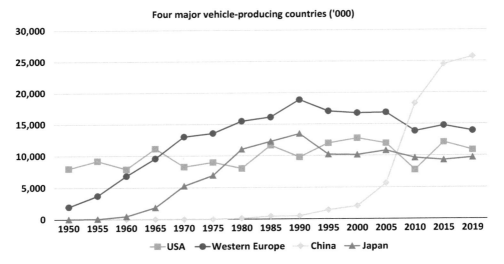

Figure 4.4 Four major vehicle-producing countries 1950–2018.
Source: Ward's data, multiple years. Reproduced with permission.

Chinese auto sector is still in its developmental stage with more than four dozen individual companies and joint ventures and annual vehicle production ranging from a low of two units (Guangzhou Fiat) to more than 2.7 million (joint ventures FAW Volkswagen and Shanghai Volkswagen) (Ward's 2020).

Figure 4.4 tracks the remarkable emergence of China as the world's largest producer of motor vehicles and Figure 4.5 displays the equally rapid rise in domestic registrations. This extraordinary increase over a relatively short time span has created significant problems with congestion and particularly urban air pollution in cities, many of which are already heavily polluted by industrial process and coal combustion. Chinese cities occupy ten places in the top twenty-four congested cities in the world (TomTom 2017) and thirty places among the top one hundred cities with air pollution measured by the annual average concentration of PM_{10} (WHO 2019).

While China's national average annual increases in the number of automobiles have ranged as high as 36 percent, these increases have been matched or exceeded in many of the country's regions. These increases are clearly unsustainable and have recently been the subject of new research and policy initiatives by the central government to reduce them. However, as of 2016, only two Chinese regions, Beijing and Tianjin, have been able to reduce recent growth rates to 1 and 0 percent respectively through a bundle of aggressive policy measures.

Table 4.2 indicates the current number of cars registered in China and the number of additional cars required if automotive density were to equal Japan, the United States, or the world. Table 4.3 repeats this exercise for Beijing, Shanghai, and Chongqing if they were to aspire to New York City's automotive density. Estimates of increased GHG emissions under a business-as-usual scenario in China have been calculated by Huo et al. (2012a and b):

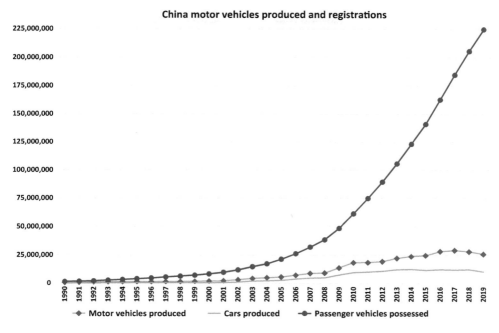

Figure 4.5 China motor vehicles produced and registrations.
Source: China Statistical Yearbook, multiple years.

Table 4.2 Car ownership projections for China based on persons per car

Country	2016		
	Registered cars	*Persons/car*	*Total population*
China	165,600,000	8.3	1,378,665,000
Japan	61,873,000	2.1	126,994,511
USA	123,552,650	2.6	323,127,513
World	973,352,643	7.2	7,008,810,000
Total cars in China if equal to car density in			
Japan	656,507,143		
USA	530,255,769		
World	191,481,250		
Increment for China			
Japan	490,907,143		
USA	364,655,769		
World	25,881,250		
Ratio to present			
Japan	296%		
USA	220%		
World	16%		

Table 4.3 Car ownership projections for three China cities based on persons per car

City	Urban area population	Cars in 2015	People per car
Los Angeles	11,901,050	6,433,000	1.85
New York City	18,106,430	7,771,000	2.33
San Francisco	2,989,610	1,769,000	1.69
Beijing	21,500,000	4,290,390	5.01
Shanghai	24,500,000	2,082,200	11.77
Chongqing	18,384,000	2,118,200	8.68

Additional cars to equal New York City car density

	Total	Net new
Beijing	9,227,468	4,937,078
Shanghai	10,515,021	8,432,821
Chongqing	7,890,129	5,771,929

Road transport in China would create 410–520 million metric tons (MMT) of oil-equivalent oil demand (three to four times the current level), 28–36 billion GJ [gigajoules] of WTW (*wheel-to-wheel or life cycle analysis*) energy demand and 1900–2300 MMT of CO_2-equivalent of WTW GHG emissions by 2050.

(Huo et al. 2012b, p. 37)

The immensity of the challenge to reduce car ownership growth rates is exacerbated by the shift among Chinese buyers towards SUVs, which now dominate market growth in this sector (Wang et al. 2017). The projections for car ownership clearly depend on the penetration of electric cars into the Chinese market, an important goal of the central government (Liang et al. 2019). Three central challenges are the material requirements needed to meet the rapidly increasing demand for automobiles, whether ICE or electric, the source of energy that will be used to power the EV sector, and the continued problem of non-GHG externalities (see chapters 7 and 9).

It would not be an overstatement to say that China's automotive sector hangs like the sword of Damocles over the global automotive industry. While most of China's current domestic production is destined for the national market, the nation's traditional manufacturing cost advantage poses a monumental threat to the continued dominance of the current major producers in Europe, North America, Japan, and Korea. Figures 4.6a and 4.6b compare hourly wage rates in the auto industry among major producing countries in 2011 and 2015. Because of China's increasing wealth, wage rates across many industries have risen in the last few years, prompting many manufacturers of labor-intensive, low-value-added products to move their production to South or Southeast Asia. However, China's determination to become a major player in the international automotive sector suggests that the production base will likely remain in China, supplemented with outsourcing of production of some components.

China's pronounced cost advantage vis-à-vis the developed countries is clearly necessary but not sufficient, however, to capture a significant share of global markets. The missing ingredient is technology. China has made a policy of attracting technology transfer not only through joint production agreements and purchase, such as the recent acquisition of

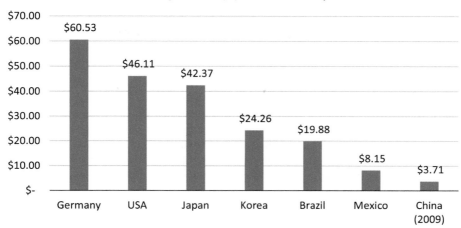

Figure 4.6a International automotive wage rates, 2011.
Source: ILO 2011.

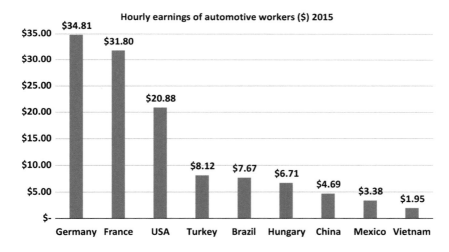

Figure 4.6b International automotive wage rates, 2015.
Source: ILO 2015 and Statista, data reproduced with permission.

Volvo, one of the global leaders of automotive technology, but also through the recruiting of foreign talent. The Chinese track record in building technological competence has already been demonstrated in such areas as high-speed computing, and solar and wind power. Their intentions to achieve similar preeminence in commercial airline production and automobiles (both internal combustion and electric) are credible in light of the fact that China has recently, in one year alone, graduated 4.7 million students in science, technology, engineering, and mathematics in contrast to 568,000 in the United States and 195,000 in Japan (*New York Times* November 1, 2017). All these initiatives are part of a concerted and powerful Chinese effort, labeled "Made in China 2035," to achieve global dominance in a broad range of high-value-added, advanced technologies (*New York Times* November 1 and 7, 2017).

Foreign car manufacturers have certainly got the message and already have a significant presence in the domestic Chinese market. There is reason to believe that some of these companies will also use the Chinese manufacturing environment as an export platform back into the global market, further jeopardizing the economic viability of their own national domestic manufacturing operations. Equally threatening to foreign manufacturers who are currently producing through joint ventures in China is a recent assessment of McKinsey (Wang et al. 2017, p. 3) that "local brands have begun to exhibit real competitiveness based on vehicle designs and quality levels" and are increasing their share of the domestic market. McKinsey conclude that "the increasing competence of local brands constitutes an urgent warning to Western original equipment manufacturers that opportunities to earn 'easy money' in China may be gone forever" (p. 3). Table 4.4 summarizes the most recent data on market shares of foreign and domestic vehicle companies in China.

Table 4.4 Market shares of major vehicle companies in China

	Model	*2019*	*Share (%)*	*Cumulative (%)*
1	Volkswagen	3,100,498	14.60	14.6
2	Honda	1,553,086	7.30	21.9
3	Toyota	1,409,198	6.60	28.5
4	Geely	1,220,832	5.70	34.2
5	Nissan	1,174,030	5.50	39.7
6	Buick	871,506	4.10	43.8
7	Changan	787,878	3.70	47.5
8	Haval	769,454	3.60	51.1
9	Hyundai	685,738	3.20	54.3
10	Audi	620,001	2.90	57.2
11	Baojun	604,204	2.80	60.0
12	Mercedes-Benz	595,486	2.80	62.8
13	BMW	544,500	2.60	65.4
14	Chevrolet	516,087	2.40	67.8
15	BYD	451,246	2.10	69.9
16	Chery	451,139	2.10	72.0
17	SAIC Roewe	426,128	2.00	74.0
18	GAC	388,364	1.80	75.8
19	Dongfeng	377,349	1.80	77.6
20	Wuling	374,878	1.80	79.4
21	BAIC	286,343	1.30	80.7
22	Kia	283,307	1.30	82.0
23	Skoda	278,378	1.30	83.3
24	SAIC MG	269,751	1.30	84.6
25	Ford	232,555	1.10	85.7
26	Mazda	224,977	1.10	86.8
27	FAW	222,188	1.00	87.8
28	Cadillac	212,506	1.00	88.8

Source: carsalesbase.com.

Table 4.5 Typology of automobile policies

Nudges and financial incentives/disincentives	Examples
Indirect carbon taxes (e.g., gasoline taxes)	Europe
Direct carbon taxes	British Columbia
Peak-load pricing on entry to urban cores	Singapore
Mobility pricing	London, Stockholm, Singapore
Lotteries to allocate license plates	Beijing
Free mass transit in urban cores	Calgary, Seattle, and others
Preferential parking for electric vehicles	Victoria, BC
Free electricity for electric vehicles	Numerous UK cities
Fiscal incentives to retire older vehicles	British Columbia
Reduction in fares for mass transit	Numerous global cities
Ride sharing	Uber, Lyft
Car sharing	All continents
Tax credits or grants for electric vehicles and hybrids	USA, Canada, UK, EU
Regulatory fiats	
Ban on urban core driving	Cambridge, UK
Alternative license plate access	Beijing
Emission control limits	Beijing
Improvement in fuel quality	National standards for sulfur content, etc.
Technological solutions	
Alternative fuels	Ethanol, biodiesel, electricity used globally
Electric vehicles	Produced and sold in Asia, North America, and Europe
Introduction and reestablishment of mass transit	Global
Autonomous vehicles	Under development and experimentally deployed in Asia, North America, and Europe

While China has increased its annual exports within recent years to approximately three-quarters of a million vehicles, its principal market is Asia, followed to a lesser extent by Europe. With the exception of Volvo, Chinese manufacturers have made no direct impact on the American market. However, several US car companies have already started to ship Chinese-made cars back to the United States under the brand names of Ford Focus, Cadillac CT6 Plug-in hybrid, and Buick Envision.

In attempting to formulate an effective response to the current challenge posed by increased automobile use, China has adopted a mixed strategy of soft policy and hard technology responses, especially in its urban areas (Huo et al. 2012a and b; Viard and Fu 2015; Yang et al. 2014; Li and Guo 2016; Wu et al. 2017). Table 4.5 presents a typology of major policy alternatives proposed or in current use in cities throughout the globe.

The real cost of gasoline

Gasoline prices vary markedly around the world as illustrated in Figure 4.7. The fundamental problem with these prices from an economics perspective is that they do not reflect the multitude of external costs associated with the production and use of gasoline. In extreme cases, the price at the pump is subsidized for social and political reasons and has no relationship whatsoever with its true social cost. Several attempts have been made to estimate the total social cost of gasoline (ICTA 2007; NRDC 1993; Shindell 2015;

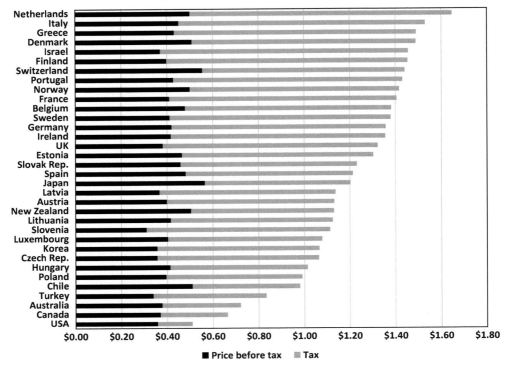

Figure 4.7 Gasoline prices and taxes.
Source: IEA 2021.

Moore and Diaz 2015) and each estimate is significantly higher than current global prices. A major attempt to reflect social costs in the price of gasoline has been in place for several years in Europe where a broad range of taxes on gasoline represent a first pass (Barde and Braathen 2007). In a sense, these taxes can be considered surrogate carbon taxes which partially internalize the cost of GHGs. Clearly, the extent to which they do so depends critically on the estimated social cost of carbon. The US EPA (2017a and b) has produced a report on this social cost with estimates as high as $212 per metric ton (MT) of CO_2 but there are numerous estimates in the literature (Moore and Diaz 2015; Bressler 2021). The determination of the true social cost of carbon is a complex task, and estimates range widely: Ricke et al. (2018) have estimated the 66 percent confidence interval of the price to range between $177 and $805 per MT of CO_2 with a median value of $417 per MT of CO_2, while a meta-analysis conducted by Wang et al. (2019) finds an extraordinary range of $50–$8,752 per MT of carbon (equivalent to $13.36–$2,386.91 per MT of CO_2) with a mean value of $200.5 per MT of carbon, ranging up to $220 per MT. While climate change is perhaps the foremost concern with automobile use at this point, any true estimate of social costs must attempt to encompass the broad range of other negative externalities cataloged earlier.

The Canadian province of British Columbia has been a leader in tackling the issue of carbon-related externalities by specifically introducing a carbon tax in 2008 on all fossil fuels. Starting at Can$10 per MT of carbon-equivalent emissions, it rose at Can$5 per year for the following four years until the annual increase was prematurely frozen by the provincial government until 2021 when it rose again by another Can$5–45 per MT (equivalent to 8.9 cents per liter of gasoline). The government intends to increase the price to Can$50 in April 2022. There are several important attributes of this initiative. It was designed to be revenue neutral by reducing personal and corporate income taxes. Attention was also paid to the distributional impact as the government issued a rebate of Can$100 to every citizen in the province. The question arose as to what impact the tax would have on gasoline consumption and ultimate GHG emissions. The results of several analyses of the impact of the tax were uniformly positive, concluding that it had induced a significant decrease in gasoline consumption with no adverse economic effects (Antweiler and Gulati 2016; Murray and Rivers 2015; Rivers and Schaufele 2012; Bernard et al. 2013; Monahan and McFatridge 2010). The results of these statistical analyses are particularly noteworthy in light of the fact that annual changes in the carbon tax are significantly lower than the short-term changes in gasoline prices due to supply and demand factors as well as opportunistic rent extraction by the oil companies (*Vancouver Sun* June 22, 2018). The current federal Liberal government in Canada has recently announced its intention to increase its carbon tax to Can$170 per MT by 2030 from Can$30 per tonne as of 2020 as part of its new energy climate plan (CBC News December 11, 2020).

There are several major options that promise to significantly reduce the environmental burden of transportation, including EVs, autonomous vehicles, mass transit, and what has been termed "the internet of motion." These are discussed in Chapter 7.

References

AMA (Automobile Manufacturers Association) (1968) *Automobiles of America*, Detroit: Wayne State University Press.

Antweiler, Werner and Sumeet Gulati (2016) "Frugal cars or frugal drivers? How carbon and fuel taxes influence the choice and use of cars," SSRN, May 11. https://ssrn.com/abstract=2778868.

Barde, Jean-Philippe and Nils Axel Braathen (2007) "Green taxes in OECD countries: An overview," in Peter N. Nemetz (ed.) *Sustainable Resource Management: Reality or Illusion*, Cheltenham: Edward Elgar.

Bernard, Jean-Thomas et al. (2013) "The BC carbon tax: Consumer response to an environmental gasoline tax," presentation, University of Ottawa, July.

Berry, R. Stephen and Margaret Fulton Fels (1972) *The Production and Consumption of Automobiles*. Report to the Illinois Institute for Environmental Quality, July.

Berry, R. Stephen and Margaret F. Fels (1973a) *Bulletin of the Atomic Scientists*, "The energy cost of automobiles," December.

Berry, R. Stephen and Margaret F. Fels (1973b) *Science and Public Affairs*, "The energy cost of automobiles," December.

Bressler, R. Daniel (2021) *Nature Communications* "The mortality cost of carbon," July 29.

Caiazzo, Fabio et al. (2013*) Atmospheric Environment*, "Air pollution and early deaths in the United States. Part I: Quantifying the impact of major sectors in 2005," November.

CBC News (2020) "Ottawa to hike federal carbon tax to $170 a tonne by 2030," December 11.

CDC (Centers for Disease Control and Prevention) (2016) "Road traffic injuries and deaths: A global problem," October 23.

CEBR (Centre for Economics and Business Research) (2014) *The Future Economic and Environmental Costs of Gridlock in 2030*, consultant report for INRIX, July.

China (multiple years) *China Statistical Yearbook*, Beijing: National Bureau of Statistics of China.

Clymer, Floyd (1950) *Treasury of Early American Automobiles 1877–1925*, New York: McGraw-Hill.

Evangeliou, N. et al. (2020) *Nature Communications*, "Atmospheric transport is a major pathway of microplastics to remote regions," July 14.

Flink, James J. (1950) *The Automobile Age*, Cambridge, MA: MIT Press.

Freund, Peter and George Martin (1993) *The Ecology of the Automobile*, Montreal; New York: Black Rose Books.

Hawkins, Troy R. (2012) *Journal of Industrial Ecology*, "Comparative environmental life cycle assessment of conventional and electric vehicles," February.

Heasley, Jerry (1977) *The Production Figure Book for U.S. Cars*, Osceola, WI: Motorbooks International.

Humes, Edward (2016a) *Door to Door: The Magnificent, Maddening, Mysterious World of Transportation*, New York: HarperCollins.

Humes, Edward (2016b) "The absurd primacy of the automobile in American life," *Atlantic*, April 12.

Huo, Hong et al. (2012a) *Energy Policy*, "Projection of energy use and greenhouse gas emissions by motor vehicles in China: Policy options and impacts," 43: 37–48.

Huo, Hong et al. (2012b) *Energy Policy*, "Vehicle-use intensity in China: Current status and future trend," 43 : 6–16.

ICTA (International Centre for Technology Assessment) (2007) *The Real Price of Gasoline, Report No. 3.*

IEA (International Energy Agency) (2019) "Commentary: Growing preference for SUVs challenges emissions reductions in passenger car market," October 15.

IEA (International Energy Agency) (2021) *Energy Prices and Taxes, 2020.*

ILO (International Labour Organization) (2011, 2015) *Global Wage Report.*

Khare, Peeyush et al. (2020) *Science Advances*, "Asphalt-related emissions are a major missing non-traditional source of secondary organic aerosol precursors," September 2.

Li, Ruimin and Min Guo (2016) *Journal of Transportation Engineering*, "Effects of odd-even traffic restriction on travel speed and travel volume: Evidence from Beijing Olympic Games," February.

Liang, Xinyu et al. (2019) *Nature Sustainability*, "Air quality and health benefits from fleet electrification in China," October.

MacLean, Heather and Lester B. Lave (1998) *Environmental Policy Analysis*, "A life-cycle model of an automobile," Carnegie Mellow University.

MacLean, Heather and Lester B. Lave (2003) *Environmental Science & Technology*, "Life cycle assessment of automobile/fuel options," October 22.

Mishan, Ezra (1967) *Journal of Transport Economics and Policy*, "Interpretation of the benefits of private transport," May, 184–89.

Mishan, Ezra (1993) *The Costs of Economic Growth*, Westport, CT: Praeger.

Monahan, Katherine and Scott McFatridge (2010) "Looking back on B.C.'s carbon tax," Smart Prosperity Institute.

Moore, Frances C. and Delavane B. Diaz (2015) *Nature Climate Change*, "Temperature impacts on economic growth warrant stringent mitigation policy," January 12.

Murray, Brian C. and Nicholas Rivers (2015) "British Columbia's revenue-neutral carbon tax: A review of the latest 'grand experiment' in environmental policy." Working paper NI WP 15-04, Duke University, May.

Musselman, Morris McNeil (2011) *Get a Horse! The Story of the Automobile in America*, Philadelphia: Lippincott Co.

NHTSA (National Highway Traffic Safety Administration) (2020) "2020 fatality data show increased traffic fatalities during pandemic," June 3.

NHTSA (National Highway Traffic Safety Administration) (2021) "Early estimates of motor vehicle traffic fatalities in 2020," *Traffic Safety Facts*, Department of Transportation, May.

New York Times (2017) "Where the STEM jobs are (and where they aren't)," November 1.

New York Times (2017) "China's technology ambitions could upset the global trade order," November 7.

New York Times (2019) "The most detailed map of auto emissions in America," October 10.

NRDC (Natural Resources Defense Council) (1993) *The Price of Mobility: Uncovering the Hidden Costs of Transportation,* October.

Ricardo.com (2011) "Ricardo study demonstrates importance of whole life vehicle CO2 emissions," June 7.

Ricke, Katharine et al. (2018) *Nature Climate Change*, "Country-level social cost of carbon", September 24.

Rivers, Nicholas and Brandon Schaufele (2012) "Carbon tax salience and gasoline demand." Working paper #1211E, Department of Economics, Faculty of Social Sciences, University of Ottawa, August.

Shindell, Drew T. (2015) *Climatic Change*, "The social cost of atmospheric release," February 25.

Smil, Vaclav (2014) "Cars weigh too much," personal blog, December 19.

SOCAAR (Southern Ontario Centre for Atmospheric Aerosol Research) (2019) *Near-Road Air Pollution Pilot Study,* University of Toronto.

Sperling, Daniel and Deborah Gordon (2009) *Two Billion Cars: Driving toward Sustainability*, Oxford, Toronto: Oxford University Press.

TomTom.com (2017) "Traffic congestion index full ranking."

Unger, Nadine et al. (2010) *PNAS*, "Attribution of climate forcing to economic sectors," February 23.

US BTS (Bureau of Transportation Statistics) (2018) *Transportation Statistics Annual Report 2018.*

US BTS (Bureau of Transportation Statistics) (2021) "U.S. energy consumption by transportation sector," March 29.

US EIA (Energy Information Administration) (2019) *Electric Power Monthly*, May.

US EPA (Environmental Protection Agency) (2017a) "Social cost of carbon: Technical documentation," accessed January 19.

US EPA (Environmental Protection Agency) (2017b) "Social cost of carbon: Fact sheet," accessed January 19.

US EPA (Environmental Protection Agency) (2020) "Fast facts on transportation greenhouse gas emissions," July 29.

US EPA (Environmental Protection Agency) (2021) "Sources of greenhouse gas emissions."

US EPA (Environmental Protection Agency) (n.d.) "Greenhouse gas emissions from a typical passenger vehicle."

Vancouver Sun (2018) "Don't blame taxes for high gas prices, blame oil companies: Economist," June 22.

Viard, V. Brian and Shihe Fu (2015) *Journal of Public Economics*, "The effect of Beijing's driving restrictions on pollution and economic activity," May.

Wang, Arthur et al. (2017) "Riding China's huge, high-flying car market," McKinsey & Company, October 18.

Wang, Pei et al. (2019) *Journal of Cleaner Production*, "Estimates of the social cost of carbon: A review based on meta-analysis," February 1.

Ward's (2010) *Motor Vehicle Facts & Figures*, Southfield, MI: Ward's Automotive Group.

Ward's (2016) *Motor Vehicle Facts & Figures*, Southfield, MI: Ward's Automotive Group.

Ward's (2017a) *Motor Vehicle Facts & Figures*, Southfield, MI: Ward's Automotive Group.

Ward's (2017b) *World Motor Vehicle Data*, Southfield, MI: Ward's Automotive Group.

Ward's (2019) *Motor Vehicle Facts & Figures*, Southfield, MI: Ward's Automotive Group.

Ward's (2020) *World Motor Vehicle Data*, Southfield, MI: Ward's Automotive Group.

WHO (World Health Organization) (2019) Ambient air pollution database, accessed August 24.

WHO (World Health Organization) (2021) "Road traffic injuries," June 21.

Winston, Clifford (2013) *Journal of Economic Literature*, "On the performance of the U.S. transportation system: Caution ahead," September.

Wu, Ye et al. (2017) *Science of the Total Environment*, "On-road vehicle emissions and their control in China: A review and outlook," 574: 332–49.

Yang, Jun et al. (2014) *Energy Policy*, "A review of Beijing's vehicle registration lottery: Short-term effects on vehicle growth and fuel consumption," 75: 157–66.

5 Unsustainable agriculture

Introduction

Arguably, the greatest transformation in the history of humankind occurred approximately 10,000 years ago with the near simultaneous emergence of an intensive system of food production in at least three separate areas of the world: Mesoamerica, southwest Asia, and China (Ponting 2007). This dramatic event, named the Neolithic Revolution, marked the beginning of the transition from a two-million-year preagricultural period marked by a dominant pattern of hunting, gathering, and herding to the emergence of initially small settlements designed to facilitate the production of select crops and the provision of pastureland for domesticated animals.

The development of a system of agriculture allowed the emergence of a large hierarchical social structure supported by, but not engaged directly in, agricultural production. The subsequent societies contained strata unprecedented in human history such as industrial-economic activity, an organized military establishment, cultural activities, organized religious orders, and governmental administrative units (see Figure 5.1). As a result, the first true cities had started to emerge by about 5000 BCE. "Human history over the last 8,000 years has been about the acquisition and the distribution of this surplus food and the uses to which it has been put. The size of that surplus has largely determined how many people can be sustained outside of agriculture" (Ponting 2007, p. 52).

Historical changes in the relative role of agricultural employment in the economic system are replicated globally today from the employment-intensive developing world to the employment-extensive developed countries (World Bank n.d. b) (see Figure 5.2). In no sense is this phenomenon static as the process of economic development is characterized by the steady shifting of employment, first from agriculture to industry and subsequently to the services sector. Figure 5.3 compares the evolution of the Chinese economy to that of the United States. By way of context, in 1952, just three years after the Communist Revolution, the percentage of the Chinese labor force in agriculture stood at 83.5 percent (China 1985) while in the United States the figure was 9.9 percent (US Department of Commerce 1975).

Yet this dramatic transformation, which forms the foundation of our modern society, did not come without costs as humanity entered into what McMichael (2017) has termed a "Faustian bargain." While preagricultural societies had formulated a system for surviving, and sometimes prospering, in the presence of a potentiality hostile natural environment, the subsequent settled generations ironically faced a more challenging environment. Early settled societies were confronted with a new and omnipresent threat of famine and death if crops failed, as well as the emergence of new diseases associated with living in relatively

DOI: 10.4324/9781003199540-7

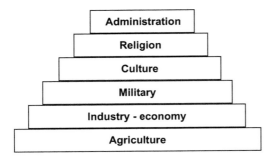

Figure 5.1 Social structure after the agricultural revolution.

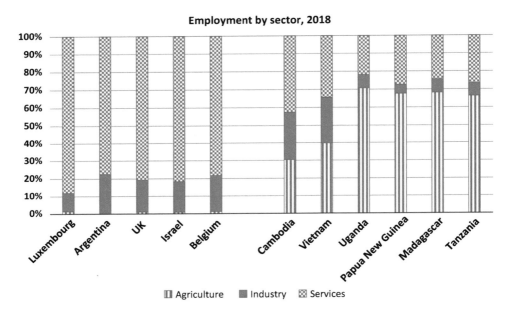

Figure 5.2 Example agricultural employment by country.
Source: World Bank n.d. b

close quarters with one another. In fact, archaeological research suggests that preagricultural societies were relatively free of the diseases that emerged with the transition to an agricultural society. Additional diseases emerged from close contact with domesticated animals where numerous pathogens were shared by both animals and humans: humans shared sixty-five pathogens with dogs, with cattle fifty, sheep forty-six, pigs forty-two, horses thirty-five, rats thirty-two, and poultry twenty-six. The citizens of the newly established agricultural societies were in many cases less well fed, of smaller stature, and prone to a vast array of infectious diseases that did not affect hunter-gatherers (see, for example, McNeill 1998; Dunn 1968; McMichael 2017; Pearce-Duvet 2006).

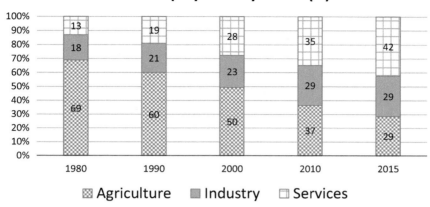

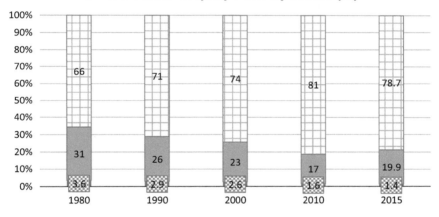

Figure 5.3 Employment by sector: China vs United States.
Note: Where percentages do not total 100, this is due to rounding.
Source: China 1985; US Department of Commerce 1975; China 2018.

The spread of agricultural systems around the world eventually led to increases in global population which, in turn, increased the reliance on the agricultural sector for survival. The historical record demonstrates a continuous struggle to provide enough food for the burgeoning population. In 1798, the Reverend Thomas Robert Malthus published his now famous treatise, *An Essay on the Principle of Population*, where he argued that population growth would inevitably outstrip food supply, leading inexorably to famine, disease, and death. It is conventional wisdom in the economics profession to view Malthus' forecast as wrong in light of historical evidence. While there are many pockets of global malnutrition today, some have argued that total available production of food is sufficient to feed all global inhabitants if problems of food storage and distribution could be overcome. For example, it is estimated that between 30–50 percent of all food produced for human consumption is lost or wasted, representing almost 30 percent of the world's agricultural land area (FAO 2011, 2013c, and 2019b; IME 2013; NAS 2019 and 2020a; UNEP 2021). A recent pathbreaking report by Chatham House (Bailey and Wellesley 2017) has identified fourteen maritime, coastal, and inland chokepoints on which global food security depends. These chokepoints are exposed to three broad categories of disruptive hazards: weather and climate hazards, security and conflict hazards, and institutional hazards such as export controls.

The somewhat sanguine view that total world food supplies are sufficient to meet global needs has been challenged by Ranganathan of the World Resources Institute (2013, p. 5). He concluded:

> We can't just redistribute food to close the food gap. Even if we took all the food produced in 2009 and distributed it evenly among the global population, the world would still need to produce 974 more calories per person per day by 2050.

Montgomery (2007, p. 240) had an equally dismal assessment: "Today, the world is living harvest-to-harvest just like Chinese peasants in the 1920s." In their latest report, the FAO (2019) reported that the number of people suffering from hunger has slowly increased and stands at more than 820 million people (Figure 5.4) (see also WHO 2019c.)

The world is faced with forecasts of population increases to as many as ten to eleven billion people by the turn of the next century, but many observers are confident that continued technological advances will be able to meet the challenge. The

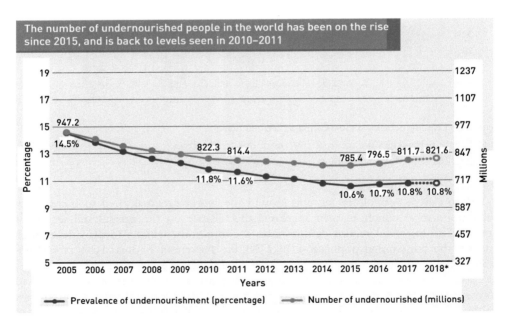

Figure 5.4 Trends in the global number of undernourished people.
Source: FAO 2019b.

most recent evidence cited to support this position is the salutary effects of the green revolution during the period 1950 to 1984. Indeed, the green revolution is one of the great periods of technological advances in agriculture and involved a concerted effort by Western industrialized nations to create a system of staple food production in Asia. The revolution was characterized by five principal components: (1) the creation of hybrid seeds, which were high yield, fast growing, and disease resistant, (2) the heavy use of fertilizer, (3) a concomitant increase in the use of pesticides, (4) mechanization and highly energy-intensive agriculture using tractors, combines, and irrigation pumps, and (5) an increase in the use of monoculture. The benefits were manifest: between 1950 and 1984 there was a 2.6 fold increase in world grain output. This represented an average increase of almost 3 percent per year and rising per capita production of more than a third. During the period 1980–85, by contrast, population growth was only 1.75 percent per year. This bounty did not come without costs, however. Among these were: land degradation, ground water contamination, social dislocation due to land aggregation and small farmer displacement, and significant additional costs (as well as direct and indirect environmental and health impacts) associated with the production and use of fertilizers, pesticides, and commercial energy products such as oil and natural gas. The success of this concerted effort to revolutionize modern agriculture is indisputable. Figures 5.5a and b show how rising grain production has so far kept pace with population growth, but further technological advances will be required on a regular basis to keep pace with not only population increase but also changing tastes of global populations experiencing rising income (FAO 2019; WHO 2019c; OWID).

Mark Bittman (2021), in his latest book, devotes a chapter to critically reexamining the effects of the green revolution. He observes that:

> the percentage of hungry people around the world has inarguably decreased since the sixties, but hunger fell nowhere as markedly in China, where there was no Green Revolution at all. There, saner land reform, distribution of (domestic) hybrid seeds, investment in irrigation, and more generous price subsidies paid direct to rural

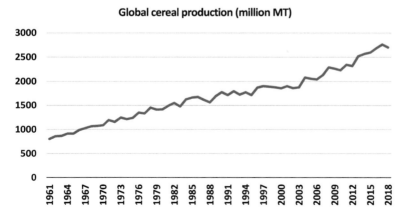

Figure 5.5a Global cereal production.
Sources: OECD–FAO 2019.

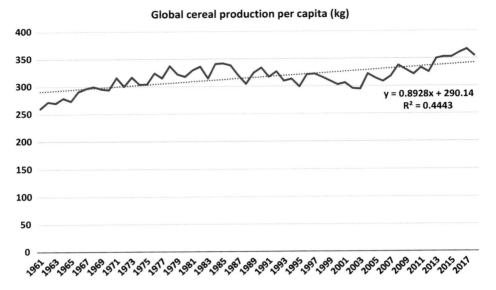

Figure 5.5b Global cereal production per capita.
Sources: OECD–FAO 2019.

peasants brought about an internal agricultural revolution that owed little or nothing to the West … If you exclude China, the number of hungry people in the world actually *increased* [emphasis added] during the heyday of the Green Revolution, despite increase in yield.

(pp. 205–6)

An interesting footnote has been added to the historical development of agriculture from the first settlements to modern times by Gosden (2003, p. 73) who states: "Despite recent massive research programs spurred by modern agro-business, almost no extra species have been added to early rosters of food animals and plants. The vast majority of what we eat was domesticated in prehistory."

The green revolution is an early example of the type of technologically sophisticated system of food production currently in widespread use in the United States and Canada. This system has been considered the model of efficiency, providing bountiful harvests not only for their own citizens but also for many less well-endowed nations of the world. Yet, this system, referred to as "industrial agriculture," represents in many respects the antithesis of sustainable development. The illusion of efficiency rests upon an exceptionally narrow concept of system boundaries. The paradox of industrial agriculture is the result of a pervasive market failure which has failed to internalize both spatial and temporal externalities. *In toto*, the social costs contained within the total boundary which encompasses the industrial agricultural system and all its offsite and temporal effects suggest that this model of "efficiency," with its harvest of "inexpensive" food, is fundamentally unsustainable (see Figure 5.6). In fact, the agricultural sector is probably the greatest generator of negative externalities of any human endeavor. The inherent large and diverse externalities are the focus of this chapter. In this respect, the current intensive agricultural system could

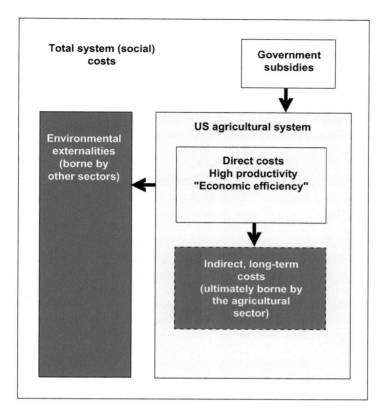

Figure 5.6 The modern industrialized agricultural system.

be conceived as a giant Ponzi scheme; it benefits present day consumers at the expense of society in the future, which will bear most of the costs of modern industrial agriculture. Bittman (2021, p. 221) observes that:

> It's most accurate to think of industrial agriculture as a form of mining—extracting soil, water, elements, fossil fuel and more, rapidly using riches that developed over eons. And, as such, it's easy to see how it can't last—how, to use contemporary language, it's not sustainable; it can't endure.

In sum, it is the view of this author that discounting Malthus as wrong is premature given the magnitude of projected population increases and the threat climate change poses to agricultural production. This issue is addressed specifically in Chapter 6.

Agricultural externalities

Settled agricultural societies provide the first examples of intensive human alteration of the environment and the major destructive impact that humans have. They also provide the first example of societies that so damaged the environment as to bring about their own collapse—an event characterized by Jared Diamond (2005) as "ecocide." The following sections summarize some of the most important agricultural externalities and their causes. These negative externalities are pervasive around the globe and, while many are characteristic of modern Western industrial agriculture, the developing world has not remained unaffected.

Soil

Global soil resources provide a multitude of vital ecological services: soil provides nutrients for plants as well as support for their roots, hosts a vast array of organisms, stores carbon, filters water, and sustains global population through the continued production of food (FAO 2015 and 2020a; Green et al. 2019). Yet this essential resource is in serious jeopardy due to loss of quantity and quality through the overapplication of chemicals, deforestation, and global warming as well as widespread erosion due to improper tillage methods and extreme weather events. Several major reports have highlighted the fact that (1) current farming practices are leading to massive rates of erosion and exhausting soils at a rate orders of magnitude greater than their rate of replenishment (Senate of Canada 1984; Clark et al. 1985; Montgomery 2007; Pimental and Burgess 2013; Amundson et al. 2015; FAO 2019a; Guerra et al. 2020; Thaler et al. 2021); (2) land degradation caused by human activity is undermining the well-being of 40 percent of humanity, driving species extinction, and intensifying climate change (IPBES 2018, 2019); and (3) only 60 years of farming may be left if soil degradation continues, and the global amount of arable and productive land per person in 2050 will be only a quarter of the level in 1960 (IPBES 2018; Arsenault 2014). As Montgomery (2007, p. 2) states:

> Unless more immediate disasters do us in, how we address the twin problems of soil degradation and accelerated erosion will eventually determine the fate of modern civilization. In exploring the fundamental role of soil in human history, the key lesson is as simple as it is clear: modern society risks repeating mistakes that hastened the demise of past civilization.

In their first report on the status of global soil resources, the FAO (2015, p. xix) stated that:

> the majority of the world's soil resources are in only fair, poor or very poor condition. Today, 33 percent of land is moderately to highly degraded due to the erosion, salinization, compaction, acidification and chemical pollution of soils. Further loss of productive soils would severely damage food production and food security, amplify food-price volatility, and potentially plunge millions of people into hunger and poverty.

Much of the world's productive agricultural land is now under cultivation and there are only a few available options for increasing production to meet future needs: (1) expanding agricultural production into marginal lands with much lower yield potential, (2) replacing forests with farms, (3) adopting more intensive farming practices, or (4) using recent advances in genetics to create new species with greater yields. Erb et al. (2018) conclude that globally converging diets may increase further the pressure on the availability of local food to meet increasing demand, thereby accelerating the need for greater food supply, especially in many developing regions.

Historically, farmers maintained soil fertility through a mix of measures including fallowing, crop rotation, mixed cropping, and the application of natural fertilizers such as livestock manure. The increasing demand for food production and adoption of more intensive production systems required the increasing use of synthetic fertilizers to compensate for declining soil fertility.

Fertilizers

Global fertilizer use has literally exploded within the last several decades to the extent that it is now having a major impact on land and water ecosystems and the natural cycling of nutrients within the global biosphere. Steffen et al. (2015) have undertaken an extensive and innovative analysis of nine planetary boundaries—a study of "the risk that human perturbations will destabilize the earth system at the planetary scale." In their analysis, anthropogenic perturbations of four processes (climate change, biosphere integrity, land system change, and biogeochemical flows) now exceed the limits of the planetary boundaries. Included in this last category is the flow of nitrogen in the global ecosystem. Figure 5.7 summarizes the rapid increase in world fertilizer production (FAO 2017). Figure 5.8 portrays the increasing application among the four largest users, most notably China (FAO 2017). While facilitating the massive increase in food production, the intensive and widespread application of fertilizers has generated several significant negative externalities. Prominent among these are the release of GHGs from the supply chain, including potent GHGs such as nitrous oxide (Wood and Cowie 2004; Wagner-Riddle et al. 2017), a GHG three hundred times more powerful than CO_2; infiltration of groundwater and drinking wells in agricultural areas with nitrates which can lead to

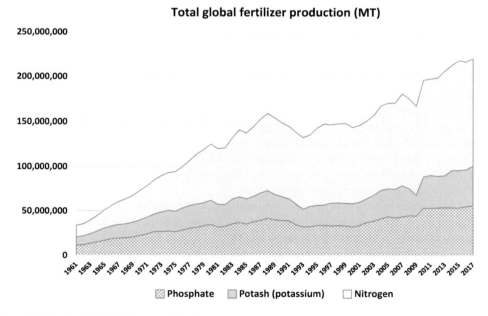

Figure 5.7 Total global fertilizer production.
Source: FAO 2017.

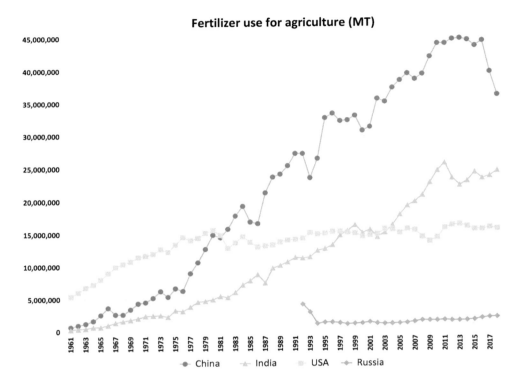

Figure 5.8 Top four fertilizer-consuming countries.
Source: FAO 2017.

methemoglobinemia or "blue baby" syndrome as well as certain types of cancer (Weyer et al. 2001; Ward et al, 2010; Jones et al. 2016; Schullehner et al. 2018); the eutrophication of lakes and rivers (Tilman et al. 2001; Sinha et al. 2017); increasing soil acidification and decreases in soil organic material (Bhattacharyya et al. 2017; Ozlu and Kumar 2018; Lavkulich 2019); and increasing number and size of hypoxic regions in coastal oceans throughout the globe, commonly referred to as dead zones, where few aquatic organisms can survive, yet it is coastal oceans which tend to have the highest biological productivity (Diaz and Rosenberg 2008; USGS 2000; NOAA 2017; Van Meter et al. 2018; Breitburg et al. 2018; *New York Times* June 3, 2020). Figure 5.9 summarizes the sources, routes, and effects of nitrate flows into the environment.

The massive increase in the use of fertilizer is but one of the major transformative changes in modern agricultural practices. Foremost among these is the emergence of monoculture as a common form of production.

Monoculture

One of the most significant components of industrial agriculture has been the wide-scale adoption of monoculture or monocropping where a single crop such as wheat, corn, or soybeans is grown over a wide geographic area, often measured in square miles. The

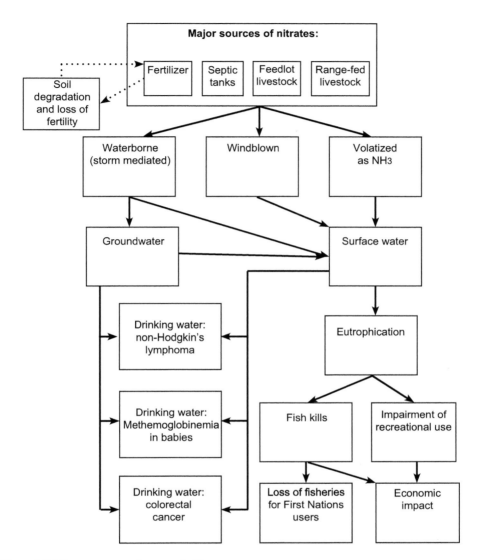

Figure 5.9 Nitrate sources, flows, and effects.

principal reason for the adoption of this technique is economies of scale, which facilitate the use of single automated harvesting methods, and generate lower costs and increased yields over conventional farming practices. While the *efficiency* of this method is cited as its principal rationale, this preconception is based on the confusion between private and social costs and benefits. The broader consideration of total social costs casts serious doubts on the claims of economic efficiency. The negative effects of monoculture are multifaceted, and include, inter alia, soil degradation and loss of nutrients, and extreme simplification of the local ecosystem, leading to the loss of biodiversity and natural biological control of pests and diseases (see for example Nordhaus 2017). In essence there is a fundamental trade-off between perceived efficiency and resilience, where resilience of an ecosystem is its ability to resist environmental perturbation and quickly recover its structure and function (Foley 2013; Hodgson et al. 2015; Willis et al. 2018). A simplified ecosystem loses its ability to respond easily to stresses, especially those associated with massive predation by insects, weeds, and disease. To overcome these serious deficiencies, farmers are forced to increase their application of synthetic products, meaning fertilizers and especially pesticides and herbicides.

Pesticides

Ever since the beginning of agriculture, humanity has faced the perennial problem of protecting its food crops from destruction by adverse weather, weeds, insects, diseases, and animals. Even today, it has been estimated that "worldwide, an annual loss of 8–10% (13 million tonnes of grains lost due to insects and 100 million tonnes due to failure to store grain properly) is estimated in stored-food commodities. Most storage losses are due to inadequate and poor storage facilities, which allow attacks by insect pests and diseases, causing enormous losses annually" (Pimental and Burgess 2014, p. 172). The classic historical example of this battle was described in the biblical tale of the ten plagues of Egypt. Modern scientific inquiry has identified the causes of these plagues as algae, bacteria, insects, viruses, and molds (Ehrenkranz and Sampson 2008). Extensive historical evidence of the fragility of food crops can also be found in the monumental research in *Science and Civilization in China* by Joseph Needham, which describes ancient Chinese efforts to protect the fruits of their agricultural economy (especially Vol. 6, parts 1 and 2, 1984, 1986).

It was not until the modern era and the development of synthetic organic pesticides and herbicides that confidence—however misplaced—emerged that the historical battle against insect pests and weeds might finally be won. From the earliest times of recorded history, humankind fought and frequently lost battles against malnutrition and famine (Ó Gráda 2009). The meager range of weapons, aside from mixed cropping to reduce the impact of crop-specific insect infestation, included some natural plant-based insecticides such as pyrethrum and artemisia (Needham, Vol. 6, Part 1) and extremely toxic elements such as arsenic (in the form of arsenic trioxide) and lead (Pimental and Burgess 2014). The use of arsenic has been documented in early China by Needham (Vol. 6, Part 2) and both arsenic and lead were in use up to the introduction of synthetic organics around the time of the Second World War. In his book *Before Silent Spring: Pesticides and Public Health in Pre-DDT America,* Whorton (1974) details the significant health risks associated with the widespread use of these two insecticides. To quote:

> Late in the nineteenth century … the British agricultural press had charged that apples imported from the United States regularly arrived with a powdery coating of arsenic and were deadly … Export fruit was required to pass the world tolerance for arsenic, while fruit kept in the United States was allowed to carry considerably more. As late as December 1926, a Bureau representative admitted that fruit bearing as much as four times the British tolerance for arsenic had been permitted on the American market. … The American food supply … was largely poisoned by lead arsenate and other arsenical insecticides. … Distribution of lead and arsenic was so complete that all members of industrialized populations carried at least traces of the metals in their tissues.
>
> (pp. 133, 137, 177)

While the application of lead and arsenic-based pesticides has long since been discontinued, significant residues of these extremely toxic elements can still be found in agricultural areas (Codling 2011). In light of this history, it is no wonder that the advent of modern organic pesticides was welcomed uncritically with open arms. Among the first and most widely used of these modern synthetic pesticides was DDT (dichlorodiphenyltrichloroe thane) because of its success in not only controlling many insects that attacked crops but also those acting as vectors for human diseases such as malaria, yellow fever, and typhus (Davis 2014). Except for its continued use in the developing world for the control of malaria, this insecticide has been largely phased out because of its indiscriminate effect on beneficial nontarget species and the emergence of genetic resistance among predatory insects. Rachel Carson's *Silent Spring*, published in 1962, did much to raise awareness of the problems inherent in the use of this pesticide. Initial beliefs in the innocuous nature of DDT led to its widespread use beyond farming, including the common practice, for example, of in-flight spraying of DDT on airline passengers just before arriving in Hawaii from the mainland in the 1950s. Recent research has found that in addition to its effects on those directly exposed to this pesticide, DDT has negative effects on human health after three generations. Granddaughters of women exposed to DDT developed earlier menarche and obesity, established risk factors for breast cancer and cardiometabolic diseases (Cirillo et al. 2021).

The history of modern pesticide use since DDT has been checkered with the development of more toxic pesticides and the concomitant process of Darwinian selection, which creates new generations of insects immune to the effects of many of them (Gould et al. 2018; *Science* August 31, 2020). Figure 5.10 illustrates the continuing and rapid rise in the global use of synthetic pesticides (World Bank n.d. b), and Figure 5.11 provides

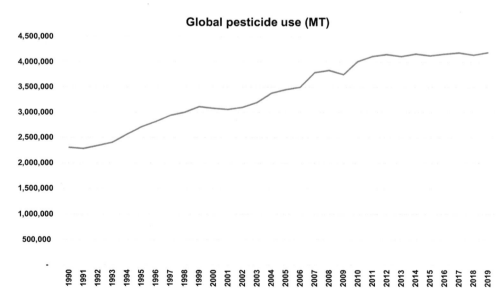

Figure 5.10 Global pesticide use.
Source: World Bank n.d. b.

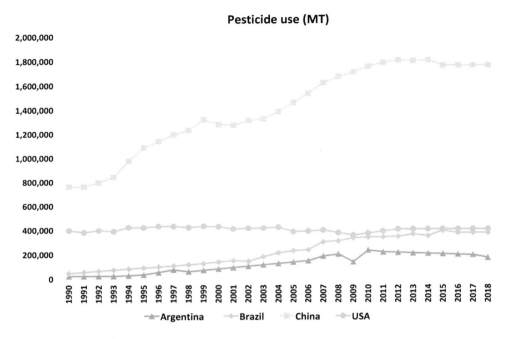

Figure 5.11 Pesticide use by four major users.
Source: World Bank n.d. b.

time series data on pesticide application among the four largest users, most notably China (FAOSTAT).

While helping to expand the use of monoculture with its attendant economies of scale, many modern pesticides entail very serious risks to both benign insect species such as bees, fish, and birds as well as aquatic ecosystems and human health since these chemicals are indiscriminate biocides (Fry 1995; *Science* September 12, 2019; Davis 2015; see also CNRS News 2018; *New York Times* September 18 and 19, 2019, Yamamuro et al. 2019; Soroye et al. 2020; Miller et al. 2020; Schulz et al. 2021). The US President's Cancer Panel (2009) reported that nearly 1,400 pesticides had been approved by the US Environmental Protection Agency (EPA) and that they contained almost 900 active ingredients, many of which are considered toxic. Evidence has emerged of wide-scale contaminant of groundwater supplies by persistent pesticides and their metabolites in regions marked by intensive agriculture (Einarson and Mackay 2001; Casado et al. 2019). Accompanying this has been the accumulation of persistent residues in soils (Silva et al. 2019), aquatic fauna, and food supplies (Winter and Katz 2011; WHO 2018).

Figure 5.12 illustrates the multiple pathways through which pesticides reach the environment, food supplies, and humans themselves (US EPA 2011). A pioneering study by the NGO Environmental Defence (2005, p. 1), found the presence of toxic chemicals in Canadians regardless of their place of residence, age, or occupation:

Laboratory tests detected 60 of the 88 chemicals in 11 volunteers: 18 heavy metals, five PBDEs, 14 PCBs, one perfluorinated chemical, 10 organochlorine pesticides,

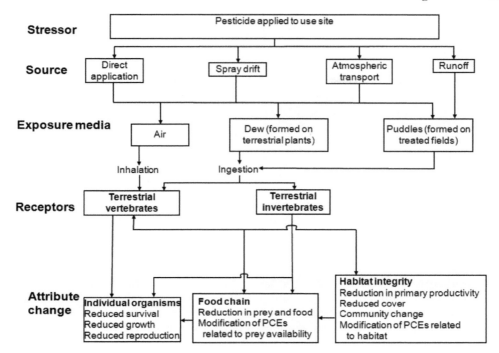

Figure 5.12 Pesticide exposure pathways.
Note: PCE is perchloroethylene.
Source: US EPA 2011.

five organophosphate insecticide metabolites, and seven VOCs [volatile organic compounds]. Nearly every chemical in each chemical group was detected. On average, 44 chemicals were detected in each volunteer, including 41 carcinogens, 27 hormone disruptors, 21 respiratory toxins and 53 reproductive/ developmental toxins.

Through a complex process of volatilization and global circulation, many of these toxic chemicals find their way to the circum-Arctic regions and can be detected at significantly elevated levels in milk fat and cord blood among northern inhabitants (Schindler 2007; Arctic Council 2004). These data are reminiscent of the era of pervasive arsenic and lead pesticides—all that has changed are the names of the chemicals.

In the end, the key question is what impact these new chemicals have not only on global fauna but also on humankind in particular. Recent epidemiological research has linked pesticide exposure to a number of human diseases including Alzheimer's (Richardson et al 2014) and Parkinson's (Richardson et al. 2009; Stetka 2014), problems with assisted pregnancies (Chiu et al. 2017), and a wide variety of cancers (Alavanja 2009; US President's Cancer Panel 2009; Bao et al. 2019). The Cancer Panel (2009, p. 45) reported that "approximately 40 chemicals classified by the International Agency for Research on Cancer as known, probable, or possible human carcinogens, are used in EPA-registered pesticides now on the market."

One of the most vexing concerns to emerge from scientific research is the pervasive use and environmental dissemination of a broad category of chemicals referred to as endocrine mimickers or disruptors (EDCs) and found in some pesticides and industrial and consumer products (EEA 2012). To quote from a major recent report (Gore et al. 2015, p. 593):

> there is strong mechanistic, experimental, animal, and epidemiological evidence for endocrine disruption, namely: obesity and diabetes, female reproduction, male reproduction, hormone-sensitive cancers in females, prostate cancer, thyroid, and neurodevelopment and neuroendocrine systems. EDCs such as bisphenol A, phthalates, pesticides, persistent organic pollutants such as polychlorinated biphenyls, polybrominated diethyl ethers, and dioxins were emphasized because these chemicals had the greatest depth and breadth of available information.

What makes these chemicals so dangerous is the fact that they are active within the human body in doses as low as several parts per trillion. (For several controversial studies focusing on EDCs and declining male sperm count and the potential significance for human reproduction see Swan et al. 1997; Swan 2020; Levine et al. 2017; Boulicault et al. 2021.)

Accompanying these medium- to long-term serious health impacts is the incidence of morbidity and mortality associated with pesticide use among agricultural workers globally. It has been estimated that there may be as many as three million cases of poisoning requiring hospital admission on an annual basis and as many as two hundred thousand deaths (BJIM 1985; Jeyaratnam 1990). Most of these are believed to occur in the developing world as the problem has been largely controlled in the industrial nations. Nevertheless, the problem has not been eliminated even here, as one study (Calvert et al. 2008, p. 883) in the United States concluded that "acute pesticide poisoning in the agricultural industry continues to be an important problem."

In light of the challenges posed by increasing resistance and the detrimental environment effects of many modern pesticides, the agrochemical industry has been engaged in a continuous effort to develop new chemicals, some of which are based on natural insecticides produced by plants for self-protection from predation. One of these classes of chemicals is neonicotinoids. These are chemically similar to nicotine and are found in the nightshade family of plants, which includes tobacco. Their introduction and rapidly increased use (Baker and Stone 2015; Foster 2018) was viewed as a positive advance in the field of pesticides since they were viewed as having lower levels of toxicity to birds, fish, and mammals than the more toxic organophosphates and carbamates they have partially replaced (Tomizawa and Casida 2005; Foster 2018).

Unfortunately, the introduction of these pesticides has become an archetypal example of revenge theory, or the law of unexpected consequences. For example, there are reports of neonicotinoids leading to significant declines in butterfly populations (Gilburn et al. 2015), insectivorous birds (Hallmann et al. 2014; Li et al. 2020), and beneficial insects (Calvo-Agudo et al. 2019). In particular, there have been increasing instances since the turn of the century of massive die-offs of bee colonies (referred to as colony collapse disorder or CCD) in the United States and elsewhere in the world, including Russia (BBC July 19, 2019). It has been reported that US beekeepers lost 40 percent of honeybee colonies in 2018 (Bruckner et al. 2019). The scientific community was at first unsure of the cause of CCD as there appeared to be a number of factors, including stress, fungi, and viruses. Conclusive evidence has, however, emerged that neonicotinoids are the primary contributing factor to this serious ecological problem (Whitehorn et al.

2012; Woodcock et al. 2016; CEH 2016; BBC August 20, 2019). One hypothesis about the etiology of CCD is that an underlying cause may be hidden by secondary factors resulting from exposure to the primary agent. In this case, it has been postulated that one such mechanism is the weakening of the bee immune system by exposure to the pesticide, leading to subsequent vulnerability to secondary infections. This is analogous to the common medical practice of distinguishing between immediate and underlying cause of death. Other hypotheses attribute the resulting mortality to disruption of bee nest behavior, social networks, and thermoregulation (Crall et al. 2018) or suppression of sperm production (Straub et al. 2016). Recent research (Siviter et al. 2021) has found increased bee mortality resulting from the synergistic interaction of agrochemicals. The authors conclude:

> Environmental risk assessment schemes that assume additive effects of the risk of agrochemical exposure may underestimate the interactive effect of anthropogenic stressors on bee mortality and will fail to protect the pollinators that provide a key ecosystem service that underpins sustainable agriculture.
>
> (p. 1)

The magnitude of the bee colony collapse has forced a reexamination of the critical role that these insects play in crop pollination. The number of bee-pollinated crops is high and includes forage and legume, fruit, vegetables, oilseed crops, and herbs and spices (Morse and Calderone 2000; Losey and Vaughan 2006; Klein et al. 2007; Stipp 2007; US White House 2014; Chaplin-Kramer et al. 2019). An estimate in 2010 of the value of US crops that rely on honeybee pollination was $19 billion (Calderone 2012). Table 5.1 reports the result of one study from 2007 which lists the percentage and value of selected crops in the United States that rely on bee pollination (Stipp 2007).

In an innovative study in South Africa, Allsopp et al. (2008) attempted to measure the value of pollination of the Western Cape deciduous fruit industry by costing alternative methods to the traditional services provided by insects. These methods include costly and labor-intensive methods such as aerial spraying or hand pollination. The resulting monetary values represent a significant proportion of the total crop value, reinforcing the

Table 5.1 Honeybee-pollinated crops

Crop	Total US crop value (million $)	Bee pollinated (%)	Value of honeybee-pollinated crops (million $)
Almonds	2,200	100	2,200
Apples	200	90	1,980
Soybeans	19,700	5	985
Cotton	5,200	16	832
Onions	868	90	781
Broccoli	653	90	588
Carrots	557	90	501
Blueberries	558	90	502
Oranges	1,800	27	486
Cherries	469	81	380

Source: Stipp 2007.

conclusion that replacing services provided normally by nature for "free" can be a costly exercise. A similar analysis conducted in the United Kingdom estimated the annual costs of hand pollination at £1.8 billion (FOEE 2012). In another study considering world agriculture as a whole, Gallai et al. (2009) estimated the total economic value of pollination at €153 billion (approximately $213 billion) and the potential loss of consumer surplus at €190–310 billion (approximately $265–425 billion; see also Aizen et al. 2009). The result of this increasing body of research has led to the near-total ban on neonicotinoids in the European Union (BBC April 27, 2018), while Canada announced in August 2018 that nicotine-based pesticides will be phased out beginning in 2021 (Canadian Press August 24, 2018). However, they are still used in the United States pending their replacement by other pesticides. In July 2019, the US EPA announced the approval of sulfoxaflor, a pesticide which the agency itself has found to be highly toxic to honeybees, prompting a lawsuit by the beekeeping industry (*New York Times* September 12, 2019). This development has come on the heels of the United States Department of Agriculture (USDA) suspending data collection on honeybee colonies in 2019, thereby losing the ability to track the state and direction of honeybee health (*Guardian* July 12, 2019). One report has suggested that it is not a coincidence that Dow Chemical, the producer of sulfoxaflor, contributed $1 million to President Donald Trump's inauguration committee (HuffPost July 15, 2019). This reflects the ongoing debate about regulatory capture within the American executive branch (WEF 2019).

One additional point is worth making concerning the indirect effects of neonicotinoids used as insecticides. While attention has been rightly focused on the detrimental impact on honeybees, Goulson (2014) has found an indirect link with a decline of bird populations in sprayed areas. While not directly toxic to birds, the loss of birds is hypothesized to be due to a marked reduction in food following the death of nontarget insects killed by this pesticide. Eng et al. (2019) find that the pesticide reduces fueling and delays migration in songbirds, with potential negative effects on reproduction and survival. This type of systems analysis, which examines indirect as well as direct effects, is the type of research sorely needed in identifying the multiple effects of human intervention in complex ecological systems.

In order to bring some perspective to the discussion of the major issues surrounding the use of pesticides in the world today, it is worthwhile reviewing briefly recent technological advances in the fight against crop-destroying insects. One of the most promising avenues of research is the rediscovery and application of what is termed integrated pest management. This is defined by Merriam-Webster as: "management of agricultural and horticultural pests that minimizes the use of chemicals and emphasizes natural and low-toxicity methods (such as the use of crop rotation and beneficial predatory insects)." Complementing biopesticides (Nollet and Rathore 2015) are techniques such as the sterilization and release of insects, and the use of natural bacteria and viruses as de facto pesticides.

It is interesting to observe that under pressure to create new methods of controlling predatory insects, the agricultural sector has resurrected techniques widely used more than two millennia ago in ancient China. In *Science and Civilization in China* (Vol. 6, Part 1, 1986) Needham reported the use of natural pest predators such as carnivorous ants, wasps, ground beetles, ladybird beetles, and carabid beetles to control infestations of plant-eating insects. Complementing these insects were frogs, ducks, and mynah birds. Some of these techniques are still in use today, including the use of insects that prey on crop-destroying pests (McFadyen 1998).

The modern scientific contributions to integrated pest management include the genetic modification of the insect genome and the creation of transgenic crops designed to produce insect–killing toxins from natural bacteria such as *Bacillus thuringiensis* (Bt). Several challenges have emerged as these techniques have gained currency. The *New York Times* (January 27, 2014) reported concern that releasing gene-silencing agents into the field could harm beneficial insects (Lundgren and Duan 2013), and could possibly harm human health (Zhang et al. 2012). The US EPA (2013, p. 23) summarized a key conceptual issue when they stated that the "environmental fate and effects of [genetic interventions] are poorly understood and present unique challenges for ecological risk assessment that have not yet been encountered in assessment for traditional chemical pesticides." Even the clever technological idea of employing natural bacteria such as Bt in transgenic crops cannot overcome the obstacle of Darwinian selection (Tabashnik et al. 2008, 2013; Tabashnik and Carriere 2017). With generation times as short as 4.7 days (Li 1995), insects have the capacity to select for resistance at an extremely rapid rate.

Other unanticipated results include cross-species effects that can directly affect human health. Pearson and Callaway (2006) report that the use of some exotic insecticides can inadvertently subsidize deer mouse populations, leading to an increased threat of hantavirus, which is present in the feces of these mice.

An additional threat has emerged in recent years which parallels the impact of intensive pesticide use on the development of insect resistance. The widespread use of fungicides has created similar selective Darwinian pressure on very serious human fungal infections such as *Candida auris* which have now developed immunity to commonly used antifungal medications (Chowdhary et al. 2013; Fisher et al. 2018, *New York Times* April 6, 2019; McKenna 2021).

All of the above suggests that attempting technological fixes to a basically unsustainable system of agricultural production is a potentially unproductive strategy and that alternative agricultural systems must be considered if humanity is going to be able to feed itself in the indefinite future. We return to this issue later in this chapter after the further discussion of agricultural externalities.

Herbicides

As with insect pests, weeds have been the bane of farming from the first days of agriculture. A wide array of techniques has been used over history to control these invasive species with varying degrees of success. Such techniques, used since the early days of Chinese agriculture (Needham 1984) have included manual removal, plowing, crop rotation, animal grazing, and mixed cropping, which can provide extensive ground cover. Today, many of these time-tested techniques have been supplemented or replaced with the use of chemical herbicides. These chemicals are in such widespread use today that traces of these compounds have been found in rainfall (Goolsby et al. 1997), groundwater, and surface waters (Water Research Center 2014.) The most common herbicide in use today is Monsanto's Roundup, the trademarked name for the chemical glyphosate. The principal problem with the application of chemical weed killers is that they are indiscriminate and fatal for most conventional domesticated crops. To address this challenge, Monsanto developed Roundup Ready crops, which have been genetically engineered to be resistant to glyphosate, thereby allowing spraying during normal crop growing seasons. This concept is similar to the genetic engineering of crops to produce Bt as described in the section on pesticides.

The use of glyphosate in the United States and globally has increased at an extraordinarily rapid rate in the last several decades. To quote the results of one recent study (Benbrook 2016, abstract):

> Since 1974 in the U.S., over 1.6 billion kilograms of glyphosate active ingredient have been applied, or 19% of estimated global use of glyphosate (8.6 billion kilograms). Globally, glyphosate use has risen almost 15-fold since so-called "Roundup Ready," genetically engineered glyphosate-tolerant crops were introduced in 1996. Two-thirds of the total volume of glyphosate applied in the U.S. from 1974 to 2014 has been sprayed in just the last 10 years. The corresponding share globally is 72%. In 2014, farmers sprayed enough glyphosate to apply ~1.0 kg/ha (0.8 pound/acre) on every hectare of U.S.-cultivated cropland and nearly 0.53 kg/ha (0.47 pounds/acre) on all cropland worldwide.

The initial optimistic assessment of the use of this herbicide has been tempered by recent research, which has revealed a number of disturbing impacts. Health Canada, the federal agency in charge of assessing the effects of products on human health in Canada, announced in November 2018 that its scientists were reviewing hundreds of documents used during the approval process for glyphosate, because of "troubling allegations" that the chemical might be a human carcinogen (CBC November 11, 2018). This follows a vote by the European Parliament in October 2017 to phase out the use of glyphosate by 2022 and Germany's decision to ban its use by 2023 (*Guardian* September 4, 2019a). Controversial research in 2017 found a link between "ultra-low doses" of Roundup herbicide and nonalcoholic fatty liver disease in laboratory rats (Mesnage 2017). More recent research (Kubsad et al. 2019) has found epigenetic transgenerational inheritance of pathologies and sperm epimutations in rats. Rodents are frequently used as a surrogate test for effects in humans for two principal reasons: (1) concern over risk and associated ethical issues associated with human testing, and (2) the existence of some genetic and somatic similarities between rats and humans which allow the frequent transferability of rat laboratory results to humans.

Other research has found the persistence of glyphosate in wild, edible plants at least one year after application (*Vancouver Sun* February 20, 2019; Wood 2019), and recent tests by the nonprofit, Environmental Working Group, found traces of glyphosate in the popular breakfast cereals Cheerios and Quaker Oats (*New York Times* August 15, 2018; Temkin 2018).

Even if these concerns over the potential carcinogenic effects of glyphosate prove to be without merit, there are several additional developments that do not bode well for its continued widespread use. First, this chemical may be contributing to the continuing decline of honeybees (Motta et al. 2018) and other insects (Goulet and Masner (2017). Second, natural selection and other processes are again operating to frustrate human control of threats to agriculture through the development of glyphosate-resistant weeds (Powles 2010; Owen 2008; *Pest Management Science*, special issue March 13, 2008; *New York Times* August 11, 2014). The resulting spread of these "super" weeds has had a perverse effect, resulting in even further use of herbicides including but not restricted to glyphosate. Benbrook (2012, abstract) reports that:

> Contrary to often-repeated claims that today's genetically-engineered crops have, and are reducing pesticide use, the spread of glyphosate-resistant weeds in

herbicide-resistant weed management systems has brought about substantial increases in the number and volume of herbicides applied. . . . Herbicide-resistant crop technology has led to a 239 million kilogram (527 million pounds) increase in herbicide use in the United States between 1996 and 2011.

Third, and perhaps most important, Mallory-Smith and Zapiola (2008) have identified a phenomenon known as gene flow. To quote:

> Gene flow, defined as the change in gene frequency in a population due to movement of gametes, individuals or groups of individuals from one place to another, has been raised consistently and repeatedly as a concern related to the introduction of genetically engineered (GE) crops. Gene flow is a natural phenomenon that is not unique to GE crops. The concerns raised relative to gene flow from GE glyphosate-resistant (GR) (Roundup Ready) crops include: the emergence of volunteer crops that are more difficult or more expensive to control, [and] *the transfer of the transgene to wild or weedy relatives* [emphasis added]. . . . Gene flow can occur via pollen and seed and, for some species, may occur via vegetative propagules.
>
> (p. 428)

All of these factors had a decidedly negative effect on the corporate image of Monsanto (Robin 2008; Gillam 2012; CBC March 11, 2019; Barber 2019; HuffPost September 14, 2019), which was finally bought by Bayer Inc in 2016 for $66 billion, creating one of the world's largest agrochemical companies. The change of ownership has not diminished the challenges facing the company, as recent court decisions have ordered Monsanto to pay up to $10.9 billion in cancer cases related to the use of Roundup (*New York Times* March 27, 2019; CBC May 14, 2019; *Guardian* May 13, 2019; Stokstad 2019; *New York Times* September 20, 2019; CTV News June 24, 2020).

Recent research has identified the emergence of what has been termed "metabolic resistance," where weeds have developed enzymes which attack and neutralize herbicides as soon as they pass through the cell's plasma membrane, allowing them to resist a herbicide to which they have never been exposed (Gullickson 2017; Brown 2021). According to Brown, "the onset of metabolic resistance marks the real dawn of the age of superweeds" (p. 31).

Biodiversity

The purpose of this section is to review briefly the role of the agricultural sector as the largest contributor to the global loss of biodiversity (Benton et al. 2021). Suffice it to say that the maintenance of a high level of biodiversity is absolutely essential for food and agriculture (Altieri 1999; FAO 2019c). As Nakhauka (2009, p. 208) has stated: "Agricultural biodiversity is the first link in the food chain, developed and safeguarded by indigenous people throughout the world and it makes an essential contribution to feeding the world."

External effects: Sanchez-Bayo and Wyckhuys (2019) identify the main drivers of species decline in order of importance: (1) habitat loss and conversion to intensive agriculture and urbanization; (2) pollution, mainly by synthetic pesticides and fertilizers; (3) biological factors, including pathogens and introduced species; and (4) climate change. Clearly the two most important of these are intimately linked to the practice of agriculture.

Dudley and Alexander (2017) list four ways agriculture, in particular, drives biodiversity loss: (1) conversion of natural ecosystems into farms and ranches; (2) intensification of management in long-established cultural landscapes; (3) release of pollutants, including GHGs; and (4) associated value chain impacts, including energy and transport use and food waste.

The adoption of monoculture practices has created vast biological deserts with grossly impaired ecosystems incapable of supporting traditional flora and fauna. The loss of beneficial insects and birds is particularly critical as it deprives the agricultural sector of natural pest control services, thereby increasing the reliance of the sector on human intervention with environmentally detrimental pesticides and herbicides. Monoculture also deprives the agricultural sector of ecosystem services, such as water flow, and weed and pest control, provided by natural mixed vegetation. Much newly created farmland has come at the expense of large natural forest areas in the developing world and has entailed the loss of the vast array of vital ecosystem services they provide, including those associated with biodiversity (Seibold et al. 2019).

What is particularly disturbing is the rate at which insect and certain bird species are decreasing (Vogel 2017; Ceballos et al. 2017; Sanchez-Bayo and Wyckhuys 2019; Hallmann et al. 2017; CNRS 2018; Inger et al. 2015; Schwagerl 2016; Powney et al. 2019; MacPhail et al. 2019). Pimm et al. (2014, p. 987) state that "current rates of extinction are about 1000 times the likely background rate of extinction." The reasons are multifaceted and complex although, as stated above, the principal driver of this phenomenon is the agricultural sector. The speed at which these changes are occurring suggests that when appropriate remedial measures are identified and implemented, it may be too late to maintain the functioning of many earth ecosystems. Delabre et al. (2021, abstract) conclude that "current food production and consumption trends are inconsistent with the Convention on Biological Diversity's 2050 vision of living in harmony with nature."

Intra-sectoral effects: Accompanying the loss of biodiversity resulting from agricultural production has been a similar loss within the agricultural sector itself driven by the necessities of modern industrial agriculture and the emergence of the agro-industrial sector. A relatively small number of crops account for a significant proportion of global terrestrial food production: sugar cane, maize (i.e. corn), wheat, rice, and potatoes. In an attempt to increase yields of these and other major crops, there has been a concerted effort to develop selected plant variants at the expense of genetic biodiversity. Several studies from the scientific community have warned that this loss of diversity threatens the integrity and resilience of future food supply (Cardinale et al. 2012; Khoury et al. 2014; FAO 2019c; IPBES 2019; Deb 2019). Dewi and Gonzalez (2015, p. 1) state:

> Over the last two decades, 75% of the genetic diversity of agricultural crops has been lost; 100 to 1000-fold decrease over time. This phenomenon results in the decrease of ecosystem abilities to provide food for people and decrease the function [sic] of other ecosystem services.

Figure 5.13 illustrates (Tomanio 2011) the decreased numbers of commercially available varieties of seeds of ten crops over the last century. McMichael (2017, p. 249) concludes that "efficiency-driven culling of the ancient diversity of strains and types of many plant foods (such as potatoes, wheat, and bananas) has lowered the resilience of agricultural systems and reduced options for the future."

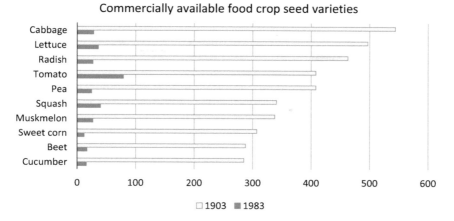

Figure 5.13 Commercially available food crop seed varieties.
Source: Tomanio 2011.

Accompanying the decline in the variety of crops under cultivation has been a marked decrease in the nutritional value of many common foods, with proportions of protein, calcium, phosphorus, iron, riboflavin, and ascorbic acid, among others, falling (*New York Times* September 12, 2015; Davis et al. 2004; Halweil 2007; Poti et al. 2015). Much of this decline has been attributed to the pursuit of increased crop yields and represents a trade-off between yield and nutrient content. Efforts to offset recent declining marginal yields as the initial salutary impacts of the green revolution play out have frequently led to trade-offs with environmental sustainability, resulting in land degradation, salinization, eutrophication, increased release of CH_4 and N_2O, groundwater pollution, and loss of biodiversity (IAASTD 2008).

Fortunately, some major efforts have been undertaken to preserve a vast variety of seeds from around the world for future generations. The most notable of these efforts is the Svalbard Global Seed Vault, an underground storage facility established by the Norwegian government in 2008 on the remote Arctic island of Svalbard at approximately 79 degrees north latitude (Norway n.d.). Drawing on contributions from twenty-three international seed banks, one million seed samples are currently stored in this facility to act as a backstop against natural disasters, climate change, or any anthropogenic activity which can lead to the loss of unique genetic information. Even this purportedly safe vault has not escaped the threat of global warming, however, as water from melting permafrost flooded the entrance tunnel in 2017 (*Guardian* May 19, 2017). Whether the development of new seeds or reuse of ancient seeds will suffice to protect global food supplies is an open question in light of climate change.

Another major development within the last few decades has been the development of biotechnology in the form of genetic engineering and the creation of genetically modified organisms, or genetically modified (GM) crops. The first of these technological innovations was Monsanto's Roundup Ready crops, which were designed to tolerate the herbicide glyphosate, as mentioned earlier in this chapter. The motivation behind the development of GM crops is multifaceted and includes, inter alia, designing crops that have higher yields; resistance to pests, plant diseases, and droughts; higher nutritional

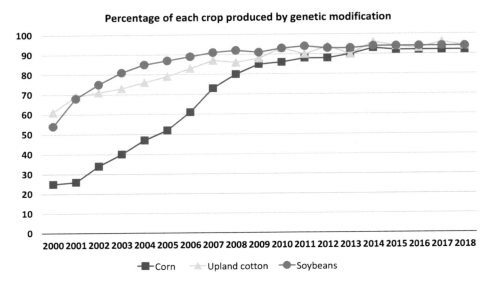

Figure 5.14 Genetically modified crops in the United States.
Source: ISAAA 2017.

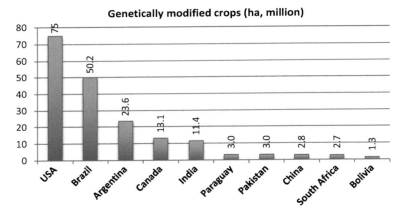

Figure 5.15 Top ten countries with genetically modified crops.
Source: ISAAA 2017.

content; lower naturally occurring toxicants; or the ability to produce medicines (USDA n.d.). To date, however, the genetic modifications have focused on insect and herbicide resistance (NAS 2016). The use of GM crops has expanded rapidly in the United States (Figure 5.14) and is centered on three crops in particular: corn, cotton, and soybeans, although much smaller crop initiatives include alfalfa, canola, sugar beets, potatoes, apples, squash, and papaya (ISAAA 2017). The use of GM crops has spread to many other nations and the top ten countries ranked by million hectares (ha) planted are shown in Figure 5.15 (ISAAA 2017).

Despite the widespread adoption of GM crops in Canada, the United States, Argentina, Brazil, and Argentina, there has been significant hesitancy about this new technology in much of Europe (WHO 2014). While European countries generally allow the importation of GM crops, most of the major agricultural producers have banned their cultivation (*New Scientist* 2015). The doubts are fostered by the unknown potential long-term detrimental effects on food supply, birds, insects, human health, and the genetic diversity of crops. The central issue is the application of the precautionary principle. Despite the extraordinary promise of this technology, several red flags have been raised. These include findings that genetic modification has not accelerated crop yield or led to an overall reduction in the use of chemical pesticides (*New York Times* October 29, 2016), and that there appears to be a decrease in wild bee abundance and pollination in fields with GM crops compared to fields containing conventional and organically produced crops (Morandin and Winston 2006).

Of particular concern is the emerging dominance in the field of GM crops of a few large agribusinesses. While these large entities are engaged in the legitimate pursuit of profit, it is essential that private benefits accruing to these corporations are compatible with social welfare. A case study of this potential divergence is provided by Monsanto, one of the world's largest producers of GM seeds and now a subsidiary of Bayer Corporation. Over the years, Monsanto gained a highly unfavorable reputation because of some of its products and its aggressive pursuit of small farmers in the court system whenever it thought its business model was under threat (Robin 2008; Barlett and Steele 2008; Thacker 2019). Society faces a difficult ethical choice between protecting corporate profits and the corporate practice of seeking, and often receiving, patent protection of products that are variants of those long considered part of the public domain. This is particularly critical in the realm of global food supply. Does the future security of food depend on increasing control by private corporations or the traditional model of open access?

A case in point is Monsanto's infamous "terminator" seeds, which are sterile and therefore farmers are forced to buy seeds from the company every year. This development marked a radical transformation of the millennium-old model of farmers using their own seed to sow the following year's crops. Monsanto's corporate record undoubtedly contributed to its eventual demise as a separate corporate entity. During the process of assuming control over Monsanto, Bayer's chief executive candidly admitted that "Monsanto's image does of course represent a major challenge for us, and it's not an aspect I wish to play down" (Reuters April 28, 2017). All of these developments suggest that society has not invested the time or resources required to truly consider all the ramifications of the direction in which the agricultural sector is heading.

Water

This chapter has already enumerated the multiple ways that agriculture leads to the contamination of surface water and groundwater due to the intensive use of fertilizers, pesticides, and herbicides. A crucial consideration is the essential role played by freshwater resources in agricultural production (Briscoe et al. 2009; UN ESCAP 2013; FAO 2003, 2015, and 2020a). In many parts of the world, supplies of water, whether from rivers or groundwater, are becoming insufficient to maintain current levels of food production (Rosa et al. 2020). Oxfam (2011) has projected that global demand for water will increase by 30 percent by 2030 and the OECD (2012b, p. 9) suggested, in a classic understatement, that "the growth and intensification of agricultural production could further heighten regional pressures on water systems in some countries." Jain et al. (2021) conclude that in India, the world's largest consumer of groundwater, given current depletion trends, cropping intensity may decrease by 28 percent nationwide and by 67 percent in groundwater-depleted regions, threatening the food security of millions of people.

In the United States, for example, competition among crops and between agriculture and urban areas for water has led to a threat to the continued viability of the Ogallala Aquifer, which sustains much of the water used for crops in the Midwest (Little 2019; Parker 2016). In parts of California, massive water withdrawals from aquifers have led to large areas of subsidence, destroying millions of dollars' worth of infrastructure (*Guardian* November 28, 2015; *New York Times* May 25, 2021). Herrera-Garcia et al. (2021) report that 19 percent of the global population may face a high probability of subsidence. Jasechko and Perrone (2021) analyzed construction records for thirty-nine million globally distributed wells and found "that millions of wells are at risk of running dry if groundwater levels decline by only a few meters." (See also Famiglietti and Ferguson 2021). Another threat to a major source of water for agriculture comes from climate change and the overuse of river water. Both the Rio Grande and the Colorado rivers have experienced a significant diminution in their flows after massive withdrawals of water over the past few decades(Udall and Overpeck 2017; Fountain 2018; *New York Times* March 19, 2019; *Guardian* February 20, 2020; Fleck and Udall 2021; *Science* July 1, 2021) and Mexico has lost most of its traditional flow from the latter (*Guardian* October 21, 2019). In addition, climate-induced drought has led to the lowest water levels in history in Lake Mead, the reservoir behind the Hoover Dam, which feeds the Colorado River (ABC News June 10, 2021; *The Hill* June 18, 2021). In mid-August 2021, the US Bureau of Reclamation issued its first ever declaration of a "tier 1" shortage for Lake Mead, forcing water cuts across those western states drawing water from the Colorado River (*Guardian* August 16, 2021). The water in Lake Mead is at 35 percent capacity, the lowest it has been since it was created in the 1930s.

Modern and intensive irrigation systems have both benefits and costs. Irrigation allows agricultural production where none could otherwise occur, increased crop yield, and multiple cropping in a year, and broadens the array of crops which can be grown in an area. Despite these benefits, irrigation has serious drawbacks, including the fact that it can raise the water table, increasing waterlogging which progressively salinizes the soil. This can lead to a gradual decline in crop production through lower yields and elimination of salt-intolerant crops such as wheat. Recent research by Kang and Eltahir (2018, p. 1) in Northern China has also identified another unanticipated effect of irrigation. The authors concluded that the:

> North China Plain is the heartland of modern China. This fertile plain has experienced vast expansion of irrigated agriculture which cools surface temperature and moistens surface air, but boosts integrated measures of temperature and humidity, and hence enhances intensity of heatwaves. Here, we project based on an ensemble of high-resolution regional climate model simulations that climate change would add significantly to the anthropogenic effects of irrigation, increasing the risk from heatwaves in this region. Under the business-as-usual scenario of greenhouse gas emissions, North China Plain is likely to experience deadly heatwaves with wet-bulb temperature exceeding the threshold defining what Chinese farmers may tolerate while working

outdoors. China is currently the largest contributor to the emissions of greenhouse gases, with potentially serious implications to its own population: continuation of the current pattern of global emissions may limit habitability in the most populous region of the most populous country on Earth.

The long-term impact of climate change on global food production is discussed in Chapter 6.

A central issue in the use of water in the agricultural sector revolves around the concept of the water footprint of various food products, whether crops (Hoekstra and Chapagain 2007; Mekonnen and Hoekstra 2011; Chapagain et al. 2005) or domesticated animals (Mekonnen and Hoekstra 2012). Figure 5.16 summarizes the water footprint of selected crops (Hoekstra and Chapagain 2007). The variation among crops raises two related issues: first, the real cost of these crops when water use is considered and, second, the appropriate location for the production of these crops, independent of political and economic distortions in the form of subsidies, quotas, and tariffs. Economic theory states that when a price of a good or service does not reflect its full social cost, too much of that product will be produced. If the product is an intermediate good, then its incorrect price will distort the mix of inputs used in production, as well as the choice of products to be produced. Water pricing, particularly by corporations in the developing world, is a highly contentious ethical issue, not the least because water is essential for human survival. In parts of the developed world water has been available for free or has been significantly underpriced, leading to market distortions and resulting inefficiencies. This is particularly the case in the US West with increased competition for limited water supplies among farming, ranching, and urban consumption (Unruh and Liverman n.d.).

An additional concept is "virtual water," which measures the embodied flow of water incorporated in the international trade in goods. Chapagain and Hoekstra (2008) have estimated that total embodied water in internationally traded commodities averages 16 percent of total global water consumption. The importance of this concept is apparent

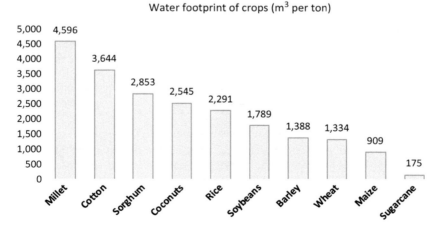

Figure 5.16 Water footprint of crops.
Source: Hoekstra and Chapagain 2007.

in those cases where water–intensive crops are produced in countries that are water poor and shipped to countries with larger supplies of fresh water. These hidden costs represent a de facto subsidy from exporting to importing nations. Depending on the relative wealth of the trading partners, this may be considered one of the ethical issues currently affecting international trade between the developing and developed world.

Energy consumption

Modern industrial agriculture is both a consumer and producer of energy products (see Figure 5.17; Hitaj and Suttles 2016). The consumption is inexorably tied to the massive use of energy resources for field preparation and seeding, harvesting, processing, heating, and lighting. In addition to these direct uses of energy products, oil and natural gas are essential feedstocks for fertilizers and agricultural chemicals such as pesticides. The extreme dependence of this sector on energy products has prompted several authors to characterize modern agriculture as *Eating Oil* (Green 1978) or *Eating Fossil Fuels* (Pfeiffer 2006). (See also Pelletier et al. 2011 and Camargo et al. 2013). As a consequence, this sector is the second largest global producer of GHGs such as carbon dioxide and nitrous oxide, following electricity and heat production by only one percentage point (see Figure 1.5). Clark et al. (2020) conclude that global food system emissions could preclude achieving

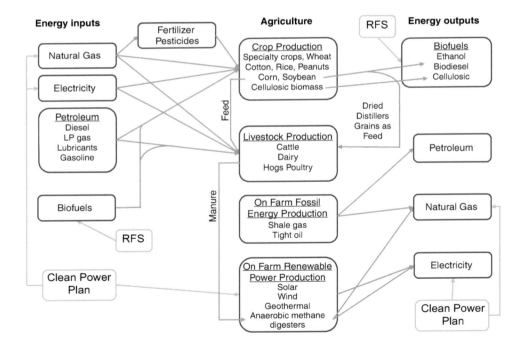

RFS = Renewable Fuel Standard.
Source: USDA, Economic Research Service.

Figure 5.17 Agriculture and energy.
Source: Hitaj and Suttles 2016.

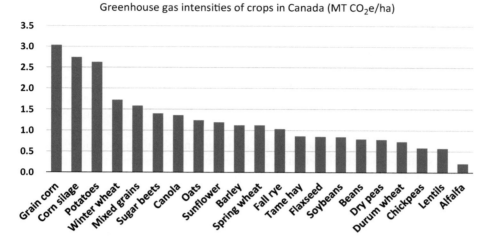

Figure 5.18 Greenhouse gas intensities of Canadian crops.
Source: Desjardins et al. n.d.

the 1.5°C and 2°C climate change targets. In its role as a major producer of GHGs, agriculture is both a contributor to and victim of global warming, and this latter issue is the focus of Chapter 6. The carbon footprint of field-grown products of the agricultural sector varies markedly by crop, as illustrated in Figure 5.18 (Desjardins et al. n.d.).

One the earliest and most insightful studies of energy use in the US food system was written by John and Carol Steinhart in 1974. Graphs in their article showed: (1) the trend in energy use in the food system compared to the caloric content of food consumed over the period 1940–70, (2) farm output as a function of energy input to the US food system over the period 1920–70, (3) the energy subsidy to the food system needed to obtain one food calorie, and (4) energy subsidies for various food crops. Two clear messages emerged from their research: first, energy subsidies varied markedly by food product, ranging from a low for wet rice cultivation in East Asia to a high associated with feedlot beef production in the United States; and second, over that period, there was a clear and marked declining marginal productivity to the continued increase in energy inputs. A similar study was performed by Pimental et al. (1973) focusing on corn as an archetypal agricultural crop in the United States. The authors found declining energy efficiency of corn production (measured by kilocalorie (kcal) return/kcal input) over the period 1945 to 1970. These two studies raise the interesting question of whether these trends have continued since that time.

Recent exhaustive research on trends in energy productivity in the agricultural sector focuses on energy input per dollar of output (Miranowski 2005). While extremely useful, these time series are not directly comparable to the results generated by Steinhart and Steinhart and Pimental since the monetary value of agricultural output can be influenced by numerous extraneous factors such as subsidies, tariffs, quotas, and other market imperfections.

Another comprehensive study funded by the European Union (Gołaszewski et al. 2012) has examined the energy efficiency of numerous agricultural products in six countries: Finland, Germany, Greece, Netherlands, Poland, and Portugal. While finding significant differences among these countries, the study was cross-sectional and no time series data were presented.

There is at least one time series study that addresses this issue. Swanton et al. (1996) examined corn and soybean crops over the period 1975 to 1991 in the Canadian province of Ontario. They found a trend of increasing energy efficiency in both crops, and attributed these results to improved crop breeding for more stress tolerance and genetic gain. Despite these somewhat encouraging findings, McMichael (2017 p. 273) concludes: "Current industrial agriculture has high immediate productivity, but very low levels of energy efficiency and resilience; it uses 10–15 units of input energy to produce one energy-unit of food."

The agricultural sector is also a significant player in the production of selected energy products such as biodiesel and ethanol. The particular issues associated with these types of products are addressed in Chapter 9, which focuses on renewable energy resources.

While total energy consumption in the US agricultural sector has remained relatively constant over the last few decades due to increases in productivity following the adoption of new technology, it is expected that the global output of one specific high energy and environmentally intense agricultural commodity, namely livestock, will continue to increase in lockstep with the increasing affluence of many countries of the developing world.

Livestock and meat production

The production of livestock imposes one of the most diverse and intensive burdens upon the environment. Its effects are felt in habitat change, land degradation, intensive water use and pollution, crop diversion for meat production, GHG production, as well as threats to biodiversity and human health (FAO 2007). The total biomass of global livestock exceeds that of the entire human population by a factor of two-thirds (Bar-On et al. 2018).

The scale of the problem

Figure 5.19 (FAO 2007) presents a graphic illustration of the relationship between living standards and meat consumption. As living standards continue to climb in much of the developing world, traditional foods such as seafood and rice have been supplemented by an increasing taste for first-world food staples, especially chicken and beef. Figures 5.20a and b track changes in demand for food products in both urban and rural China over the period from 1990 to 2010 (National Bureau of Statistics of China 2015). While grains and vegetables continued to dominate the diet in both geographic regions, there was a noticeable shift to a greater consumption of meat, reflecting the changes in taste accompanying a rising standard of living in both rural and urban areas. Even incremental changes in diet can have profound effects when spread over a population of 1.25 billion people. More recent research (Bai et al. 2018) indicates that this trend has continued, if not accelerated, in the last decade with its concomitant impact on the environment. McKinsey (2018) has reported that the past ten years has witnessed a marked increase in the demand for meat globally. Almost half of this comes from China (*Guardian* December 5 2015). Figure 5.21 presents Chinese projections for domestic meat consumption to 2029 (China 2020).

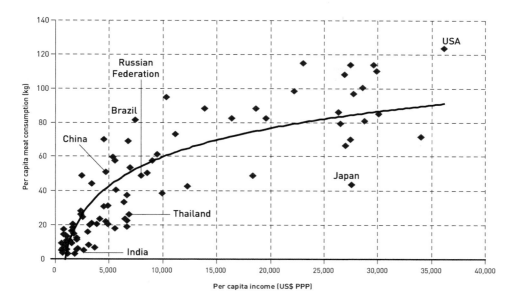

Note: National per capita based on purchasing power parity (PPP).

Figure 5.19 Meat consumption and per capita income.
Source: FAO 2007.

This shift in diet is not confined to China and is reflected in the growing number of farm animals at the global level. As Monbiot (2015) has stated: "Human numbers are rising at roughly 1.2% a year, while livestock numbers are rising at around 2.4% a year. By 2050 the world's living systems will have to support about 120m tonnes of extra humans, and 400m tonnes of extra farm animals." Recent estimates of global livestock numbers from the Food and Agriculture Organization (FAO 2018) of the United Nations include: 22.7 billion chickens, 1.47 billion cattle, 1.24 billion ducks, 1.17 billion sheep, and 1.0 billion goats. Figure 5.22 presents FAO historical and projected meat production in both developed and developing countries to 2050 (FAO 2007, p.15).

Fossil fuel use and greenhouse gases

The production of meat for human consumption is very energy intensive and, as a consequence, plays a major role in anthropogenic GHG emissions (FAO 2007; Pew Commission 2008; McMichael et al. 2007; UK CCC 2018). The livestock sector accounts for 18 percent of global GHG releases, representing a higher share than transportation (FAO 2007; Greenpeace 2020; and see Jackson et al. 2020 and Frank et al. 2019). In addition to the ecological impact of meat production, the dairy sector makes a significant contribution to GHG emissions. One researcher claims that these emissions exceed some of the major international mining and fossil fuel companies (Sharma 2020). Viewing the animal production system as a whole, these GHGs include carbon dioxide, methane, ammonia, and nitrous oxide. David Pimentel of Cornell University has been one of the most prolific

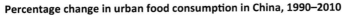

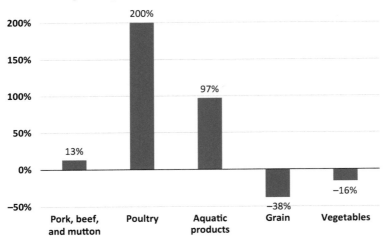

Percentage change in urban food consumption in China, 1990–2010

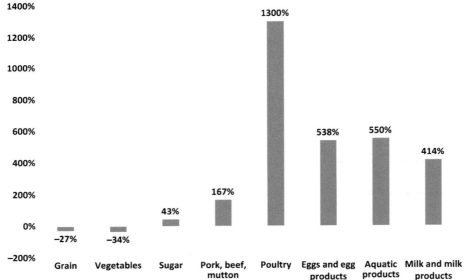

Percentage change in rural food consumption in China, 1978–2010

*Figure 5.20*a and b China urban and rural diet changes.
Source: National Bureau of Statistics of China 2015.

researchers on the environmental burden of the agricultural sector. In his research on
fossil fuel requirements, he has found:

On average, animal protein production in the U.S. requires 28 kilocalories (kcal)
for every kcal of protein produced for human consumption. Beef and lamb are the

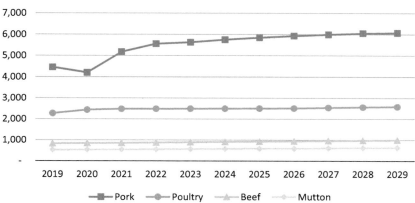

Figure 5.21 Chinese meat consumption projections.
Source: China 2020.

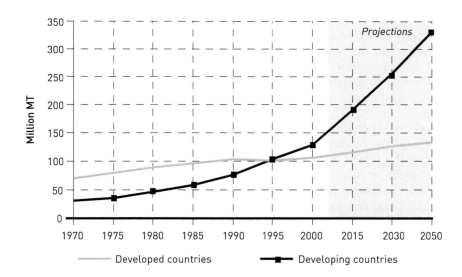

Figure 5.22 Trends in global meat consumption.
Source: FAO 2007.

most costly, in terms of fossil fuel energy input to protein output at 54:1 and 50:1, respectively. Turkey and chicken meat production are the most efficient (13:1 and 4:1, respectively). Grain production, on average, requires 3.3 kcal of fossil fuel for every kcal of protein produced.

(*Cornell Chronicle* August 7, 1997)

In a somewhat tongue-in-cheek assessment, Jamais Cascio (n.d.) created a cheeseburger footprint as a variant of carbon footprinting. His study used detailed data on energy use in the food sector—codeveloped by Stockholm University and the Swiss Federal Institute of Technology—to construct an approximate picture of the magnitude of the GHGs associated with this ubiquitous American product. His research concluded that "the greenhouse gas emissions arising every year from the production and consumption of cheeseburgers is roughly the amount emitted by 6.5 million to 19.6 million SUVs. There are now approximately 16 million SUVs currently on the road in the U.S." Supporting evidence for this informal calculation has been provided in a report from the Center for International Forestry Research (Kaimowitz et al. 2004) entitled "Hamburger connection fuels Amazon destruction."

Land-use changes

According to the FAO (2007, p. xxi):

> The livestock sector is by far the single largest anthropogenic user of land. The total area occupied by grazing is equivalent to 26 percent of the ice-free terrestrial surface of the planet. In addition, the total area dedicated to feedcrop production amounts to 33 percent of total arable land. In all, livestock production accounts for 70 percent of all agricultural land and 30 percent of the land surface of the planet. Expansion of livestock production is a key factor in deforestation, especially in Latin America where the greatest amount of deforestation is occurring—70 percent of previous forested land in the Amazon is occupied by pastures, and feedcrops cover a large part of the remainder. About 20 percent of the world's pastures and rangelands, with 73 percent of rangelands in dry areas, have been degraded to some extent, mostly through overgrazing, compaction and erosion created by livestock action.

Global forest loss, especially in the developing world, has reached epidemic proportions within the last few decades (Nepstad et al. 2006; the Global Forest Watch website, globalforestwatch.org; Curtis et al. 2018; *New York Times* April 25, 2019). These losses have occurred in Southeast Asia, Africa, and Latin America. Brazil is one of the most prominent examples of deforestation, and this has been driven largely by agricultural requirements for pasture for cattle farming for beef and leather as well as farmland for crops such as soybeans, a major source of food for livestock (Morton et al. 2006; Nepstad et al. 2006; Barona et al. 2010; Cederberg et al. 2011; *Guardian* July 2, 2019 and November 17, 2021; *New York Times* November 18 and 19, 2021; Brasil Ministerio da Ciencia, Tecnologia e Inovacoes 2021). Brazil is the world's largest exporter of soybeans and among the top three exporters of beef after the United States and Australia. Recent efforts within Brazil to control the rate of deforestation are being undermined by the 2018 election of a right-wing president devoted to continued exploitation of the Amazon's resources (*New York Times* July 28, 2019; *Guardian* July 3 and August 1, 2019).

A life-cycle analysis of the carbon footprint of the Brazilian beef industry by Cederberg et al. (2011) includes the effects of land-use changes in the calculations. The result is a much more pessimistic assessment of the overall climatic effect of this industry. To quote:

> Expansion of cattle ranching for beef production is a major cause of deforestation in the LAR (Legal Amazon Region). The carbon footprint of beef produced on

newly deforested land is estimated at more than 700 kgCO$_2$-equivalents per kg car-cass weight if direct land use emissions are annualized over 20 years. This is orders of magnitude larger than the figure for beef production on established pasture on non-deforested land. While Brazilian beef exports have originated mainly from areas outside the LAR, i.e. from regions not subject to recent deforestation, we argue that increased production for export has been the key driver of the pasture expansion and deforestation in the LAR during the past decade and this should be reflected in the carbon footprint attributed to beef exports. We conclude that carbon footprint standards must include the more extended effects of land use changes to avoid giving misleading information to policy makers, retailers, and consumers.

(p. 1773)

This is an excellent example of the type of systems analysis required to create an accurate assessment of the carbon footprint of all anthropogenic activities, not just agricultural.

Water use and water pollution

The livestock sector accounts for more than 8 percent of global human water use, prin-cipally for irrigation of feed crops (FAO (2007). Mekonnen and Hoekstra (2012) have produced an extensive assessment of the water footprint of farm animal products (see Table 5.2). They have found that the production of animal products represents almost one-third of total water use in the agricultural sector and that this footprint is consid-erably larger than that associated with crop products. For example, they found that the average water footprint per calorie for beef is twenty times that for cereals and starchy

Table 5.2 Water footprint of selected animal products

Product	Farming system	Total (m³ of water/ton product)
Beef	Grazed	21,829
	Mixed	15,712
	Industrial	10,244
	Weighted average	15,415
Mutton and lamb	Grazed	16,311
	Mixed	8,335
	Industrial	5,623
	Weighted average	10,412
Pork	Grazed	8,724
	Mixed	6,226
	Industrial	5,225
	Weighted average	5,988
Chicken	Grazed	9,370
	Mixed	4,987
	Industrial	2,873
	Weighted average	4,325

Source: Data extracted from Mekonnen and Hoekstra 2012.

roots. The principal reason for this discrepancy is the unfavorable feed conversion efficiency for animal products.

Livestock has major negative impacts on water quality from several sources: grazing, feedlots, and processing. The FAO produced a comprehensive report on the environmental effect of livestock under the title *Livestock's Long Shadow: Environmental Issues and Options* (2007; see also FAO 2013a). With respect to water, they concluded:

> In the United States sediments and nutrients are considered to be the main water-polluting agents. The livestock sector is responsible for an estimated 55 percent of erosion and 32 percent and 33 percent, respectively, of the N [nitrogen] and P [phosphorus] load into freshwater resources. The livestock sector also makes a strong contribution to water pollution by pesticides (37 percent of the pesticides applied in the United States), antibiotics (50 percent of the volume of antibiotics consumed in the United States), and heavy metals (37 percent of the Zn [zinc] applied on agricultural lands in England and Wales).
>
> (p. 167)

Table 5.3 summarizes their findings. The waste streams from meat processing operations are shown in Figure 5.23 (FAO 2007). Perhaps the most insidious effects of livestock production flow from the use of feedlots and the questionable economics used to justify their utilization.

Feedlots

As of 2019, there were 30,320 feedlots in the United States. While 85.8 percent of these have fewer than 1,000 head per feedlot, feedlots with more than 1,000 head account for 81 percent of all cattle on feed (NCBA 2016). Feedlots have been in existence for the last few decades and are designed to feed and slaughter large numbers of livestock within one confined location. The rationale is lower economic cost due to economies in feeding and processing. Unfortunately, there are several major negative externalities which call into question the economic case for their continued existence (UCS 2008; Kirby 2010; Genoways 2014; Lymbery and Oakeshott 2014). The first problem is the concentration and disposal of waste products, particularly urine and feces. It has been estimated that feedlots produce about 65 percent of the manure from all American animal operations. The estimated quantity of three hundred million tons per year is twice that produced by the country's entire human population (UCS 2008). Because of its high nutritional, chemical, and bacterial content, this waste must be contained on site, either stored in large manure piles, which pose a risk of runoff and leaching, or stored in large lagoons. This presents serious challenges for containment as any untoward escape into the environment can lead to the eutrophication of water bodies, with their attendant effect on flora and fauna, as well as the spreading of pollution to downstream water supplies, posing a potential threat to human health. A graphic example of these risks was provided by the effects of Hurricane Florence on North Carolina's hog waste lagoons in 2018. Estimates suggest that upwards of 110 lagoons in the state released pig manure into the environment (*New York Times* September 19, 2018). The *New York Times* reported that North Carolina has 9.7 million pigs, which produce 10 billion gallons of manure annually, mostly on large-scale farms. Stored manure can also lead to airborne pollution such as ammonia, which can cause increased rates of respiratory disease in local communities (UCS 2008).

Table 5.3 Livestock's Long Shadow: Summary on water

Water use			
Drinking and servicing water		Global	0.6% of water use
		United States	1% of water use
		Botswana	23% of water use
Meat and milk processing, tanning		Global	0.1% of water use
Irrigated feed production (excluding forage)		Global	7% of water use
Water depletion			
Water evaporation by feed crops (excluding grassland and forage)		Global	15% of water evapotranspired in agriculture
Nutrient contamination	Nitrogen	Thailand (pig waste)	14% of nitrogen (N) load
		Vietnam (pig waste)	38% of N load
		Guangdong, China (pig waste)	72% of N load
		United States	3% of N load
	Phosphorus	Thailand (pig waste)	61% of phosphorus (P) load
		Vietnam (pig waste)	92% of P load
		Guangdong, China (pig waste)	94% of P load
		United States	32% of P load
Biological contamination		N.A.	
Antibiotic consumption		United States	50% of antibiotics consumed
Pesticide (for corn and soybean as feed) applied		United States	37% of pesticides applied
Erosion from agricultural land		United States	55% of erosion process
Heavy metals applied	Zinc	England and Wales	37% of zinc applied
	Copper	England and Wales	40% of copper applied

Source: UN FAO 2007.

A potentially much more serious problem emerges from the unique ecological issues associated with feedlot structure and management—the widespread use of antibiotics in these facilities. A recent research study detected airborne bacteria with antibiotic-resistant genes downwind of feedlots in Texas (McEachran et al. 2015). Antibiotics are widely used in the industry for both growth promotion and disease control. In the latter case, antimicrobials are used to counteract natural forces that increase the likelihood of bacterial infection in animals due to artificially high stocking density in a feedlot environment. Mathematical epidemiological models of disease spread (Anderson and May 1979; May and Anderson 1979) identify density as one of the critical determining factors in the development of epidemics, their spread, and endurance. There is strong evidence that one of the major causes of emerging bacterial resistance to antibiotics is overuse of these pharmaceuticals in livestock (AAM 2002; FAO 2007; FAO, WHO, and OIE 2008; Hawkey and Jones 2009; Mellon et al. 2001; Neyra et al. 2012; Pereira et al. 2014; Tang et al. 2017; Davis et al. 2011; Pew Commission 2008; US HHS 2010; Hall et al. 2018; OIE-WOAH 2018).

The reason that antibiotic use in the production of livestock for food is so important is because of its potential negative effect on human health. The practice of medicine was

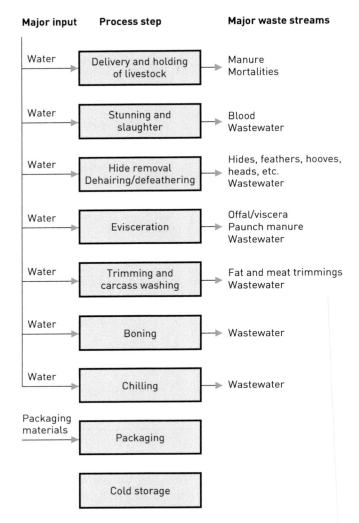

Figure 5.23 Meat processing flow diagram.
Source: FAO 2007.

changed dramatically with the introduction of antibiotics during and after the Second World War. Prior to that time, infectious bacterial diseases were responsible for a large share of mortality. By way of illustration, Figure 5.24 shows the changing face of mortality in the United States over the last century (US NCHS mortality data). The principal causes of death today in the industrialized world are cancer and cardiovascular diseases such as heart disease and stroke. The advent of antibiotics revolutionized modern medicine by permitting a broad range of procedures such as orthopedic surgery, transplantation, and cancer treatments. As Hall et al. (2018, pp. 2, 9) state: "a lack of effective antibiotics could effectively end much of modern medicine," plunging us back into an era "when a scratch could kill" (see also CCA-CAC 2019; Kwon and Powderly 2021).

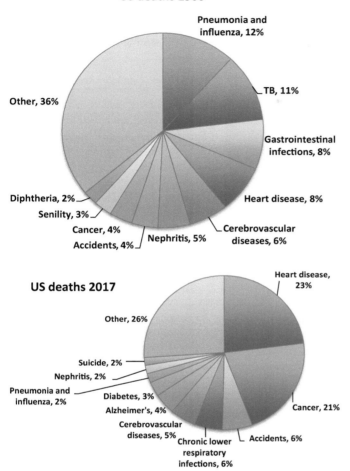

Figure 5.24 US deaths 1900 versus 2017.
Source: US NCHS mortality data.

The reason for this concern is the emergence of antibiotic-resistant bacteria and their impact on the incidence of morbidity and mortality (*New York Times* November 13, 2019). Several causes have been advanced to explain this phenomenon. The first is the overuse of antibiotics in human health, either through inappropriate prescribing or the incorrect use of these drugs by patients. In some countries, such as Mexico and Kenya, these drugs are available over the counter (*New York Times* October 17, 1988 and April 7, 2019). The inappropriate use of antibiotics facilitates the emergence of bacterial resistance through the process of Darwinian selection. The second cause is linked inexorably to the widespread use of antibiotics in the agricultural sector for the same reasons as pertain to humans. In fact, agricultural use of these drugs may account for as much as 80 percent of all prescriptions in North America (Slaughter 2011), although this number has been disputed because of the absence of comprehensive data. Nevertheless, the use of antibiotics in agriculture is expected to increase rapidly in such countries as Brazil, Russia, India, and China (Boeckel et al. 2015). The same mechanisms of natural selection apply here as well. The problem is compounded by the fact that many of the antibiotics used for the treatment of livestock are the same drugs used in human medicine (NRDC 2016; US FDA 2016). The CDC (2013) reported that the estimated costs of antibiotic resistance in the United States may be as high as $55 billion per year (2008 dollars).

Figure 5.25 illustrates how antibiotic resistance emerges and spreads to the human population (US CDC 2013). Recent research has found antibiotics in sewage, streams, groundwater, aquatic fauna, and drinking water sources and antibiotic-resistance genes in estuarine environments (Miller et al. 2019; Parnanen et al. 2019; Hendriksen et al. 2019; Givens et al. 2016; Casado et al. 2019; Aarestrup and Woolhouse 2020; Guo et al. 2020). Antibiotic-resistant bacteria have been found in fish and meat in the United States, Canada, and the United Kingdom (CBC News March 15, 2019; *New York Times* April 16, 2013; EWG 2013; *Guardian* January 15, 2018; Jorgensen et al. 2016). Antibiotic resistance is accelerated whenever animals, including humans, are exposed to subtherapeutic doses of antibiotics which are, by definition, insufficient to kill all the bacteria in an infected animal. This permits the survival of the subset of bacteria with resistance. A disturbing trend has been the emergence of several strains of bacteria that are resistant to all or virtually all classes of antibiotics (Hall et al. 2018). Some of this resistance is facilitated by horizontal gene transfer between bacteria (Bello-Lopez et al. 2019). In recent years, few new antibiotics have been discovered as the research incentives have changed for the pharmaceutical industry (WHO 2019a and b). With an aging population, it is more economically attractive to devote research funds to the development of drugs that treat long-lasting chronic conditions (Hall et al. 2018).

The threat to population health is so severe that several national and international bodies have raised the alarm: the United Kingdom (O'Neill 2016); the Council of Canadian Academics (CCA-CAC 2019); the US CDC (2013); the World Health Organization (WHO 2017b), the United Nations (IACG 2019); the World Bank (2017); and a special high-level committee convened by the UK government (UK Review on Antimicrobial Resistance 2016). This committee estimated that there are at least seven hundred thousand deaths per year attributable to drug-resistant infections and that this figure may rise to as high as ten million by 2050 unless serious remedial measures are undertaken (see also AACC 2016.) Hall et al. (2018) estimate that the current number of deaths that can be attributed to antimicrobial resistance could be as high as 1.5 million people. In 2017, the US FDA banned the use of antibiotics for growth promotion, but their use for prophylactic and therapeutic purposes continues in the United States (*New York Times* May 25, 2018). Despite the concern over the widespread use of antibiotics in livestock expressed by both national and international agencies, the industry has continued to promote their use, although they are much more guarded in their terminology. For example, in one pamphlet entitled "Pig Zero" distributed at a swine industry trade show, the pharmaceutical company that published it (*New York Times* June 7, 2019) recommended feeding antibiotics to pigs on a daily basis as a prophylactic and only incidentally mentioned that the pigs have a "3.5 lb heavier final weight" on the recommended drug regimen (Elanco 2018). This is all in the face of WHO recommendations (2017a):

We recommend an overall reduction of all classes of medically important antimicrobials in food-producing animals; (2) we recommend complete restriction of use of all

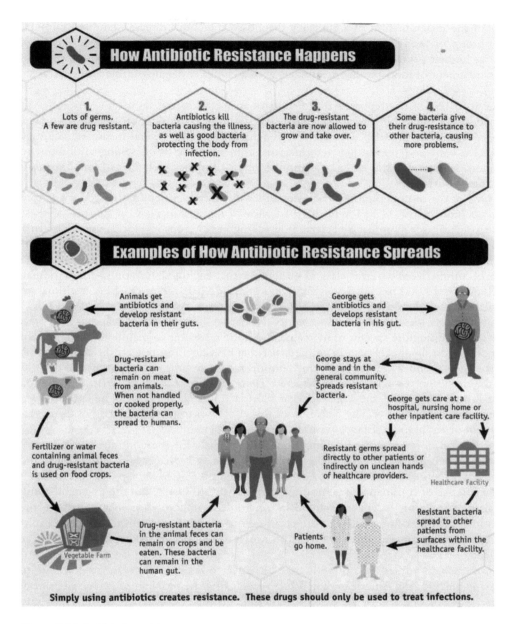

Figure 5.25 Antibiotic resistance.
Source: US NCHS 2013.

classes of medically important antimicrobials in food-producing animals for growth promotion; (3) we recommend complete restriction of use of all classes of medically important antimicrobials in food-producing animals for prevention of infectious disease that have not yet been clinically diagnosed; (4) we suggest that antimicrobials classified as critically important for human medicine should not be used for control of the dissemination of a clinically diagnosed infectious disease identified within a group of food-producing animals; and (5) we suggest that antimicrobials classified as highest priority critically important for human medicine should not be used for treatment of food-producing animals with a clinically diagnosed infectious disease.

Aarestrup (2012) has reported that Denmark managed to cut its use of antibiotics by 60 percent while achieving a 50 percent increase in pork production (see also *New York Times* December 6, 2019). This result was achieved through several measures including selective bans and preventing veterinarians from profiting from selling antibiotics to farmers. Transferring this latter regulation to other countries such as the United States is a contentious issue.

One of the most egregious misuses of antibiotics in the agricultural sector arises from the decision of the US EPA in 2019 to allow a massive increase in the use of these pharmaceuticals to combat a bacterium attacking citrus crops in Florida and California. The EPA decided to allow up to 650,000 pounds of streptomycin and oxytetracycline to be sprayed on crops on an annual basis. To put this in perspective, the total annual US use of aminoglycosides, the class of antibiotics that includes streptomycin, for human medicine is 14,000 pounds (*New York Times* May 17, 2019). The US EPA decision was vehemently criticized by both the US Food and Drug Administration and the CDC. Unfortunately, these drugs are also used to combat syphilis, tuberculosis, and urinary tract infections, raising the specter of increased antibiotic resistance in mainline drugs used for major human illnesses. It can be argued that this EPA decision reflects the reorientation of the agency under the former Trump administration towards a focus on private benefits to the exclusion of social costs. A *New York Times* article of August 16, 2019 reported on research findings from the University of Florida (Li et al. 2019) that the spraying was deemed to be ineffective. The net result of this effort was to further the risk of the development of antibiotic resistance with no appreciable benefit.

A critical question emerges concerning the rationale for the continued existence of feedlots given the magnitude of the threat they pose to human health both locally and globally. A report by the Union of Concerned Scientists (UCS 2008, p. 1) concludes that the existence of confined animal feeding operations (CAFOs) is "not the inevitable result of market forces; it has been fostered by misguided public policy." They attribute the continued existence of feedlots to direct subsidies for pollution control and indirect subsidies to grain farmers, which are passed through to feedlots in the artificially low price of feed.

Others have argued that there is no alternative to feedlots if we are to continue to provide meat for the American diet. While recognizing the problem of externalities from these types of operations, the gist of the argument for maintenance of the status quo is based on the theory of risk-risk trade-offs. Simply stated, this theory states that any action or policy to curtail or prevent the use of a product or technology that is motivated by the desire to reduce potential risks—invoking the precautionary principle—must be tempered by the consideration of the risks associated with abandoning or not adopting such technology. Clearly enunciated in a book by Graham and Wiener (1997) entitled *Risk vs. Risk: Tradeoffs in Protecting Health and the Environment*, the theory has been applied to several case studies by other authors. Marchant and Mossman (2005) examine the use of the precautionary principle in the European Union courts, focusing, by way of example, on the use of antibiotics in animal feed. This is a controversial subject that has received a large degree of scientific scrutiny. The position advanced by Marchant and Mossman is that discontinuing the use of these drugs in current modes of livestock production poses a greater threat than their continued use because of the increased chances that human consumers will be exposed to a greater level of bacteria from the food production system. This risk–risk trade-off is part of a generic argument that presumably could apply in other cases where the precautionary principle is being considered.

There is a logical fallacy with the argument advanced in this particular case study because of an incorrect definition of system boundaries. In essence, the argument is that the current system of livestock production achieves significant economic efficiencies but has some inherent risks that require offsetting actions such as the use of antibiotics. Cessation of this preventative measure will expose consumers to the inherent system risk. The implicit assumption—and logical pitfall—is that the current system of meat production is a given, and that no other alternatives are possible or economically desirable. If one expands the range of alternatives to include grass-fed, integrated crop–livestock systems (ICLSs) or smaller scale production systems rather than CAFOs, then a comprehensive life-cycle systems analysis that recognizes and incorporates all externalities might suggest that the feedlot system is less economically efficient from a societal perspective than the alternatives. The major study of the hidden costs of feedlots by the Union of Concerned Scientists (2008, p. 1) focuses on market distortions which tilt the simple economics trade-offs in favor of CAFOs. To quote:

> alternatives are at a competitive disadvantage because CAFOs have reduced their costs through subsidies that come at the public's expense, including (until very recently) low cost feed. CAFOs have also benefited from taxpayer supported pollution cleanup programs and technological "fixes" that may be counterproductive, such as the overuse of antibiotics. … Subsidies have included payments to grain farmers that historically supported unrealistically low animal feed prices, and payments to CAFOs to prevent water pollution.

The logical conclusion is that any situation with a potential risk–risk trade-off should be considered on a case-by-case basis with a clear delineation of the appropriate system boundaries to avoid the logical inconsistencies inherent in too narrow an analysis of alternatives.

It should be noted that the emerging threat of antibiotic resistance resulting from factory farming in the United States is not the only pathogenic threat to society. A report by a nongovernmental organization (NGO), Compassion in World Farming (2007, p. 2), states that "the development of highly pathogenic strains of bird flu lies at the door of factory farming … An intensive poultry farm provides the optimum condition for viral mutation and transmission. … Intensive farming is creating highly virulent flu strains." Historically Chinese farmers have lived in close proximity to poultry and animals and, with the increase in rapidly conducted international trade, new and deadly mutant strains of influenza can move around the globe in a matter of days (Harrison 2012). Similar breeding grounds for swine flu have been found in intensive pig farms in North Carolina (*Science* March 7, 2003), and such viruses have the potential to move across species and pose a direct threat to human health (Willyard 2019).

In sum, the extent of negative externalities associated with agricultural production is immense, and a comprehensive effort to cost these effects presents a monumental challenge. Nevertheless, two studies have generated initial estimates. Pretty et al. (2000,

p. 113) estimated total external costs of agriculture in the United Kingdom at £1.15–3.91 billion with the caveat that the study "has only estimated those externalities that give rise to financial costs, so is likely to underestimate the total negative impacts of modern agriculture." A comparable study for the United States (Tegtmeier and Duffy 2004, pp. 14, 16) estimated annual external costs at $5.7–16.9 billion. This study also comes with a serious caveat:

> these numbers are conservative, considering we are limited by the complexities of assigning monetary values to environmental and health impacts and the lack of related data. Comparing our findings with a more comprehensive list of agricultural externalities illustrates the incomplete nature of our national tally. . . . Furthermore, the estimates presented in this paper are conservative for reasons beyond the need for more valuation data. Many industrial agricultural practices present us with environmental risks that have unknown potential consequences. Potentialities are difficult to define because effects are diffuse in time and location. Some of these risks have been acknowledged scientifically but not necessarily politically.

One innovative initiative has been undertaken within a market context to at least incrementally move the sector away from its current unsustainable path. FAIRR (2019) has developed a Protein Producer Index which analyzes the largest global meat, dairy, and aquaculture producers by combining nine environmental, social, and governance risk factors with the Sustainable Development Goals of the United Nations (UN). The purpose of this index is to create a benchmark which can be a resource for institutional investors and other organizations interested in reassessing their relationship with the livestock sector. While only a small step towards sustainability, it can act as a bridging mechanism while more systematic solutions are identified and applied in practice (*Guardian* September 4, 2019b).

In sum, the modern industrial agricultural model has produced a bountiful harvest of food at low cost. This has come, however, with a panoply of significant negative externalities. An examination of one crop, in particular, presents a cogent illustration of the fundamental problems with this model from the perspective of sustainability.

Coffee—a case study in cultivating externalities

Coffee is one of the world's most popular beverages, with more than four hundred billion cups consumed each year (Coffee Facts n.d.). Total exports in 2018 reached a high of 169,063 thousand 60 kg bags with a value of $30.6 billion (ICO 2018c; WTEx 2019). Coffee is produced by more than four dozen countries in Africa, Asia, and Central and South America, and the sector employs more than twenty-five million people (Clay 2004). For some of these countries (Burundi, Colombia, Ethiopia, Guatemala, Honduras, Kenya, Nicaragua, Rwanda, Timor-Leste, and Uganda) coffee is either their most important export or among the top four major export earning commodities (UN 2017). Traditionally, Brazil has been the world's largest exporter (with 13.3 percent of global exports by value in 2017) but, within the last several decades, Vietnam has emerged as the second largest global exporter, accounting for 9.7 percent (ICO 2018a). While this beverage is consumed around the world, the European Union and the United States dominate global imports (with 39 percent and 23 percent respectively in 2018) (ICO 2018b).

Two principal species of coffee dominate global production and trade: arabica and robusta. They differ in taste, aroma, caffeine content, and disease resistance. Which type is more appropriate for cultivation depends on local differences in soil, insolation, moisture, slope, disease, and pests (Clay 2004). Over the last several years, the production of arabica has been slightly greater than that of robusta (with approximately a 60–40 split) (BaristaJoy 2021). The principal uses for these two types of coffee tend to differ, with robusta feeding the instant, flavorings, and mass-produced brands, while arabica finds a market in high-quality brands and specialty coffees (Clay 2004).

Coffee has been traditionally cultivated in what is referred to as a shade-grown production system characterized by the dominance of existing forest cover with a mix of plant species. Farmers tended to glean their income from this essentially polycultural environment from coffee and a mix of other plant products. A major change occurred in the 1970s with the acceleration in Brazil of a new production system, sun-grown, which is based on techniques developed in the green revolution (Fridell 2014). The conversion of shade-grown to sun-grown coffee has continued over the past few decades, largely driven by economic factors. While the costs of production are higher in the latter system, the yield is much greater, giving a higher overall return and cost advantage (de Graaff 1986).

There are major differences between the two principal production systems and these differences have a profound impact on the issue of sustainability. Sun-grown coffee essentially applies the green revolution, capital-intensive model of monocultural plantations with high planting densities, often as high as fifteen thousand trees per hectare (Clay 2004). Inherent in this agricultural system is the almost complete removal of forest cover accompanied by the intensive use of irrigation, fertilizers, pesticides, and herbicides. Donald (2004, p. 24) provides one strong reason for the emergence of this system:

> Intensification of production has, in most Latin American countries, been supported and encouraged by government, trade, and international aid organizations in a bid to raise production. Such support has been mediated largely through the provision of subsidies, many originating in the United States (the U.S. Agency for International Development has been a major supporter of the modernization of coffee production in Latin America).

One report (Rice 1998) stated that throughout Latin America as much as 40 percent of 6.5 million acres of coffee land had been converted to sun-grown systems. In Southeast Asia, virtually all coffee produced in Vietnam is sun-grown.

Not surprisingly, this industrial model of production entails significant negative externalities. One of the most important consequences is the massive loss of biodiversity (Gobbi 2000; Perfecto et al. 2005) among such diverse biota as trees and epiphytes, mammals, birds, reptiles, amphibians, and arthropods (Moguel and Toledo 1999; UNCTAD and IISD n.d.). In drawing a contrast between sun-grown and shade-grown coffee, a major report by the Smithsonian Migratory Bird Center (Rice and Bedoya 2010) reviewed more than fifty studies on biodiversity in shade-grown farms in Central and South America and Southeast Asia. Their conclusion was unequivocal:

> The Smithsonian Migratory Bird Center (SMBC) can now make the case that shade-grown coffee production is the next best thing to a natural forest, and put to rest any arguments about the sustainability of a sun-coffee system. In study after

study, habitat on shade-grown coffee farms outshone sun-grown coffee farms with increased numbers and species of birds as well as and [sic] improved bird habitat, soil protection/erosion control, carbon sequestration, natural pest control and improved pollination. While sun-grown systems can have higher yields, the shaded farms easily outperform them in sustainability measurements with the trees providing an array of ecological services that offer both direct and indirect "income/payback" to farmers and the environment. The "hidden yield" in the shade versus sun comparison is that of the non-coffee products and opportunities coming from the shaded system. In addition to ecotourism on several shade coffee farms, firewood, fruits, building materials and medicinal plants are all resources harvested to varying degrees by shade coffee farmers and used and/or sold by farmers.

(p. 1)

The list of negative externalities associated with sun-grown coffee is not limited to the loss of biodiversity. Other negative externalities include: significantly lower carbon sequestration in soils (UNCTAD and IISD n.d.), a high water footprint owing to the use of irrigation, increased susceptibility to disease such as leaf rust (Donald 2004; Fridell 2014), the requirement for nitrogen fertilizer to replace the nutrients normally produced by dead leaves from overstory trees and nitrogen-fixing legumes in shade-grown coffee farms, the requirement for herbicides for weeds found in much less abundance in shade-grown farms due to shade and mulch from fallen leaves, erosion of topsoil and leaching of chemicals into local water bodies, and soil acidification (Craves 2006). Coffee trees in full-sun plantations have productive lives of six to eight years in contrast to the eighteen to twenty-four years in a shade-grown system. This represents additional costs to the former as it necessitates replacing the growing stock much more frequently (Clay 2004). In addition, the tendency for an overreliance on a limited number of high-producing tree varieties raises the risk of a narrowing of the genetic stock. Recent research suggests that long-term coffee monoculture may not be sustainable for yet another reason. Zhao et al. (2018) found that over time, long-term monoculture of coffee reduced yields and resulted in serious economic losses in China because continuous cropping with this system of production decreased soil pH, organic matter content, and potentially beneficial microbes while increasing soil electrical conductivity, a measure of soil salinity.

In contrast to the ecological disadvantages of sun-grown coffee, research in Mexico (Jha and Dick 2008, p. R1126) has found that traditional coffee farms "maintain genetic connectivity with adjacent habitats and can serve as foci for forest regeneration," in essence promoting the genetic diversity of native trees.

In fact, shade-grown and full-sun cultivation are at opposite ends of a spectrum of production systems. Moguel and Toledo (1999) have described at least five different coffee production systems, which can be summarized (Craves 2006, pp. 1–2) as:

Rustic: Often used on small family farms. Coffee is grown in the existing forest with little alteration of native vegetation. Tree species are diverse, with an average of twenty-five species. Three or more shade strata (layers of vegetation). Shade cover is 70–100 percent.

Traditional polyculture: Coffee is grown under a combination of native forest trees and planted tree and plant species, including fruit and vegetables both for the farmer and for market, fuel wood, and medicinal plants, among others. Trees under which coffee is frequently grown include species of Inga, Grevillea, Acacia, Erythrina, and Gliricidia. Shade cover is 60–90 percent.

Commercial polyculture: More trees removed in order to increase the number of coffee plants, and shade is provided mostly by planted timber and fruit trees. Canopy trees are regularly pruned, and epiphytes are typically removed. More often involves use of fertilizers and pesticides due to the lack of vegetative cover which helps prevent loss of soil nutrients, etc. Typically only two vegetation layers, the canopy and the coffee. Shade cover is 30–60 percent.

Shaded monoculture: Dense plantings of coffee under an overstory of only one or two tree species (usually Inga), which are heavily pruned. Epiphytes are removed. Shade cover is 10–30 percent.

Full sun: Lacks a tree canopy, or has a few isolated trees. No shade cover.

While sun-grown coffee is usually considered "technified" in contrast to natural shade-grown systems, the existence of the multiple variants of production creates a more subtle distinction. As Rice (1998, p.2) states:

> Equating technification directly with sun coffee poses some problems, however. Certain countries, such as El Salvador, grow much of their coffee beneath a forestlike canopy. At the ground level, though, high-yielding varieties and agrochemicals dominate the production process, often with a good shade canopy composed of a single species. For this reason, it makes more sense to talk in terms of high-diversity/low-input versus low-diversity/high-input coffee farms when referring to traditional shade and technified (sun) coffee, respectively. "High diversity" refers to a rich mix of shade tree species that form the canopy in traditional coffee systems. "Low input" reflects the low levels of agro-chemicals used in producing the coffee. A technified farm, whether completely open to the sun or not, would have a low diversity of shade trees and be dependent upon high levels of chemical inputs.

Despite this more nuanced description of alternative farming systems, the fact remains that the coffee industry has undergone a massive transformation which has moved a significant proportion of its production towards a much less sustainable model with massive negative externalities. In classic economics, the standard remedy for such negative impacts is through the rubric of internalizing externalities, for example by increasing the price of inputs and other final products with negative environmental impacts, thereby forcing the producer to alter the production system, mix of inputs, or level of production in response to changing price signals. What is happening in the case of coffee is essentially the opposite and might be called *externalizing internalities*; unpriced externalities are generated where none existed before. The result, of course, is an artificially low price and high quantity of production of an unsustainable product, the price of which does not reflect its true social cost.

Despite this trend, there is some good news. Consumer attitudes and tastes are changing. There is an emerging, albeit still small, market for higher-quality, specialty coffees from shade-grown farms and frequently sold under the banner of organic or free trade coffee. Whether this will make an impact on the increasing demand for coffee (IndexBox 2019) remains to be seen however.

Table 5.4 Circular economy objectives, strategies, and practices in the agri-food industry

Objectives	Strategies	Practices
Reduced resource consumption	Eco-design	Agroecology
		Energy efficiency
		Zero waste grocery stores
		Zero waste grocery delivery
	Process optimization	Shorter supply chains
		Agrimetrics yield tracking
		Digital tracking of food waste
		Quality control
	Responsible consumption and procurement	Consumer awareness
		Sustainable food choices
		Discounting soon-expiring food
		Sustainable procurement
	Sharing economy	Cooperative supermarkets
		Food sharing
Extending life of products and components	Donating and reselling	Surplus food recovery
		Reappropriation of surplus food
	Performance economy	Meal subscription service
Giving resource new life	Industrial ecology	Agricultural industrial eco-park
	Recycling and composting	Green bins
		Nutrient recovery
		Reappropriation of food waste
	Energy recovery	Biogas and electricity
		Biofuel

Source: Smart Prosperity Institute 2021.

AGRICULTURAL EXTERNALITIES: ALTERNATIVE SOLUTIONS AND GENERAL CONCLUSIONS

The Smart Prosperity Institute has produced several *Circular Economy Sectoral Roadmaps* including one on the agri-food industry (2021). In this latest study on the application of circular economy principles, the Institute applies their analytical template to objectives, strategies, and practices in the agri-food industry. These are summarized in Table 5.4.

In summary, given the vast array and seriousness of the negative externalities generated by modern industrial agriculture, there is a strong case to be made that this production system is not sustainable. Gliessman (2015a) lists the central elements of modern industrial agriculture, many of which lead to unsustainable food production: intensive tillage, monoculture, application of synthetic fertilizers, extensive irrigation, chemical pest and weed control, manipulation of plant and animal genomes, and factory farming of animals. The negative consequences are numerous and include soil degradation, overuse of water and damage to hydrological systems, pollution of the environment, destruction of natural habitat, dependence on external inputs and nonrenewable resources, production of GHGs and loss of carbon sinks, loss of genetic diversity, loss of local control over agricultural production, increasing vulnerability and risk, and global inequality. Several major recent reports have emphasized these findings (Government Office for Science 2011; IPCC 2014; Lloyd's 2015; IPCC 2019).

There is a burgeoning literature suggesting numerous innovative approaches and changes which may alleviate some, but not all, of these problems (NRC 1989; Kimbrell

2002b; Filson 2004; Ribaudo 2005; UNCTAD and UNEP 2008; Pretty 2008; Wojtkowski 2008; Godfray et al. 2010; Foley 2011; Bello and Babatunde 2012; Tuomisto et al. 2012; Garnett et al. 2013; UCS 2013; Blandford et al. 2013; Godfray and Garnett 2014; Pimental and Burgess 2014; Godfray and Garnett 2014; Isaacson 2015; Rockstrom et al. 2017; Shennan et al. 2017; Seufert and Ramankutty 2017; Berners-Lee et al. 2018; Stanley et al. 2018; BBC *Science Focus Magazine* 2019; NAS 2019 and 2020b; Land Institute 2019; Handelsman 2021; Wittwer et al. 2021). The solutions include:

- Changing tillage methods
- Increasing the use of green and regular manure
- Changing from monoculture to mixed/interplanted systems and polyculture
- Moving from synthetic pesticides to integrated pest management
- Changing area irrigation systems to drip irrigation where possible
- Increasing the use of crop rotations and cover crops
- Growing crops only in ecologically appropriate areas
- Restricting the feeding of human-edible crops to animals
- Moving towards increased use of renewable energy, with the possible exception of current forms of biofuels (see Chapter 9)
- Increasing the use of kitchen and yard recycled material for composting
- Advancing research into perennial food crops
- Moving from feedlots with grain-fed livestock to grass-fed open range
- Use of intensive regenerative grazing and adaptive multi-paddock grazing
- Eliminating the use of antibiotics for growth promotion
- Reducing unnecessary subsidies and trade barriers to cut overproduction of certain commodities
- Promoting change in diets to healthier foods with less reliance on red meat
- Using price signals to internalize negative externalities so that price includes the social cost
- Increasing the use of organic farming where appropriate
- Adopting chain of ownership systems to track sources
- Pursuing research into artificial meat
- Increasing the use of third-party certification
- Devoting more resources to the reintroduction of greater biodiversity to reduce the recent historical trend to fewer more specialized phenotypes (e.g., Deb 2019)
- Applying principles from the circular economy literature in such areas as regenerative practices, designing out food waste, and creating transparent value chains (Gravis 2020)
- Assessing the potential for payment for ecosystem services in livestock-inclusive production systems (Silvestri et al. 2012)
- Adopting integrated crop-livestock systems (Peterson et al. 2020)

More detailed recommendations are found in NRC (1989) and Gliessman (2015a). In general, the organizing principle behind most of these recommendations, aside from fixing the economic problem of market failure, is to shift to a more resilient system of what is termed *agroecology*, which is based on the integration of ecological, social, and economic goals. Among these multifaceted goals are concern over social and economic equity, and recognition of the fundamental role of biodiversity and the serious deficiencies of monocultural systems of production (Altieri 1999; OECD 2012; Wijeratna

2012; DeLonge et al. 2016; Gliessman 2015a, b, and 2016; Rosset and Altieri 2017; Patel 2021).

In a report published in 2020, the UN FAO outlined the ten elements of agroecology (FAO 2020b, p.1) :

> What makes agroecology distinct?
> Agroecology is fundamentally different from other approaches to sustainable development. It is based on bottom-up and territorial processes, helping to deliver contextualized solutions to local problems. Agroecological innovations are based on the co-creation of knowledge, combining science with the traditional, practical and local knowledge of producers. By enhancing their autonomy and adaptive capacity, agroecology empowers producers and communities as key agents of change. Rather than tweaking the practices of unsustainable agricultural systems, agroecology seeks to transform food and agricultural systems, addressing the root causes of problems in an integrated way and providing holistic and long-term solutions. This includes an explicit focus on social and economic dimensions of food systems. Agroecology places a strong focus on the rights of women, youth and indigenous peoples.

The ten elements are:

> Diversity—Diversification is key to agroecological transitions to ensure food security and nutrition while conserving, protecting and enhancing natural resources.
>   Co-creation and sharing of knowledge—Agricultural innovations respond better to local challenges when they are co-created through participatory processes.
>   Synergies—Building synergies enhances key functions across food systems, supporting production and multiple ecosystem services.
>   Efficiency—Innovative agroecological practices produce more using less external resources.
>   Recycling—More recycling means agricultural production with lower economic and environmental costs.
>   Resilience—Enhanced resilience of people, communities and ecosystems is key to sustainable food and agricultural systems.
>   Human and social values—Protecting and improving rural livelihoods, equity and social well-being is essential for sustainable food and agricultural systems.
>   Culture and food traditions—By supporting healthy, diversified and culturally appropriate diets, agroecology contributes to food security and nutrition while maintaining the health of ecosystems.
>   Responsible governance—Sustainable food and agriculture requires responsible and effective governance mechanisms at different scales—from local to national to global.
>   Circular and solidarity economy—Circular and solidarity economies that reconnect producers and consumers provide innovative solutions for living within our planetary boundaries while ensuring the social foundation for inclusive and sustainable development.

Organic farming can be one of the components of agroecology, and concerns about possible lower yields in this type of farming compared to conventional farming have been addressed in a large meta-dataset assembled by Ponisio et al. (2015). They found that with the application of agroecological techniques such as multicropping, intercropping, and crop rotations, the organic–conventional yield gap is reduced or eliminated. Similar results have been reported from case studies in NRC (1989) and Altieri (2004). However, in those cases where yields from organic farming are lower, they are "usually more than offset by the advantage gained in reduced dependence on external inputs and an accompanying reduction in adverse environmental impacts" (Gliessman 2015a, p. 288).

Similar conclusions have been reached with respect to ICLSs. Peterson et al. (2020) conducted a meta-analysis of sixty-six studies and concluded that "annual cash crops in ICLS averaged similar yields (−7 percent to +2 percent) to crops in comparable non-integrated systems," (abstract). Gliessman (2015a) provides a more detailed discussion of the array of benefits flowing from ICLSs. These include producing protein-rich food and other products, putting crop residues and byproducts to use, returning nutrients to the soil in manure and compost, improving soil health, using animals to aid with cultivation and transport, managing vegetation and controlling weeds, increasing subsequent crop yields with rotation, and providing ecosystem services in the form of carbon sequestration, erosion control, maintenance of watershed health, and biodiversity protection (pp. 245–247). Gliessman quotes Clark (2004) who defines an integrated farm as one in which livestock are incorporated into farm operation "specifically to capture positive synergies among enterprises—to perform tasks and supply services to other enterprises—not just as a marketable commodity," (p. 242). In sum, Gliessman describes the "ecological complementarity" of livestock and forage plants.

> Plants feed animals, and animal excrement provides, in concentrated form, the nutrients plant require. Thus, an integrated system—as opposed to one that is merely diversified—harnesses this complementarity to move energy and nutrients between the crop component and the animal component. When animals are integrated into agroecosystems in this way, more of the ecosystem processes operating in natural systems can be incorporated into the functioning of the agroecosystem, increasing its resilience and sustainability.
>
> (p. 242)

A clear benefit associated with agroecology in contrast to modern industrial agriculture is the salutary impact on GHG emissions through reduced emissions and sequestration. Lin et al. (2011, p. 1) describe three ways in which reductions in GHGs are achieved in comparison to industrial agricultural systems:

> (1) a decrease in materials used and fluxes involved in the release of GHGs based on agricultural crop management choices; (2) a decrease in fluxes involved in livestock production and pasture management; and (3) a reduction in the transportation of agricultural inputs, outputs and products through an increased emphasis on local food systems.

One clear message that emerges from many of the studies on agriculture and sustainability is the necessity to lower the consumption of beef in global diets because of the magnitude of the environmental impact of its production. A recent study (Xu et al. 2021) has found that GHG emissions from animal-based foods are twice those of plant-based foods. One superficially bizarre recommendation that attempts to address this issue is the production and consumption of insects as a source of protein (Oonincx et al. 2010;

Belluco et al. 2013; Huis 2013; FAO n.d. b). Strange as this may sound, many groups already practice entomophagy, especially in developing nations (Ramos-Elorduy 2009). Although this concept would be unlikely to resonate in developed nations, the UN FAO (2013c, p. 2) concludes that entomophagy can be useful for three reasons:

Health

- Insects are healthy, nutritious alternatives to mainstream staples such as chicken, pork, beef, and even fish (from ocean catch).
- Many insects are rich in protein and good fats and high in calcium, iron, and zinc.
- Insects already form a traditional part of many regional and national diets.

Environmental

- Insects promoted as food emit considerably fewer GHGs than most livestock (methane, for instance, is produced by only a few insect groups, such as termites and cockroaches).
- Insect rearing is not necessarily a land-based activity and does not require land clearing to expand production. Most land is used for food production.
- The ammonia emissions associated with insect rearing are also far lower than those linked to conventional livestock, such as pigs.
- Because they are cold-blooded, insects are very efficient at converting feed into protein (crickets, for example, need twelve times less feed than cattle, four times less than sheep, and half as much as pigs and broiler chickens to produce the same amount of protein).
- Insects can be fed on organic waste streams.

Livelihoods (economic and social factors)

- The harvesting/rearing of insects, also known as minilivestock, is a low-tech, low-capital investment option that offers entry even to the poorest sections of society, such as women and the landless.
- Minilivestock offers livelihood opportunities for both urban and rural people.
- Insect rearing can be low-tech or very sophisticated, depending on the level of investment.

A more modern, mainstream concept known as smart farming has been advanced as a partial solution to the issue of agricultural externalities (IAEA 2021). It involves the application of modern information and communication technologies in agriculture. In particular:

> Following the plant breeding and genetics revolutions, this Third Green Revolution is taking over the agricultural world based upon the combined application of ICT [information and communications technology] solutions such as precision equipment, the Internet of Things (IoT), sensors and actuators, geo-positioning systems, Big Data, Unmanned Aerial Vehicles (UAVs, drones), robotics, etc.
>
> (SmartAKIS n.d., p. 1)

Despite its potential to reduce some of the negative externalities associated with modern agriculture, smart farming runs the risk of serving as a mere high-tech add-on to a system of industrial agriculture which is itself ultimately unsustainable.

An allied and somewhat broader term, "climate-smart agriculture" (CSA), involves a mixture of high tech and some principles of agroecology. The FAO (2021, p. 1) defines it as:

> an approach that helps to guide actions needed to transform and reorient agricultural systems to effectively support development and ensure food security in a changing climate. CSA aims to tackle three main objectives: sustainably increasing agricultural productivity and incomes; adapting and building resilience to climate change; and reducing and/or removing greenhouse gas emissions, where possible.

Both smart farming and CSA have been the subject of numerous articles and research studies by a diverse range of agencies and consultants describing both their theoretical contributions and actual achievements and challenges in the field (Braimoh 2014; McKinsey 2020a, b, and c; WEF 2020; World Bank 2021 and n.d. a; Rainforest Alliance 2020; FAO n.d. c; IAEA 2021; Terdoo and Adekola 2014; Chandra et al. 2017; Richards et al. 2019; IFAD 2011 and 2019). It should be noted that some concerns have been raised about the conceptualization and application of CSA (Lilliston 2015; IATP 2015a and b; Helllin and Fisher 2019; Idel and Beste 2020) focusing on potential trade-offs with some of the Sustainable Development Goals (SDGs) (i.e. SDG 1 no poverty, SDG 5 gender equality, and SDG 10 reduced inequalities), the appropriate role for soils in storing carbon, and the extensive role of big agribusiness. Hellin and Fisher (2019, p. 493) observe that:

> CSA efforts are targeted at climate change hotspots based on climate modelling. Less attention is paid to the heterogeneity of farmers and farming conditions in these hotspots, including the vulnerabilities of specific groups, or to how CSA relates to broader development challenges facing these farmers, which may be rooted in unequal power relations and entrenched inequalities. Many farmers have benefited from CSA but there is limited evidence that CSA adoption has enabled significant numbers of very poor farmers to escape poverty, even though it is the poor who are most impacted by climate change.

In some respects, components of both smart farming and CSA may not be compatible with the philosophy and practices of agroecology and may delay the comprehensive reorganization of agriculture to achieve sustainability across its three interrelated dimensions of ecology, economics, and society. Table 5.5 compares several key characteristics of natural ecosystems with sustainable agroecosystems and industrial agriculture (Gliessman 2015a, p. 288). Gliessman advances the following principle: "*the greater the structural and functional similarity of an agroecosystem to the natural ecosystems in its biogeographic region, the greater the likelihood that the agroecosystem will be sustainable*" (Gliessman's emphasis).

As stated earlier in this chapter, there is continuing controversy over the role of GM foods in guaranteeing future food supplies. Attitudes are country-specific and vary particularly between the United States and several European countries. Suffice it to say that at this moment it is unclear how this approach fits into the agroecological model.

The practice of agriculture aligned with ecological principles is not a new phenomenon. There are several civilizations in the ancient world that employed an agroecological

Table 5.5 Comparison of natural ecosystems with sustainable and industrial agroecosystems

Property	Natural ecosystems	Sustainable agroecosystems	Industrial agroecosystems
Production (yield)	Low	Low to high	High
Productivity (process)	Medium	Medium/high	Low/medium
Diversity	High	Medium	Low
Resilience	High	Medium	Low
Output stability	Medium	Low to high	High
Flexibility	High	Medium	Low
Human displacement of ecological processes	Low	Medium	High
Reliance on external human inputs	Low	Medium	High
Autonomy	High	High	Low
Interdependence	High	High	Low
Sustainability	High	High	Low

Source: Gliessman 2015a. Reproduced with permission.

Table 5.6 Ancient Chinese innovations in agriculture

Innovation	Earliest recorded use in China	European delay to adoption (years)
Row cultivation of crops and intensive hoeing	6th century BCE	2,200
Iron plow	6th century BCE	2,200
Efficient horse harness—trace	4th century BCE	500
Efficient horse harness—collar	3rd century BCE	1,000
Rotary winnowing fan	2nd century BCE	2,000
Multi-tube ("modern") seed drill	2nd century BCE	1,800

Source: Temple 2007.

approach which sustained their food supply for generations. Foremost among these are China and the Incan civilization of ancient Peru. Temple (2007) describes how several early Chinese agricultural practices and tools preceded their European introduction by anywhere from 500 to more than 2,000 years. Table 5.6 lists these innovations by first recorded dates of use in both China and Europe. Most of these advances were essential to the practice of an efficient and productive agricultural system. As Temple observes: "there was simply no comparison between the primitive and hopeless agriculture of Europe before the eighteenth century and the excellent and advanced agriculture of China after the fourth century BC" (pp. 19–20).

The ability of China to support its growing population over 7,000 years has been credited to a system of agriculture which was made both resilient and sustainable by integrating agricultural practices with an intimate knowledge of local ecology (Liu et al. 2011; Gong et al. 2003; IIED 2015). Central to this approach were pioneering techniques including use of legume crops for nitrogen fixation, organic manure, crop rotations, intercropping, use of diverse crop varieties to reduce vulnerability to pests and diseases, use of terraces in mountainous regions to prevent erosion and maximize the amount of land available for food production, irrigation engineering systems, rice seeding, transplant and greenhouse planting, and recycling of human and animal waste to maintain soil fertility.

One of the most important elements of this broad and diverse system of agriculture was the practice of intensive farming systems that combined crop growing, animal husbandry, and fisheries to form a "stable and yet structurally complex ecosystem [which] enables it to deliver services like natural pest control, sustainable high yield and ideal micro-climate conditions in a resource-efficient manner" (ANU 2013, p. 2).

The Chinese also pioneered the use of mixed species aquaculture (i.e. polyculture) as early as the Chou Dynasty from 1122 BCE (FAO n.d. a). For example, Wu (2016, p. 1) describes the benefits of raising fish in rice paddies as one common form of aquaculture: "the unique symbiotic rice–fish aquaculture system sees rice plants providing fish shelter from the sun and predators such as egrets, while fish fertilize the rice and eat the larvae and weeds that harm rice."

The definitive study of the vast array of innovative agricultural practices in ancient China was written by Joseph Needham (1984) in his monumental, multivolume account, *Science and Civilization in China*. Volume Six, coauthored with Francesca Bray and running to 724 pages, is almost exclusively devoted to the practice of agriculture. Needham observed that:

> It was Chinese farmers and economists too who laid the foundations of pedology or the science of soils, for many different kinds of soils are described in the *Yugong* chapter *Shujing* which can hardly be later than the early . . . 5th century B.C., as also in the *Guanzi*, which may be dated in the 4th B.C. By comparison we show how the Roman agriculturalists practically gave up the attempt to classify soil types. This is why we make so bold as to say that along with oecology and plant geography, pedology too was born in China.
>
> (Quoted in Gong et al. 2003, p. 12)

Needham describes in detail field systems, agricultural implements, techniques, and crop systems. Unfortunately, some of these principles and practices fell by the wayside in light of the apparent economic benefits of industrial agriculture in the modern world. More detail is provided in the section of this chapter devoted to pesticides, which describes how ancient Chinese agriculture was already employing the benign and sustainable practice of integrated pest management.

The Incan empire in Peru of 1438–1533 faced the challenge of changing climate and vastly different geoclimatic zones, including deserts, mountainous terrain, and river basins. Each zone required its own agricultural solution for the successful growing of food to feed an expanding empire. To achieve this goal, the Incans established living laboratories to test the viability and productivity of numerous crops in each locale. Using this form of agroecological experimentation allowed the Incas to develop more than 4,000 types of potatoes suitable to the diverse growing conditions the encountered. Most famous of these experimental laboratories is perhaps the Incan agricultural circles (Quechua *muyu*) found in the Sacred Valley between Cusco and Machu Picchu (see Figure 5.26). Each level of the circular terraces provided a different temperature and moisture gradient for crop testing.

Plachetka (2105) describes these terraces as a form of restorative ecology in the context of agroecology. And as Halloy and Seimon (2005, p. 1) state:

> High Andean cultures constitute one of the best examples of long-term, large scale experimentation in sustainable land use. The Central Andes have a temperate to cool

Figure 5.26 Inca agricultural circles.

climate and tubers are the crops grown at the highest altitudes, e.g., potato (possibly the highest altitude crop in the world), ulluco, oca and mashua. We compare the effect of a range of cultural elements in different regions on criteria of sustainability. Yields are lower than maximum yields obtained with intensive agriculture as there is a tradeoff between productivity, risk management, external subsidies and degradation. Key elements of Andean experimentation are: distributed research and development for hundreds to thousands of years, during which climates and cultures have changed dramatically; high native biodiversity; a culture of careful observation, selection, breeding, conservation and exchange of genetic varieties; and a knowledge inten- sive management strategy taking advantage of biodiversity and three-dimensional landscape, and cultural heterogeneity, maintaining a high temporal and spatial gamma diversity (dynamic turnover of crop diversity). These elements have led to the development of land use management strategies resilient to environmental variability.

Several ancient civilizations in Mesoamerica, such as the Maya and Aztecs, were also practicing elements of agroecology, some of which, such as intercropping or *milpa*, are still in use today (Miller et al. 2010; mayansandtikal.com 2021; Cartwright 2015; aztecsandtenochtitlan.com (n.d); Gliessman 2015b; Bittman 2021).

Finally, it is worth mentioning the emergence of indoor urban farms and vertical farms (Despommier 2009; Beacham et al. 2019) as possible solutions to the problems of field-grown crops. While there are some marginal contributions to food supply from such undertakings, there are several empirical and theoretical challenges. Specifically,

> closed-system urban farming based on electrically generated photosynthetic light would result in food production with high cost, large energy use, a giant carbon footprint and incompatibility with some forms of renewable energy.
>
> (Shackford 2014, p. 2)

And:

> Too often, farmers struggle to turn bumper crops of salad greens into sufficient revenue to keep the farm gates open. And those that do often have to prioritize ways to stay financially viable over achieving social goals.
>
> (Helmer 2019, p. 3)

A somewhat tongue-in-cheek characterization of the distinction between field-grown food and vertical farms might look as follows:

> **System A (field cultivation):** grow food on the land and put people in high-rises
> versus
> **System B (vertical greenhouses):** put people on the land and grow food in high-rises.

All of the potential remedial measures outlined above will be for naught if GHGs from other major sectors remain on their current track and global warming continues to increase. The most critical issue facing the future of global agriculture is the vulnerability of food production in the face of continuing climate change. This forms the subject of the following chapter.

References

AACC (American Association for Clinical Chemistry) (2016) "UN tackles drug-resistant infections," October 20.

AAM (American Academy of Microbiology) (2002) *The Role of Antibiotics in Agriculture*.

Aarestrup, Frank (2012) *Nature*, "Get pigs off antibiotics," June 28.

Aarestrup, Frank M. and Mark E.J. Woolhouse (2020) *Science*, "Using sewage for surveillance of antimicrobial resistance," February 7.

ABC News (2021) "Lake Mead hits lowest water levels in history amid severe drought in the West," June 10.

Aizen, M.A. et al. (2009) *Annals of Botany*, "How much does agriculture depend on pollinators: Lessons from long-term trends in crop production," June, 1579–88.

Alavanja, Michael C.R. (2009) *Reviews on Environmental Health*, "Pesticides use and exposure extensive worldwide," October–December.

Allsopp, M.H. et al. (2008) PloS One, "Valuing insect pollination services with cost of replacement," September.

Altieri, Miguel A. (1999) *Agriculture, Ecosystems and Environment*, "The ecological role of biodiversity in agroecosystems," 74: 19–31.

Altieri, Miguel A. (2004) *Genetic Engineering in Agriculture: The Myths, Environmental Risks, and Alternatives*, second edition, Oakland, CA: Food First Books.

Amundson, Ronald et al. (2015) *Science*, "Soil and human security in the 21st century," May 8.

Anderson, Roy M. and Robert M. May (1979) *Nature*, "Population biology of infectious diseases: Part I," August 2.

ANU (Australian National University) (2013) "Agri-environmental practices in ancient China." Student blog, June 4.

Arctic Council (2004) *Persistent Toxic Substances, Food Security and Indigenous Peoples of the Russian North*. Final report, November.

Arsenault, Chris (2014) *Scientific American*, "Only 60 years of farming left if soil degradation continues," December 5.

Aztecsandtenochtitlan.com (n.d.) "Aztec farming and agriculture."

Bai, Zhaohai (2018) *Science Advances*, "China's livestock transition: Driving forces, impacts, and consequences," July 18.

Bailey, Rob and Laura Wellesley (2017) "Chokepoints and vulnerabilities in global food trade," Chatham House, June 27.

Baker, N.T. and W.W. Stone (2015) *Estimated Annual Agricultural Pesticide Use for Counties of the Conterminous United States 2008–12*, United States Geological Survey.

Bao, Wei et al. (2019) *JAMA Internal Medicine*, "Association between exposure to pyrethroid insecticides and risk of all-cause and cause-specific mortality in the general US adult population," December 30.

Barber, Dan (2019) "Save our food. Free the seed," *New York Times*, June 9.

BaristaJoy (2021) "Arabica vs. robusta (the two types of coffee beans)," September 25.

Bar-on, Yinon et al. (2018) *PNAS*, "The biomass distribution on earth," June 19.

Barlett, Donald L. and James B. Steele (2008) "Monsanto's harvest of fear," *Vanity Fair*, May.

Barona, Elizabeth et al. (2010) *Environmental Research Letters*, "The role of pasture and soybean in deforestation of the Brazilian Amazon," April 16.

BBC (2018) "EU member states support near-total neonicotinoids ban," April 27.

BBC (2019) "Russia alarmed by large fall in bee populations," July 19.

BBC (2019) "Why 500 million bees have died in Brazil in three months," August 20.

BBC Science Focus Magazine (2019) "The artificial meat factory—the science of your synthetic supper," May 23.

Beacham, Andrew M. et al. (2019) *The Journal of Horticultural Science and Biotechnology*, "Vertical farming: A summary of approaches to growing skywards," February 14.

Bello, Segun R. and Balogun R. Babatunde (eds.) (2012) *Sustainable Agriculture: Challenges & Prospects*, Createspace.com.

Bello-Lopez, J. Manuel et al. (2019) *MDPI Microorganisms*, "Horizontal gene transfer and its association with antibiotic resistance in the genus *Aeromonas* spp.," September 18.

Belluco, Simone et al. (2013) *Comprehensive Reviews in Food Science and Food Safety*, "Edible insects in a food safety and nutritional perspective: A critical review," April.

Benbrook, Charles M. (2012) *Environmental Sciences Europe*, "Impacts of genetically engineered crops on pesticide use in the U.S.: The first sixteen years," December.

Benbrook, Charles M. (2016) *Environmental Sciences Europe*, "Trends in glyphosate use in the United States and globally," February 2.

Benton, Tim G. et al. (2021) "Food system impacts on biodiversity loss: Three levers for food system transformation in support of nature." Research paper, Chatham House, February.

Berners-Lee, M. et al. (2018) *Elementa Science of the Anthropocene,* "Current global food production is sufficient to meet human nutritional needs in 2050 provided there is radical societal adaptation," July 18.

Bhattacharyya, R. et al. (2017) "Nitrogen and soil quality," in Yash P. Abrol et al. (eds.) *The Indian Nitrogen Assessment: Sources of Reactive Nitrogen, Environmental and Climate Effects, and Management Options and Policies,* Amsterdam: Elsevier.

Bittman, Mark (2021) *Animal, Vegetable, Junk: A History of Food, from Sustainable to Suicidal,* New York: Houghton Mifflin Harcourt.

BJIM (*British Journal of Industrial Medicine*) (1985) "Health problems of pesticide usage in the third world," August, 505–6.

Blandford, David et al. (2013) *Eurochoices,* "Extensification versus intensification in reducing greenhouse gas emissions in agriculture: Insights from Norway," December.

Boeckel, Thomas P. van et al. (2015) *PNAS,* "Global trends in antimicrobial use in food animals," May 5.

Boulicault, Marion et al. (2021) *Human Fertility,* "The future of sperm: A biovariability framework for understanding global sperm count trends," March.

Braimoh, Ademola (2014) "What is climate-smart agriculture?" World Economic Forum.

Brasil Ministerio da Ciencia, Tecnologia e Inovacoes (2021) "Estimativa de desmatamento por corte raso na Amazonia legal papra 2021 e de 13.235 km2."

Breitburg, Denise (2018) *Science,* "Declining oxygen in the global ocean and coastal waters," January 5.

Briscoe, John et al. (2009) "Water and agriculture: Implications for development and growth," Paul H. Nitze School of Advanced International Studies and Center for Strategic and International Studies, November.

Brown, H. Claire (2021) "Attack of the superweeds," *New York Times Magazine,* August 22.

Bruckner, Selina et al. (2019) "Honey bee colony losses 2018–2019: Preliminary results," Bee Informed Partnership, June 19.

Calderone, Nicholas W. (2012) *PloS One,* "Insect pollinated crops, insect pollinators and US agriculture: Trend analysis of aggregate data for the period 1992–2009," May 22.

Calvert, Geoffrey M. et al. (2008) *American Journal of Industrial Medicine,* "Acute pesticide poisoning among agricultural workers in the US, 1998–2005," December.

Calvo-Agudo. Miguel et al. (2019) *PNAS,* "Neonicotinoids in excretion product of phloem-feeding insects kill beneficial insects," August.

Camargo, Gustavo G. et al. (2013) *BioScience,* "Energy use and greenhouse gas emissions from crop production using the farm energy analysis tool," April.

Canadian Press (2018) "Pesticides linked to death of the bees to be phased out of Canada within three years, sources say," August 24.

Cardinale, Bradley J. et al. (2012) *Nature,* "Biodiversity loss and its impact on humanity," June.

Carson, Rachel (1962) *Silent Spring,* Boston: Houghton Mifflin Harcourt.

Cartwright, Mark (2015) "Maya food & agriculture," World History Encyclopedia, April 24.

Casado, Jorge, (2019) *Science of the Total Environment,* "Screening of pesticides and veterinary drugs in small streams in the European Union by liquid chromatography high resolution mass spectrometry," June 20.

Cascio, Jamais (n.d.) "The cheeseburger footprint," www.openthefuture.com.docx

CBC News (2018) " 'Troubling allegations' prompt Health Canada review of studies used to approve popular weed-killer," November 11.

CBC News (2019) "Shrimp containing antibiotic-resistant bacteria found in Canadian grocery stores," March 15.

CBC News (2019) "Monsanto's Roundup under siege as courts award more damages against popular weed killer," May 14.

CCA-CAC (Council of Canadian Academies) (2019) *When Antibiotics Fail*, November 12.

CDC (Centers for Disease Control and Prevention) (2013) "Antibiotic resistance threats in the United States, 2013."

Ceballos, Gerardo et al. (2017) *PNAS*, "Biological annihilation via the ongoing sixth mass extinction signaled by vertebrate population losses and declines," July 10.

Cederberg, Christel et al. (2011) *Environmental Science & Technology*, "Including carbon emissions from deforestation in the carbon footprint of Brazilian beef," January 31.

CEH (Centre for Ecology & Hydrology) 2016 "New study: Neonicotinoid insecticides linked to wild bee decline across England."

Chandra, Alvin (2017) *World Development*, "A study of climate-smart farming practices and climate-resiliency field schools in Mindanao, the Philippines," October, 214–30.

Chapagain, Ashok K. and Arjen Y. Hoekstra (2008) *Water International*, "The global component of freshwater demand and supply: An assessment of virtual water flows between nations as a result of trade in agricultural and industrial products," March.

Chapagain, A.K. et al. (2005) *The Water Footprint of Cotton Consumption*, UNESCO-IHE Institute for Water Education, September.

Chaplin-Kramer, R. et al. (2019) *Science*, "Global modeling of nature's contributions to people," October 11.

China (1985) *Statistical Yearbook of China 1985*, Beijing: State Statistical Bureau.

China (2018) *Statistical Yearbook*, Beijing: China Statistics Press.

China (2020) *China Agricultural Outlook (2020–2029)*, Beijing: China Agricultural Science and Technology Press.

Chiu, Yu-Han (2017) *JAMA Internal Medicine*, "Association between pesticide residue intake from consumption of fruits and vegetables and pregnancy outcomes among women undergoing infertility treatment," October 30.

Chowdhary, Anuradha et al. (2013) *PloS Pathogens*, "Emergence of azole-resistant *Aspergillus fumigatus* strains due to agricultural azole use creates an increasing threat to human health," October.

Cirillo, Piera M. et al. (2021) *Cancer Epidemiology, Biomarkers, and Prevention*, "Grandmaternal perinatal serum DDT in relation to granddaughter early menarche and adult obesity: Three generations in the child health and development studies cohort," April 14.

Clark, E.A. (2004) "Benefits of re-integrating livestock and forages in crop production systems," in D. Clements and A. Shrestha (eds.) *New Dimensions in Agroecology*, Binghamton, NY: Food Products Press, pp. 405–36.

Clark, Edwin H. et al. (1985) *Eroding Soils, The Off-Farm Impacts*, Washington, DC: The Conservation Foundation.

Clark, Michael A. et al. (2020) *Science*, "Global food system emissions could preclude achieving the 1.5° and 2° climate change targets," November 6.

Clay, Jason (2004) *World Agriculture and the Environment: A Commodity-by-Commodity Guide to Impacts and Practices*, Washington, DC: Island Press.

CNRS News (2018) "Where have all the farmland birds gone?" April 19.

Codling, Eton (2011) "Environmental impact of residual lead and arsenic pesticides in soil," in Margarita Stoytcheva (ed.) *Pesticides in the Modern World: Risks and Benefits*, IntechOpen, pp. 169–80.

Coffee Facts (n.d.) "HowStuffWorks.com"

Compassion in World Farming (2007) "The role of the intensive poultry production industry in the spread of avian influenza," February.

Cornell Chronicle (1997) "U.S. could feed 800 million people with grain that livestock eat, Cornell ecologist advises animal scientists," August 7.

Crall, James D. et al. (2018) *Science*, "Neonicotinoid exposure disrupts bumblebee nest behavior, social networks, and thermoregulation," November 9.

Craves, Julie (2006) *Coffee & Conservation*, "What is shade-grown coffee?" February 6.

CTV (2020) "Bayer to pay up to US$10.9 billion to settle Monsanto case," June 24.

Curtis, Philip G. et al. (2018) *Science*, "Classifying drivers of global forest loss," September 14.

Davis, Donald R. et al. (2004) *Journal of the American College of Nutrition*, "Changes in USDA food composition data for 43 garden crops, 1950–1999," 23(6).

Davis, Frederick Rowe (2014) *Banned: A History of Pesticides and the Science of Toxicology*, New Haven, CT: Yale University Press.

Davis, Mark (2015) "Highly hazardous pesticides: Finding alternatives and reducing risk by 2020," International Institute for Sustainable Development, April 13.

Davis, Meghan F. et al. (2011) *Current Opinion in Microbiology*, "An ecological perspective on U.S. industrial poultry production: The role of anthropogenic ecosystems on the emergence of drug-resistant bacteria from agricultural environments," June.

De Graaff, J. (1986) *The Economics of Coffee*, Wageningen: Pudoc.

Deb, Debal (2019) "Restoring rice biodiversity," *Scientific American*, October.

Delabre, Izabela et al. (2021) *Science Advances*, "Actions on sustainable food production and consumption for the post-2020 global biodiversity framework," March 19.

DeLonge, Marcia S. et al. (2016) *Environmental Science & Policy*, "Investing in the transition to sustainable agriculture," 55: 266–73.

Desjardins, R.L. et al. (n.d.) "Carbon footprint of agriculture products—a measure of the impact of agricultural production on climate change." Presentation, Agriculture and Agri-food Canada.

Despommier, Dickson (2009) "The rise of vertical farms," *Scientific American*, November.

Dewi, Gusti Ayu and Veronica Argelis Gonzalez (2015) "Conserving traditional seed crops diversity." Brief for the UN's *Global Sustainable Development Report*, State University of New York College of Environmental Science and Forestry.

Diamond, Jared (2005) *Collapse: How Societies Choose to Fail or Succeed*, New York: *Penguin Books*.

Diaz, Robert J. and Rutger Rosenberg (2008) *Science*, "Spreading dead zones and consequences for marine ecosystems," August 15.

Donald, Paul F. (2004) *Conservation Biology*, "Biodiversity impacts of some agricultural commodity production systems," February.

Dudley, Nigel and Sasha Alexander (2017) *Biodiversity*, "Agriculture and biodiversity: A review," July 28.

Dunn, Frederick L. (1968) "Epidemiological factors: Health and disease in hunter-gatherers," in Richard B. Lee (ed.), *Man the Hunter*, Chicago: Aldine Publishing Co, 221–8.

EEA (European Environment Agency) (2012) *The Impacts of Endocrine Disruptors on Wildlife, People and Their Environments*. EEA Technical Report No. 2/2012.

Ehrenkranz, N. Joel and Deborah A. Sampson (2008) *Yale Journal of Biology and Medicine*, "Origin of the Old Testament plagues: Explications and implications," March.

Einarson, Murray D. and Douglas M. Mackay (2001) *Environmental Science & Technology*, "Water contamination," February 1.

Elanco (2018) "Pig Zero: Singling him out is never this easy."

Eng, Margaret L. et al. (2019) *Science*, "A neonicotinoid insecticide reduces fueling and delays migration in songbirds," September 13.

Environmental Defence (2005) *Toxic Nation: A Report on Pollution in Canadians*, November.

Erb, Karl-Heinz et al. (2018) "Unexpectedly large impact of forest management and grazing on global vegetation biomass," *Nature*, January 4.

EWG (Environmental Working Group) (2011) *Meat Eater's Guide to Climate Change + Health*, July.

EWG (Environmental Working Group) (2013) *Meat and Antibiotics: Meat Eaters Guide*.

FAIRR (2019) "Protein Producer Index 2019".

Famiglietti, James S. and Grant Ferguson (2021) *Science*, "The hidden crisis beneath our feet," April 23.

FAO (2003) *Agriculture Food and Water*.

FAO (2007) *Livestock's Long Shadow: Environmental Issues and Options*.

FAO (2011) *Global Food Losses and Food Waste.*

FAO (2013a) *Tackling Climate Change through Livestock.*

FAO (2013b) *World Apparel Fiber Consumption Survey.*

FAO (2013c) *Edible Insects: Future Prospects for Food and Feed Security.* FAO Forestry Paper 171.

FAO (2015) *Status of the World's Soil Resources.*

FAO (2017) *World Fertilizer Trends and Outlook.*

FAO (2019a) *Soil Erosion.*

FAO (2019b) *The State of Food Security and Nutrition in the World: Building Climate Resilience for Food Security and Nutrition.*

FAO (2019c) *The State of the World's Biodiversity for Food and Agriculture.*

FAO (2020a) *The State of Food and Agriculture 2020.*

FAO (2020b) *The 10 Elements of Agroecology: Guiding the Transition to Sustainable Food and Agricultural Systems.*

FAO (2021) *Climate-Smart Agriculture.*

FAO (n.d. a) "Framework for aquaculture development in China," in *The Study Tour and the People's Republic of China.*

FAO (n.d. b) *The Contribution of Insects to Food Security, Livelihoods and the Environment.*

FAO (n.d. c) "What is happening to agrobiodiversity?"

FAO, WHO, and OIE (2008) *Joint FAO/WHO/OIE Expert Meeting on Critically Important Antimicrobials: Report of the FAO/WHO/OIE Expert Meeting; FAO Headquarters, Rome, 26–30 November 2007.*

FAOSTAT, Food and Agriculture Organization database accessible on the fao.org website.

Filson, Glen C. (2004) *Intensive Agriculture and Sustainability: A Farming Systems Analysis*, Vancouver: UBC Press.

Fisher, Matthew C. et al. (2018) *Science*, "Worldwide emergence of resistance to antifungal drugs challenges human health and food security," May 18.

Fleck, John and Brad Udall (2021) *Science*, "Managing Colorado River risk," May 28.

FOEE (Friends of the Earth Europe) (2012) "UK faces annual bill of £1.8 billion without bees," April 11.

Foley, Jonathan (2013) *Ensia*, "It's time to rethink America's corn system," March 5.

Foley, Jonathan A. (2011) "Can we feed the world and sustain the planet?" *Scientific American*, November.

Foster, Leonard (2018) "Are bees really dying? Are we the cause or the solution?" Address to the Vancouver Institute, November 24.

Fountain, Henry (2018) "In a warming West, the Rio Grande is drying up," *New York Times*, May 24.

Frank, Stefan et al. (2019) *Nature Climate Change*, "Agricultural non-CO_2 emission reduction potential in the context of the 1.5°C target," January.

Fridell, Gavin (2014) *Coffee*, Cambridge: Polity Press.

Fry, D. Michael (1995) *Environmental Health Perspectives*, "Reproductive effects in birds exposed to pesticides and industrial chemicals," October 1.

Gallai, Nicola et al. (2009) *Ecological Economics*, "Economic valuation of the vulnerability of world agriculture confronted with pollinator decline," January 15.

Garnett, T. et al. (2013) *Science*, "Sustainable intensification in agriculture: Premises and promises," July 5.

Genoways, Ted (2014) *The Chain: Farm, Factory, and the Fate of Our Food*, New York; London: HarperCollins.

Gilburn, Ander S. et al. (2015) *PeerJ*, "Are neonicotinoid insecticides driving declines of widespread butterflies?" November 24.

Givens, Carrie E. et al. (2016) "Antimicrobial resistance in the environment." Presentation, United States Geological Survey, June 22.

Gliessman, Stephen R. (2015a) *Agroecology: The Ecology of Sustainable Food Systems*, third edition, Boca Raton, FL: CRC Press.

Gliessman, Steve (2015b) *Agroecology and Sustainable Food Systems*, "Agroecology: A growing field," November 17.

Gliessman, Steve (2016) *Agroecology and Sustainable Food Systems*, "Transforming food systems with agroecology," January 26, 187–9.

Gobbi, Jose A. (2000) *Ecological Economics*, "Is biodiversity-friendly coffee financially viable? An analysis of five different coffee production systems in western El Salvador," May.

Godfray, H. Charles and Tara Garnett (2014) *Philosophical Transactions of the Royal Society B*, "Food security and sustainable intensification," February 20.

Godfray, H. Charles et al. (2010) *Science*, "Food security: The challenge of feeding 9 billion people," February 12.

Gołaszewski, Janusz and Chris de Visser (2012) *State of the Art on Energy Efficiency in Agriculture, AgrEE*, European Union, January.

Gong, Zitong et al. (2003) *Geoderma*, "Origin and development of soil science in ancient China," 115:3–13.

Goolsby, Donald A. et al. (1997) *Environmental Science & Technology*, "Herbicides and their metabolites in rainfall: Origin, transport, and deposition patterns across the Midwestern and Northeastern United States, 1990–1991," 31(5).

Gore, A.C. et al. (2015) *Endocrine Reviews*, "The Endocrine Society's second scientific statement on endocrine-disrupting chemicals," December 1.

Gosden, Chris (2003) *Prehistory: A Very Short Introduction*, Oxford: Oxford University Press.

Gould, Fred et al. (2018) *Science*, "Sociobiological dilemma of pesticide resistance," May 18.

Goulet, Henri and Lubomir Masner (2017) *Biodiversity*, "Impact of herbicides on the insect and spider diversity in eastern Canada," July.

Goulson, Dave (2014) *Nature*, "Ecology: Pesticides linked to bird declines," July 12.

Government Office for Science (2011) *The Future of Food and Farming: Challenges and Choices for Global Sustainability*.

Graham, John D. and Jonathan Baert Wiener (eds.) (1997) *Risk vs. Risk: Tradeoffs in Protecting Health and the Environment*, Cambridge, MA: Harvard University Press.

Gravis, Lena (2020) *Building a Healthy and Resilient Food System*, Ellen MacArthur Foundation, May 27.

Green, Julia K. et al. (2019) *Nature*, "Large influence of soil moisture on long-term terrestrial carbon uptake," January 24.

Green, Maurice B. (1978) *Eating Oil: Energy Use in Food Production*, Boulder, CO: Westview Press.

Greenpeace (2020) *Farming for Failure*, September.

Guardian (2015) "The Central Valley is sinking: Drought forces farmers to ponder the abyss," November 28.

Guardian (2015) "China's cloned cows: Meat on the table or environmental disaster?" December 5.

Guardian (2017) "Arctic stronghold of world's seeds flooded after permafrost melts," May 19.

Guardian (2018) "British supermarket chickens show record levels of antibiotic-resistant superbugs," January 15.

Guardian (2019) "Monsanto must pay couple $2bn in largest verdict yet over cancer claims," May 13.

Guardian (2019) "Revealed: Rampant deforestation of Amazon driven by global greed for meat," July 2.

Guardian (2019) "Brazil: Huge rise in Amazon destruction under Bolsonaro, figures show," July 3.

Guardian (2019) "Trump administration to approve pesticide that may harm bees," July 12.

Guardian (2019) "Amazon deforestation: Bolsonaro government accused of seeking to sow doubt over data," August 1.

Guardian (2019a) "Germany to ban use of glyphosate weedkiller by end of 2023," September 4.

Guardian (2019b) "Global food producers 'failing to face up to role' in climate crisis," September 4.

Guardian (2019) "The lost river: Mexicans fight for the mighty river taken by the U.S.," October 21.

Guardian (2020) "Colorado River flow shrinks from climate crisis, risking 'severe water shortages'," February 20.

Guardian (2021) "Biggest US reservoir declares historic shortage, forcing water cuts across west," August 16.

Guerra, Carlos A. et al. (2020) *Landscape Ecology*, "Global vulnerability of soil ecosystems to erosion," March 10.

Gullickson, Gil (2017) *Successful Farming*, "Meet metabolic resistance," March 20.

Guo, Xing-pan et al. (2020) *Science of the Total Environment*, "Antibiotic resistance genes in biofilms on plastic wastes in an estuarine environment," July 18.

Hall, William et al. (2018) *Superbugs: An Arms Race against Bacteria*, Cambridge, MA: Harvard University Press.

Hallmann, Caspar A. et al. (2014) *Nature*, "Declines in insectivorous birds are associated with high neonicotinoid concentrations," July 17.

Hallmann, Caspar A. et al. (2017) *PLoS ONE*, "More than 75 percent decline over 27 years in total flying insect biomass in protected areas," October 18.

Halloy, Stephan Roland Pierre and Anton Seimon (2005) *Acta Horticulturae*, "Traditional Andean cultivation systems and implications for sustainable land use," April.

Halweil, Brian (2007) "Still no free lunch: Nutrient levels in U.S. food supply eroded by pursuit of high yields," The Organic Center, September.

Handelsman, Jo (2021) "How dirt could help save the planet," *Scientific American*, July.

Harrison, Mark (2012) *Contagion: How Commerce Has Spread Disease*, New Haven, CT: Yale University Press.

Hawkey, Peter M. and Annie M Jones (2009) *Journal of Antimicrobial Chemotherapy*, "The changing epidemiology of resistance," September.

Hellin, Jon and Eleanor Fisher (2019) *Nature Climate Change*, "The Achilles heel of climate-smart agriculture," July.

Helmer, Jodi (2019) HuffPost, "Urban farms are supposed to solve our food woes. The reality is not so simple," November 11.

Hendriksen, Rene S. et al. (2019) *Nature Communications*, "Global monitoring of antimicrobial resistance based on metagenomics analyses of urban sewage," March 8.

Herrera-Garcia, Gerardo et al. (2021) *Science*, "Mapping the global threat of land subsidence," January 1.

Hill (2021) "Lake Mead's decline points to scary water future in West," June 18.

Hitaj, Claudia and Shellye Suttles (2016) *Trends in U.S. Agriculture's Consumption and Production of Energy: Renewable Power, Shale Energy, and Cellulosic Biomass*, USDA Economic Research Service, Economic Information Bulletin, No. 159, August.

Hodgson, Dave et al. (2015) *Trends in Ecology and Evolution*, "What do you mean by resilience?" September.

Hoekstra, A.Y. and A.K. Chapagain (2007) *Water Resources Management*, "Water footprints of nations: Water use by people as a function of their consumption pattern," June 27.

HuffPost (2019) "EPA approves bee-killing pesticide after U.S. quits tracking vanishing hives," July 15.

HuffPost (2019) "Monsanto's spies," September 14.

Huis, Arnold van (2013*) Annual Review of Entomology*, "Potential of insects as food and feed in assuring food security," January.

IAASTD (International Assessment of Agricultural Knowledge Science and Technology for Development) (2008) "Context, conceptual framework and sustainability indicators."

IACG (Interagency Coordination Group on Antimicrobial Resistance) (2019) *No Time to Wait: Securing the Future from Drug-Resistant Infections*, Report to the Secretary-General of the United Nations, April.

IAEA (International Atomic Energy Agency) (2021) "Development of smart agriculture practices."

IATP (Institute for Agriculture and Trade Policy) (2015a) "Food system scholars and scientists pen second letter to FAO Director-General supporting agroecology," June 24.

IATP (Institute for Agriculture and Trade Policy) (2015b) "More than 350 organizations from around the world oppose greenwashing and false solutions of 'climate smart agriculture'," press release, September 21.

ICO (International Coffee Organization) (2018a) "Exports of all forms of coffee by all exporting countries, 1990–2017."

ICO (International Coffee Organization) (2018b) "World coffee consumption."

ICO (International Coffee Organization) (2018c) *Coffee Market Report,* December.

Idel, Anita and Andrea Beste (2020) *The Belief in Technology and Big Data: The Myth of Climate Smart Agriculture—Why Less Bad Isn't Good,* The Greens/EFA in the European Parliament.

IFAD (International Fund for Agricultural Development) (2011) *Climate-Smart Smallholder Agriculture: What's Different?* Occasional Paper 3.

IFAD (International Fund for Agricultural Development) (2019) *Opportunities, Challenges and Limitations of Climate-Smart Agriculture: The Case of Egypt,* June 21.

IIED (International Institute for Environment and Development) (2015) "Sustainable agriculture in China: Then and now," March 26.

IME (Institution of Mechanical Engineers) (2013) *Global Food: Waste Not, Want Not.*

IndexBox (2019) "World—coffee (green)—market analysis, forecast, size, trends and insights."

Inger, Richard et al. (2015) *Ecology Letters,* "Common European birds are declining rapidly while less abundant species' numbers are rising," January.

IPBES (Intergovernmental Science-Policy Platform on Biodiversity and Ecosystem Services) (2018) *Summary for Policymakers of the Thematic Assessment of Land Degradation and Restoration,* United Nations, March 24.

IPBES (Intergovernmental Science-Policy Platform on Biodiversity and Ecosystem Services) (2019) *Summary for Policymakers of the Global Assessment Report on Biodiversity and Ecosystem Services of the Intergovernmental Science-Policy Platform on Biodiversity and Ecosystem Services,* May 29.

IPCC (Intergovernmental Panel on Climate Change) (2014) *AR5 Synthesis Report: Climate Change 2014.*

IPCC (Intergovernmental Panel on Climate Change) (2019) *The Ocean and Cryosphere in a Changing World,* September 25.

ISAAA (International Service for the Acquisition of Agribiotech Application) (2017) "Global status of commercialized biotech/GM crops in 2017: Biotech crop adoption surges as economic benefits accumulate in 22 years." ISAAA Briefs, Brief 53.

Isaacson, Betsy (2015) "To feed humankind, we need the farms of the future today," Newsweek, October 22.

Jackson, R.B. et al. (2020) *Environmental Research Letters,* "Increasing anthropogenic methane emissions arise equally from agricultural and fossil fuel sources," July 15.

Jain, Meha et al. (2021) *Science Advances,* "Groundwater depletion will reduce cropping intensity in India," February 24.

Jasechko, Scott and Debra Perrone (2021) *Science,* "Global groundwater wells at risk of running dry," April 23.

Jeyaratnam, J. (1990) *World Health Statistics Quarterly,* "Acute pesticide poisoning: A major global health problem," 43(3): 139–44.

Jha, Shalene and Christopher W. Dick (2008) *Current Biology,* "Shade coffee farms promote genetic diversity of native trees," December 23.

Jones, Rena R. et al. (2016) *Environmental Health Perspectives,* "Nitrate from drinking water and diet and bladder cancer among postmenopausal women in Iowa," November 1.

Jorgensen, Frieda et al. (2016) *Antibiotic Resistance Report for FS241044,* Public Health England, September.

Kaimowitz, David et al. (2004) "Hamburger connection fuels Amazon destruction," Center for International Forestry Research.

Khoury, Colin K. et al. (2014) *PNAS,* "Increasing homogeneity in global food supplies and the implications for food security," March 18.

Kimbrell, Andre (ed.) (2002a) *Fatal Harvest: The Tragedy of Industrial Agriculture*, Washington, DC: Island Press.

Kimbrell, Andre (ed.) (2002b) *The Fatal Harvest Reader: The Tragedy of Industrial Agriculture*, Washington, DC: Island Press.

Kirby, David (2010) *Animal Factory*, New York: St. Martin's Press.

Klein, Alexandra-Maria et al. (2007) *Proceedings of the Royal Society B*, "Importance of pollinators in changing landscapes for world crops," February.

Kubsad, Deepika et al. (2019) *Scientific Reports*, "Assessment of glyphosate induced epigenetic transgenerational inheritance of pathologies and sperm epimutations: Generational toxicity," April 23.

Kwon, Jennie H. and William G. Powderly (2021) *Science*, "The post-antibiotic era is here," July 30.

Land Institute (2019) *Perennial Crops: New Hardware for Agriculture*.

Lavkulich, Les (2019) Personal communication.

Levine, Hagai et al. (2017) *Human Reproductive Update*, "Temporal trends in sperm count: A systematic review and meta-regression analysis," July 25.

Li, Tang (1995) "Shortest generation time," in T.J. Walker (ed.) *University of Florida Book of Insect Records*, Gainesville, FL: University of Florida.

Li, Yijia et al. (2020) *Nature Sustainability*, "Neonicotinoids and decline in bird biodiversity in the United States," December.

Lilliston, Ben (2015) "What's wrong with 'climate smart' agriculture?" Institute for Agriculture & Trade Policy, September 30.

Lin, Brenda B. et al. (2011) *CAB Reviews: Perspectives in Agriculture, Veterinary Science, Nutrition and Natural Resources*, "Effects of industrial agriculture on climate change and the mitigation potential of small-scale agro-ecological farms," July.

Little, Jane Braxton (2019) *Scientific American Earth 3.0*, "Saving the Ogallala Aquifer," June 3.

Liu, Yunhui et al. (2011) *Agriculture Ecosystems & Environment*, "Agricultural landscapes and biodiversity in China," January.

Losey, John E. and Mace Vaughan (2006) *BioScience*, "The economic value of ecological services provided by insects," April.

Lundgren, Jonathan G. and Jian J. Duan (2013) *BioScience*, "RNAI-based insecticidal crops: Potential effects on nontarget species," August.

Lymbery, Philip and Isabel Oakeshott (2014) *Farmageddon: The True Cost of Cheap Meat*, London: Bloomsbury.

MacPhail, Victoria J. et al. (2019) *Journal of Insect Conservation*, "Incorporating citizen science, museum specimens, and field work into the assessment of extinction risk of the American Bumble bee (*Bombus pensylvanicus* De Geer 1773) in Canada," April 17.

Mallory-Smith, Carol and Maria Zapiola (2008) *Pest Management Science*, "Gene flow from glyphosate-resistant crops," April 1.

Malthus, Robert (1798) *An Essay on the Principle of Population*, republished in New York by Penguin Classics, 2015.

Marchant, G. and K. Mossman (2005) *Arbitrary and Capricious: The Precautionary Principle in the European Union Courts*. Washington, DC: AEI Press.

May, Robert M. and Roy M. Anderson (1979) *Nature*, "Population biology of infectious diseases. Part II," August 9.

Mayansandtikal.com (2021) "Mayan agriculture."

McEachran, Andrew D. et al. (2015) *Environmental Health Perspectives*, "Antibiotics, bacteria, and antibiotic resistance genes: Aerial transport from cattle feed yards via particulate matter," April.

McFadyen, Rachel E. Cruttwell (1998) *Annual Review of Entomology*, "Biological control of weeds," January.

McKenna, Maryn (2021) "Deadly kingdom," *Scientific American*, June.

McKinsey (2018) "How the global supply landscape for meat protein will evolve," October.

McKinsey (2020a) "Agriculture and climate change: Reducing emissions through improved farming practices," April.

McKinsey (2020b) "Creating value in digital-farming solutions," October.

McKinsey (2020c) "Feeding the world sustainably," June.

McMichael, Anthony J. et al. (2007) *Lancet*, "Food, livestock production, energy, climate change, and health," September 13.

McMichael, Anthony J. et al. (2017) *Climate Change and the Health of Nations: Famines, Fevers, and the Fate of Populations*, New York: Oxford University Press.

McNeill, William H. (1998) *Plagues and People*, New York: Anchor Books.

Mekonnen, M.M. and A.Y. Hoekstra (2011) *Hydrology and Earth System Sciences*, "The green, blue and grey water footprint of crops and derived crop products," May.

Mekonnen, Mesfin M. and Arjen Y. Hoekstra (2012) *Ecosystems*, "A global assessment of the water footprint of farm animal products," 15: 401–15.

Mellon, Margaret et al. (2001) *Hogging It: Estimates of Antimicrobial Abuse in Livestock*. Cambridge, MA: Union of Concerned Scientists.

Mesnage, Robin et al. (2017) *Scientific Reports*, "Multiomics reveal non-alcoholic fatty liver disease in rats following chronic exposure to an ultra-low dose of Roundup herbicide," January 9.

Miller, Frederic P. et al. (2010) *Agriculture in Mesoamerica*, Mauritius: Alphascript Publishing.

Miller, Janet L. et al. (2020) *Science Advances*, "Common insecticide disrupts aquatic communities: A mesocosm-to-field ecological risk assessment of fipronil and its degrades in U.S. streams," October 23.

Miller, Thomas H. et al. (2019) *Environment International*, "Biomonitoring of pesticides, pharmaceuticals and illicit drugs in a freshwater invertebrate to estimate toxic or effect pressure," August.

Miranowski, John A. (2005) "Energy consumption in US agriculture," in J. Outlaw et al. (eds.) *Agriculture as a Producer and Consumer of Energy*, Wallingford: CABI Publishing.

Moguel, Patricia and Victor M. Toledo (1999) *Conservation Biology*, "Review: Biodiversity conservation in traditional coffee systems of Mexico," February.

Monbiot, George (2015) "There's a population crisis all right. But probably not the one you think," *Guardian*, November 19.

Montgomery, David (2007) *Dirt: The Erosion of Civilizations*, Berkeley, CA: University of California Press.

Morandin, Lora A. and Mark L. Winston (2006) *Agriculture Ecosystems & Environment*, "Pollinators provide economic incentive to preserve natural land in agroecosystems," September.

Morse, Roger A. and Nicholas W. Calderone (2000) "The value of honey bees as pollinators of U.S. crops in 2000," Cornell University.

Morton, Douglas C. et al. (2006) *PNAS*, "Cropland expansion changes deforestation dynamics in the southern Brazilian Amazon," September 26.

Motta, Erick V.S. et al. (2018) *PNAS*, "Glyphosate perturbs the gut microbiota of honey bees," October 9.

Nakhauka, Ekesa Beatrice (2009) International Journal of Biodiversity and Conservation, "Agricultural biodiversity and nutrient security: The Kenyan perspective," November.

NAS (National Academies of Sciences, Engineering and Medicine) (2016) *Genetically Engineered Crops: Experiences and Prospects*.

NAS (National Academies of Sciences, Engineering and Medicine) (2019) *Science Breakthroughs to Advance Food and Agricultural Research by 2030*, March.

NAS (National Academies of Sciences, Engineering and Medicine) (2020a) *A National Strategy to Reduce Food Waste at the Consumer Level*, October.

NAS (National Academies of Sciences, Engineering and Medicine) (2020b) *Building a More Sustainable, Resilient, Equitable, and Nourishing Food System: Proceedings of a Workshop—in Brief*, December 2.

National Bureau of Statistics of China (2015) *China Yearbook of Household Survey*, Department of Household Surveys, Beijing: China Statistics Press.

National Foundation for Infectious Diseases (n.d.) "What is antibiotic resistance?"

NCBA (National Cattlemen's Beef Associations) (2016) NCBA.org.webarchive.

Needham, Joseph (1984, 1986) *Science and Civilization in China*, Volume 6, parts 1 and 2, Cambridge: Cambridge University Press.

Nepstad, Daniel C. et al. (2006) *Conservation Biology*, "Globalization of the Amazon soy and beef industries: Opportunities for conservation," December.

New Scientist (2015) "More than half of EU officially bans genetically modified crops," October 5.

New York Times (1988) "Health care on the border: Poor go to Mexico," October 17.

New York Times (2013) "Report on U.S. meat sounds alarm on 'superbugs'," April 16.

New York Times (2014) "Genetic weapon against insects raises hope and fear in farming," January 27.

New York Times (2014) "Invader batters rural America, shrugging off herbicides," August 11.

New York Times (2015) "A decline in the nutritional value of crops," September 12.

New York Times (2016) "Broken promises of GM crops," October 29.

New York Times (2018) "Antibiotics in meat could be damaging our guts," May 25.

New York Times (2018) "Report finds traces of a controversial herbicide in Cheerios and Quaker Oats," August 15.

New York Times (2018) "Lagoons of pig waste are overflowing after Florence. Yes, that's as nasty as it sounds," September 19.

New York Times (2019) "Amid 19-year drought, states sign deal to conserve Colorado River water," March 19.

New York Times (2019) "Monsanto ordered to pay $80 million in Roundup cancer case," March 27.

New York Times (2019) "What you need to know about Candida auris," April 6.

New York Times (2019) "In a poor Kenyan community, cheap antibiotics fuel deadly drug-resistant infections," April 7.

New York Times (2019) "A respite from record losses, but tropical forests are still in trouble," April 25.

New York Times (2019) "Citrus farmers facing deadly bacteria turn to antibiotics, alarming health officials," May 17.

New York Times (2019) "Warning of 'pig zero': One drugmaker's push to sell more antibiotics," June 7.

New York Times (2019) "Under Brazil's far-right leader, Amazon protections slashed and forests fall," July 28.

New York Times (2019) "Spraying antibiotics to fight citrus scourge doesn't help, study finds," August 16.

New York Times (2019) "Beekeepers confront the E.P.A. over pesticides," September 12.

New York Times (2019) "A revolution in Brittany. Mayors defy French state to ban pesticides," September 18.

New York Times (2019) "Roundup weedkiller is blamed for cancers, but farmers say it's not going away," September 20.

New York Times (2019) "New York identifies hospitals and nursing homes with deadly fungus," November 13.

New York Times (2019) "Denmark raises antibiotic-free pigs. Why can't the U.S.?" December 6.

New York Times (2020) "Gulf of Mexico 'dead zone' will be large this summer, scientists predict," June 3.

New York Times (2021) "The central California town that keeps sinking," May 25.

New York Times (2021) "Destroying the Amazon for leather auto sales," November 18.

New York Times (2021) "Amazon deforestation soars to 15-year high," November 19.

Neyra, Ricardo Castillo et al. (2012) *Safety and Health at Work*, "Antimicrobial-resistant bacteria: An unrecognized work-related risk in food animal production," June.

NOAA (National Oceanic and Atmospheric Administration) (2017) "Gulf of Mexico 'dead zone' is the largest ever measured," August 2.

Nollet, Leo M. and Hamir Singh Rathore (eds.) (2015) *Biopesticides Handbook*, London: CRC Press.

Nordhaus, Hannah (2017) "Cornboy vs. the billion-dollar bug," *Scientific American*, March.

Norway (n.d.) "Svalbard global seed vault history," at seedvault.no.

NRC (National Research Council) (1989) *Alternative Agriculture*, Washington, DC: National Academy Press.

NRDC (Natural Resources Defense Council) (2016) *Livestock Antibiotics Surging Up, Up, Up*, December 2.

OECD (Organisation for Economic Co-operation and Development) (2012a) *Building Resilience for Adaptation to Climate Change in the Agricultural Sector*. Proceedings of a joint FAO/OECD workshop, April 23–24.

OECD (Organisation for Economic Co-operation and Development) (2012b) *Water Quality and Agriculture: Meeting the Policy Challenge*.

OECD–FAO (Organisation for Economic Co-operation and Development; Food and Agriculture Organization)(2019) *Agricultural Outlook 2019–2028*.

Ó Gráda, Cormac (2009) *Famine: A Short History*, Princeton, NJ: Princeton University Press.

OIE-WOAH (World Organization for Animal Health) (2018) *Annual Report on Antimicrobial Agents Intended for Use in Animals: Better Understanding of the Global Situation; Third Report*.

O'Neill, Jim (2016) *Tackling Drug-Resistant Infections Globally: Final Report and Recommendations; The Review on Antimicrobial Resistance*, commissioned by the UK government and Wellcome Trust, May.

Oonincx, Dennis G.A.B. et al. (2010) *PLoS ONE*, "An exploration on greenhouse gas and ammonia production by insect species suitable for animal or human consumption," December 29.

Owen, Michael D.K. (2008) *Pest Management Science*, "Weed species shifts in glyphosate-resistant crops," January 30.

OWID (Our World In Data) ourworldindata.org, Oxford University, Martin School.

Oxfam (2011) *Growing a Better Future*.

Ozlu, Ekrem and Sandeep Kumar (2018) *Soil Society of America Journal*, "Response of soil organic matter to fertilizer," September 13.

Parker, Laura (2016) "To the last drop," *National Geographic*, August.

Parnanen, Katariina M.M. et al. (2019) *Science Advances*, "Antibiotic resistance in European wastewater treatment plants mirrors the pattern of clinical antibiotic resistance prevalence," March 27.

Patel, Raj (2021) "The power of agroecology," *Scientific American*, November.

Plachetka, Uwe Christian (2015) "The significance of Andean terraces for indigenous knowledge on agro-ecology: The Moray puzzle," personal webpage, March 31.

Pearce-Duvet, Jessica M.C. (2006) *Biological Reviews*, "The origin of human pathogens: Evaluating the role of agriculture and domestic animals in the evolution of human disease," August, 369–82.

Pearson, Dean E. and Ragan M. Callaway (2006) *Ecology Letters*, "Biological control agents elevate hantavirus by subsidizing deer mouse populations," April.

Pelletier, Nathan et al. (2011) *Annual Review of Environment and Resources*, "Energy intensity of agriculture and food systems," November.

Pereira, R.V. et al. (2014) *Journal of Dairy Science*, "Effect of on-farm use of antimicrobial drugs on resistance in fecal *Escherichia coli* of preweaned dairy calves," October 11.

Perfecto, Ivette et al. (2005) *Ecological Economics*, "Biodiversity, yield and shade coffee certification," September.

Pest Management Science (2008) *Special Issue: Glyphosate-Resistant Weeds and Crops*, April.

Peterson, Caitlin A. et al. (2020) *PLoS One*, "Commercial integrated crop-livestock systems achieve comparable crop yields to specialized production systems: A meta-analysis," May 7.

Pew Commission on Industrial Farm Animal Production (2008) *Putting Meat on the Table: Industrial Farm Animal Production in America*.

Pfeiffer, Dale Allen (2006) *Eating Fossil Fuels: Oil, Food and the Coming Crisis in Agriculture*, Gabriola Island, BC: New Society Publishers.

Pimental, David and Michael Burgess (2013) *Agriculture*, "Soil erosion threatens food production," August.

Pimental, David and Michael Burgess (2014), "Environmental and economic benefits of reducing pesticide use," in D. Pimental and R. Peshan (eds.) *Integrated Pest Management*: Pesticide Problems; *Volume 3*, Berlin: Springer.

Pimental, David et al. (1973) *Science*, "Food production and the energy crisis," November 2.

Pimm, S.L. et al. (2014) *Science*, "The biodiversity of species and their rates of extinction, distribution, and protection," May 30.

Ponisio, LC. et al. (2015) *Proceedings of the Royal Society B*, "Diversification practices reduce organic to conventional yield gap," January 22.

Ponting, Clive (2007) *A New Green History of the World: The Environment and the Collapse of Great Civilizations*, London: Penguin.

Poti, Jennifer M. et al. (2015) *American Journal of Clinical Nutrition*, "Is the degree of food processing and convenience linked with the nutritional quality of foods purchased by US households?" June, 1251–62.

Powles, Stephen B. (2010) *PNAS*, "Gene amplification delivers glyphosate-resistant weed evolution," January 19.

Powney, Gary D. et al. (2019) *Nature Communications*, "Widespread losses of pollinating insects in Britain," March.

Pretty, J.N. et al. (2000) *Agricultural Systems*, "An assessment of the total external costs of UK agriculture," February.

Pretty, Jules (2008) *Philosophical Transactions of the Royal Society B*, "Agricultural sustainability: Concepts, principles and evidence," February.

Rainforest Alliance (2020) "What is climate-smart agriculture?" January 21.

Ramos-Elorduy, Julieta, (2009) *Entomological Research*, "Anthropo-entomophagy: Cultures, evolution and sustainability," September.

Ranganathan, Janet (2013) "The global food challenge explained in 18 graphics," World Resources Institute, December 3.

Reuters (2017) "Bayer CEO says Monsanto's reputation is a 'major challenge'," April 28.

Ribaudo, Marc (2005) "Managing manure to improve air and water quality." Presentation to the USDA agricultural air quality task force meeting, November 15, Wailea-Maui, Hawaii.

Rice, Robert (1998) "A rich brew from the shade," Organization of American States.

Rice, Robert and Mauricio Bedoya (2010) "The ecological benefits of shade-grown coffee: The case for going bird friendly," Smithsonian Migratory Bird Center, September.

Richards, Meryl et al. (2019) "Climate change mitigation potential of agricultural practices supported by IFAD investments: An ex ante analysis." IFAD Research Series 35, International Fund for Agricultural Development, March.

Richardson, Jason R. et al. (2009) *Archives of Neurology*, "Elevated serum pesticide levels and risk of Parkinson disease," July.

Richardson, Jason R. et al. (2014) *JAMA Neurology*, "Elevated serum pesticide levels and risk for Alzheimer disease," March.

Robin, Marie-Monique (2008) *The World According to Monsanto: Pollution, Corruption and the Control of Our Food Supply*, New York: The New Press.

Rockstrom, Johan et al. (2017) *Ambio*, "Sustainable intensification of agriculture for human prosperity and global sustainability," February.

Rosa, Lorenzo et al. (2020) *Science Advances*, "Global agricultural economic water scarcity," April 29.

Rosa, Marcos R. et al. (2021) *Science Advances*, "Hidden destruction of older forests threatens Brazil's Atlantic forest and challenges restoration programs," January 20.

Rosset, Peter M. and Miguel A. Altieri (2017) *Agroecology: Science and Politics*, Black Point, NS: Fernwood Publishing.

Sanchez-Bayo, Francisco and Kris A.G. Wyckhuys (2019) *Biological Conservation*, "Worldwide decline of the entomofauna: A review of its drivers," April.

Schindler, David (2007) "A life with pesticides." Address to the Vancouver Institute, November 3.

Schullehner, Jorg et al. (2018) International Journal of Cancer, "Nitrate in drinking water and colorectal cancer risk: A nationwide population-based cohort study," July 1.

Schulz, Ralf et al. (2021) *Science*, "Applied pesticide toxicity shifts toward plants and invertebrates, even in GM crops," April 2.

Schwagerl, Christian (2016) *Yale Environment 360*, "What's causing the sharp decline in insects, and why it matters," July 6.

Science (2003) "Chasing the fickle swine flu," March 7.

Science (2019) "Common pesticide makes migrating birds anorexic," September 12.

Science (2020) "Some mosquitoes already have resistance to the latest weapon against malaria," August 31.

Science (2021) "The Colorado River is shrinking: Hard choices lie ahead, this scientist warns," July 1.

Seibold, Sebastian et al. (2019) *Nature*, "Anthropod decline in grasslands and forests is associated with landscape-level drivers," October 30.

Senate of Canada (1984) Soil at Risk: Canada's Eroding Future; *A Report on Soil Conservation by the Standing Committee on Agriculture, Fisheries and Forestry*.

Seufert, Verena and Navin Ramankutty (2017) "Many shades of gray: The context-dependent performance of organic agriculture," March 10.

Shackford, Stacey (2014) "Indoor urban farms called wasteful, 'pie in the sky'," *Cornell Chronicle*, February 19.

Sharma, Shefali (2020) *Milking the Planet: How Big Dairy is Heating Up the Planet and Hollowing Rural Communities,* Institute for Agriculture and Trade Policy, June 15.

Shennan, Carol et al. (2017) *Annual Review of Environment and Resources*, "Organic and conventional agriculture: A useful framing?" October.

Silva, V. et al. (2019) *Science of the Total Environment*, "Pesticide residues in European agricultural soils: A hidden reality unfolded," February 25.

Silvestri, Silvia et al. (2012) "Greening livestock: Assessing the potential of payment for environmental services in livestock inclusive agricultural production systems in developing countries," CGIAR.

Sinha, E. et al. (2017) *Science*, "Eutrophication will increase during the 21st century as a result of precipitation changes," July 28.

Siviter, Harry et al. (2021) *Nature*, "Agrochemicals interact synergistically to increase bee mortality," August 4.

Slaughter, Congresswoman Louise (2011) "Confirmed: 80 percent of all antibacterial drugs used on animals, endangering human health," press release, February 23.

Smart Prosperity Institute (2021) *Background Materials for Circular Economy Sectoral Roadmaps: Agrifood*, Circular Economy Global Sector Best Practices Series, February.

SmartAKIS (n.d.) "What is smart farming?"

Soroye, Peter et al. (2020) *Science*, "Climate change contributes to widespread declines among bumble bees across continents," February 7.

Stanley, Paige L. et al. (2018) *Agricultural Systems*, "Impacts of soil carbon sequestration on life cycle greenhouse gas emissions in Midwestern USA beef finishing systems," May.

Steffen, Will et al. (2015) *Science*, "Planetary boundaries: Guiding human development on a changing planet," February 13.

Steinhart, John S. and Carol E. Steinhart (1974) *Science,* "Energy use in the U.S. food system," April 19.

Stetka, Bret (2014) "Parkinson's disease and pesticides: What's the connection?" *Scientific American*, April 8.

Stipp, David (2007) "Flight of the honey bee," *Fortune*, 156(5): 108–16.

Stokstad, Erik (2019) *Science*, "Costly cancer lawsuits may spur search to replace world's most common weed killer," May 22.

Straub, Lars et al. (2016) *Proceedings of the Royal Society B*, "Neonicotinoid insecticides can serve as inadvertent insect contraceptives," July 27.

Swan, Shanna H. (2020) *Countdown: How Our Modern World Is Threatening Sperm Counts, Altering Male and Female Reproductive Development, and Imperiling the Future of the Human Race*, New York: Scribner.

Swan, Shanna H. et al. (1997) *Environmental Health Perspectives*, "Have sperm densities declined? A reanalysis of global trend data," November.

Swanton, Clarence et al. (1996) *Agricultural Systems*, "Recent improvements in the energy efficiency of agriculture: Case studies from Ontario, Canada," December.

Tabashnik, Bruce E. and Yves Carriere (2017) *Nature Biotechnology*, "Surge in insect resistance to transgenic crops and prospects for sustainability," October 11.

Tabashnik. Bruce E. et al. (2008) *Nature Biotechnology*, "Insect resistance to Bt crops: Evidence vs theory," February 7.

Tabashnik, Bruce E. et al. (2013) *Nature Biotechnology*, "Insect resistance to Bt crops: Lessons from the first billion acres," June.

Tang, Karen L. et al. (2017) *Lancet*, "Restricting the use of antibiotics in food-producing animals and its associations with antibiotic resistance in food-producing animals and human beings: A systematic review and meta-analysis," November.

Tegtmeier, Erin M. and Michael D. Duffy (2004) *International Journal of Agricultural Sustainability*, "External costs of agricultural production in the United States," 2(1).

Temkin, Alexis (2018) "Breakfast with a dose of Roundup?" Environmental Working Group, August 15.

Temple, Robert (2007) *The Genius of China: 3,000 Years of Science, Discovery & Invention*, Rochester, VT: Inner Traditions.

Terdoo, Fanen and Olalekan Adekola (2014) *African Journal of Agricultural Research*, "Assessing the role of climate smart agriculture in northern Nigeria," April 10.

Thacker, Paul D. (2019) "An inside look at how Monsanto, a PR firm and a reporter give readers a warped view of science," HuffPost, August 6.

Thaler, Evan et al. (2021) *PNAS*, "The extent of soil loss across the US corn belt," February 23.

Tilman, David et al. (2001) *Science*, "Forecasting agriculturally driven global environmental change," April 13.

Tomanio, John (2011) graphic from https://thesocietypages.org/socimages/2011/07/19/loss-of-genetic-diversity-in-u-s-food-crops/.

Tomizawa, Motohiro and John E. Casida (2005) *Annual Review of Pharmacology & Toxicology*, "Neonicotinoid insecticide toxicology: Mechanisms of selective action."

Tuomisto, H.L. et al. (2012) *Journal of Environmental Management*, "Does organic farming reduce environmental impacts? A meta-analysis of European research," September 1.

UCS (Union of Concerned Scientists) (2008) *CAFOs Uncovered: The Untold Costs of Confined Animal Feeding Operations*.

UCS (Union of Concerned Scientist) (2013) *The Healthy Farm: A Vision for U.S. Agriculture*.

Udall, Bradley and Jonathan Overpeck (2017) *Water Resources Research*, "The twenty-first century Colorado River hot drought and implications for the future," March 24.

UK CCC (Committee on Climate Change) (2018) *Land Use: Reducing Emissions and Preparing for Climate Change*, November.

UK Review on Antimicrobial Resistance (2016) *Tackling Drug-Resistant Infections Globally: Final Report and Recommendations*, May.

UN (United Nations) (2017) *International Trade Statistics Yearbook*.

UN ESCAP (United Nations Economic and Social Commission for Asia and the Pacific) (2013) "Water, food and energy nexus in Asia and the Pacific." Discussion paper, Economic and Social Commission for Asia and the Pacific, United Nations.

UNCTAD (United Nations Conference on Trade and Development) and IISD (International Institute for Sustainable Development) (n.d.) "Sustainability in the coffee sector: Exploring opportunities for international cooperation," Background paper.

UNCTAD (United Nations Conference on Trade and Development) and UNEP (United Nations Environment Programme) (2008) *Organic Agriculture and Food Security in Africa*, UNEP–UNCTAD Capacity Building Task Force on Trade, Environment and Development.

UNEP (United Nations Environment Programme) (2021) *Food Waste Index Report 2021.*

Unruh, Jon and Diana Liverman (n.d.) "Changing water use and demand in the Southwest," United States Geological Survey.

US CDC (Centers for Disease Control and Prevention) (2013) *Antibiotic Resistance in the United States, 2013.*

US EPA (Environmental Protection Agency) (2011) *Guidance for the Development of Conceptual Models for Problem Formulation Developed for Registration Review,* March 10.

US EPA (Environmental Protection Agency) (2013) "White paper on RNAi technology as a pesticide: Problem formulation for human health and ecological risk assessment," October 29.

US FDA (Food and Drug Administration) (2016) "Antimicrobials sold or distributed for use in food-producing animals," December.

US HHS (US Department of Health and Human Services), Food and Drug Administration, Center for Veterinary Medicine (2010) "The judicious use of medically important antimicrobial drugs in food-producing animals," June 28.

US NCHS (National Center for Health Statistics) (2013). mortality data (multiple years) Leading Causes of Death, Centers for Disease Control and Prevention.

US President's Cancer Panel (2009) *Reducing Environmental Cancer Risk.*

US White House (2014) "Fact sheet: The economic challenge posed by declining pollinator populations," June 20.

USDA (n.d.) "Biotechnology FAQs."

USGS (United States Geological Survey) (2000) "Restoring life to the dead zone: Addressing Gulf hypoxia, a national problem," June.

Van Meter, K.J. et al. (2018) *Science,* "Legacy nitrogen may prevent achievement of water quality goals in the Gulf of Mexico," April 27.

Vancouver Sun (2019) "The herbicide glyphosate persists in wild, edible plants: B.C. study," February 20.

Vogel, Gretchen (2017) *Science,* "Where have all the insects gone?" May 12.

Wagner-Riddle, Claudia et al. (2017) *Nature Geoscience,* "Climate change and soil thaw-freezing cycles," April.

Ward, Mary H. et al. (2010) *Epidemiology,* "Nitrate intake and the risk of thyroid cancer and thyroid disease," May.

Water Research Center (2014) "Pesticides and herbicides in drinking water and groundwater," Dallas, TX.

WEF (World Economic Forum) (2019) "The speed of the energy transition," September.

WEF (World Economic Forum) (2020) "How carbon-smart farming can feed us and fight climate change," August 3.

Weyer, Peter J. et al. (2001) *Epidemiology,* "Municipal drinking water nitrate level and cancer risk in older women: The Iowa Women's Health Study," May.

Whitehorn, Penelope R. et al. (2012) *Science,* "Neonicotinoid pesticide reduces bumble bee colony growth and queen production," April 20.

WHO (World Health Organization) (2014) "Frequently asked questions on genetically modified foods," May.

WHO (World Health Organization) (2017a) "Web annex A. Evidence base" in *Guidelines on Use of Medically Important Antimicrobials in Food-Producing Animals.*

WHO (World Health Organization) (2017b) "Stop using antibiotics in healthy animals to prevent the spread of antibiotic resistance," press release, November 7.

WHO (World Health Organization) (2018) "Pesticide residues in food," February 19.

WHO (World Health Organization) (2019a) *Antibacterial Agents in Clinical Development: An Analysis of the Antibacterial Clinical Development Pipeline.*

WHO (World Health Organization) (2019b) *Antibacterial Agents in Preclinical Development: An Open Access Database*.

WHO (World Health Organization) (2019c) "World hunger is still not going down after three years and obesity is still growing," July 15.

Whorton, James (1974) *Before Silent Spring: Pesticides and Public Health in Pre-DDT America*, Princeton: Princeton University Press.

Wijeratna, Alex (2012) *Fed Up: Now's the Time to Invest in Agro-ecology*, International Food Security Network, June.

Willis, Kathy J. et al. (2018) *Science*, "What makes an ecosystem resilient," March 2.

Willyard, Cassandra (2019) "Flu on the farm," *Scientific American*, September 18.

Winter, Carl K. and Josh M. Katz (2011) *Journal of Toxicology*, "Dietary exposure to pesticide residues from commodities alleged to contain the highest contamination levels," May.

Wittwer, Raphael A. et al. (2021) *Science Advances*, "Organic and conservation agriculture promote ecosystem multifunctionality," August 20.

Wojtkowski, Paul (2008) *Agroecological Economics: Sustainability and Biodiversity*, Amsterdam: Elsevier.

Wood, Lisa J. (2019) *Canadian Journal of Forest Research*, "The presence of glyphosate in forest plants with different life strategies one year after application," June.

Wood, Sam and Annette Cowie (2004) *A Review of Greenhouse Gas Emission Factors for Fertilizer Production*, Research and Development Division, State Forests of New South Wales, Cooperative Research Centre for Greenhouse Accounting, June.

Woodcock, Ben A. et al. (2016) *Nature Communications*, "Impacts of neonicotinoid use on long-term population changes in wild bees in England," August 16.

World Bank (2017) *Drug-Resistant Infections: A Threat to Our Economic Future*, March.

World Bank (2021) "Climate-smart agriculture," April 5.

World Bank (n.d. a) "Climate-smart agriculture in Mexico."

World Bank (n.d. b) World Development Indicators, https://databank.worldbank.org/source/world-development-indicators.

WWF (World Wildlife Fund) (n.d.) *Living Waters: Thirsty Crops*.

WTEx (World's Top Exports) (2019) "Coffee exports by country," April 17.

Wu, Yan (2016) *China Daily*, "1,000-year-old agricultural practice, China's solution to sustainable farming," June 7.

Xu, Xiaoming et al. (2021) "Global greenhouse gas emissions from animal-based foods are twice those of plant-based foods," *Nature Food*, September 13.

Yamamuro, Masumi et al. (2019) *Science*, "Neonicotinoids disrupt aquatic food webs and decrease fishery yields," November 1.

Zhang, Lin et al. (2012) *Cell Research*, "Exogenous plant MIR168a specifically targets mammalian LDLRAP1: Evidence of cross-kingdom regulation by microRNA," January.

Zhao, Qingyun et al. (2018) *Scientific Reports*, "Long-term coffee monoculture alters soil chemical properties and microbial communities," April 17.

6 Agriculture and the existential threat of climate change

In Chapter 5, Figure 5.1 portrayed the hierarchical development of society after the Neolithic Revolution. The pyramidal shape with the large base representing employment in the agricultural sector remains a common phenomenon in many countries in the developing world. In contrast, Figure 6.1 is an inverted pyramid typical of a modern, Western-style economy where the percentage of total employment devoted to agricultural production is very low (see figures 6.2 and 6.3). In addition to providing a literal representation of the modern economy, Figure 6.1 has a profound figurative interpretation: every economy, regardless of its stage of development, is ultimately dependent on agricultural production to maintain the complex infrastructure that characterizes its society. Viewed in this way, the vulnerability of all societies to the vicissitudes of food production becomes apparent. There is an inherent fragility here which only becomes apparent in times of stress—whether ecological, political, economic, or social.

Until fairly recently little serious attention had been given to the vulnerability of our food supplies to climate change. Even if such vulnerability was acknowledged, a common refrain was that the sector could adapt. It is the hypothesis of this book that such faith is misplaced and that food supply is the Achilles' heel of adaptation. This section is divided into two parts: the first discusses the role of increased atmospheric carbon dioxide on plant growth, and the second addresses the medium- to long-term threats to global agriculture from all the manifestations of climate change.

Carbon dioxide and plant growth

In the face of political inertia and the lagged effects of global warming, one of the few bright sides was the *apparent* positive impact of increased levels of atmospheric carbon dioxide on the growth of plants, including food crops (Kimball 1983; Cure and Acock 1986; Lu et al. 2016; Uddling et al. 2018). The suggestion was that continued global warming might not have posed as great a threat to food supplies as feared. Unfortunately, this misimpression was generated by a simple extrapolation. As discussed in Chapter 2, too often such extrapolations are made when in fact the relationship is curvilinear. Such appears to be the case with respect to the CO_2–plant nexus. Recent more nuanced research has demonstrated that as CO_2 levels continue to rise past their early positive impacts on plant growth, the opposite effect can materialize and plant growth is significantly lower than expected (Ainsworth and Long 2005) or is retarded due to a combination of factors (Tai et al. 2014; Reich et al. 2018; Chandler and LePage 2007; NASA 2016; Diaz et al. 1993; Yuan et al. 2019; Ortiz-Bobea at al. 2021). The entire growth–response phenomenon may

DOI: 10.4324/9781003199540-8

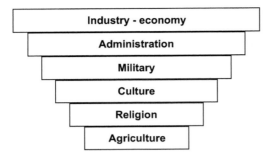

Figure 6.1 The modern industrialized economy.

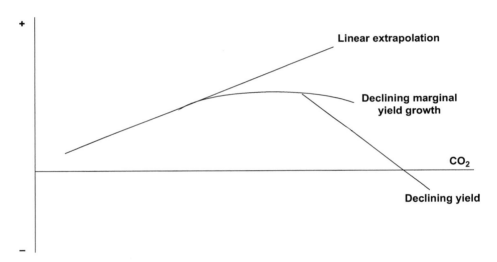

Figure 6.2 CO_2-plant growth function.

in extremis be a curvilinear function that is concave to the x-axis (see Figure 6.2). As such, the projected continued increase in atmospheric carbon dioxide does not bode well for our food supply.

Increasing levels of carbon dioxide have an additional impact on plants, particularly leaf thickness. Kovenock and Swann (2018) have found that higher CO_2 levels cause plants to thicken their leaves—by as much as one-third in mass per area—reducing their efficiency in sequestering atmospheric carbon. They estimate that this can result in a decline in global net primary productivity of 5.8 petagrams of carbon per year (PgC/year), representing a decreased CO_2 sink of similar magnitude to current fossil fuel emissions of 8 PgC/year.

The next section explores in more detail what further impacts continued climate change can be expected to have on the agricultural sector generally and food crops in particular.

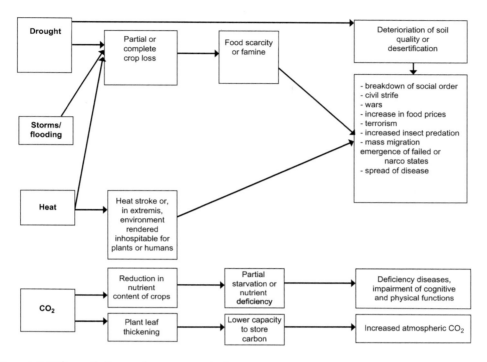

Figure 6.3 Effects of climate change on agriculture.

Climate change and agriculture

Climate change can affect agriculture in several significant ways, alone or in combination: through drought, heat, the direct effect of greenhouse gases (GHGs) on plant nutritional content, and water and storms. Recent research has established a direct link between anthropogenic activity manifested in climate change and extremes in precipitation, resulting in floods or drought (Madakumbura et al. 2021). Figure 6.3 displays the first, second, and third order effects of these factors and a more detailed discussion of each follows.

Drought

Few, if any, natural phenomena have posed a greater threat to the survival of civilizations than drought. Table 6.1 lists some major past civilizations from the second millennium BCE onwards, each of which has fallen in part due to drought (Cullen et al. 2000; Diamond 2005; Sheffield and Wood 2011; Evans et al. 2018; Yancheva et al. 2007; Ortloff and Kolata 1993; Sinha et al. 2019; Hodell et al. 1995 and 2001). But drought is not confined to distant history. Within the last century, the world has experienced, and continues to experience, crippling national and regional droughts. Included among these are:

- 1930s US Dust Bowl (McLeman et al. 2013)
- 1959–61 China (Ó Gráda 2009)

Table 6.1 Drought and civilization collapse

Civilization	Period
Akkadian Empire in Syria	2334 BCE–2193 BCE
Old Kingdom of Ancient Egypt	4200 to 4000 cal. yr BP
Mycenaean, Hittites, and New Kingdom of Egypt	Late 13th and 12th centuries BCE
Mayan Empire in Central America	750–910 CE
Tang Dynasty in China	700–907 CE
Tiwanaku Empire in Bolivia	1000–1100 CE
Anasazi culture in the southwest United States	1090–1200 CE
Khmer/Angkor civilization in Cambodia	802–1431 CE
Ming Dynasty in China	1368–1644 CE

Source: Cullen et al. 2000; Diamond 2005; Sheffield and Wood 2011; Evans et al. 2018; Yancheva et al. 2007; Ortloff and Kolata 1993; Sinha et al. 2019.

Note: Cal. yr BP is an abbreviation of calibrated years before the present.

- 1972 Russia (UNICEF 2010)
- 1972–73 India and Ethiopia (Ó Gráda 2009)
- 1980–81 Uganda (Ó Gráda 2009)
- 1984–85 Sudan (Ó Gráda 2009)
- 1991–92 Somalia (Ó Gráda 2009)
- 1998 Sudan (Ó Gráda 2009)
- 2001–9 Southeast Australia (Dijk et al. 2013)
- 2002 Malawi (Devereux 2002)
- 2003 Europe (Ciais et al. 2005)
- 2005 South Darfur (UNICEF 2005)
- 2005 Niger (Ó Gráda 2009)
- 2010 Amazon (Lewis et al. 2011)
- 2010 Russia, Ukraine, and Kazakhstan (USDA 2011)
- 2011–12 East Africa (Taylor 2011)
- 2012 US Southern Tier (Rippey 2015)
- 2017 Northern and Northeast China (Wang et al. 2018)
- 2017 US northern Great Plains (Hoell et al. 2018)
- 2017 East Africa (Funk et al. 2018)
- 2018 Southern Guatemala (*New York Times* June 29, 2018)
- 2018 Cape Town and southern South Africa (*USA Today* January 22, 2018)
- 2019 Australia (*Guardian* May 15, 2019)
- 2019 Somalia (*Guardian* June 6, 2019)
- 2019 India (*Guardian* June 12, 2019)
- 2021 Madagascar (UN OCHA 2021)
- 2021 California and the American West (*Guardian* May 10, 2021; *New York Times* July 20, 2021)
- 2021 Canadian Prairies (CBC News May 15, 2021)
- 2021 Taiwan (*New York Times* May 27, 2021)

Recent research has raised the specter of continuing or worsening drought events in North and South America, Europe, Asia, the Middle East, and Africa with significant effects on future crop yields (Romm 2011; Büntgen et al. 2021; Dosio 2017; Glotter and

Elliott 2016; Liang et al. 2018; Earth Institute 2018; Su et al. 2018; WMO 2019; Williams et al. 2020; Cowan et al. 2020; *Science* April 17, 2020; Alizadeh et al. 2020; Cook et al. 2020; Haile et al. 2020; *New York Times* July 8, 2020; Markonis et al. 2021; HuffPost April 17 and April 21, 2021; *New York Times* June 21, 28, and 29, 2021; CNN June 23 and August 22, 2021).

The consequences of drought are multifaceted and include, within any one country or region, partial or complete loss of crops as the most immediate result, followed by food shortages, price increases, and possibly famine. These can be accompanied by a further diverse range of disastrous results including the breakdown of government and civil society, civil strife, terrorism, civil war, increased insect predation, disease, mass migration, desertification, and the potential emergence of failed states (see, for example, Brown 2009; Ó Gráda 2009; Cribb 2010; Soysa and Gleditsch 1999; Dyer 2011; Mohtadi 2012; Ebi and Bowen 2016; World Bank 2016; UK Ministry of Defence 2018; Park et al. 2018; Parenti 2011; Feng et al. 2019; Winsemius et al. n.d.; White House 2021). Many of these consequences are not confined to the region under stress. Out-migration, the spread of disease, civil war, and the transformation of formerly stable national governments to criminal enterprises all can have profound effects on neighboring states and the global community (Desai et al. 2021).

One study (Lesk et al. 2016) estimated that drought and extreme heat reduced global cereal production by 9–10 percent over the period 1964 to 2007. While drought is frequently the result of excessive heat, heat waves of short to medium length may not necessarily lead to drought conditions and, as such, heat is addressed as a separate category. Ultimately, aridity can have profound impacts on ecosystems including "abrupt decays in plant productivity, soil fertility and plant cover and richness" (Berdugo et al. 2020, p. 787). Berdugo et al. predict that "more than 20% of the terrestrial surface will cross one or several of these [global] thresholds by 2100". Potential global tipping points threaten the continued growth and stability of global food production. By way of example, a recent study by Ritchie et al. (2021) using data from Great Britain concluded that economic and land-use impacts of crossing a tipping point with the potential collapse of the Atlantic Meridional Overturning Circulation, the conveyor current, are "likely to include widespread cessation of arable farming" (p. 76).

What has saved many countries from disaster from the loss of food supplies has been the international safety net whereby global grain exporters provide food relief directly or through international agencies. Two factors may threaten this safety net in the future as the world experiences increasing temperatures and accompanying drought (NASA 2015). First, is the potential loss of domestic grain surpluses among the world's major grain exporters. For example, in 2019, Australia, the third largest exporter of wheat in 2017 after Russia and the United States (IndexBox 2019), was forced to import due to drought across its eastern states (*Guardian* May 15, 2019). In fact it has been reported that increases in Australian wheat yields have stalled since 1990 due to climate change (Hochman et al. 2017). The outlook is not particularly encouraging, as the country's national science agency (CSIRO 2018) has predicted that warming trends will continue into the future with increases in the frequency and/or intensity of heat events, fire weather, and drought. Equally disturbing was the effect of the drought of 2001–10 on rice production in Australia. Output dropped from a high of 1,643 kilotons (kt) in 2000–01 to 17.6 kt in 2007–08 (Dijk et al. 2013; Australia Department of Agriculture, accessed 2019; Trnka et al. 2019).

Second, the possibility exists that future warming with accompanying drought will increase the probability of synchronized losses to certain global crops such as maize, wheat, and soybeans (Lunt et al. 2016; Anderson et al. 2019; Tigchelaar et al. 2018; Mehrabi and Ramankutty 2019). To quote Tigchelaar et al. (p. 6644):

> For the top four maize-exporting countries, which account for 87% of global maize exports, the probability that they have simultaneous production losses greater than 10% in any given year is presently virtually zero, but it increases to 7% under 2°C warming and 86% under 4°C warming. Our results portend rising instability in global grain trade and international grain prices, affecting especially the ~800 million people living in extreme poverty who are most vulnerable to food price spikes.

When global commodity markets are tight, any slight change in supply can have an outsized impact on price. This applies to food crops in particular. The 1972 partial failure of the wheat crop from Russia, which produces 21 percent of the global total, caused grain prices to hit 125-year highs, while soybeans increased in price from $3.30 to $12.90 per bushel, and food prices around the world rose 50 percent in 1973 (Businessinsider.com 2010). A similar phenomenon was observed after the 2012 drought in the United States and is predicted to only worsen in the next few decades (Oxfam 2012). Figure 6.4 displays wheat prices from 1961 to 2019. As with many commodities, prices tend to be volatile and are influenced by a mixture of ecological, political, economic, and social factors. At least five price peaks are apparent in this time series: 1974, 1980, 1996, 2008, and 2012. Peaks in 1974 and 2012 were driven by drought in Russia and the United States respectively. The increased prices of 1996 were attributed to crop losses from cold weather in the United States (US BLS 1998), and 2008 was due to a multitude of causes, including poor

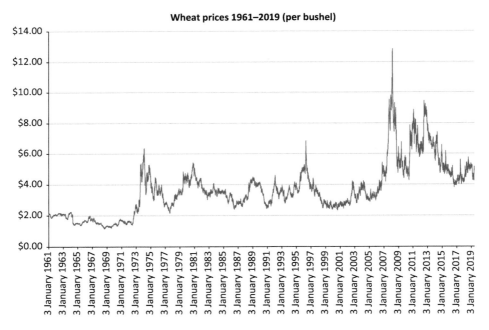

Figure 6.4 Wheat price trends 1961–2019.
Source: www.macrotrends.net.

wheat harvests in Australia and the Ukraine (Wiggins et al. 2010). Whenever these price spikes occur, undue financial pressure is placed upon those developing countries relying heavily on the importation of grains, and wheat in particular. By way of example, in 1996 wheat was Egypt's most valuable import valued at $1.2 billion. Wheat has remained a crucial import, valued at $1.9 billion in 2008 and $4.7 billion in 2020, second only to refined petroleum products (UN, various years). Egypt and several of its Middle Eastern neighbors are extremely sensitive to food prices and have experienced potentially destabilizing food riots over the past few decades (*New York Times* March 3, 1992, and February 25, 2008).

Confidence that watersheds can completely recover after drought, thereby reestablishing an important source of water for crops, may be misplaced. Peterson et al. (2021, p. 745) report on Australia's experience in a post-drought period and observe that "watersheds can have a finite resilience to disturbances … [H]ydrological droughts can persist indefinitely after meteorological droughts." These findings could have implications for food supply far beyond Australia as the authors cite other research which found that prolonged droughts have caused unexpectedly large reductions in stream flows in the United States and China (Tian et al. 2018; Avanzi et al. 2020).

A significant proportion of the potential increased mass migration, a source of anxiety for the West, can ultimately be tied to conflict and climate change manifesting in the form of drought, heat, and flooding (Hsiang et al. 2011; CARE et al. 2009). To many countries, such events entail potentially serious risks to national order and security. The UNHCR (2018) has reported that more than seventy million people were forcibly displaced in 2018, primarily due to a variety of political and economic causes. Munich Re (Laczko 2008; and see also CRO Forum 2016) has identified mass migration as an emerging issue in the next few years with risks and potential benefits for countries with aging populations and in need of new labor. (See also World Bank 2014a). But, clearly, the impact of conflict and mass migration linked to climate change transcends mere economics. Several recent articles have attributed upheavals such as the Arab Spring (Perez 2013) and its consequences in Darfur (Biello 2009), Egypt (Biello 2011), and Syria (Fischetti 2015), as well as upheavals in Mexico (Center for Global Development 2012; Climate Reality Project 2018) to global climate change within the boundaries of a country or its neighbors. Several other studies have examined the relationship between climate change and human conflict but have found conflicting evidence (Hsiang et al. 2013; Hsiang and Burke 2014; Forsyth and Schomerus 2013; Missirian and Schlenker 2017).

It should also be noted that compound drought and heat events may have the potential to sufficiently reduce the carbon sequestering ability of soils that they become net carbon sources, creating yet another positive feedback loop in the global warming cycle (Zhou et al. 2019). Alizadeh et al. (2020) have identified an "alarming" increase in the number of these compound events with the number of geographic areas experiencing these occurrences also increasing.

Several scientific reports have projected an increasing frequency and severity of drought over the rest of this century (Rind et al. 1990; Burke et al. 2006; Seager et al. 2007; Solomon et al. 2009; Dai 2011; Romm 2011; Cook et al. 2014; Underwood 2015; Park et al. 2018; Zhou et al. 2019). This and other similar projections have moved climate change considerations into discussions on national security. The US Department of Defense (Schwartz and Randall 2003; US DoD 2014a and b, 2015, and 2021) and other American agencies (NIC 2021; US DHS 2021) have now clearly tied the threat of future climate change, including events such as drought, to American security interests

(see also Holland 2016). The importance of drought across economic, social, and ecological dimensions has prompted the development of continuously updated monitoring
databases at both the international (Standardized Precipitation-Evapotranspiration Index
[SPEI] Global Drought Monitor at spei.csic.es) and US levels (US Drought Monitor at
droughtmonitor.unl.edu).

Heat

While excessive heat has many of the same consequences of its frequent sequela, drought,
it also has several distinct effects of its own. In particular, *in extremis*, it can make a region
totally uninhabitable for humans, thus compounding the difficulty of any residual efforts
to produce crops. For example, one scientific study (Pal and Eltahir 2015) forecast that
given the current trajectory of global warming, the Persian Gulf region will be unable to
support human habitation within this century due to predicted *wet-bulb* temperatures (i.e.
combining *dry-bulb* temperatures, or conventional thermometer readings, with humidity)
in excess of 35 degrees Celsius (°C). At this temperature, the human body is incapable of
maintaining a homeostatic temperature balance and faces death in a short period of time
(Sherwood and Huber 2010; Raymond et al. 2020). Vicedo-Cabrera et al. (2021) have
found that more than one-third of heat-related deaths in forty-three countries surveyed
can be attributed to anthropogenic climate change. Recent dry-bulb temperatures in the
Gulf region have already surpassed historical records; during the summer of 2017 in the
Iranian city of Ahvaz readings reached 54°C or 129.2 degrees Fahrenheit (°F) (*Independent*
June 30, 2017). Concerns have also been voiced over the future habitability of Pakistan's
Indus Valley, considered one of the areas of the world most vulnerable to climate change.
In June 2021, the city of Jacobabad reached a temperature of 52°C (126°F). To quote the
report in the *Telegraph* (June 28, 2021):

> This city of some 200,000 in Pakistan's Sindh province has long been renowned for
> its fierce heat, but recent research has conferred an unwelcome scientific distinction.
> Its mixture of heat and humidity has made it one of only two places on earth to
> have now officially passed, albeit briefly, a threshold hotter than the human body can
> withstand.

A similar dire situation faces major agricultural and densely populated regions in South
Asia and China, specifically around the Ganges and Indus river basins (Im et al. 2017)
and the North China Plain (Kang and Eltahir 2018; see also Chen et al. 2018; Zhou et al.
2018). Diffenbaugh (2020, abstract) has suggested that "21st century global warming has
substantially increased the probability of unprecedented hot and wet events" (see also Li
et al. 2020.) Xu et al. (2020, p. 11350) have forecast that "over the coming 50 [years], 1 to
3 billion people are projected to be left outside the climate conditions that have served
humanity well over the past 6,000 [years]."

The issue is not only high average temperatures; it is the occurrence of heat waves
of short duration or sustained periods which can have devastating impacts on crops and
human health. In statistical terms, this is the distinction between mean and variance but,
in this case, the increased variance of temperature under global warming is asymmetrical,
with a much greater probability of extreme heat rather than cold (Bathiany et al. 2018;
New York Times July 28, 2017; Coumou and Robinson 2013; Fisher and Knutti 2015).
A recent risk study of global urban centers (Verisk Maplecroft 2021) concludes that of 576

cities studied, Asian urban areas represent 99 of the 100 most vulnerable to extreme heat stress as well as pollution, dwindling water supplies, and other natural hazards associated with climate change (see also Rogers et al. 2021 and *Science* October 4, 2021).

Such events are not restricted to the developing world, however. Within the past few years, and particularly during the summer of 2017, southern Europe sustained an elevated rate of mortality due to excessive heat (Kew et al. 2018) and California declared a state of emergency during a heat wave in mid-2021 (BBC June 18, 2021). The world is now seeing twice as many days over 50°C as in the 1980s (BBC September 13, 2021). In August 2021, Sicily experienced the highest ever temperature in Europe at 48.8°C, surpassing the record of 48°C in Athens in 1977 (*Guardian* August 11, 2021). A recent in-depth study has attempted to quantify the number of excess deaths due to heat waves in twenty developed and developing countries under various climate change scenarios (Guo et al. 2018). The findings tend to support other recent observations that global warming has a disproportionality greater effect on the poorer regions of the world (*New York Times* March 12, 2018).

Some historical data have already provided evidence of the negative effect of extreme heat on crop yields (World Bank 2014b). Lesk et al. (2016) examined data on weather and crop yields over the period 1964–2007 and found that droughts and extreme heat significantly reduced global cereal production by 9–10 percent. Another study covering the period 1980–2008 (Lobell 2011) concluded that weather events contributed to a global maize and wheat production decline of 3.8 percent and 5.5 percent respectively. Battisti and Naylor (2009) reviewed the effects of severe heat in Europe during the summer of 2003 and reported that Italian maize yields dropped 36 percent, while France experienced significant decreases in several commodities: maize and fodder (down 30 percent), fruit (down 25 percent), and wheat (down 21 percent). These observations of past events have been complemented by the development of several models that attempt to predict future crop declines in the face of rising global temperatures. Liu et al. (2016) predict that a 1°C increase in global temperature will lead to declines in wheat yields of between 4.1 percent and 6.4 percent. Zhao et al. (2017) broaden their focus to cover the four major crops, including wheat, which provide two-thirds of human caloric intake. Their results predict reductions in yields for each degree Celsius increase in global mean temperatures as follows: wheat, down 6 percent; rice, down 3.2 percent, maize, down 7.4 percent; and soybeans, down 3.1 percent. Additional evidence on the negative effect of heat on crop yields has been provided by Schauberger et al. (2017) and Tack et al. (2017).

More detailed research has examined crop yields on the basis of night and day temperatures and assumptions of linearity in temperature–yield functions. Mohammed and Tarpley (2009, p. 999) observe that:

> although the global increase in nighttime temperature is at a faster rate than daytime temperature and it is well-known that high temperatures are a major constraint to crop productivity especially when temperature extremes coincide with critical stages of plant development, most of the studies on crop growth and grain yield are based on daily mean air temperature, which assumes no difference in the influence of day versus night temperatures.

They cite the work of Peng et al. (2004) who found that a decline in rice yields could be attributed to increased nighttime temperature associated with global warming.

Of particular note is evidence to support the theory that ecological processes are frequently not linear. Lobell et al. (2011) used historical data on African maize yields to demonstrate that the effect of heat on these yields was nonlinear. These results are even more pronounced under drought conditions than under optimal rain-fed management. Schlenker and Roberts (2009) conducted a similar analysis of US corn, soybean, and cotton yields and found that the resulting curvilinear function is concave to the x-axis whereby yields increase up to a full day 29–32°C and then decline steeply above these levels. Their conclusions, derived from scenario-based modeling, are not encouraging as they conclude that "area-weighted average yields are predicted to decrease by 30–46% before the end of the century under the slowest warming scenario and decrease by 63–82% under the most rapid warming scenario."

Unfortunately, the significant negative direct effects of rising temperatures on crop yields are accompanied by at least one major indirect effect: insect predation. Deutsch et al. (2018) use a spatially explicit insect population metabolism model to estimate losses to rice, maize, and wheat. Insect consumption of crops is driven by metabolic rates and population size, both of which are functions of temperature. Projected global yield losses are estimated to increase by 10 to 25 percent per degree Celsius of global mean surface warming, with the highest losses expected in the grain-producing regions of the northern hemisphere. Riegler (2018) concludes that this pessimistic assessment may be an underestimate as many insect pests are vectors of plant pathogens, which could further increase crop losses due to global warming. Other research on past and recent infestations of locusts also suggests causal links with short-term changes in weather patterns such as levels of precipitation (*Guardian* June 8, 2020; *East African* January 31, 2020; Tian et al. 2011; see also FAO 2019, chapter 2.4).

None of these findings is particularly encouraging in light of expected global population growth and increased incomes with their concomitant changes in taste towards more ecologically damaging foods. Principal among these is meat, the production of which relies heavily on grain as an input. Optimistic assessments that heat-stressed grain production could simply move further north towards a more benign environment are problematic for several reasons: first, the regions no longer hospitable for crop production will face increased economic hardships; second, as global temperatures continue to rise, geographic limits to further northern progression will be reached; and finally, not all soils at more northerly latitudes may be capable of supporting large-scale intensive crop production. As Overpeck and Conde observe (2019, p. 807), "absent climate change mitigation, adaptation strategies will in many cases become overwhelmed, leading to unacceptable costs to both human and natural systems."

A potentially portentous milestone was reached in late June and early July 2021 with the heat wave that afflicted the Pacific Northwest of North America, particularly Washington State, Oregon, Montana, and British Columbia. There were four distinguishing characteristics of the heat dome: first, daily heat records were exceeded not by small increments, but by large increases in the order of 9°F (BBC July 7, 2021), a surprising result considered virtually impossible without climate change (WWA 2021b). Portland Oregon reached 115°F and the town of Lytton in British Columbia set a new Canadian record of 121°F (*New York Times* June 29, 2021; CBC News June 30, 2021). Unfortunately, the town was subsequently completely destroyed by a forest fire. Second, there was significant damage to crops in both Washington State and British Columbia (CBC News July 6, 2021; *New York Times* July 3, 2021), with up to 75 percent of some fruit crops too damaged to be harvested. It has also been estimated that the heat dome might have killed as many as one billion small marine animals, such as mussels, snails, sea stars, and clams, on Canada's west coast, as well as threatening the region's iconic salmon fisheries (*Guardian* July 8, 2021a; *New York Times* July 9, 2021). A parallel threat has materialized in Montana with drought endangering the state's trout industry (*New York Times* July 23, 2021). Third, almost one thousand deaths in the human population of the Pacific Northwest have been attributed to the heat dome (CBC News July 2, 2021; *Guardian* July 8, 2021b). The fourth factor, potentially the most important, is the speculative hypothesis—as yet unproven— that a threshold has been crossed in the relationship between climate change and heat waves "where just a relatively small rise in global temperatures could greatly increase the likelihood of a big jump in [isolated events of] extreme heat" (*New York Times* July 7, 2021). This de facto tipping point was unanticipated as recently as July 2021 (*Guardian* July 7, 2021). Unfortunately, the heat event was not confined to the Pacific Northwest in North America, as California, Nevada, and Arizona subsequently experienced a similar problem, which exacerbated wildfires and threatened the operation of electric power grids.

Accompanying the heat wave in western North America have been massive forest fires in Oregon and British Columbia, unprecedented fires in Siberia, devastating flooding in Europe and British Columbia, and record rainfall in China (CNN July 16, 17, and 18, 2021; *New York Times* July 17, 21, and 22, and November 29, 2021; *Guardian* July 20, 2021). The distinguishing characteristic of all these events is the unmistakable fingerprint of climate change (CNN July 16, 2021). Unfortunately these types of events are likely to increase in frequency and severity until climate change is stabilized or reversed at some indeterminate time in the future (*Guardian* July 21, 2021; Kahraman et al. 2021). Clearly, if these types of record-breaking events become the norm they could represent a major threat to human health and global food supplies. Scientific support for this possibility has been provided by Fischer et al. (2021) who conclude: "In high-emission scenarios, week-long heat extremes that break records by three or more standard deviations are two to seven times more probable in 2021–2050 and three to 21 times more probable in 2051–2080, compared to the last three decades" (p. 1).

The occurrence of unprecedented extreme heat, drought, and excessive precipitation all pose a major threat to global food supply. While the quantity of food produced is the key to human survival, attention must also be paid to food quality, particularly its nutritional content.

Greenhouse gases and crop nutritional quality

To the prospect of future decreases in food output resulting from drought, heat, predation, and disease must be added the threat to the nutritional value of crops. One of the first studies to systematically survey and report on research findings was published by Loladze in 2002. The author found increasing ambient carbon dioxide led to decreases of up to 20 percent in a broad array of nutrients, including nitrogen, phosphorus, potassium, calcium, sulfur, magnesium, iron, zinc, manganese, and copper (see also Weyant et al. 2018). A string of more recent research has expanded on Loladze's analysis, predicting:

- lower concentrations of zinc and iron in grains and legumes (Myers et al. 2014; Weyant et al. 2018)
- increasing zinc deficiency, particularly in Africa and South Asia (Myers et al. 2015)
- significantly lower iron concentrations in wheat, rice, barley, legumes, and maize (Smith et al. 2017)

- reduced protein content of crops such as rice and wheat (Medek et al. 2017)
- reduction in protein, micronutrients, and vitamin content of rice (Zhu et al. 2018)
- decreased crop nitrogen and protein concentrations (Uddling et al. 2018)

These are worrying trends considering the current widespread extent of malnutrition among many developing nations (WMO 2018; WHO 2019).

Storms and floods

It is ironic that the process of global warming, which exacerbates drought and heat, can also cause increased rainfall and cooler temperatures depending on locale and time of year. A fundamental characteristic of climate change is the increased incidence of weather extremes, rainfall and heat, and the frequency and severity of storms (WWA 2021a). While some governments remain reluctant to acknowledge the existence and full ramifications of climate change, the phenomenon has not escaped the notice of the insurance industry. Major reinsurers such as Munich Re (n.d.) and Swiss Re (2020) have identified strong causal linkages between our warming planet and natural disasters and are predicting that events will worsen. While some experts are reluctant to link any one event to climate change, the overall pattern is clear—anthropogenic global warming is real and will get worse barring any major changes to our patterns of production and consumption. Each year, both major reinsurance companies produce reports on the extent and cost of natural disasters including, but not limited to, storms and floods.

While necessary for crop growth and survival, water can be devastating for agriculture if it occurs out of season or in too large a quantity over too short a time. Flooding can delay planting, destroy crops during the growing season, or prevent their expeditious harvesting. Serious storms entailing high winds, torrential rain, or hail can also damage or destroy crops in the fields, in greenhouses, or in storage (Iowa State University 2010; Purdue University Department of Agronomy 2019). The scientific literature and media have provided detailed descriptions of such events in diverse major food-producing areas of China (Sun et al. 2018), Northern Europe and Russia (Lehmann et al. 2018), sub-Saharan Africa (Müller et al. 2014), Africa (Kendon et al. 2019), the Mekong Delta (Kuenzer et al. 2013; Padilla 2011), Bangladesh (Rimi et al. 2018), Uruguay River basin (Abreu et al. 2018), and the US Midwest (CTV News March 19, 2019; *New York Times* March 18, 2019; Molten 2019).

A detailed analysis of the impact of floods on food security was performed by Pacetti et al. (2017) by integrating remote sensing with agricultural statistics and water footprint values. The authors focused on two major emblematic case studies: Bangladesh in 2007 and Pakistan in 2010. They concluded:

> In Bangladesh, the estimated lost rice is around 12.5% of the total potential production, which implies a 5.3% calories loss with respect to the total potential energy provided by rice and 4.4% of total WF [water footprint] associated to national food supply. In Pakistan, the results show a crops loss of 19% for sugarcane and 40% for rice, with a related calories loss of 8.5% and a WF loss of 13.5%. The results highlighted the countries vulnerability to flood, . . . [as] both countries [are] strongly dependent on local agricultural production. The 2007 flood event reflected badly upon Bangladeshi food security, almost doubling the existing food deficit. The same happened in Pakistan where an already scarce food supply has been worsened by the 2010 flood.
> (p. 503)

Table 6.2 Summary of billion–dollar disasters 1980–2019

Disaster type	Number of events	Percentage of all disasters	CPI-adjusted losses ($, billion)	Percentage of total losses	Average event cost ($, billions)	Deaths
Drought	26	10.60	247	14.60	9.5	2,993
Flooding	30	12.20	124.7	7.40	4.3	546
Freeze	9	3.70	30.2	1.80	3.4	162
Severe storm	106	43.10	232.6	13.80	2.2	1,630
Tropical cyclone	42	17.10	927.5	54.90	22.1	6,487
Wildfire	16	6.50	79.5	4.70	5	344
Winter storm	17	6.90	48.9	2.90	2.9	1,048
All disasters	246	100	1690.4	100	49.4	13,210

Source: NOAA 2019.

Note: Where percentages do not total 100, this is due to rounding.

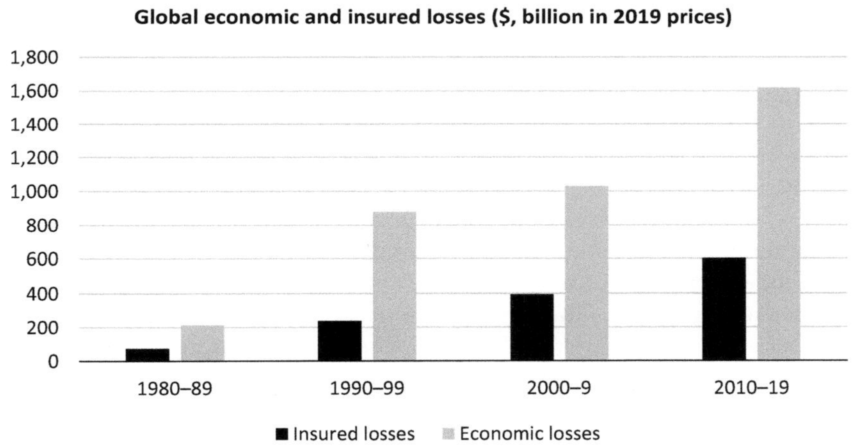

Global economic and insured losses ($, billion in 2019 prices)

Figure 6.5 Global economic and insured losses.
Source: Swiss Re 2020.

Some of the most extensive and detailed records of the cost of weather and climate disasters are available from the US National Centers for Environmental Information for the period 1980 to 2019 (NOAA 2019). Summary results are reproduced in Table 6.2, which shows costs totaling $1.69 trillion over these four decades. Clearly, this includes much more than crop damage. Further, a detailed examination of the data allows more precise identification of flood disasters in the United States. The following estimates of monetary damage include an agricultural component as part of the total cost: 1993 in the Midwest—$37.3 billion; 1997 in the Northern Plains—$5.9 billion; 2000 in South Florida—$1.4 billion; 2009 in the Mississippi River area—$3.4 billion; 2017 and Hurricane Maria— $92.7 billion; 2018 and Hurricane Michael—$25.2 billion; 2019 and the Midwest—costs to be determined (see also Figure 6.5).

At the global level, Munich Re and Swiss Re have assembled databases of more than 34,000 natural disasters that have occurred since 1974 (see Munich Re (n.d.) NatCatSERVICE; Swiss Re 2020; Hoeppe n.d.). Figure 6.5 summarizes economic and insured losses from weather-related disasters since 1980 (Swiss Re 2020). Over a decade ago, Munich Re (2010) had already identified an ominous trend:

> The long-term trend towards ever higher natural catastrophe costs continues. . . . the number and intensity of weather-related catastrophes is expected to increase in the coming decades, largely on account of climate change.
>
> (p. 1)

A recent study by Kummu et al. (2021) concluded that one-third of global food production is at risk from climate change. The authors introduce the concept of safe climate space (SCS), which incorporates the key variables that determine agricultural production: precipitation, temperature, and aridity. They conclude (p.1) that:

> rapid and unhalted growth of greenhouse gas emissions could force 31% of the global food crop and 34% of livestock production beyond the SCS by 2081–2100. The most vulnerable areas are South and Southeast Asia and Africa's Sudano-Sahelian Zone, which have low resilience to cope with these changes.

In conclusion, the principal message about the future of agriculture in the face of climate change is somber. There is mounting evidence, as detailed above, to suggest that even if major changes in food production systems were undertaken to reduce the array of negative externalities and make these systems more sustainable, continuing releases of GHGs and resulting global warming, if left unabated, would inevitably create a crisis which would seriously, if not irreparably, threaten global food supplies and the continued viability of modern civilization as we know it. These pessimistic conclusions have been reaffirmed by a recent report of the Intergovernmental Panel on Climate Change (IPCC 2019) on climate change and land; the IPCC concludes that our current system of industrial agriculture is unsustainable. We have pursued a narrow vision of efficiency at the expense of resilience. But the challenge facing our agricultural system transcends the multitude of problems associated with the myriad of negative externalities. Intensified efforts to develop new hybrid strains of crops that are resistant to flood, drought, salinity, and pest infestation will not alleviate the profound risk from increasing global temperatures. In fact, if the NASA projections of future temperatures prove to be correct, much of current agricultural production may not be possible. *In extremis*, our modern societies may regress from the social structure depicted in Figure 6.1 with its inverted pyramid shape to the pyramidal structure typical of the early years post agricultural revolution represented in Figure 5.1. In these circumstances, we could return to a dystopian world where the majority of the population, possibly much fewer in number, devotes most of its time to eking out a bare existence from the land.

References

Abreu, Rafael C. de et al. (2018) *Bulletin of the American Meteorological Society*, "Contribution of anthropogenic climate change to April–May 2017 heavy precipitation over the Uruguay River basin," December.

Ainsworth, Elizabeth A. and Stephen P. Long (2005) *The New Phytologist*, "What have we learned from 15 years of free-air CO_2 enrichment (FACE): A meta-analytic review of the responses of photosynthesis, canopy properties and plant production to rising CO_2," February.

Alizadeh, Mohammad Reza et al. (2020) *Science*, "A century of observations reveals increasing likelihood of continental-scale compound dry-hot extremes," September 8.

Anderson, W.B. et al. (2019) *Science Advances*, "Synchronous crop failures and climate-forced production variability," July 3.

Australia Department of Agriculture (accessed 2019) "Summary of Australia statistics for rice."

Avanzi, Francesco et al. (2020) *Hydrology and Earth System Sciences*, "Climate elasticity of evapotranspiration shifts the water balance of Mediterranean climates during multi-year droughts," September 3.

Bathiany, S. et al. (2018) *Scientific Reports*, "Abrupt climate change in an oscillating world," March 22.

Battisti, David S. and Rosamond L. Naylor (2009) *Science*, "Historical warnings of future food insecurity with unprecedented seasonal heat," January 9.

BBC (2021) "California declares state of emergency amid heatwave," June 18.

BBC (2021) "Record June temperatures point to more 'extraordinary' extremes," July 7.

BBC (2021) "Climate change: Europe's extreme rains made more likely by humans," August 24.

BBC (2021) "Climate change: World now sees twice as many days over 50C," September 13.

Berdugo, Miguel et al. (2020) *Science*, "Global ecosystem thresholds driven by aridity," February 15.

Biello, David (2009) "Can climate change cause conflict? Recent history suggests so," *Scientific American*, November 23.

Biello, David (2011) "Are high food prices fueling revolution in Egypt?" *Scientific American*, February 1.

Brown, Lester R. (2009) *Environment*, "Could food shortages bring down civilization?" May.

Büntgen, Ulf et al. (2021) *Nature Geoscience*, "Recent European drought extreme beyond Common Era background variability," April.

Burke, Elanor J. et al. (2006) *Journal of Hydrometeorology*, "Modeling the recent evolution of global drought and projections for the twenty-first century with the Hedley Centre Climate Model," October.

Businessinsider.com (2010) "Russia's wheat problem could be just the beginning of a global food crisis," The Daily Reckoning, August 10.

CARE et al. (2009) *In Search of Shelter: Mapping the Effects of Climate Change on Human Migration and Displacement.*

CBC News (2021) " 'Extreme drought' is threatening parts of the prairies, says Agriculture Canada," May 15.

CBC News (2021) "For 3rd straight day, B.C. village smashes record for highest Canadian temperature at 49.6 C," June 30.

CBC News (2021) "B.C.'s heat wave likely contributed to 719 sudden deaths in a week, coroner says—triple the usual number," July 2.

CBC News (2021) "B.C. heat wave 'cooks' fruit crops on the branch in sweltering Okanagan and Fraser valleys," July 6.

Center for Global Development (2012) "Pinpoint climate studies flag trouble for Mexico, CenAm farmers," December 20.

Chandler, David and Michael Le Page (2007) *New Scientist*, "Climate myths: Higher CO2 levels will boost plant growth and food production," May 16.

Chen, Yang et al. (2018) *Bulletin of the American Meteorological Society*, "Anthropogenic warming has substantially increased the likelihood of July 2017-like heat waves over central Eastern China," December.

Ciais, Ph. et al. (2005) *Nature*, "Europe-wide reduction in primary productivity caused by the heat and drought in 2003," September 22.

Climate Reality Project (2018) "How is climate change affecting Mexico?" February 15, Climaterealityproject.org

CNN (2021) "Climate change has pushed a million people in Madagascar to the 'edge of starvation,' UN says," June 23.

CNN (2021) "'Climate change has arrived,' European officials say, as deadly floods engulf entire towns," July 16.

CNN (2021) "Desperate search for survivors as Western Europe reels from a 'catastrophe of historic proportion'," July 17.

CNN (2021) "Europe floods: Enormous scale of destruction is revealed as water subsides," July 18.

CNN (2021) "The Middle East is running out of water, and parts of it are becoming uninhabitable," August 22.

Cook, B.I. et al. (2020) *Earth's Future*, "Twenty-first century drought projections in the CMIP6 forcing scenarios," April 19.

Cook, Benjamin I. et al. (2014) *Climate Dynamics*, "Global warming and 21st century drying," March.

Coumou, Dim and Alexander Robinson (2013) *Environmental Research Letters*, "Historic and future increase in the global land area affected by bimonthly heat extremes," September.

Cowan, Tim et al. (2020) *Nature Climate Change*, "Present-day greenhouse gases could cause more frequent and longer Dust Bowl heatwaves," May 18.

Cribb, Julian (2010) *The Coming Famine: The Global Food Crisis and What We Can Do to Avoid It*, Berkeley; Los Angeles; London: University of California Press.

CRO Forum (2016) *Emerging Risks Initiative. Risk Radar update*, October.

CSIRO (Commonwealth Scientific and Industrial Research Organisation) (2018) *State of the Climate 2018*, Australian Government Bureau of Meteorology.

CTV News (2019) "U.S. floodwaters threaten millions in crop and livestock losses," March 19.

Cullen, H.M. et al. (2000) *Geology*, "Climate change and the collapse of the Akkadian empire: Evidence from the deep sea," April 1.

Cure, Jennifer and Basil Acock (1986) *Agriculture and Forest Meteorology*, "Crop responses to CO2 doubling: A literature survey," October 1.

Dai, Aiguo (2011) *Climate Change*, "Drought under global warming - a review," January–February.

Desai, Bina et al. (2021) "Addressing the human cost in a changing climate," *Science*, June 18.

Deutsch, Curtis A. et al. (2018) *Science*, "Increase in crop losses to insect pests in a warming climate," August 31.

Devereux, Stephen (2002*) IDS Bulletin*, "The Malawi famine of 2002," October 1.

Diamond, Jared (2005) *Collapse: How Societies Choose to Fail or Succeed*, New York: Penguin.

Diaz, S. et al. (1993) "Evidence of a feedback mechanism limiting plant response to elevated carbon dioxide," *Nature*, August 12.

Diffenbaugh, Noah S. (2020) *Science Advances*, "Verification of extreme event attribution: Using out-of-sample observations to assess changes in probabilities of unprecedented events," March 18.

Dijk, Albert I.J.M. van et al. (2013) *Water Resources Research*, "The millennium drought in southeast Australia (2001–2009): Natural and human causes and implications for water resources, ecosystems, economy and society," 49: 1040–57.

Dosio, Alessandro (2017) *Climate Dynamics*, "Projection of temperature and heat waves for Africa with an ensemble of CORDEX Regional Climate Models," September 17.

Dyer, Gwynn (2011) *Climate Wars: The Fight for Survival as the World Overheats*, London, Oneworld Publications.

Earth Institute (2018) "Current megadrought in the West could be one of the worst in history," Columbia University, December 13.

East African (2020) "Climate change linked to African locust invasion," January 31.

Ebi, Kristie L. and Kathryn Bowen (2016) *Weather and Climate Extremes*, "Extreme events as sources of health vulnerability: Drought as an example," March.

Evans, Nicholas P. et al. (2018) *Science*, "Quantification of drought during the collapse of the classic Maya civilization," August 3.

FAO (Food and Agriculture Organization) (2019) *Food Systems at Risk: New Trends and Challenges.*

Feng, Qi et al. (2019) *Nature Sustainability*, "Domino effect of climate change over two millennia in ancient China's Hexi Corridor", October.

Fischer, E.M. et al. (2021) *Nature Climate Change,* "Increasing probability of record-shattering climate extremes," July 26.

Fischetti, Mark (2015) "Climate change hastened Syria's civil war," *Scientific American*, March 2.

Fisher, E.M. and R. Knutti (2015) *Nature Climate Change*, "Anthropogenic contribution to global occurrence of heavy-precipitation and high-temperature extremes," April 27.

Forsyth, Tim and Mareike Schomerus (2013) *Climate Change and Conflict: A Systematic Evidence Review*, The Justice and Security Research Programme," September.

Funk, Chris et al. (2018) *American Meteorological Society*, "Examining the potential contributions of extreme 'western V' sea surface temperatures to the 2017 March–June East African drought," December.

Glotter, Michael and Joshua Elliott (2016) *Nature Plants*, "Simulating Dust Bowl agriculture in a modern Dust Bowl drought," December 12.

Guardian (2019) "Australia to import wheat for first time in 12 years as drought eats into grain production," May 15.

Guardian (2019) "Indian villages lie empty as drought forces thousands to flee," June 12.

Guardian (2019) "Two million people at risk of starvation as drought returns to Somalia," June 6.

Guardian (2020) " 'Rolling emergency' of locust swarms decimating Africa, Asia and Middle East," June 8.

Guardian (2021) "California declares drought emergency across vast swath of state," May 10.

Guardian 2021) "World 'must step up preparations for extreme heat'," July 7.

Guardian (2021a) " 'Heat dome' probably killed 1bn marine animals on Canada coast, experts say," July 8.

Guardian (2021b) "Record-breaking US Pacific north-west heatwave killed almost 200 people," July 8.

Guardian (2021) " 'Everything is on fire': Siberia hit by unprecedented burning," July 20.

Guardian (2021) "Catastrophic floods could hit Europe far more often, study finds," July 21.

Guardian (2021) "Highest recorded temperature of 48.8C in Europe apparently logged in Sicily," August 11.

Guo, Yuming et al. (2018) *PLoS Medicine*, "Quantifying excess deaths related to heatwaves under climate change scenarios: A multicountry time series modelling study," July 31.

Haile, Gebremedhin Gebremeskel et al. (2020) *Earth's Future*, "Projected impacts of climate change on drought patterns over East Africa," May 26.

Hochman, Zvi et al. (2017) *Global Change Biology*, "Climate trends account for stalled wheat yields in Australia since 1990," January 24.

Hodell, David A. et al. (1995) *Nature*, "Possible role of climate in the collapse of Classic Maya civilization," June 1.

Hodell, David A. et al. (2001) *Science*, "Solar forcing of drought frequency in the Maya lowlands," May 18.

Hoell, Andrew et al. (2018) *Bulletin of the American Meteorological Society,* "Anthropogenic contributions to the intensity of the 2017 United States Northern Great Plains drought," December.

Hoeppe, Peter (n.d.) "Trends of natural disasters: The role of global warming." Presentation, Munich Re.

Holland, Andrew (2016) "Preventing climate wars," *Scientific American*, May 17.

Hsiang, Solomon M. and Marshall Burke (2014) *Climate Change,* "Climate, conflict and social stability: What does the evidence say?" 123: 39–55.

Hsiang, Solomon M. et al. (2011) *Nature*, "Civil conflicts are associated with the global climate," August 25.

Hsiang, Solomon M. et al. (2013) *Science*, "Quantifying the influence of climate on human conflict," September 13.

HuffPost (2021) "US West prepares for possible first water shortage declaration," April 17.

HuffPost (2021) "Parts of California given emergency drought declaration," April 21.

Im, Eun-Soon et al. (2017) *Science Advances*, "Deadly heat waves projected in the densely populated agricultural regions of South Asia," August 2.

Independent (2017) "Temperatures in Iranian city of Ahvaz hit 129.2F (54C), near hottest on Earth in modern measurements," June 30.

IndexBox (2019) *World—Wheat—Market Analysis, Forecast, Size, Trends and Insights*.

Iowa State University (2010) "Floods and your crops: Natural disasters," June.

IPCC (Intergovernmental Panel on Climate Change) (2019) *Climate Change and Land*.

Kahraman, Abdullah et al. (2021) *Geophysical Research Letters*, "Quasi-stationary intense rainstorms spread across Europe under climate change," June 30.

Kang, Suchul and Elfatih A.B. Eltahir (2018) *Nature Communications*, "North China plain threatened by heat waves due to climate change and irrigation," July 31.

Kendon, Elizabeth J. et al. (2019) *Nature Communications*, "Enhanced future changes in wet and dry extremes over Africa to convection-permitting scale," June.

Kew, Sarah F. et al. (2018) *Bulletin of the American Meteorological Society*, "The exceptional summer heat wave in Southern Europe 2017," December.

Kimball, B.A. (1983) *Agronomy Journal*, "Carbon dioxide and agricultural yield: An assemblage and analysis of 430 prior observations," September 1.

Kovenock, Marlies and Abigail L.S. Swann (2018) *Global Biogeochemical Cycles*, "Leaf trait acclimation amplifies simulated climate warming in response to elevated carbon dioxide," October 1.

Kuenzer, Claudia et al. (2013) *Remote Sensing*, "Flood mapping and flood dynamics of the Mekong Delta: ENVISAT-ASAR-WSM based time series analyses," February 5.

Kummu, Matti et al. (2021) *One Earth*, "Climate change risks pushing one-third of global food production outside the safe climatic space," May 21.

Laczko, Frank (2008) "Migration and the environment: We need policy-oriented research," Munich Re.

Lehmann, J. et al. (2018) *Geophysical Research Letters*, "Increased occurrence of record-wet and record-dry months reflect changes in mean rainfall," December 12.

Lesk, Corey et al. (2016) *Nature*, "Influence of extreme weather disasters on global crop production," January 7.

Lewis, Simon L. et al. (2011) *Science*, "The 2010 Amazon drought," February 4.

Li, Dawei et al. (2020) Environmental Research Letters, "Escalating global exposure to compound heat-humidity extremes with warming," May 19.

Liang, Yulian et al. (2018) *Theoretical and Applied Climatology*, "Projection of drought hazards in China during the twenty-first century," July.

Liu, Bing et al. (2016) *Nature Climate Change*, "Similar estimates of temperature impacts on global wheat yield by three independent methods," September 12.

Lobell, David B. (2011) *Science Express*, "Climate trends and global crop production since 1980", May 5.

Lobell, David B. et al. (2011) *Nature Climate Change*, "Nonlinear heat effects on African maize as evidenced by historical yield trials," April.

Loladze, Irakli (2002) *Trends in Ecology & Evolution*, "Rising atmospheric CO2 and human nutrition: Toward globally imbalanced plant stoichiometry," October.

Lu, Xuefei et al. (2016) *Scientific Reports*, "Elevated CO2 as a driver of global dryland greening," February 12.

Lunt, Tobias et al. (2016) *Climate Risk Management*, "Vulnerabilities to agricultural production shocks: An extreme, plausible scenario for assessment of risk for the insurance sector," 13(1–9).

Madakumbura, Gavin d. et al. (2021) *Nature Communications*, "Anthropogenic influence on extreme precipitation over global land areas seen in multiple observational datasets," July 6.

Markonis, Yannis et al. (2021) *Science Advances*, "The rise of compound warm-season droughts in Europe," February 3.

McLeman, Robert A. et al. (2013) *Population and Environment*, "What we learned from the Dust Bowl: Lessons in science, policy, and adaptation," August 28.

Medek, Danielle E. et al. (2017) *Environmental Health Perspectives*, "Estimate effects of future atmospheric CO_2 concentrations on protein intake and the risk of protein deficiency by country and region," August 2.

Mehrabi, Zia and Navin Ramankutty (2019) *Nature Ecology & Evolution*, "Synchronized failure of global crop production," April 15.

Missirian, Anouch and Wolfram Schlenker (2017) *Science*, "Asylum applications respond to temperature fluctuations," December 21.

Mohammed, A.R. and L. Tarpley (2009) *Agricultural and Forest Meteorology*, "High nighttime temperatures affect rice productivity through altered pollen germination and spikelet fertility," June.

Mohtadi, Shahrzad (2012) *Bulletin of the Atomic Scientists*, "Climate change and the Syrian uprising," August 16.

Molten, Megan (2019) *Wired*, "For the Midwest, epic flooding is the face of climate change," May 24.

Müller, Christoph et al. (2014) *Global Change Biology*, "Hotspots of climate change impacts in sub-Saharan Africa and implications for adaptation and development", May 5.

Munich Re (2010) "Munich Re sees unbroken upward trend in natural catastrophe costs, Chile earthquake loss forecast raised," June 8.

Munich Re (n.d.) NatCatSERVICE (natural catastrophe statistics online at Munichre.com).

Myers, Samuel S. et al. (2014) *Nature*, "Increasing CO_2 threatens human nutrition," May 7.

Myers, Samuel S. et al. (2015) *Lancet*, "Effect of increased concentrations of atmospheric carbon dioxide on the global threat of zinc deficiency: A modelling study," October.

NASA (National Aeronautics and Space Administration) (2015) "NASA releases detailed global climate change projections," June 9.

NASA (National Aeronautics and Space Administration) (2016) "CO2 is making Earth greener—for now," April 26.

NIC (National Intelligence Council) (2021) *National Intelligence Estimate: Climate Change and International Responses Increasing Challenges to US National Security through 2040*, NIC-NIE-2021-10030-A.

New York Times (1992) "Patient old Egypt can't go on like this," March 3.

New York Times (2008) "Rising inflation creates unease in Middle East," February 25.

New York Times (2017) "It's not your imagination. Summers are getting hotter," July 28.

New York Times (2018) "Hotter, drier, hungrier: How global warming punishes the world's poorest," March 12.

New York Times (2018) "A warming world creates desperate people," June 29.

New York Times (2019) "'It's probably over for us': Record flooding pummels Midwest when farmers can least afford it," March 18.

New York Times (2020) "In parched Southwest, warm spring renews threat of 'megadrought'," July 8.

New York Times (2021) "Severe drought, worsened by climate change, ravages the American west," May 19.

New York Times (2021) "Taiwan prays for rain and scrambles to save water," May 27.

New York Times (2021) "Brazil, besieged by Covid, now faces a severe drought," June 21.

New York Times (2021) "It's some of America's richest farmland, but what is it without water?" June 28.

New York Times (2021) "Pacific Northwest heat wave shatters temperature records," June 29.

New York Times (2021) "'Let the birds eat them': Crops shrivel as heat wave hits Washington," July 3.

New York Times (2021) "Climate change drove Western heat wave, analysis finds," July 7.

New York Times (2021) "Like 'postapocalyptic movies': heat wave killed marine wildlife en masse," July 9.

New York Times (2021) "As frozen land burns, Siberia trembles," July 17.

New York Times (2021) "Drought in Utah town halts growth," July 20.

New York Times (2021) "The bootleg fire is now generating its own weather," July 21.

New York Times (2021) "A somber toll as record rain swamps China," July 22.

New York Times (2021) "Montana's famed trout under threat as drought intensifies," July 23.

New York Times (2021) "After the floods, British Columbia picks up the pieces," November 29.

NOAA (National Oceanic and Atmospheric Administration) (2019) Database of billion-dollar weather and climate disasters 1980–2019.

Ó Gráda, Cormac (2009) *Famine: A Short History*, Princeton: NJ: Princeton University Press.

Ortiz-Bobea, Ariel et al. (2021) *Nature Climate Change*, "Anthropogenic climate change has slowed agricultural productivity growth," April 1.

Ortloff, Charles R. and Alan L. Kolata (1993) *Journal of Archaeological Science*, "Climate and collapse: Agro-ecological perspectives on the decline of the Tiwanaku state," March.

Overpeck, Jonathan T. and Cecilia Conde (2019) *Science*, "A call to climate action," May 31.

Oxfam (2012) "Food crises doomed to repeat until leaders find courage to fix problems," media advisory, August 15.

Pacetti, Tommaso et al. (2017) *Advances in Water Resources*, "Floods and food security: A method to estimate the effect of inundation on crops availability," June 28.

Padilla, Katie (2011) *ICE Case Studies*, "The impacts of climate change on the Mekong delta," December.

Pal, Jeremey S. and Elfatih A.B. Eltahir (2015) *Nature Climate Change*, "Future temperature in southwest Asia projected to exceed a threshold for human adaptability," October 26.

Parenti, Christian (2011) *Tropic of Chaos: Climate Change and the New Geography of Violence*, New York: Bold Type Books.

Park, Chang-Eui et al. (2018) *Nature Climate Change*, "Keeping global warming within 1.5°C constrains emergence of aridification," January 1.

Peng, Shaobing et al. (2004) *PNAS*, "Rice yields decline with higher night temperature from global warming," July 6.

Perez, Ines (2013) "Climate change and rising food prices heightened Arab Spring," *Scientific American*, March 4.

Peterson, Tim J. et al. (2021) *Science*, "Watersheds may not recover from drought," May 14.

Purdue University Department of Agronomy (2019) "Crops and floods: Crop damage by excessive rain, ponding, and floods."

Raymond, Colin et al. (2020) *Science Advances*, "The emergence of heat and humidity too severe for human tolerance," May 8.

Reich, Peter B. et al. (2018) *Science*, "Unexpected reversal of C3 versus C4 grass response to elevated CO2 during a 20-year field experiment," April 20.

Riegler, Markus (2018) *Science*, "Insect threats to food security", August 31.

Rimi, Ruksana H. et al. (2018) *Bulletin of the American Meteorological Society*, "Risks of pre-monsoon extreme rainfall events of Bangladesh: Is anthropogenic climate change playing a role?" December.

Rind, D. et al. (1990) *Journal of Geophysical Research*, "Potential evapotranspiration and the likelihood of future drought," June 20.

Rippey, Bradley R. (2015) *Weather and Climate Extremes*, "The U.S. drought of 2012," December.

Ritchie, Paul D.L. et al. (2021) *Nature Food*, "Shifts in national land use and food production in Great Britain after a climate tipping point," January.

Rogers, Cassandra D.W. et al. (2021) *Geophysical Research Letters*, "Recent increase in exposure to extreme humid-heat events disproportionately affect populated regions," September 17.

Romm, Joseph (2011) *Nature*, "The next dust bowl," October 27.

Schauberger, Bernhard et al. (2017) *Nature Communications*, "Consistent negative response of US crops to high temperatures in observations and crop models," January 19.

Schlenker, Wolfram and Michael J. Roberts (2009) *PNAS*, "Nonlinear temperature effects indicate severe damages to U.S. crop yields under climate change," September 15.

Schwartz, Peter and Doug Randall (2003) *An Abrupt Climate Change Scenario and Its Implications for United States National Security*, Jet Propulsion Laboratory, Pasadena, CA, October.

Science (2020) "Deep deficit," April 17.

Science (2021) "Extreme heat is broiling people in developing cities," October 4.

Seager, Richard et al. (2007) *Science*, "Model projections of an imminent transition to a more arid climate in southwestern North America," May 25.

Sheffield, Justin and Eric F. Wood (2011) *Drought: Past Problems and Future Scenarios*, Abingdon, Oxford: Earthscan, Routledge.

Sherwood, Steven C. and Matthew Huber (2010) *PNAS*, "An adaptability limit to climate change due to heat stress," May 25.

Sinha, Ashish et al. (2019) *Science Advances*, "Role of climate in the rise and fall of the Neo-Assyrian Empire," November 14.

Smith, M.R. et al. (2017) *GeoHealth*, "Potential rise in iron deficiency due to future anthropogenic carbon dioxide emissions," August 2.

Solomon, Susan et al. (2009) *PNAS*, "Irreversible climate change due to carbon dioxide emissions," September 2.

Soysa, Indra de and Nils Petter Gleditsch (1999) *Environmental Change & Security Project Report*, "To cultivate peace: Agriculture in a world of conflict," Issue 5, Summer.

Su, Buda et al. (2018) *PNAS*, "Drought losses in China might double between the 1.5°C and 2.0°C warming," October 16.

Sun, Ying, et al. (2018) *Bulletin of the American Meteorological Society*, "Anthropogenic influence on the heaviest June precipitation in Southeastern China since 1961," December.

Swiss Re (2020) *Natural Catastrophes in Times of Economic Accumulation and Climate Change*, Sigma No. 2.

Tack, Jesse et al. (2017) *PNAS*, "Disaggregating sorghum yield reductions under warming scenarios exposes narrow genetic diversity in US breeding programs," August 29.

Tai, Amos P.K. et al. (2014) *Nature Climate Change*, "Threats to future global food security from climate change and ozone air pollution," July.

Taylor, Alan (2011) *The Atlantic*, "Famine in East Africa," July 27.

Telegraph (2021) "Hotter than the human body can handle: Pakistan city broils in world's highest temperatures," June 28.

Tian, Huidong et al. (2011) *PNAS* "Reconstruction of a 1,910-y-long locust series reveals consistent associations with climate change fluctuations in China," August 30.

Tian, Wei et al. (2018) *Journal of Hydrology*, "Investigation and simulation of changes in the relationship of precipitation–runoff in drought years," August 15.

Tigchelaar, Michelle et al. (2018) *PNAS*, "Future warming increases probability of globally synchronized maize production shocks," June 26.

Trnka, Miroslav et al. (2019) *Science Advances*, "Mitigation efforts will not fully alleviate the increase in water scarcity occurrence probability in wheat-producing areas," September 25.

Uddling, Johan et al. (2018) *Current Opinion in Plant Biology*, "Crop quality under rising atmospheric CO_2," October.

UK Ministry of Defence (2018) *Global Strategic Trends: The Future Starts Today*, sixth edition.

UN (United Nations) (various years) *International Trade Statistics Yearbook*.

UN OCHA (United Nations Office for the Coordination of Humanitarian Affairs) (2021) "Madagascar: Humanitarian snapshot—March 2021," March 31.

Underwood, Emily (2015) *Science*, "Models predict longer, deeper U.S. droughts," February 13.

UNHCR (United Nations High Commissioner for Refugees) (2018) "Global trends: Forced displacement in 2018."

UNICEF (United Nations Children's Fund) (2005) "Drought exacerbates crisis in South Darfur," July 25.

US BLS (Bureau of Labor Statistics) (1998) "Three factors led to 1996 grain price shock," *TED:The Economics Daily*, November 2.

US DHS (Department of Homeland Security) (2021) *DHS Strategic Framework for Addressing Climate Change*, October 21.

US DoD (Department of Defense) (2014a) *Quadrennial Defense Review 2014.*

US DoD (Department of Defense) (2014b) *2014 Climate Change Adaptation Roadmap.*

US DoD (Department of Defense) (2015) *National Security Implications of Climate-Related Risks and a Changing Climate*, July 23.

US DoD (Department of Defense) (2021) *Climate Risk Analysis*, report to the National Security Council, October.

USA Today (2018) "Cape Town could be the first major city in the world to run out of water," January 22.

USDA (United States Department of Agriculture) (2009) "Egypt grain and feed annual," Global Agriculture Information Network, GAIN Report number EG9002, March 10.

USDA ERS (2011) "Why Another Commodity Price Spike?" September 1.

Verisk Maplecroft (2021) *Environmental Risk Outlook 2021.*

Vicedo-Cabrera, A.M. et al. (2021) "The burden of heat-related mortality attributable to recent human-induced climate change," *Nature Climate Change*, May 31.

Wang, Shanshan et al. (2018) *Bulletin of the American Meteorological Society,* "Attribution of the persistent spring-summer hot and dry extremes over Northeast China in 2017," December.

Weyant, Christopher et al. (2018) *PLoS Medicine*, "Anticipated burden and mitigation of carbon-dioxide-induced nutritional deficiencies and related diseases: A simulation modeling study," July 3.

White House (2021) *Report on the Impact of Climate Change on Migration*, October.

WHO (World Health Organization) (2019) "World hunger is still not going down after three years and obesity is still growing," July 15.

Wiggins, Steve et al. (2010) *What Caused the Food Price Spike of 2007–08? Lessons for World Cereal Markets*, UK Overseas Development Institute, March.

Williams, A. Park et al. (2020) *Science*, "Large contribution from anthropogenic warming to an emerging North American megadrought," April 17.

Winsemius, Hessel et al. (n.d.) "Global exposure analysis on floods/drought and poverty." Presentation, World Bank and Institute for Environmental Studies, University Amsterdam.

WMO (World Meteorological Organization) (2018) *Global Nutrition Report*.

WMO (2019) *State of the Climate in Africa 2019.*

World Bank (2014a) *Groundswell: Preparing for Internal Climate Migration.*

World Bank (2014b) *Turn Down the Heat: Confronting the New Climate Normal.*

World Bank (2016) *High and Dry: Climate Change, Water, and the Economy.*

WWA (World Weather Attribution) (2021a) "Heavy rainfall which led to severe flooding in Western Europe made more likely by climate change," August 23.

WWA (World Weather Attribution) (2021b) "Western North American extreme heat virtually impossible without human-caused climate change," July 7.

Xu, Chi et al. (2020) *PNAS*, "Future of the human climate niche," May 4.

Yancheva, Gergana et al. (2007*) Nature*, "Influence of the intertropical convergence zone on the East Asian monsoon," January 4.

Yuan, Wenping et al. (2019) *Science Advances*, "Increased atmospheric vapor pressure deficit reduces global vegetation growth," August 14.

Zhao, Chuang et al. (2017) *PNAS*, "Temperature increase reduces global yields of major crops in four independent estimates," August 29.

Zhou, Chunlue, et al. (2018) *Bulletin of the American Meteorological Society,* "Attribution of a record-breaking heatwave event in summer 2017 over the Yangtze River Delta," December.

Zhou, Sha et al. (2019) *Science Advances,* "Projected increase in intensity, frequency, and terrestrial carbon costs of compound drought and aridity events," January 23.

Zhu, Chunwu et al. (2018) *Science Advances,* "Carbon dioxide (CO_2) levels this century will alter the protein, micronutrients, and vitamin content of rice grains with potential health consequences for the poorest rice-dependent countries," May 23.

Part III

Quid nunc? Solutions, conditional solutions, and nonsolutions

In light of the multifaceted challenges to environmental and resource sustainability outlined in Part II of this book, a diverse range of new technologies and production processes have been adopted or proposed. Prominent among these are electric cars, autonomous vehicles, nuclear power, renewable energy, carbon capture and storage, and geoengineering. Each is reviewed in Part III.

DOI: 10.4324/9781003199540-9

7 Hi-tech transportation

Several potential game changers have emerged, each of which holds out the promise of revolutionizing the field of personal transport: electric cars and autonomous vehicles (AVs). Each is discussed in turn, followed by a review of the state and promise of mass transit, and what has been called the Internet of Motion.

Electric cars

Electric vehicles (EVs) are now considered the technology of choice by several major countries as they attempt to address the pressing problem of climate change (see Figures 7.1 and 7.2). For example, Germany has announced its intention to ban the sale of internal combustion engines (ICEs) by 2030, both the United Kingdom and France have proposed similar bans to come into effect by 2040, California will ban all sales of new gas-powered cars by 2035, and the Biden administration has budgeted $174 billion to encourage the adoption of EVs (Inside EVs 2016; *Guardian* July 6, 2017; BBC July 26, 2017; *New York Times* September 23, 2020 and March 31, 2021). For its part, China, now the world's largest market for EVs (at 40 percent of global sales), has called for 20 percent of all vehicles sold in the country to run on alternative fuels by 2025 and plans eventually to eliminate all ICEs in new cars (*New York Times* October 9, 2017; *Independent* September 10, 2017). Bloomberg (April 12, 2019 and December 16, 2020) has forecast that battery-powered EVs will be cheaper than ICE vehicles in 2025 and more than half of all global light-duty vehicles sold will be electric by 2040. This prediction of cost parity has been reaffirmed by the investment bank UBS (2020), which expects the total cost gap with conventional cars will close fully by 2024. Sales of EVs have been accelerating, increasing by 43 percent globally in 2020, and some analysts feel that the adoption of these vehicles is nearing a tipping point (IEA 2020; *New York Times* September 20, 2020; *Guardian* January 22, 2021). While China and the United States have the largest number of EVs in operation (IEA 2020), in 2020 Norway became the first country where sales of EVs outstripped all other types of propulsion (*Guardian* January 5, 2021). Nevertheless, it appears that China may achieve major dominance in the global production of EVs because of government policy promoting the development of technological expertise and the control and processing of vital minerals used in EVs (Ward's 2019; McKinsey 2020; *New York Times* January 29, May 6, October 31, November 20 and 21 2021, and May 4, 2021b; IEA 2021).

In recognition of this emerging trend towards EVs, several major automobile manufacturers including GM, Volvo, Volkswagen, and Ford have already announced their intention to shift part or all of production to EVs (CNN February 17, 2021; *New York Times* January 28, February 17, March 2, March 16, April 23 and October 5, 2021; ABC

DOI: 10.4324/9781003199540-10

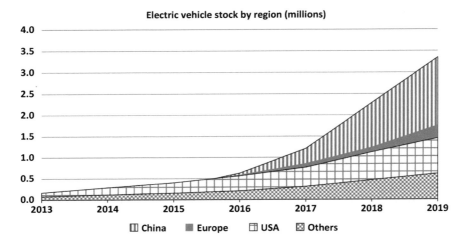

Figure 7.1 Electric vehicle stock by region.
Source: IEA 2020.

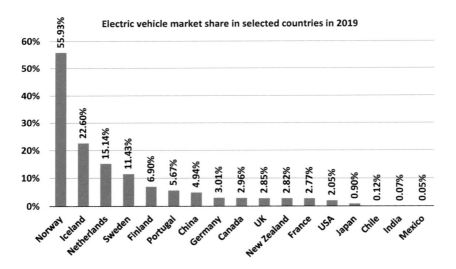

Figure 7.2 Electric vehicle market share in selected countries, 2019.
Source: IEA 2020.

News August 5, 2021). Symbolic of this shift is that the market value of electric car manu-facturer Tesla has risen above that of ExxonMobil "in a sign that investors are increasingly betting on a global energy transition away from fossil fuels" (Bloomberg Green June 30, 2020).

There are three principal variants of EVs: gasoline-electric hybrids, either plug-in or onboard generated, and pure plug-in. From the point of view of addressing cli-mate change, only the pure EV satisfies the criterion of eliminating fossil fuel as a direct fuel. The International Energy Agency (IEA 2020) has estimated that given the right circumstances the global stock of EVs could reach as many as 140–245 million by 2030. Bloomberg's estimates (Bloomberg New Energy Finance May 21, 2018) suggest as many as 600 million by 2040.

Electric vehicles may be a conceptually appealing answer to the dilemma posed by the rapidly surging dissemination of ICEs, but they come with several critical issues:

1. First is the familiar "chicken-and-egg" problem where the widespread adoption of EVs requires extensive infrastructure (principally charging stations), but the incentive for building such stations is influenced by the number of EVs on the road. The adoption rate will also be constrained by a fleet turnover problem as new ICE vehicles sold today could last one or two decades before trade-ins or disposal (*New York Times* January 29 and March 13, 2021).
2. There are questions concerning battery capacity and miles between charges as well as charging times (*New York Times* May 4, 2021a). However, Toshiba has announced that it is developing a solid-state battery with fast charging capability, which can reduce recharge times to as little as six minutes, while researchers at Penn State University have developed technology for a ten-minute recharge, comparable to refueling times for ICE cars (Toshiba 2017; Messer 2019). The battery challenge has become a central focus of the auto industry with the prospect of major technological advances in the near to medium-term future (*New York Times* February 16 and September 8, 2021; Pomerantseva et al. 2019; Yang et al. 2019). Ford has predicted that the successful development of a solid-state battery could increase battery energy density by at least 25–30 percent, leading to a comparable increase in driving range with the same size battery (*US News & World Report* May 5, 2021).
3. While EVs are generally found to have a lower environmental impact (Patterson et al. 2011; IEA and ICCT 2019; Knobloch et al. 2020; *New York Times* March 2, 2021b) there are some concerns: for example, the absence of any major reductions in total material use and weight versus ICE cars. Hawkins et al. (2012) conducted a comparative life-cycle assessment of the materials content of a standard ICE vehicle and an EV and concluded that "EVs exhibit the potential for significant increases in human toxicity, freshwater eco-toxicity, freshwater eutrophication, and meta depletion impacts, largely emanating from the vehicle supply chain. Results are sensitive to assumption regarding electricity source, use phase energy consumption, vehicle lifetime, and battery replacement schedules" (p. 53). These conclusions have been reaffirmed by a major study by the consulting firm Arthur D. Little (Brennan and Barder 2016). A study by McKinsey (2018) anticipates increased demand and price rises for commodities currently essential to EV technology, such as cobalt and lithium (*New York Times* May 6, 2021). However, the future development and rollout of solid-state batteries may reduce and change the nature of material requirements (Bloomberg New Energy Finance May 21, 2018). Building, repairing, recycling, and disposal of EV-related material will pose new challenges that have to be addressed (Harper et al. 2019; *New York Times* March 31, 2021) as well as the geopolitical, ethical, and environmental issues of sourcing exotic metals and conflict minerals (*New York Times* May 6, 2021; IEA 2021). As mentioned, a downside of the extensive adoption of batteries is the problem of disposal; Morse (2021) reports that there is a concerted push to develop better recycling methods. However, one positive note is that the average battery cell composition of several of these metals and materials is projected

to decrease within the next decade (Transport & Environment 2021). An additional challenge is highlighted by Melin et al. (2021) who call for clear global standards for battery regulation to avoid investment distortions, material leakage where the outflow of recycled products across national borders deprives a country of sufficient recycled content for its industries, and investment slowdown.

4. Three recent British reports (Eyre and Killip 2019; CCC 2019a and b) have identified another potential problem with the wide-scale adoption of EVs. Since EVs are cheaper to run than ICE cars, the net result might be an increase, rather than decrease, in vehicle use, reflecting a typical downward sloping demand curve.

5. There is a potential risk of fire associated with batteries in EVs. The *Washington Post* (August 4, 2021) recently reported on a fire in a Tesla electric car parked overnight in an owner's garage. To quote:

> Automakers including General Motors, Audi and Hyundai have recalled EVs over fire risks in recent years and have warned of the associated dangers. Chevrolet last year advised owners not to charge their vehicles overnight or keep their fully charged vehicles in garages. It recalled more than 60,000 of its Bolt electric vehicles over concerns about the cars spontaneously combusting while parked with full batteries or charging, after reports of five fires without prior impact damage. The company issued another recall last month covering the same vehicles after two reports of battery fires in repaired vehicles.

6. The most important issue is the source of the electricity used to power EVs. From the point of view of GHGs, the wide-scale adoption of EVs may replace the multitude of individual cars generating GHGs with fewer but much larger individual sources of GHGs, in other words, centralized power plants. This is critically dependent on the fuel used (i.e. fossil versus non-fossil) to generate the electricity and this, in turn, will vary markedly by geographic location (Holdway et al. 2010). Table 7.1 reports the current mix of carbon-based and non-carbon-based fuel sources for selected countries in 2017 as reported by the IEA (2017a). Biofuels and waste are broken out as a separate category since as much as 50 percent of such fuels is carbon based. As such, there may be a critical time lapse between combustion of biofuels, with the concomitant release of CO_2, and the subsequent uptake of CO_2 through plant regrowth.

Assuming, for the sake of argument, that countries were somehow able to convert all their existing automotive stock to electric power, then the question arises as to how much additional national power capacity would be required (*New York Times* March 2, 2021a and August 3, 2021). Table 7.2 illustrates the derivation of these estimates and shows the wide range of increases in electricity capacity needed depending on national car stock and total installed capacity. These values range from a low of 1 percent in Denmark to 33 percent in Croatia and the United Kingdom. One research study concluded that a shift to EVs may have little overall system-wide effect on GHGs if the national grid is dominated by coal-fired generation (Wilson 2013), although other researchers are less pessimistic about the net impact on total emissions (Knobloch et al. 2020).

Clearly, the current mix of fuel sources is less important than the nature of new sources brought on line at the margin. As a case in point, China has made it national policy to lead the world in the introduction of renewably sourced power. Despite this fact, however,

Table 7.1 Electricity mix in 2015 by country

TWh

Country	Fossil fuels	Nuclear	Hydro	Geothermal	Solar/wind	Biofuel and waste	Total
Australia	217.56	0	16.29	0	20.67	3.5	258.02
Austria	15.71	0	42.25	0	7.86	5.51	71.33
Belgium	25.5	42.23	1.4	0	10.33	7.16	86.62
Canada	124.71	101.11	392.65	0	32.58	7.35	658.4
China	4678.33	248.07	1189.84	0.13	425.72	92.82	6634.91
Denmark	8.4	0	0.02	0	15.53	7.09	31.04
Finland	12.7	22.48	14.77	0	5.24	12.34	67.53
France	62.89	398.36	55.11	0.13	35.48	10.17	562.14
Germany	346.08	76.32	26.16	0.16	146.8	58.22	653.74
Greece	41.39	0	4.04		9.53	0.31	55.27
Iceland	0	0	14.06	5.17	0.01	0	19.24
Ireland	21.63	0	0.9	0	7.46	0.89	30.88
Israel	65.74	0	0	0	1.93	0	67.67
Italy	186.97	0	38.02	6.2	42.78	21.85	295.82
Japan	819.9	32.91	90.16	2.46	81.96	40.93	1068.32
Korea	393.25	148.43	7.01	0	11.3	6.9	566.89
Netherlands	94.61	3.4	0.06	0	12.9	6.29	117.26
New Zealand	8.27	0	25.18	7.91	2.27	0.59	44.22
Norway	2.74	0	142.99	0	3.13	0.5	149.36
Portugal	34.84	0	7.63	0.22	13.24	3.5	59.43
Spain	126.15	58.04	21.07	0	63.62	6.85	275.73
Sweden	1.79	65.7	65.17	0	17.84	13.76	164.26
Switzerland	0.76	20.38	37.03	0	1.82	3.1	63.09
Turkey	209.17	0	58.22	6.13	21.64	2.12	297.28
United Kingdom	161.64	70.34	8.8	0	61.53	36.02	338.33
United States	2691.54	838.86	325.11	18.73	333.67	78.52	4286.43

Source: IEA 2017a.

the country is still adding coal-based capacity at a significant rate in order to meet rapidly expanding demand (*New York Times* July 1, 2017). McKinsey (2018) has estimated that if half the cars on the roads in the United States were EVs, daily natural gas demand would increase by more than 20 percent. Electric vehicles would have to be charged largely off peak in order to avoid creating peaking problems in electricity demand, which would require significantly more generating capacity. As far as the United States is concerned, a hopeful sign is that much of the recent incremental additions to generating capacity have been renewable (US EIA 2018 and 2020), suggesting that the increased adoption of EVs is not making a major contribution to GHG emissions. In fact, green power accounted for more than 50 percent of global net additional electricity capacity in 2015 (*Guardian* October 25, 2016). The IEA (2021) reported: "Renewable energy use increased 3% in 2020 as demand for all other fuels declined. The primary driver was an almost 7% growth in electricity generation from renewable sources."

Another game-changing breakthrough has been the introduction of an electric version of Ford's iconic and bestselling F-150 Lightning truck (*New York Times* May 19, 2021b).

' *Table 7.2* Anticipated electricity demand for electric vehicles

Country	km/car/year	Cars	'000 total km	km per kWh		Annual kWh		Annual TWh		Electricity generated	Increment required (%)	
				Min	Max	Min	Max	Max	Min	TWh	Max	min
Australia	13,800	13,297,260	183,502,188,000	4	6	45,875,547,000	30,583,698,000	45.88	30.58	248.26	18	12
Austria	12,600	4,694,921	59,156,004,600	4	6	14,789,001,150	9,859,334,100	14.79	9.86	61.6	24	16
Belgium	14,000	5,511,080	77,155,120,000	4	6	19,288,780,000	12,859,186,667	19.29	12.86	71.46	27	18
Bulgaria	600	3,017,000	1,810,200,000	4	6	452,550,000	301,700,000	0.45	0.30	46.927	1	1
Canada	15,200	21,729,596	330,289,859,200	4	6	82,572,464,800	55,048,309,867	82.57	55.05	656.11	13	8
China (est.)	16,900	120,724,000	2,040,235,600,000	4	6	510,058,900,000	340,039,266,667	510.06	340.04	5665.745	9	6
Croatia	12,100	1,466,000	17,738,600,000	4	6	4,434,650,000	2,956,433,333	4.43	2.96	13.436	33	22
Czech Republic	7,600	4,893,562	37,191,071,200	4	6	9,297,767,800	6,198,511,867	9.30	6.20	84.97	11	7
Denmark	500	2,329,578	1,164,789,000	4	6	291,197,250	194,131,500	0.29	0.19	32.18	1	1
Finland	12,600	3,172,735	39,976,461,000	4	6	9,994,115,250	6,662,743,500	9.99	6.66	68.09	15	10
France (est.)	18,000	31,800,000	572,400,000,000	4	6	143,100,000,000	95,400,000,000	143.10	95.40	556.98	26	17
Germany	13,500	44,403,124	599,442,174,000	4	6	149,860,543,500	99,907,029,000	149.86	99.91	621.94	24	16
Iceland	11,700	216,000	2,527,200,000	4	6	631,800,000	421,200,000	0.63	0.42	18.12	3	2
India (est.)	20,500	27,174,000	557,067,000,000	4	6	139,266,750,000	92,844,500,000	139.27	92.84	1041.53	13	9
Ireland	16,900	1,933,000	32,667,700,000	4	6	8,166,925,000	5,444,616,667	8.17	5.44	26.04	31	21
Israel	17,700	2,445,000	43,276,500,000	4	6	10,819,125,000	7,212,750,000	10.82	7.21	60.81	18	12
Italy	1,500	37,080,753	55,621,129,500	4	6	13,905,282,375	9,270,188,250	13.91	9.27	278.12	5	3
Japan	7,900	60,667,517	479,273,384,300	4	6	119,818,346,075	79,878,897,383	119.82	79.88	1035.53	12	8
Korea	12,600	15,747,162	198,414,241,200	4	6	49,603,560,300	33,069,040,200	49.60	33.07	545.87	9	6
Latvia	1,400	657,799	920,918,600	4	6	230,229,650	153,486,433	0.23	0.15	5.141	4	3
Lithuania	1,500	1,869,000	2,803,500,000	4	6	700,875,000	467,250,000	0.70	0.47	3.708	19	13
Luxembourg	1,300	372,538	484,299,400	4	6	121,074,850	80,716,567	0.12	0.08	1.91	6	4
Netherlands	14,500	8,192,570	118,792,265,000	4	6	29,698,066,250	19,798,710,833	29.70	19.80	103.42	29	19
New Zealand	12,300	2,767,000	34,034,100,000	4	6	8,508,525,000	5,672,350,000	8.51	5.67	43.55	20	13
Norway	11,100	2,539,552	28,189,027,200	4	6	7,047,256,800	4,698,171,200	7.05	4.70	141.59	5	3
Slovak Republic	1,500	1,949,000	2,923,500,000	4	6	730,875,000	487,250,000	0.73	0.49	27.15	3	2

Slovenia	9,700	1,076,962	4	10,446,531,400	6	2,611,632,850	1,741,088,567	2.61	1.74	17.16	15	10
Sweden	9,200	4,585,520	4	42,186,784,000	6	10,546,696,000	7,031,130,667	10.55	7.03	153.55	7	5
Switzerland	10,600	4,384,490	4	46,475,594,000	6	11,618,898,500	7,745,932,333	11.62	7.75	70.1	17	11
Turkey	6,200	9,857,915	4	61,119,073,000	6	15,279,768,250	10,186,512,167	15.28	10.19	251.96	6	4
United Kingdom	13,700	32,612,782	4	446,795,113,400	6	111,698,778,350	74,465,852,233	111.70	74.47	336.04	33	22
United States	18,309	120,983,811	4	2,215,092,595,599	6	553,773,148,900	369,182,099,267	553.77	369.18	4319.16	13	9
Indicator	—	—	—	—	—	—	—	—	—	Max	33	—
										Min	—	1

There are several critical characteristics which distinguish EVs, including the Lightning, from internal combustion vehicles (Motor1.com 2013 p. 1):

- An ICE vehicle can never be made to operate as efficiently as an EV.
- An ICE vehicle will always require more maintenance than an EV.
- The number of moving/breakable parts in an ICE will always be higher than in an EV.
- No ICE will ever come with free gas for life. An EV is offered today with free "fuel" for life (Tesla Model S Supercharging).
- No ICE will ever offer the immediate torque and smooth power delivery of an EV.
- If AWD [all-wheel drive] is your cup of tea, EVs, with their infinitely controllable electric motors, beat ICE [sic] hands down.

The new F-150 Lightning has several noteworthy features. To quote Ford's advertising (Ford website):

> **The Front Trunk Has Power.** The front trunk features four Pro Power Onboard 120V outlets for a total of 2.4kW of exportable power, plus one USB-C and one USB-A outlet. You can run power tools and a TV when you're off the clock.
>
> **Ford Intelligent Backup Power.** Have a power outage at home? No problem. Because the all-electric F-150 Lightning features available Ford Intelligent Backup Power that can provide full-home power for up to three days on a fully charged battery, or as long as ten days if rationing power. Combined with the available 80-amp Ford Charge Station Pro, this control over your home energy is good at the best of times, but essential when power outages are a reality.

Perhaps, most importantly, the potentially widespread appeal of the F150 Lightning holds the promise of moving EVs into the mainstream of the US automotive market, attracting a large number of buyers who might have been indifferent or hostile to the use of electric automobiles.

In sum, the net contribution to the amelioration of climate change by the widespread adoption of EVs remains an open question at the moment, pending major new advances in battery and related technologies. Even if such obstacles were to be overcome, many of the negative effects of automobile use, such as material use, pollution from tire, brake, and road wear, congestion, the need for supporting road infrastructure, and accidents, among others, would remain unaddressed. As Farhad Manjoo concludes in his *New York Times* column (February 18, 2021) on technology: "There's one big problem with electric cars. They're still cars. Technology can't cure America of its addiction to the automobile." Nevertheless, there are already signs that urban mobility modes and design are being reimagined and some public policies related to permitted automotive density and street use are being adjusted in light of the emergence of EVs (Statista July 19, 2019; Manjoo 2020; *Daily Telegraph* June 26, 2020; *New York Times* November 14, 2019, and March 3, May 27, and October 3 2021; CNN February 9, 2021).

Autonomous vehicles

While the emergence of the electric car as a viable alternative to the traditional fossil-fueled vehicle is, in many ways, a landmark development, it is by no means revolutionary, as EVs were in production and use in the early nineteenth century. In contrast, the development of the self-driving car promises to revolutionize not only the private and commercial vehicle sectors, but also drastically to change the economic, social, and political context in which this new technology will exist. Arbib and Seba (2017, p. 6) feel that "we are on the cusp of one of the fastest, deepest, most consequential disruptions of transportation in history."

Echoing the problem of linear extrapolation in the face of exponential growth discussed in Chapter 1 of this volume, Arbib and Seba state that there is overwhelming evidence that:

> Mainstream analysis is missing, yet again, the speed, scope and impact of technology disruption. Unlike those analyses, which produce linear and incremental forecasts, our modeling incorporates systems dynamics, including feedback loops, network effects and market forces that better reflect the reality of fast-paced technology-adoption S-curves.
>
> (p. 6)

At present, there are several variants of AV technology, some operational, others in development. Mervis (2017) lists five levels describing the degree of automotive self-driving and current status: (1) accelerates, brakes, *or* steers—present fleet; (2) accelerates, brakes, *and* steers—now in testing; (3) assumes full control within narrow parameters, such as when driving on the freeway, but not during merges or exits—might never be deployed; (4) everything, only under certain conditions (e.g., specific locations, speed, weather, time of day)—where the industry wants to be; and (5) everything—goes everywhere, any time, and under all conditions—somewhere in the next half-century. As Mervis observes, only level five represents a true AV vehicle (see also US EIA 2017).

While some of the benefits of this new technology remain speculative at this time, there are several purported benefits which have received wide-scale publicity: (1) AVs will reduce congestion by removing cars from the road, reducing air pollution; (2) AVs could help create more public space because they would eliminate the need for parking structures; and (3) AVs will be shared, meaning fewer cars on the road, thereby also promising significant reduction in greenhouse gas (GHG) emissions (Arieff 2017). Additional benefits might include fewer traffic accidents, injuries, and deaths and more free time for the pursuit of work or leisure.

Because the introduction and testing of AVs has occurred only recently (Mervis 2017), there is little empirical evidence to support any of these promised benefits at this time. The general tenor of these assumed positive effects follows a long history of promised benefits accompanying the introduction of any new technology with little consideration of possible short-term and long-term costs or disadvantages (*New York Times* May 24, 2021; Norton 2021). In many respects, the automobile is the archetypal example of revenge theory. Despite all its manifest benefits, the private vehicle has created enormous negative externalities, not the least of which is its significant contribution to global warming and the concomitant threat to human civilization. While the self-driving vehicle promises to alleviate many of these externalities, there is little evidence at this point to support this optimistic conclusion. In fact, several researchers have hypothesized that the AV may worsen, rather than alleviate, the problems such as traffic volume and accidents that we so desperately need to address (Harb et al. 2018; Schaller Consulting 2017; ABC News October 25, 2021).

In the short run, there are several critical technological challenges which must be addressed: resolution of intersensor conflict, interpretation of and response to roadworks and other animate and inanimate obstacles, unusual weather conditions, and interactions with human-driven vehicles (*Guardian* July 5, 2016). The complex nature of interaction between humans and automated machines has been illustrated in the context of air travel by a US FAA report (2013, p. 26) which found:

> "Automation behavior is unexpected or unexplained" . . . was present in about 46% of the accident reports, 60% of major incident reports, and 38% of ASRS [Aviation Safety Reporting System] incidents. The general issue "Understanding of automation is inadequate" was present in about 34% of the accident reports, 30% of the major incident reports, and 5% of the ASRS incidents. Also included in this set is the issue "Automation is too complex" because complex systems are often difficult to understand.

Similar concerns have been raised in the context of nuclear power (see Chapter 8). While automotive automation differs in multiple respects from both aviation and nuclear technology, the generic issue of how humans respond to automated systems transcends specific technologies.

New issues will have to be addressed such as the increased potential for motion sickness (Sivak and Schoettle 2015), accident liability (Popper 2017), and hacking and security threats (Lu 2017). In a special issue of the *New York Times Magazine* (November 7, 2017), the newspaper asked several authors to imagine the future of a world dominated by AVs. The short essays ranged in content from the fantastic to the macabre. In one tongue-in-cheek essay by Mark O'Connell (2017) entitled "Get ready for D.O.A.s," the author posited that "the saddest part about self-driving cars will be all the times people die mid-trip and then our dinner guests or pizza guy will arrive dead." He concludes that

> self-driving cars bearing the earthly remains of the recently deceased—automated Ubers, say, with heart-attack victims sprawled incredulously across the rear seat—are, in a sense, an extreme metaphor for the near future of capitalism. The technology will be miraculous, yes; but if it functions as intended, it will serve as an uncanny vector of human obsolescence.

Despite this somewhat far-fetched and dystopian imagined future, there are several serious concerns raised in the research literature about the utopian vision of an AV future. Sivak and Schoettle (2016) anticipate no significant increase in occupant productivity despite promises to this effect. Arieff (2017) argues that AVs will not reduce congestion and that given the American love for cars, few will be willing to give them up for car sharing. Walker (2018) has used a simulation model to predict that not only will congestion not be reduced, but that vehicle miles will increase despite a potential decrease in the total vehicle fleet. But perhaps the most serious prediction has been generated by the US National Renewable Energy Laboratory (NREL 2013) which concluded that under one scenario, total fuel demand by light-duty vehicles could increase by as much as 217 percent, thereby leading to a worsening of global warming rather than its alleviation.

One tantalizing promise of the new technology is a reduction in the enormous human cost of road accidents in the form of injuries and fatalities. The number of both fatal and nonfatal injuries could increase significantly in the next decade as the adoption of automobiles continues to spread, especially in the developing world. The associated economic costs are enormous, estimated at $518 billion and representing as much as

3–5 percent of GDP (CDC 2016; WHO 2021). Clearly any new technology, such as autonomous automobiles, delivering on promises to drastically reduce these numbers would be a benefit. This is clearly a goal yet to be achieved in light of a few recent fatalities due to AVs *(New York Times* December 7, 2020, and March 25 and July 5, 2021; CNN April 19, 2021).

Arbib and Seba (2017) present a grand utopian vision of the changes that AVs will bring about. To quote:

> By 2030, within 10 years of regulatory approval of autonomous vehicles (AVs), 95% of U.S. passenger miles traveled will be served by on-demand autonomous electric vehicles owned by fleets, not individuals, in a new business model we call "transport-as-a-service" (TaaS). The TaaS disruption will have enormous implications across the transportation and oil industries, decimating entire portions of their value chains, causing oil demand and prices to plummet, and destroying trillions of dollars in investor value—but also creating trillions of dollars in new business opportunities, consumer surplus and GDP growth.
>
> (p. 6)

Here again, some caution is warranted. Captain Sully Sullenberger, pilot of the airplane that made a dramatic landing on the Hudson River in 2009, had the following comment about new technology employing increased automation:

> When automation became possible in aviation, people thought, "We can eliminate human error by automating everything." We've learned that automation does not eliminate errors. Rather, it changes the nature of the errors that are made. And it makes possible new kinds of errors.
>
> (Wachter 2015)

A more general articulation of this phenomenon was proposed by Charles Perrow in his 1984 book entitled *Normal Accidents: Living with High-Risk Technologies.* While much has been made of the inevitable role of human error (see Chapter 8 on nuclear power and the evolution of modern risk analysis), Perrow's central thesis is that accidents are inevitable—that is, they are "normal"—in modern complex technologies and cannot be engineered out.

Perrow's theory concentrates on the properties of systems themselves, rather than on the errors that owners, designers, and operators make. In other words, he seeks a more basic explanation for accidents than operator error, faulty design or equipment, inadequately trained personnel, or that the system might be too big, underfinanced, or mismanaged. In fact, some accidents can be ascribed to safety systems themselves.

Technology is, in theory, value neutral. However, its implementation raises philosophical challenges, and ethical judgments in particular. Yuval Noah Harari, author of the imaginative and controversial book on the future of humankind, *Homo Deus: A Brief History of Tomorrow* (2017), illustrates this problem with a modern interpretation of the classic philosophical problem of the runaway tram car (Greene et al. 2001). He offers the following scenario: an automated automobile finds itself about to run over five pedestrians unless it engages in extreme evasive action, in this case driving over a cliff and killing the occupant. Clearly, the software in the car must make a determination of which course of action is preferable. The algorithm that makes this decision must be the result of a deep and challenging ethical thought process by the computer programmers who created it. In a somewhat tongue-in-cheek resolution to this problem, Harari suggests that we could let the market determine the answer. Toyota, for example, could design two variants of its cars: a Toyota Altruist and a Toyota Egotist. The car buyer could choose which model to buy. The former would save the five pedestrians at the expense of the car occupant; the latter would do the opposite (*CBC Ideas in the Afternoon*, May 7, 2018). Clearly the larger implications of moving to automated cars are not as simple as they may appear.

In a recent paper in *Nature* (Awad et al. 2018), an international group of academics reported on an innovative research project which attempted to determine public perceptions of appropriate ethical guidelines for AVs. As the authors note:

> Never in the history of humanity have we allowed a machine to autonomously decide who should live and who should die, in a fraction of a second, without real-time supervision. We are going to cross that bridge any time now, and it will not happen in a distant theatre of military operations; it will happen in that most mundane aspect of our lives, everyday transportation.
>
> (p. 63)

One particularly distinguishing feature of this research was the use of the web to gather opinions from several million people in more than two hundred countries. The survey focused on nine specific trade-offs, by asking for preferences for: (1) sparing humans versus pets; (2) sparing passengers versus pedestrians; (3) sparing more versus fewer lives; (4) sparing men versus women; (5) sparing the young versus the elderly; (6) sparing pedestrians who cross legally versus those who jaywalk; (7) sparing the fit versus the less fit; (8) sparing those with higher versus lower social status; and (9) staying on course versus swerving.

The analysis was conducted at four different levels: global preferences, individual variation, cultural clusters and country-level predictors. In general, the strongest preferences were observed for sparing humans over animals, more lives rather than fewer, and young lives. There were strong cultural variations, but "the fact that broad regions of the world displayed relative agreement suggests that our journey to consensual machine ethics is not doomed from the start" (p. 63).

Despite Awad's relatively optimistic assessment, we cannot rely on the utopian vision of a future dominated by AVs to solve the increasing threat of global warming. Society must look elsewhere for real solutions. We must avoid the age-old temptation to jump on the technology treadmill and assume that new technology will solve the problems generated by past technology. Car-based solutions are probably not the answer to car-based problems of this magnitude.

Several economic and regulatory initiatives have been contemplated or implemented in the hope of providing at least short-term relief from some of the negative externalities associated with private passenger vehicles. One such approach involves the use of mobility pricing. Unfortunately such innovative pricing schemes can be a lightning rod for anti-tax sentiment. It is interesting to note, however, that Stockholm introduced congestion charges in 2006 for a seven-month trial period which was followed by a referendum. Somewhat surprisingly, a majority voted to retain the charges (CTS 2014). A recent government-sponsored report in British Columbia details how such a system might be implemented (MPIC 2018). Whether the public acceptance demonstrated in Sweden can be replicated in North America remains an open question in light of the significantly different national attitudes to the role of government in promoting social welfare. However, as recently as April 2019, New York City opted to implement a system of congestion pricing, joining London, Stockholm, and Singapore (*New York Times* March 26, 2019).

One recently proposed technological solution suggests a hybrid of AVs and mass transit, called "autonomous rail rapid transit." Calthorpe and Walters (2017) describe how the technology works: "Autonomous rapid transit proposes the application of AV technology in shared vehicles in dedicated transit lanes similar [to] those used in bus rapid transit (BRT) systems" (p. 3).

They cite a study by Fehr & Peers (2014) which

> looked at replacing the buses with a fleet of four-person AVs that would gather at least three passengers before proceeding directly to the destination. In addition to skipping all the typical bus stops along the way to a passengers' [sic] destination, the cars would travel in a platoon and trigger green lights at intersections for better traffic flow. The analysis found that such a system would reduce travel time by 35 percent compared with BRT and by 50 percent compared with the private vehicles traveling alongside in the nondedicated lanes.
>
> (p. 4)

Calthorpe and Walters conclude with an optimistic but tempered conclusion:

> AV technology ultimately will find its way forward in different forms in different places. The unintended consequences of its use should be kept in mind as policy makers and manufacturers apply these new capabilities. In both the short and long terms, simulations show that the best application of AV technology is a network of ART [autonomous rapid transit] lines combined with high-capacity metro transit systems. This will avoid degradation of AV performance due to mixed flow, encourage people to share rides, and prompt drivers to reduce their use of private autos. This can then easily evolve into complete ART districts in which private cars are eliminated. The urban form that ultimately emerges is compelling: a city with almost no on-street parking, housing that is free of garage costs, abundant pedestrian zones, ubiquitous bike lanes, and no ugly surface parking lots. What's more, each step along the way will improve existing communities.
>
> (p. 4)

In sum, the era of driverless cars has yet to arrive (*New York Times* May 12, 2020; *Guardian* January 3, 2021). Part of the problem is the mixed attitudes by potential users. A report by the Boston Consulting Group (Lang et al. 2016) found that while many individuals welcomed the introduction of AVs, many were also concerned about safety. Ten factors for hesitation were identified in the survey:

- I do not feel safe if the car is driving itself (50 percent)
- I want to be in control at all times (45 percent)
- I do not want the car to make any mistakes (43 percent)
- Driving is a pleasure for me (30 percent)
- I don't know enough about self-driving technology (27 percent)
- I like a vehicle to be proven and tested for some time (27 percent)
- I wouldn't trust being in mixed traffic with a self-driving car (26 percent)

- I am not willing to pay extra for self-driving functionalities (25 percent)
- I am concerned that the car could be hacked (23 percent)
- I fear that the car could break down (20 percent)

In light of all these diverse factors, it is useful to examine other components of a mixed transportation strategy for the future which place much greater emphasis on mass transit.

Mass transit

There are numerous advantages to mass transit as a major form of transportation in an urban setting. First and foremost, it represents a much more efficient form of transportation than the individual automobile and, as such, has significantly fewer of the negative effects associated with automotive use including, but not limited to, the contribution to total GHGs. Of particular importance, mass transit facilitates the densification of the urban environment, drastically reducing the massive infrastructural requirements of individual automotive travel.

It is ironic that most North American cities had, at one time, substantial mass transit networks in the form of at-grade and above-grade systems. Figure 7.3 presents historical data to illustrate this point. There was a steady decline in ridership from 1920 to 1940, a brief increase in the war years, and then a precipitous decline following the end of the Second World War. What had happened to cause this decline? First and foremost was undoubtedly the increasing popularity of the private automobile and the construction of the infrastructure necessary to support it. However, in a landmark court decision in 1949, a federal court in California found five corporations (Firestone Tire, Standard Oil of California, Phillips Petroleum, General Motors, and Mack Trucks) guilty of a conspiracy

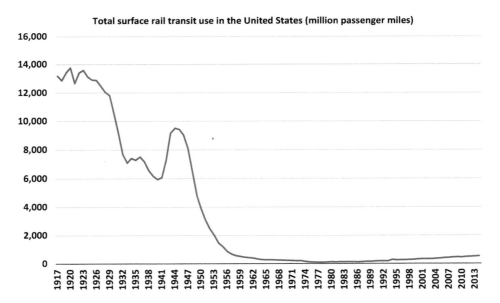

Figure 7.3 Trends in surface rail transit ridership in the United States.
Source: APTA, multiple years.

to create a transportation monopoly by buying up transit systems throughout the United States over the period 1938 to 1950 and retiring them from operation (USSC 1948). The common interest binding these entities together was their mutual goal to advance the use of automobiles and their associated products, such as tires and petroleum. The final result was a fine of $5,000 levied on General Motors and $1 levied on its treasurer. It is clear that the outcome of this case posed no significant barrier to the continued surge in automobile ownership.

To be perfectly fair, it is likely that, absent this conspiracy, the massive growth of automobile usage would have proceeded anyway, albeit at a slightly slower pace. The multifaceted benefits of the modern automobile presented an irresistible attraction for the typical consumer and few, if any, individuals could have anticipated the long-term ecological impact of their choices. Even if they had, the fundamental and common disconnect between private and social costs and benefits would have militated against any other logical choice during the postwar decades.

Ezra Mishan's depiction of options being foreclosed by path dependence poses an extraordinary challenge (Mishan 1967 and 1969). In the short run, one obvious solution is to accelerate the adoption and spread of mass transit, which de facto shrinks city size by reducing total travel time in and out of the urban core. The construction of more mass transit is a necessary but not sufficient answer to the problem. What is required is a systems approach which includes reconstructing consumers' choices by altering the relative prices of alternative transportation modes using such innovative polices as carbon taxes and mobility pricing. The effectiveness of carbon taxes has been described in Chapter 4 and their political acceptability has been enhanced by their revenue neutrality. The move by several cities in North America and Europe to make public transit free has had a positive impact on usage while increasing equality and reducing pollution (*New York Times* August 15, 2020; HuffPost February 22, 2020). Unfortunately, the advent of COVID-19 has had a seriously detrimental effect on ridership and has threatened several urban transit companies with bankruptcy (Gelinas 2020; *New York Times* December 6, 2020). When and if this situation will ameliorate itself remains to be seen. An additional threat to urban mass transit has become apparent with the flooding of subway systems in China, New York, and London during the extreme weather of summer 2021 (*New York Post* July 8, 2021; *New York Times* July 24, 2021)). The shift in weather patterns threatens other infrastructure as well, including roads, bridges, and rail networks, illustrating the emerging problem of unexpected risks accompanying climate change (CNN July 25, 2021; *New York Times* July 25, 2021; *Guardian* July 26, 2021).

The Internet of Motion

Tom Standage, deputy editor of *The Economist*, in his recent work, *A Brief History of Motion* (2021), provides an insightful overview of transportation from 3500 BCE to modern times. In contemplating the future, he asks: "What will be the dominant mode of urban transport in the postcar era? Will it be buses, trains, taxis, ride hailing, car clubs, bike sharing, or scooters? The answer is yes—to all of the above." He visualizes an "Internet of Motion" made feasible by the advent of the smartphone, which would provide individuals with a menu of options—single or combined—for moving from point A to point B. Under this model, mobility is a service, potentially replacing or supplementing individual ownership of the means of transit. This concept is redolent of Ray Anderson's reconceptualization of business outlined in Chapter 3 of this volume.

The emergence of this phenomenon will force a major reorientation of strategy among the world's major automotive manufacturers. In fact, such a strategic adjustment is already underway. To quote:

> Given that such programs explicitly aim to provide an alternative to car ownership, it may seem odd that car makers are also moving into the field. After all, a future in which different modes of transport can seamlessly be combined will involve fewer cars and less private ownership. But carmakers hope to provide vehicles (and later autonomous vehicles) for ride-hailing and car-sharing fleets. In some cases they are also dabbling with providing mobility services themselves . . . Carmakers claim that the new model provides an opportunity for them to shift from selling cars into the potentially more profitable business of selling rides. Total car sales each year add up to around $2 trillion; but the personal transport market, which includes vehicles, services, and software, is worth more like $10 trillion, according to industry estimates. The stage is therefore set for a brutal fight between carmakers, ride-hailing giants, and mobility start-ups in the coming years, as the emphasis shifts from car ownership to mobility services.
>
> (p. 212)

A version of Standage's vision has already been introduced in several cities in Europe and Tokyo under the rubric MaaS (mobility as a service) and a version has been proposed for Pittsburgh and a new suburb outside Phoenix. The results have been mixed because of the difficulties of assembling all mobility providers under one umbrella, the advent of COVID-19, and the difficulty of coaxing people out of their private automobiles (*New York Times* December 5, 2024). Yet, this may indeed be the wave of the future as governments, companies, and the general public become more sensitive to the necessity of greening our transportation systems.

Peter Norton, a professor in the Department of Engineering and Society at the University of Virginia, adopts a similar and broader view of options available to the public in pursuit of mobility. In his recent book, *Autonorama: The Illusory Promise of High-Tech Driving* (2021), Norton focuses in particular on the misplaced promise of AVs, citing an eighty-year history of unfulfilled promises. In his view, the automobile industry has succeeded in narrowing the perceived range of options to a choice between the status quo of car dependency and the futuristic promise of high-tech car dependency. To Norton, this is a blind alley as "applied to complex systems, high-tech innovations never just solve problems—they change problems, disrupting balances and introducing new problems" (p. 223). Norton specifically criticizes the industry and many policymakers who describe the public's love of driving as a rationale for continuing down the path of car dependency. To Norton, this narrow choice set reflects the elimination from consideration of a broad of range of mobility alternatives which are cheaper, more efficient, safer, and currently available. While other jurisdictions, such as the Netherlands, have a multi-modal solution to mobility in place, the range of choices in the United States, for example, has been narrowed by past actions of the automobile industry (e.g., the purchase and elimination of urban tram lines), and government decisions to expand the highway system and redesign urban spaces to accommodate automobiles: "Since the 1930s, US transportation policy—local, state and national—has prioritized the least efficient mode at the expense of all others" (p. 201). To Norton, the view that AVs are the inevitable future "interprets the loss of choices as a choice, and driving in the absence of good choices as a preference to drive," (p. 200). He states: "Whenever alternatives to driving have been attractive possibilities, people have taken advantage of them, to the benefit of not just the individual but also the community" (p. 235).

Concluding comments

In conclusion, the automobile has made an indelible impact upon modern industrialized economies and is poised to do the same in the rapidly developing nations of the world. This remarkable and pervasive phenomenon prompts the following thought experiment in the area of environmental design: If we knew at the beginning of the automobile era what we know now, would we have pursued the same course of action? Would we have entered into the same Faustian bargain typical of so many of humankind's fateful technological choices? Would we have chosen a path that would lead us away from, rather than towards, an economic sector which has contributed so much to the development of the modern city but is now a major contributor to climate change?

Of course, it is virtually impossible to conduct a controlled experiment in the true scientific sense, since so much of our modern urban infrastructure tied to the use of automobiles is locked-in and resistant to significant change. It is possible to get a glimpse, however, of what this alternative world might look like in those few cases where cities are in the process of being born. In the mid-1990s, the Chinese government commissioned the late Bing Thom, one of Canada's foremost architects, to create a city from the ground up using all the best concepts of how to design a truly workable and livable urban area. Dalian New Town, an instant port city, was to be built on the coast of the Yellow Sea over a period of thirty years with the explicit goal of showcasing an ideal urban design to house one million people at a cost of over $700 billion (Thom 1998). Population mobility was a central factor and, not surprisingly, automobility was de-emphasized in favor of pedestrian-based and mass transit options. Unfortunately, all did not turn out as planned, as the original concepts had to be modified as the target population was increased to over six million inhabitants, posing a serious challenge to the achievement of the initial design goals. More recent initiatives undertaken by China include a new smart city inside Shenzhen which, among its numerous technological innovations, will have fewer streets for cars and expanded use of AVs (*Daily Telegraph* June 26, 2020).

Despite the inability to start afresh, several global cities have recently tried to retrofit or reestablish more efficient transportation systems onto existing urban infrastructure. Los Angeles, long considered the epitome of car-based urban congestion, has recently constructed the first phase of a multibillion dollar subway system across its massive urban area. Other cities in the United States in the process of following suit include Honolulu, Indianapolis, Denver, Seattle, and Phoenix. One particularly noteworthy North American example is the city of Vancouver, which is determined to be the greenest city on the continent. Starting in 1985, in anticipation of the World Expo in that city in the following year, the city and province constructed the longest fully automated, electric and driverless mass transit system in the world. With 4 major lines, more than 50 miles of track, and more than five dozen stations, it posted a record 453 million total boardings in 2019 just prior to the outbreak of COVID-19.

Constrained by geography and subject to high rates of in-migration because of the urban amenities and lifestyle it offers, Vancouver is in serious need of densification to offset its large proportion of single-family detached housing stock, despite high residential population density in its urban core. The SkyTrain has made a significant contribution to addressing the problem of density, as most of the lines have attracted the construction of high-density, multistorey apartment and condominium complexes. This outcome has been unambiguously positive but, so typical of the modern city, the number of automobiles on its congested streets continues to increase and the city has only recently produced a draft transportation strategy to address this and related traffic problems (Translink 2021).

In sum, with the prospect of two billion motor vehicles on the planet within the next few decades, coupled with the remaining multifaceted and unresolved problems, even with the widespread adoption of EVs it appears that the transport sector has little prospect of becoming sustainable in the immediate to medium-term future. Three critical questions emerge from this analysis: (1) Can mass transit or the Internet of Motion succeed in replacing the widespread use of automobiles? (2) Is it possible to reduce total distance traveled by encouraging densification to locate individuals closer to their place of work? (3) Can we foresee a future where work-related travel is eliminated through such mechanisms as telecommuting? Already a part of business practice, and further promoted by the recent pandemic, telecommuting is the modern re-creation of the disseminated artisan workshops of the pre-Industrial Revolution era.

At a minimum, it is essential that future urban planning tightly integrates transportation options with urban form issues such as zoning and building design. Other solutions remain beyond the visible horizon. To put it starkly, it is difficult to imagine a sustainable world where an increasing number of global citizens consider it desirable to be accompanied by two thousand pounds of metal, plastic, glass, and rubber whenever and wherever they travel.

In the long run, it appears clear that we must totally reconceptualize the concept of the city—the location of work, residence, and leisure. In this respect, the methodology of backcasting seems particularly relevant: we imagine the city we desire at some point in the future and then determine how we get there from here. This is no mean task, but one undoubtedly superior to the fruitless search for new uni-dimensional, high-tech answers that promise quick but ephemeral fixes in the absence of longer-term systems-based solutions.

Addendum 1: The essential duality of technological progress

In his book, *The Fate of the Species: Why the Human Race May Cause Its Own Extinction and How We Can Stop It,* Fred Guterl (2012), the former executive editor of the *Scientific American,* made the following observation about the Manichean role of technology in human history: "We have climbed out on a technological limb, and turning back is a disturbing option. We are dependent on our technology yet our technology now presents the seeds of our destruction" (p. 5).

The development of new technology has a long history of promised benefits with little consideration of possible short-term and long-term costs or disadvantages. This unshakable faith in the power of new technology to cure all ills—especially those created by old technology—is often referred to as "technophilia" or "technofundamentalism." The reason for the imbalance between perceived benefits and costs is that many benefits are easily measured, concentrated, and attainable in a relatively short time span, while costs and risks may be diffuse, delayed, ignored, or unknown and, as a consequence, no careful and definitive decision calculus can be accomplished. It is probably safe to say that with few exceptions, most new technologies have had both positive and negative impacts. Even if the costs are known before wide-scale adoption, society may have decided to proceed on the basis of a reasoned but myopic cost-benefit or risk-benefit analysis (Huesemann and Huesemann 2011). The globe is filled with the remnants of technologies that have had unanticipated accident sequences, have failed, or have generated significant negative consequences (for example, Medvedev 1979; Petroski 1994; Freiman and Schlager 1994; Biello 2007; Brown 2013; Green Cross and Pure Earth 2016; Higginbotham 2019; Chiles 2002; Farvar and Milton 1972; Steinberg and Hamm 1983).

One of the earliest articulations of the challenge posed by untempered optimism in technology was the conference volume edited by Farvar and Milton (1972), entitled *The Careless Technology: Ecology and International Development*. This work contained fifty case studies by international authors describing the unintended and invariably detrimental effects of development projects that had been were erroneously deemed "progress." A more recent expansion of this type of critique was presented by Edward Tenner in his 1996 book *Why Things Bite Back: Technology and the Revenge of Unintended Consequences*. Tenner's survey of what he terms "revenge" effects spans the disciplines including such disparate areas as medicine, environmental control, agriculture, energy production, computers, and sports. In 2001 and 2013, the European Environment Agency (EEA) published the results of extensive research on almost three dozen case studies of technologies introduced with great promise and measurable benefits but which have led to significant negative and largely unforeseen or underestimated consequences (Harremoes et al. 2001; EEA 2013). Table 2.2 listed these technologies and their revenge effects. The principal message was the need for greater use of the precautionary principle.

Ironically, one of the most transformative and beneficial technologies of the last few decades with potentially enormous revenge effects is digital technology and, in particular, the internet and social media platforms. Recent evidence has emerged that documents the vast negative effects on human behavior, civil discourse, democratic institutions and processes, public safety, corporate business, national security, and electricity demand, as well as the reach and power of organized crime and independent and state-sponsored hackers, and cyberwarfare (US CRS 2017; Vosoughi et al. 2018; *New York Times* March 15, 2018; US CERT accessed March 15, 2108; Nichols 2017; *Guardian* May 7, 2017; Mounk 2018; *New York Times* March 18, 2018; *New York Times* March 27, 2018; Foer 2017; NIC 2021; BBC February 8, 2021; *New York Times* January 30, 2021; *New York Times* May 19 2021a; *New York Times* June 1 and 3, 2021; *Hill* July 1, 2021; *New York Times* July 20, 2021). Guterl (2012) describes a chilling scenario where cyber warfare on domestic electric power grids could result in catastrophic consequences with millions of lives at risk. The American energy secretary has echoed this sentiment by stating that US adversaries are capable of shutting down the country's power grid (HuffPost June 7, 2021).

Perhaps the most persuasive discussion of the potential dystopian effects of new technology is provided by Harari (2018) in his latest book, which focuses in part on the confluence of two new and radically disruptive technologies: biotechnology and artificial intelligence (AI). In this study, the revenge effects include potential threats to nothing less than the continued existence of the socioeconomic-political structure of modern society (see also Harari 2017 and July 25, 2017; Walsh 2019). In recognition of these risks, the European Union has proposed strict new rules for AI in what are deemed high-risk areas: (1) biometric identification and categorization of natural persons; (2) management and operation of critical infrastructure; (3) education and vocational training; (4) employment, management of workers and access to self-employment; (5) access to and enjoyment of essential private services and public services and benefits; (6) law enforcement;

(7) migration, asylum, and border control; and (8) administration of justice and democratic processes (European Commission 2021a and specifically Annex III in EC 2021b).

One of the most recent illustrations of the risks of new technology has been provided by the two crashes of Boeing's new 737 MAX airplane (*New York Times* March 14, 2019), exemplifying the delicate trade-off between complexity and resilience. It is disturbing that the failure of one component designed to prevent a catastrophic accident of this highly complex machine was sufficient to cause total system failure, resulting in over 300 deaths. In a remarkably insightful study, Petroski (1994) created a conceptual framework for the analysis of design errors in engineering projects from ancient days until modern times. His conclusions are that many of these errors have been, and continue to be, a common feature of new technological developments. Two of the lessons he highlights apply to the case of the 737 MAX. Citing Galileo's work *Two New Sciences*, published in 1638, he quotes the author who states: "A circumstance … is worthy of your attention as indeed are all events which happen contrary to expectation, especially when a precautionary measure turns out to be a cause of disaster" (p. 49). Petroski also cites the work of a Roman named Vitruvius who wrote *The Ten Books on Architecture* in the first century BCE. In that work, Vitruvius describes a famous case study of a fundamental mistake made by a Roman contractor, Paconius, in the design of a modified vehicle for transporting architectural columns. In interpreting this story, Petroski observes that (p.16):

> How easily a design concentrating on satisfying one kind of objective in detail can overlook modifications that in retrospect prove to be disastrous to the functioning of the machine, structure, or process that is the primary purpose of the design.

This lesson appears to capture the essence of the problem faced by Boeing in attempting to modify its 737 by adding new, more powerful engines. Instead of taking the time to redesign the airplane as a whole to accommodate this major change, Boeing chose to mount these larger engines closer to the fuselage and further in front of the wing, creating a new and more powerful source of lift. This modification changed the aerodynamic characteristics of the airplane. This was the source of the problem that Boeing was attempting to compensate for with the creation of the Maneuvering Characteristics Augmentation System software (*New York Times* March 14, April 8, and June 1, 2019). It is the ultimate irony that the problems that befell this aircraft were conceptually similar to problems that have affected engineering designs since antiquity.

One of the principal challenges accompanying the design and application of new technologies is the human-machine interface, especially in the presence of automated systems (Reason 1990, 2008). Christine Negroni, an international expert on aviation disasters, has conducted countless interviews with pilots, regulators, and designers in an attempt to understand this phenomenon (Negroni 2016). Her insights and those of her interviewees have a relevance far beyond air transport (see Chapter 8 on nuclear energy). Some of her observations are reproduced below:

- What has not changed is how difficult it is for designers to know in advance all the ways an idea on the drawing board will function in reality (p. 137).
- Engineers are so embedded into the system, they know the design so well, they can't see its flaws (p. 163).
- When you push the envelope, you open a greater area of risk (p. 165).
- Automation's downside is that it creates both complexity and complacency (p. 226).

- When automation reduces the workload too much, vigilance suffers (p. 228).
- [With respect to] the human or the machine what is emerging is that each does the job differently. The computer is a rule-based system . . . What it means to be human is to break the rules. A computer will continue to do its computing while the building burns around it. A human will adapt to the situation (p. 230).
- Machines do not improvise, and computers are not creative. What pilots bring to the cockpit is their humanity. It is their greatest contribution (p. 238).

The particular risk enunciated by many pilots is described as "automation dependency," which entails a pilot's overreliance on the autopilot (and other automated systems) (Schiff 2015; St. George 2016). All of these comments on automation are particularly relevant to the discussions on automobiles and nuclear technology. In August, the US National Highway Traffic Safety Administration authorized an investigation into Tesla's autopilot system after at least eleven accidents with it (*New York Times* August 16, 2021).

In an insightful article, Bostrom (2002) discussed the unique threats posed by existential risks arising from accelerating technological progress. The potential threats posed by these meta-risks "could cause our extinction or destroy the potential of Earth-originating intelligent life. ... Existential risks have a cluster of features that make ordinary risk management ineffective" (p. 1). (The development and current state of risk analysis is discussed in greater length in Chapter 8 on nuclear power). The dual nature of technological development raises at least two fascinating questions: What technologies have been unambiguously positive? Are there some technologies which humanity would be better off without?

Another recent event in the United States provides an archetypal example of the trade-off between efficiency and resilience. Much of American infrastructure has entered the digital age with significant efficiency gains associated with the complex array of high-tech monitoring and control systems. The vulnerability of these complex system was demonstrated by the cyberattack on a major pipeline which supplies petroleum products to the US East Coast (*New York Times* May 13, 2021). The delay in rectifying the damage caused by this attack has led to demands for a comprehensive reevaluation of US infrastructure security focusing on pipelines, electric grids and power plants (*Forbes* May 10, 2021; SecurityInfowatch.com May 10, 2021, *New York Times* May 13, 2021).

Guterl (2012) describes the "dark potential of biotechnology." This modern science promises to deliver humanity from many of its most dangerous afflictions, and yet "this knowledge is 'dual use'—it can also reveal ways of disrupting the process of life, turning it off like a switch. It could lead to bio-weapons of startling effectiveness that work in ways we can only dimly imagine now" (p. 98; see also NAS 2019). Walsh (2019) observes that "the dual use dilemma is really the dilemma of science" (p. 211) and concludes that "biotechnology poses the single greatest existential risk human humans will face in the year to come" (pp. 233–4). One of the most comprehensive studies of the benefits and risks of advanced biotechnology comes from the US National Intelligence Council (NIC 2021), which publishes regular assessments of positive and negative long-term trends that can affect national security and other critical areas. Threats from the innocent or intentional use of biotechnology have attracted particular attention, especially with respect to possible bioterrorism (Cronin 2019; NIC 2021). Such is the nature of the Pandora's box opened by the rapid advance of new technology. The challenges posed by new technologies continue to pervade most of modern human activities and affect such diverse areas as medicine, defense, agriculture, fisheries, transportation, nuclear power, fossil fuels, responses to global warming, and renewable energy. This complex interrelated array of issues flowing from the development of modern technology has prompted numerous calls for greater oversight and regulation (Harris 2016; NAS 2019; *Science* February 19, 2020).

An interesting footnote to the myriad and sometimes counterproductive applications of modern technology has been provided by the current rage for cryptocurrencies based on blockchain technology. It has been reported that mining for bitcoin has a nontrivial effect on climate as the electricity need is "more than used by entire countries" although the magnitude of its total energy requirements is a source of some disagreement (*Guardian* February 27, 2021; BBC February 10, 2021; *New York Times* March 10, 2021; Cambridge Centre for Alternative Finance 2021; Koomey and Masanet 2021; *Smart Prosperity* 2021). On July 8, 2021 the Cambridge Bitcoin Electricity Consumption Index estimated that bitcoin network power requirements ranged from 2.96 to 19.85 gigawatts (GW). Over the period 2014–21, the highest estimated annualized energy requirements occurred on May 13, 2021 with 519.964 terawatt hours (tWh) (Cambridge Centre for Alternative Finance 2021). In May 2021, it was reported that Iran had banned cryptocurrency mining for four months after it had contributed to a blackout in the nation's electricity grid (BBC May 26, 2021). Similarly, bans have been either put in place or proposed in China and India (*New York Times* September 24, 2021; BBC November 24, 2021).

To some observers, cryptocurrency is basically a modern, high-tech version of speculative bubbles that have characterized societies since the time of the Dutch Tulip Mania of 1636 and the South Sea Bubble of 1720 (Mackay 1932; Galbraith 1990). Another controversial use of blockchain technology with potentially significant GHG emissions has been the recent emergence of nonfungible tokens (NFTs) in the form of digital art (*New York Times* April 16, 2021). In one example, Chris Preecht, an Austrian architect and artist, discovered to his dismay that "creating the 300 items of digital art that he had planned to sell, 100 each of three art pieces, would have burned through the same amount of electricity that an average European would otherwise use in two decades." Clearly, these two examples provide an archetypal illustration of the fact that not all new technologies are unambiguously beneficial.

Addendum 2: The flying car; A case study in pathological techno-optimism

The recent mainstream media has highlighted the ongoing development and imminent deployment of flying cars (CTV News April 21, 2017; *Globe and Mail* May 30, 2018, *USA Today* December 24, 2019; Bernhard 2020; *Guardian* June 3 and 29, 2021; *MotorTrend* January 12, 2021; *Daily Mail* June 11, 2021; *New York Times* June 12, 2021; *Telegraph* June 30, 2021; Global News June 30, 2021). CNN has reported (June 30, 2021) that one company had conducted a thirty-five-minute test flight in Slovakia between the city of Nitra and the capital, Bratislava. There are essentially two divergent visions of the future of flying cars. The first would be a market limited to the wealthy, creating "the equivalent of on-demand helicopter travel to a wider circle of elites" (DeGood 2020). This would add only another layer to an already crowded and energy-intensive personal transportation network.

The second and much more ambitious vision would be to create a mass market for these hybrid vehicles. The logistic and aesthetic complexities of this conceptualization move the concept into the realm of science fiction. There would be no point in attempting to replicate the current road grid in the air for flying cars. This would achieve nothing to alleviate the current degree of road congestion, one of the key selling points of this invention. Users would be able to travel directly from point A to point B, cutting time and distance from their normal travel routes. This would create a vast array of intersecting travel routes at several hundred to a thousand feet or more above the ground. This would require several fundamental technological challenges: First, all vehicles would have to be vertical takeoff and landing to eliminate the need for runways. Second, they would have to be autonomous in order to prevent accidents. One could not rely on the ability of a large number of drivers to avoid the multiple collision challenges. In this respect, the current experience with autonomous cars is a sobering reminder of the difficulties that might be encountered (*New York Times* June 29, 2021). Third, the requirement to maintain both horizontal and vertical distance between vehicles would severely limit the capacity of this system in relationship to conventional on-ground traffic. Fourth, the cars would probably have to be electric in order to reduce the combustion of fossil fuel, although this would still place an additional burden on a nation's energy supply system in order to meet the requirements of keeping vehicles airborne (Stone 2017). Fifth, there would be a need for a complex and widespread computer-controlled system for collision avoidance. Given the potential magnitude of this challenge, it is likely that numerous supercomputers would have to be deployed across most urban areas. Sixth, the vision and acoustic pollution would be unpalatable to most urban residents. Seventh, any accidents could rain debris down on people and property below. Even Elon Musk, known for his highly creative inventions, thinks that flying cars are a bad idea (*Business Insider* February 16, 2017).

In sum, the concept of a flying car is the antithesis of sustainability and yet the temptation, if not de facto imperative, to deploy new technology is irresistible regardless of its effects.

References

ABC News (2021) "US automakers pledge huge increase in electric vehicles," August 5.
ABC News (2021) "NTSB chair wants Tesla to limit where autopilot can operate," October 25.
APTA (American Public Transportation Association) (multiple years) *Report on Transit Ridership*.
Arbib, James and Tony Seba (2017) *Rethinking Transportation 2020–2030*, RethinkX.
Arieff, Allison (2017) "Automated vehicles can't save cities," *New York Times*, February 27.
Awad, Edmond et al. (2018) *Nature*, "The moral machine experiment," November 1.
BBC (2017) "New diesel and petrol vehicles to be banned from 2040 in UK," July 26.
BBC (2021) "Hacker tries to poison water supply of Florida city," February 8.
BBC (2021) "Bitcoin consumes 'more electricity than Argentina'," February 10.
BBC (2021) "Iran bans cryptocurrency mining for four months after blackouts," May 26.
BBC (2021) "Ford announces $11.4bn investment in electric vehicle plants," September 28.
BBC (2021) "Indian government set to ban cryptocurrencies," November 24.
Bernhard, Adrienne (2020) "The flying car is here—and it could change the world," Future Inc, November 11.
Biello, David (2007) "World's top 10 most polluted places," *Scientific American*, September 13.
Bloomberg (2019) "Electric vehicle battery shrinks and so does the total cost," April 12.
Bloomberg (2020) "Electric cars closing in on gas guzzlers as battery costs plunge," December 16.
Bloomberg Green (2020) "Tesla overtakes Exxon's market value in symbolic energy shift," June 30.
Bloomberg New Energy Finance (2018) "Long-term electric vehicle outlook 2018," May 21.
Bostrom, Nick (2002) *Journal of Evolution and Technology*, "Existential risks: Analyzing human extinction scenarios and related hazards," March.
Brennan, John W. and Timothy R. Barder (2016) *Battery Electric Vehicles vs. Internal Combustion Engine Vehicles*, Arthur D. Little, November.

Brown, Kate (2013) *Plutopia: Nuclear Families, Atomic Cities, and the Great Soviet and American Plutonium Disasters*, New York: Oxford University Press.

Business Insider (2017) "Elon Musk says flying cars are a bad idea," February 16.

Calthorpe, Peter and Jerry Walters (2017) *Urban Land*, "Autonomous vehicles: Hype and potential," March 1.

Cambridge Centre for Alternative Finance (accessed July 8, 2021) *Cambridge Bitcoin Electricity Consumption Index*.

CCC (Committee on Climate Change) (2019a) *Net Zero: Technical Report*, May.

CCC (Committee on Climate Change) (2019b) *Net Zero: The UK's Contribution to Stopping Global Warming*, May.

CDC (Centers for Disease Control and Prevention) (2016) "Road traffic injuries and deaths: A global problem," October 23.

Chiles, James R. (2002) *Inviting Disaster: Lessons from the Edge of Technology*, New York: Harper Business.

CNN (2021) "New 'future city' to rise in southwest China," February 9.

CNN (2021) "Ford is investing $1 billion in Germany as it goes electric in Europe," February 17.

CNN (2021) "Police say no one was in driver's seat in fatal Tesla crash," April 19.

CNN (2021) "Flying car completes 35-minute test flight between cities," June 30.

CNN (2021) "Thunderstorms cause flash flooding in London, submerging roads and some train stations," July 25.

Cronin, Audrey Kurth (2019) *Power to the People: How Open Technological Innovation Is Arming Tomorrow's Terrorists*, New York: Oxford University Press.

CTS (Centre for Transport Studies) (2014) *The Stockholm Congestion Charges: An Overview*. CTS Working Paper 2014:7, Stockholm.

CTV News (2017) "Is it a bird? Is it a plane? Flying car to go on sale," April 21.

CTV News (2021) "Are electric cars really as eco-friendly as people say?" November 10.

Daily Mail (2021) "Take-off for air taxis! Richard Branson's Virgin Atlantic and Rolls-Royce back £3billion British plan to roll out 1,000 'near silent' zero emissions flying cars in 2024," June 11.

Daily Telegraph (2020) "Beijing steals a march as its smart metropolis is West's forbidden city," June 26.

DeGood, Kevin (2020) "Flying cars will undermine democracy and the environment," Center for American Progress, May 28.

EEA (European Environment Agency) (2013) Late Lessons from Early Warnings: Science, Precaution, Innovation. EEA Report No. 1/2013.

Erhardt, Gregory D. et al. (2019) *Science Advances*, "Do transportation network companies decrease or increase congestion?" May 18.

European Commission (2021a) "Proposal for a Regulation of the European Parliament and of the Council laying down harmonised rules on artificial intelligence (Artificial Intelligence Act) and amending certain Union legislative acts," April 21.

European Commission (2021b) "Annexes to the proposal for a Regulation of the European Parliament and of the Council laying down harmonised rules on artificial intelligence (Artificial Intelligence Act) and amending certain Union legislative acts," April 21.

Eyre, Nick and Gavin Killip (eds.) (2019) *Shifting the Focus: Energy Demand in a Net-Zero Carbon UK*, Centre for Research into Energy Demand Solutions, July 5.

Farvar, M. Taghi and John P. Milton (1972) *The Careless Technology: Ecology and International Development*, Garden City, NY: Natural History Press.

Fehr & Peers (2014) "Effect of next-generation vehicles on travel demand & highway capacity," February.

Foer, Franklin (2017) *World Without Mind: The Existential Threat of Big Tech*, New York: Penguin.

Forbes (2021) "Pipeline cyber attack demands reevaluation of U.S. infrastructure security," May 10.

Freiman, Fran Locher and Neil Schlager (1994) *Failed Technology: True Stories of Technological Disaster*, Gale Research.

Galbraith, John Kenneth (1990) *A Short History of Financial Euphoria*, New York: Whittle Books.

Gelinas, Nicole (2020) "The coronavirus could destroy mass transit: Federal aid can help," *New York Times*, July 3.

Global News (2021) "Flying car completes 35-minute test flight between cities in Slovakia," June 30.

Globe and Mail (2018) "Flying cars may become a reality sooner than you think," May 30.

Green Cross and Pure Earth (2016) *World's Worst Pollution Problems: The Toxics Beneath Our Feet.*

Greene, Joshua et al. (2001) *Science*, "An fMRI Investigation of emotional engagement in moral judgment," September 14.

Guardian (2016) "Why self-driving cars aren't safe yet: Rain, roadworks and other obstacles," July 5.

Guardian (2016) "Renewables made up half of net electricity capacity added last year," October 25.

Guardian (2017) "The great British Brexit robbery: How our democracy was hijacked," May 7.

Guardian (2017) "France to ban sales of petrol and diesel cars by 2040," July 6.

Guardian (2021) " 'Peak hype': Why the driverless car revolution has stalled," January 3.

Guardian (2021) "Electric cars rise to record 54% market share in Norway," January 5.

Guardian (2021) "Electric vehicles close to 'tipping point' of mass adoption" January 22.

Guardian (2021) "Electricity needed to mine bitcoin is more than used by 'entire countries'," February 27.

Guardian (2021) "Flying cars? Electric jets? Five things you need to know about the future of transport," June 3.

Guardian (2021) "Flying cars will be a reality by 2030, says Hyundai's Europe chief," June 29.

Guardian (2021) "Flash floods will be more common as climate crisis worsens, say scientists," July 26.

Guterl, Fred (2012) *The Fate of the Species: Why the Human Race May Cause Its Own Extinction and How We Can Stop It*, New York: Bloomsbury.

Harari, Yuval (2017) "The age of disorder: Why technology is the greatest threat to humankind," *New Statesman America*, July 25.

Harari, Yuval Noah (2017) *Homo Deus: A Brief History of Tomorrow*, Toronto: Signal.

Harari, Yuval Noah (2018) *CBC Ideas in the Afternoon*, interview, May 7.

Harb, M. et al. (2018) *Transportation*, "Projecting travelers into a world of self-driving vehicles. Estimating travel behavior implications via a naturalistic experiment," November.

Harper, Gavin et al. (2019) *Nature*, "Recycling lithium-ion batteries from electric vehicles," November 6.

Harremoes, Poul et al. (2001) *Late Lessons from Early Warnings: The Precautionary Principle 1896– 2000*, European Environmental Agency.

Harris, Elisa D. (ed.) (2016*) Governance of Dual-Use Technologies: Theory and Practice*, American Academy of Arts and Sciences.

Hawkins, Troy R. et al. (2012) *Journal of Industrial Ecology*, "Comparative environmental life cycle assessment of conventional and electric vehicles," October 4.

Higginbotham, Adam. (2019) *Midnight in Chernobyl: The Untold Story of the World's Greatest Nuclear Disaster,* New York: Simon & Schuster.

Hill (2021) "US, UK agencies warn Russian hackers using 'brute force' to target hundreds of groups," July 1.

Holdway, Aaron R. et al. 2010) Energy & Environmental Science, "Indirect emissions from electric vehicles: Emissions from electricity generation," September 22.

Huesemann, Michael and Joyce Huesemann (2011) *Techno-Fix: Why Technology Won't Save Us or the Environment,* Gabriola Island, BC: New Society Publishers.

HuffPost (2020) "Here's what happens when public transit is free," February 22.

HuffPost (2021) "Energy secretary says U.S. adversaries are capable of shutting down power grid," June 7.

IEA (International Energy Agency) and ICCT (International Council on Clean Transportation) (2019) "Fuel economy in major car markets: Technology and policy drivers 2005–2017." Working paper 19, March 2.

IEA (International Energy Agency) (2017a) *Electricity 2017.*

IEA (International Energy Agency) (2017b) *Global EV Outlook 2017.*

IEA (International Energy Agency) (2020) *Global EV Outlook 2020: Entering the Decade of Electric Drive?*

IEA (International Energy Agency) (2021) *The Role of Critical Minerals in Clean Energy Transitions.*

Independent (2017) "China to ban petrol and diesel cars, state media reports," September 10.

Inside EVs (2016) "Germany moves to ban ICE vehicle sales by 2030, electric-only from 2030 on," October 10.

Knobloch, Florian et al. (2020) *Nature Sustainability*, "Net emissions reductions from electric cars and heat pumps in 59 world regions over time," March 23.

Koomey, Jonathan and Eric Masanet (2021) *Joule*, "Does not compute: Avoiding pitfalls assessing the internet's energy and carbon impacts," July 21.

Lang, Nikolaus et al. (2016) *Self-Driving Vehicles, Robo-Taxis, and the Urban Mobility Revolution*, Boston Consulting Group, July 21.

Lu, Yiren (2017) *New York Times Magazine*, "The blind spot of A.I. cars," November 7.

Mackay, Charles (1932) *Extraordinary Popular Delusions and the Madness of Crowds*, Boston: L.C. Page.

Manjoo, Farhad (2020) "I've seen a future without cars, and it's amazing," *New York Times*, July 9.

Manjoo, Farhad (2021) "There's one big problem with electric cars," *New York Times*, February 18.

McKinsey (2018) "Three surprising resource implications from the rise of electric vehicles," May 23.

McKinsey (2020) "How to drive winning battery-electric-vehicle design: Lessons from benchmarking ten Chinese models," June.

Medvedev, Zhores A. (1979) *Nuclear Disaster in the Urals*, New York: W.W. Norton.

Melin, Hans Eric et al. (2021) *Science,* "Global implications of the EU battery regulation," July 23.

Mervis, Jeffrey (2017*) Science*, "Not so fast," December 20.

Messer, Andrea Elyse (2019) "In and out with 10-minute electric vehicle recharge," Penn State University.

Mishan, Ezra (1967) *The Costs of Economic Growth*, New York: Praeger.

Mishan, Ezra (1969) *Technology and Growth: The Price We Pay*, New York: Praeger.

Morse, Ian (2021) "A dead battery dilemma," *Science* May 21.

Motor1.com (2013) "Why electric vehicles are fundamentally superior to ICE," November 3.

MotorTrend (2021) "Cadillac has a flying car? Not exactly, but it has a preview of one," January 12.

Mounk, Yascha (2018) *The People vs. Democracy: Why Our Freedom Is in Danger & How To Save It*, Cambridge, MA: Harvard University Press.

MPIC (Mobility Pricing Independent Commission) (2018) *Metro Vancouver Mobility Study*, May.

NAS (National Academy of Sciences) (2018) *Biodefense in the Age of Synthetic Biology*, Washington, DC: National Academies Press.

NAS (National Academy of Sciences) (2019) "Strategies for identifying and addressing vulnerabilities posed by synthetic biology." Proceedings of a workshop in brief, November.

Negroni, Christine (2016) *The Crash Detectives: Investigating the World's Most Mysterious Air Disasters*, New York: Penguin.

New York Post (2021) "New Yorkers wade through underground lakes as subway stations flood," July 8.

New York Times (2017) "As Beijing joins climate fight, Chinese companies build coal plants," July 1.

New York Times (2017) "China hastens the world toward an electric-car future," October 9.

New York Times (2018) Cyberattacks put Russian fingers on the switch at power plants, U.S. says," March 15.

New York Times (2018) "Facebook and Cambridge Analytica: What you need to know as fallout widens," March 19.

New York Times (2018) "Cambridge Analytica whistle-blower contends data-mining swung Brexit vote," March 27.

New York Times (2019) "The Boeing 737 Max and the problems autopilot can't solve," March 14.

New York Times (2019) "Over $10 to drive in Manhattan? What we know about the congestion pricing plan," March 26.

New York Times (2019) "Boeing's 737 Max: 1960s design, 1990s computing power and paper manuals," April 8.

New York Times (2019) "Boeing built deadly assumptions into 737 Max, blind to a late design change," June 1.

New York Times (2019) "Cities worldwide are reimagining their relationship with cars," November 14.

New York Times (2020) "This was supposed to be the year driverless cars went mainstream," May 12.

New York Times (2020) "Should public transit be free? More cities say, why not?" August 15.

New York Times (2020) "The age of electric cars is dawning ahead of schedule," September 20.

New York Times (2020) "California plans to ban sales of new gas-powered cars in 15 years," September 23.

New York Times (2020) "Public transit faces huge service cuts across U.S.," December 6.

New York Times (2020) "Uber is giving self-driving car project to a start-up," December 7.

New York Times (2021) "G.M. will sell only zero-emission vehicles by 2035," January 28.

New York Times (2021) "G.M. wants to make electric cars. China dominates the market," January 29.

New York Times (2021) "Electric cars are coming, and fast. Is the nation's grid up to it?" August 3.

New York Times (2021) "The auto industry bets its future on batteries," February 16.

New York Times (2021) "Ford says it will phase out gasoline-powered vehicles in Europe," February 17.

New York Times (2021a) "Volvo plans to sell only electric cars by 2030," March 2.

New York Times (2021b) "How green are electric vehicles?" March 2.

New York Times (2021) "The city where cars are not welcome'" March 3.

New York Times (2021) "Bitcoin's climate change impact is under scrutiny," March 10.

New York Times (2021) "Electric cars are coming. How long until they rule the road?" March 13.

New York Times (2021) "Volkswagen aims to use its size to head off Tesla," March 16.

New York Times (2021) "Carmakers strive to stay ahead of hackers," March 18.

New York Times (2021) "Tesla's autopilot technology faces fresh scrutiny," March 25.

New York Times (2021) "Biden's push for electric cars: $174 billion, 10 years and a bit of luck." March 31.

New York Times (2021) "NFTs are shaking up the art world. They may be warming the planet, too," April 16.

New York Times (2021) "Three electric S.U.V.s with Tesla in their sights," April 23.

New York Times (2021a) "The auto industry bets its future on batteries," May 4.

New York Times (2021b) "As cars go electric, China builds a big lead in factories," May 4.

New York Times (2021) "The lithium gold rush: Inside the race to power electric vehicles," May 6; reprinted as "Lithium mining projects may not be green friendly," May 6.

New York Times (2021) "Pipeline hack points to growing cybersecurity risk for energy systems," May 13.

New York Times (2021a) "Hackers and climate change threaten U.S. energy independence," May 19.

New York Times (2021b) "Ford's electric F-150 pickup aims to be the Model T of E.V.s," May 19.

New York Times (2021) "The costly pursuit of self-driving cars continues on. And on. And on," May 24.

New York Times (2021) "Can removing highways fix America's cities?" May 27.

New York Times (2021) "Ransomware disrupts meat plant in latest attack on critical U.S. business," June 1.

New York Times (2021) "Secret chats show how cybergang became a ransomware powerhouse," June 3.

New York Times (2021) "What is a flying car?" June 12.

New York Times (2021) "Crashes involving Teal Autopilot and other driver-assistance systems get new scrutiny," June 29.

New York Times (2021) "Tesla says autopilot makes its cars safer, crash victims say it kills," July 5.

New York Times (2021) "Constant but camouflaged, flurry of cyberattacks offers glimpse of new era," July 20.

New York Times (2021) "Climate crisis turns world's subways into flood zones," July 24.

New York Times (2021) "As China boomed, it didn't take climate change into account. Now it must," July 25.

New York Times (2021) "Tesla autopilot faces U.S. inquiry after series of crashes," August 16.

New York Times (2021) "Your batteries are due for disruption," September 8.

New York Times (2021) "China declares all cryptocurrency transactions illegal," September 24.

New York Times (2021) "Trams, cable cars, electric ferries: How cities are rethinking transit," October 3.

New York Times (2021) "Ford will build 4 factories in a big electric vehicle push," October 5.

New York Times (2021) "LG to pay G.M. $1.9 billion over Bolt battery recall," October 12.

New York Times (2021) "Old power gear is slowing use of clean energy and electric cars," October 28.

New York Times (2021) "China's popular electric vehicles have put Europe's automakers on notice," October 31.

New York Times (2021) "A power struggle over cobalt rattles the clean energy revolution," November 20.

New York Times (2021) "How the U.S. lost ground to China in the contest for clean energy," November 21.

New York Times (2021) "Is an all-encompassing mobility app making a comeback?" December 5.

New York Times Magazine (2017) "Tech and design issue: The car did what?" November 7.

NIC (National Intelligence Council) (2021) *Global Trends 2040: A More Contested World*, March.

Nichols, Tom (2017) *The Death of Expertise: The Campaign against Established Knowledge and Why It Matters*, New York: Oxford University Press.

Norton, Peter (2021) *Autonorama: The Illusory Promise of High-Tech Driving*, Washington: Island Press.

NREL (National Renewable Energy Laboratory) (2013) "Autonomous vehicles have a wide range of possible energy impacts," July 16.

O'Connell, Mark (2017) *New York Times Magazine*, "Get Ready for D.O.A.s," *The Tech & Design Issue: Life After Driving*; *The Rev-up—Imagining a 20% self-driving world*, November 7.

Patterson, Jane et al. (2011) *Preparing for a Life Cycle CO$_2$ Measure*, Ricardo, May 20.

Perrow, Charles (1984, second edition 1999) *Normal Accidents: Living with High-Risk Technologies*, Princeton, NJ: Princeton University Press.

Petroski, Henry (1994) *Design Paradigms: Case Histories of Error and Judgment in Engineering*, Cambridge: Cambridge University Press.

Pomerantseva, Ekaterina et al. (2019) *Science*, "Energy storage: The future enabled by nanomaterials," November 22.

Popper, Nathaniel (2017) *New York Times Magazine*, "The liability conundrum," November 7.

Reason, James (1990) *Human Error*, Cambridge, UK: Cambridge University Press.

Reason, James (2008) *The Human Contribution: Unsafe Acts, Accidents and Heroic Recoveries*, Boca Raton, FL: Routledge.

Recharge (2021) "Zinc-ion batteries: 'Up to 50% cheaper than lithium-ion, with no raw-materials concerns'," January 11.

Schaller Consulting (2017) *Unsustainable? The Growth of App-Based Ride Services and Traffic, Travel and the Future of New York City*, February 27.

Schiff, Capt. Brian (2015) "Automation dependency," *Lift Magazine*, Spring.

Science (2020) "Europe plans to strictly regulate high-risk AI technology," February 19.

SecurityInfowatch.com (2021) "Colonial pipeline cyberattack is a chilling reminder of U.S. infrastructure vulnerability," May 10.

Sivak, Michael and Brandon Schoettle (2015) "Motion sickness in self-driving vehicles," University of Michigan, Transportation Research Institute, April.

Sivak, Michael and Brandon Schoettle (2016) "Would self-driving cars increase occupant productivity?" University of Michigan, Transportation Research Institute, September.

Smart Prosperity (2021) "The carbon footprint of cryptocurrency," August 23.

St. George, David (2016) *SAFE*, "Expand your aviation comfort zone," ww2.safepilots.org, January.

Standage, Tom (2021) *A Brief History of Motion: From the Wheel, to the Car, to What Comes Next*, New York: Bloomsbury.

Statista (2019) "Mobility Berlin: Get around sustainably," July 19.

Steinberg, Rolf and Manfred Hamm (1983) *Dead Tech: A Guide to the Archaeology of Tomorrow*, San Francisco: Sierra Club Books.

Stone, Mike (2017) "Flying cars could happen. But they'll probably create more problems than they solve," Greentech Media, June 12.

Telegraph (2021) "'New era' for transport as convertible car completes first flight," June 30.

Tenner, Edward (1996) *Why Things Bite Back: Technology and the Revenge of Unintended* Consequences, New York: Vintage.

Thom, Bing (1998) "From the ground up: Designing and building a new city in China," in Peter N. Nemetz (ed.) *The Vancouver Institute: An Experiment in Public Education*, Vancouver, BC: JBA Press.

Toshiba (2017) "Toshiba develops next-generation lithium-ion battery with new anode material," press release, October 3.

Translink (2021) *Transport 2050*, Vancouver, B.C.

Transport & Environment (2021) "Key transport trends in Q1 2021," March 30.

UBS (2020) "Q-Series: Tearing down the heart of an electric car lap 2; Cost parity a closer reality?" July 17.

US CERT (Computer Emergency Readiness Team, Cybersecurity and Infrastructure Security Agency, Department of Homeland Security) (2018) information on multiple threats, accessed March 15.

US CRS (Congressional Research Service) (2017) *Dark Web*, March 10.

US EIA (Energy Information Administration) (2017) *Study of the Potential Energy Consumption Impacts of Connected and Automated Vehicles,* March.

US EIA (Energy Information Administration) (2018) *Today in Energy: Natural Gas and Renewables Make Up Most of 2018 Electric Capacity Additions*, May 7.

US EIA (Energy Information Administration) (2020) "New electric generating capacity in 2020 will come primarily from wind and solar," January 14.

US FAA (Federal Aviation Administration) (2013) *Operational Use of Flight Path Management Systems*. Report of the Performance-Based Operations Aviation Rulemaking Committee.

US News & World Report (2021) "Ford is betting that solid-state batteries will cut EV costs," May 5.

USA Today (2019) "Possibility or pipe dream: How close are we to seeing flying cars?" December 24.

USSC (United States Supreme Court) (1948) United States v. National City Lines, No. 544.

Visual Capitalist (2016) "The extraordinary raw materials in a Tesla Model S," March 7.

Vosoughi, Soroush et al. (2018) *Science*, "The spread of true and false news online," March 9.

Wachter, Bob (2015) "My interview with Capt. Sully Sullenberger: On Aviation, Medicine, and Technology," blog, The Hospital Leader: Official Blog of the Society of Hospital Medicine, February 23.

Walker, Joan (2018) "The traffic jam of robots: Implications of autonomous vehicles on trip-making," Automated Vehicle Symposium 2016, University of California, Berkeley, July 9–12.

Walsh, Bryan (2019) *End Times: A Brief Guide to the End of the World; Asteroids, Supervolcanoes, Rogue Robots, and More*, London: Hachette Books.

Ward's (2019) *China's New Energy Vehicle Future.*

Washington Post (2021) "Tesla Model S garage fire follows pattern prompting warnings for other EVs," August 4.

WHO (World Health Organization) (2021) "Traffic injuries," June 21.

Wilson, Lindsay (2013) *Shades of Green: Electric Cars' Carbon Emissions around the Globe,* Shrink That Footprint, February.

Yang, Xiao-Guang et al. (2019) *Joule,* "Asymmetric temperature modulation for extreme fast charging of lithium-ion batteries," December 10.

8 Nuclear power

No form of energy production elicits such strong emotions as nuclear power. The industry is established in at least 30 countries with 443 operating reactors as of May 2021. Fifty-four reactors are currently under construction, another 101 are planned, and 325 are proposed (WNA 2021). Nuclear power is considered by some as the only feasible means of meeting future energy demand without generating greenhouse gases (GHGs). While the *operation* of nuclear reactors generates no carbon dioxide, an assessment of nuclear power's total contribution to climate change requires the measurement of carbon dioxide production from the construction and operation of all facilities and equipment used in the nuclear fuel cycle. In fact, only this type of comprehensive systems analysis will reveal the differences among all energy sources, be they nuclear, fossil, or renewable.

Emotions run strong on both sides of this debate, and it is noteworthy that the environmental movement is split, with some environmental nongovernmental organizations now suggesting that nuclear power may be an acceptable transition source of power while other longer-term solutions are identified and implemented. Nuclear power accounted for about 10 percent of total global electricity production in 2019 (WNA 2021), but the importance of nuclear power in a nation's overall power production varies markedly by country. While nuclear power contributes 15.6 and 19.7 percent of all UK and US electricity production respectively, it represents 70.6 percent of France's total electricity output. Table 8.1 lists the number of reactors by country as well as the contribution of nuclear power to total energy production as of August 2020 (WNA 2020).

The United States opened its first commercial reactor in 1957, following closely on the heels of the United Kingdom. The first years of the new nuclear power era were filled with optimism, as characterized by the remark of Lewis Strauss, then chair of the US Atomic Energy Commission (AEC), that electricity from nuclear reactors would be "too cheap to meter" (Strauss 1954). The construction of nuclear reactors in the United States largely came to a halt with the last commercial reactor to go critical in 1997. The reasons are multifaceted and complex and, in many respects, are still relevant today, challenging the growth or even survival of the industry. In essence, the critical issue is one of risk, whether it is financial, technological, environmental, or national security. The development of the modern discipline of risk analysis has been intimately connected to the creation and expansion of the commercial nuclear power sector.

The coevolution of risk analysis and nuclear power

The transformation of nuclear power from military to civilian use required the development of more sophisticated analytical methodologies to assess the potential risks of

DOI: 10.4324/9781003199540-11

Table 8.1 Nuclear reactors as of August 2020

Country	Units	Net capacity MW(e)	Percentage of total installed capacity	Under construction	Added MW(e)
Argentina	3	1,641	5.9	1	25
Armenia	1	375	27.8		
Belgium	7	5,930	47.6		
Brazil	2	1,884	2.7	1	1,245
Bulgaria	2	2,006	37.5		
Canada	19	13,554	14.9		
China	48	46,498	4.9	11	10,926
Czech Republic	6	3,932	35.2		
Finland	4	2,794	34.7	1	1,630
France	56	61,370	70.6	1	1,630
Germany	6	8,113	12.4		
Hungary	4	1,902	49.2		
India	22	6,255	3.2	7	4,824
Iran	1	915	1.8	1	915
Japan	33	31,679	7.5	2	2,653
Korea, Rep. of	24	23,172	26.2	4	5,360
Mexico	2	1,552	4.5		
Netherlands	1	482	3		
Pakistan	5	1,318	6.6	2	2,028
Romania	2	1,300	18.5		
Russia	38	28,437	19.7	4	4,424
Slovakia	4	1,814	53.9	2	880
Slovenia	1	688	37		
South Africa	2	1,860	6.7		
Spain	7	7,121	21.4		
Sweden	7	7,740	34		
Switzerland	4	2,960	23.9		
Taiwan	4	3,844	13.4	2	2,600
United Kingdom	15	8,923	15.6	2	3,260
Ukraine	15	13,107	53.9	2	2,070
United States	95	97,154	19.7	2	2,234
Total	**440**	**390,320**		**45**	**46,704**

Source: IAEA 2018.

the nuclear power cycle. There are two principal variants of risk analysis: probabilistic risk assessment (PRA) and risk–benefit analysis (RBA), the latter a melding of PRA and cost-benefit analysis. In principle the definition of risk is beguilingly simple: Risk (R) is defined as the product of accident consequences (C) and accident probability (P). In other words, (R) = C x P. For example, if the probability of an accident is 10^{-1}/year, and the average number of deaths per accident is 100, then the risk is 1/10 x 100 = 10 deaths/year. Table 8.2 presents some crucial concepts and terminology in the field of risk analysis. This table builds upon the work of Frank Knight (1921) by dividing the nature of risks into four categories: (1) certainty—which is not technically risk per se—where we are aware of the consequences of an event or decision and know that consequence is certain to occur. In other words, its probability is 1.0; (2) risk—where the consequences of an event or decision are known but not with precision. In this case, a probability distribution is used to define the outcomes; (3) uncertainty—a situation where the consequences are known but the probability of occurrence is unknown; (4) "wicked problems"—a series

Table 8.2 Risk terminology

	Consequences (single or multiple)	Probability of occurrence
Certainty	Known	1
Risk	Known	Probability distribution
Uncertainty	Known	Unknown
"Wicked" problems	Unknown	Unknown

of outcomes that society does not even know the existence of, let alone their probability (Balint et al. 2011).

There are a number of ways to ascertain the probability estimates to be used in PRA:

(1) **The actuarial method** is used in cases where there is substantial recorded experience, and the accident probability can be determined directly from these data.

(2) **Fault trees** start with the definition of the undesired event, the probability of which is to be determined. The analysis works backwards to examine all possible contributory causes (US NRC 1981). Figure 8.1 is a highly simplified fault tree depicting the possible precursors to the release of radioactive wastes to the biosphere (McGrath 1974). The final probability can be computed from the probabilities assigned to each of the preceding risk factors. Because much of the data used to construct fault trees is the result of expert opinion, which is subjective in nature, and because uncertainties can be compounded by the serial multiplication of probabilities throughout the fault tree, the results can have a significant degree of imprecision.

(3) **Event trees** are similar to fault trees but the logic flows in reverse; the event tree starts with an initiating event and asks to what results it might lead. Figure 8.2 is a highly simplified version of the most probable sequence for a catastrophic failure in a nuclear pressurized water reactor (PWR) (Crouch and Wilson 1980; Wilson and Crouch 1982). The overall probability of the accident is the product of all probabilities along the branches of the tree. In this example, probabilities are derived from a number of sources, including actuarial data on pipe breaks and unfavorable weather from past experience, and expert opinion where a sufficiently accurate actuarial database cannot be constructed. There are two basic assumptions in event tree analysis: (i) the analysis is assumed to be complete, meaning that the event trees include all possible accident paths, or at least all those with a major contribution to risk; and (ii) the probabilities are assumed to be unrelated to one another (e.g., p_1, p_2, p_3, and p_4 are in fact independent). If interdependencies are known they can be formally incorporated into the analysis. The validity of PRA can be compromised by the existence of unknown correlation between paths, commonly referred to as "common mode failures."

While these methodologies appear conceptually straightforward, their successful application can be complex and controversial. Despite the powerful tools that both PRA and RBA bring to decision-making, there are numerous conceptual difficulties, or pathologies, with both methodologies (Fairley 1977): (1) neither assigns probabilities to credible threats that are difficult to quantify; (2) both give inadequate treatment of multiple risks and possible synergistic effects; (3) both are susceptible to the problem of not choosing the most appropriate measure of risk; (4) both are susceptible to common mode failures; (5) both

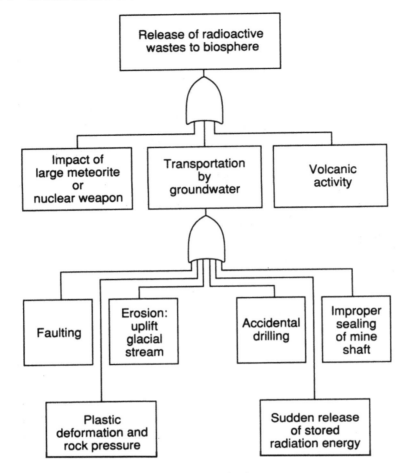

Figure 8.1 Example fault tree for the release of radioactive waste.
Source: McGrath (1974).

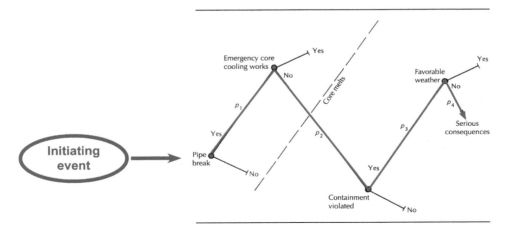

Figure 8.2 Example event tree for catastrophic nuclear failure.
Source: Crouch and Wilson (1980).

may incorporate past analytical errors or oversights in the data; (6) neither determines the correct dose-response relationships in measuring the effect on biological entities such as humans; (7) neither is able to anticipate all accident scenarios; and (8) both inaccurately estimate probabilities of anticipated accident scenarios (in particular, they underestimate).

Many of these complexities have dogged the application of PRA to nuclear power and the distinct steps of the nuclear fuel cycle: mining, processing, enrichment (where required), fabrication, operation, decommissioning, and waste storage. Each of the major concerns and risks is summarized briefly below.

Design risk: While not universally used, the predominant technology in modern nuclear reactors is a light water system (LWR) with either pressurized water (PWR) or boiling water (BWR). A large amount of cooling water is required to prevent the radioactive core from becoming overheated; overheating can lead to a meltdown and potentially catastrophic release of radioactive material. The design adopted by the United States for its commercial reactors, and replicated in most other nations, was based on the original reactors developed to power the American navy's atomic submarines and other vessels. As an historical footnote, the original development of nuclear propulsion for US submarines was due to the determination of one person, Admiral Hyman Rickover, who had to overcome fierce resistance from the naval establishment, which was wedded to the continued use of petroleum-based fuels (Oliver 2018).

The adaptation of the submarine-based atomic reactor for civilian purposes was deemed the most effective and rapid route to commercialization. In retrospect, some experts feel this decision was problematic, as it has led to a class of reactors that is not inherently safe, meaning that human control is required (in the form of technological add-ins or actual human intervention) in order to forestall major risks such as meltdown. In recognition of this design problem, research has been ongoing for several years to design a technologically and economically viable reactor that is inherently safe—one that will shut itself down and not lead to the large-scale release of radionuclides even if a major system failure occurs (Cooper 2014). The most prominent designs have included the Westinghouse Advanced Passive 1000 (AP1000) reactor; General Electric's Economic Simplified Boiling Water Reactor; the AREVA EPR, the product of a joint French-German collaboration; and an innovative design referred to as a pebble-bed reactor in which the fuel is enclosed in many small graphite-based spheres instead of conventional fuel rods (McCullum 2019). Of these new "Gen III+" reactor designs, the AP1000 is the closest to being added to the US grid, as two prototype reactors are under construction in the American state of Georgia (NEI 2018). It is estimated, however, that the costs could balloon to $20 billion (POWER 2017). However, several major setbacks have occurred recently which have cast a pall over the future of nuclear power in both the United States and the United Kingdom: Westinghouse Electric Company, a major developer of commercial reactors, filed for bankruptcy in 2017 (*New York Times* March 29, 2017) and two advanced-design reactors in South Carolina were abandoned in 2017 despite incurred costs of $9 billon (Benzinga.com 2017).

The situation in other countries remains mixed. In January 2019, Hitachi announced the abandonment of plans to build its Advanced Boiling Water Reactor in Wales (*New York Times* January 18, 2019). While Japan and several countries in Europe have been reexamining their commitment to nuclear power (*New York Times* October 2, 2013 and December 6, 2016), China appears committed to a major expansion of its nuclear industry in its attempt to drastically reduce the GHG footprint of its massive power

Table 8.3 China's nuclear reactors

Year	In operation							Under construction
	1995	2000	2005	2010	2015	2017	2020	
Reactors	3	3	9	13	31	39	48	11
MW(e)	2,188	2,188	6,587	10,065	26,774	34,514	46,498	10,926

Source: WNA, various years.

sector (see Table 8.3). In addition to the continued installation of traditional PWRs, four AP1000 reactors are planned in China. Even with this new generation of reactors, however, there is a continuing debate over their inherent safety (Fairewinds Associates 2010; *New York Times* April 21, 2010, March 8, 2011 and May 20, 2011).

The US Department of Energy has recently decided to support the development of smaller, newer modular reactors with about 10 percent of the output of a conventional reactor (*Science* October 16, 2020). One proposed by NuScale Power, an American company founded in 2007, has been specifically designed to shut down automatically without explicit human intervention although a special advisory committee of the Nuclear Regulatory Commission (NRC), the US government agency responsible for nuclear safety, raised concerns that this unique design might not work as planned in all circumstances (*Science* August 28, 2020). Two other smaller reactor designs have also received funding from the Department of Energy: the first would use molten sodium as a coolant rather than water; the second would use helium (*Science* October 16, 2020). There are at least two issues of concern: First, the use of sodium as a coolant in the Natrium reactor from TerraPower Inc requires extra measures to prevent leaks as this metal will burn on contact with air and explode on contact with water (*Scientific American* October 13, 2014). Leaks of molten sodium can, as a consequence, pose serious safety hazards. Both France and Japan experienced sodium leakage with their fast breeder reactors. The second potential concern is that the Natrium reactor and the Xe-100 reactor from X-Energy, a "nuclear energy solution company" based in Maryland (x-energy.com), rely on uranium fuel, which is enriched to as much as 20 percent. This is far in excess of the 3.5 percent enrichment of conventional light water reactors and the unenriched uranium used in Canada's CANDU (Canadian Deuterium Uranium) reactor. While still far short of the more than 90 percent enrichment required for atomic weapons, this creates an elevated risk of theft or diversion by terrorist groups or rogue governments (Lyman 2021).

Operating safety and technological risk: Cognizant of the non-zero risk of a loss of coolant accident (LOCA)—the most serious accident sequence in a light water reactor, which could lead to a meltdown of the reactor core—the US AEC, the precursor to the US NRC, undertook a study in 1957 designated as WASH-740 and entitled *Theoretical Possibilities and Consequences of Major Accidents in Large Nuclear Power Plants.* The study focused on the severity of accident consequences determined by four principal factors: (1) the type and quantity of fission products released (major/minor); (2) the release temperature (hot/cold); (3) the distribution of particle size (1 micron / 7 microns); and (4) meteorological variations such as night/day, where the central issue is the existence of atmospheric inversions; and rain / dry weather, where the central issue is particle

Table 8.4 WASH-740 worst-case scenarios

	Urgent evacuation	Total evacuation	Restrictions on land and outdoor activity	Restrictions on farming, use of crops
Radius (miles)	0 to 100	0 to 335	0 to 1,200	5.6 to 3,100
Area (square miles)	0 to 92	0 to 760	0 to 8,200	2.3 to 150,000
Persons affected	0 to 85,000	0 to 460,000	0 to 3,000,000	n/a

Source: US AEC 1957.

washout. Because of the analytical approach adopted, attention was focused on the most extreme cases (see Table 8.4).

The most significant criticism of the report was that it dealt only with consequences and not probabilities and, as a result, did not meet the definition of a PRA. The sub-title of the work did, however, explicitly recognize the significance of probability, as it read *A Study of Possible Consequences If Certain Assumed Accidents, Theoretically Possible but Highly Improbable, Were to Occur in Large Nuclear Power Plants*. To remedy the omission of explicit probability estimates in WASH-740, the AEC published a second study in 1973 labeled WASH-1250 and entitled *The Safety of Nuclear Power Reactors (Light-Water Cooled) and Related Facilities*. This represented the first organized attempt to incorporate accident probabilities into the analysis of possible reactor accidents. The results of this study demonstrated the expected inverse correlation between accident severity and probability (see figures 6-8 and 6-9 in the report, pp. 6–31).

In 1974, the US AEC was abolished because of concern over its dual role as regulator and promoter of nuclear power. In its stead, the NRC was established and formally began operations on January 19, 1975 (NRC 2019b). The NRC produced its first compre-hensive assessment of risks at nuclear power plants entitled *WASH-1400: Reactor Safety Study; An Assessment of Accident Risks in U.S. Commercial Nuclear Power Plants*, a massive multivolume work which firmly established event and fault tree analysis as the *sine qua non* of PRA. The report estimated the likelihood of a core-melt accident at one in twenty thousand per reactor-year. This stands in marked contrast to the challenges faced by the authors of the WASH-740 study in eliciting expert views on the probability of reactor accidents. To quote:

> As to the probabilities of major reactor accidents, some experts held that numerical estimates of a quantity so vague and uncertain as the likelihood of occurrence of major reactor accidents have no meaning. They declined to express their feeling about the probability in numbers. Others, though admitting similar uncertainty, neverthe-less ventured to express their opinions in numerical terms. Estimations so expressed of the probability of reactor accidents having major effects on the public ranged from a chance of one in 100,000 to one in a billion per year for each large reactor.
>
> (US AEC 1957, p. viii)

The monumental effort that generated WASH-1400 was not without controversy, however, and the NRC commissioned a risk assessment report in 1978 (US NRC 1978, called the Lewis Report) to reexamine the methodology and conclusions of WASH-1400. This subsequent report was critical of several aspects of WASH-1400. It alleged: (1) inad-equate treatment of common mode failure, (2) an inadequate database, (3) poor statistical

Table 8.5 WASH–1400 worst-case scenarios plus update

	WASH-1400 (1975)	1982 revisions
Deaths	3,300 early	102,000 early (Salem NJ plant on Delaware River)
Property damage	$14 billion	$314 billion (Indian Point No. 3 reactor located 25 miles north of New York City)

Sources: NRC 1975 and 1982.

treatment, (4) inconsistent propagation of uncertainties throughout the calculation, and (5) that the Executive Summary was a "poor description of the contents of the report." The Lewis Report concluded that the Executive Summary should not be portrayed as a description of the contents of the report, and has "lent itself to misuse in the discussion of reactor risk" (p. vii). In fact, some experts felt that the Executive Summary was written as a public statement that reactors were safe compared to other risks to which the public is exposed.

Shortly after the publication of the Lewis Report, the NRC issued a formal statement on January 18, 1979 entitled "NRC statement on risk assessment and the *Reactor Safety Study Report* (WASH-1400)." The following comments are quoted from this statement: (1) "the Commission withdraws any explicit or implicit past endorsement of the Executive Summary," (2) "the Executive Summary does not adequately indicate the full extent of the consequences of reactor accidents and, as a result, the reader may be left with a . . . more favourable impression of reactor risks in comparison with other risks than warranted by the study", and (3) "the Commission does not regard as reliable the Reactor Safety Study's numerical estimate of the overall risk of reactor accident (pp. 2 and 3 of Attachment 1)."

Both WASH-1250 and WASH-1400 were generic studies in that they examined American reactors as a class. In 1982, the NRC published a report (known as the CRAC-II report and with simulations conducted by Sandia Labs) which drastically revised the worst-case scenarios of an atomic reactor accident. Part of the methodology involved examining the risks associated with individual plants rather than plants generically or in the abstract. Table 8.5 compares the WASH-1400 estimates of deaths and property damage with the 1982 revisions. In a further attempt to refine their analysis of a severe accident in a nuclear power plant, the NRC published another report in 1990 numbered NUREG-1150, which focused on potential accident sequences in five American reactors (see also NRDC 2011). Still not confident in the results of these analyses, the NRC subsequently initiated yet another research project in 2007 entitled *State-of-the-Art Reactor Consequence Analyses (SOARCA) Report*, which was published in 2012 with the designation NUREG-1935. The general results of this more recent study suggested a much more optimistic picture of potential accidents in US nuclear reactors. The key results are listed:

- When operators are successful in using available on-site equipment during the accidents analyzed in the SOARCA, they can prevent the reactor from melting, or can delay or reduce releases of radioactive material to the environment.
- Analyses in the SOARCA indicate that all modeled accident scenarios, even if operators are unsuccessful in stopping the accident, progress more slowly and release much smaller amounts of radioactive material than indicated in earlier studies.

- As a result, public health consequences from severe nuclear power plant accidents modeled in the SOARCA are smaller than previously calculated.
- The delayed releases calculated provide more time for emergency response actions such as evacuating or sheltering for affected populations. For the scenarios analyzed, the SOARCA shows that emergency response programs, if implemented as planned and practiced, reduce the risk of public health consequences.
- Both mitigated (operator actions are successful) and unmitigated (operator actions are unsuccessful) cases of all modeled severe accident scenarios in the SOARCA cause essentially no risk of death during or shortly after the accident.
- The SOARCA's calculated longer-term cancer fatality risks for the accident scenarios analyzed are millions of times lower than the general US cancer fatality risk.

These conclusions appear unduly optimistic in light of the Fukushima disaster, which had not been fully evaluated by the date of publication. In fact, the NRC was still issuing reports on this accident as of June 2018 (US NRC 2018a and b; US NRC 2014). Three initial conclusions emerge from this use of PRA. First, it is much more complex than even those involved in its use realized; second, it is sometimes difficult to separate the production and interpretation of scientific studies from the underlying value judgments of those intimately involved in the analysis, the US NRC being a case in point; and third, the more site- and situation-specific the analysis, the better.

Recent nuclear accident history

Over the course of commercial nuclear power history, there have been three major accidents in the commercial nuclear power industry out of a total of 17,430 reactor-years of operation: the partial meltdown of the reactor core at Three Mile Island in Pennsylvania in 1979, the Chernobyl catastrophe of 1986, and the Fukushima disaster of 2011. To advocates of nuclear power, this is proof of a remarkably safe record in comparison to other sources of power. There are several major qualifications which must be addressed. First, the history of nuclear power has been marked by a number of unanticipated near misses (UCS various years; BBC September 12, 2011) and other less serious problems (Greenpeace 2006; UCS 2016). Some of these have been related to the inadequate understanding of how metallurgical reactor components age in the presence of radiation. Gregory Jaczko, former chair of the US NRC, wrote a short book in 2019 entitled *Confessions of a Rogue Nuclear Regulator*. In that work, Jaczko describes at least three other incidents that could have led to catastrophic nuclear accidents. These situations occurred at the Davis-Besse plant near Toledo, Ohio, the Fort Calhoun plant on the Missouri River in Nebraska, and the Brown's Ferry plant in Alabama.

A significant concern that has only recently emerged is referred to as a "fat-tail" distribution in risk analysis. While the probability of accidents may be low, there is a class of such risks—as demonstrated by the Chernobyl disaster—with truly catastrophic consequences. While an industrial accident at a fossil-fueled plant may endanger some workers and cause localized environmental pollution, a similar accident at a nuclear reactor can essentially remove a large swath of land—in the order of hundreds of square miles—from long-term cultivation and human habitation. It can also cause an increased number of cancers among the general public. Three of the most dangerous radionuclides released from nuclear reactor accidents include cesium-137, strontium-90, and iodine-131. The general rule of thumb within the nuclear safety community is that the public must be protected from these radioactive elements for ten to thirteen half-lives, where a half-life is the time it takes for the radioactive emissions from an isotope to fall by 50 percent from the previous level. The half-lives for these three isotopes are 30.0 years, 29.12 years, and 8.04 days respectively. This suggests that a geographic area seriously contaminated with these isotopes should remain off limits to human habitation for up to three hundred years. These qualitative and quantitative risks are unique to the nuclear power industry. It is somewhat ironic that the renewed interest in extreme nuclear events among governments, academics, and the general public is reminiscent of the early focus of WASH-740 on such occurrences, despite the shortcomings of that report from 1957.

Three Mile Island accident

On March 28, 1979, the Three Mile Island reactor complex in Pennsylvania suffered a major LOCA, which led to the melting of 35–40 percent of the fuel and the collapse of 70 percent of the core structure (Mahaffey 2014). The US NRC attributed this accident to "a combination of equipment malfunctions, design-related problems and worker errors" (NRC 2018c, p. 1). The existence of an external containment structure prevented release of much of the radioactive material produced by the meltdown. Mahaffey termed it the world's worst industrial accident in which not one person was harmed. This somewhat bright assessment could not be applied to the entire American nuclear industry, however, and public perception of nuclear power has shifted significantly. The cleanup operation, completed in 1993, cost approximately $1 billion (Mahaffey 2014). The reactor was finally shut down on September 20, 2019 (CBC September 20, 2019),

The Chernobyl accident

The meltdown accident that occurred in the Ukrainian town of Chernobyl on April 26, 1986, as a consequence of an ill-conceived test of the reactor's safety systems, was much more serious and indeed deemed catastrophic. Without an external containment structure, the massive release of radioactive material escaped unimpeded and spread throughout Europe for up to ten days. Numerous books and reports have now been written on this incident, including by the International Atomic Energy Agency (IAEA 2005), Alexievich and Gessen (2005), Petryna (2013), Leatherbarrow (2016), Plokhy (2019), Kostenko (2019), and Higginbotham (2019). Despite these extensive studies, one of the most instructive and exhaustive reports of this disaster was early research conducted by a Russian nuclear scientist, Zhores Medvedev (1990), who described the extent of radioactive contamination. To quote:

> Fallout from Chernobyl was registered in every country of the northern hemisphere, but it was only in the Soviet Union and Europe that levels were high enough to affect human health and agriculture. . . . However, some areas in a number of countries were affected more seriously. In many hot spots in Europe (such as Lapland, parts of southern Germany, the Austro-Hungarian border, east Poland) the mean exposure from Chernobyl fallout was up to 50 or even 100 times higher than average.
>
> (pp. 220 and 222)

Evacuations were ordered in some areas up to 150–200 kilometers (km) from the immediate exclusion zone around the reactor, but the author felt that the greatest long-term impact would be on agriculture. Medvedev stated that "if international standards were being applied for the use of agricultural land, nearly 1 million hectares would be considered lost for a century, and about 2 million hectares would be lost for 10–20 years" (p. 11). The principal pathway of exposure for humans was eating contaminated food, and the recognition of this risk led several countries to withdraw from the market their supplies of fresh milk, vegetables, and selected milk and meat products such as lamb (Simmonds 1987).

The total impacts of the Chernobyl accident on human health are still to be researched and there is a great deal of uncertainty about the long-term effects. The most immediate concern was the occurrence of thyroid cancers from the uptake of radioactive iodine and the longer-term impact from several longer lasting radioactive elements such as strontium-90, which is preferentially absorbed by the body instead of calcium. To quote Zhores Medvedev (1990): "Since plutonium and strontium remain fixed in the body for decades, it is clear that the medical history of Chernobyl will continue well into the next century" (p. 182). The World Health Organization (WHO 2005) concluded that while fewer than fifty people, mostly rescue workers, died as a result of radiation exposure, up to four thousand people could die as a result of the accident. Medvedev quoted one report which stated that six hundred thousand people were classified as having been significantly exposed to radiation. As Medvedev states, "cancer only accounts for a third of the cases of 'radiation shortening of life span'" (p. 166), with the remainder due to hormonal disorders, infections, negative impact on the immunological system, cardiovascular disease, and renal failure (Medvedev 1990).

More recent exhaustive studies supported many of Medvedev's earlier conclusions about the potential extent of cancer and non-cancer morbidity and mortality (e.g., Yablokov 2009). Greenpeace (2006) assembled a scientific panel of fifty-two scientists from seven countries to reexamine the scientific literature published since the accident at Chernobyl. Drawing on over 500 scientific papers, the report concluded: "The most recently published figures indicate that in Belarus, Russia and Ukraine alone the accident resulted in an estimated 200,000 additional deaths between 1990 and 2004. . . . These data indicate that 'official' figures (e.g., the IAEA 2005 evaluation) . . . may grossly underestimate both the local and international impact of the accident" (p. 9). Of particular note was the report's observations that: first, the long latency period of certain cancers such as thyroid cancer may delay their early recognition; second, that "endocrine system pathology is a highly important and significant impact observed in those populations exposed to Chernobyl radiation, given the importance of the endocrine system in the modulation of whole body function" (p. 14). This can lead to a reduced ability to fight infectious and noninfectious diseases; and third, an increased frequency in chromosomal aberrations in contaminated areas of Ukraine, Belarus, and Russia.

In 2019, Professor Kate Brown of the Massachusetts Institute of Technology published a work summarizing her extensive research as the first Western historian to access archives in Ukraine, Russia, and Belarus related to this accident. Her research essentially corroborated Medvedev's earlier estimates of the extent of potential morbidity and mortality, in sharp contrast to the prevailing opinion among Western health agencies, which focused on the figure of fifty deaths. One estimate provided on fatalities in Ukraine alone was as high as 150,000 and did not include Russia or Belarus where 70 percent of the fallout landed (p. 310). Other studies have projected between 17,000 and 93,000 deaths due to cancer alone (Dorfman et al. 2013).

More recent research has produced mixed results. Yeager et al. (2021) conclude that "evidence is lacking for a substantial effect on germline DNMs [*de novo* mutations] in humans, suggesting minimal impact on health of subsequent generations," (p. 725), while the results of Morton et al. (2021) "point to DNA double-strand breaks as early carcinogenic events that subsequently enable PTC [papillary thyroid cancer] growth following environmental radiation exposure" (abstract).

The intense retrospective analysis of this disaster led to a serious reconsideration of the nature and practice of risk analysis itself. It is unclear if a formal PRA had ever been conducted prior to the accident but, if it had, it would have provided no indication of the probability or consequences of the accident. Figure 8.3 illustrates what a risk analysis might have looked at and what it would have missed given the state of the science at the time. None of the seven major events or consequences was, or could have been, anticipated in a formal risk analysis. The Soviet reactor design is unique, but this is nonetheless a sobering message for risk assessments of other currently operating reactors worldwide with different designs.

1. ***Initiating event:*** Until or if AI can advance to the stage where it can substitute for all the capabilities of the human mind, human interaction with technology will be a continuing necessity. In several major accidents, and especially in the case of the Chernobyl disaster, operator error was a crucial factor in causing and exacerbating the computer meltdown (Medvedev 1990). As Mahaffey has stated: "the most difficult problem to handle is the reactor operator" (2014, p. 101). Recent research has

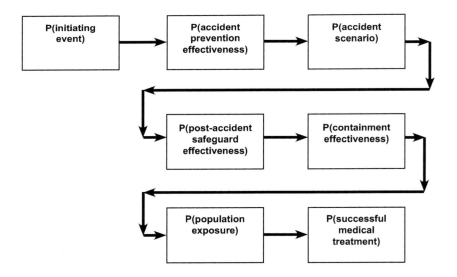

1. Initiating event: operator error—unanticipated
2. Accident prevention: failure of control rod reinsertion—unanticipated
3. Accident mode: steam explosion + core disintegration—unanticipated
4. Post-accident safeguard: lack of effectiveness of water pool for steam—unanticipated
5. Containment: inability to contain steam explosion—unanticipated
6. Population exposure: wind dispersion patterns—unanticipated
7. Medical treatment success: poor success of bone marrow transplants—unanticipated

Figure 8.3 Chernobyl hypothesized a priori risk analysis.

focused on how to address operator missteps in forestalling and controlling accident sequences in this and other complex technologies (see, for example, Negroni 2016).

2. ***Accident prevention***: Despite the design of systems to respond to potential runaway reactor accidents by rapidly inserting control rods back into the reactor core, this was not possible as the guide-pipes at Chernobyl had twisted and warped as the reactor began to melt (Mahaffey 2014, p. 365).

3. ***Accident mode***: An unanticipated combination of steam and hydrogen explosions accompanied the process of core disintegration in the reactor (Medvedev 1990; Mahaffey 2014).

4. ***Post–accident safeguards***: Professor Richard Wilson of Harvard University described the failure of the water pool at the base of the reactor, designed to relieve excessive steam pressure, and the implications of this design deficiency for American reactors: "I'm just a little nervous that we have the same design and it didn't work" (*New York Times* May 19, 1986).

5. ***Containment***: Mahaffey (2014) has described the Soviet graphite-moderated reactor system as "the most dangerous method for making power using fission. . . . There was no practical way to construct a sealed containment building over this tall machine, so the world is protected from fission products in the reactor by a single barrier, a round, concrete lid, eight feet thick, held by gravity in the reactor room floor" (p. 358). It was this lid that was blasted off by the subsequent explosions.

6. ***Population exposure***: As Makhijani and Saleska (1999, p. 155) observed:

> One of the most important, unanticipated features of the Chernobyl accident was the ten-day duration of the fire, accompanied by a correspondingly long time during which large releases of radioactivity continued. As Medvedev points out, the modeling of nuclear power plant accidents generally assumes a single, short-term release of radioactivity. Weather conditions during such short releases can reasonably be assumed to be constant. As a result, severe accidents are assumed to have a fallout trace that forms a single elongated, cigar-shaped pattern, much like the typical fallout patterns from a nuclear bomb explosion near ground level. . . . But it was not valid for the Chernobyl accident. During the ten days of the fire, which was accompanied by huge releases of radioactivity, wind directions and the weather changed many times.

The French Institut de Radioprotection et de Sûreté Nucléaire (IRSN) has produced a report and graphic video which displays the changing drift of the radioactive cloud over the ten days of release (2011). Grigori Medvedev (1990, p. 79), the chief engineer at the time of the plant's construction, estimated that the reactor ended up releasing almost 50 short tons of evaporated fuel in contrast to only 4.5 short tons released by the Hiroshima atomic bomb. However, a major difference between the two events was the much wider distribution of radionuclides from Chernobyl, leading to lower *average* doses.

7. ***Medical treatment success***: Baranov et al. (1989) reported only a modest level of success in treating several victims of acute radiation poisoning, citing the comorbidities which can complicate this process following a reactor accident. This was despite the unreasonably optimistic prognosis for bone marrow transplants forecast by Dr. Robert Gale from the University of California, Los Angeles who performed these operations shortly after the accident (Brown 2019, pp. 23–25).

Mahaffey (2014, p. 375) has described in detail the serious design flaws that contributed to the Chernobyl accident, but is also less optimistic about the state of American reactor engineering after the explosion of American-designed reactors at Fukushima in 2011. To quote:

> It seems unfortunate, but nothing was learned from the Chernobyl disaster. It did not, for example, lead to a better understanding of reactor accidents or an improvement in reactor design. . . . The next disaster, though, would involve American engineering, and there would be no excuse for it.
>
> (p. 375)

It appears that major risks from the Chernobyl reactor remain even thirty-five years after the accident. In an online posting on May 5, 2021, *Science* magazine reported:

> Fission reactions are smoldering again in uranium fuel masses buried deep inside a mangled reactor hall. "It's like the embers in a barbecue pit," says Neil Hyatt, a nuclear materials chemist at the University of Sheffield. Now, Ukrainian scientists are scrambling to determine whether the reactions will wink out on their own—or require extraordinary interventions to avert another accident. Sensors are tracking a rising number of neutrons, a signal of fission, streaming from one inaccessible room, Anatolii Doroshenko of the Institute for Safety Problems of Nuclear Power Plants (ISPNPP) in Kyiv, Ukraine, reported last week during discussions about dismantling the reactor. "There are many uncertainties," says [the] ISPNPP's Maxim Saveliev. "But we can't rule out the possibility of [an] accident." The neutron counts are rising slowly, Saveliev says, suggesting managers still have a few years to figure out how to stifle the threat. Any remedy he and his colleagues come up with will be of keen interest to Japan, which is coping with the aftermath of its own nuclear disaster 10 years ago at Fukushima, Hyatt notes. "It's a similar magnitude of hazard."

The Fukushima accident

The most recent example of the serious risks posed by nuclear technology is the Fukushima accident of March 11, 2011. Significant quantities of radioactive isotopes were released into the atmosphere and ocean, forcing the large-scale evacuation of a large area of countryside. At one point, the Japanese government was seriously considering evacuating Tokyo—a monumental if not impossible task (*Independent* January 27, 2012).

There are several noteworthy characteristics of this accident which pose a challenge to the current state of thinking in reactor safety. First, the accident was a common mode failure. As described above, the validity of an a priori PRA can be compromised by common mode failures where there are unknown correlations between ostensibly independent paths of an event tree outlining the sequence of possible events from an accident and their attendant probabilities.

Japan's Fukushima reactors had been designed to withstand the shock from an earthquake and had an independent diesel backup power system outside the reactor building to provide emergency electrical power in the case that power was lost. The unanticipated common mode failure was the combined effect of the direct earthquake shock to the reactor, which disabled the primary power source, and the indirect effect of the earthquake, which induced a tsunami, disabling the backup diesel power system. The massive ocean wave breeched protective seawalls, inundating the diesel power units, which had been constructed close to the shore at too low an elevation, and thus depriving the reactors of the power necessary to maintain the stability of the radioactive reactor cores. The second noteworthy characteristic of the Fukushima accident was the occurrence of several other unanticipated accident sequences, including but not limited to hydrogen explosions, fuel meltdown in three of the reactors, and the loss of external containment before the subsequent breach of several internal containment structures including three of the four reactor core vessels (*New York Times* May 24, 2011). Third, the accident demonstrated once again the inherent and unavoidable contributing causes from human error in design, operation, and regulatory oversight. Fourth, it became apparent that the reactors themselves were not the sole source of risk from radioactive releases. Large quantities of spent reactor fuel, stored on site—as with most reactors worldwide—pose an equal if not greater risk of radioactive contamination (see discussion of issues facing waste storage). And, finally, the accident demonstrated that certain safety features used in the American reactor industry, such as vents for hydrogen release, did not operate as planned at Fukushima (*New York Times* May 18, 2011a). Figure 8.4 details a hypothetical chain of events that could lead to a serious reactor accident with deviations from the standard risk model as a consequence of a common mode failure. The *New York Times* reported on March 11, 2017 that Japan was still struggling to control the nuclear waste generated by the accident. This includes both on-site and near-site contamination plus continuing release of radioactive water into the ocean. (*New York Times* March 10, 2016; *Japan Times* March 29, 2018; *Guardian* March 11, 2019; BBC September 10, 2019 and October 16, 2020; *Science* August 7, 2020 and March 5, 2021).

In a report on lessons from the Fukushima disaster, the US National Academy of Sciences (NAS 2014) concluded that:

> Four decades of analysis and operating experience have demonstrated that nuclear plant core-damage risks are dominated by beyond-design-basis accidents. Such accidents can arise, for example, from multiple human and equipment failures, violations of operational protocols, and extreme external events. Current approaches for regulating nuclear plant safety, which have been traditionally based on deterministic concepts such as the design–basis accident, are clearly inadequate for preventing core-melt accidents and mitigating their consequences.
>
> (p. 10)

While the American nuclear power industry and the NRC have voiced confidence in the safety of the US nuclear power system, several reports have raised concerns that the US system could possibly face similar types of risks as Fukushima (UCS 2011; Markey 2011; *New York Times* March 13 and May 18, 2011a, b, and c; NAS 2014 and 2016). Concerns over the implications of the Fukushima disaster prompted the NRC to set up a Japan Task Force to study the accident at Fukushima and the effectiveness of the plant's safety systems. Their report proposed improvements in areas ranging from loss of power to earthquakes, flooding, spent fuel pools, venting, and preparedness, and concluded that a "'patchwork of regulatory requirements' developed 'piece-by-piece over the decades' should be replaced with a 'logical, systematic and coherent regulatory framework' to further bolster reactor safety in the United States" (US NRC 2011, p. 1; see also NAS 2014 and 2016).

While the three major nuclear reactor accidents in commercial reactors occurred in large developed economies—the US, Japan, and the former Soviet Union—the diffusion

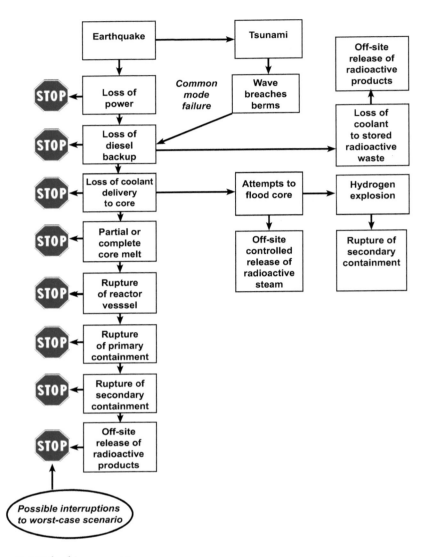

Figure 8.4 Fukushima event tree.

of similar technology into countries with less advanced supporting environments, whether technological, institutional, economic, or political, raises the prospect of additional risks. In some cases, less developed countries have an excessive reliance on nuclear power and may not be able to afford to take these machines off-line for regular and essential maintenance. National electricity systems such as those of Slovenia or Armenia, which rely for a large percentage of their power on a single reactor, have systems with very low levels of resilience.

As early as 1979, an article in *Nature* (Agarwal 1979) warned of the inherent dangers associated with the adoption of nuclear power by countries with insufficient technological expertise to handle this technology. To quote:

Unlike the US, no developing country can suddenly afford to lose a billion-dollar plant because of an accident. In some countries, a large power plant can form as much as 10% of the electrical grid. The loss of such a plant could plunge the country into an energy crisis that could cripple its growing economy. Once a developing country has an unsafe plant therefore these economic pressures could persuade it to continue dangerous operations.

(pp. 468–469)

The article went on to describe a bizarre occurrence in one reactor where defective fuel bundles led to widespread contamination of the plant and extremely high radioactivity levels. The reactor was so heavily contaminated

that it [was] impossible for maintenance jobs to be performed without the maintenance personnel exceeding the fortnightly dose of 400 mrem [millirem] in a matter of minutes. Thus the maintenance worker . . . holding a spanner in one hand and a pencil dosimeter in the other, turning a nut or two, three rotations and rushing out of the work area [was] a common phenomenon.

(p. 469)

The issue of engineering safety systems into advanced and complex technologies such as nuclear power was the subject of an innovative study by Charles Perrow in 1999. Entitled *Normal Accidents: Living with High Risk Technologies*, the central hypothesis of the book is that accidents are inevitable, or normal, in systems characterized by what Perrow terms "interactive complexity" and "tight coupling." The former term (as opposed to "linear interactions") describes a situation where one component can interact with any other system component outside the normal production sequence. The latter (as opposed to "loose coupling") describes a situation in which two elements are joined in such a manner that there is no slack or buffer between them. Perrow found that most manufacturing can be characterized as loose coupling and linear interactions, but a nuclear power plant is exactly the opposite. What Perrow is describing is a trade-off between efficiency and resilience. While complex systems, such as nuclear power, are more efficient than linear systems, there is a greater inherent risk of failure independent of conventional risk factors such as operator error, faulty design, poorly trained personnel, or other forms of mismanagement (see also Casti 2012).

Security risk: Nuclear reactors may be an enticing target for terrorist attack or as a source of radioactive material and there is no easy way of estimating the probability of this threat (*New York Times* April 4, 2016; Allison 2004). Bob Woodward, in his book *Obama's Wars* (2011), has stated that one of the predominant concerns of the US government and military is the possibility that a terrorist group obtains a nuclear weapon and uses it against an American city. Terrorist groups might obtain such a weapon in several ways: by stealing it, purchasing a weapon or low-to-weapons-grade uranium or plutonium on the black market, or from a rogue or failed state. The International Panel on Fissile Materials (IPFM) (2021) estimated that the global stockpile of civilian plutonium was 316 short tons in 2020. This is a particularly attractive target for terrorists since this element can be made into an atomic device without enrichment (see McPhee 1973; Willrich and Taylor 1974).

It is impossible to overestimate the catastrophic impact of an atomic device exploded in a major city. The immense impact on economic, social, and political systems would have global ramifications, threatening the continued existence of open, democratic societies. In fact, it might not require the use of a rudimentary atomic bomb. The potential of dirty bombs—radioactive material dispersed by conventional explosives—to disrupt modern societies is also a credible threat.

The emergence of unstable or failed states is sufficient reason to view with concern the spread of nuclear reactors to such nations (particularly in the developing world). The examples of Iraq and Syria and their past plans for reactor construction come immediately to mind. In addition, some nations have sought nuclear power plants with the intention of supplementing power production with the retrieval of bomb-grade plutonium. It has been suggested that India produced its first bomb-grade fuel from a research reactor supplied by Canada (CBC May 20, 1974; see also IPFM 2015, p. 26). Both Iraq and Syria were suspected of similar intentions, prompting the destruction of their reactors by Israeli air strikes (*New York Times* March 21, 2018). In essence, nuclear power and nuclear weapons have been termed two sides of the same coin (NIS 2014). In the aftermath of the Fukushima accident, eight European nonnuclear countries (Austria, Greece, Ireland, Latvia, Liechtenstein, Luxembourg, Malta, and Portugal) issued a joint declaration in Vienna on May 25, 2011 (Austria et al. 2011), stating that "the very significant safety, security, environmental and proliferation risks associated with [the] nuclear power option remain, and need to be addressed by the international community, including cooperation between nuclear and non-nuclear states" (p. 2). Several recent reports (Kovacic et al. 2018; Rockwood et al. 2019; NAS 2021) have highlighted concerns over the potential for diversion of potential bomb-grade material from current operating reactors as well as from new designs such as molten salt reactors and pebble-bed modular reactors, "both of which are associated with features that can pose challenges to safeguards" (Rockwood et al. 2019, p. 35).

Environmental risk: The necessity for nuclear reactors to be located near large supplies of cooling water—rivers, lakes, or oceans—exposes these installations to the risk of flooding. In some parts of the world, including the United States, reactors have been located on or near seismic faults. Both of these circumstances bring the threat of common mode failures, significantly increasing the difficulty of reducing the overall level of potential risks.

Financial risk: Three factors in particular have been cited as reasons for the cessation of most nuclear power construction in the United States. First is what is termed NIMBY, or the "not-in-my-backyard" phenomenon, where citizens object to the placement of reactors in or near their neighborhoods, slowing the process of regulatory approval. Even more important has been the escalation of costs associated with the construction of the reactors themselves. As safety standards have become stricter, builders face increasing costs. A major part of this problem is that each reactor is essentially unique; there has been no single template for reactor construction in the United States. This makes the entire process from initial design to final completion much more costly. One remedy for this problem is to adopt the French system whereby a standardized design is used throughout the country, thereby significantly reducing the time and cost of construction. This approach is characterized by a trade-off between efficiency and resilience. The downside of a uniform design and lack of diversity is that if an unexpected and serious problem is found in one reactor, it may affect all, thereby transforming *localized* risk into *systemic* risk with all its attendant cost consequences.

The issue of the cost of nuclear power in comparison with other power sources is controversial due to several technology-specific issues affecting nuclear power. First, the use of market prices may distort the comparison with alternative electricity technology. The global nuclear industry, and particularly the United States, has been the recipient of significant subsidies, tilting the playing field. Subsidies include the establishment of a ceiling on liability, established by the US Price-Anderson Nuclear Industries Indemnity Act of 1957, which caps the level of private sector liability from an accident at $12.6 billion (US NRC 2010 and n.d.). Sovacool (2011) has estimated the combined property and health costs of 105 nuclear accidents from 1942 to 2011 at over $175 billion. The federal government has also provided loan guarantees, funds for reactor decommissioning, and government-funded experimental waste storage facilities. In addition to all these de facto subsidies, the cost of the initial development of modern PWR reactors was absorbed by military expenditure associated with the development of nuclear propulsion systems for ships. Where nuclear accidents have occurred, such as at Fukushima, it has been estimated that the decommissioning and cleanup process could last at least another thirty years and cost as much as $76 billion, most of which would be borne by government. To place this in context, the four units at Fukushima cost $2.2 billion to construct over a period of ten years (*Science* March 5, 2021). The cleanup entails both long-term disposal of highly radioactive material, and short- to medium-term challenges of dealing with such things as large quantities of water used to cool the melted reactors (BBC September 10, 2019). The utility that operated the Fukushima reactor has announced plans to release large quantities of contaminated water into the sea in order to reduce the inventory of radioactive wastewater stored on site (CNN October 24, 2020; *Guardian* April 13, 2021). While initial concerns focused on the levels of "relatively harmless" radioactive tritium in the water, more recent revelations suggest the presence of much more dangerous isotopes, especially ruthenium-106, cobalt-60, and strontium-90 (*Science* August 7, 2020). Several of Japan's neighbors, namely China, South Korea, and Taiwan, have already expressed "grave concerns" about this intended action by Japan (*New York Times* April 13, 2021).

A similar litany of decommissioning challenges for Chernobyl could take as long or longer. In one half-serious, tongue-in-cheek comment about the financial problems facing the industry, Koplow (2011, p. 1) observed that:

> subsidies to the nuclear fuel cycle have often exceeded the value of the power produced. This means that buying power on the open market and giving it away for free would have been less costly than subsidizing the construction and operation of nuclear power plants. Subsidies to new reactors are on a similar path.

Waste disposal risks: Waste from nuclear reactors generally falls into three categories: low-, medium-, or high-level depending on the intensity and duration of the radiation from the waste products. Fission products with high levels of radioactivity but relatively short half-lives are stored on site until their radiation levels decrease to what are deemed safe levels. A major problem arises from actinides, or very long-lived radioactive elements, which are mixed with the fission products. Some of these products, such as plutonium-239, have half-lives in excess of 25,000 years. This, in turn, suggests a required period of complete isolation of approximately 250,000 years. In 1972, Alvin Weinberg (1972), one of the fathers of modern atomic power, stated that humanity had entered into a Faustian bargain with the development of atomic power, as the sequestration of the radioactive byproducts would create the necessity for a special nuclear priesthood to guard these wastes in perpetuity (see also Kneese 1973). This requirement entails extraordinary political and social challenges. Throughout human history, there has been no single dynasty that has lasted more than one thousand years. According to the Russian Academician, Alexander Kazhdan (1984), the only dynasty that survived one thousand years was the Byzantine Empire of the fourth to fifteen centuries. The second longest lasting in human history appears to be China's Chou Dynasty, which was in place for less than 900 years—from 1122–255 BCE. Historical transitions between dynasties have usually been tumultuous, and it is difficult to imagine that the de facto priesthood could remain a functioning entity for such a long period of time. If such a priesthood were to disappear, some other effective mechanism would have to be found to guarantee that sequestered radioactive waste would not be disturbed by future human intervention. Linguists have pondered the question as to whether future civilizations would understand the languages we now speak and write, raising the interesting challenge of how our generation could signal to those living in the far future that the wastes are dangerous and should not be approached or excavated. Are there symbols that are independent of language that could be used? This is somewhat similar to efforts by NASA to create a method of communication with other advanced civilizations in the universe should they exist and intercept one of NASA's interspatial probes.

While several proposals have been advanced for disposing of high-level wastes, many have been discarded because of their inherent risks. These include attempting to shoot waste into space or carrying wastes deep into the earth's core via subduction zones on the ocean's floor. The solution felt to be most practical and safe is the underground storage of such wastes in various types of geological formation (Birkholzer et al. 2012). The proposal that has received the longest study and most funding has been that relating to Yucca Mountain in Nevada. Over the past several decades, the US Department of Energy has spent in excess of $4.5 billion in an attempt to prove that this site is geologically secure now and for the indefinite future. Unfortunately, the project is well over budget and well behind schedule. In one critique, Pilkey and Pilkey-Jarvis (2007) demonstrated that the conceptual and empirical models developed to demonstrate the safety of this site have failed and that the United States is no closer to finding and developing a waste disposal site now than it was in the 1980s when the project was originally envisaged. The US government has recently decided to abandon this option for waste disposal and is favoring some form of stabilization such as vitrification. The scientific feasibility and safety of this proposed alternative remain to be demonstrated.

At the moment, large quantities of highly radioactive isotopes are kept in on-site waste storage pools in close proximity to working reactors (IPFM 2015). Global spent fuel inventories were estimated at 289,000 metric tons (MT) of uranium in 2018, and this is expected to reach 449,000 in 2033 (Greene 2020). In some cases, the radioactive inventory of these pools exceeds that of their associated reactors by an order of magnitude. A study by nuclear scientists von Hippel and Schoeppner (2016) suggests that current high-density storage configurations of spent fuel pose a far greater threat than the radioactive release from Fukushima (see also *New York Times* March 17, 2011). In fact, they report that a catastrophic spent fuel pool accident almost occurred following a loss of coolant at Fukushima. In light of this near miss, the US NRC performed a simulation analysis of an earthquake-triggered accidental fire and loss of coolant in a spent pool at the Peach Bottom nuclear plant in Pennsylvania. The worst-case scenario would require the displacement of 4.1 million people from 24,000 km² of contaminated land and would cause as many as 20,000 deaths from cancer (von Hippel and Schoeppner 2016, p 152; US NRC 2013). In fact, von Hippel and Schoeppner felt that the NRC estimates did not include the most severe scenario, which could force relocation of 18.21 million people from 101,000 km² (Stone 2016). They concluded that "a fire in a high-density spent fuel pool in the United States that displaced on the order of ten million people for years … would be an extraordinary peacetime catastrophe" (p. 160).

After deeming the probability of such an accident to be extremely low (i.e. less than one in ten million years or lower) (US NRC 1989 and 2001), the NRC performed a cost-benefit analysis which concluded that the cost of requiring changes to storage at all US reactors was not warranted. von Hippel and Schoeppner (2016) took issue with the results of the cost-benefit analysis on the basis of several contestable assumptions and factors omitted from consideration (pp. 158–159). Foremost among these was the exclusion of the possibility of a terrorist-caused release despite the fact that these pools would be a very tempting target with potentially enormous consequences if such an attack was successful.

The potential for terrorism in general poses a particular challenge to conventional risk assessment and RBA because of the difficulty of assigning a probability to its occurrence. In 1977, Fairley and Mosteller wrote a seminal book on the application of statistics to public policy. They suggested six major guidelines for the estimation of accident probabilities. The first of these, and the one most relevant to the discussion of terrorism is "estimates of the probability of an accident must include, explicitly or implicitly, contributions from all the possible sources of the accident" (p. 334). While this is the intent of event and fault trees in risk analysis, the analyses can lead to seriously misleading results if the probability of an event is omitted or not known. The authors provide the following analogy from the game of poker to make their point:

1. What is the probability of randomly drawing a royal flush from a deck of cards? The answer is 1 chance in 649,740.
2. The following question can then be asked: What is the chance of seeing a royal flush in a real game of poker with strangers? It turns out that this is an entirely different question.
3. Suppose for example that the probability of cheating is assigned a tentative probability of 1 in 10,000. What then is the answer to the second question?
4. It is then equal to 1/10,000 plus 1/649,740, which is just a little over 1 in 10,000.

Clearly the estimated probability of cheating is a guess, but it may not be an unreasonable estimate. The point is that some reasonable probability estimate of cheating may be significantly higher than the probability of a natural occurrence and therefore its probability would be the dominant and relevant one to consider.

Such an analogy is directly relevant to the case of terrorism, as the NRC's failure to consider such an occurrence in a PRA could lead to results that are essentially misleading if not meaningless (*New York Times* January 7, 2003). Just because it is difficult to estimate the probability of a terrorist attack does not justify its omission if such an occurrence is possible. Several recent reports have specifically highlighted the need for a more exhaustive analysis of the risk of terrorist attacks on waste storage facilities (NAS 2006; NRC 2019a).

In a major critique of the use of risk analysis for nuclear power, the European Environment Agency (EEA) (Dorfman et al. 2013) concluded that:

> Given the degree of uncertainty and complexity attached to even the most tightly framed and rigorous nuclear risk assessment, attempts to weight the magnitude of accident by the expected probability of occurrence have proven problematic, since these essentially theoretical calculations can only be based on sets of pre-conditioning assumptions. This is not an arcane philosophical point but rather a very practical issue with significant implications for the proper management of nuclear risk. With its failure to plan for the cascade of unexpected beyond[-]design-base accidents, the regulatory emphasis on risk-based probabilistic assessment has proven very limited. An urgent reappraisal of this approach and its real-life application seems overdue.
>
> (p. 432)

More specifically, drawing on the work of Ramana (2009) and Maloney 2011) they concluded that:

> [Probabilistic risk assessment] has proven structurally limited in its ability to conceive and capture the outcomes and consequences of a nuclear accident resulting from a cascading series of events, as described in the Fukushima disaster and all previous major nuclear accidents. This implies that relatively simplified chain-of-event fault-tree models may not be sufficient to account for the indirect, non-linear, and feedback relationships common for accidents in complex systems. Here, modeled common-cause, common-mode, and dependent failures have proved problematic; partly due to data limitation (since major failures occur infrequently), and because failure mechanisms are often plant specific (Ramana, 2009). Most PRAs assume failure likelihood can be captured through identical, independent log-normal failure distributions. Since strong independence assumptions employed in PRAs assume that reactor safety systems are duplicated and reliable, core damage frequency estimates are typically very low. Because of this, there may be good reason to question the conceptual and theoretical completeness, and empirical and practical reliability of PRA models. This is partly because PRA is prone to undercounting accident scenarios—since risk is estimated for enumerated reactor states, failure to account for unknown and serially cascading beyond design-base accident scenarios leaves an un-measurable model error in the core damage frequency estimate (Maloney, 2011).
>
> (p. 447)

Commercial reactors and climate change

One of the principal arguments advanced by proponents of nuclear power is that it is an essential bridge energy source to move from fossil fuels to renewable sources due to its lack of GHG emissions. While superficially appealing, the case for nuclear power is more complicated than it appears. In the first place, there is a complex interdependence of climate change warming and nuclear power. For nuclear plants relying on proximate rivers or lakes to provide necessary cooling water, the occurrence of drought and

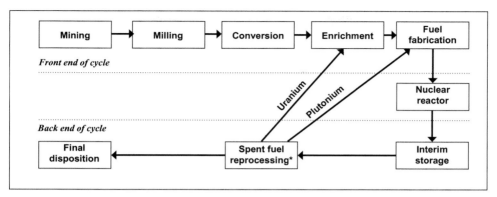

* Spent fuel reprocessing is omitted by most countries.

Figure 8.5 Nuclear fuel cycle.

low water levels or unusually high water temperatures can compromise their ability to operate. While similar problems can affect any other thermal-based electricity production such as coal, oil, and natural gas, nuclear power has an additional disadvantage because nuclear plants produce less electricity per pound of circulating steam, thereby necessitating larger cooling water requirements per megawatt hour (MWh) of capacity (EPRI 2002, Vol. 3, pp. 3–1 to 3–2). It has been reported that a series of heat waves in 2003 forced French and German reactors to reduce their output levels (Faeth et al. 2014, p. 47).

There is an even more fundamental challenge to the potential role of nuclear power as a bridge to renewable energy sources, and that concerns its GHG footprint. While the *operation* of a nuclear power plant produces no carbon dioxide, a systems analysis of nuclear power must include the entire nuclear fuel cycle. As illustrated in Figure 8.5, the nuclear fuel cycle is composed of up to nine distinct steps, all the way from the original mining of uranium ore to the disposal of radioactive fission products.

Most of these steps have a carbon footprint. In separate meta-studies, estimates of these emissions have been found to vary widely depending on the nature of assumptions and included or excluded factors (Sovacool 2008 and 2011; Beerten et al. 2009). These estimates range from a low of 1.4 grams (g) to a high of 288 g CO_2e per kilowatt-hour (kWh). To put these in context, Table 8.6 lists the results of a meta-analysis by Nugent and Sovacool (2013), who present the mean estimated life-cycle carbon footprints for a wide variety of power sources. It is clear from these data that while nuclear power emits considerably less CO_2e than fossil fuels, its per kWh emissions are 32–560 percent higher than renewables.

One ostensible advantage of nuclear power over renewables is the ability to provide continuous baseload power for an electric power grid. However, recent technological advances hold promise that baseload power could be provided by a network of integrated renewable energy sources as well, thus removing one of the few remaining arguments in favor of atomic power (see Chapter 9).

One of the most surprising assessments of nuclear power has come from Gregory Jaczko (2019), former chair of the US NRC. He begins his recent book with the following

Table 8.6 Life-cycle estimates of CO_2e emissions by energy technology

Technology	Capacity/configuration/fuel	Mean estimate (g CO2e/kWh)
Hydroelectric	3.1 MW, reservoir	10
Biogas	Anaerobic digestion	11
Hydroelectric	300 kW, run-of-river	13
Solar thermal	80 MW, parabolic trough	13
Biomass	Forest wood co-combustion with hard coal	14
Biomass	Forest wood steam turbine	22
Biomass	Short rotation forestry co-combustion with hard coal	23
Biomass	Forest wood reciprocating engine	27
Biomass	Waste wood steam turbine	31
Wind	Various sizes and configurations	34
Biomass	Short rotation forestry steam turbine	35
Geothermal	80 MW, hot dry rock	38
Biomass	Short rotation forestry reciprocating engine	41
Solar photovoltaic	Various sizes and configurations	50
Nuclear	Various reactor types	66
Natural gas (conventional)	Various combined cycle turbines	443
Natural gas (fracking)	Combined cycle turbines using fuel from hydraulic fracturing	492
Natural gas (LNG)	Combined cycle turbines utilizing LNG	611
Fuel cell	Hydrogen from gas reforming	664
Diesel	Various generator and turbine types	778
Heavy oil	Various generator and turbine types	778
Coal	Various generator types with scrubbing	960
Coal	Various generator types without scrubbing	1,050

Source: Nugent and Sovacool 2013. Reproduced with permission.

statement: "I know nuclear power is a failed technology. This is the story of how I came to this belief" (p. ix). He continues:

> No one can design a safety system that will work perfectly. Reactor design is inherently unsafe because a nuclear plant's power—if left unchecked—is sufficient to cause a massive release of radiation. So nuclear power plan accidents *will* happen. . . . I now believe that nuclear power is more hazardous than it is worth. Because the industry relies too much on controlling its own regulation, the continued use of nuclear power will lead to catastrophe in this country or somewhere else in the world. This is a truth we all must confront.
>
> (pp. 20 and 22)

Conclusion

As stated above, the joint declaration by eight European nonnuclear countries on May 25, 2011 (Austria et al. 2011) concluded that "the risks of nuclear power outweigh any potential benefit [and] . . . nuclear power is not compatible with the concept of sustainable development and . . . does not provide a viable option to combat climate change" (p. 1). On balance, the sum of all the enumerated costs and risks associated with nuclear power represents a serious challenge to proposals to adopt atomic energy as a bridge to a sustainable energy future.

References

Agarwal, Anil (1979) *Nature*, "This nuclear power plant is contaminated: India's demand for energy means it cannot be shut down," June 7.

Alexievich, Svetlana and Keith Gessen (2005) *Voices from Chernobyl*, London: Dalkey Archive Press.

Allison, Graham (2004) *Nuclear Terrorism: The Ultimate Preventable Catastrophe*, New York: Times Books.

Austria et al. (2011) Joint declaration issued in Vienna, May 25.

Balint, Peter J. et al. (2011) *Wicked Environmental Problems: Managing Uncertainty and Conflict*, Washington, DC: Island Press.

Baranov, A. et al. (1989) *New England Journal of Medicine*, "Bone marrow transplantation after the Chernobyl nuclear accident," July 27.

BBC (2011) "Timeline: Nuclear plant accidents," September 12.

BBC (2019) "Fukushima: Radioactive water may be dumped in Pacific," September 10.

BBC (2020) "Fukushima: Japan 'to release contaminated water into sea'," October 16.

Beerten, Jef et al. (2009) *Energy Policy*, "Greenhouse gas emissions in the nuclear life cycle: A balanced appraisal," August 4.

Benzinga.com (2017) "$9 billion later, US abandons 2 nuclear facilities only 40% complete," August 1.

Birkholzer, Jens et al. (2012) *Annual Review of Environment and Resources*, "Geological disposal of high-level radioactive waste: Status, key issues and trends," November.

Brown, Kate (2019) *Manual for Survival: A Chernobyl Guide to the Future*, New York: W.W. Norton.

Casti, John (2012) *X-events: The Collapse of Everything*, New York: William Morrow.

CBC (1974) "Canada blamed for India's 'peaceful' bomb,'" *As It Happens*, radio broadcast, May 20.

CBC (2019) "Three Mile Island nuclear plant closes down," September 20.

CNN (2020) "Fukushima water release could change human DNA, Greenpeace warns," October 24.

Cooper, Mark (2014) *Energy Research & Social Science*, "Small modular reactors and the future of nuclear power in the United States," September.

Crouch, Edmund and Richard Wilson (1980) "Estimates of risks," in Peter N. Nemetz (ed.) *Resource Policy: International Perspectives*, Montreal: Institute for Research on Public Policy, 299–318.

Dorfman, Paul et al. (2013) "Late lessons from Chernobyl, early warnings from Fukushima," in European Environment Agency (EEA), *Late Lessons from Early Warnings: Science, Precaution, Innovation*, January.

EPRI (Electric Power Research Institute) (2002) Water & Sustainability *(Volume 3): U.S. Water Consumption for Power Production; The Next Half Century*, March.

Faeth, Paul et al. (2014) *A Clash of Competing Necessities: Water Adequacy and Electric Reliability and Electricity in China, India, France, and Texas*. CNA Corporation, July.

Fairewinds Associates (2010) "Post accident AP1000 containment leakage: An unreviewed safety issue," April 21.

Fairley, William B. (1977) "Evaluating the 'small' probability of a catastrophic accident from the marine transportation liquefied natural gas," in William B. Fairley and Frederick Mosteller, *Statistics and Public Policy*, Reading, MA: Addison-Wesley, 331–354.

Fairley, William B. and Frederick Mosteller (1977) *Statistics and Public Policy*, Reading, MA: Addison-Wesley.

Greene, Carlyn (2020) "Global spent fuel overview," UxC, LLC, January 28.

Greenpeace (2006) *The Chernobyl Catastrophe: Consequences on Human Health*, April 15.

Guardian (2019) "Fukushima grapples with toxic soil that no one wants," March 11.

Guardian (2021) "Fukushima: Japan announces it will dump contaminated water into sea," April 13.

Higginbotham, Adam (2019) *Midnight in Chernobyl: The Story of the World's Greatest Nuclear Disaster*, London: Simon & Schuster.

Independent (2012) "Revealed: Secret evacuation plan for Tokyo after Fukushima," January 27.

IAEA (International Atomic Energy Agency) (2005) *Chernobyl: The True Scale of the Accident,* December.

IAEA (International Atomic Energy Agency) (2018) *Nuclear Power Reactors in the World.*

IPFM (International Panel on Fissile Materials) (2021) "Fissile Material Stocks," September 4.

(IRSN) Institut de Radioprotection et de Sûreté Nucléaire (2011) "Chernobyl 25 years on," April.

Jaczko, Gregory (2019) *Confessions of a Rogue Nuclear Regulator,* New York: Simon & Schuster.

Japan Times (2018) "Seven years on, radioactive water at Fukushima plant still flowing into ocean, study finds," March 29.

Kazhdan, Alexander (1984) "Byzantine culture." Lecture delivered to the Vancouver Institute, September 29.

Kneese, Allen V. (1973) *Resources,* "The Faustian bargain," Resources for the Future, September.

Knight, Frank (1921) *Risk, Uncertainty and Profit,* Boston: Houghton Mifflin.

Koplow, Doug (2011) *Nuclear Power: Still Not Viable without Subsidies,* Union of Concerned Scientists, Cambridge, MA, February.

Kostenko, Svetlana (2019) *Chernobyl: The Dawn After; Apocalyptic Aftermath of a Nuclear Disaster (Vol. II),* independently published.

Kovacic, Donald N. et al. (2018) "Safeguards challenges for molten salt reactors." Presentation to the Institute of Nuclear Materials Management Annual Meeting, August 1, Baltimore, MD.

Leatherbarrow, Andrew (2016) *Chernobyl 01:23:40: The Incredible True Story of the World's Worst Nuclear Disaster,* self-published on Amazon.

Lyman, Edwin (2021) *"Advanced" Isn't Always Better: Assessing the Safety, Security, and Environmental Impacts of Non-light-water Nuclear Reactors,* Union of Concerned Scientists, March.

Mahaffey, James (2014) *Atomic Accidents: A History of Nuclear Meltdowns and Disasters from the Ozark Mountains to Fukushima,* New York; London: Pegasus Books.

Makhijani, Arjun and Scott Saleska (1999) *The Nuclear Power Deception: US Nuclear Mythology from Electricity "Too Cheap to Meter" to "Inherently Safe" Reactors,* Blue Ridge Summit, PA: Rowman & Littlefield.

Maloney, Stephen (2011) "Assessing nuclear risk in the aftermath of Fukushima," Risk.net, July 11.

Markey, Congressman Edward J. (2011) *Fukushima Fallout: Regulatory Loopholes at U.S. Nuclear Plants,"* May 12.

McCullum, Rod (2019) "Reactor redo," *Scientific American,* May.

McGrath, P.E. (1974) *Radioactive Waste Management: Potentials and Hazards from a Risk Point of View."* Report EURFNR-1204 (KFK 1992), US-EURATOM Fast Reactor Exchange Program, June 1.

McPhee, John (1973) *The Curve of Binding Energy,* New York: Farrar, Strauss and Giroux.

Medvedev, Grigori (1990) *The Truth about Chernobyl,* New York: Basic Books.

Medvedev, Zhores (1990) *The Legacy of Chernobyl,* New York; London: W. W. Norton.

Morton, Lindsay M. et al. (2021) *Science,* "Radiation-related genomic profile of papillary thyroid cancer after the Chernobyl accident," April 22.

NAS (National Academy of Sciences) (2006) *Safety and Security of Commercial Spent Nuclear Fuel Storage: Public Report.*

NAS (National Academy of Sciences) (2014) *Lessons Learned from the Fukushima Nuclear Accident for Improving Safety of U.S. Nuclear Plants,* National Research Council.

NAS (National Academy of Sciences) (2016) *Lessons Learned from Fukushima PHASE 2.*

NAS (National Academy of Sciences) (2021) *Nuclear Proliferation and Arms Control Monitoring, Detection and Verification: A National Security Priority; Interim Report.*

Negroni, Christine (2016) *The Crash Detectives: Investigating the World's Most Mysterious Air Disasters,* New York: Penguin.

NEI (Nuclear Energy Institute) (2018) "Vogtle co-owners vote to continue AP1000 construction project," September 27.

New York Times (1986) "Chernobyl design found to include new safety plans," May 19.

New York Times (2003) "Threats and responses: Domestic security," January 7.

New York Times (2010) "Critics challenge safety of new reactor design," April 21.

New York Times (2011) "Westinghouse's reactor design approaches N.R.C. approval," March 8.

New York Times (2011) "U.S. nuclear plants have same risks as Japan plants," March 13.

New York Times (2011) "Danger of spent fuel outweighs reactor threat," March 17.

New York Times (2011a) "U.S. was warned on vents before failure at Japan's plant," May 18.

New York Times (2011b) "Regulators find design flaws in new reactors," May 18.

New York Times (2011c) "In Japan reactor failings, danger signs for the U.S.," May 18.

New York Times (2011) "Westinghouse nuclear reactor design flaw is found," May 20.

New York Times (2011) "Company believes 3 reactors melted down in Japan," May 24.

New York Times (2013) "Former Japanese leader declares opposition to nuclear power," October 2.

New York Times (2016) "Fukushima keeps fighting radioactive tide 5 years after disaster," March 10.

New York Times (2016) "Could there be a terrorist Fukushima?" April 4.

New York Times (2016) "German court upholds nuclear exit but orders compensation for power companies," December 6.

New York Times (2017) "Struggling with Japan's nuclear waste, six years after disaster," March 11.

New York Times (2017) "Westinghouse files for bankruptcy, in blow to nuclear power," March 29.

New York Times (2018) "Ending secrecy, Israel says it bombed Syrian reactor in 2007," March 21.

New York Times (2019) "Hitachi to cease work on nuclear power plant in north Wales," January 18.

New York Times (2021) "Japan's plan for Fukushima wastewater meets a wall of mistrust in Asia," April 13.

NIS (Nuclear Information Service) (2014) "Nuclear power and the proliferation of nuclear weapons: Two sides of the same coin," October 15.

NRDC (Natural Resources Defense Council) (2011) "Nuclear accident at Indian Point: Consequences and costs," October.

Nugent, Daniel and Benjamin K. Sovacool (2013) *Energy Policy*, "Assessing the lifecycle greenhouse gas emissions from solar PV and wind energy: A critical meta-survey," November 12.

Oliver, Rear Adm. Dave (2018) *Against the Tide: Rickover's Leadership and the Rise of the Nuclear Navy,* Annapolis, MD: Naval Institute Press.

Perrow, Charles (1999) *Normal Accidents: Living with High Risk Technologies*, Princeton, NJ: Princeton University Press.

Petryna, Adriana (2013) *Life Exposed: Biological Citizens after Chernobyl*, Princeton, NJ: Princeton University Press.

Pilkey, Orrin H. and Linda Pilkey-Jarvis (2007) *Useless Arithmetic: Why Environmental Scientists Can't Predict the Future,* New York: Columbia University Press.

Plokhy, Serhii (2019) *Chernobyl: History of a Tragedy*, Great Britain: Penguin.

POWER (2017) "Cost to complete Vogtle AP1000 nuclear units could balloon to $20B," August 4.

Ramana, M.V. (2009) *Annual Review of Environment and Resources*, "Nuclear power: Economic, safety, health, and environmental issues of near-term technologies," November 21.

Rockwood, Laura et al. (2019) *IAEA Safeguards: Staying Ahead of the Game,* Swedish Radiation Security Authority, January.

Science (2020) "Opening the floodgates at Fukushima," August 7.

Science (2020) "Critics question whether novel reactor is 'walk-away safe'," August 28.

Science (2020) "Department of Energy picks two advanced nuclear reactors for demonstration projects," October 16.

Science (2021) "Endless cleanup," March 5.

Science (2021) "'It's like the embers in a barbecue pit.' Nuclear reactions are smoldering again at Chernobyl," May 5.

Scientific American (2014) "Can sodium save nuclear power?", October 13.

Simmonds, Jane (1987) "Europe calculates the health risk," *New Scientist*, April 23.

Sovacool, Benjamin (2008) *Energy Policy*, "Valuing the greenhouse gas emissions from nuclear power: A critical survey," August.

Sovacool, Benjamin K. (2011) *GAIA,* "Questioning the safety and reliability of nuclear power: An assessment of nuclear incidents and accidents," 20 (2): 95–103.

Stone, Richard (2016) *Science,* "Near miss at Fukushima is a warning for U.S.," May 27.

Strauss, Lewis L. (1954) Remarks prepared for delivery at the Founders' Day dinner, National Association of Science Writers, US Atomic Energy Commission, September 16.

UCS (Union of Concerned Scientists) (2011) *The NRC and Nuclear Plant Safety in 2010,* March.

UCS (Union of Concerned Scientists) (2016, various years) *The NRC and Nuclear Power Plant Safety.*

US AEC (Atomic Energy Commission) (1957) *WASH-740: Theoretical Possibilities and Consequences of Major Accidents in Large Nuclear Power Plants: A Study of Possible Consequences If Certain Assumed Accidents, Theoretically Possible but Highly Improbable, Were to Occur in Large Nuclear Power Plants,* March.

US AEC (Atomic Energy Commission) (1973) *WASH-1250: The Safety of Nuclear Power Reactors (Light-Water Cooled) and Related Facilities.*

US NRC (Nuclear Regulatory Commission) (1975) *WASH-1400: Reactor Safety Study; An Assessment of Accident Risks in U.S. Commercial Nuclear Power Plants,* October.

US NRC (Nuclear Regulatory Commission) (1978) *NUREG/CR-0400: Risk Assessment Review Group Report to the U.S. Nuclear Regulatory Commission.*

US NRC (Nuclear Regulatory Commission) (1979) "NRC statement on risk assessment and the *Reactor Safety Study Report* (WASH-1400)," January 18.

US NRC (Nuclear Regulatory Commission) (1981) *Fault Tree Handbook.*

US NRC (Nuclear Regulatory Commission) (1982) *Calculation of Reactor Accident Consequences for US Nuclear Power Plants* (CRAC-II Report). Simulations conducted by Sandia Labs, New Mexico.

US NRC (Nuclear Regulatory Commission) (1989) *NUREG-1353: Regulatory Analysis for the Resolution of Generic Issue 82,* "Beyond Design Basis Accidents in Spent Fuel Pools," April.

US NRC (Nuclear Regulatory Commission) (1990) *NUREG-1150 Vol. 3: Severe Accident Risks; An Assessment for Five U.S. Nuclear Power Plants—Appendices D&E,* January.

US NRC (Nuclear Regulatory Commission) (2001) *NUREG-1738: Technical Study of Spent Fuel Pool Accident Risk at Decommissioning Nuclear Power Plants,* February.

US NRC (Nuclear Regulatory Commission) (2010) "Nuclear insurance and disaster relief funds," fact sheet, August.

US NRC (Nuclear Regulatory Commission) (2011) "NRC's Japan task force recommends changes to defense in depth measures at nuclear plants; cites station blackout, seismic, flooding and spent fuel pools as areas for improvement," press release no. 11–127, July 13.

US NRC (Nuclear Regulatory Commission) (2012) *State-of-the-Art Reactor Consequence Analyses (SOARCA) Report (NUREG-1935); Part 2.*

US NRC (Nuclear Regulatory Commission) (2013) *NUREG 2161: Consequence Study of a Beyond-Design-Basis Earthquake Affecting the Spent Fuel Pool for a U.S. Mark I Boiling Water Reactor.*

US NRC (Nuclear Regulatory Commission) (2014) *Reflections on Fukushima: NRC Senior Leadership Visit to Japan, 2014.*

US NRC (Nuclear Regulatory Commission) (2018a) "Post Fukushima order implementation status," June 29.

US NRC (Nuclear Regulatory Commission) (2018b) "Post Fukushima flooding and seismic hazard reevaluation status," June 29.

US NRC (Nuclear Regulatory Commission) (2018c) "Backgrounder on the Three Mile Island accident," June.

US NRC (Nuclear Regulatory Commission) (2019a) "Backgrounder on nuclear security."

US NRC (Nuclear Regulatory Commission) (2019b) "History," January 28.

US NRC (Nuclear Regulatory Commission) (n.d.) "Backgrounder: Nuclear insurance; Price-Anderson Act."

von Hippel, Frank and Michael Schoeppner (2016) *Science & Global Security,* "Reducing the danger from fires in spent fuel pools," 24(3): 141–73.

Weinberg, Alvin (1972) *Science,* "Social institutions and nuclear energy," July 7, 4043, 27–34.

WHO (World Health Organization) (2005) "Chernobyl: The true scale of the accident," September 5.

Willrich, Mason and Theodore B. Taylor (1974) *Nuclear Theft: Risks and Safeguards.* Report to the Energy Policy Project of the Ford Foundation.

Wilson, Richard and Edmund Crouch (1982) *Risk/Benefit Analysis,* Cambridge, MA: Ballinger Publishing.

WNA (World Nuclear Association) (various years and 2020) *World Nuclear Performance Report,* August.

WNA (World Nuclear Association) (2021) "World nuclear power reactors & uranium requirements," May.

Woodward, Bob (2011) *Obama's Wars,* New York: Simon & Schuster.

Yablokov, Alexey et al. (2009) *Annals of the New York Academy of Sciences,* "Chapter III: Consequences of the Chernobyl catastrophe for the environment," November 30.

Yeager, Meredith et al. (2021) *Science,* "Lack of transgenerational effects of ionizing radiation exposure from the Chernobyl accident," April 22.

9 Renewable energy

Prospects and challenges

While nuclear power is considered by many as a transition fuel away from reliance on fossil fuels, it is generally agreed that the ultimate goal must be to convert global energy to renewable sources. The principal advantage of renewable fuels is their zero net operational contribution to the global greenhouse gas (GHG) burden. Included in the list of renewables are such diverse sources as hydropower, solar thermal, solar photovoltaic (solar PV), geothermal, wind, biogas, solid and liquid biomass, tidal, wave power, ocean thermal gradients, and municipal and industrial waste. Virtually all these renewable sources, with the exception of tidal power and geothermal energy, are directly or indirectly the result of solar insolation. While some renewable technologies are under continuing development others, such as wind, falling water, and biomass, have been in use for centuries.

Global renewable installed energy capacity has grown dramatically from 1,136 gigawatts (GW) in 2009 to 2,799 GW in 2020, and total production has experienced a similar jump from 3,898 terawatt-hours (TWh) in 2009 to 6,586 TWh in 2018 (IRENA 2020b and 2021a). In 2020, approximately 29 percent of all global electricity generated was renewable (OWID) and more than 80 percent of all new global electricity generating capacity was renewable (IRENA 2021a). Capacity varies markedly by country and technology as illustrated in Table 9.1, which lists the top five countries in each category (REN21 2019). Figure 9.1a places these numbers in context by showing the contribution of each power source to total world primary energy supply in 2017 (IEA 2019c) and Figure 9.1b tracks the relative shares over the period 1985–2019 (OWID). McKinsey (2019) has made the optimistic prediction that renewables will account for 50 percent of electricity generation by 2035.

While the broad range of renewable alternatives offers the prospect that these sources will make a major contribution to global energy supply in the mid to distant future (IEA 2019b and 2021f), there are several critical issues affecting their development and application: (1) providing instantaneous on-demand availability, (2) lack of efficient electricity storage media, (3) distance of renewable sources from markets and integration into existing grids, (4) current per kilowatt (kW) costs, (5) uninternalized externalities of conventional energy sources, (6) climatic feedback effects, and (7) scale-up time for a renewable energy economy. Part A of this chapter addresses these issues, and Part B provides an overview of the four major renewable sources: hydropower, solar, wind, and biofuels.

DOI: 10.4324/9781003199540-12

Table 9.1 Top five countries by installed renewable capacity (MW in 2018)

Bio-power	Brazil	United States	China	India	Germany	World
	14,782	12,712	13,235	10,271	9,457	117,828
Geothermal	United States	Indonesia	Philippines	Turkey	New Zealand	World
	2,541	1,946	1,944	1,283	966	13,277
Hydro	China	Brazil	United States	Canada	Russia	World
	352,261	104,195	102,847	81,004	53,935	1,295,317
Solar photovoltaic	China	Japan	United States	Germany	India	World
	175,016	55,500	49,692	45,277	26,887	480,619
Concentrated solar thermal	Spain	United States	South Africa	Morocco	India	World
	2,304	1,758	400	530	229	5,466
Wind power	China	United States	Germany	India	Spain	World
	184,665	94,295	58,982	35,288	23,436	563,659

Source: REN21 2019.

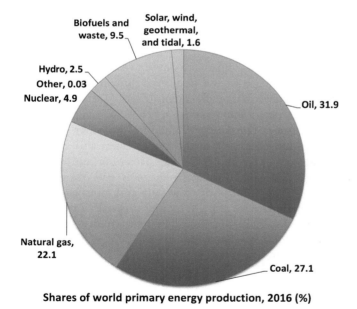

Shares of world primary energy production, 2016 (%)

Figure 9.1a Shares of world primary energy production.
Source: IEA 2019a.

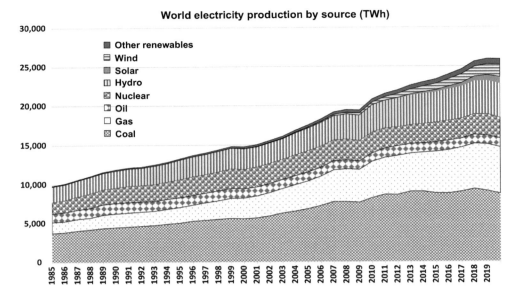

Figure 9.1b World electricity production by source 1985–2019.
Source: OWID.

Renewable challenges

Short-term, on-demand availability

All electric supply utilities must maintain a relatively constant baseload; this has traditionally been provided by coal, oil, nuclear, and large hydropower installations. The
intermittent nature of many renewables has made them generally unsuitable for this
function, essentially establishing an upper limit of system renewables capacity to avoid
jeopardizing a utility's ability to meet constantly fluctuating customer demand. For
Germany, one of the most advanced countries in the use of renewable energy, clean
energy sources accounted for up to 46 percent of total electricity consumption in 2020
(*Financial Post* February 10, 2021), largely in the form of solar PV and wind power.
Germany still relies, however, on a supply of both nationally and internationally available, nonrenewable power to compensate for the fluctuating shortfall. There are several
major approaches to advance the global use of renewables: first, the development of an
array of media to store power; second, giving access to currently installed electricity
grids; and third, the construction of an integrated national or international grid capable
of overcoming local supply constraints.

Storage media

Several alternatives have been proposed to act as effective storage media for energy
generated from intermittent sunshine and wind. These include batteries for the direct
storage of electricity, heat stored in such media as molten salt, or as hydrogen, compressed

air, or pumped storage, so that power is available on demand from these sources. Significant technological and economic barriers remain to the large-scale, effective commercialization of all of these alternatives, although pumped hydro storage is already being used in several countries (IHA 2019 and 2020). Prominent among these are China (32.1 GW), Japan (28.5 GW), and the United States (24.2 GW) out of a global total of 133.1 GW (IRENA 2017). A proposal has recently been floated in the United States to use the reservoir behind the Hoover Dam as a de facto storage medium for energy (*New York Times* August 4, 2018), although water levels have been dropping in this reservoir over the last few years. Battery technology has advanced rapidly within the last few decades with the advent of lithium-ion batteries and other advanced systems in research and development, including electro-chemical and electro-mechanical storage (IRENA 2017; *New York Times* September 26, 2018; *Science* May 18, June 29, July 31, and August 23, 2018, and March 12, July 11, and April 10, 2019; IEA 2020c). The US National Renewable Energy Laboratory (NREL 2019) has conducted extensive research on lithium-ion batteries in particular, and has generated projections of cost estimates to the turn of this century. Costs have declined rapidly in the past few years and currently have a capital expenditure in utility-scale applications of approximately $1,500 per installed kW. These costs are projected to decline to as low as $300 per kW by 2050.

An interesting development with respect to batteries was provided by California in the summer of 2020 when the state was faced with a major heat wave which taxed the electrical power system's capacity to service state-level demand. The *New York Times* (September 3, 2020) reported that "during the state's recent electricity crisis, more than 30,000 batteries supplied as much power as a midsize natural gas plant," and one utility "delivered 50 megawatts—enough to power 20,000 homes—from batteries it had installed at businesses, local governments and other customers."

It has also been suggested that electric vehicles (EVs) could act as backup storage for power grids during the night when they are not on the road, as that is when storage is needed most. As noted in Chapter 7, not all characteristics of the modern EV are environmentally benign. There are issues associated with the exotic metals and conflict minerals used in construction of EVs (*New York Times* November 20 and 29, 2021) and the looming e-waste timebomb is an additional problem; we will face the challenge of recycling lithium from spent batteries from the increasing number of EVs expected on global roads in the next decade (Oberhaus 2020; see also IEA 2021c). One possible alternative currently under development is the use of zinc rather than lithium since zinc is potentially cheaper and safer (Recharge 2021; Service 2021).

Integration into existing grids

Most jurisdictions with renewable power have had few problems integrating new renewable sources into their existing grid as long as there remains sufficient traditional baseload power and the proportion of renewables does not exceed levels where they pose logistical problems of integration and system stability and/or threaten the revenue base of electric utilities. Two milestones have been reported out of Europe within the last few years. On one day in 2016 Germany was able to supply 100 percent of electricity demand from renewables (REW 2016) and, over the first five months of 2019, the United Kingdom was able to meet 48 percent of all demand with renewables (BBC June 21, 2019). This landmark was exceeded in April 2021 when the United Kingdom produced 60 percent of its electricity with wind and solar power (BBC April 7, 2021).

Nevertheless, the task of integration presents several technological and economic challenges (REN21 2019; IEA 2011 and n.d.; *New York Times* December 26, 2017). Where the provision of renewables is dominated by the major utilities, there are still requirements to allow two-way access to the grid by individual consumers or corporations producing their own renewable power and wishing to sell some or all of it to the grid. There are two categories of supplier: small-scale commercial producers of wind, solar, or biomass who seek to sell their entire product, and individual homeowners with small-scale wind or solar installations which may produce more than the homeowners require. In this case, the government, in concert with the utilities, must establish appropriate prices for purchasing this power. An example drawn from the state of Hawaii is provided in the section devoted to solar power.

Smart grids

Integrated smart grids could successfully incorporate a diverse range of energy sources within or between individual nations. The advantage of this technological solution is the ability to compensate for the lack of consistent power from both solar and wind power. Under this scenario, power from one local source could be available to the grid even if another location—at some distance—was not able to generate power. This type of highly interconnected grid system could emulate the baseload provision of current energy supply systems (Fthenakis et al. 2008; Jacobson and Delucchi 2009; Pfenninger et al. 2014; Barthelmie and Pryor 2014; Fairley 2018), thereby allowing renewable sources to assume the dominant if not exclusive role in a nation's electrical power system. One report (Carbon Tracker 2019) has concluded that renewable electricity is the cheapest source of new baseload. An integral part of this type of technological solution is the willingness of conventional power companies to buy excess power from many small, disseminated renewable sources at a reasonable price. This area has been the subject of new rules and regulations (called feed-in tariffs) in several jurisdictions in both Europe and the United States.

One of the most comprehensive studies of the challenge of integrating variable renewables into established electric power grids was published by the International Energy Agency (IEA 2011). Their assessment examines eight case studies to determine the ability of any one national grid to accommodate renewables using dispatchable plant, storage, interconnection, and demand-side management. They conservatively estimated the percentage of renewable power each country could accommodate easily: Japan 19 percent, Spain and Portugal 27 percent, Mexico 29 percent, Great Britain and Ireland 31 percent, the Canadian Maritimes 37 percent, the US West 45 percent, the Nordic market 48 percent, and Denmark 63 percent (see also REN21 2013; Ernst & Young Global Ltd 2013).

A major challenge yet to be addressed is the vulnerability of the electrical grid systems to climate change. Stone et al. (2021) raise the possibility of critical infrastructure failures during extreme weather events, and an article by Plumer (2021) concludes that "systems are designed to handle spikes in demand, but the wild and unpredictable weather linked to global warming will very likely push grids beyond their limits." One example is the recent heat wave in Oregon which melted power cables for Portland's streetcar system (*Newsweek* June 28, 2021; see also *New York Times* August 13, 2021).

Costs

One of the principal arguments against the expanded deployment of renewables has been the cost compared to conventional energy sources such as coal, oil, natural gas, and nuclear. However, the cost of renewables has undergone a major shift within the last decade. Most renewable technologies have been moving rapidly down the learning curve and, with the benefit of extensive research and development and economies of scale, have been able to realize substantial decreases in per unit cost of electricity (IRENA 2019b, 2020a, 2021b and d). Our World in Data (2020) reports that since 2009, costs of new solar PV have come down by 89 percent and wind by 70 percent. Lazard (2020) reports the following range of levelized cost data (levelized cost of energy; LCOE) for unsubsidized renewable power over the period 2009–2020: wind $101–$169 LCOE per megawatt-hour (MWh) in 2009 versus $26–$54 in 2020; and solar $323–$394 in 2009 versus $31–$42 in 2020.

A report from IRENA in 2019 (2019b) has found that onshore wind and solar PV are now frequently less expensive than any fossil fuel option without financial assistance. The *New York Times* (April 7, 2020) has reported that wind turbines and solar panels produce electricity more cheaply than natural gas and coal in California and Texas, while Bloomberg Green (April 28, 2020) found that both solar and wind are the cheapest sources of power in most of the world. The International Renewable Energy Agency (IRENA) (2021b) has provided estimates of global renewable electricity costs as of 2020 (Table 9.2). Table 9.3 presents estimates from the US Energy Information Administration (US EIA 2021a) of levelized costs for new renewable and conventional generation entering service in 2026, and Table 9.4 presents Lazard's estimates of levelized cost of energy comparisons on an unsubsidized basis for 2019 (Lazard 2020).

Jaccard (2020, p. 209) does provide a word of caution in simple comparisons of the costs of renewables and nonrenewables. To quote:

> we cannot conclude that wind, water, and solar are economically superior to fossil fuels for generating electricity based solely on their relative costs per kilowatt-hour. Our comparison must include the value of their production or the cost of adding backup storage so that their output is dispatchable.

This cautionary note may be losing some of its relevance in light of the rapidly falling costs of battery storage (US EIA 2020) and the acceleration in the international installation of renewable energy sources, a process that would not continue without a cost advantage.

Table 9.2 Estimates of renewable electricity costs ($/kWh)

	Global weighted-average levelized cost of electricity	
	2010	*2020*
Biomass	0.076	0.076
Geothermal	0.049	0.071
Hydro	0.038	0.044
Solar PV	0.381	0.057
Concentrating solar power	0.340	0.108
Offshore wind	0.162	0.084
Onshore wind	0.089	0.039

Source: IRENA 2020.

Table 9.3 US cost projections by energy source ($ per MWh)

	Cost projections, 2026 ($)
Dispatchable technologies	
Ultra-supercritical coal	72.78
Combined cycle	37.11
Combustion turbine	106.62
Advanced nuclear	69.39
Geothermal	36.40
Biomass	89.21
Battery storage	119.84
Nondispatchable technologies	
Wind, onshore	36.93
Wind, offshore	120.52
Solar, standalone	32.78
Solar, hybrid	47.67
Hydroelectric	55.26

Source: US EIA 2021a.

Table 9.4 Lazard estimates of unsubsidized levelized costs of electricity, 2019

	$/MWh		
	Low	*Midpoint*	*High*
Renewable energy			
Solar PV—rooftop residential	150	—	227
Solar PV—rooftop commercial and industrial	74	—	179
Solar PV—community	63	—	94
Solar PV—crystalline utility scale	31	—	42
Solar PV—thin film utility scale	29	—	38
Soar thermal tower with storage	126	—	156
Geothermal	59	—	101
Wind	26	—	54
Wind offshore	—	86	—
Conventional			
Gas peaking	151	—	198
Nuclear	129	—	198
Coal	65	—	159
Gas combined cycle	44	—	73–127

Source: Lazard 2020.

Uninternalized externalities of conventional power sources

Systems theory informs us that renewable and conventional power sources are not competing on the same playing field. The critical issue is one of comparable total cost, and this implies a formal accounting of externalities as well as present and past subsidies for each type of energy (Koplow and Dernbach 2001). Table 9.5 presents estimates of the cost of externalities for air pollution and climate change for 2005 and 2030 (NAS 2009); see also Alberici et al. 2014). Figure 9.2, based on data from four sources (US EIA 2019a; NAS

Table 9.5 Cost of externalities (US cents per kWh, 2007)

	Air pollution 2005			Air pollution 2030	Climate change (2005/2030)		
	5th%	*Mean*	*95th%*	*Mean*	*Low*	*Mid*	*High*
	Weighted by net generation						
Coal	0.19	3.2	12.0	1.7	1.0 / 1.6	3.0 / 4.8	10.0 / 16.0
Natural gas	0.001	0.16	0.55	0.13	0.5 / 0.8	1.5 / 2.4	5.0 / 8.0
	Equally weighted						
Coal	0.53	4.4	13.2				
Natural gas	0.004	0.43	1.7				

Source: NAS 2009; Delucchi and Jacobson 2011.

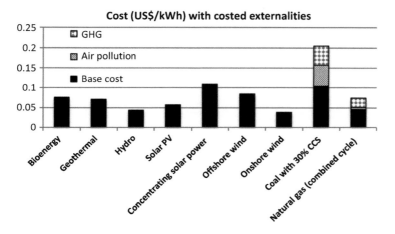

Figure 9.2 Cost of electricity with costed externalities.
Sources: US EIA 2019a; NAS 2009; Delucchi and Jacobson 2011; Alberici et al. 2014.

2009; Delucchi and Jacobson 2011; Alberici et al. 2014), displays an inflation-adjusted estimate of costs of major electricity-producing systems with externalities included.

In fact, Figure 9.2 is somewhat incomplete, as it suggests that GHGs are only associated with fossil fuel–based energy systems. While renewable sources operate without producing carbon dioxide, the inputs into these systems are not free of GHGs. Systems analysis that looks at the entire system from cradle to grave is required to identify the total GHG emissions of any one system of energy production. Life-cycle analysis is the foremost method of so doing (Nugent and Sovacool 2014). In 2004, the World Energy Council (WEC) commissioned a life-cycle analysis report to compare major energy systems. To quote: "The objective of [life-cycle analysis] is to describe and evaluate the overall environmental impacts of a certain action by analyzing all stages of the entire process from raw materials supply, production, transport, and energy generation to recycling and disposal stages" (p. 3). This type of analysis can be conducted for a variety of pollutants, including SO_2, NOx, volatile organic compounds (VOCs), and particulates. Here we focus on the system-wide production of carbon dioxide as reported by the WEC. Figure 9.3 is derived

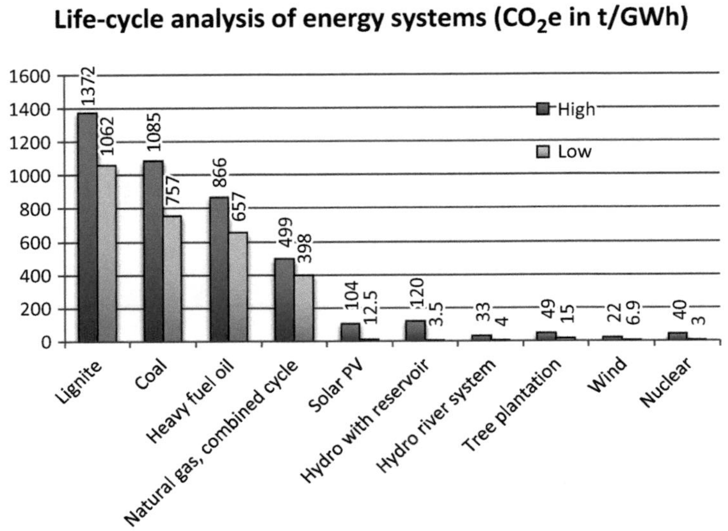

Life-cycle analysis of energy systems (CO$_2$e in t/GWh)

Figure 9.3 Life-cycle analysis of energy systems (CO$_2$ only).
Source: WEC 2004.

from their analysis. It should be noted that fossil fuel plants produce the bulk of their GHG emissions during operation; in contrast, GHG emissions from renewables, including nuclear, originate in the pre-operation stages.

In 2013, the International Monetary Fund (IMF) published a report estimating the implicit subsidies of the economic damage caused by fossil fuels. This totaled $800 billion in 2011 alone. A later study from the University of Cambridge (Hope et al. 2015) estimated implicit climate subsidies at $883 billion in 2012. The authors observed that "for all companies the implicit subsidy exceeds their post-tax profit (averaged over five years). For all pure coal companies, the implicit subsidy exceeds their total revenue" (p. 1).

While there can be a significant margin of uncertainty concerning estimates of externalities, it should be apparent that market-based comparisons of per kilowatt-hour (kWh) cost can seriously misrepresent the relative costs of alternative electricity generating sources. By way of example, a comprehensive full-cost accounting study of coal used for electricity production estimated the cost of externalities to be double or even triple the price of coal-fired power with a range of 9.36 to 26.89 cents per kWh in 2008 US dollars (Epstein et al. 2011).

What market-based cost studies also omit is the distorting effect of historical and current subsidies for fossil fuels and nuclear power (Alberici et al. 2014). While many renewables currently receive government subsidies, they are not of the same order of magnitude as the direct and indirect grants, tax concessions, depletion allowances, and other forms of de facto subsidies received by fossil fuels over the past many decades. The case of nuclear power is another case in point, as this industry has profited from extensive historical co-research and development with military programs, and the extraordinary limited liability provided by the US Price-Anderson Act of 1957. Under this legislation, overall pooled industry liability is capped at $12 billion and liability limits for individual operators are between $400 million and $500 million (US EIA 2007; US NRC 2019).

The fact that the nuclear industry lobbied hard for this legislation and that the insurance industry is unwilling to assume unlimited exposure suggests that they take seriously the risk of a major catastrophe even if the probability is considered very low. As noted in Chapter 8, an early report by the US Nuclear Regulatory Commission (US NRC 1982), which estimated the potential financial costs of a nuclear disaster by individual US plants, posited a worst-case scenario of $314 billion damages at the Indian Point Unit 3 reactor in New York State. A subsequent study by the NRDC (2011) estimated that the costs could range from $600 billion to $6 trillion.

It is not an easy task to measure the historical magnitude of such subsidies to fossil fuels and nuclear power, but several studies have tried to do so (see Table 9.6). The remarkable range of these estimates is the consequence of cost categories included or excluded from the calculations (Koplow and Dernbach 2001; Koplow 2011). One estimate from the Overseas Development Institute (ODI) of global subsidies (total over time) for oil and gas production placed the value in excess of $650 billion (ODI 2013) while another more recent study (Coady et al. 2019) estimated total global fossil fuel subsides over time at $5.2 trillion. A second report from the ODI (2019) found that the G20 countries had increased their subsidies to coal from $17.2 billion to $63.9 billion from 2013/14 to 2019 despite their commitment to address the challenge of climate change. The most recent report on subsidies from the IMF (Parry et al. 2021) concludes that:

> Globally, fossil fuel subsidies were $5.9 trillion in 2020 or about 6.8 percent of GDP [gross domestic product] and are expected to rise to 7.4 percent of GDP in 2025. Just 8 percent of the 2020 subsidy reflects undercharging for supply costs (explicit subsidies) and 92 percent for undercharging for environmental costs and foregone consumption taxes (implicit subsidies). Efficient fuel pricing in 2025 would reduce global carbon dioxide global carbon dioxide emissions 36 percent below baseline levels, which is in line with keeping global warming to 1.5 degrees, while raising revenues worth 3.8 percent of global GDP and preventing 0.9 million local air pollution deaths per year.

An accompanying spreadsheet lists the magnitude of these subsidies for two dozen countries. China provides the largest subsidy at $2,203 billion, representing 14.7 percent of GDP; followed by the United States ($662 billion or 3.1 percent of GDP), and Russia $523 billion, representing 34.8 percent of GDP).

Table 9.6 Estimates of subsidies to fossil fuels and nuclear power

Commodity	Average estimated subsidy range
Oil (annual 1999$)	$562 million–$367 billion–$1.7 trillion
Coal (annual 1999$)	$438 million–$10.5 billion
Natural gas (annual 1999$)	$1.35 billion–$6.60 billion
Nuclear (cents/kWh)	0.74 (ongoing)–11.42 (new)

Sources: Koplow and Dernbach 2001; Koplow 2011.

In light of the uninternalized economic externalities associated with the nuclear fuel cycle and fossil fuel production, the superficial comparison of costs per kW or kWh becomes meaningless. Some forms of renewable energy are not only competitive at current market prices, they have an even greater cost advantage when the comparison is cast—as it should be—in terms of total social cost.

In sum, renewable sources of energy clearly have a much smaller ecological and economic impact, including a lesser impact on the climate, than fossil fuels; however, that does not mean they have no environmental impacts at all. In a recent study, the International Energy Agency (IEA 2021c) concluded that "the rapid deployment of clean energy technologies as part of energy transitions implies a significant increase in demand for minerals" (p. 6). The report listed eleven minerals in particular that play a major role in wind and solar energy and EVs: copper, lithium, nickel, manganese, cobalt, graphite, chromium, molybdenum, zinc, rare earths, and silicon. The IEA recommends greater scrutiny of social and environmental factors related to their extraction, processing, use, and disposal. However, they conclude that "emissions along the mineral supply chain do not negate the clear climate advantages of clean energy technologies" (p. 15).

Climatic feedback effects

There is one additional threat to the long-run viability of renewable sources resulting, ironically enough, from the problem these sources are designed to address. A study coauthored by the Harvard Medical School, Center for Health and the Global Environment (2005) has projected an increase in both the mean and variance of extreme weather events. The increased frequency and severity of regional droughts may deprive hydroelectric power stations of sufficient water (e.g., CNN August 21, 2021), and the increased intensity of marine- and land-based wind storms and flooding may threaten the structural integrity of installed wind farms, solar PV installations, and electrical transmission grids. All of these threats must be considered in assessing the risks and benefits of new renewable energy sources.

Scale-up to an economy based on renewable power

There is at least one major technological constraint to such a massive transformation of energy systems. Smil (2010) has pointed out that historical energy transformations—from wood to coal to oil—have all taken fifty to sixty years, and he posits that a move to renewables will take no less a period of time, particularly in light of the magnitude of global energy supply and demand (see also Temple 2018 and *New York Times* November 7, 2017). The percentage of global energy use derived from fossil fuels has remained relatively constant at approximately 80 percent since 1971 (World Bank, accessed October 2019). The increased use of renewables has apparently been matched by comparable increases in the use of fossil fuels. Many developing countries still rely on coal for a major proportion of their electricity production for two principal reasons: ubiquity and low cost (IEA 2019c, d, and f). China presents an excellent example of this conundrum. Despite the country's efforts to expand the use of renewable energy sources, it still relies on coal for most of its electricity production and continues to build coal-fired power stations in an attempt to keep up with rapidly expanding demand (*New York Times* October 13 and 28, 2021; *Globe and Mail* October 11, 2021; see Figure 9.4). Nevertheless, Texas, the leading US producer of both oil and natural gas, completed a $7 billion investment in 2014 for

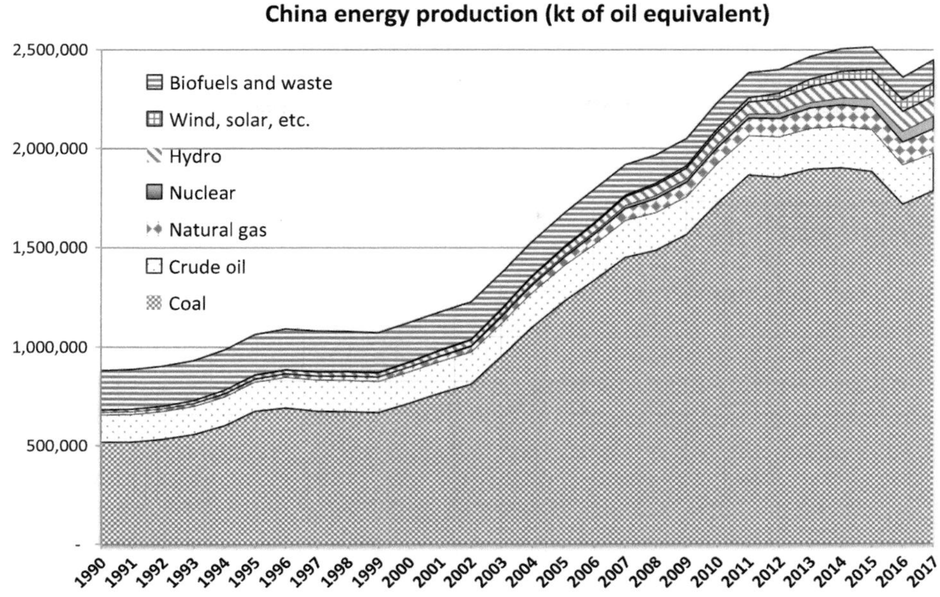

China energy production (kt of oil equivalent)

Figure 9.4 Chinese energy production.
Source: China National Bureau of Statistics, multiple years.

3,600 miles of new transmission lines to connect wind farms in the Panhandle to major urban demand centers (*New York Times* July 23, 2014). The US EIA (2021b) reports that

> Texas leads the nation in wind-powered generation and produced about 28 percent of all US wind-powered electricity in 2020. Wind power surpassed the state's nuclear generation for the first time in 2014 and produced more than twice as much electricity as the state's two nuclear power plants combined in 2020.

Even Wyoming, a state with a major coal industry, may soon become home to one of the largest wind farms in the United States, despite its continued reliance on coal for employment and revenue (*New York Times* March 5, 2021; Associated Press May 2, 2021). While the transition to renewables is proceeding apace in the developed countries, major initiatives have also been taken among the developing nations, but there is a clear need for new financing from the global economy (IEA 2021d). This was one of the major topics of discussion at COP21 (see Chapter 10).

Major renewable energy sources

Hydroelectricity

The use of water for power has a long history, stretching back to the second century BCE in China where water was used to pound and hull grain, break ore, and assist the process of papermaking. It was not until the nineteenth century that the genesis of modern hydroelectric power occurred. As illustrated in Figure 9.1a, hydro provides 2.5 percent of world primary energy; however, its role in the production of electricity is much more significant with a 16.3 percent share, the largest renewable contributor to electric power (IEA 2019c). In 2020 hydropower achieved a record 4,370 TWh (IHA 2021; see also IEA 2020b). The size of hydropower installations varies markedly, from micro hydro with capacities ranging from 5–100 kW to large reservoir-based dams up to 22,500 megawatts (MW). Table 9.1 lists the five countries with the largest installed hydro capacity, but the role this source plays in domestic electricity production depends on the availability of alternative fuels, suitable sites, cost, and distance from markets. By way of example, the contribution of hydro to total electricity supply in the United States is only 7 percent, but Brazil and Canada have a much higher dependence, with 63 percent and 60 percent respectively (IEA 2019c and g). In an extreme case, a country such as Nepal, 99.9 percent of total electricity production is supplied by hydro, mostly small-scale.

Hydroelectricity has several distinct advantages. Once built, it is relatively inexpensive, can serve as baseload power, and has been labeled a green source of energy as its operation produces no GHGs. There are several qualifications to its green credentials, however, as there can be unanticipated negative social, economic, and environmental costs (Ackermann et al. 1973; Goldsmith and Hildyard 1984; Scudder 2005; Ansar et al. 2014) as illustrated by the cases of the Aswan Dam in Egypt and the more recent Three Gorges Dam in China described in Chapter 2. Most of the important effects of hydropower are associated with the construction and operation of reservoirs behind the dams themselves. Significant effects of hydropower include:

- Flooding of agricultural land and forests
- Mobilization of toxic minerals such as mercury (*New York Times* November 10, 2016)
- Displacement of population
- Blockage of navigation and fisheries, which occasionally can require the eventual removal of a dam (*Science* November 18, 2011)
- Fragmentation of local habitat and ecosystem (*Science* February 2, 2018)
- Induced seismicity and landslides (Hvistendahl 2008)
- Change to regional water tables (*New York Times* May 19, 2011)
- Reservoirs can become a repository for industrial and municipal wastes (*New York Times* May 19, 2011)
- Loss of natural amenities such as rivers
- Detrimental downstream effects on biodiversity, agriculture, human health, fisheries, infrastructure, and coastlines (Ezcurra et al. 2019)
- Potential eutrophication behind the dam leading to loss of fisheries
- Possible silting up of the reservoir, reducing the electrical output of the dam
- Changes in precipitation and runoff due to climate change in some regions, which may pose a threat to the viability of hydropower (Kao et al. 2015). This possibility has already arisen with respect to power generated by the Hoover Dam, a major supplier of electricity to the American West (*New York Times* August 21, 2021).

And, finally, the issue of contributions to climate change arises: while the operation is GHG free, a systems analysis of the inputs associated with construction finds GHGs emissions from the significant use of concrete—one of the world's most GHG-intensive products—in many of these structures. In addition, if the land to be flooded has not been adequately cleared, there may be sizable emissions of methane from rotting vegetation as well as flooded soil (IRN 2006; Cullenward and Victor 2006). Even run–of–river hydro-power may contribute to GHG emissions, as evidenced by measurement data from the Amazon basin (Bertassoli et al. 2021).

Despite these complexities, hydroelectric power still plays, and will continue to play, an essential role in displacing fossil fuels in the production of electricity. Numerous sites remain to be developed and the World Bank has increased its financial support for large hydro projects in the developing world to promote a process of continued economic development that is less GHG intensive (Hydro Review 2007). Power Technology (2019) reports that of the world's ten largest power plants recently under construction, the majority were hydroelectric, representing an addition of almost 37 GW of new capacity to current global capacity of 1,330 GW (IHA 2018 and 2021). One of the largest under-developed sources of potential hydropower has been the Mekong River basin and, up until 2020, plans were in place to construct several major dams on the river. These plans were recently suspended for at least a decade over fears of several major detrimental effects on fisheries and the delivery of beneficial sediments to the lower Mekong (Schmitt et al. 2019). It is estimated that sixty million people depend on the river and its resources, and both people and resources could be jeopardized by major dam construction (*Guardian* March 20, 2020).

Wind

Wind power, like water power, has ancient origins (Turbinegenerator.org n.d.). Its first recorded use was by Heron of Alexandria in the first century to power an organ. Several centuries later, both the Persians and Chinese were using windmills to grind grains and pump water (Needham 1994). The beginning of the modern era using wind to generate electricity occurred in Ohio in 1887 (turbinegenerator.org). Globally, 744 GW of wind capacity is now installed, accounting for 7 percent of global renewable energy production (WWEA 2021). As indicated in Table 9.1, the top five countries account for 70 percent of all installed capacity. However, national reliance on wind power varies markedly by country. Wind energy accounted for only 4 percent of Chinese electricity production in 2018 (China National Bureau of Statistics 2020) and 8.4 percent of electricity output in 2020 in the United States (US EIA 2021c), where it exceeded hydropower output. In contrast, wind power represents almost half of Denmark's electricity supply, followed by almost 30 percent of supply in Uruguay and Ireland, and approximately 20 percent in Germany, Portugal, and Spain (REN21 2019). Because wind is currently nondispatchable, capacity factors will vary by time and location. US domestic utility-scale wind generators have had a 35 percent capacity factor in the last few years (US EIA 2021d; Life by Numbers n.d.).

While there are few environmental issues with wind power, some concerns have been raised about background noise, bird kills, and aesthetic impacts, although there is dis-agreement on the extent or severity of these effects (US DoE accessed October 2019a). Partly in response to these issues and a desire to find locations with greater reliability of wind speed and duration, there has been a concerted push to install wind farms offshore, particularly in the UK, Germany, and China (IEA 2019e). As of 2018, the total installed global offshore capacity was 23,706 MW, representing only 4 percent of all wind capacity (IRENA 2019a). After "conducting a state-of-the-art geospatial analysis of the speed and quality of wind along hundreds of thousands of kilometers [km] of coastline around the world," the IEA now feels that the potential growth of offshore wind over the next two decades will be huge with a potential value of $1 trillion (IEA 2019a, b, and c). Several countries in Europe have made significant commitments to this technology, including the UK, Netherlands, Denmark, and Germany, and the Biden administration has announced a major offshore wind plan (McKinsey 2020b; BBC February 4, 2021; *New York Times* March 29, May 12 and 25, October 15, 2021). Sherman et al. (2020) have suggested that offshore wind could make a significant impact on decarbonizing China's economy, with a potential 5.4 times larger than the current Chinese coastal demand for power.

The key to further development of wind power is evolution in the size and power of the turbine blades, allowing greater output at lower per unit cost (*New York Times* March 20, 2014 and April 23, 2018). The largest wind turbines now exceed 10 MW capacity, and wind farms composed of multiple turbines can now make a significant contribution to a national electricity grid (Power Technology 2014). General Electric has announced plans for a giant 13 MW turbine in excess of 850 feet (ft) in height (*New York Times* January 1, 2021). The IEA has forecast that wind energy could supply as much as 18 percent of global energy demand by 2050. In order to achieve these ambitious goals, Veers et al. (2019, p. 1) have identified three major challenges that need to be addressed: "the first is the need for a deeper understanding of the physics of atmospheric flow in the critical zone of plant operation. The second involves science and engineering of the largest dynamic, rotating machines in the world. The third encompasses optimization and control of fleets of wind plants working synergistically within the electricity grid. Addressing these challenges could enable wind power to provide as much as half of our global electricity needs." A somewhat controversial issue is the potential existence of an upper limit to the amount of energy that wind farms can draw from the atmosphere (*New Scientist* March 30, 2011). If such a limit does exist, there appears to be little chance that it will be reached at any time soon, guaranteeing that wind power will continue to make an increasing contribution to global renewable energy supply. The issue of cost-competitiveness no longer seems a barrier to adoption of this technology on a wider scale as cost decreases are expected to continue over the next few decades (Jansen et al. 2020; Wiser et al. 2021).

One final issue is the disposal of old wind turbine blades, as it has been estimated that in the United States alone about eight thousand blades will be removed in 2021 (Golden 2021). To quote:

> Primarily made from reinforced fiberglass composite, blades are difficult to crush or recycle. They're massive—some are longer than a Boeing 747 wing—and they're strong, built to withstand hurricane-force winds. The most common solution today is to cut them down (using a diamond encrusted industrial blade) and bury them in a mass blade grave. The European Union, which has strict regulations about what can go into landfills, has turned to burning blades in power plants. This practice arguably makes an even larger environmental problem, as incineration emits greenhouse gases and air pollutants. Burying the blades is relatively benign. They don't leach into soils or emit other harmful chemicals, as other waste products can. "This is the least problematic waste in terms of environmental concerns that we've ever gotten," said Cindie Langston, manager of the solid waste division for Casper, Wyo., a home to a blade graveyard. "We get tires, asbestos, contaminated soil, pretty nasty stuff." But the practice is a conspicuous waste of materials and is at odds with sustainability Ideals.

(pp. 1–2)

Solar energy

It should come as no surprise that solar energy, as with wind and hydropower, had its genesis in ancient civilization. Aside from human and animal power, these were the principal energy sources available to humanity prior to the fossil fuel era. Passive solar heating played an important role in house and town design in ancient China, Greece, and Rome. In 533 CE, solar rights were included in the digest of Roman civil law prepared by Justinian, emperor of the eastern Roman Empire, with access to sunlight and rights to solar heat guaranteed (Butti and Perlin 1980).

The modern use of solar energy is represented by two principal technologies: solar water heating in flat plate collectors, and arrays of PV cells, which convert sunlight to electricity based on the photoelectric effect first enunciated by Albert Einstein in 1905. In 2020, there were 623 GW of solar PV installed globally, representing 3.3 percent of global electricity demand, while the PV sector was valued at $135 billion in 2019 (IEA 2020d). A third form of solar energy utilization is concentrated solar power, where an array of mirrors tracks the sun and focuses its energy on a collector which converts this energy to electricity (US DoE accessed 2019b and c). Global installed capacity is much lower than solar PV, at 5,466 MW in 2018 due in part to its higher cost and reliance on direct solar radiation, restricting its geographic location.

Solar water heating is found throughout the world, frequently in the form of rooftop collectors on individual homes and apartment buildings. Solar PV, however, holds the promise of major contribution to global electricity production, as costs continue their rapid decline (IRENA 2016 and 2021a; NREL 2017) and with the expectation of continuing advances in conversion efficiency, which already ranges from 24 percent up to 47 percent (Jeong et al. 2020; Kim et al. 2020; NREL 2020; Juarez-Perez and Marta Haro 2020; Kohler et al. 2021). As indicated in Table 9.1, the top five producing countries, led by China, account for 73 percent of the global total. As with wind power, the current state of the technology and related infrastructure of solar power forces it to act as a nondispatchable source with a capacity factor of 26.1 percent in 2018 in the United States. Solar PV faces many of the same challenges as wind power if it is to make a significant contribution to national electricity supply. The most important challenges are to develop further in-service improvements in efficiency (Polman et al. 2016), an expanded smart grid that can integrate storage with multiple producers, and innovative technological modifications and applications (Trieb et al. 2012), and to transform significantly electric utility business models (Biello 2014). Together, it has been estimated that solar and wind energy potential could be one hundred times greater than global energy demand (Carbon Tracker 2021a).

If these issues can be successfully addressed, solar power could achieve the breakthrough required to supply much of the US demand for electricity (Fthenakis et al. 2009; Zweibel et al. 2007). In 2019, it was predicted that solar power would experience "spectacular growth in the next 5 years" (Electrek 2019; see also IEA 2020a). In particular, the IEA has focused on distributed PV systems in home, commercial buildings, and industry and made the following observations:

- Distributed solar PV systems in homes, commercial buildings, and industry are set to take off, bringing significant changes in power systems.
- China is forecast to account for almost half of global distributed PV growth.
- Contrary to conventional wisdom, distributed PV growth is dominated by commercial and industrial applications rather than residential.

- Some one hundred million solar rooftop systems for homes could be operating worldwide by 2024.
- Rapid cost reductions could lead to a distributed PV boom.
- Major policy and tariff reforms are required to make distributed PV growth sustainable.

The most recent prediction on the potential for solar power was enunciated by the US Department of Energy (DoE) in their 2021 *Solar Futures Study*, which provided a blueprint for a zero-carbon grid. The study envisioned solar power providing as much as 40 percent of US electricity by 2035 and 45 percent by 2050. The end of this section includes a short case study on the use of distributed solar power in the state of Hawaii.

In sum, the prospects for the further development and utilization of solar power appear excellent. There are at least two environmental issues to be addressed, however. First, solar farms tend to be land-intensive and can compete with agriculture. To address this issue, Miskin et al. (2019, p. 972) propose the concept of "aglectric farming," where agricultural land is shared for food and energy co-production by "adjusting the intensity, spectral distribution and duration of shading [which] allows innovative photovoltaic systems to achieve significant power generation without potentially diminishing agricultural output." Second, the production of PV cells is a high-tech process involving a number of toxic chemicals during production and eventual disposal (Fthenakis et al. 2008; Nguyen 2018). It is essential for firms to control these emissions during the life cycle of solar panels, and the ability to do so depends on the willingness and ability of all participants in the supply chain from cradle to grave. While a majority of producers in Silicon Valley are making a concerted effort to address this problem (Silicon Valley Toxics Coalition accessed October 21, 2019), in some countries, such as China, some of these precautions have not been taken, leading to threats to the local environment and human health (*Washington Post* March 9, 2008). The adoption of solar power has been encouraged by initiatives such as solar mandates for new buildings in California (*New York Times* September 8, 2021) and economic incentives in Hawaii.

Case study: Renewable energy in the state of Hawaii

While the Trump Administration showed little enthusiasm for tackling, let along recognizing, climate change, several states and cities took the lead in this area. No state felt the need to do so more than Hawaii, which has no fossil fuel reserves. Fortunately, the state is endowed with a range of renewable resources and has made a major policy commitment to move to 100 percent renewable power by 2045. As of 2021, Hawaiian Electric produced 34.5 percent of its electricity from renewables (Hawaiian Electric 2021). Figure 9.5 displays the mix of energy sources for electricity production in the state in 2019 (Hawaii State Energy Office 2020). Note that geothermal, associated with Hawaii's volcanic resources, is currently off-line, although in 2017 it accounted for approximately 4 percent of total state electricity production (Hawaii State Energy Office 2020). Petroleum still plays a dominant role in the state's total energy supply, with 23.6 percent of petroleum devoted to electric power production but, more importantly, 65.3 percent required for transportation. Requirements for air transportation have dominated the use of petroleum; air transportation accounts for the largest share at 33.9 percent, principally because of the geographic isolation of the state.

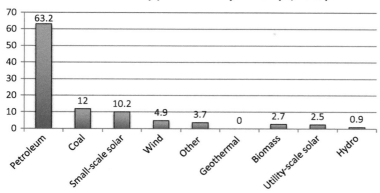

Figure 9.5 Hawaii electricity production by source in 2019.
Source: Hawaii State Energy Office 2020.

Table 9.7 Hawaiian electricity resources by island

	Oahu (%)	Hawaii island (%)	Maui county (Maui, Lanai, and Molokai) (%)	Kauai (%)
Geothermal	n.a.	31.0	n.a.	n.a.
Customer-sited solar	9.0	12.0	12.0	n.a.
Grid-scale solar	2.0	0.4	1.0	n.a.
Total solar	11.0	12.4	13.0	26.4
Waste to energy	6.0	0.0	0.0	n.a.
Wind	3.0	10.5	21.0	n.a.
Hydro	n.a.	3.0	0.1	8.8
Biofuels	1.0	n.a.	0.1	9.0
Nonrenewable	79.0	43.0	66.0	55.8

Source: Hawaiian Electric et al. 2018b.

Hawaii faces a number of challenges, some unique to its geography. Hawaii is composed of six islands and there is a mismatch between island-specific energy resources and the main market of Oahu where the majority of the population lives. Table 9.7 describes recent total and island-specific uses of energy sources for electricity production (Hawaiian Electric et al. 2018b; Kauai Island Utility Cooperative accessed October 2019; Maui Electric n.d.). Because of its location in the middle of the Pacific Ocean, there is no opportunity for interstate electrical interchange. Achievement of the 2045 goal of total reliance on renewables will require new technological developments in the area of energy storage, including advanced batteries. Other challenges are more typical and include the necessity to create a more resilient grid (Maui Electric n.d.) and transform the transportation sector to EVs fueled by renewables. The state has produced a roadmap (Hawaiian Electric et al. 2018a) to achieve this goal. It involves five steps: "(1) increasing electric vehicle adoption by helping to lower costs and educating customers; (2) accelerating the buildout of EV charging infrastructure; (3) supporting the electrification of buses and

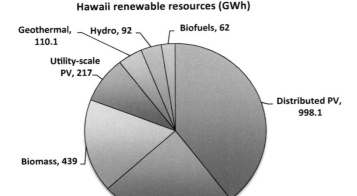

Hawaii renewable resources (GWh)

Geothermal, 110.1 — Hydro, 92 — Biofuels, 62

Utility-scale PV, 217

Distributed PV, 998.1

Biomass, 439

Wind, 602

Figure 9.6 Hawaii renewable resources.
Source: Hawaii State Energy Office 2020.

other heavy equipment; (4) incentivizing EV charging to align with grid needs and save drivers and utility customers money; and (5) coordinating with ongoing grid modernization and planning efforts to help maximize the use of renewable resources." In June 2021, the state governor signed into law a mandate that Hawaii change 100 percent of its light-duty passenger vehicles to electric by 2030 and the rest of its light-duty fleet by 2035 (*Maui News* June 27, 2021).

The largest contribution to Hawaii's renewable energy comes from distributed solar PV, in line with the IEA's emphasis on the emerging role of this source (Figure 9.6). Hawaii has already actively pursued the development of distributed solar PV and energy storage using a variety of policy and economic instruments in both the residential and commercial sectors (*Maui News* January 21 and November 12, 2021). Hawaiian Electric Company has recently instituted a cash incentive for residential and commercial customers to install batteries to either use or discharge power during peak hours (*PV Magazine* July 20, 2021). In the state, 173,000 structures have PV installations, including one-third of homes. Several innovative proposals have recently been advanced on Maui and Molokai. Hawaiian Electric is proposing a program which would allow customers without rooftop solar to benefit from renewable energy cost savings (*Maui News* July 28, 2021b) and Maui County is proposing to require that new one- or two-family residential buildings over 5,000 ft^2 be net-zero-energy homes (*Maui News* August 17, 2021). In 2020 two companies submitted proposals to the state public utility commission to install combined solar power battery storage to address the inherent problem of matching supply to demand (*Maui News* September 17, 2020; *Honolulu Star Advertiser* May 14, 2021). As of June 2021, there were plans on Maui for the addition of 215 MW in solar power, accompanied by 860 MW of battery storage (*Maui News* June 26, 2021 and July 28, 2021a). In July, a 370-acre solar and battery project on the slopes of Haleakala volcano received approval (*Maui News* July 28, 2021) and a 450-acre solar installation was approved for central Maui in November (*Maui News* November 12, 2021).

Biofuels

Throughout history, humanity has used wood, plant, and animal waste to supply heat for cooking and warming the home. This remains common in developing countries and will continue in the absence of available and affordable commercial fuel. The IEA (2019c) has reported that biofuels and waste currently account for 9.2 percent of world total primary energy supply. What has changed in the last few decades is the emergence of industrial-scale production of electricity using wood, as well as production of liquid fuels for the transportation sector using crops such as corn, wheat, sugarcane, and plant products such as palm oil. The driving force for these developments has been governmental policy designed to address the challenge of global warming. Each of these processes is described along with their system-wide ecological effects. The principal conclusion of this discussion is that, as currently practiced, each of these systems is ill-conceived and potentially counterproductive.

Electricity production from wood

At this point in time, many of the wood products used for electricity production are derived from wood waste converted into wood pellets for combustion in thermal power plants. Much of current US production is currently being shipped to Europe, which is the world's largest market for pellets and woody biomass and is expected to grow strongly for the next few years (Giuntoli et al. 2021; International Forest Industries 2021). However, concerns have been raised about the supposed environmental benefits of this product (*New York Times* April 21, 2021). Specific concerns focus on the fact that "wood releases more carbon dioxide per unit of electricity than coal … and a newly planted tree can take decades to reabsorb the carbon dioxide emitted by burning."

There is also increasing interest in growing or harvesting trees for bioenergy purposes (Natural Resources Canada 2016). Booth (2014) states that more than seventy new woodburning plants have been built since 2005 or were under construction, while another seventy-five were proposed and in various stages of development in the United States at the time of her report. Because this source of energy is considered renewable, it qualifies for tax credits, subsides, and incentives (Cho 2011, updated 2016). Interest in this technology is not confined to North America, however; as of 2015 nearly half of Europe's renewable energy was coming from wood (Upton 2015). The push to advance this technology is based on the stated assumption that combustion of wood is carbon neutral, as any carbon dioxide released will be taken up by tree growth. This would permit an endless source of green energy.

There are several major problems associated with this process. First, the combustion of this type of biomass can emit large quantities of conventional air pollutants, posing a threat to human health (Buonocore et al. 2021). Included in these emissions are particulates, CO, NOx, and VOCs depending on the temperature of combustion. And as stated earlier in this section, wood produces more GHGs on combustion than coal, since wood has a lower energy density. This, however, is not a problem if using wood as fuel is indeed carbon neutral. However, third, and most important, there is a profound temporal difference between the release and reabsorption of carbon dioxide by growing trees. The release occurs instantaneously upon combustion, but the reabsorption of this CO_2 may take several decades as trees grow slowly. It has been estimated that achievement of true carbon neutrality might not occur for at least forty years (RSPB et al. n.d.). The net result of this fundamental accounting error is that wood combustion for electricity will increase rather than decrease GHG emissions over a lengthy period of time, rendering this technology indisputably counterproductive (Greenpeace 2011; Upton 2015; Bitov and Booth 2014; RSPB et al. n.d.).

Production of ethanol from food crops

While renewable energy sources appear more environmentally benign and cost-competitive when market distortions such as subsidies and externalities are accounted for, there is one prominent case where the opposite is true. After adjustments for net energy output (Pimental and Patzek 2005; Patzek and Pimental 2005) and total system impacts on GHG production (Fargione et al. 2008; Searchinger et al. 2008; Grafton et al. 2014), it appears that most government initiatives for the production of ethanol as a transportation fuel have been counterproductive. This experience provides a note of caution about the necessity for a systematic study of all environmental, social, and economic ramifications of any new energy technology, even renewables.

Biofuel production has been rising steadily in the last few decades, but both production and consumption are currently dominated by the United States and Brazil, although significant production is occurring in China, Europe, and India largely as a result of government support policies through subsidies or mandated production (OECD 2008). Figure 9.7 shows biofuel production by major country in 2017, and Figure 9.8 displays the rapid run-up in US production of ethanol over the last several decades. The OECD and FAO estimate that by 2027 China will have become the world's third largest producer (OECD–FAO 2019). It has been reported that in 2011, 98 percent of Thailand's cassava chips were destined for biofuel production in China (*New York Times* April 6, 2011). Prices

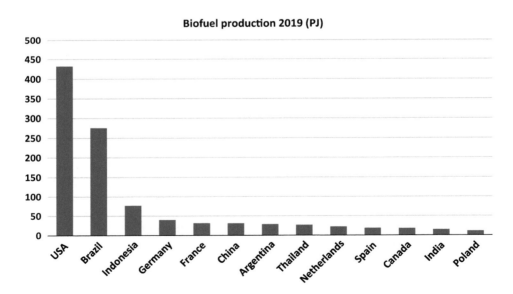

Figure 9.7 Biofuel output by major producing country in 2017.
Source: IEA 2019h.

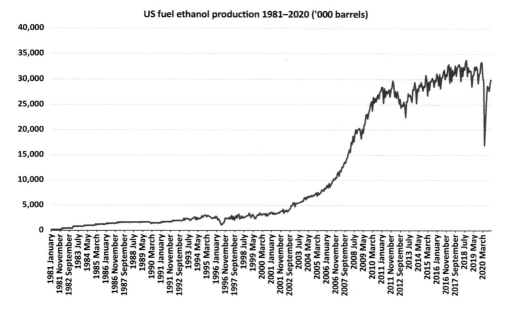

Figure 9.8 US annual ethanol production.
Source: US EIA 2021d.

for cassava doubled in the preceding three-year period as demand increased fourfold. The OECD and FAO (OECD–FAO 2019, p. 39) predict that:

> Global use of ethanol is expected to grow around 18% or an additional 21 bln L [billion liters] by 2028 with greater use expected mostly in China (+5.4 bln L). In 2017, the Chinese government announced the goal of a 10% ethanol blending share for 2020, which is expected to be filled through domestic production coming from domestic maize and imported cassava.

Biofuels take two forms: ethanol, largely derived from grain and sugar cane, and bio-diesel derived from vegetable oils. The rationale for the production of biofuels is beguil-ingly simple. Biofuels are supposed to be carbon neutral since the emissions of carbon dioxide during their combustion in the automotive sector, for example, are offset by carbon take-up during plant growth. In fact, concern has been raised that oil sold as "waste cooking oil" imported from East Asia as a biofuel feedstock in the European Union may not actually be waste and may in fact be contributing to deforestation and the loss of animal feed (Grinsven et al. 2021; BBC April 21, 2021). Equally important, the World Bank concluded in 2008 that the large increase in biofuel production in the United States and the European Union was the most important driver of rising global food prices over the period 2002–8, imposing an increasing burden on the poor in developing countries. This and other purported benefits of biofuel production and use raise a number of major conceptual problems. A cautionary tale is provided by US experience with the produc-tion of ethanol.

AMERICAN ETHANOL PRODUCTION

Over the past few decades, the United States has implemented several major policy initiatives to introduce alternative fuels into the domestic gasoline supply using a combination of tax subsidies and minimum production mandates (*New York Times* November 30, 2015). Foremost among these fuels is "gasohol," a blend of gasoline and plant-based ethanol. Within the United States, four major normative rationales have been advanced for this policy: to reduce GHG emissions, to reduce dependence on foreign oil supplies (now somewhat moot in light of recent advances in oil extraction from nonconventional sources), to reduce air pollution in cities, and to provide additional income to the farm sector. In the United States the feedstock of choice has been corn, in Canada, wheat and, in Brazil, sugarcane. The production of ethanol is an energy-intensive process involving the distillation of fermented sugars to achieve a water-free alcohol suitable for blending with conventional gasoline. To grasp the chemical and economic significance of this process, it is necessary to understand the concept of net energy analysis.

Net energy analysis focuses on the relationship between the energy required to produce an energy product and the energy available for use after the production process. The crucial characteristic of this analysis is that it is conducted at the system level; in other words, it includes inputs at all relevant stages of the production process. Included is not only energy used in the production of the final energy product, but also energy used in the production of the capital goods employed in the recovery or production of the energy product. The net energy ratio is defined as:

> (the energy output from the fuel produced) / (the energy input required to extract the energy plus the energy embodied in the capital equipment required to extract the energy).

Note that this is a variant of Hall's (2017) energy return on investment (EROI), the calculation of which is:

> (energy output—energy input) / (energy input).

Net energy ratios have been calculated for a broad range of energy products and Figure 9.9 summarizes the results of one early comprehensive study conducted by the Canadian government (Winstanley et al. 1977). As evident from these data, domestic and conventional natural gas have the highest ratio. What is noteworthy, however, are the values for gasohol, which range from a high of 1.8 to a low of 0.8. Put simply, a ratio less than 1.0 means that more energy is required to produce the product than is available for consumption. In other words, ethanol in North America has no positive net energy balance if produced by standard agricultural production techniques and conventional distillation technology. There may be a modest net positive energy balance only if: (1) energy-conserving farm practices are developed, (2) energy-conserving industrial technology is used, and (3) crop residues are used to replace conventional fuels, such as the oil used in distillation, the most energy-intensive part of the production process. However, from a systems perspective, the use of crop residues deprives the field of nutrients, necessitating the increasing application of fertilizers, which are themselves energy intensive. Based on extensive research undertaken by Pimental and Patzek (2005), it is possible to conduct a precise net energy analysis of ethanol produced in the United

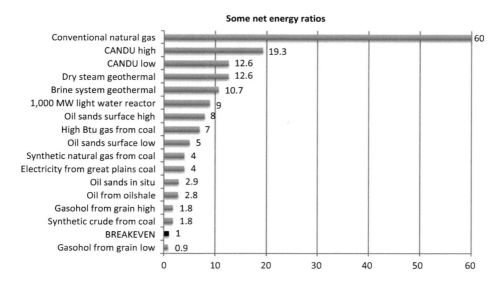

Figure 9.9 Net energy ratios.
Source: Winstanley et al. 1977.

States. Figure 9.10 summarizes the results of their analysis. DeCicco et al. (2016) report that additional carbon uptake by crops offsets only 37 percent of biofuel-related biogenic CO_2 emissions. These results suggest a net increase, rather than decrease, in GHGs based on a systems analysis including displacement effects and land-use changes.

Hall and Day (2009; see also Murphy et al. 2011) conducted an updated comparison of EROIs for American energy sources. Their results differ somewhat from those of Winstanley et al., with domestic oil producing the highest EROI, but ethanol/gasohol still at the bottom of the list at an average of 1.07. However, after accounting for several factors, including statistical error and geographic differences in data values, the authors concluded that they were "unable to assert whether the true value of the EROI of corn ethanol is greater than one… . In light of this work, we conclude that production of corn ethanol within the United States is unsustainable and requires energy subsidies from the larger oil economy" (Murphy et al. 2011, p. 179.)

The inability of corn-based ethanol to achieve a positive net energy balance has prompted researchers to consider other agricultural and nonagricultural feedstocks (Table 9.8). While some may hold promise with further development in the technology of conversion, this remains a work in progress.

A GASOHOL SCORECARD

Under the normative theory of government, the principal reason for government intervention in the economy is to correct market failure where markets fail to achieve efficient resource allocation. For example, a government may intervene where prices do not reflect social costs. The US federal government charges no sales tax on ethanol, thereby creating a large de facto subsidy for its production and use in gasohol.

Energy inputs and cost of corn per hectare

Inputs	Quantity	kcal x 1,000	Costs $
Labour	11.4 hrs	462	$ 148.20
Machinery	55 kg	1,018	$ 103.21
Diesel	88 L	1,003	$ 34.76
Gasoline	40 L	405	$ 20.80
Nitrogen	153 kg	2,448	$ 94.86
Phosphorus	65 kg	270	$ 40.30
Potassium	77 kg	251	$ 23.87
Lime	1,120 kg	315	$ 11.00
Seeds	21 kg	520	$ 74.81
Irrigation	8.1 cm	320	$ 123.00
Herbicides	6.2 kg	620	$ 124.00
Insecticides	2.8 kg	280	$ 56.00
Electricity	13.2 kWh	34	$ 0.92
Transport	204 kg	169	$ 61.20
Total		**8,115**	**$ 916.93**

Corn yield	8,655 kg/ha
kcal/kg	0.937608

Inputs per 1,000 liters of 99.5% ethanol produced from corn

Input	Quantity	kcal x 1,000	Dollars ($)
Corn grain (@ 0.937608 kcal/kg)	2,690 kg	2,522	$ 284.25
Corn transport	2,690 kg	322	$ 21.40
Water	40,000 L	90	$ 21.16
Stainless steel	3 kg	12	$ 10.60
Steel	4 kg	12	$ 10.60
Cement	8 kg	8	$ 10.60
Steam	2,546,000 kcal	2,546	$ 21.16
Electricity	392 kWh	1,011	$ 27.44
95% ethanol to 99.5%	9 kcal/L	9	$ 40.00
Sewage effluent	20 kg BOD	69	$ 6.00
Total		**6,597**	**$ 453.21**

	Corn
Input	6,597
Output	5,130
Product	Ethanol
Units	kcal per 1,000 liters of ethanol
I/O ratio:	1.29
O/I ratio:	0.78

Figure 9.10 Energy analysis of corn–based ethanol.
Source: Pimental and Patzek 2005.

Table 9.8 Energy balances of alternative feedstocks

	Corn	Switchgrass	Wood cellulose	Soybeans	Sunflower
Input	6,597	7,455	8,061	11,878	19,599
Output	5,139	5,130	5,130	9,000	9,000
Product	Ethanol	Ethanol	Ethanol	Biodiesel	Biodiesel
Units	kcal per 100 liters of ethanol			kcal per 100 liters of biodiesel	
Input/output ratio	1.28	1.45	1.57	1.32	2.18
Output/input ratio	0.78	0.69	0.64	0.76	0.46

Source: Pimental and Patzek 2005.

The product is gaining acceptance by the consumer because it is price-competitive at the pump. One should be circumspect about this policy because of at least one red flag: the fact that a massive de facto subsidy has been required to keep this product viable. While the government has backed off a direct financial subsidy, the same result has been achieved by government mandates requiring the production of a given amount of ethanol every year.

The question arises as to what prices at the pump (i.e., the market price) are not telling us. Net energy balances tell us that this entire venture does not make any sense from the perspective of energy analysis. We are putting in more energy than we are getting out. Net energy analysis confirms the suspicion that if the federal government was not heavily subsidizing or mandating its production, ethanol would be a dead duck. Why is the government following a policy that seems so ill-advised? This requires the application of the *positive* theory of government, which attempts to explain why government behavior may deviate from the normative model. Of the four posited reasons for promoting the use of gasohol, only the environmental reduction of some air pollutants (excluding GHGs) seems plausible, although weak. We can hypothesize about government motives: (1) they originally wanted to appear to be tackling the problem of foreign oil dependence, (2) they want to appear to be tackling the problem of urban air pollution—although there may be better ways of achieving this end, (3) they want to appear to be tackling the issue of global warming, (4) the government is ignorant of the systems implications of their policy, or (5) the government may be responding to special interest groups.

The relevant US special interest groups in gasohol policy include corn farmers who represent a powerful lobby in the United States. Promoting the use of gasohol increases the demand for their products and raises the prices they receive for their grain. This is an indirect and less obvious way of subsidizing this sector of the economy. The US Department of Agriculture (USDA) has reported that as much as 34 percent of the American corn crop was devoted to the production of ethanol in 2020, down from 39 percent in 2019 (USDA 2021). A similar economic rationale relating to farm-based interest groups may explain continued European support for ethanol-blended gasoline. Within the United States, there has been a strong lobbying effort by the American agribusiness giant, Archer Daniels Midland Ltd, which controlled 60–75 percent of US ethanol production until the advent of the COVID-19 pandemic.

In the 1992 US federal election and in subsequent elections, Archer Daniels Midland made significant monetary contributions to both the Republicans and the Democrats in order to maintain tax policies favorable to the continued production of ethanol and use of gasohol. In sum, the widespread support for ethanol production, at least in the United States, represents a victory of political power over economics and sustainable agriculture and transportation. According to one research study published in 2015 (Manhattan Institute for Policy Research), the Renewable Fuel Standard, which mandates the blending of ethanol into gasoline, has cost American motorists more than $10 billion per year in extra fuel costs. In essence this is a massive rent (i.e., nonproductive) transfer from the driving public to special interests such as farmers, distillers, and marketers who profit from the production of corn, ethanol, and gasohol. The American federal government has recently reaffirmed its commitment to the use of ethanol as a vehicle to maintain farm incomes for what, one suspects, may be primarily political reasons (*New York Times* October 4 and 7, 2019).

OTHER COUNTRIES AND ISSUES

The only country where ethanol-based automotive fuel is being widely used and appears to have a positive net energy balance is Brazil, which uses sugar cane as a feedstock. A systems analysis would suggest, however, that there are notable externalities associated with its production in Brazil, including rampant forest destruction in the Amazon with the loss of biodiversity and other forest ecosystem services, degradation or loss of soils, water contamination or depletion, and lower levels of food security for indigenous tribes and other Brazilians (Goldemberg et al. 2008; *Guardian* August 17, 2007 and July 3, 2019).

There are several broader issues to be addressed in the production of ethanol fuels: (1) the question of net GHG production, and (2) the system-wide impacts on the agricultural sector, both domestic and foreign. Because there is usually no net energy output, there is rarely a net reduction in GHG production (*New York Times* September 14, 2011). Even if there is some net reduction in GHG emissions from the ethanol production process per se, there is another issue—more GHGs are being produced by the net conversion of forests and grasslands for the production of ethanol-producing crops (Searchinger et al. 2008; Searchinger and Heimlich 2015) (see Table 9.9). Using a worldwide agricultural model to estimate emissions from land-use change, the authors found that corn-based ethanol, instead of producing a 20 percent saving, nearly doubles GHG emissions over 30 years and increases GHGs for 167 years. Fargione et al. (2008) refer to a "biofuel carbon debt" where rainforests, peatlands, savannahs, and grasslands are converted to biofuel production leading to the release of 17 to 420 times more CO_2 than the annual GHG reductions that biofuels provide through the displacement of fossil fuels.

With respect to system-wide impacts on other components of the agricultural sector, crops grown for ethanol production are replacing food crops, thereby limiting their supply and driving up food prices domestically and internationally (Mitchell 2008). This can also have a significant impact on consumer prices for commodities using corn as a component (Figure 9.11). Corn is a major component of numerous products, especially the food we eat—both directly as an additive, and indirectly as a major feed source for livestock (see tables 9.10 and 9.11). Rosegrant and Msangi (2014) ascribe the reduction in the availability of calories and increase in malnutrition in developing countries to the negative effects of food price increases there. In many such countries, the effects can be devastating: for example, the average Mexican relies on tortillas made of corn to provide 40 percent of their protein. The increase in corn prices has created a major problem in that country (*New York Times* January 19, 2007).

Table 9.9 Systems analysis of ethanol with land-use changes

Fuel	Making feedstock	Refining fuel	Vehicle operation (burning fuel)	Net land-use effects			
				Feedstock carbon uptake from atmosphere	Land-use change	Total GHGs	Change in net GHGs versus gasoline (%)
Gasoline	4	15	72	0	0	92	
						74	−20
Corn ethanol	24	40	71	−62		Without feedstock credit	Without feedstock credit
Corn ethanol plus land-use change	24	40	71	−62	104	177	93
Biomass ethanol	10	9	71	−62		27	−70
Biomass ethanol plus land-use change	10	9	71	−62	111	138	50

Source: Searchinger et al. 2008. Reproduced with permission.

Note: Units are grams of GHG CO_2 equivalent per megajoule of energy in fuel.

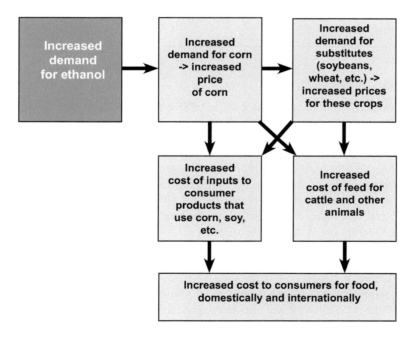

Figure 9.11 Effects of ethanol production.

Table 9.10 Nonfood products that use corn

Adhesives (glues, pastes, mucilages, gums, etc.)	Ink for stamping prices in stores
Aluminum	Insecticides
Antibiotics (penicillin)	Insulation, fiberglass
Asbestos insulation	Latex paint
Aspirin	Leather tanning
Automobiles (everything on wheels)	Livestock feed
Batteries, dry cell	Paper board, (corrugating, laminating, cardboard)
Calcium magnesium acetate	Paper manufacturing
Coatings on wood, paper, and metal	Paper plates and cups
Color carrier in paper, textiles, printing	Pharmaceuticals
Cosmetics	Powders
Cough syrups	Rugs, carpets
Crayons and chalk	Shaving cream and lotions
Cylinder heads	Shoe polish
Degradable plastics	Soaps and cleaners
Dessert powders	Spark plugs
Dextrose (intravenous solutions, icing sugar)	Stamps
Disposable diapers	Starch and glucose
Dyes	Starched clothing
Envelopes	Synthetic rubber finishes
Ethanol—fuel and windshield washer fluid	Talcums
Ethyl and butyl alcohol	Textiles
Explosives, firecrackers	Tires
Finished leather	Toothpaste
Fuel ethanol	Wallpaper
Gypsum wallboard	

Palm oil: A case study in systems theory

Among all the world's vegetable oils, palm oil has the highest levels of production and consumption (USDA 2019). Because of its relatively low cost and physicochemical properties (Tan and Nedhi 2012; *Guardian* December 17, 2014), it is used in a vast array of products including processed food, cosmetics, soap and shampoos, lubricants, paints, and pesticides (Martin 2012). Since 2009, palm oil has found a major use as biodiesel fuel after the European Union established a minimum target of 10 percent for renewable energy consumed by the transport sector (USDA 2018). Palm oil was perceived as being carbon neutral, and hence was classified as a renewable fuel and adopted. European Union subsidies also supported the uptake of palm oil, as did the oil's ability to provide the highest level of energy intensity among all vegetable oils when combusted (*New York Times* January 31, 2007).

The world's largest producers are Indonesia and Malaysia, representing 58 percent and 26 percent respectively of a global market of 73 million metric tons (MT) worth $23.2 billion in 2019 (USDA 2019; see also Harvard Atlas of Economic Complexity and WTEx for related data). Indonesia's exports of palm oil began to rise rapidly in the mid to late 1990s and were the country's largest export in 2016, representing 7.8 percent of total export earnings. In 2017, this percentage had jumped to 9.6 percent, second only to the export of coal briquettes at 10 percent (OEC accessed 2019). The International Union

Table 9.11 Foods containing corn

Alcohol	Gelatin desserts
Ale	Graham crackers
Baby food	Gravies
Bacon	Gum
Baking mixes	Hominy grits
Baking powders	Ice cream
Batters for frying	Infant formula
Beer	Instant coffee and tea
Beverages (sweetened)	Jams, jellies, and preserves
Bleached white flour	Licorice
Breads and pastries	Malted products
Breakfast cereals	Margarine
Cakes	Mayonnaise
Candies	Meats (bologna, sausage)
Canned vegetables	Mustard, prepared
Carbonated beverages	Oleo margarine
Catsup/ketchup	Peanut butter
Cheese spreads	Popcorn
Chewing gum	Potato chips
Chocolate products	Powdered sugar
Cookies	Preserves
Corn chips	Puddings
Corn flakes	Salad dressings
Corn meal	Soft drinks
Cream pies	Soups
Edible oil	Soybean milks
Flour and grits	Syrups
Fritos	Tacos
Frostings	Tortillas
Frozen foods	Vinegar, distilled
Fructose	Vitamins
Fruit (canned)	Wheat bread
Fruit drinks	Whiskey
Gelatin capsules	Wine

Source: Institute for Responsible Technology 2017

for Conservation of Nature (IUCN) (Meijaard et al. 2018) estimated the total area of palm oil plantations (industrial scale and smallholders) at 25 million hectares (ha), equivalent to the area of the United Kingdom (*Guardian* June 26, 2018).

Much of the Indonesian and Malaysian palm oil production comes from large monoculture estates ranging up to 729 km^2 in size (Clay 2004). These vast plantations have been created through the massive logging and burning of forests, particularly in Indonesia. This has entailed significant environmental effects ranging from habitat destruction, biodiversity loss, and soil erosion, to pollution of water sources—surface, drinking and groundwater—loss of ecosystem function and degradation of downstream environments (Danielsen et al. 2009; Strona et al. 2018; Clay 2004; Nellemann et al. 2007; IPBES 2019). Perhaps the most important impact, however, has been the massive release of carbon dioxide from forest removal. The majority of the forested land deemed most desirable for palm oil production lies over vast peat bogs, which are among the largest reservoirs of global stored carbon, holding twelve times as much carbon as other rainforests (Greenpeace 2007). As a consequence, when they are disturbed or burned along with their forest cover, the resulting release of GHGs makes a significant contribution to total world emissions. The IUCN (2021) estimated that the forest and peatland fires in Indonesia in 2015 released more CO_2 than the entire United States that year.

An earlier study by Page et al. (2002, p. 61), focusing on emissions during 1997, estimated that widespread fires throughout the peatlands of Indonesia produced emissions "equivalent to 13–40% of the mean annual global carbon emissions from fossil fuels, and contributed greatly to the largest annual increase in atmospheric CO_2 concentration detected since records began in 1957." In addition to the massive contribution to global atmospheric carbon dioxide, one study estimated that the resulting haze, which blanketed Southeast Asia, in one year alone contributed to the deaths of more than one hundred thousand people (Koplitz et al. 2016). Accompanying mortality effects from a large-scale release of particulates from massive forest fires in Southeast Asia are other numerous effects on food production, tourism, and nonfatal health impacts such as reduced–activity days and respiratory-related disorders with or without hospitalization (*Guardian* October 26, 2015; Harrison et al. 2009; *New York Times* September 20, 2016). Until recently, these unconventional sources of GHGs had not been factored into estimates of global total releases. A subsequent recalculation found that Indonesia was the third largest producer of GHGs after China and the United States (*Independent* October 26, 2009).

The ironic and unfortunate consequence of the massive development of palm oil plantations for the production of biodiesel is the misplaced assumption that this fuel is carbon neutral. After factoring in the carbon dioxide produced by the loss of forest cover due to logging and burning as well as the combustion of peat bogs, the nominal benefit of using this fuel totally disappears. In a major systems-based analysis of total carbon released during the palm oil production and use cycle, Danielsen et al. (2009, p. 348) conclude that

> it would take between 75 and 93 years for the carbon emissions saved through use of biofuel to compensate for the carbon lost through forest conversion, depending on how the forest was cleared. If the original habitat was peatland, carbon balance would take more than 600 years.

In other words, the production of palm oil as currently practiced is completely counterproductive from a global warming perspective as it makes the GHG situation much worse than before.

Once the contribution of palm oil production to global warming was realized, the EU decided to amend its original mandate. However, the new policy will not be fully implemented until 2030 at the earliest (Oxfam 2018; Deutsche Welle 2018). As with any industry with vested interests and large sums of money at stake, it is extremely difficult to alter established patterns of ownership and investment (Lustgarten 2018). The production of this commodity has become so valuable that a large illegal sector has emerged in company with the legal sector (FOEE 2013). With increasing negative feedback from nongovernmental organizations (NGOs) and civil society actors, the industry established the Roundtable on Sustainable Palm Oil (RSPO) in 2004 to promote "the growth and use of sustainable oil palm products through credible global standards and engagement of stakeholders" (RSPO website, rspo.org). Unfortunately, several organizations and reports have raised serious questions about whether the RSPO will alter the situation appreciably (Danielsen et al. 2009; Greenpeace 2007; Strona et al. 2018; Martin 2012; Nellemann et al. 2007; FOEE 2010 and 2013; Carlson et al. 2018). In an attempt to address some of these issues, the United Nations Environment Programme (UNEP) signed an agreement with the RSPO to promote sustainable practices within the industry (UNEP 2014). Illustrative of the difficulty of enforcing sustainable practices in palm oil, however, it has been recently revealed that a Korean company has been systematically burning forests in order to create palm oil plantations (BBC November 12, 2020). As a consequence of an investigation by the BBC, the company has been rejected by the Forest Stewardship Council, the world's leading green certification body (BBC July 15, 2021). Nelson et al. (2014) in their study of deforestation in Papua New Guinea concluded that "most of the developers are clearing forest with no intention of cultivating palm oil, and that a large-scale land grab is therefore occurring in Papua New Guinea under the guise of oil palm development," p. 188.

Approximately 5–10 percent of palm oil is devoted to energy use (Rainforest Rescue n.d.; Palm Oil Investigations n.d.). Even if palm oil is phased out as a source of biodiesel (see, for example, NNFCC 2019) its use in a myriad other products is forecast to increase over the next decade (OECD–FAO 2018; IndexBox 2019). The recent emergence of this new and previously unrecognized contribution to climate change represents, at its simplest, the absence of a meaningful systems analysis to capture all relevant costs and benefits of new products and technologies.

It is ironic that the IUCN has given begrudging approval to the continued production of palm oil, despite its profoundly negative effect on biodiversity in general, and wildlife in particular, as long as the industry makes a concerted effort to increase its level of sustainability (IUCN 2018; see also Rochmyaningsih 2019). It has reached this painful conclusion after assessing the greater potential environmental impact of alternative oil crops. It is a sad commentary on the complex and difficult choices the world faces in trying to reverse the slide to greater unsustainability when a leading agency for the preservation of biodiversity is reconciled to the continued production of an ecologically disastrous crop because it is perceived to be the least bad of a broad range of alternatives.

Other possible technological innovations

Several innovative technologies for generating electricity, such as wave power and tidal power, have also been the object of research. While wave power is still in experimental stages (US EIA n.d. a), tidal has reached a more advanced stage of research and application (CNBC April 22, 2021; US EIA n.d. b) with operating plants in South Korea (254 MW), La Rance Estuary in France (240 MW), Nova Scotia, Canada (20 MW), and smaller plants in China and Russia.

Perhaps the most promising innovation, however, is hydrogen, which has been touted for many years as a major vehicle for fighting climate change by replacing other fossil fuels in a multitude of uses (*New York Times* November 11 and December 28, 2020; Fairley 2020). In at least one respect hydrogen is an ideal fuel. When it is burned (i.e., rapidly oxidized), the only product is water. The major issue is that hydrogen is a secondary fuel and relies on other energy sources to produce it. It can be extracted from natural gas and other fossil fuels by reforming, and this is the principal source of the fuel (CTV August 28, 2021). Alternatively, it can be extracted from water through an energy-intensive process of electrolysis, which splits the water molecule into its two components: oxygen and hydrogen. Recent research advances have held out the promise of other possible sources as well as significantly lower costs of electrolysis for hydrogen generation, opening up a potentially vast market for the gas (Hauch et al. 2020; Tong et al. 2020; *Science* March 10, 2020 and March 10, 2020; Xu 2020). Despite these potential technological breakthroughs, a sustainable solution would require the use of renewable energy for electrolysis, as the process of producing hydrogen from natural gas creates more GHG emissions than the burning of natural gas by itself (Howarth and Jacobson 2021). An economy-wide transformation to the use of hydrogen would still require major changes to infrastructure to facilitate hydrogen's storage, transport, and use (Fairley 2020). Some concern has been raised that using hydrogen fuels could lock in reliance on fossil fuels (Ueckerdt et al. 2021) since it is

> unlikely that e-fuels [i.e. electrofuels, powerfuels, or electricity-based synthetic fuels, which are hydrocarbon fuels synthesized from hydrogen and CO_2] will become cheap and abundant early enough. Neglecting demand-side transformations threatens to lock in a fossil fuel dependency if e-fuels fall short of expectations,
>
> (p.1)

In the same study, the authors note that using electricity to power automobiles and heat houses would be more energy efficient.

Considering lower-tech solutions, scientists at Purdue University have developed an ultra-white paint which reflects 98 percent of sunlight (BBC April 16, 2021). This is a marked improvement over many current paints which reflect between 80–90 percent of sunlight. Several states, such as New York and California, have already implemented policies to use ultra-white paint to address climate issues. Professor Xiulin Ruan of Purdue has stated that "if you were to use our paint to cover a roof area of about 1,000 sq ft (93 sq m), we estimate you could get a cooling power of 10 kilowatts. That's more powerful than the central air conditioners used by most houses."

Summary

Clearly, the hope of stabilizing global temperatures ultimately rests on phasing out carbon-based fuels and replacing them with a range of non-carbon-based alternatives, principally renewable energy sources. This is the main message of a major new report by the IEA (2021e) entitled *Net Zero by 2050: A Roadmap for the Global Energy Sector*. While such a transformation in the developed world may ultimately be a political decision, the challenge facing the developing world is one of available capital. There is a clear need for changes to the international aid policies of the developed world, as well as changes to the incentive structure in global capital markets (IEA 2021e), but the IEA feels that action on emissions in emerging and developing economies is very cost effective.

In their recent work (*Empowering the Great Energy Transition*), Valentine et al. (2019, p. 4) identify ten forces favoring the further development of renewables: (1) growing evidence of declining fossil fuel stocks and rising prices, (2) capricious fluctuation patterns of fossil fuel prices, (3) the strategic need to diversify, (4) political instability and conflict due to fossil fuels, (5) improved understanding of the health and environmental costs of fossil fuels, (6) sobering evidence of climate change impacts, (7) the contested politics of nuclear power, (8) innovations in performance and cost within the renewable energy sector, (9) the rise of government and market support for renewable energy, and (10) first-mover advantages amid a new energy boom.

Having identified factors conducive to the transition to renewable energy sources, Valentine et al. raise the pertinent question of why progress is not faster in this direction. In this regard, they describe at least six interrelated challenges that still remain (p. 35): (1) scientific uncertainty regarding climate change impacts, (2) resistance from powerful entrenched interests, (3) difficulties in fostering and financing a transition, (4) difficulties in reshaping market dynamics with the right policy mix, (5) consumer apathy, and (6) failure in politics and governance. The bulk of their book is devoted to resolving and/or removing each of these impediments. Additional concerns about the process of transition have been raised by other authors: specifically, the currently existing massive natural gas infrastructure already in place (Webber 2021), as well as the small percentage of global utilities prioritizing renewable energy in their investment decisions (Alova 2020).

Several recent reports present a very optimistic assessment of the continued growth of the renewable energy sector. MarketWatch (2021) forecasts a growth in this market from approximately $1.49 billion in 2017 to an expected $2.15 billion by 2025. A similar upbeat assessment has been presented by the IEA (2020a), which notes in particular the resilience of the sector to the COVID-19 pandemic. Among their main conclusions are: (1) the resilience of renewables is driven by the electricity sector, (2) renewable power additions have defied COVID-19 to set a new record, (3) Europe and India will lead a renewables surge in 2021, (4) increasing policy certainty in key markets could significantly boost renewables deployment, (5) renewables are set to lead the global electricity sector, and (6) recent policy momentum has the potential to give renewable energy use an extra boost. A follow-up report by the IEA on world energy investment (2021g, p. 9) echoes many of these conclusions but adds the observation that "clean energy investment is on a moderate upswing, but remains far short of what is required to avoid severe impacts from climate change."

Even if renewables assume a dominant position in energy combustion, there remains the issue of petrochemicals and the significant energy use and environmental effects associated with their production (CIEL 2019a and b). The fossil fuel industry is a major player in the production of plastics and the output of this product is expected to continue to grow over the next few decades (CIEL n.d. a and b). Plastics have become a central part of modern manufacturing and are ubiquitous, yet they pose a major environmental threat to planetary ecosystems. Recent research, however, has raised the prospect of using both wind and solar energy to produce plastics and fertilizers, eliminating many of the current environmental effects associated with the petrochemical industry (*Science* May 8, 2020).

A successful transition to the wide-scale adoption of renewable energy could be facilitated by the removal of subsidies to fossil fuels to level the playing field, changes in attitudes among the investment community (discussed in Chapter 10), and the promise of numerous new employment opportunities. This last factor can play an important role in shaping public attitudes towards renewables since there is mounting concern that a shift away from fossil fuels will result in significant job losses throughout the supply chain. Fortunately, this concern is largely misplaced as the US renewable sector is reported to have as many as ten times more jobs than the fossil fuel industry (*New Scientist* October 15, 2019; see also McKinsey 2020a). This phenomenon is replicated in Canada (CBC December 2, 2014; Clean Energy Canada 2019). At the global scale, IRENA (2021c) reports that employment in renewable energy was estimated at twelve million in 2020 and it is expected that this number will continue to grow. A recent study (Pai et al. 2021) estimates that by 2050 around 84 percent of all energy jobs could be in solar and wind manufacturing and generation. To underline the relative attractiveness of these jobs, the US Bureau of Labor Statistics (US BLS 2019a, b, and c) has reported that the fastest growing occupations expected over the period 2018–28 are solar PV installers and wind turbine service technicians, with growth rates of 63 percent and 57 percent respectively. The former had a median pay in 2019 of $44,890 per year, the latter $52,910 per year. Clearly, the expected shift in employment out of the fossil fuel industry requires time and retraining for new occupations. It is noteworthy that President Biden's budget proposal of April 2021 contains the sum of $100 billion for workforce training programs (Bloomberg Law April 1, 2021). In Canada, renewable energy and retrofits have been proposed as job-creating alternatives to the challenges facing the domestic oil sector (CBC April 20, 2020).

One signal of the shift away from fossil fuels to renewables has been the recent difficulty faced by the coal industry with plummeting stock values and increased bankruptcies. However, despite the fact that financing costs for coal mining have increased dramatically (Zhou et al. 2021), coal demand has rebounded strongly in 2021 driven by the power sector, principally in China (IEA 2021a and b). As of 2020, China consumed 51.7 percent of the world's coal, followed by India at 11.8 percent, and the United States at 7.2 percent (BP 2020).

It would not be an overstatement to say that shifting China's reliance on coal power would be a major step in helping to control global GHG emissions. This will be no easy task as the country is experiencing increased urbanization with higher energy use per capita, a major concern with economic and social stability based on the ability to meet the increasing expectations of its population of a better standard of living, and a historical challenge of aligning the goals of China's disparate regions with those of the central government in Beijing (*New York Times* March 16, 2021). On an optimist note, one recent report has suggested that China could save upwards of $1.6 trillion by closing six hundred coal-fired plants (TransitionZero 2021, p. 12), finding that:

> independent of climate, water and air issues, the vast majority of China's coal fleet could be shut and replaced at a saving. We come to this conclusion by comparing the cost to replace the power generated from the coal plants with the lowest cost zero carbon alternative. The calculation is based on the value adjusted levelised cost of electricity (VALCOE) of either wind or solar, minus the long run marginal cost (LRMC) of coal over a 20-year period. The lowest cost clean energy alternatives in China are currently wind and solar, which are variable energy generation sources. To compensate for the variability of wind and solar we adjust the levelised cost based on the value it adds to the grid. VALCOE is a concept developed by the International Energy Agency (IEA) and aims to incorporate grid flexibility and capacity. Due to the intrinsically deflationary nature of wind and solar, we found replacing the coal fleet with clean energy could save China $1.6 trillion or cost negative $20/tCO$_2$.

The announcement by China's President Xi Jinping in September 2020 that the country is committed to cutting its net carbon emissions to zero by 2060 (*Science* September 29, 2020) appears to be extraordinarily ambitious but at least indicates that China may have decided that decisive action is required. The determination to address the problem of coal power was reaffirmed by President Xi at President Biden's international virtual climate summit in April 2021 (*South China Morning Post* April 22, 2021), although China is continuing to build coal-fired power plants (Standaert 2021).

The IEA issued a "dire warning" (IEA 2021b) about the trend to increased production of coal-fired electricity as reported in its 2021 *Global Energy Review* (2021a). To quote the press release with the report:

> "economic recovery from the Covid crisis is currently anything but sustainable for our climate," said Fatih Birol, the IEA Executive Director. "Unless governments around the world move rapidly to start cutting emissions, we are likely to face an even worse situation in 2022 … The expected rise in coal use dwarfs that of renewables by almost 60%, despite accelerating demand for renewables."
>
> (IEA2021b)

If Smil's (2010, 2014) observation still holds true that major energy transformations have historically taken fifty to sixty years, this reinforces the perception that emissions from fossil fuels will continue for some time, even at lower rates of use. Unfortunately, fifty to sixty years may be too long to forestall even more dramatic shifts in global climate.

On a more positive note, a recent report from Carbon Tracker (2021b) has identified a process of energy "leapfrogging" where "emerging markets are about to leapfrog fossil fuels to generate all the growth in their electricity supply from renewables" (p. 1). To quote:

> **The emerging markets are key to the global transition**. 88 percent of the growth in electricity demand between 2019 and 2040 is expected to come from the emerging markets. If they do not leapfrog to renewables, there will be no global energy transition.
>
> **Leapfrog means growth**. While a total transition is hard, the leapfrog is more achievable because it requires emerging markets to generate the increase in their domestic demand from renewable electricity, improving energy security.
>
> **There are four key groups of emerging markets.** These are: China, which is nearly half the electricity demand, and 39 percent of the expected growth; other importers of coal and gas such as India or Vietnam, which are a third of the demand and nearly half the growth; coal and gas exporters such as Russia or Indonesia, which are 16 percent of demand but only around 10 percent of the growth; and 'fragile' states such as Nigeria or Iraq which are 3 percent of demand and around the same share of growth.
>
> **Many countries have already leapfrogged**. Developed market demand for fossil fuels for electricity generation peaked in 2007, and is down 20 percent since then; 99 percent of developed markets have already seen a peak. Meanwhile, South African fossil fuel demand for electricity peaked in 2007, Chile in 2013, Thailand in 2015, Turkey in 2017. India's double leapfrog—connecting nearly all households to electricity and its renewable energy rollout—is one of the most revolutionary in scale. While its fossil fuel demand for electricity has plateaued for now, it could rise again as the economy recovers unless energy storage prices fall rapidly. (p. 1)

At least three additional reports present an optimistic assessment of the future of renewables: it has been reported (*Guardian* September 1, 2021) that OPEC has urged its member states to focus more on renewable energy; over the past three years, "all of the Clean Energy Leaders experienced growth in their market capitalization, whereas the Oil Majors all declined" (Clean Edge 2021); and the Asian Development Bank announced at the COP26 Conference in Glasgow in November 2021 a fund to help retire coal plants in Asia and replace them with solar and wind power installations (*Science* November 2, 2021). Finally, some of the key factors influencing the current and future energy transition are explored further in Chapter 10 of this book.

References

Ackermann, William C. et al. (1973) *Man-Made Lakes: Their Problems and Environmental Effects*, American Geophysical Union.

Alberici, Sacha et al. (2014) *Subsides and Costs of EU Energy: An Interim Report*, European Commission.

Alova, Galina (2020) *Nature Energy*, "A global analysis of the progress and failure of electric utilities to adapt their portfolios of power-generation assets to the energy transition," August 31.

Ansar, Atif et al. (2014) *Energy Policy*, "Should we build more large dams? The actual costs of hydropower megaproject development," January.

Associated Press (2021) "Wyoming backs coal with $1.2M threat to sue other states," May 2.

Barthelmie, R.J. and S.C. Pryor (2014) *Nature Climate Change*, "Potential contribution of wind energy to climate change mitigation," June 8.

BBC (2019) "Clean energy overtaking fossil fuels in Britain," June 21.

BBC (2020) "The burning scar: Inside the destruction of Asia's last rainforests, November 12.

BBC (2021) "Denmark to build 'first energy island' in North Sea," February 4.

BBC (2021) "Britain's electricity system 'greenest ever' over Easter," April 7.

BBC (2021) "'Whitest ever' paint reflects 98% of sunlight," April 16.

BBC (2021) "Climate change: Growing doubts over chip fat biofuel," April 21.

BBC (2021) "Korindo: Korean palm oil giant stripped of sustainability status," July 15.

Bertassoli, Dailson J. et al. (2021) *Science Advances*, "How green can Amazon hydropower be? Net carbon emission from the largest hydropower pant in Amazonia," June 25.

Biello, David (2014) "Solar wars," *Scientific American*, November.

Bitov, Kelly and Mary S. Booth (2014) *Climate of Deception: Why Electricity Consumers Who Care about Global Warming and Air Pollution Need FTC Protection from Biomass Industry Greenwashing*, Partnership for Policy Integrity.

Bloomberg Green (2020) "Solar and wind cheapest sources of power in most of the world," April 28.

Bloomberg Law (2021) "Biden targets $100 billion in plan to aid downturn-hit workers," April 1.

Booth, Mary S. (2014) *Trees, Trash and Toxics: How Biomass Energy Has Become the New Coal*, Partnership for Policy Integrity, April 2.

BP (British Petroleum) (2020) *Statistical Review of World Energy 2020*, June.

Buonocore, Jonathan J. et al. (2021) *Environmental Research Letters*, "A decade of the U.S. energy mix transitioning away from coal: Historical reconstruction of the reductions in the public health burden of energy," May 5.

Butti, Ken and John Perlin (1980) *A Golden Thread: 2500 Years of Solar Architecture and Technology*, Palo Alto, CA; New York: Cheshire Books.

Carbon Tracker (2019) *The Trillion Dollar Energy Windfall*, September.

Carbon Tracker (2021a) *The Sky's the Limit: Solar and Wind Energy Potential is 100 Times As Much As Global Energy Demand*, April.

Carbon Tracker (2021b) *Reach for the Sun: The Emerging Market Electricity Leapfrog*, July.

Carlson, Kimberly et al. (2018) *PNAS*, "Effect of oil palm sustainability certification on deforestation and fire in Indonesia," January 2.

CBC (2014) "Clean energy provides more jobs than oilsands, report says," December 2.

CBC (2020) "Renewable energy, retrofits touted as job-creating alternative to oil sector devastation," April 20.

China National Bureau of Statistics (2020, multiple years) *China Statistical Yearbook*.

Cho, Renee (2011, updated 2016) "Is biomass really renewable? State of the planet," Earth Institute, Columbia University, October 19.

CIEL (Center for International Environmental Law) (2019a) *Plastic & Health: The Hidden Costs of a Plastic Planet*, February.

CIEL (Center for International Environmental Law) (2019b) *Plastic & Climate: The Hidden Costs of a Plastic Planet*, May.

CIEL (Center for International Environmental Law) (n.d. a) "Fueling plastics: Fossils, plastics, & petrochemical feedstocks."

CIEL (Center for International Environmental Law) (n.d. b) "Fueling plastics: How fracked gas, cheap oil, and unburnable coal are driving the plastics boom."

Clay, Jason (2004) *World Agriculture and the Environment: A Commodity-by-Commodity Guide to Impacts and Practices*, Washington, DC: Island Press.

Clean Edge (2021) "Q3 2021 Review."

Clean Energy Canada (2019) "Missing the bigger picture," May.

CNBC (2021) "'World's most powerful tidal turbine' gears up for operation," April 22.

CNN (2021) "The Southwest's looming water battle," August 21.

CNN (2021) "China and India face a deepening energy crunch," October 12.

Coady, David et al. (2019) "Global fossil fuel subsidies remain large: An update based on country-level estimates." IMF working paper WP/19/89, International Monetary Fund, May 2.

CTV (2021) "Green hydrogen could be the fuel of the future. Here's why it's not yet a silver bullet," August 28.

Cullenward, D. and D.G. Victor (2006) *Climatic Change*, "The dam debate and its discontents," April 25.

Danielsen, Finn et al. (2009) *Conservation Biology*, "Biofuel plantations on forested lands: Double jeopardy for biodiversity and climate," April.

DeCicco, J.M. et al. (2016) *Climatic Change*, "Carbon balance effects of U.S. biofuel production and use," October.

Delucchi, Mark A. and Mark Z. Jacobson (2011) *Energy Policy*, "Providing all global energy with wind, water, and solar power, Part II: Reliability, system and transmission costs, and policies," March.

Deutsche Welle (2018) "Despite EU palm oil ban, biofuel problems will continue," January 23.

Electrek (2019) "Global solar PV market to see 'spectacular growth' over next 5 years," October 21.

Epstein, Paul R. et al. (2011) *Annals of the New York Academy of Sciences*, "Full cost accounting for the life cycle of coal," February.

Ernst & Young Global Ltd (2013) "EY RECAI: Renewable energy country attractiveness index," November.

Ezcurra, E. et al. (2019) *Science Advances*, "A natural experiment reveals the impact of hydroelectric dams on the estuaries of tropical rivers," March 13.

Fairley, Peter (2018) "Building a weather-smart grid," Scientific American, July.

Fairley, Peter (2020) "The H2 solution," *Scientific American*, February.

Fargione, Joseph et al. (2008) *Science Express*, "Land clearing and the biofuel carbon debt," February 7.

Financial Post (2021) "Is Germany making too much renewable energy?" February 10.

FOEE (Friends of the Earth Europe) (2010) *Commodity Crimes: Illicit Land Grabs, Illegal Palm Oil and Endangered Orangutans*.

FOEE (Friends of the Earth Europe) (2013) "Financiers of palm oil must stop deforestation and illegal activity," November 20.

Fthenakis, Vasilis et al. (2009) *Energy Policy*, "The technical, geographical, and economic feasibility for solar energy to supply the energy needs of the US," February.

Giuntoli, Carnia A. et al. (2021) *The Use of Woody Biomass for Energy Production in the EU*, JRC Science for Policy Report, European Commission.

Globe and Mail (2021) "In China, a worsening energy crisis highlights the country's dependence on coal as it tries to transition to green sources," October 11.

Goldemberg, Jose et al. (2008) *Energy Policy*, "The sustainability of ethanol production from sugarcane," 36: 2086–97.

Golden, Sarah (2021) *Energy Weekly*, "What to do about wind turbine blades?" June 10.

Goldsmith, Edward and Nicholas Hildyard (1984) *The Social and Environmental Effects of Large Dams*, San Francisco: Sierra Club Books.

Grafton, R. Quentin et al. (2014) *Energy Policy*, "US biofuels subsidies and CO2 emissions: An empirical test for a weak and strong green paradox," May.

Greenpeace (2007) *How the Palm Oil Industry is Cooking the Climate*, November.

Greenpeace (2011) *Fuelling a BioMess: Why Burning Trees for Energy Will Harm People, the Climate and Forests*.

Grinsven, Anouk van et al. *Transport & Environment* (2021) "Used cooking oil (UCO) as biofuel feedstock in the EU," April.

Guardian (2007) "Biofuels menace rainforests," August 17.

Guardian (2014) "Why does palm oil still dominate the supermarket shelves?" December 17.

Guardian (2015) "Indonesia's fires labelled a 'crime against humanity' as 500,000 suffer," October 26.

Guardian (2018) "Palm oil 'disastrous' for wildlife but here to stay, experts warn," June 26.

Guardian (2019) "Brazil: Huge rise in Amazon destruction under Bolsonaro, figures show," July 3.

Guardian (2020) "Cambodia scraps plans for Mekong hydropower dams," March 20.

Guardian (2021) "Opec member urges oil producers to focus more on renewable energy," September 1.

Hall, Charles A.S. (2017) *Energy Return on Investment*, Cham: Springer.

Hall, Charles A.S. and John W. Day Jr. (2009) "Revisiting the limits to growth after peak oil," *American Scientist*, May–June.

Harrison, Mark E. et al. (2009) *Biologist*, "The global impact of Indonesian forest fires," August.

Harvard (various years) Atlas of Economic Complexity, Growth Lab.

Harvard Medical School, Center for Health and the Global Environment (2005) "Climate change futures. Health, ecological and economic dimensions," sponsored by Swiss Re and the United Nations Development Programme.

Harvard University (n.d.) "What did Malaysia export in 2016," Atlas of Economic Complexity, Growth Lab.

Hauch, A. et al. (2020) *Science,* "Recent advances in solid oxide cell technology for electrolysis," October 9.

Hawaii State Energy Office (2020) *Hawai'i's Energy Facts & Figures*.

Hawaiian Electric (2021) "Our clean energy portfolio."

Hawaiian Electric et al. (2018a) "Electrification of transportation: Strategic roadmap," March.

Hawaiian Electric et al. (2018b) *Sustainability Report*.

Honolulu Star Advertiser (2021) "Public Utilities Commission agrees to modify conditions for Hawaiian Electric's battery storage project," May 14.

Hope, Chris et al. (2015) "Quantifying the implicit climate subsidy received by leading fossil fuel companies." Working paper no. 02/2015, Judge Business School, University of Cambridge.

Howarth, Robert W. and Mark Z. Jacobson (2021) *Energy Science & Engineering*, "How green is blue hydrogen?" July 26.

Hvistendahl, Mara (2008) "China's Three Gorges Dam: An environmental catastrophe?" Scientific American, March 25.

Hydro Review (2007) "World Bank boosts hydro, other renewables funding," October 24.

IEA (International Energy Agency) (2011) *Harnessing Variable Renewables: A Guide to the Balancing Challenge*, Paris.

IEA (International Energy Agency) (2019a) *Offshore Wind Outlook*, October 25.

IEA (International Energy Agency) (2019b) *World Energy Outlook*, November 13.

IEA (International Energy Agency) (2019c) *World Energy Statistics 2019*.

IEA (International Energy Agency) (2019d) *Coal Information 2019*.

IEA (International Energy Agency) (2019e) *Offshore Wind Outlook 2019*.

IEA (International Energy Agency) (2019f) *World Energy Balances 2019*.

IEA (International Energy Agency) (2019g) *Electricity Information 2019*.

IEA (International Energy Agency) (2019h) *Renewables 2019: Analysis and Forecast to 2024*, October.

IEA (International Energy Agency (2020a) *Trends in Photovoltaic Applications 2020*.

IEA (International Energy Agency (2020b) *Hydropower Status Report*.

IEA (International Energy Agency (2020c) *Innovation in Batteries and Electricity Storage*.

IEA (International Energy Agency (2020d) *Renewables 2020: Analysis and Forecast to 2025*.

IEA (International Energy Agency (2021a) *Global Energy Review 2021: Assessing the Effects of Economic Recoveries on Global Energy Demand and CO2 Emissions*.

IEA (International Energy Agency) (2021b) "Global carbon dioxide emissions are set for their second-biggest increase in history," press release, April 20.

IEA (International Energy Agency (2021c) *The Role of Critical Minerals in Clean Energy Transitions*.

IEA (International Energy Agency (2021d) *Financing Clean Energy Transitions in Emerging and Developing Economies*.

IEA (International Energy Agency (2021e) *Net Zero by 2050: A Roadmap for the Global Energy Sector*.

IEA (International Energy Agency (2021f) *Renewable Energy Market Update 2021: Outlook for 2021 and 2022; Fuel Report*, May.

IEA (International Energy Agency) (2021g) *World Energy Investment 2021*.

IEA (International Energy Agency) (2021h) "Executive summary" in *Renewables*.

IEA (International Energy Agency) (n.d.) (accessed October 18, 2019) "System integration of renewables."

IHA (International Hydropower Association) (2018) *Hydropower Status Report: Sector Trends and Insights*.

IHA (International Hydropower Association) (2019) "Pumped storage hydropower."

IHA (International Hydropower Association) (2020) "Let's get flexible: Pumped storage and the future of power systems," September 9.

IHA (International Hydropower Association) (2021) *Hydropower Status Report: Sector Trends and Insights*.

IMF (International Monetary Fund) (2013) *Energy Subsidy Reform: Lessons and Implications*, January 28.

Independent (2009) "Illegal logging responsible for loss of 10 million hectares in Indonesia," October 26.

IndexBox (2019) *World Palm Oil Market Analysis 2019*.

Institute for Responsible Technology (2017) "Corn products and derivatives list," June 6.

International Forest Industries (2021) "The forecasted growth in wood pellet production in Europe will increase competition for wood fiber & require new feedstock sources," April 14.

IPBES (Intergovernmental Science-Policy Platform on Biodiversity and Ecosystem Services) (2019) *Global Assessment Report on Biodiversity and Ecosystem Services of the IPBES: Summary for Policymakers*.

IRENA (International Renewable Energy Agency) (2016) *The Power to Change: Solar and Wind Cost Reduction Potential to 2025*, June.

IRENA (International Renewable Energy Agency) (2017) *Electricity Storage and Renewables: Costs and Markets to 2030*, October.

IRENA (International Renewable Energy Agency) (2019a) *Renewable Energy Statistics*.

IRENA (International Renewable Energy Agency) (2019b) *Renewable Power Generation Costs in 2018*.

IRENA (International Renewable Energy Agency) (2020a) *Power Generation Costs 2019*.

IRENA (International Renewable Energy Agency) (2020b) *Renewable Energy Statistics 2020*.

IRENA (International Renewable Energy Agency) (2021a) "World adds record new renewable energy capacity in 2020," press release, April 5.

IRENA (International Renewable Energy Agency) (2021b) *Renewable Power Generation Costs in 2020*.

IRENA (International Renewable Energy Agency) (2021c) *Renewable Energy and Jobs Annual Review 2020*.

IRENA (International Renewable Energy Agency) (2021d) "Renewable power generation costs in 2020," infographic.

IRN (International Rivers Network) (2006) *Fizzy Science: Loosening the Hydro Industry's Grip on Reservoir Greenhouse Gas Emissions Research*, November.

IUCN (International Union for Conservation of Nature) (2018) "Palm oil and biodiversity," Issues Brief, June.

IUCN (International Union for Conservation of Nature) (2021) "Peatlands and climate change," November.

Jaccard, Mark (2020) *The Citizen's Guide to Climate Success: Overcoming Myths that Hinder Progress*, New York: Cambridge University Press.

Jacobson, Mark Z. and Mark A. Delucchi (2009) "A path to sustainable energy by 2030," *Scientific American*, November.

Jansen, Malte et al. (2020) *Nature Energy*, "Offshore wind competitiveness in mature markets without subsidy," August.

Jeong, Mingyu et al. (2020) *Science*, "Stable perovskite solar cells with efficiency exceeding 24.8% and 0.3-V voltage loss," September 26.

Juarez-Perez, Emilio J. and Marta Haro (2020) *Science*, "Perovskite solar cells take a step forward," June 19.

Kao, Shih-Chieh et al. (2015) *Energy*, "Projecting changes in annual hydropower generation using regional runoff data: An assessment of the United States federal hydropower plants," February.

Kauai Island Utility Cooperative (n.d.) (accessed October 2019) "Renewables."

Kim, Gwisu et al. (2020) *Science*, "Impact of strain relaxation on performance of alpha-formamidinium lead iodide perovskite solar cells," October 2.

Kohler, Malte et al. (2021) *Nature Energy*, "A silicon carbide-based highly transparent passivating contact for crystalline silicon solar cells approaching efficiencies of 24%" April 15.

Koplitz, Shannon N. et al. (2016) *Environmental Research Letters*, "Public health impacts of the severe haze in Equatorial Asia in September–October 2015. Demonstration of a new framework for informing fire management strategies to reduce downwind smoke exposure," September 19.

Koplow, Doug and John Dernbach (2001) *Annual Review of Energy and the Environment*, "Fossil fuel subsidies and greenhouse gas emissions: A case study of increasing transparency for fiscal policy," November.

Koplow, Douglas (2011) *Nuclear Power: Still Not Viable without Subsidies*, Union of Concerned Scientists, Cambridge, MA, February.

Lazard (2020) *Lazard's Levelized Cost of Energy Analysis: Version 14.0*, October.

Life by Numbers (n.d.) "Capacity and capacity factor of wind energy."

Lustgarten, Abrahm (2018) "Palm oil was supposed to help save the planet. Instead it unleashed a catastrophe," *New York Times*, November 20.

Manhattan Institute for Policy Research (2015) *The Hidden Corn Ethanol Tax*, March.

MarketWatch (2021) "Renewable energy market size research report growth forecast 2025," press release, March 25.

Martin, Ben (2012) *Ecologist*, "Palm oil: The hidden ingredient causing an ecological disaster," March 14.

Maui Electric (n.d.) (accessed October 2019) "Empowering you. A more resilient grid."

Maui News (2020) "Two solar power, battery storage projects are submitted to PUC," September 17.

Maui News (2021) "New program will speed up rooftop solar projects," January 21.

Maui News (2021) "Hawaii options for green energy abound," June 26.

Maui News (2021) "State drives effort toward electric," June 27.

Maui News (2021a) "Pulehu Solar project moves forward," July 28.

Maui News (2021b) "Feedback sought on Molokai shared solar program," July 28.

Maui News (2021) "Larger homes would be net-zero under new bill," August 17.

Maui News (2021) "State's largest solar project gets green light," November 12.

McKinsey (2019) *Global Energy Perspective 2019: Reference Case*, January.

McKinsey (2020a) "How a post-pandemic stimulus can both create jobs and help the climate," May 27.

McKinsey (2020b) "Orsted's renewable-energy transformation," July 10.

Meijaard, E. et al. (2018) *Oil Palm and Biodiversity: A Situation Analysis by the IUCN Oil Palm Task Force.*

Miskin, Caleb K. et al. (2019) *Nature Sustainability*, "Sustainable co-production of food and solar power to relax land-use constraints," October.

Mitchell, Donald (2008) "A note on rising food prices." Policy Research Working Paper 4682, World Bank, July.

Murphy, David J. et al. (2011) *Environment, Development and Sustainability*, "New perspectives on the energy return on (energy) investment (EROI) of corn ethanol," February.

NAS (National Academy of Sciences) (2009) *Hidden Costs of Energy: Unpriced Consequences of Energy Production and Use.*

Natural Resources Canada (2016) "Forest bioenergy," February 4.

Needham, Joseph (1994) *The Shorter Science and Civilization in China.* An abridgment of Joseph Needham's original text by Colin A. Ronan, Cambridge, UK: Cambridge University Press.

Nellemann, Christian et al. (2007) *The Last Stand of the Orangutan*, United Nations Environment Programme.

Nelson, Paul N. et al. (2014) *Conservation Letters*, "Oil palm and deforestation in Papua New Guinea," May/June.

New Scientist (2011) "Wind and wave farms could affect Earth's energy balance," March 30.

New Scientist (2019) "US green economy has 10 times more jobs than the fossil fuel industry," October 15.

New York Times (2007) "Cost of corn soars, forcing Mexico to set price limits," January 19.

New York Times (2007) "Once a dream fuel, palm oil may be an eco-nightmare," January 31.

New York Times (2011) "Rush to use crops as fuel raises food prices and hunger fears," April 6.

New York Times (2011) "China admits problems with Three Gorges Dam," May 19.

New York Times (2011) "Serious error found in carbon savings for biofuels," September 14.

New York Times (2014) "Wind industry's new technologies are helping it compete on price," March 20.

New York Times (2014) "Texas is wired for wind power, and more farms plug in," July 23.

New York Times (2015) "E.P.A. rule requires a big jump in biofuel use," November 30.

New York Times (2016) "Blazes in Southeast Asia may have led to deaths of over 100,000, study says," September 20.

New York Times (2016) "Canada's big dams produce clean energy, and high levels of mercury," November 10.

New York Times (2017) "Wind and solar power advance, but carbon refuses to retreat," November 7.

New York Times (2017) "Power prices go negative in Germany, a positive for energy users," December 26.

New York Times (2018) "How windmills as wide as jumbo jets are making clean energy mainstream," April 23.

New York Times (2018) "Tropical forests suffered near-record tree losses in 2017," June 28.

New York Times (2018) "The $3 billion plan to turn Hoover Dam into a giant battery," August 4.

New York Times (2018) "Cheaper battery is unveiled as a step to a carbon-free grid," September 26.

New York Times (2019) "Trump, facing farmers' discontent, plans help for ethanol," October 4.

New York Times (2019) "A Trump policy shift gives farmers in key 2020 states 'exactly what we wanted'," October 7.

New York Times (2020) "Oil companies are collapsing due to coronavirus, but wind and solar energy keep growing," April 7.

New York Times (2020) "Its electric grid under strain, California turns to batteries," September 3.

New York Times (2020) "California is trying to jump-start the hydrogen economy," November 11.

New York Times (2020) "The gospel of hydrogen power," December 28.

New York Times (2021) "A monster wind turbine is upending an industry," January 1.

New York Times (2021) "Wyoming coal country pivots, reluctantly, to wind farms," March 5.

New York Times (2021) "China's climate ambitions collide with its coal addiction," March 16.

New York Times (2021) "Biden administration announces a major offshore wind plan," March 29.

New York Times (2021) "There's a booming business in America's forests. Some aren't happy about it," April 21.

New York Times (2021) "Biden administration approves nation's first major offshore wind farm." May 12.

New York Times (2021) "Biden opens California's coast to wind farms," May 25.

New York Times (2021) "Seattle and Portland aren't built for extreme heat waves," August 13.

New York Times (2021) "The Southwest's most important river is drying up," August 21.

New York Times (2021) "California solar panel mandate for new buildings advances," September 8.

New York Times (2021) "China's power problems expose a strategic weakness," October 13.

New York Times (2021) "Biden administration plans wind farms along nearly the entire U.S. coastline," October 15.

New York Times (2021) "China digs more coal for power needs, despite climate change," October 28.

New York Times (2021) "A power struggle over cobalt rattles the clean energy revolution," November 20.

New York Times (2021) "Hunt for the 'blood diamond of batteries' impedes green energy push," November 29.

Newsweek (2021) "Extreme heat melts streetcar cable in Portland, service suspended for days," June 28.

Nguyen, David H. (2018) *Science*, "Toxic chemicals in solar panels," April 30.

NNFCC (2019) "Implications of imported used cooking oil (UCO) as a biodiesel feedstock," May.

NRDC (Natural Resources Defense Council) (2011) *Nuclear Accident at Indian Point: Consequences and Costs*, New York, October.

NREL (National Renewable Energy Laboratory) (2017) *U.S. Solar Photovoltaic System Cost Benchmark: Q1 2017.*

NREL (National Renewable Energy Laboratory) (2019) "Annual technology baseline: Electricity."

NREL (National Renewable Energy Laboratory) (2020) "Best research-cell efficiencies."

NREL (National Renewable Energy Laboratory) (2020) "NREL six-junction solar cell sets two world records for efficiency," press release, April 13.

Nugent, Daniel and Benjamin K. Sovacool (2014) *Energy Policy*, "Assessing the lifecycle greenhouse gas emissions from solar PV and wind energy: A critical meta-survey," February.

Oberhaus, Daniel (2020) *Wired,* "The race to crack battery recycling—before it's too late," November 20.

ODI (Overseas Development Institute) (2013) *Time to Change the Game: Fossil Fuel Subsidies and Climate*, London, November.

ODI (Overseas Development Institute) (2019) "G20 coal subsidies: Tracking government support to a fading industry," June.

OEC (Observatory of Economic Complexity) (accessed 2019) oec.world.

OECD (Organisation for Economic Co-operation and Development) (2008) *Biofuel Support Policies: An Economic Assessment*, August.

OECD–FAO (Organisation for Economic Co-operation and Development; Food and Agriculture Organization) (2019) *OECD–FAO Agricultural Outlook 2019–2028:* Special Focus; Latin America, July.

OWID (Our World in Data) www.ourworldindata.org, Oxford Martin School, Oxford University.

OWID (Our World in Data) (2020) "Why did renewables become so cheap so fast?" Oxford Martin School, Oxford University, December 1.

Oxfam (2018) "New EU biofuel rules not enough to help people or the planet," June 14.

Page, Susan E. et al. (2002) *Nature*, "The amount of carbon released by peat and forest fires in Indonesia during 1997," November 7.

Pai, Sandeep et al. (2021) *One Earth*, "Meeting well-below 2°C target would increase energy sector jobs globally," July 23.

Palm Oil Investigations (n.d.) "What is palm oil?"

Parry, Ian et al. (2021) "Still not getting energy prices right. A global and country update of fossil fuel subsidies." Working paper WP/21/236, International Monetary Fund, September 24.

Patzek, Tad W. and David Pimental (2005) *Critical Reviews in Plant Sciences*, "Thermodynamics of energy production from biomass," January 18.

Pfenninger, Stefan et al. (2014) *Nature Climate Change*, "Potential for concentrating solar power to provide baseload and dispatchable power," June 22.

Pimental, David and Tad W. Patzek (2005) *Natural Resources Research*, "Ethanol production using corn, switchgrass, and wood; biodiesel production using soybean and sunflower," March.

Plumer, Brad (2021) "A glimpse of America's future: Climate change means trouble for power grids," New York Times, June 15.

Polman, Albert (2016) *Science*, "Photovoltaic materials: Present efficiencies and future challenges," April 15.

Power Technology (2014) "The world's 10 biggest wind turbines," January 1.

Power Technology (2019) "The world's biggest under-construction power plants by capacity," April 3.

PV Magazine (2021) "Hawaiian Electric battery cash incentive goes live," July 20.

Rainforest Rescue (n.d.) (accessed May 2019) "Palm oil: Facts about the ingredient that destroys the rainforests."

Recharge (2021) "Zinc-ion batteries: 'Up to 50% cheaper than lithium-ion, with no raw-materials concerns'," January 11.

REN21 (Renewable Energy Policy Network) (2013 and 2019) *Renewables: Global Status Report*.

REW (Renewable Energy World) (2016) "Germany achieves milestone: Renewables supply nearly 100 percent energy for a day," May 16.

Rochmyaningsih, Dyna (2019) *Science*, "Courting controversy, scientists team with industry to tackle one of the world's most destructive crops," July 11.

Rosegrant, Mark W. and Siwa Msangi (2014) *Annual Review of Environment and Resources*, "Consensus and contention in the food-versus-fuel debate," October.

RSPB (Royal Society for the Protection of Birds) et al. (n.d.) (accessed October 2019) *Dirtier than Coal? Why Government Plans to Subsidise Burning Trees Are Bad News for the Planet*.

RSPO (Roundtable on Sustainable Palm Oil) (n.d.) "About us."

Schmitt, R.J.P. et al. (2019) *Science Advances*, "Planning dam portfolios for low sediment trapping shows limits for sustainable hydropower in the Mekong," October 23.

Science (2011) "Will busting dams boost salmon?" November 18.

Science (2018) "Dams nudge Amazon's ecosystems off-kilter," February 2.

Science (2018) "Chemical storage of renewable energy," May 18.

Science (2018) "See-through solar cells could power offices," June 29.

Science (2018) "This 'flow battery' could power green homes when the sun goes down and the wind stops blowing," July 31.

Science (2018) "Powerful new battery could help usher in a green power grid," August 23.

Science (2019) "New fuel cell could help fix the renewable energy storage problem," March 12.

Science (2019) "Marrying two types of solar cells draws more power from the sun," April 10.

Science (2019) "Giant batteries and cheap solar power are shoving fossil fuels off the grid," July 11.

Science (2020) "Next generation water splitter could help renewables power the globe," March 10.

Science (2020) "Without fossil fuels, reactors churn out chemicals," May 8.

Science (2020) "Can China, the world's biggest coal consumer, become carbon neutral by 2060?" September 29.

Science (2021) " 'A rather beautiful concept': Plan aims to replace Asia's coal plants with renewable energy," November 2.

Scudder, Thayer (2005) *The Future of Large Dams*: Dealing with Social, Environmental, Institutional and Political Costs, London; Sterling, VA: Earthscan.

Searchinger, Tim and Ralph Heimlich (2015) "Avoiding bioenergy competition for food crops and land." Working paper, World Resources Institute, January.

Searchinger, Timothy et al. (2008) *Science*, "Use of U.S. croplands for biofuels increases greenhouse gases through emissions from land-use change," February 29.

Service, Robert F. (2021) *Science*, "Zinc aims to beat lithium batteries at storing energy," May 28.

Sherman, Peter et al. (2020) *Science Advances*, "Offshore wind: An opportunity for cost-competitive decarbonization of China's energy economy," February 21.

Silicon Valley Toxics Coalition (accessed October 21, 2019) "2016–17 solar scorecard."

Smil, Vaclav (2010) *Energy Transitions: History, Requirements, Prospects*, Santa Barbara, CA: Praeger.

Smil, Vaclav (2014) "The long slow rise of solar and wind," Scientific American, January.

South China Morning Post (2021) "Global climate summit: US sets emissions target for 2030; China offers no new commitments," April 22.

Standaert, Michael (2021) *Yale Environment 360* "Despite pledges to cut emissions, China goes on a coal spree," March 24.

Stone, Brian Jr. et al. (2021) *Environmental Science & Technology*, "Compound climate and infrastructure events: How electrical grid failure alters heat wave risk," April 30.

Strona, Giovanni et al. (2018) *PNAS*, "Small room for compromise between oil palm cultivation and primate conservation in Africa," August 28.

Tan, Chin-Ping and Imededdine Arbi Nehdi (2012) "The physicochemical properties of palm oil and its components," in Lai Oi-Ming et al. (eds.) *Palm Oil: Production, Processing, Characterization, and Uses*, Urbana, IL: AOCS Press.

Temple, James (2018) *MIT Technology Review*, "At this rate, it's going to take nearly 400 years to transform the energy system," March 14.

Tong, Wenming et al. (2020) *Nature Energy*, "Electrolysis of low-grade and saline surface water," May.

TransitionZero (2021) "Turning the supertanker: Powering China's coal to clean transition with actionable analytics," April 15.

Transport & Environment (2021) "Used cooking oil demand likely to double, and EU can't fully ensure sustainability," April.

Transport & Environment (2021) "Used cooking oil (UCO) as biofuel feedstock in the EU," December.

Trieb, Franz et al. (2012) *Energy Policy*, "Solar energy imports from the Middle East and North Africa to Europe," 42: 341–53.

Turbinegenerator.org (n.d.) (accessed October 2019) "The history of wind power."

Ueckerdt, Falko et al. (2021) *Nature Climate Change*, "Potential and risks of hydrogen-based e-fuels in climate change mitigation," May 6.

UNEP (United Nations Environment Programme) (2014) "UNEP and Roundtable on Sustainable Palm Oil sign new agreement," November 14.

Upton, John (2015) "Pulp fiction: The European accounting error that's warming the planet," ClimateCentral.org.

US BLS (Bureau of Labor Statistics) (2019a) "Wind turbine technicians," in *Occupational Outlook Handbook*.

US BLS (Bureau of Labor Statistics) (2019b) "Fastest growing occupations," in *Occupational Outlook Handbook*.

US BLS (Bureau of Labor Statistics) (2019c) "Solar photovoltaic installers," in *Occupational Outlook Handbook*.

US DoE (Department of Energy) (accessed October 2019a) "Wind energy myths."

US DoE (Department of Energy) (accessed October 2019b) *Concentrating Solar Power*.

US DoE (Department of Energy) (accessed October 2019c) *Solar Research Spotlight: Concentrating Solar-Thermal Power*, Office of Energy Efficiency and Renewable Energy.

US DoE (Department of Energy) (2021) *Solar Futures Study*, September.

US EIA (Energy Information Administration) (2007) *Federal Financial Interventions and Subsidies in Energy Markets*, Washington, DC, April.

US EIA (Energy Information Administration) (2019a) *Levelized Cost and Levelized Avoided Cost of New Generation Resources,*" February.

US EIA (Energy Information Administration) (2019b) *Short-Term Energy Outlook (STEO),* January.

US EIA (Energy Information Administration) (2020) "Utility-scale battery storage costs decreased nearly 70% between 2015 and 2018," *Today in Energy,* October 23.

US EIA (Energy Information Administration) (2021a) *Levelized Costs of New Generation Resources in the* Annual Energy Outlook 2021, February.

US EIA (Energy Information Administration) (2021b) "Texas: State profile and energy estimates."

US EIA (Energy Information Administration) (2021c) "Wind explained: Electricity generation from wind," March 17.

US EIA (Energy Information Administration) (2021d) *Monthly Energy Review,* February.

US EIA (Energy Information Administration) (n.d. a) "Tidal power."

US EIA (Energy Information Administration) (n.d. b) "Wave power."

US NRC (Nuclear Regulatory Commission) (1982) *Calculation of Reactor Accident Consequences for US Nuclear Power Plants,* CRAC-II Report. Simulations conducted by Sandia Labs, New Mexico.

US NRC (Nuclear Regulatory Commission) (2019) "Nuclear Insurance: Price-Anderson Act," April.

USDA (US Department of Agriculture) (2018) *Biofuel Mandates in the EU by Member States in 2018,* GAIN Report GM 18024, June 19.

USDA (US Department of Agriculture) (2019) Crop Explorer. "Oil palm 2019," Foreign Agricultural Service.

USDA (US Department of Agriculture) (2021) "U.S. corn production and portion used for fuel ethanol," Alternative Fuels Data Center, June.

Valentine, Scott et al. (2019) *Empowering the Great Energy Transition: Policy for a Low-Carbon Future,* New York: Columbia University Press.

Veers, Paul et al. (2019) *Science,* "Grand challenges in the science of wind energy," October 10.

Washington Post (2008) "Solar energy firms leave waste behind in China," March 9.

Webber, Michael E. (2021) *Scientific American,* "What to do about natural gas," April.

WEC (World Energy Council) (2004) *Comparison of Energy Systems Using Life Cycle Assessment: A Special Report of the World Energy Council,* July.

Winstanley, Gil et al. (1977) *Energy Requirements Associated with Selected Canadian Energy Developments,* Research report No. 13, Office of Energy Conservation, Energy, Mines and Resources Canada, Ottawa, March.

Wiser Ryan et al. (2021) *Nature Energy,* "Expert elicitation survey predicts 37% to 49% declines in wind energy costs by 2050," April 15.

World Bank (accessed October 2019) "World development indicators."

WTEx (World's Top Exports) (2018) "Palm oil exports by country," October 24.

WWEA (World Wind Energy Association) (2021) "Worldwide wind capacity reaches 744 gigawatts: An unprecedented 93 gigawatts added in 2020," March 24.

Xu, Hui (2020) "High-temperature alkaline water electrolysis." Presentation to the 2020 DOE H_2 and Fuel Cell Annual Merit Review Meeting, Giner, Inc, Newton, MA, May 20.

Zhou, Xiaoyan et al. (2021) *The Energy Transition and Changing Financial Costs,* Oxford Sustainable Finance Programme, April.

Zweibel, Ken et al. (2007) "By 2050 solar power could end U.S. dependence on foreign oil and slash greenhouse gas emissions," *Scientific American,* December 16.

10 Conclusion

The narrowing path to sustainability

At the international climate summit held in Paris in December 2015, 196 nations agreed on a goal to limit global temperature increases to no more than 2 degrees Celsius (°C), and preferably 1.5°C, above preindustrial levels. In light of a variety of complex factors, including continued economic development, lagged effects of greenhouse gases (GHGs), political inertia, emplaced capital, and entrenched vested interests, it is becoming increasingly likely that this goal will not be attained (UNEP 2021a and b; SEI et al. 2020; Raftery et al. 2017; BBC October 11, 2019; WMO 2020). Indeed, temperature increases may end up exceeding 2°C. A recent report from the World Meteorological Organization (WMO 2021) concludes that "it is about as likely as not (40% chance) that at least one of the next 5 years will be 1.5°C warmer than preindustrial levels and the chance is increasing with time" (p. 2).

The US Fourth National Climate Assessment (US Global Change Research Program 2018), Chapter 2, p. 2) states that "without significant reductions, annual average global temperatures could increase by 9°F (5°C) or more by the end of this century compared to preindustrial temperatures." To put this in context, Australia's Climate Council (2015) concluded that even the 2°C limit agreed to in Paris is no longer considered safe. Steffen et al. (2018) have concluded that even if the Paris goals are achieved, "we cannot exclude the risk that a cascade of feedbacks could push the Earth System irreversibly onto a "Hothouse Earth' pathway" (p. 8254). This could be accompanied by sea levels 10–60 meters higher than today (Stockholm Resilience Centre 2018). Under this scenario, current land, forest, and ocean sinks could be transformed into carbon sources through a process of self-reinforcing feedback loops. Solomon et al. (2009, p. 1704) show that "climate change that takes place due to increases in carbon dioxide concentration is largely irreversible for 1,000 years after emissions stop." Even if emissions can be stabilized, the concentration of carbon in the atmosphere will continue to rise until an equilibrium is reached (*New York Times* June 26, 2017).

There is ample evidence to suggest that the path we are on is profoundly self-destructive. A recent report by the US National Intelligence Council (NIC 2021) highlights the multifaceted threats faced by the global community over the next two decades. Just with respect to the environment, the report observes:

> The physical effects of climate change are likely to intensify during the next two decades, especially in the 2030s. More extreme storms, droughts, and floods; melting glaciers and ice caps; and rising sea levels will accompany rising temperatures. The impact will disproportionately fall on the developing world and poorer regions and [will] intersect with environmental degradation to create new vulnerabilities and

DOI: 10.4324/9781003199540-13

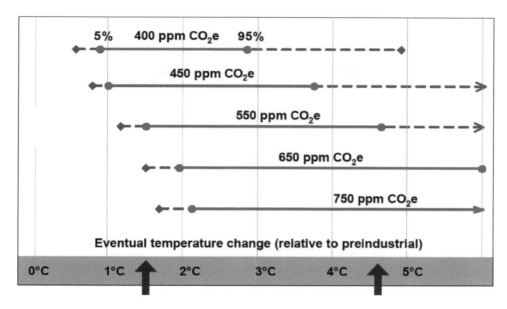

Figure 10.1 Relationship between atmospheric CO_2 levels and temperature change.
Source: Stern 2007, p. 330.

exacerbate existing risks to economic prosperity, food, water, health, and energy security.

(pp. 6–7)

Three graphs in particular demonstrate the nature and magnitude of the associated risks. The first, by NASA (see book cover) shows the degree to which the earth's temperature will rise over the next few decades. The second and third graphs are from the Stern Review (2007) and show, respectively, the relationship between atmospheric CO_2 and global temperature (Figure 10.1), and the prediction of the massive negative effects associated with each additional degree of temperature (Figure 10.2).

In light of the ominous forecast, it is highly likely that most suggested forms of adaptation will fail, especially with respect to food production. This has led members of the scientific community to suggest several advanced and speculative technological solutions to carbon releases and solar insolation. These solutions are included under the rubric of negative-emission technologies (Minx et al. 2018; Fuss et al. 2018). The following sections describe two of the most prominent of these technological solutions: geoengineering in the form of solar radiation management and carbon capture and storage. This is followed by a brief discussion of the more nature-based proposal for global reforestation.

Geoengineering

The concept of geoengineering encompasses a range of major interventions in the global ecosystem. The belief that such interventions may be needed is founded on the assumption that increasing GHG production is a given and emissions cannot be reduced significantly.

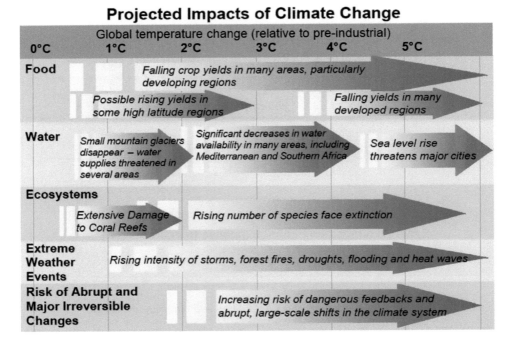

Figure 10.2 Projected effects of temperature rise.
Source: Stern 2007, p. 330.

There are two basic variants of this technology: (1) carbon dioxide removal from the atmosphere (CDR); and (2) solar radiation management (SRM), which entails reflecting solar radiation back into space. This relatively new area of engineering has come under intense scrutiny over the last decade, with a broad diversity of scientific assessments, ranging from resigned acceptance through counseling caution to severe criticism (Crutzen 2006; Kunzig 2008; Kunzig and Broecker 2008; Dean 2008; Robock 2008; *Scientific American* 2008; Royal Society [UK] 2009; Hegerl and Solomon 2009; Blackstock et al. 2009; Keith 2010; UNEP 2010; Fleming 2010; Kintisch 2010; US GAO 2011; Hamilton 2013; Keller et al. 2014; Cusack et al. 2014; *Earth's Future* 2016; Trisos et al. 2018; Proctor et al. 2018; Irvine et al. 2019; CIEL 2019; McKibben 2021; Kolbert 2021; NAS 2021; Keith 2021). The nature of the scientific criticism rests on five critical concerns: first, there is a fundamental uncertainty about the effectiveness of these techniques; second, if some of the techniques work, they would have to be continued for the indefinite future, for failure to do so would lead to a potentially catastrophic surge in GHGs; third, many of these technological solutions would fail to address, or would contribute to, equally serious problems such as the acidification of the world's oceans; fourth, most of these technologies entail unacceptable levels of risk since our knowledge of the complex functioning of ecosystems remains seriously incomplete; and fifth, some of the proposed technologies would entail enormous costs. Table 10.1 summarizes some of the most prominent of the recent proposals and their inherent risks. Robock (2020, p. 65) outlines twenty-eight risks or concerns with geoengineering under the headings of: physical and biological

Table 10.1 Geoengineering and its risks

Solar radiation management (SRM)	Risks
A. Injecting sulfate aerosols into the stratosphere	Potentially large hydrological effects, including, *in extremis*, megadroughts. May also lead to reduced precipitation, soil moisture, and river flow at regional levels. May lead to accelerated destruction of the ozone layer. May alter the carbon cycle. Could shift atmospheric optical properties from blue towards whitish. Would attenuate little of global agricultural danger from climate change. Could make oceans more acidic. Would allow atmospheric GHG concentrations to continue increasing.
B. Cloud brightening at sea	Potentially large regional changes in precipitation, evaporation, and runoff.
C. Injection of sea water aerosol into the atmosphere, conducted at sea	Some effects could be similar to A and B above.
D. Giant reflectors in orbit	Would require constant monitoring and maintenance, depending on the number and size of the reflectors. Depending on the size, misalignment could have large unanticipated consequences, including unknown effects on ocean currents, temperature, precipitation, and wind.
E. Cloud seeding	See B above.
General risks for SRM	No reduction in CO_2 production, thereby leading to continued acidification of entire ocean biological chain. This would threaten sea-life and oxygen production. Less insolation for photosynthesis and solar energy production. Continual upkeep required to forestall sudden cessation which could lead to rapid climate warming in a short period of time. Must be maintained indefinitely. None has an experimental proof of concept.

Carbon dioxide removal (CDR)	Risks
F. Iron fertilization of the ocean	Could potentially disrupt the ocean food web and biogeochemical cycles. Could lead to anoxic conditions in large regions of the ocean, leading to methane production. Could potentially lead to increased acidification of deep ocean.
G. Pumping CO_2 into subsea geological formations	Any loss of CO_2 from such formations would accelerate ocean acidification leading to potentially catastrophic consequences for both marine and land-based life.
H. Pumping CO_2 into underground geological formations (carbon capture and storage; CCS)	See discussion of CCS in this chapter.
I. Capturing CO_2 from the air and subsequent sequestration	Likely to be much less efficient and more expensive than CO_2 capture from concentrated point sources. Faces many of the same issues as CCS.
J. Afforestation/ reforestation	Would require a massive reversal in current accelerating trends in deforestation, especially in the developing world. Potential loss of agricultural land.

(continued)

Table 10.1 Cont.

Solar radiation management (SRM)	Risks
K Irrigation of desert regions to promote vegetative growth	Significant new requirements for scarce water resources. An increase in biological productivity in desert regions could have negative effects on productivity elsewhere because of induced changes in atmospheric circulation and precipitation and temperature patterns.
L. Converting roofs and pavements to a light, reflective color	Would have to be of an extraordinarily large scale, entailing massive costs and logistical issues.
M. Genetic crop modification	Potentially unanticipated effects on food production.

climate system; human impacts; aesthetics; governance; ethics; and unknowns, especially human error during implementation and unexpected consequences or revenge effects. By proposing to conduct experiments on such a grand scale and which impact the entire global ecosystem, humankind is running the risk of fat-tail (Weitzman 2009) or zero-infinity events (i.e., low probability events with massive consequences). With only one Earth, a failed experiment of this magnitude could be disastrous. As such, it may be safer to consider a technology, a version of which already exists, such as carbon capture and storage (CCS).

Carbon capture and storage

One potential technology that has received a great deal of international attention is CCS, also referred to as CCUS (carbon capture, utilization, and storage) (IPCC 2005; IEA 2020; Conniff 2020; Biniek et al. 2020; *New York Times* March 8, 2021; *Science* March 26, 2021). There are two general approaches: recovery of CO_2 from flue gases or directly from the atmosphere. Several flue-gas recovery projects are currently in operation worldwide and are associated with power plants, fertilizer and steel production, and oil sands and biofuels (Carbonbrief 2014; CCSA n.d.). In the energy sector, the carbon dioxide is generally injected into underground fossil fuel reservoirs to promote recovery of oil and natural gas. In other industrial sectors, the carbon is captured at the point of emission and then injected into the earth where the goal is to isolate the gas indefinitely. Dowell et al. (2017, p. 243) argue that carbon utilization in industries outside of the oil and gas industry is a "costly distraction, financially and politically, from the real task of mitigation, since this potential market for the chemical conversion of CO_2 would account for no more than 1 percent of the mitigation challenge."

Several critical criteria must be met before flue-gas recovery can be considered a major contributor to CO_2 removal at the global level. First, the technology would only be useful for large single-point emission sources and inappropriate for distributed sources or fugitive emissions. Second, there must be reasonably proximate favorable geological formations for carbon dioxide injection. Third, the costs must be a relatively small proportion of the total cost of energy production. And, finally, there must be some assurance that the geological formations designed to contain the injected CO_2 are stable and able to hold the gas indefinitely.

One report (Thomson 2009, p. 46) concluded that "by one estimate the United States would have to construct 300,000 injection wells at a cost of $3 trillion by 2030 just to keep emissions at 2005 levels." Smil (2010) has calculated that governments will have to construct CO_2 infrastructure about twice the size of the world's crude oil industry just to bury 25 percent of the world's emissions. These scale-up issues pose among the most imposing challenges to this technology even if other scientific questions were to be resolved satisfactorily.

A fundamental uncertainty remains about the ultimate effectiveness and safety of such a system. It is not known with any certainty how long the CO_2 would stay underground and, if it were to escape, the consequence could be an environmental crisis of potentially greater magnitude than the original problem. This type of risk is an archetypal example of revenge theory. A US EPA study (2008) stressed the multitude of scientific uncertainties associated with CCS, focusing on the vulnerability of the geological system to unanticipated migration of gas, leakage, and undesirable pressure changes, and the possible negative consequences of system failure on human, plant, and animal life.

While research continues into the scientific and economic feasibility of this technology, several dozen commercial-scale facilities are in operation (Global CCS Institute 2020), but several high-profile projects in the United States, Britain, and Canada have been cancelled (*New Scientist* October 24, 2011; *Globe and Mail* April 26, 2012; *Guardian* October 19, 2011; *New York Times* July 13, 15, and 31, 2011, January 16 and May 19, 2012), although proposals from the oil and gas sector continue to be advanced (*Vancouver Sun* July 13, 2021; see also Chapter 3). This technology may prove viable in the future, but its recent track record and current level of uncertainty suggest that any corporate or governmental plans to rely extensively on it for carbon dioxide control entails an unacceptable risk (Kirchsteiger 2008; Wilday et al. 2011; Rochon et al. 2008; Smil 2010). A report from the National Academy of Sciences (NAS 2019, p. 4) cautions that:

> negative emissions technologies are best viewed as a component of the mitigation portfolio, rather than a way to decrease atmospheric concentrations of carbon dioxide only after anthropogenic emissions have been eliminated ...The committee recognizes that there is a possibility that large negative emissions in the future could result in a moral hazard, by reducing humanity's will to cut emissions in the near term. Reducing emissions is vital to addressing the climate problem.

This view is echoed by Anderson and Peters (2016, p. 183) who conclude that reliance on negative-emission concepts locks in humankind's carbon addiction. To quote: "negative-emission technologies are not an insurance policy, but rather an unjust and high-stakes gamble."

Other studies reinforce ongoing concerns by focusing on direct costs (Biello 2016), air pollution and total social costs including intergenerational ethical issues (Lenzi et al. 2018; Jacobson 2019), possible obstruction of mitigation (Lenzi 2018), and the incentive to maintain "dangerous habits" by allowing industry to continue business as usual (Plumer and Flavelle 2021; see also CBC November 29, 2019).

A major step towards the achievement of viable direct air capture and storage (Mulligan et al. 2018) has been achieved by several demonstration projects (BBC June 7, 2018 and April 3, 2019; Keith et al. 2018). However, this potential solution must still overcome some of the fundamental challenges facing flue-gas recovery: scale-up, number of global units required to achieve significant levels of atmospheric CO_2 reduction, energy inputs required, cost, and the issue of carbon dioxide disposition. For example, a Swiss company has recently installed a direct air capture machine for carbon in Iceland, which can capture about 4,000 short tons of CO_2 per year and store it underground. Unfortunately, this represents only a "tiny fraction of the 33 billion tons of the gas forecast by the International Energy Agency to be emitted worldwide this year" (Inside Climate News September 9, 2021).

In light of the economic and technological challenges facing the direct recovery of CO_2 from combustion sources, a second major approach has been proposed: the direct removal of carbon dioxide from the atmosphere. Broecker and Kunzig (2008, p. 211) conclude that "we cannot solve the CO_2 problem without tacking small and mobile sources. Right now, Lackner and Wright's invention [scrubbing the gas directly from the air] offers the only hope." (See Earth Institute, Columbia University, n.d.) However, James Hansen et al. (2017 pp. 577–578) have concluded that:

> continued high fossil fuel emissions today place a burden on young people to undertake massive technological CO_2 extraction if they are to limit climate change and its consequences. Proposed methods of extraction such as bioenergy with carbon capture and storage (BECCS) or air capture of CO_2 have minimal estimated costs of USD 89–535 trillion this century and also have large risks and uncertain feasibility. Continued high fossil fuel emissions unarguably sentences young people to either a massive, implausible cleanup or growing deleterious climate impacts or both.

In contrast to these high-tech solutions with their attendant risks, *natural* climate solutions (NCSs) can increase carbon storage and/or avoid GHG emissions through conservation, restoration, and improved management practices across global forests, wetlands, grasslands, and agricultural lands (see, for example, Drever et al. 2021). Griscom et al. (2017) studied twenty possible NCSs and concluded (p. 11645):

> We show that NCS can provide over one-third of the cost-effective climate mitigation needed between now and 2030 to stabilize warming to below 2 °C. Alongside aggressive fossil fuel emissions reductions, NCS offer a powerful set of options for nations to deliver on the Paris Climate Agreement while improving soil productivity, cleaning our air and water, and maintaining biodiversity.

Reforestation and forest preservation

A major alternative to the use of technology to remove carbon from the atmosphere is the adoption of a natural climate solution which includes reforestation (Bastin et al. 2019). Along with oceans and soils, forests are among the principal global sinks for carbon and prevent the concentration of GHGs in the atmosphere from becoming even higher. While this undertaking can, in theory, make a difference, there are several qualifications to the extent of its potential success.

(1) It has been estimated that foresting enough area to seriously address climate change would require land areas significantly in excess of what are available. In fact, if implemented as a global solution to climate change, the area would probably eliminate virtually all natural ecosystems. To quote one research report on the limits to global warming mitigation by terrestrial carbon removal (Boysen et al. 2017, p. 463):

Our results show that those tCDR [terrestrial carbon dioxide removal] measures are unable to counteract "business-as-usual" emissions without eliminating virtually all natural ecosystems. Even if considerable (Representative Concentration Pathway 4.5 [RCP4.5]) emissions reductions are assumed, tCDR with 50% storage efficiency requires >1.1 Gha [giga hectares] of the most productive agricultural areas or the elimination of >50% of natural forests. In addition, >100 MtN/yr [million metric tons of nitrogen per year] fertilizers would be needed to remove the roughly 320 GtC [gigatons of carbon] foreseen in these scenarios. Such interventions would severely compromise food production and/or biosphere functioning. Second, we reanalyze the requirements for achieving the 160–190 GtC tCDR that would complement strong mitigation action (RCP2.6) in order to avoid 2°C overshoot anytime. We find that a combination of high irrigation water input and/or more efficient conversion to stored carbon is necessary. In the face of severe trade-offs with society and the biosphere, we conclude that large-scale tCDR is not a viable alternative to aggressive emissions reduction.

(2) Planting the billions of trees needed would require an extensive effort to continuously monitor seedlings to guarantee they received enough water and nutrients to survive and thrive and escape any human or animal predation for domestic, commercial, or industrial purposes.

(3) If carbon dioxide emissions continue unabated, there will be an ongoing requirement to plant more trees, regardless of whether the land for such expansion is available or even exists.

(4) A prerequisite to this massive undertaking is the stabilization of the current stock of forests being removed annually by human activity.

(5) Climate change is already contributing to the loss of forest cover by insect predation, drought, and forest fire and this also requires immediate remediation as some large global forests have been converted from carbon sinks into carbon sources (Natural Resources Canada 2007; Baccini et al. 2017; Sierra Club of BC 2019; CBC February 12, 2019). The interaction of climate change and forests has become another item in the list of threatening positive feedback loops that can accelerate global warming.

(6) Even if forests remain standing, climate change is affecting the quality of growth and the capacity to absorb carbon (Matricardi et al. 2020).

(7) The expansion of forestland should not come at the expense of other crucial land uses, most notably agriculture.

One study has found that as many as 58.9 million hectares (ha) of natural forest have grown back since 2000 with little or no intervention (Force of Nature 2021). However, global data reveal that this regrowth has been more than offset by global levels of deforestation as tropical forest destruction has accelerated in recent years (*New York Times* March 31, 2021). To counter this overall trend, several countries have embarked on major reforestation efforts. Most notable among these has been China's effort to reverse the pronounced negative economic and ecological effects of deforestation by undertaking a massive program of reforestation beginning in 1978 following the passage of the Natural Forest Conservation Program (Vina et al. 2016; NASA Earth Observatory 2019). As a result of this effort, China has sought to compensate for its loss of forests for domestic use and export by increasing the importation of both lumber and round wood from global sources, including Russia, South America, Africa, and Southeast Asia (Katsigris et al. 2004;

Hoang and Kanemoto 2021; *New York Times* April 9, 2019). These imports have been both legal and illegal (Mir and Fraser 2003; Johnson 2003; Global Witness 2015; Siriwat and Nijman 2018; Environmental Investigation Agency 2019a and b). For example, a report by Chatham House (Hoare 2015) concluded that "half of all the trade in illegal wood-based products is now destined for China" (p. viii). They report that most of this illegal timber comes from Indonesia, Brazil, and Malaysia, and that while some other countries produce less timber overall, they have a much higher share of illegal timber in their production. For example, virtually 100 percent of the timber produced by the Democratic Republic of Congo is illegal.

A systems analysis of China's overall success in addressing global warming and its own ecological requirements clearly needs an accounting of the loss of other forests sacrificed for the Chinese market to determine if there has been any net gain at the global level. At issue is not only the total loss of forest cover but also the loss of biodiversity as highly productive forests are replaced with reduced biodiversity in exporting countries. However, consideration of biodiversity and other vital ecological functions is not confined to exporters. Hua et al. (2018) reported on the results of China's new forest policy:

> We found that while the region's gross tree cover grew by 32%, this increase was entirely due to the conversion of croplands to tree plantations, particularly monocultures. Native forests, in turn, suffered a net loss of 6.6%. Thus, instead of truly recovering forested landscapes and generating concomitant environmental benefits, the region's apparent forest recovery has effectively displaced native forests, including those that could have naturally regenerated on land freed up from agriculture.
>
> (p. 493)

A study by Ahrends et al. (2017) suggested that "China's forest cover gains are highly definition-dependent" (p.1) and are an order of magnitude less than reported. In some cases, shrubs have been mistaken for trees; in other cases,

> most of China's afforestation investment targets environments . . . our model classes as unsuitable for trees. Here, gains detectable via satellite imagery are limited. Conversely, the regions where modest gains are detected are environmentally suitable but have received little afforestation investment due to conflicting land-use demands for agriculture and urbanization. This highlights the need for refined forest monitoring, and greater consideration of environmental suitability in afforestation programmes.

The *New York Times* (December 2, 2021) recently published an assessment of the efforts of the corporate sector, particularly Coca-Cola, Kellogg, Walmart, and Mars, to achieve net-zero deforestation. The conclusion was that despite the best of intentions, none of these companies could completely identify the extent of deforestation in their complex supply chains.

None of these qualifications should deter efforts by governments or the private sector to use as many natural ecological processes as possible to stabilize or even reduce global warming. However, what should be apparent from the discussion of both technological and natural systems for removing carbon from the atmosphere is that there is absolutely no substitute for the decarbonization of the global economy. That must be the singular and principal focus of both national and international efforts.

Alternative economic models

Several innovative economic concepts have emerged in an attempt to facilitate the transformation of our complex economic system to a sustainable model. Professor Rebecca Henderson of the Harvard Business School is one of a number of academics reexamining the role of our modern capitalist system in the current climate crisis. In her most recent work entitled *Reimagining Capitalism in a World on Fire* (2021), she concludes that the current form of our capitalist system is "broken" and the single-minded pursuit of profit has led to climate change, inequality and hatred, polarization and distrust. This is an extremely powerful critique, but the author sees a potential solution in the form of a reimagined model of business which maintains the central role of business in our society but focuses on a realignment of corporate values to include social goals. The book is replete with case studies of companies that have already made the effort to seriously reorient their corporate strategy in a more socially effective manner. A fundamental component of her prescription is a concomitant "rewiring" of our global and financial system. The author advances the concept of enlightened industry self-regulation in coordination with government, the entity ultimately responsible for society's well-being. To quote:

> We need governments to provide either the economic incentives that will move firms to action, or the regulations that will force everyone to do the right thing. Business, in its own interest, must take the lead. Without good government and free politics, the free market will not survive.
>
> (p. 203)

What distinguishes this proposal from the traditional laissez-faire model of self-regulation is the coordination with government and the role of leading companies in inducing others to adopt a broader interpretation of their mission through a combination of targeted purchasing and investment decisions. This is a more expanded version of the Walmart model (see Chapter 3) where the company uses its role as a de facto private regulator to induce its suppliers to adopt more sustainable means of production.

In fact, some of what Henderson is espousing is already underway. Numerous banks, investment houses, insurance companies, and pension funds are now increasingly sensitive to climate risk in investment decisions and this is having a direct impact on corporate decision-making. Examples abound:

- The emergence of green and clean energy and innovation indexes (CNN April 23, 2021; Clean Edge 2021)
- Pension funds dropping fossil fuel stocks (*New York Times* December 9, 2020)
- An investment house's decision to overhaul their investment strategy to incorporate climate risk (RFF 2020) and another's decision to cease funding of oil projects
- Research that has identified increased profitability from divestment (Institute for Energy Economics and Financial Analysis 2021 and BlackRock n.d.)
- Several reports from national and international agencies, universities, and research institutes highlighting the need for revised risk analysis in light of climate change (US CFTC 2020; NGFS 2020; Kedward et al. 2020; Datamaran 2021; Harvard Law School Forum on Corporate Governance 2020; Ceres 2020).

- The decision by the US Federal Reserve to join a network of global financial regulators focused on the systems risks of climate change and their management (*New York Times* December 15, 2020b)
- Several major reports by international agencies identifying the gains from climate-related investment and renewable energy (OECD 2017)
- An initiative by at least one Western government to require banks to disclose their climate risk (CNN April 13, 2021)
- Funds such as mutual funds and stock exchange–traded funds that focus on environmental, social, and governance principles (ESG funds) have gained popularity with investors over time (SEC 2021).
- The US Securities and Exchange Commission (SEC) is enhancing its focus on climate-related disclosure in public company filings. In 2010 it provided guidance to public companies regarding existing disclosure requirements as they apply to climate change matters. As part of its enhanced focus in this area, staff will review the extent to which public companies address the topics identified in the 2010 guidance, assess compliance with disclosure obligations under the federal securities laws, engage with public companies on these issues, and absorb critical lessons on how the market is currently managing climate-related risks (SEC 2021).

It can be argued that the solution to the existential threat of climate change is ultimately political rather than relying on the development of radically new technology. Several authoritative studies have already concluded that the necessary technology already exists and, in partnership with NCS, can address the social, economic, and ecological effects of climate change (Allwood et al. 2019; WEF 2021; Princeton University 2020). This does not mean that the necessary changes will come easily. The Princeton report describes the six crucial pillars necessary to support the transition to net zero. These are: (1) end-use energy efficiency and electrification, (2) clean energy in the form of wind and solar generation with transmission infrastructure and firm power, (3) bioenergy and other zero-carbon fuels and feedstocks, (4) carbon dioxide capture, utilization, and storage, (5) reduced non-CO_2 emissions such as methane, N_2O, and fluorocarbons, and (6) enhanced land sinks. *The New York Times* (December 15, 2020a) also illustrates the nature of the challenge by providing at least six examples of what must be done:

- This year, energy companies will install 42 gigawatts (GW) of new wind turbines and solar panels, smashing records. But that annual pace would need to nearly double over the next decade, and then keep soaring, transforming the landscapes in states like Florida or Missouri.
- The capacity of the nation's electric grid would have to expand roughly 60 percent by 2030 to handle vast amounts of wind and solar power, which would mean thousands of miles of new power lines crisscrossing the country.
- Car dealerships would look radically different. Today, electric vehicle (EV) models are just 2 percent of new sales. By 2030, at least 50 percent of new cars sold would need to be battery powered, with that share rising thereafter.
- Most homes today are heated by natural gas or oil. But in the next ten years, nearly one-quarter would need to be warmed with efficient electric heat pumps, double today's numbers.
- Virtually all of the two hundred remaining US coal-burning power plants would have to shut down by 2030.

- Today, there are no cement plants that bury their emissions underground, and there are no facilities sustainably producing hydrogen, a clean-burning fuel. By the mid-2020s, several such plants would need to be operating to prepare for wider deployment.

Only government in a leading role, in concert with business, can act effectively using a combination of economic incentives and regulation to address this historic challenge. Most governments around the world need to significantly up their game as current national proposals to curtail emissions fall significantly short of what is required to achieve a meaningful impact on climate change (SEI et al. 2019). Failing that, it has been estimated that climate change could cut the world economy by as much as $23 trillion in 2050 (Swiss Re Institute 2021). One major emitter, India, has already labeled the achievement of net-zero targets as "pie in the sky," stating that poor nations want to continue using fossil fuels and the rich countries "can't stop it" (BBC March 31, 2021).

Reengineering global financial systems

Perhaps the most definitive and authoritative assessment of the need to reengineer financial systems has been provided by Mark Carney, the former governor of the Bank of Canada and Bank of England, in his 2021 book, *Value(s): Building a Better World for All*.

Carney identifies two types of risk related to climate change: physical/ecological risks and transition risks. Transition risks arise:

> as a result of the adjustment towards a lower carbon economy. Changes in policies, technologies and physical risk will prompt reassessment of the value of a large range of assets, as the costs and opportunities of the transition become apparent. The longer meaningful adjustment is delayed, the more transition risks will increase.
>
> (p. 278)

Carney describes effort to address climate change as a "struggle between urgency and complacency" (p. 300). The urgency flows from three interrelated phenomena: (1) the urgency of carbon budgets that could be consumed within a decade, (2) the urgency of the sixth mass extinction, and (3) the urgency to reorient the financial system to finance the tens of trillions of dollars of investment needed over the next three decades for the transition to a sustainable economy.

Several other reports have also suggested financial needs in the trillions of dollars. A report by the United Nations Environment Programme (UNEP) entitled *State of Finance for Nature* (2021c) concludes there will be a $4.1 trillion financing gap for nature by 2050 (including climate change, biodiversity, and land degradation targets). The International Renewable Energy Agency (IRENA 2021) concludes that "USD 131 trillion will need to flow into an energy system over the period to 2050 that prioritizes technology avenues compatible with a 1.5°C Pathway" (p. 28).

Carney is reasonably optimistic that humanity can rise to the challenges, but solving the climate crisis requires three "technologies": engineering, political, and financial. "All are within our grasp." The required engineering entails three priorities: building a zero-carbon economy by greening the generation of electricity, decarbonizing transportation, and reducing emissions. The political aspect requires setting the right goals and a major step in this direction has been taken with the creation of the United Nations' Sustainable Development Goals (see Chapter 2).

The principal focus of Carney's work is an emphasis on the creation of financial technology to ensure that every financial decision takes climate change into account. This requires "a new sustainable *financial* system to fund private sector innovation, amplify the effectiveness of government climate polices and accelerate the transition" (p. 317). He envisages three fundamental building blocks:

- Reporting: disclosure of climate-related financial impacts must become comprehensive
- Risk: climate risk management needs to be transformed
- Returns: investing for a net-zero world must go mainstream.

Table 10.2 summarizes the key components of these building blocks.

The author's final plea is for global climate equity where a new sustainable financial system helps emerging developing economies in at least three ways (pp. 329–330): (1) by financing investments in sustainable infrastructure; (2) comprehensive reporting by companies in advanced economies of their scope 1, 2, and 3 emissions will encourage them to minimize climate risks and maximize opportunities across their supply chains since developing countries are where most scope 3 emissions are generated or outsourced, and (3) the transition to net zero will require new market structures that could substantially increase capital flows to developing and emerging economies.

This new focus on climate issues within the financial sector is already being reflected in several recent reports and initiatives within both the private and public sectors. For example:

Table 10.2 Components of Mark Carney's building blocks

Reporting

Disclosure of governance, strategy, and risk management
Consistent and comparable metrics applicable across all sectors, as well as specific metrics for the most carbon-intense sectors
Use of scenario analysis so as to consider dynamically the potential impacts of the risks and opportunities of the transition to a low-carbon economy on strategy and financial planning

---

Risks

Disclosures need to go beyond the static to the strategic (that is, what the plans of the private sector are for their future emissions and the associated financial impact.)
Climate stress tests that differ from normal stress tests. These stress tests, which are being developed, will include outcomes as well as more traditional macro and financial impacts aspects. Specifically, they need to assess physical and transition risk together, because businesses and our economies will face both.

Returns

Emerging best-practice transition plans include:
  defining a net-zero objective in terms of scope 1, 2, and 3
  outlining clear short-term milestones and metrics for senior management to use to monitor progress and gauge success
  board level governance
  embedding metrics in executive compensation.

Source: Carney 2021.

- The *New York Times* (December 5, 2021a) has reported that in the United Kingdom, government policy is focusing on the financial industry to play a central role in meeting climate goals.
- The US Financial Stability Oversight Council (FSOC 2021) has published a report on climate-related financial risk with recommendations the FSOC and its members "can adopt to strengthen the financial system and make it more resilient to climate-related shocks and vulnerabilities" (p. 4).
- The European Central Bank (ECB 2020) has published a guide on climate-related and environmental risks which lists thirteen supervisory expectations of institutions supervised by the ECB. Specifically, the guide "outlines the ECB's understanding of the safe and prudent management of climate-related and environmental risks under the current prudential framework. It describes how the ECB expects institutions to consider climate-related and environmental risks—as drivers of existing categories of risk—when formulating and implementing their business strategy and governance and risk management frameworks. It further explains how the ECB expects institutions to become more transparent by enhancing their climate-related and environmental disclosures" (p. 3).
- The investor service company, Moody's, has published research (2021) concluding that "financial firms that take rapid, predicable pace to zero financed emissions will win the race."

Other major proposals

There is a broad array of other proposals ranging from reengineering our industrial systems of production to abandoning growth as the central tenet of our economic systems. Three of the most noteworthy are the concepts of the circular economy, the steady-state economy, and degrowth.

Circular economy

The concept of the circular economy has been championed by the Ellen MacArthur Foundation (2021; see also sustainability.com 2021). According to Stahel (2016, p. 435):

> A "circular economy" would turn goods that are at the end of their service life into resources for others, closing loops in industrial ecosystems and minimizing waste. It would change economic logic because it replaces production with sufficiency: reuse what you can, recycle what cannot be reused, repair what is broken, remanufacture what cannot be repaired. A study of seven European nations found that a shift to a circular economy would reduce each nation's greenhouse gas emissions by up to 70% and grow its workforce by about 4%!—the ultimate low-carbon economy.

According to the Ellen MacArthur Foundation (2021), a number of factors indicate that the traditional linear model of production (i.e., cradle to cradle) has issues and is being questioned. Issues include economic losses and structural waste, price risks, supply risk, natural systems degradation, regulatory trends, advances in technology, acceptance of alternative business models, and urbanization.

But despite the emerging recognition by both governments and many corporations of the need to circularize economies, a recent report (Circle Economy 2020) has found that the world economy is only 8.6 percent circular and is getting worse. The major reasons for this shortfall have been resource extraction, which increased twelvefold between 1900 and 2015, ongoing stock buildup, and low levels of end-of-use processing and cycling. To quote from Circle Economy's 2018 report:

> increased and accelerated material use is to a large extent driven by rising prosperity levels globally. Whilst elevating people out of poverty is a desirable, even essential outcome, the associated material use is not. The circular economy has a key role to play in decoupling growth from material extraction, thereby creating the conditions for sustainable development to deliver more prosperity for a larger population, but with diminishing use of primary resources.
>
> (p. 11)

Steady-state economies and degrowth

There is a fundamental paradox at the center of our modern capitalist system. The perceived success or failure of this system is measured by the extent of economic growth, yet it is this growth that is ultimately unsustainable in a closed ecological system such as planet Earth. The theoretical solution to this critical problem is to achieve development without a concomitant increase in the growth of energy and material throughput. This is a meta version of the delinkage challenge posed by the growth of national carbon emissions along with gross domestic product (GDP). Research cited in a companion volume (Nemetz 2021) suggests that this type of delinkage appears to be presently beyond our grasp, at least at the planetary level—which is clearly the most critical level.

Over the past few decades, there have been numerous books articulating conceptualizations of alternative economic systems under the rubrics of steady state, zero growth, and degrowth (Daly 1973, 1991, and 2014; Victor 2019; Jackson 2009; Heinberg 2011; Rubin 2012; Czech 2013; D'Alisa et al. 2015; Washington and Twomey 2016; Pilling 2018).

Steady-state economics: In many respects, this concept is associated largely with the work of Herman Daly, former senior economist at the World Bank. He provides the following definition of the term (Daly 2014, p. 78ff):

> A steady-state economy is one that develops qualitatively (by improvement in science, technology and ethics) without growing quantitatively in physical dimensions; it lives on a diet—a constant metabolic flow of resources from depletion to pollution (the entropic throughput) maintained at a level that is within the assimilative and regenerative capacities of the ecosystem of which the economy is a subsystem.

He has proposed ten measures as key components of a transition to a steady-state economy:

(1) Cap-auction-trade systems for basic resources
(2) Ecological tax reform, involving a shift in the tax base from labor and capital towards resources extracted from nature and returned to nature in the form of pollution
(3) Limiting the range of inequality in income distribution
(4) Freeing up part of the working day, week, and year
(5) Reregulating international commerce, moving away from free trade, free capital mobility, and globalization.

(6) Downgrading the World Trade Organization, World Bank, and International Monetary Fund (IMF) to something like Keynes's original plan for a multilateral payments clearing union

(7) Moving away from fractional reserve banking towards a system of 100 percent reserve requirements

(8) Stopping treating the scarce as if it were nonscarce (e.g., the atmosphere, electromagnetic spectrum, and public lands), and the nonscarce (e.g., the nonrival commonwealth of knowledge and information) as if it were scarce

(9) Stabilizing population

(10) Reforming national accounts

Despite the fact that some of these proposals would seem radical to mainstream economists, Daly observes that:

> The conceptual change in vision from the norm of a growth economy to that of a steady-state economy is radical, but the policies advocated are subject to gradual application. . . . These measures are based on the impeccably conservative institutions of private property and decentralized market allocation. The policies advocated simply recognize that: (1) private property loses its legitimacy if too unequally distributed; (2) markets lose their legitimacy if prices do not tell the truth about opportunity costs; and (3) that the macroeconomy becomes an absurdity if its scale is required to grow beyond the biophysical limits of the earth.
>
> (p. 86)

Three questions come immediately to mind: (1) Is growth actually required in a capitalist system? (2) Is growth unique to such a system? (3) How realistic is it to expect that a transition to a steady-state economy is feasible in the near- to medium-term future?

With respect to the first and second questions, the growth imperative is not confined to modern capitalist systems. Communist economies face the same imperative to grow in order to maintain and/or increase the living standards of their citizens. Lawn (2011) makes the argument that a steady-state economy is perfectly compatible with capitalism. He observes that:

> a capitalist system can exist in a wide variety of forms. Unfortunately, many observers fail to recognize that the current "growth imperative" is the result of capitalist systems everywhere being institutionally designed to grow. They need not be designed this way to survive and thrive. Indeed, because continued growth is both existentially undesirable and ecologically unsustainable, redesigning capitalist systems through the introduction of Daly-like institutions would prove to be capitalism's savior. What's more, it would constitute humankind's best hope of achieving sustainable development.
>
> (p. 1)

The third question is not easily answered. Even if renewable energy were to replace fossil fuels, the pressures of increasing population and wealth would continue to drive the extraction of increasing quantities of renewable and nonrenewable resources, with their unsustainable impact on global ecosystems. The response of techno-optimists is that continued advances in technology will allow us to achieve the transition from an economy depending on quantity to one focused on quality. There are several outstanding examples of this type of transition, including Anderson's model of focusing on services provided by goods rather than goods per se, and the development of the modern information economy with accompanying technology. One need only visit the poorer nations of Africa, such as Tanzania, to see how the advent of cellular phone networks has revolutionized the economy and society as there were limited ground-based phone networks. These new networks have brought about a revolution in local market economies where women in the workforce, particularly in rural areas, can now bypass traditional local and constrictive financial trading institutions and deal directly with a global market.

The emergence of the information age has also had a profound impact on our economic systems, creating a much more efficient system of production, communication, and trade. Questions have been raised however, about the proposed shift from the paperless office to electronic records. Global production of paper and cardboard has continued to rise despite the technological revolution of digital storage (FAO 2020). As for the predicted savings in energy associated with production of paper, this has been at least partially offset by the enormous energy requirements associated with data storage. It has been reported that the internet will use a fifth of all the world's electricity by 2025, but technological advances may significantly reduce this percentage in the future through increased efficiency and conversion to renewable power sources. Despite the promise of technology, questions remain as to whether technology advances will be fast enough to offset the world's increased demands for material throughput, and if such developments will entail revenge effects that offset any benefits the technology might offer.

Degrowth: Because of the recognition within the disciplines of ecology and ecological economics that continued growth is not possible (e.g. NEF 2010), a new concept called degrowth has emerged which shares many critical characteristics with steady-state economics but entails a broader philosophical rationale. Kallis et al. (2015, pp. 3–4) provide a summary description of this concept:

> Degrowth signifies, first and foremost, a critique of growth. It calls for the decolonization of public debate from the idiom of economism and for the abolishment of economic growth as a social objective. Beyond that, degrowth signifies also a desired direction, one in which societies will use fewer natural resources and will organize and live differently than today. 'Sharing', 'simplicity', 'conviviality', 'care' and the 'commons' are primary significations of what this society might look like. Usually, degrowth is associated with the idea that smaller can be beautiful. Ecological economists define degrowth as an equitable downscaling of production and consumption that will reduce societies' throughput of energy and raw materials. However, our emphasis here is on different, not only less. Degrowth signifies a society with a smaller metabolism, but more importantly, a society with a metabolism which has a different structure and serves new functions. Degrowth does not call for doing less of the same. The object is not to make an elephant leaner, but to turn an elephant into a snail. In a degrowth society everything will be different: different activities, different forms and uses of energy, different relations, different gender roles, different allocations of time between paid and non-paid work, different relations with a non-human world. . . . Degrowth is not the same as negative GDP growth. Still, a reduction in GDP, as currently counted, is a likely outcome of actions promoted in the name of degrowth. A green, caring and communal economy is likely to secure the good life, but unlikely to increase gross domestic activity two or three percent per year.

Kallis et al. (2018) review research on degrowth and identify a limited number of historical and recent cases of small societies which have deemphasized growth. However, for the modern developed world and rapidly developing nations, the concept of degrowth is clearly an aspirational goal and, like the concept of a steady-state economy, raises critical questions over the timing, feasibility, and acceptability of its realization.

National and international initiatives

With accelerating climate change becoming increasingly obvious, a majority of Western industrialized nations have begun to propose serious steps to address the issue. England has promised to "halt the decline of nature" in what has been billed as a "net zero" equivalent for nature (BBC May 18, 2021). This initiative accompanies the UK government's plan to cut GHG emissions by 78 percent by 2035, three-quarters of the way to net zero by 2050 (Gov.UK 2021). In the United States, the Biden administration has established a goal of reducing GHG emissions by 50 percent by 2030 compared to 2005 levels by "leading a clean energy revolution" with the ultimate aim of achieving net-zero emissions by 2050 (White House 2021). The federal budget plan included a tax on imports from countries lagging in climate change responses in line with a similar European proposal, a clean energy standard, and tax breaks for renewables and EVs, all with the intention of creating a transformed economy with numerous high-paying jobs in a renewables-based environment.

But perhaps the most ambitious plan has recently been announced by the European Union (EU), which plans aggressive new laws to phase out fossil fuels under the rubric "Fit for 55" (EU 2021a, b, and c; *New York Times* July 14a and b, July 19, 2021). Major policy proposals to achieve a targeted reduction of 55 percent GHG emissions by 2030 and climate neutrality by 2050 fall into seven principal categories: the EU Emissions Trading System (ETS); energy efficiency; renewable energy; road transport CO_2 emissions; agriculture; land use, land-use change, and forestry; and effort sharing. A synopsis of major initiatives is presented in Appendix 1. Despite these dramatic policy proposals, several caveats are warranted. First, all twenty-seven EU member states must ratify the agreement and, even then, it may take several years to become law. Second, the EU accounts for only approximately 8 percent of global GHG emissions. And third, there is a built-in escape clause for the automotive sector allowing it to postpone achievement of the zero-emission target to 2040 (Fasken 2021).

China has also announced plans to address global warming. Given its role as the world's largest emitter of GHGs, any success in this endeavor will have a major impact on climate change. However, while the country is a global leader in the development and installation of wind and solar energy technology, it still relies on an extensive network of coal-fired power stations. Internal economic and political considerations pose a major challenge to the achievement of China's ambitious plans (see, for example, CNN June 30, 2021).

Similar challenges face some of the world's other major economies. The achievement of the Biden administration's ambitious goals depends on the delicate balance of power in the Congress and the outcome of the 2022 midterm and 2024 presidential elections. Norway, the United Kingdom, and Canada have been termed "climate hypocrites" for promising ambitious GHG reductions but engaging in activity that is inconsistent with the achievement of these goals (Kottasova 2021). Principal among these inconsistencies is the fact that all three countries continue to be major producers and/or exporters of fossil fuels. One policy analyst has accused the Canadian government of "cooking the books" by incorrectly claiming that the country's forests are carbon sinks, that energy-intensive CCS is a viable solution, and that international carbon offsets can substitute for real reductions in GHG emissions (Lee 2021).

The most exhaustive study of governmental and corporate plans for achieving net zero has been published by the Energy and Climate Intelligence Unit and Oxford Net Zero (Black et al. 2021). The study included 4,000 entities: 202 countries, all of the 806 states and regions in the world's 25 largest emitting countries, all 1,170 cities with populations above 500,000, and the 2,000 largest publicly traded companies by sales. They found that 124 countries, 73 states and regions, 155 cities, and 417 companies in their sample have made some form of commitment to net zero. The authors concluded that "a significant proportion of political and business leaders now accept the case for reaching net zero by mid-century" (p. 24), but they caution that "many nations with mid-century net zero pledges have NDCs [nationally determined contributions, which set targets to 2030] that do not match up in ambition" (p. 4).

Even if the Western industrialized countries achieve a modicum of success in lowering their GHG emissions in an attempt to achieve the Paris goals of limiting global temperature increase by 1.5–2°C, one study suggested that three countries in particular pose a serious threat to achieving these goals. Paris Equity Check (accessed July 26, 2021) concluded that Russia, Brazil, and China all have energy policies associated with 5°C rises in atmospheric temperature by 2100. This projection is consistent with the US EIA's (2019) forecast that all increases in global energy-related carbon dioxide emissions will be generated by countries that are not members of the Organisation for Economic Co-operation and Development (OECD).

COP26 and future directions

One of the most hopeful signs has been the outcome of the international conference held in Glasgow during November of 2021. Almost two hundred nations attended the conference, which was designed to build on the promises of the Paris Conference of 2015. Designated as COP26, the recent conference produced several remarkable results: a final statement (UN 2021a), accompanied by twenty-nine declarations and statements (UN 2021b, c, and d; see Appendix 2). The following summary of the results has been provided by the United Nations (UN 2021e) under the title of "What was agreed":

> Recognizing the emergency
> Countries reaffirmed the Paris Agreement goal of limiting the increase in the global average temperature to well below 2°C above pre-industrial levels and pursuing efforts to limit it to 1.5 °C. And they went further, expressing "alarm and utmost concern that human activities have caused around 1.1 °C of warming to date, that impacts are already being felt in every region, and that carbon budgets consistent with achieving the Paris Agreement temperature goal are now small and being rapidly depleted." They recognized that the impacts of climate change will be much lower at a temperature increase of 1.5 °C compared with 2 °C.

> Accelerating action
> Countries stressed the urgency of action "in this critical decade," when carbon dioxide emissions must be reduced by 45 per cent to reach net zero around mid-century. But with present climate plans—the Nationally Determined Contributions—falling far

short on ambition, the Glasgow Climate Pact calls on all countries to present stronger national action plans next year, instead of in 2025, which was the original timeline. Countries also called on the UNFCCC [United Nations Framework Convention on Climate Change] to do an annual NDC Synthesis Report to gauge the present level of ambition.

Moving away from fossil fuels

In perhaps the most contested decision in Glasgow, countries ultimately agreed to a provision calling for a phase-down of coal power and a phase-out of "inefficient" fossil fuel subsidies—two key issues that had never been explicitly mentioned in decisions of UN climate talks before, despite coal, oil and gas being the main drivers of global warming. Many countries, and NGOs [nongovernmental organizations], expressed dissatisfaction that the language on coal was significantly weakened (from phase-out to phase-down) and consequently, was not as ambitious as it needs to be.

Delivering on climate finance

Developed countries came to Glasgow falling short on their promise to deliver US$100 billion a year for developing countries. Voicing "regret," the Glasgow outcome reaffirms the pledge and urges developed countries to fully deliver on the US$100 billion goal urgently. Developed countries, in a report, expressed confidence that the target would be met in 2023.

Stepping up support for adaptation

The Glasgow Pact calls for a doubling of finance to support developing countries in adapting to the impacts of climate change and building resilience. This won't provide all the funding that poorer countries need, but it would significantly increase finance for protecting lives and livelihoods, which so far made up only about 25 per cent of all climate finance (with 75 per cent going towards green technologies to mitigate greenhouse gas emissions). Glasgow also established a work programme to define a global goal on adaptation, which will identify collective needs and solutions to the climate crisis already affecting many countries.

Completing the Paris rulebook

Countries reached agreement on the remaining issues of the so-called Paris rulebook, the operational details for the practical implementation of the Paris Agreement. Among them are the norms related to carbon markets, which will allow countries struggling to meet their emissions targets to purchase emissions reductions from other nations that have already exceeded their targets. Negotiations were also concluded on an Enhanced Transparency Framework, providing for common timeframes and agreed formats for countries to regularly report on progress, designed to build trust and confidence that all countries are contributing their share to the global effort.

Focusing on loss & damage

Acknowledging that climate change is having increasing impacts on people especially in the developing world, countries agreed to strengthen a network—known as the Santiago Network —that connects vulnerable countries with providers of technical assistance, knowledge and resources to address climate risks. They also launched a new "Glasgow dialogue" to discuss arrangements for the funding of activities to avert, minimize and address loss and damage associated with the adverse effects of climate change.

New deals and announcements
There were many other significant deals and announcements—outside of the Glasgow Climate Pact—which can have major positive impacts if they are indeed implemented. These include:

Forests
137 countries took a landmark step forward by committing to halt and reverse forest loss and land degradation by 2030. The pledge is backed by $12bn in public and $7.2bn in private funding. In addition, CEOs from more than 30 financial institutions with over $8.7 trillion of global assets committed to eliminate investment in activities linked to deforestation.

Methane
103 countries, including 15 major emitters, signed up to the Global Methane Pledge, which aims to limit methane emissions by 30 per cent by 2030, compared to 2020 levels. Methane, one of the most potent greenhouse gases, is responsible for a third of current warming from human activities.

Cars
Over 30 countries, six major vehicle manufacturers and other actors, like cities, set out their determination for all new car and van sales to be zero-emission vehicles by 2040 globally and 2035 in leading markets, accelerating the decarbonization of road transport, which currently accounts for about 10 per cent of global greenhouse gas emissions.

Coal
Leaders from South Africa, the United Kingdom, the United States, France, Germany, and the European Union announced a ground-breaking partnership to support South Africa—the world's most carbon-intensive electricity producer—with $8.5 billion over the next 3-5 years to make a just transition away from coal, to a low-carbon economy.

Private finance
Private financial institutions and central banks announced moves to realign trillions of dollars towards achieving global net zero emissions. Among them is the Glasgow Financial Alliance for Net Zero, with over 450 firms across 45 countries that control $130 trillion in assets, requiring its member to set robust, science-based near-term targets.

This extraordinary and complex negotiation raised hopes for the future but not without serious reservations about several important issues: the impact of lobbying to water down the recommendations, insufficient attention to the threats to small island nations, the ability and willingness of political leaders to make the hard choices necessary to implement the recommendations, and the apparent inability to limit warming to 1.5°C, with the world possibly reaching a temperature increase of 2.4°C (*Globe and Mail*, November 10 and 13, 2021; O'Grady 2021; Caldwell 2021; Ou et al. 2021; CNN November 14, 2021; NPR November 14, 2021; *Guardian* November 1, 2021; BBC November 9 and 17, 2021; Carter and Dowler 2021; Climate Action Tracker 2021).

All these exemplary goals must be viewed in the context of recent history. A recent study of the resource use of 150 countries over the last 30 years (O'Neill et al. 2018) concludes that:

> no country meets basic needs for its citizens at a globally sustainable level of resource use. Physical needs such as nutrition, sanitation, access to electricity and the elimination of extreme poverty could likely be met for all people without transgressing planetary boundaries. However, the universal achievement of more qualitative goals (for example, high life satisfaction) would require a level of resource use that is 2–6 times the sustainable level, based on current relationships. Strategies to improve physical and social provisioning systems, with a focus on sufficiency and equity, have the potential to move nations towards sustainability, but the challenge remains substantial.

As the *Guardian* (November 18, 2021) succinctly summarizes the research: "No country has met welfare goals in past 30 years 'without putting [the] planet at risk.'" These findings represent a major roadblock to the dual and fundamentally interrelated goals of providing for the welfare of a nation's citizens and protecting the earth's climate and ecosystems.

Final comment

In summary, the earth appears headed towards significantly higher temperatures with all their potentially devastating consequences. No single technological solution has been demonstrated as of yet that can reverse or significantly slow this progression in the immediate future. Nothing less than an extraordinary coordinated effort by civil society, business, and government can stem this tide. This will require us to overcome the economic, political, and social inertia that characterizes modern society and achieve a profound change in patterns of production and consumption at the global level. Such change will require an integrated array of new and creative economic instruments, regulations, and off-the-shelf technologies and the pursuit of new technologies contingent upon the application of the precautionary principle, with the ultimate aim of decarbonization of our economic systems (McDonough and Braungart 1988, 2002; Pacala and Socolow 2004; Socolow 2011; Griscom et al. 2017; LSE 2018; Davis et al. 2018; Falk et al. 2019; IMF 2019; World Bank 2019; Paul et al. 2019; Lempert et al. 2019; Quantis 2019; Stern 2021).

As the IPCC report of 2019 (p. 17) concluded:

> Pathways limiting global warming to 1.5°C with no or limited overshoot would require rapid and far-reaching transitions in energy, land, urban and infrastructure (including transport and buildings), and industrial systems (high confidence). These systems transitions are unprecedented in terms of scale, but not necessarily in terms of speed, and imply deep emissions reductions in all sectors, a wide portfolio of mitigation options and a significant upscaling of investments in those options.

In August 2021, the Spanish online magazine CTXT leaked text from a draft IPCC report scheduled to be released in March 2022. The conclusions in this report were startling, but not totally unexpected. The recommendations suggested that to stabilize the earth's climate, several momentous changes had to occur: (1) GHG emissions had to peak before 2025, (2) no more coal or natural gas power plants should be built and existing plants should be closed within the next decade, (3) major shifts are required in global diets to a greater reliance on vegetables rather than meat, and (4) major changes are required in the nature of our current transportation systems, presumably moving away from internal combustion engines (ICEs) and towards relocation of places of work and greater use of mass transit. Most critically, the report suggests that a radical change is required in our economic system, abandoning the preoccupation with continued economic growth, focusing on inter alia reduced material throughput. This recommendation is in line with the concepts of steady state and degrowth described above. On a cautiously positive note, the report observes that fighting climate change need not necessarily be incompatible with alleviating poverty, as the top ten percent of the richest nations emit ten times more GHGs than the bottom ten percent. However, if we fail at this unprecedented and daunting undertaking, the worst-case scenario suggests that the earth will be faced with increasing frequency and magnitude of climate-related disasters with devastating storms, fires and floods, heat and drought rendering large areas of the globe uninhabitable, and a Malthusian era of food scarcity and disease.

References

Ahrends, A. et al. (2017) Proceedings of the Royal Society B, "China's fight to halt tree cover loss," May 17.

Allwood, J.M. et al. (2019) *Absolute Zero: Delivering the UK's Climate Change Commitment with Incremental Changes to Today's Technologies*, UK FIRES, November 29.

Anderson, Kevin and Glen Peters (2016) *Science*, "The trouble with negative emissions," October 14.

Baccini, A. et al. (2017) *Science*, "Tropical forests are a net carbon source based on aboveground measurements of gain and loss," October 13.

Bastin, Jean-Francois et al. (2019) *Science*, "The global tree restoration potential," July 5.

BBC (2018) "Key 'step forward' in cutting cost of removing CO2 from air," June 7.

BBC (2019) "Climate change: 'Magic bullet' carbon solution takes big step," April 3.

BBC (2019) "Climate change: Big lifestyle changes are the only answer," October 11.

BBC (2021) "Climate change: Net zero targets are 'pie in the sky'," March 31.

BBC (2021) "Green light for 'net zero' equivalent for nature," May 18.

BBC (2021) "COP26: Document leak reveals nations lobbying to change key climate report," October 21.

BBC (2021) "COP26: World headed for 2.4C warming despite climate summit—report," November 9.

BBC (2021) "Climate change: What did the scientist make of COP26?" November 17.

Biello, David (2016) "Carbon capture may be too expensive to combat climate change," Scientific American, January 1.

Biniek, Krysta et al. (2020) "Driving CO2 emissions to zero (and beyond) with carbon capture, use, and storage," *McKinsey Quarterly*, June.

Black, Richard et al. (2021) *Taking Stock: A Global Assessment of Net Zero Targets*, The Energy and Climate Intelligence Unit and Oxford Net Zero, March.

BlackRock (n.d.) *Investment and Fiduciary Analysis for Potential Fossil Fuel Divestment: Phase 1; Survey of Divestments of Fossil Fuel Reserve Owners and Identification of Securities Issued by Fossil Fuel Reserve Owners*, report draft.

Blackstock, J.J. et al. (2009) *Climate Engineering Responses to Climate Emergencies*, Santa Barbara, CA, Novim, July 29.

Boysen, Lena R. et al. (2017) *Earth's Future*, "The limits to global-warming mitigation by terrestrial carbon removal," May 17.

Broecker, Wallace S. and Robert Kunzig (2008) *Fixing Climate: What Past Climate Changes Reveal about the Current Threat—And How to Counter It*, New York: Hill and Wang.

Brooks, David B. (1981) Zero *Energy* Growth for Canada, Toronto: McClelland and Stewart.

Caldwell, Christopher (2021) "Bankers took over the climate change summit: That's bad for democracy," New York Times, November 25.

Carbonbrief (2014) "Around the world in 22 carbon capture projects," October 7.

Carney, Mark (2021) *Value(s): Building a Better World for All*, Toronto: Penguin Random House.

Carter, Lawrence and Crispin Dowler (2021) "Leaked documents reveal the fossil fuel and meat producing countries lobbying against climate action," Unearthed, October.

CBC (2019) "Canada's forests actually emit more carbon than they absorb—despite what you've heard on Facebook," February 12.

CBC (2019) "Carbon capture and storage: Hasn't Alberta learned its lesson," November 29.

CCSA (Carbon Capture and Storage Association) (n.d.) "International CCS projects."

Ceres (2020) *Addressing Climate as a Systemic Risk: A Call to Action for U.S. Financial Regulators*, June.

CIEL (Center for International Environmental Law) (2019) *Fuel to the Fire: How Geoengineering Threatens to Entrench Fossil Fuels and Accelerate the Climate Crisis*, February.

Circle Economy (2018) The Circularity Gap Report: An Analysis of the Circular State of the Global Economy, January. Circle Economy (2020) *The Circularity Gap Report 2020: When Circularity Goes from Bad to Worse; The Power of Countries to Change the Game*.

Clean Edge (2021) "Q3 2021 review," March.

Climate Action Tracker (2021) "COP26 initial assessment: Glasgow sectoral initiatives currently close the 2030 emissions gap by 9%," November.

Climate Council (2015) *Climate Change 2015: Growing Risks, Critical Choices*.

CNN (2021) "New Zealand bill would require banks to disclose climate risks, in a world first," April 13.

CNN (2021) "The world is waking up to the climate crisis. Just look at Wall Street," April 23.

CNN (2021) "China is facing its worst power shortage in a decade. That's a problem for the whole world," June 30.

CNN (2021) "COP26 ended with the Glasgow Climate Pact. Here's where it succeeded and failed," November 14.

Conniff, Richard (2020) "The last resort: Can we remove enough CO_2 from the atmosphere to slow or even reverse climate change? Scientific American, summer.

Crutzen, Paul (2006) *Climate Change*, "Albedo enhancement by stratospheric sulfur injections: A contribution to resolve a policy dilemma?" July 25.

CTXT (2021) "El IPCC considera que el decrecimiento es clave para mitigar el cambio climatico" (The IPCC considers degrowth to be key to mitigating climate change), August 7.

Cusack, Daniela F. et al. (2014) *Frontiers in Ecology*, "An interdisciplinary assessment of climate engineering strategies," June.

Czech, Brian (2013) *Supply Shock: Economic Growth at the Crossroads and the Steady State Solution*, Gabriola Island, BC: New Society Publishers.

D'Alisa, Giacomo et al. (eds.) (2015) *Degrowth: A Vocabulary for a New Era*, New York: Routledge.

Daly, Herman E. (ed.) (1973) *Toward a Steady-State Economy*, San Francisco: W.H. Freeman & Co.

Daly, Herman E. (1991) *Steady-State Economics*, second edition, Washington, DC: Island Press.

Daly, Herman E. (2014) *From Uneconomic Growth to a Steady-State Economy*, Cheltenham, UK; Northampton, MA: Edward Elgar.

Datamaran (2021) "A first look at the EU sustainability standards: 10 top highlights from the new EFRAG's report," March 18.

Davis, Steven J. et al. (2018) *Science*, "Net-zero emissions energy systems," June 29.

Dean, Cornelia (2008) "Handle with care," New York Times, August 11.

Dowell, Niall Mac et al. (2017) *Nature Climate Change*, "The role of CO2 capture and utilization in mitigating climate change," April.

Drever, C. Ronnie et al. (2021) *Science Advances*, "Natural climate solutions for Canada," June 4.

Earth Institute, Columbia University (n.d.) "Klaus S. Lackner, director of the Lenfest Center for Sustainable Energy."

Earth's Future (2016) "Crutzen +10: Reflecting upon 10 years of geoengineering research," special issue, May 16, updated February 2, 2018.

Ellen MacArthur Foundation (2021) Completing the Picture: How the Circular Economy Tackles Climate Change.

Environmental Investigation Agency (2019a) *State of Corruption: The Top-Level Conspiracy behind the Global Trade in Myanmar's Stolen Teak*, February.

Environmental Investigation Agency (2019b) *Ban-boozled: How Corruption and Collusion Fuel Illegal Rosewood Trade in Ghana*, July 30.

EU (European Union) (2021a) "2030 climate target plan."

EU (European Union) (2021b) "EU climate target plan 2030: Building a modern, sustainable and resilient Europe."

EU (European Union) (2021c) "EU climate target plan 2030: Key contributors and policy tools."

EU (European Union) (2021d) "European Green Deal: Commission proposes transformation of EU economy and society to meet climate ambitions," press release, July 14.

European Central Bank (2020) *Guide on Climate-Related and Environmental Risks*, November.

Falk, Johan et al. (2019) "Future Earth: Scaling 36 solutions to halve emissions by 2030," Exponential Roadmap 1.5.

FAO (Food and Agriculture Organization) (2020) Pulp and Paper Capacities.

Fasken (2021) "A bold step: The EU accelerates targets for zero-emission vehicles," Vancouver, July 27.

Fleming, James Rodger (2010) *Fixing the Sky: The Checkered History of Weather and Climate Control*, New York: Columbia University Press.

Force of Nature (2021) "Mapping forest regeneration hotspots."

FSOC (Financial Stability Oversight Council) (2021) Report on Climate-Related Financial Risk 2021.

Fuss, Sabine et al. (2018) *Environmental Research Letters*, "Negative emissions: Part 2; Costs, potential and side effects," May 22.

Gelenbe, Erol and Yves Caseau (2015) *Ubiquity*, "The impact of information technology on energy consumption and carbon emissions," June.

Global CCS Institute (2020) Global Status of CCS 2020.

Global Witness (2015) *The Cost of Luxury: Cambodia's Illegal Trade in Precious Wood with China*, February.

Globe and Mail (2012) "Alberta's carbon capture efforts set back," April 26.

Globe and Mail (2021) "COP26: World to warm at least 2.4 C, climate analysis shows," November 10.

Globe and Mail (2021) "COP26 summit ends with agreement endorsed by almost 200 countries, but skepticism remains," November 13.

Gov.UK (2021) "UK enshrine new target in law to slash emissions by 78% by 2035," April 20.

Griscom, Bronson W. et al. (2017) *PNAS*, "Natural climate solutions," October 31.

Guardian (2011) "Longannet carbon capture project cancelled," October 19.

Guardian (2021) "Climate optimism is an illusion, UN chief tells Cop26," November 1.

Guardian (2021) "No country has met welfare goals in past 30 years 'without putting planet at risk'," November 18.

Hamilton, Cline (2013) *Earthmasters: The Dawn of the Age of Climate Engineering*, New Haven, CT: Yale University Press.

Hansen, James et al. (2017) *Earth System Dynamics*, "Young people's burden: Requirement of negative CO2 emissions," July 18.

Harvard Law School Forum on Corporate Governance (2020) "Addressing climate as a systemic risk: A call to action for financial regulators," June 28.

Hegerl, Gabriele C. and Susan Solomon (2009) *Science*, "Risks of climate engineering," August 21.

Heinberg, Richard (2011) *The End of Growth: Adapting to Our New Economic Reality*, Gabriola Island, BC: New Society Publishers.

Henderson, Rebecca (2021) *Reimagining Capitalism in a World on Fire*, New York: Hachette Book Group.

Hoang, Nguyen Tien and Kelichiro Kanemoto (2021) *Nature Ecology & Evolution*, "Mapping the deforestation footprint of nations reveals growing threat to tropical forests," March 29.

Hoare, Alison (2015) *Tackling Illegal Logging and the Related Trade: What Progress and Where Next?* Chatham House, July.

Hua, Fangyuan et al. (2018) *Biological Conservation*, "Tree plantations displacing native forests: The nature and drivers of apparent forest recovery on former croplands in Southwestern China from 2000 to 2015," June.

IEA (International Energy Agency) (2020) *Energy Technology Perspectives 2020: Special Report on Carbon Capture Utilisation and Storage; CCUS in Clean Energy Transitions*.

IMF (International Monetary Fund) (2019) *Mitigating Climate Change*.

Inside Climate News (2021) "Biggest "direct air capture" plant starts pulling in carbon, but involves a fraction of the gas in the atmosphere," September 9.

Institute for Energy Economics and Financial Analysis (2021) "Major investment advisors BlackRock and Meketa provide a fiduciary path through the energy transition," March 22.

IPCC (Intergovernmental Panel on Climate Change) (2005) Carbon Dioxide Capture and Storage.

IPCC (Intergovernmental Panel on Climate Change) (2019) *Special Report: Global Warming at 1.5C*, October 21.

IRENA (International Renewable Energy Agency) (2021) *World Energy Transitions Outlook: 1.5°C Pathway*.

Irvine, Peter et al. (2019) *Nature Climate Change*, "Halving warming with idealized solar geoengineering moderates key climate hazards," March 11.

Jackson, Tim (2009) *Prosperity Without Growth: Economics for a Finite Planet*, London: Earthscan.

Jacobson, Mark Z. (2019) *Energy & Environmental Science*, "The health and climate impacts of carbon capture and direct air capture," December 1.

Johnson, S. (2003) *International Forestry Review*, "Estimating the extent of illegal trade of tropical forest products," September.

Kallis, Giorgos et al. (2015) "Introduction: Degrowth," in Giacomo D'Alisa et al. (eds.) *Degrowth: A Vocabulary for a New Era*, New York: Routledge.

Kallis, Giorgos et al. (2018) Annual Review of Environment and Resources, "Research on degrowth," October.

Katsigris, E. et al. (2004) *International Forestry Review*, "The China forest products trade: Overview of Asia-Pacific supplying countries, impacts and implications," December.

Kedward, Katie et al. (2020) "Managing nature-related financial risks: A precautionary policy approach for central banks and financial supervisors," Working paper: IIPP WP 2020-09, UCL Institute for Innovation and Public Purpose, August 18.

Keith, David W. (2010) *PNAS*, "Photophoretic levitation of engineered aerosols for geoengineering," September 21.

Keith, David W. (2021) Science, "Toward constructive disagreement about geoengineering," November 12.

Keith, David W. et al. (2018) *Joule*, "A process for capturing CO2 from the atmosphere," August 15.

Keller, David P. et al. (2014) *Nature Communications*, "Potential climate engineering effectiveness and side effects during a high carbon dioxide–emission scenario," February 25.

Kintisch, Eli (2010) *Hack the Planet: Science's Best Hope—or Worst Nightmare—for Averting Climate Catastrophe*, Hoboken, NJ: John Wiley & Sons.

Kirchsteiger, C. (2008) *Safety Science*, "Carbon capture and storage-desirability from a risk management point of view," August.

Kolbert, Elizabeth (2021) *Under a White Sky: The Nature of the Future*, New York: Random House.

Kottasova, Ivana (2021) "Norway, the UK and Canada are not climate champions, they are climate hypocrites," CNN, February 17.

Kunzig, Robert (2008) "A sunshade for planet earth," Scientific American, November.

Kunzig, Robert and Wallace S. Broecker (2008) *Fixing Climate: The Story of Climate Science—and How to Stop Global Warming*, London: Green Profile Press.

Lawn, Philip (2011) Annals of the New York Academy of Sciences, "Is steady-state capitalism viable?" February.

Lee, Marc (2021) "Road to zero carbon emissions full of potholes," Vancouver Sun, June 24.

Lempert, Robert et al. (2019) "Pathways to 2050: Alternative scenarios for decarbonizing the U.S. economy," RAND Corporation, May.

Lenzi, Dominic (2018) *Global Sustainability*, "The ethics of negative emissions," May 8.

Lenzi, Dominic et al. (2018) *Nature*, "Weigh the ethics of plans to mop up carbon dioxide," September 20.

LSE (London School of Economics) (2018) "What is a carbon price and why do we need one?" May 17.

Matricardi, Eraldo Aparaecido Trondoli et al. (2020) *Science*, "Long-term forest degradation surpasses deforestation in the Brazilian Amazon," September 11.

McDonough, William and Michael Braungart (1998) *Atlantic Monthly*, "The next industrial revolution," October, 82–92.

McDonough, William and Michael Braungart (2002) *Cradle to Cradle: Remaking the Way We Make Things*, New York: North Point Press.

McKibben, Bill (2021) "The enormous risk of atmospheric hacking," New Yorker, February 18.

Minx, Jan C. et al. (2018) *Environmental Research Letters*, "Negative emissions: Part 1; Research landscape and synthesis," May 22.

Mir, J. and A. Fraser (2003) *International Forestry Review*, "Illegal logging in the Asia-Pacific region: An ADB perspective," September.

Moody's (2021) "Financial firms that take rapid, predictable pace to zero financed emissions will win the race," October 12.

Mulligan, James et al. (2018) "Technological carbon removal in the United States." Working paper, World Resources Institute, September.

NAS (National Academy of Sciences) (2019) *Negative Emissions Technologies and Reliable Sequestration: A Research Agenda*.

NAS (National Academy of Sciences) (2021) *Reflecting Sunlight: Recommendations for Solar Geoengineering Research and Research Governance*.

NASA Earth Observatory (2019) "China and India lead the way in greening."

Natural Resources Canada (2007) "Is Canada's forest a carbon sink or source?" October.

NEF (New Economics Foundation) (2010) Growth Isn't Possible: Why We Need a New Economic Direction, January.

Nemetz, Peter N. (2021) *The Economics and Business of Sustainability*, Abingdon, UK; New York: Routledge.

New Scientist (2011) "UK's carbon-capture failure is part of a global trend," October 24.

New York Times (2011) "Utility shelves ambitious plan to limit carbon," July 13.

New York Times (2011) "AEP move to stop carbon capture and sequestration project shocks utilities, miners," July 15.

New York Times (2011) "Obstacles to capturing carbon gas," July 31.

New York Times (2012) "Growing doubts in Europe on future of carbon storage," January 16.

New York Times (2012) "With natural gas plentiful and cheap, carbon capture projects stumble," May 19.

New York Times (2017) "Carbon in atmosphere is rising, even as emissions stabilize," June 26.

New York Times (2019) "China's voracious appetite for timber stokes fury in Russia and beyond," April 9.

New York Times (2020) "New York's $226 billion pension fund is dropping fossil fuel stocks," December 9.

New York Times (2020a) "To cut emissions to zero, U.S. needs to make big changes in next 10 years," December 15.

New York Times (2020b) "Fed joins climate network, to applause from the left," December 15.

New York Times (2021) "Oil giants prepare to put carbon back in the ground," March 8.

New York Times (2021) "Tropical forest destruction accelerated in 2020," March 31.

New York Times (2021a) "How Europe's ambitious new climate agenda will affect businesses," July 14.

New York Times (2021b) "Europe unveils plan to shift from fossil fuels, setting up potential trade spats," July 14.

New York Times (2021) "Europe plans aggressive new laws to phase out fossil fuels," July 19.

New York Times (2021) "Hundreds of companies promised to help save forests. Did they?" December 2.

New York Times (2021a) "Britain enlists banks to fight climate change," December 5.

New York Times (2021b) "Is an all-encompassing mobility app making a comeback?" December 5.

NGFS (Network for Greening the Financial System) (2020) "Overview of environmental risk analysis by financial institutions," September and October 9.

NIC (National Intelligence Council) (2021) *Global Trends 2040: A More Contested World*, March.

NPR (2021) "An island nation's representative says COP26 failed to set actionable response plan," November 14.

OECD (Organisation for Economic Co-operation and Development) (2017) *Investing in Climate, Investing in Growth*, May 23.

O'Grady, Cathleen (2021) *Science*, "The new climate path is more ambitious. But hopes dim for limiting warming to 1.5°C," November 16.

O'Neill, Daniel W. et al. (2018) Nature Sustainability, "A good life for all within planetary boundaries," February.

Ou, Yang et al. (2021) *Science*, "Can updated climate pledges limit warming well below 2°C," November 5.

Pacala, S. and R. Socolow (2004) *Science*, "Stabilization wedges: Solving the climate problem for the next 50 years with current technologies," August 13.

Paris Equity Check (accessed July 26, 2021) "Pledged warming map."

Paul, Mark et al. (2019) *Decarbonizing the US Economy: Pathways toward a Green New Deal*, Roosevelt Institute, June.

Pilling, David (2018) The Growth Delusion, London: Bloomsbury.

Plumer, Brad and Christopher Flavelle (2021) "Businesses aim to pull greenhouse gases from the air. It's a gamble," New York Times, June 18.

Princeton University (2020) *Net-Zero America: Potential Pathways, Infrastructure, and Impacts*, December 15.

Proctor, Jonathan et al. (2018) *Nature*, "Estimating global agricultural effects of geoengineering using volcanic eruptions," August 23.

Quantis (2019) *The Quantis Food Report 2020*.

Raftery, Adrian E. et al. (2017) *Nature Climate Change*, "Less than 2°C warming by 2100 unlikely," September.

RFF (Resources For the Future) (2020) "Lessons from COVID-19 on air pollution, managing climate risk in investments, and more," May 15.

Robock, Alan (2008) *Bulletin of the Atomic Scientists*, "20 reasons why geoengineering may be a bad idea," May/June.

Robock, Alan (2020) *The Bridge*, "Benefits and risks of stratospheric solar radiation management for climate intervention (geoengineering)," spring.

Rochon, Emily et al. (2008) *False Hope: Why Carbon Capture and Storage Won't Save The Climate*, Greenpeace, May.

Royal Society (UK) (2009) *Geoengineering the Climate: Science, Governance and Uncertainty*, September.

Rubin, Jeff (2012) The *End of Growth*, Toronto: Random House Canada.

Science (2021) "Carbon capture marches toward practical use," March 26.

Science (2021) "Can updated climate pledges limit warming well below 2°C?" November 5.

Science (2021) "The new climate pact is more ambitious. But hopes dim for limiting warming to 1.5°C," November 18.

Scientific American (2008) "The hidden dangers of geoengineering." October 3.

SEC (Securities and Exchange Commission) (2021) "SEC response to climate and ESG risks and opportunities," April 9.

SEI (Stockholm Environment Institute) et al. (2019) *The Production Gap Report: The Discrepancy between Countries' Planned Fossil Fuel Production and Global Production Levels Consistent with Limiting Warming to 1.5°C or 2°C.*

SEI (Stockholm Environment Institute) et al. (2020) *The Production Gap Report.*

Sierra Club of BC (2019) "Hidden, ignored and growing: B.C.'s forest carbon emissions," January.

Siriwat, Pewnthai and Vincent Nijman (2018) *Environmental Conservation*, "Using online media-sourced seizure data to assess the illegal wildlife trade in Siamese rosewood," January 13.

Smil, Vaclav (2010) *Energy Myths and Reality: Bringing Science to the Energy Policy Debate,* Washington, DC: AEI Press.

Socolow, Robert (2011) *Bulletin of the Atomic Scientists*, "Wedges reaffirmed: A short essay and ten solicited comments on the essay," September 27.

Solomon, Susan et al. (2009) *PNAS*, "Irreversible climate change due to carbon dioxide emissions," February 10.

Stahel, Walter R. (2016) *Nature*, "Circular economy," March 24.

Steffen Will et al. (2018) *PNAS*, "Trajectories of the Earth system in the Anthropocene," August 14.

Stern, Nicholas (2007) The Economics of Climate Change: The Stern Review, Cambridge: Cambridge University Press.

Stern, Nicholas (2021) "A time for action on climate change and a time for change in economics." Working paper based on address to Royal Economic Society Conference, past president's address, Centre for Climate Change Economics and Grantham Research Institute on Climate Change and the Environment, October.

Stockholm Resilience Centre (2018) "Planet at risk of heading towards 'Hothouse Earth' state," August 6.

Sustainability.com (2021) *Circularity: From Theory to Practice*, December.

Swiss Re Institute (2021) *The Economics of Climate Change: No Action Not an Option*, April.

Thomson, Graham (2009) *Burying Carbon Dioxide in Underground Saline Aquifers: Political Folly or Climate Change Fix?* Munk Centre for International Studies, University of Toronto, September 23.

Trisos, Christopher H. et al. (2018) *Nature Ecology & Evolution*, "Potentially dangerous consequences for biodiversity of solar engineering implementation and termination," January.

UN (United Nations) (2021a) "Climate Change Conference UK 2021: COP26; The Glasgow Climate Pact."

UN (United Nations) (2021b) "Outcomes 1: UN Climate Change Conference (COP26) at the SEC; Glasgow 2021."

UN (United Nations) (2021c) "Outcomes 2: UN Climate Change Conference (COP26) at the SEC; Glasgow 2021."

UN (United Nations) (2021d) "Outcomes 3: UN Climate Change Conference (COP26) at the SEC; Glasgow 2021."

UN (United Nations) (2021e) COP26: Together for Our Planet.

Unearthed (2021) "Leaked documents reveal the fossil fuel and meat producing countries lobbying against climate action," October.

UNEP (United Nations Environment Programme) (2010) *Emerging Issues*: *Environmental Consequences of Ocean Acidification: A Threat to Food Security*, Nairobi.

UNEP (United Nations Environment Programme) (2021a) *Adaptation Gap Report 2020.*

UNEP (United Nations Environment Programme) (2021b) *Emissions Gap Report*, November.

UNEP (United Nations Environment Programme) (2021c) *State of Finance for Nature*.

US CFTC (Commodity Futures Trading Commission) (2020) *Managing Climate Risk in the U.S. Financial System*. Report of the Climate-Related Market Risk Subcommittee, Market Risk Advisory Committee of the US Commodity Futures Trading Commission, September 30.

US EIA (Energy Information Administration) (2019) "EIA projects nearly 50% increase in world energy usage by 2050, led by growth in Asia," September 25.

US EPA (Environmental Protection Agency) (2008) *Vulnerability Evaluation Framework for Geologic Sequestration of Carbon Dioxide*, Washington, DC, July 10.

US GAO (General Accountability Office) (2011) "Climate engineering: Technical status, future directions and potential response," July.

US Global Change Research Program, *US Fourth National Climate Assessment* (2018) especially Chapter 2, "Our changing climate," revised March 2021.

US White House (2021) "Fact sheet: Present Biden's leaders summit on climate," April 23.

Vancouver Sun (2021) "Shell Alberta refinery carbon capture plan part of net-zero goal," July 13.

Victor, Peter A. (2019) *Managing without Growth: Slower by Design, Not Disaster*, second edition, Cheltenham: Edward Elgar.

Vina, Andres et al. (2016) *Science Advances*, "Effects of conservation policy on China's forest recovery," March 18.

Washington, Haydn and Paul Twomey (eds.) (2016) *A Future Beyond Growth: Towards a Steady State Economy*, London: Routledge.

WEF (World Economic Forum) (2021) *Consultation: Nature and Net Zero*, January.

Weitzman, Martin L. (2009) *Review of Economics and Statistics*, "On modeling and interpreting the economics of catastrophic climate change," 91(1): 1–19.

Wilday, Jill et al. (2011) *Process Safety and Environmental Protection*, "Hazards from carbon dioxide capture, transport and storage," November.

WMO (World Meteorological Organization) (2021) *State of the Global Climate 2020*.

WMO (World Meteorological Organization) (2021) *Global Annual to Decadal Climate Update: Target years; 2021 and 2021–2025*.

World Bank (2019) *State and Trends of Carbon Pricing*.

Appendix 1

European Commission climate proposals of July 14, 2021 (EU 2021d)

EU Emissions Trading System: The European Commission is proposing to lower the overall emissions cap even further and increase its annual rate of reduction. The Commission is also proposing to phase out free emission allowances for aviation and align with the global Carbon Offsetting and Reduction Scheme for International Aviation, and to include shipping emissions for the first time in the EU ETS. To address the lack of emissions reductions in road transport and buildings, a separate new emissions trading system is set up for buildings and fuel distribution for road transport.

Effort Sharing Regulation: This assigns strengthened emissions reduction targets to each member state for buildings, road, and domestic maritime transport, agriculture, waste, and small industries.

Regulation on Land Use, Forestry and Agriculture: This sets an overall EU target for carbon removal by natural sinks at a level equivalent to 310 million tonnes of CO_2 emissions by 2030. By 2035, the EU should aim to reach climate neutrality in the land-use, forestry, and agriculture sectors, including also agricultural non-CO_2

emissions, such as those from fertilizer use and livestock. The EU Forest Strategy aims to improve the quality, quantity, and resilience of EU forests. It supports foresters and the forest-based bioeconomy while keeping harvesting and biomass use sustainable, preserving biodiversity, and setting out a plan to plant three billion trees across Europe by 2030.

Renewable Energy Directive: This will set an increased target to produce 40 percent of EU energy from renewable sources. To meet both EU climate and environmental goals, sustainability criteria for the use of bioenergy are strengthened and member states must design any support schemes for bioenergy in a way that respects the cascading principle of uses for woody biomass.

Energy Efficiency Directive: This will set a more ambitious binding annual target for reducing energy use at EU level. It will guide how national contributions are established and will almost double the annual energy saving obligation for member states. The public sector will be required to renovate 3 percent of its buildings each year to drive the renovation wave, create jobs, and bring down energy use and costs to the taxpayer.

Stronger CO2 emissions standards for cars and vans: These will accelerate the transition to zero-emission mobility by requiring average emissions of new cars to come down by 55 percent from 2030 and 100 percent from 2035 compared to 2021 levels. As a result, all new cars registered as of 2035 will be zero emission. To ensure that drivers are able to charge or fuel their vehicles at a reliable network across Europe, the revised **Alternative Fuels Infrastructure Regulation** will require member states to expand charging capacity in line with zero-emission car sales, and to install charging and fueling points at regular intervals on major highways: every 60 kilometers for electric charging and every 150 kilometers for hydrogen refueling.

Aviation and maritime fuels cause significant pollution and also require dedicated action to complement emissions trading. The Alternative Fuels Infrastructure Regulation requires that aircraft and ships have access to clean electricity supply in major ports and airports. The **ReFuelEU Aviation Initiative** will oblige fuel suppliers to blend increasing levels of sustainable aviation fuels in jet fuel taken onboard at EU airports, including synthetic low-carbon fuels, known as e-fuels. Similarly, the **FuelEU Maritime Initiative** will stimulate the uptake of sustainable maritime fuels and zero-emission technologies by setting a maximum limit on the GHG content of energy used by ships calling at European ports.

A revision of the Energy Taxation Directive: This revision proposes to align the taxation of energy products with EU energy and climate policies, promoting clean technologies and removing outdated exemptions and reduced rates that currently encourage the use of fossil fuels.

New Carbon Border Adjustment Mechanism: This will put a carbon price on imports of a targeted selection of products to ensure that ambitious climate action in Europe does not lead to "carbon leakage." This will ensure that European emission reductions contribute to a global emissions decline, instead of pushing carbon-intensive production outside Europe.

Appendix 2

COP26 list of statements and declarations

Adaptation Research Alliance, Joint Statement on Launch, 9 November 2021

Agricultural Commodity Companies, Corporate Statement of Purpose

Breakthrough Agenda, Launching an annual Global Checkpoint Process in 2022

Chair's Summary, Policy Dialogue on Accelerating Transition to Sustainable Agriculture through Redirecting Public Policies and Support and Scaling Innovation

Clydebank Declaration for Green Shipping Corridors

Co-Chairs Conclusions of Education and Environment Ministers Summit at COP26

COP26 Congo Basin Joint Donor Statement

COP26 Declaration on Accelerating the Transition to 100% Zero Emission Cars and Vans

COP26 Health Programme

COP26 IPLC Forest Tenure Joint Donor Statement

COP26 World Leaders Summit: Presidency Summary

COP26 World Leaders Summit: Statement on the Breakthrough Agenda

Focus of Energy Transition Council

Forests, Agriculture and Commodity Trade

Glasgow Leaders' Declaration on Forests and Land Use

Global Action Agenda for Innovation in Agriculture

Global Coal to Clean Power Transition Statement

Global Forest Finance Pledge

Green Grids Initiative: One Sun One World One Grid: One Sun Declaration

International Aviation Climate Ambition Coalition

Joint statement in support of the UK–IEA Product Efficiency Call to Action to raise global ambition through the Super-Efficient Equipment and Appliance Deployment (SEAD) initiative

MDB Joint Climate Statement

MDB Joint Nature Statement

Mission Innovation: Breakthrough Energy Collaboration Agreement

New Mission Innovation Missions

Political Declaration on the Just Energy Transition in South Africa

Statement on International Public Support for the Clean Energy Transition

Supporting the Conditions for a Just Transition Internationally

---

Note that the full text of these documents can be found at UN 2021b, c and d.

11 Pandemics and sustainability

Humanity has been afflicted with disease throughout history, but especially following the agricultural revolution of ten thousand years ago with the subsequent dramatic transformation in human economic, social, and political institutions. Driving the emergence of these new diseases, which were largely absent from hunter-gatherer societies (see Chapter 2), were such factors as the domestication of animals, acting as a conduit of diseases from wild animals, and settlement patterns involving increased population density. Much has been written about the role that disease has played in human history (Cartwright 1972; Cohen 1989; Nikiforuk 1991; McNeill 1998; Cantor 2001; Oldstone 2010; Harrison 2012; Quammen 2012; Shah 2016; Skwarecki 2016; Snowden 2020; Harper 2021). In many cases, the impact has been dramatic, determining the outcome of battles and the fate of nations and empires (Winegard 2019). An archetypal example is provided by the vicissitudes of the Roman Empire over its long history, which was influenced to no small degree by disease and climate change (Harper 2017). While epidemics have been relatively common in history, pandemics have had the most dramatic consequences. The Black Death of the fourteenth century was responsible for as many as two hundred million deaths, killing as much as one-third of the world's population (Meacham 2020). This momentous event is posited to have destroyed the old feudal order and begun the long transition into modernity (Johnson and Mueller 2002; Alfani 2020).

Prior to the emergence of COVID-19 in 2019–20, the most recent global experience of pandemics dated to the Spanish flu of 1918, which afflicted a world exhausted from the First World War. It affected as much as one-third of the global population with estimates of mortality ranging as high as 50–100 million (Hagemann 2020). As of the writing of this book, confirmed global COVID-19 cases have reached more than 318 million with 5.5 million deaths (WHO Coronavirus Dashboard accessed January 16, 2022). However, the WHO has expressed the opinion that the real toll of this disease could be as high as six to eight million cases due to widespread underreporting (*Hill* May 21, 2021). One example, in particular, is illustrative of this problem. The *New York Times* (May 25, 2021) conducted its own study of Indian epidemiological data with the help of experts. Official case numbers suggested 26.9 million reported cases with 307,231 deaths. The newspaper created three additional scenarios: a conservative scenario, a more likely scenario, and a worse scenario. In this last scenario, cases were estimated at 700.7 million with 4.2 million fatalities. A companion study by Anand et al. (2021) has produced an estimate of mortality as high as 4.9 million. These are much more reasonable estimates than the official death toll in light of findings of a recent serosurvey which estimated that 21.4 percent of the population had been exposed to the virus (BBC February 5, 2021). In fact, India is not the only country that appears to have significantly undercounted its COVID-19

DOI: 10.4324/9781003199540-14

cases. It seems to be an endemic problem across African countries in no small part due to overstretched and underfunded national health care systems (Wild 2021). Even in the United States it has been estimated that cases may have been undercounted by as much as 60 percent (Irons and Raftery 2021).

A recent comparison of the COVID-19 and 1918 flu pandemics has found that excess deaths in 2020 surpassed those of 1918 (*New York Times* April 23, 2021). Not all countries have been impacted by COVID-19 to the same degree. For example, while the United States has approximately 4 percent of the world's population, at one point it had experienced 25 percent of the cases and 20 percent of the deaths (WHO and US CDC websites, accessed February 16, 2021).

The COVID-19 virus has been devastating, affecting all spheres of human activity. The virus has had a major impact on international trade (WTO 2020) and has been particularly severe among developing nations (World Bank 2020a; Egger et al. 2021) with the cumulative effects of COVID-19, conflict, and climate change leading to a reversal in gains in poverty eradication for the first time in a generation (World Bank 2020b). While the developed nations have more resilience than their southern counterparts, none has escaped the economic, social, and political impacts of the virus. For example, the US Congressional Budget Office (CBO 2020) has projected that over an eleven-year time horizon, the United States could lose as much as $7.9 trillion in gross domestic product (GDP). Socially and politically, many industrialized nations have experienced the rise of right-wing extremism, threatening the post Second World War democratic consensus. In the United States, the pandemic is considered a contributing factor to the change in government during the federal election of November 2020.

Fortunately, it is conceivable that the virus may face eventual control through the widescale acceptance of rules on social distancing, mask wearing, personal sanitation measures in the form of hand washing, avoidance of large social gatherings, the development of vaccines at unprecedented speed, and the achievement of herd immunity. The only issue with this optimistic assumption is the continued evolution of new virus variants which may ultimately create a semi-permanent chronic disease requiring yearly booster shots much like influenza (see, for example, *New York Times,* October 14, 2021).

Foremost among the responses of the medical community has been a series of scientific breakthroughs which have led to the development of nontraditional treatments such as messenger RNA (mRNA) vaccines to complement more traditional vaccines based on viral DNA (*Science* December 16, 2020). These new vaccine types may hold the promise of an effective medical response to new virus variants which evolve from a continuous process of mutation. The challenge still remains of how to address the problem of the development of these new COVID variants; these may elude current vaccines and continue to bind to the angiotensin-converting enzyme 2 (ACE2) receptors found on most human organs. One promising avenue of research is the use of engineered human ACE2 injected into the body to act as a decoy, binding to the spike protein of the SARS coronavirus 2 and thereby reducing or eliminating its capacity to infect human cells (Chan et al. 2020). Clinical trials of this novel approach are currently underway (ImmunityBio 2021).

Table 11.1 is an initial summary of some of the most significant effects of this most recent pandemic, understanding that data are incomplete and much remains to be learned as the pandemic plays out. The table is constructed as follows: the first column identifies the affected sector, the second describes the immediate impact of the virus, the third attempts to assess the effect of the virus on three components of sustainability, and the fourth speculates on the possible medium- to long-term effects in each area.

Table 11.1 The multifaceted effects of COVID-19

Area of concern	Current effects	Immediate effect on sustainability			Possible medium-to long-term effects
		Ecological	Economic	Social	
Mass transit	Pronounced reduction in use and shift to alternative modes of transport	Negative effect	Negative effect	Negative effect	Slow recovery
Automobile sales and use	Overall reduced use	Positive effect	Negative effect	—	Probable recovery of use post COVID-19
Air travel	Reduced use	Positive effect	Negative effect	—	Probable recovery post COVID-19 for pleasure, less so for business with increase in video conferencing and virtual meetings
Retail trade	Reduced employment and bankruptcies	Positive effect	Negative effect	Negative effect	Slow and partial recovery of in-person shopping in light of replacement by e-commerce (e.g., online shopping) and mega-retailers like Amazon
Employment	Down, especially among women and minorities; increased stress and health risks for essential workers	—	Negative effect	Negative effect	Slow recovery although some jobs gone forever and certain groups remain at disadvantage
Trade and supply chains	Disrupted	Positive effect	Negative effect	—	Potential disruption in manufacturing due to delays in sourcing parts and materials; increase in domestic sourcing
Creative arts: theaters, movies, concerts, museums, art galleries	Reduced attendance and bankruptcies	—	Negative effect	Negative effect	Some will not survive as digital access increases
Social gatherings: weddings, funerals, parties	Smaller and fewer in number	—	Negative effect	Negative effect	Eventual recovery
Sporting events	Fewer events and smaller in-person events	—	Negative effect	Negative effect	Eventual recovery
Religious gatherings	Fewer events and smaller in-person events	—	—	Negative effect	Eventual recovery

Outdoor recreation	Positive effect	Negative effect	Negative effect	Full recovery but may be delayed; potential overuse of local areas and resources
Educational sector	—	Negative effect	Negative effect	Probable return to full attendance despite parallel online learning but lost opportunities with potential lifelong effects for affected cohorts
Food production and transportation	—	Negative effect	Negative effect	Expected to eventually return to normal after the pandemic, but with possible changes to labor supply and supply chains
Fossil fuel use	Positive effect	Positive and negative effect	—	May not achieve previous levels because changing competitive environment for alternative fuels is leading to changing energy industry structure; but atmospheric levels of CO_2 will continue to rise for some time even with severe cutbacks in fossil fuel use
Greenhouse gases	Positive effect	Positive effect	—	May recover if world returns to business as usual
Air pollution	Positive effect	Positive effect	—	May recover if world returns to business as usual
Ambient noise	Positive effect	—	—	May recover if world returns to business as usual
Restaurants and cafes	—	Negative effect	Negative effect	Many will be permanently out of business
Mental health	—	Negative effect	Negative effect	Long road to recovery, increased resource needs
General health	—	Negative effect	Negative effect	Only partial recovery for those affected and possible long-term negative effects on personal and public health
Family relationships	—	—	Positive and negative effect	Permanent benefits as well as damage

(continued)

Table 11.1 Cont.

Area of concern	Current effects	Immediate effect on sustainability			Possible medium-to long-term effects
		Ecological	Economic	Social	
Urban structure	Less traffic, more people seek suburban and exurban space and isolation	Positive and negative effect	Positive and negative effect	Positive and negative effect	Loss of inhabitants and working population may be difficult to reverse; potential increase in livability through urban redesign, but lower conurban density may lead to greater infrastructure requirements; possible revitalization of rural areas
Work environment	Increased work at home but less social contact, less commuting, increased office space vacancies; greater level of job satisfaction and efficiency	Positive effect	Positive and negative effect	Negative effect	May represent a permanent change accompanied by increased use of digital communication
Tourism and ecotourism	Reduced tourism accompanied by major fiscal impacts on airlines, charter buses, cruise companies, travel agents and tour groups, and ecotourism sector	Positive and negative effect	Negative effect	Negative effect	Less stress on many local environments but loss of jobs for locals and fewer funds for conservation and ecological protection
Personal and household finances	Increased levels of poverty, loss of homes and poorer diet	—	Negative effect	Negative effect	Long-term detrimental personal financial consequences and more limited future opportunities
Health care sector	Increasing stress on limited resources with greater need for vaccines, public health education, and resources to overcome backlog in diagnostic and surgical procedures	—	Negative effect	Negative effect	Possible future employment opportunities and remuneration due to increased funding of public health, but possible long-term system recovery

As stated, this table is a work in progress and must await the continuing development of events and consequences. It is necessarily speculative, but certain general observations can be made at this point. First, the foremost question is whether human society—involving government, business, and individuals—will seize this opportunity to create new economic, political, and social structures more consistent with the goal of achieving global sustainability. This process will entail a complex mix of policies, instruments, and technologies, many of which do in fact already exist, but some that do not (see chapter 12). There is considerable inertia in all these areas, and the achievement of this goal is by no means certain.

Second, and equally important, is the strong possibility that pandemics will be a reoccurring feature of our global society (Settele et al. 2020; UNEP 2020; *Guardian* March 18, April 27, May 7, and June 17 , 2020; Snowden 2020). A scientific consensus is emerging that several fundamental changes at the global level are drivers of this possibility. These include: ecological change, continued increases in population and urbanization, increased wealth and its concomitant need for great material inputs, intensification of animal husbandry in the developing world (e.g., *Science* June 29, 2020), continuing cross-species transmission of mutated viruses, factory farming in the developed world (e.g., Walters 2003; Gorman 2021; Pew Commission on Industrial Farm Animal Production 2008; Munnink et al. 2020), and increased interaction of humans with currently remote or undeveloped natural environments, thereby exposing the population to a wide range of localized and relatively dormant viruses through the process of economic development. While the current rapid global transportation networks increase the speed and capacity for dispersion of disease, this is merely a modern manifestation of the historical role of commerce and trade in the spread of diseases (Harrison 2012). Several candidates of such emerging viruses include, inter alia, Ebola, SARS, MERS, Zika, chikungunya, Avian influenza, Nipah, dengue, and Marburg, but the potential reservoir of latent or dormant viruses that could pose a significant threat to human health may number in the hundreds or more (Watsa and WDSFG 2020; King 2021; *New York Times* May 20, 2021; Shi and Gao 2021).

In a landmark epidemiological study, Grange et al. (2021) identified and ranked 887 wildlife viruses for their potential to infect humans using 31 host, viral, and environmental risk factors. They found that the top twelve were known zoonotic viruses but several newly detected wildlife viruses ranked higher than known zoonotic viruses. The virus with the highest score on their ranking system was Lassa fever, which is endemic in parts of West Africa and whose principal animal vector is the multimammate rat (CDC 2019). The next eleven viruses on the ranking are SARS-CoV-2, Ebola, Seoul virus, Nipah virus, hepatitis E, Marburg virus, SARS-CoV, simian immunodeficiency virus, rabies, lymphocytic choriomeningitis virus, and simian foamy virus.

A particularly disturbing discovery has been made by Souilmi et al. (2021) of a coronavirus epidemic in East Asia twenty thousand years ago. To quote one report on this study (*New York Times* June 28, 2021):

> Researchers have found evidence that a coronavirus epidemic swept East Asia some 20,000 years ago and was devastating enough to leave an evolutionary imprint on the DNA of people alive today. The new study suggests that an ancient coronavirus plagued the region for many years, researchers say. The finding could have dire implications for the Covid-19 pandemic if it's not brought under control soon through vaccination. "It should make us worry," said David Enard, an evolutionary biologist at the University of Arizona who led the study, which was published on

Thursday in the journal *Current Biology*. "What is going on right now might be going on for generations and generations."

Over the past half century, the developed world has been lulled into a false sense of security through the widespread adoption of certain critical public health measures such as the provision of clean water and the separation of drinking water sources and disposal of wastewater. Adding to this complacency has been the reliance on antibiotics to cure many bacterial diseases once considered fatal. This optimistic view is being challenged by the wide-scale development of antibiotic resistance, which is propelled largely by overuse and misuse among both the human population and the agricultural sector (US HHS 2010; Davis et al. 2011; Neyra et al. 2012; Pereira et al. 2014; Tang et al. 2017; Hall et al. 2018; WOAH–OIE 2018, WHO 2020; and see Chapter 6). Despite the widespread toll of COVID-19, some epidemiologists and virologists feel that future rates of mortality could be significantly higher for localized or as yet undiscovered emerging viruses (Snowden 2020). As Snowden states:

> Many of the central features of a global modern society continue to render the world acutely vulnerable to the challenge of pandemic disease. The experience of SARS and Ebola—the two major "dress rehearsals" of the new century—serve as a sobering reminder that our public health and biomedicine defences are porous. Prominent features of modernity—population growth, climate change, rapid means of transportation, the proliferation of megacities, with inadequate urban infrastructure, warfare, persistent poverty, and widening social inequalities—maintain the risk.
>
> (p. 7)

The problem, as defined by Harper (2021), is what he terms the "paradox of plenty" fueled by our technological advances. To quote:

> Our success as a species has been a boon for our parasites. [p. 9] . . . The paradox of plenty is a common pattern in the human past: the material forces that enable population growth and human connectivity also create new ecologies of infectious disease and stimulate the emergence of new pathogens.
>
> (p. 419)

The one note of optimism in this regard is that the optimal strategy for a successful virus is to maximize the opportunity for reproduction, transmission, and ultimate survival. As a general principle, viruses that are too lethal run the risk of killing their host before there is a chance to be transmitted to a new host (Christakis 2020). On balance, this provides only modest solace for a civilization facing large numbers of sick and dying. However, concern has been raised by several biologists that this constraint on increasing virulence of COVID may not be relevant at this stage in the evolution of the virus as "death occurs weeks after the transmission ceases" (*Telegraph* November 29, 2021).

The prospect of future pandemics suggests that some of the environmental, social, and economic changes that have occurred in response to the current pandemic may become more common in our societies. Not all these changes will necessarily be negative, particularly if they lead to a world of great sustainability. Within the business sector, we may experience what Joseph Schumpeter (1942) has termed "creative destruction," where forces that cause the demise of some companies and industries may open up opportunities for new and innovative models of business. However, initial drops in air pollution and global carbon dioxide emissions have reversed, accompanied by a rebound in energy demand in 2021, suggesting that fundamental change in our economic system may be very difficult to achieve (CNN March 16, 2021; Fyfe et al. 2012; IEA 2021a; WMO 2021; IEA 2021b).

There have been, and may continue to be, significant opportunity costs associated with future pandemics and our responses to them. For example, the diversity of scarce resources devoted to combating and treating COVID-19 has led to reductions in progress against other diseases. These effects may be manifested in reduced inoculations, increased numbers of childhood diseases, delayed surgeries, premature deaths, and other public health measures being allocated insufficient funding. Much of the developing world is characterized by serious underfunding of public health measures and institutions, but a similar problem affects the developed world as well. For more than three decades, Laurie Garrett (1994, 2000) has been warning of the chronic underfunding of public health. We are suffering the consequence of this profound lapse in social and economic priorities. Harrison (2012, p. xvi) concludes that:

> Public health measures are best understood as unstable compromises between disparate and sometimes conflicting interests. Governments have always balanced the prospect of infection against the losses that may result from curtailment of commerce.

This profound dilemma has been recognized globally today in the difficult political, social, and economic decisions around lockdowns and curfews intended to slow the spread of COVID-19. This disease has been called an "SOS signal for the human enterprise" (*Guardian* June 5, 2020), and unless we abandon a business-as-usual model, the continued acceleration of climate change will facilitate the generation and spread of new pandemics (NPR March 24, 2020; Van Kerkhove et al. 2021). By way of example, recent research on the impacts of climate change has projected that the increased range of mosquitoes, which carry malaria and dengue fever, could increase the global population at risk by as many as 4.7 billion people within semitropical, tropical, and temperate regions of the world (Colon-Gonzalez 2021). These are just two of the many endemic and emerging diseases which could experience a new expansion of their global reach in the next few decades as a result of climate change.

As Harper (2021, p. 469) states:

> As human control of the environment has expanded, Darwinian evolution has continued, or even accelerated. The evolution of new pathogens is not an anomaly but rather the strictest obedience to the laws of nature. COVID-19 was the evolution of the product of the ecological conditions we have created—numbers, density, and connectivity, especially in the age of jet travel. The ongoing pandemic has been a jarring reminder that humanity's control over nature is necessarily incomplete and unstable.

This somber view of the future is reinforced by the recent work of Rob Dunn (2021) in his book entitled *The Natural History of the Future: What the Laws of Biology Tell Us About the Destiny of the Human Species*. To quote:

> Collectively, these laws of the living world and our place in it offer a vision for what is and is not possible with regard to the natural history of the future and our place

in it. Only by keeping life's laws in mind can we imagine a sustainable future for our species, a future in which our cities and towns are not flooded again and again by the consequences of our failed attempts to manage life—flooded not only by water but also by pests, parasites and hunger. We will fail again and again if we ignore these laws. The bad news is that our default approach to nature seems to be to try to hold it back. We tend to fight nature at our own expense and then blame vengeful gods . . . when things don't work out. The good news is that it doesn't have to be that way: if we pay attention to a set of relatively simple laws of life, we have a much better chance of surviving a hundred years, a thousand years, or even a million years. But if we don't, well, ecologists and evolutionary biologists together actually have a pretty good idea of the trajectory of life in our absence.

(p. 18)

References

Alfani, Guido (2020) "The economic consequence of large-scale pandemics: lessons from the history of plague in Europe and the Mediterranean." Working paper, University of Warwick, April 27.

Anand, Abhishek et al. (2021) "Three new estimates of India's all-cause excess mortality during the COVID-19 pandemic." Working paper 589, Center for Global Development, July 20.

BBC (2021) "ICMR sero survey: One in five Indians exposed to Covid-19," February 5.

Cantor, Norman F. (2001) *In the Wake of the Plague: The Black Death and the World It Made*, New York: Simon & Schuster.

Cartwright, Frederick F. (1972) *Disease and History*, New York: Dorset Press.

Chan, Kui K. et al. (2020) "Engineering human ACE2 to optimize binding to the spike protein of SARS coronavirus 2," *Science*, September 4.

Christakis, Nicholas, A. (2020) *Apollo's Arrow: The Profound and Enduring Impact of Coronavirus*, New York; Boston; London: Little, Brown Spark.

CNN (2021) "Satellite images show air pollution returning to pre-pandemic levels as restrictions loosen," March 16.

Cohen, Mark Nathan (1989) *Health and the Rise of Civilization*, New Haven, CT: Yale University Press.

Colon-Gonzalez, Felipe J. et al. (2021) *The Lancet*, "Projecting the risk of mosquito-borne diseases in a warmer and more populated world: A multi-model, multi-scenario intercomparison modelling study," July 1.

Davis, Meghan F. et al. (2011) *Current Opinion in Microbiology*, "An ecological perspective on U.S. industrial poultry production: The role of anthropogenic ecosystems on the emergence of drug-resistant bacteria from agricultural environments," June.

Dunn, Rob (2021) *The Natural History of the Future: What the Laws of Biology Tell Us About the Destiny of the Human Species*, New York: Basic Books.

Egger, Dennis et al. (2021) *Science*, "Falling living standards during the COVID-19 crisis: Quantitative evidence from nine developing countries," February 5.

Fyfe, J.C. et al. (2021) *Science Advances*, "Quantifying the influence of short-term emission reductions on climate, March 5.

Garrett, Laurie (1994) *The Coming Plague: Newly Emerging Diseases in a World out of Balance*, New York: Farrar, Straus and Giroux.

Garrett, Laurie (2000) *Betrayal of Trust: The Collapse of Global Public Health*, New York: Hyperion.

Gorman, James (2021) "A new bird flu jumps to humans: So far, it's not a problem," *New York Times*, April 26.

Grange, Zoe L. et al. (2021) "Ranking the risk of animal-to-human spillover for newly discovered viruses," April 13.

Guardian (2020) " 'Tip of the iceberg': Is our destruction of nature responsible for COVID-19?" March 18.

Guardian (2020) "Halt destruction of nature or suffer even worse pandemics, say world's top scientists," April 27.

Guardian (2020) " 'Promiscuous treatment of nature' will lead to more pandemics—scientists," May 7.

Guardian (2020) "Coronavirus is an 'SOS signal for the human enterprise'," June 5.

Guardian (2020) "Pandemics result from destruction of nature, say UN and WHO," June 17.

Hagemann, Hannah (2020) "The 1918 flu pandemic was brutal, killing more than 50 million people worldwide," NPR, April 2.

Hall, William et al. (2018) *Superbugs: An Arms Race against Bacteria*, Cambridge, MA: Harvard University Press.

Harper, Kyle (2017) *The Fate of Rome: Climate, Disease, & the End of an Empire,* Princeton, NJ: Princeton University Press.

Harper, Kyle (2021) *Plagues Upon the Earth: Disease and the Course of Human History,* Princeton, NJ: Princeton University Press.

Harrison, Mark (2012) *Contagion: How Commerce Has Spread Disease*, New Haven, CT: Yale University Press.

Hill (2021) "WHO: COVID-19 deaths likely two to three times higher than reported," May 21.

IEA (International Energy Agency) (2021a) "After steep drop in early 2020, global carbon dioxide emissions have rebounded strongly," March 2.

IEA (International Energy Agency) (2021b) Global Energy Review 2021.

ImmunityBio (2021) "ImmunityBio announces novel ACE2 decoy COVID-19 therapeutic that shows high binding to SARS-CoV-2 variants and neutralizes live viruses," March 11.

Irons, Nicholas J. and Adrian E. Raftery (2021) *PNAS*, "Estimating SARS-CoV-2 infections from deaths, confirmed cases, tests, and random surveys, August 3.

Johnson, Niall P.A.S. and Juergen Mueller (2002) *Bulletin of the History of Medicine*, "Updating the accounts: Global mortality of the 1918–1920 'Spanish' influenza pandemic," 76:105–115.

King, Anthony (2021) *Science*, "Two more coronavirus may infect people," May 28.

McNeill, William H. (1998) *Plagues and People*, New York: Anchor Books.

Meacham, Jon (2020) *New York Times*, "Pandemics of the past," May 7.

Munnink, Bas B. Oude et al. (2020) *Science*, "Transmission of SARS-Co-V-2 on mink farms between humans and mink and back to humans," November 10.

New York Times (2021) "'Excess deaths' in 2020 surpassed those of 1918 flu pandemic," April 23.

New York Times (2021) "The latest coronavirus comes from dogs," May 20.

New York Times (2021) "Just how big could India's Covid toll be?" May 25.

New York Times (2021) "A coronavirus epidemic hit 20,000 years ago, new study finds," June 28.

New York Times (2021) "Covid will be an era, not a crisis that fades," October 14.

Neyra, Ricardo Castillo et al. (2012) *Safety and Health at Work*, "Antimicrobial-resistant bacteria: An unrecognized work-related risk in food animal production," June.

Nikiforuk, Andrew (1991) *The Fourth Horseman: A Short History of Plagues, Scourges and Emerging Viruses*, Toronto: Penguin.

NPR (2020) "How climate change increases our risk for pandemics," March 24.

Oldstone, Michael B.A. (2010) *Viruses, Plagues, & History*, Oxford; New York: Oxford University Press.

Pereira, R.V. et al. (2014) *Journal of Dairy Science*, "Effect of on-farm use of antimicrobial drugs on resistance in fecal *Escherichia coli* of preweaned dairy calves," December.

Pew Commission on Industrial Farm Animal Production (2008) *Putting Meat on the Table: Industrial Farm Animal Production in* America.

Quammen, David (2012) *Spillover: Animal Infections and the Next Human Pandemic*, New York: W.W. Norton.

Schumpeter, Joseph (1942) *Capitalism, Socialism, and Democracy*, reissued in 2008, New York: Harper Perennial Modern Classics.

Science (2020) "Swine flu strain with human pandemic potential increasingly found in pigs in China," June 29.

Science (2020) "Messenger RNA gave us a COVID-19 vaccine: Will it treat diseases, too?" December 16.

Settele, Josef et al. (2020) "COVID-10 stimulus measures must save lives, protect livelihoods, and safeguard nature to reduce the risk of future pandemics," IPBES guest article, April 27.

Shah, Sonia (2016) *Pandemic,* New York: Sara Crichton Books.

Shi, Weifeng and George F. Gao (2021) *Science,* "Emerging H5N8 avian influenza viruses," May 21.

Skwarecki, Beth (2016) *Outbreak! 50 Tales of Epidemics that Terrorized the World*, Avon, MA: Adams Media.

Snowden, Frank M. (2020) *Epidemics and Society: From the Black Death to the Present*, New Haven, CT: Yale University Press.

Souilmi, Yassine et al. (2021) *Current Biology,* "An ancient viral epidemic involving host coronavirus interacting genes more than 20,000 years ago in East Asia," August 23.

Tang, Karen L. et al. (2017) *The Lancet*, "Restricting the use of antibiotics in food-producing animals and its associations with antibiotic resistance in food-producing animals and human beings: A systematic review and meta-analysis," November 1.

Telegraph (2021) "Will the new omicron variant cause severe disease or just a runny nose?" November 29.

UNEP (United Nations Environment Programme) et al. (2020) *Preventing the Next Pandemic: Zoonotic Disease and How to Break the Chain of Transmission.*

US CBO (Congressional Budget Office) (2020) "Re: Comparison of CBO's May 2020 interim projections of gross domestic product and its January 2020 baseline projections." Letter to the Honorable Charles E. Schumer, June 1.

US CDC (Centers for Disease Control and Prevention) (2019) "Lassa fever."

US CDC (Centers for Disease Control and Prevention), (accessed February 16, 2021), website, www.cdc.gov/.

US HHS (Department of Health and Human Services) (2010) "The judicious use of medically important antimicrobial drugs in food-producing animals," June 28.

Van Kerkhove, Maria D. et al. (2021) *Science* "Preparing for 'Disease X'," October 13.

Walters, Mark Jerome (2003) *Six Modern Plagues and How We Are Causing Them*, Washington, DC: Island Press.

Watsa, Mrinalini and WDSFG (Wildlife Disease Surveillance Focus Group) (2020) *Science*, "Rigorous wildlife disease surveillance," July 10.

WHO (World Health Organization) (2020) "Antibiotic resistance: Key facts," July 31.

WHO (World Health Organization) Coronavirus Dashboard (accessed February 16 and November 28, 2021), website, www.who.int/.

Wild, Sarah (2021) *Scientific American*, "Hidden toll of COVID in Africa threatens global pandemic progress," March 25.

Winegard, Timothy C. (2019) *The Mosquito: A Human History of Our Deadliest Predator,* Toronto: Allen Lane, Pengin Random House Canada.

WMO (World Meteorological Organization) (2021) *State of the Global Climate 2020.*

WOAH–OIE (World Organization for Animal Health) (2018) *OIE Annual Report on Antimicrobial Agents Intended for Use in Animals: Third Report.*

World Bank (2020a) Brief, "Understanding poverty/topics/poverty," June 8.

World Bank (2020b) *Reversals of Fortune: Poverty and Share Prosperity.*

WTO (World Trade Organization) (2020) "WTO goods barometer flashes red as COVID-19 disrupts world trade," May 20.

Index